Merchant Shipping Law

Development of National and Customary Law for Safety of Life at Sea

By

J. N. K. Mansell

Merchant Shipping Law: Development of National and Customary Law for Safety of Life at Sea

By J. N. K. Mansell

This book first published 2023

Ethics International Press Ltd, UK

British Library Cataloguing in Publication Data

A catalogue record for this book is available from the British Library

Print Book ISBN: 978-1-80441-274-9

eBook ISBN: 978-1-80441-275-6

The difficulties which our sailors now have to encounter are not those which met their ancestors, who battled with the elements in small shallops no bigger than a modern fishing-smack, amid the dangers of unknown and uncharted seas. Rather is the modern difficulty that of dealing with the splendid instruments of commerce now in the vogue, and the immense increase in traffic, especially in the narrower seas - conditions which require in those who have the responsibility a higher scientific training and a greater alertness in the avoidance of accidents than was needed at any previous period of our history

Edward Blackmore*

---

* Master Mariner; Shipmaster; Shipowner; Associate of Naval Architects; Formerly a resident Justice of the Peace for the County of Renfrew, New Brunswick; and a Member of the Institution of Engineers and Shipbuilders in Scotland

Dedication

To the memory of the countless thousands lost at sea throughout the nineteenth century due to unseaworthy ships, long forgotten shipwrecks and the intransigence of politicians

Contents

Introduction

Throughout the nineteenth century Great Britain was the predominant maritime nation, leading the world in matters of tonnage, trade, technology and development of national and customary maritime law. In 1800 there were no commercial steamships and British merchant ships were entirely unregulated in matters of safety and seaworthiness. By the end of the century steamships had reached degrees of size, power, speed and sophistication unimaginable 100 years earlier. The Merchant Shipping Act, 1894, set the standard for many maritime nations and consolidated a vast body of merchant shipping law. A comprehensive regulatory regime was in place to determine whether ships were safe, seaworthy, and not overloaded. This account sets out to provide a previously unpublished authoritative record of the development of that law in the context of the political, economic, technical, and societal issues of the time, including many tragic and long forgotten shipwrecks.

At least 1,000 seafarers were lost at sea per year throughout the nineteenth century. Some years experienced far greater losses of ships along with their crews and passengers through collision, shipwreck, fire, overloading, unseaworthiness and often, errors of navigation or judgement of those in control or command. For the first half-century there was very little attempt by Parliament to enact legislation to address these issues. Statistics on shipwreck were compiled from the early 1830's and, along with public pressure, forced the appointment of a Select Committee on Shipwreck in 1836. Although the committee found that the causes of shipwrecks were many and various and confirmed the parlous state of the unregulated shipping industry, no legislation ensued. It was not until a public outcry arose in 1838 over proven allegations of cannibalism amongst the crews of waterlogged and unseaworthy timber ships that politicians were galvanized to enact the first, very limited, legislation for the safety of those particular seafarers. This legislation was arbitrarily and quietly repealed twenty-three years later in spite of annual statistics that had clearly demonstrated its efficacy.

For most of the century politicians took an extreme laissez faire approach to the shipping industry, believing that the shipowner knew best and that any attempt to legislate in detail would transfer his responsibility to the Government; a view enthusiastically supported by a very active and influential shipowners lobby amongst Members of the House of Commons. Regulation was freely referred to by politicians as 'evil', 'vicious' and 'mischievous' throughout the century and although Parliament enthusiastically regulated other dangerous industries such as mining and railways, the most dangerous industry of all, seafaring, was literally out of sight and out of mind.

The Colonial Office had been proactive from 1803 in passing the first of many Passenger Acts dealing principally with the welfare of tens of thousands of emigrants to British colonies. The term 'seaworthy' was first enshrined in legislation through a Passenger Act in 1835 with the Controller of Customs having the power to require the ship to be surveyed if her seaworthiness was in doubt. In 1842 a Passenger Act was the first to legislate for carriage of a certain number of boats aboard passenger ships, powered by sail or steam.

For the first half of the nineteenth century no British seafarers in positions of responsibility were required to hold certificates of competency, unlike their counterparts aboard ships of other principal maritime nations. An 1836 report identified this lack of competency as one of the prime causes of shipwreck and recorded some alarming examples of incompetent and drunken masters. A further Select Committee on Shipwreck in 1843 heard vehement evidence from shipowners who were "decidedly hostile to the enforcement of examination by Act of Parliament considering such compulsion an unnecessary interference in the selection of persons as they think most likely to serve them best in the various duties they have to perform', in spite of evidence of children as young as fourteen being appointed by shipowners as masters of their ocean-going sailing ships. The committee made a strong recommendation that compulsory examinations should be held for prospective officers and masters but the Government introduced them, unsuccessfully, on a voluntary basis.

Steam was a significant driver for change. Marine steam engines slowly improved in efficiency and reliability over the first few decades of the century, operating at first solely in coastal trades with limited cargo capacity due to the large quantity of coal required for fuel. The catalyst for regulation of ships was the development of steam engines in the late 1830's suitable to propel heavily subsidised paddle steamers across the North Atlantic on scheduled services. With very limited cargo carrying ability they carried only high value cargoes, royal mail and a limited number of first class passengers. The very few existing iron ocean-going steamships were first regulated in 1846 and required to carry boats to a different scale to those required under the Passenger Acts; a result of fractured and diverse administration of merchant ships which came under the umbrella of a number of different Government departments and offices.

Mid-century was a turning point in regulation and administration of merchant ships and in their ability to trade. In the late 1840s a ground swell of opposition built up against the archaic Navigation Laws that restricted trade between Britain and her colonies to British owned and crewed ships, stifling competition and, through outdated tonnage rules, ship design. This culminated with their repeal in 1849 introducing a new era of competition and resulting in a dramatic expansion of trade. In 1850 the Government addressed the vexed issue of oversight of ships and seafarers and created a Naval Department of the Board of Trade to be responsible for 'superintendence of matters relating to the British Mercantile Marine'. The Act also stipulated that examinations be instituted for persons intending to be masters or mates of foreign-going ships. A further Steam Navigation Act in 1851 included a table for the number of boats to be carried by sailing vessels and steam vessels based upon the registered tonnage of the ship rather than the total number of people aboard; a fatal flaw that was to have far reaching consequences. This folly was compounded when the Colonial Office introduced yet another Passenger Act the following year with different requirements to the 1851 Act for the carriage of boats for 'every passenger ship'. Mid-century also covered the tragic period when tens of thousands of emigrants fleeing the Irish famine died of typhoid or cholera (ship fever) while making their westbound passage in very unhygienic conditions aboard sailing ships usually employed in the timber trade from North America to Britain. Such emigrant ships were also often lost with their entire complement through foundering, stranding or unseaworthiness.

Competition increased between steam passenger ships in the North Atlantic trade, with associated issues of achieving fast passages to meet the terms of their lucrative mail contracts regardless of adverse weather, fog and icebergs. This recklessness resulted in some disastrous collisions, groundings and total disappearance of ships, often with great loss of life. The situation was heightened by unprecedented increases in size, power and passenger capacity that continued for the remainder of the century. Collisions continued throughout the century in spite of the development, principally by Great Britain and France, of customary law observed by all principal maritime nations for prevention of collision. Many stern warnings from Judges on the dangers of excessive speed in conditions of fog and ice did little to remedy matters.

The year 1854 saw the greatest number of ships and people lost at sea between 1848 and 1878, and enactment of one of the most comprehensive consolidations of merchant shipping law during the nineteenth century and the principal merchant shipping Act for the following forty years; the Merchant Shipping Act, 1854. Concerns about the quality of chain cables and anchors, the last resort for a vessel being driven onto a lee shore, led to regulation of the manufacturing and marking process in 1862 which, with a subsequent Act, was consolidated into the last merchant shipping legislation enacted during the nineteenth century, in 1899.

The term 'coffin ship' was coined in the 1830s to label the overladen and unseaworthy ships carrying timber principally from Canada to Great Britain, and also used during the Irish exoduses in the 1830s and mid-century. The lack of any limitation upon how much cargo could be loaded aboard a ship allowed some shipowners to operate unseaworthy, overladen and over-insured ships, in the expectation of losing the ship and its crew, to gain an insurance payout. This greed, exploitation and callous disregard for life also attracted the label of coffin ships. Seamen were frequently jailed for refusing to go to sea in such ships. There was a great reluctance amongst shipowners and politicians to address this issue until Samuel Plimsoll entered Parliament in 1868 and made it his mission in life to remedy the situation through legislation. Largely as a result of his efforts, by 1876 ships were required to be marked with a load line, which could however be placed where the shipowner thought appropriate for a particular cargo. It was not until 1890, long after Plimsoll had left Parliament, that the exact location of the load line was laid down in law.

Watertightness, integral to the safety and buoyancy of a ship, particularly when damaged through stranding or collision, could only be achieved as ships became larger through effective subdivision by watertight bulkheads. A Parliamentary shipwreck committee in 1843 correctly noted that 'watertight divisions in steam vessels are calculated to prevent loss of vessel and machinery, and to ensure the preservation of life, by affording time for the preparation of boats for passengers and crew'. In 1846 iron passenger steamers of 100 ton and upwards were required to have watertight divisions fore and aft of the engine room. In 1854 this requirement was extended to all steamships which had to be 'divided by such partitions into not less than three equal parts'. The provisions of the 1854 Act were quietly repealed in 1862. The matter of whether any ship should have watertight bulkheads was left to the discretion of shipowners as it was their view, along with that of the Board of Trade, that 'the law concerning bulkheads in iron ships had proved mischievous'. However, as such bulkheads also served to provide transverse strength, particularly as ships became significantly longer and narrower during the second half of the century, it was necessary for transverse bulkheads to be designed into the structure of the ship to what were often subjectively deemed by Board of Trade inspectors to be 'effective' and 'satisfactory' standards as decreed by a Bulkheads Committee of experts in 1890.

By the early 1870s there was widespread concern that, in spite of increasingly comprehensive safety legislation, casualties to ships and loss of life were not diminishing. A summary of official inquiries into wrecks and casualties, excluding collisions, showed that from the year 1856 to 1872 inclusive, while 60 ships were known to have been lost from defects in the vessel or in the stowage, 711 ships were lost from neglect or bad navigation. After a lengthy investigation looking into matters such as load line, survey, remedial legislation, casualty inquiries and under-manning a Royal Commission on Unseaworthy Ships stated in 1877 that '...we have been anxious throughout our Report not to transfer responsibility from the shipowner to the executive government. It is the duty of the shipowner to keep his ship in a seaworthy condition, and to select competent officers and crew. We believe that under the arrangements suggested in our Report, the Board of Trade will have the means of ascertaining how far this duty has been fulfilled, and will then have the power to punish those persons who have been neglectful'.

In spite of this recommendation disasters at sea continued unabated, to the extent that, by 1884 a Royal Commission to Investigate the Saving of Life at Sea was established. From 1874 to 1883 inclusively '...No less than 699 vessels, with 8475 crew on, were reported as missing, with the cause of their loss unknown'. Statistics showed that many of these ships were carrying bulk grain or coal, both cargoes prone to shifting if not properly stowed, with coal having the added risk of fire. Once again, the conclusions of a Royal Commission were inconclusive. The general outcome of their inquiry was the Life-Saving Appliances Act, 1888, which 'did not touch the root of all evil, but only makes provision for the saving of life when accidents do occur'. Attention was paid by scientists to the dangers of bulk grain and coal with new stowage requirements being regulated for the former. New scientific advice addressing fires in bulk cargoes of coal determined that the accepted method of ventilating such cargoes was causing the fires.

The last decade of the century saw more legislation for merchant ships including the Merchant Shipping Act, 1894, at the time the largest statute ever enacted by the British parliament, and a consolidation of all British merchant shipping and mercantile shipping law. The 1894 Act became the template for shipping law throughout the British Empire until well into the twentieth century.

During the long course of the nineteenth century the ratio of crew to tonnage had steadily decreased to the point where it had been identified as a direct cause of loss of ships in a large number of accidents. A Manning Committee of the Board of Trade agreed in 1896 that there was a definite association between under-manning and unseaworthiness. Accordingly, the Merchant Shipping Act, 1897 made under-manning a detainable deficiency, applicable to British ships and to foreign ships in British ports. In spite of comprehensive rules for the prevention of collision there were three very serious collisions during the 1890's, involving British, German and French passenger ships, resulting in the loss of 1,443 passengers and crew.

The influence of a shipowners lobby group in the House of Common was effective throughout the nineteenth century and was nowhere more evident than in the matters of watertight bulkheads and provision of lifeboats. The 1894 Act provided that ships of 12,000 gross tons and upwards were to carry 16 lifeboats under davits with the remainder of boat capacity in 'additional wood, metal, collapsible, or other boats or life-rafts, all of approved pattern, as conveniently placed for putting into the water as the ship's arrangements admit of'. This legislation took no account of the existing rapid growth in size of passenger ships and was outdated before it was enacted. There was no encouragement to fit more boats under davits due to legislation giving the shipowner the discretion to 'avoid encumbrance of the deck'. If effective watertight bulkheads were fitted that would enable the ship to remain afloat with two adjacent compartments flooded, the number of boats not under davits could be reduced by half (the Bulkhead Committee had recommended that no extra boats would be so required). By the end of the century the upper tonnage of 12,000 gross tons had been long overtaken. The Board of Trade stated in 1896 that they saw no reason to increase this limit and were not to even consider doing so until well into the twentieth century.

The entrenched laissez faire belief of Parliamentarians, Government officials and shipowners that 'the State should stand aside', and their misplaced concerns regarding their assumption of responsibility for the safety of ships were eventually allayed through a realisation that, due to the great size and complexity of the shipping industry and its importance to the British economy, prescriptive legislation for safety of life at sea was very necessary. This sea change in attitudes was helped by a pragmatic legislative model of consolidation which slowly developed whereby the parent legislation dealt with broad principals and responsibilities while frequently changing technical details were embodied in flexible secondary legislation; rules, regulation and Orders in Council.

The rising tide of loss of life at sea finally slackened and started to turn in the very last decade of the century.

Chapter 1

Seaworthiness

Central to the concept of seaworthiness is that a ship must be well enough constructed and equipped to withstand the perils of the sea and be adequately and efficiently crewed and operated to safely load, carry and deliver the cargoes entrusted to it by shippers. It must be seaworthy.

Today's world of more than 60,000 ships trading internationally, crewed by more than one and a half million seafarers, operate under a comprehensive regulatory regime of internationally agreed standards for safety and seaworthiness. These standards, which emanate from the United Nations Convention on the Law of the Sea[1], are codified through statutory instruments by the member States of the International Maritime Organization and brought into effect by those States through their national law. Ships are required to meet 'generally accepted international regulations, procedures and practices governing, inter alia, the construction, equipment and seaworthiness of ships, as well as the manning of ships and the training of crews'[2]. Ships trading internationally are required to carry a number of mandatory certificates issued by their country of registration that attest to their seaworthiness and compliance with statutory IMO instruments. If found to be deficient in these standards, by their flag State or by other States, including lack of or out-of-date certificates, ships are unseaworthy and eligible for detention until deficiencies that affect the safety and security of the ship, its crew, and the marine environment are rectified.

In yesterday's very long world of shipping it is only in the very recent past that ships have suffered any form of city or State control. In the Middle Ages, as ships became larger, ventured further and carried more valuable cargoes, both States and private organisations began to use or adopt empirical standards to ensure seaworthiness, safe carriage of cargoes, and prevention of overloading. Some ships were subject to inspections and surveys to ensure those standards were met, both in construction of the ship and sometimes during the loading and discharging processes.

Records exist from the activities of the Hanseatic League in Northern Europe in 1412, 1417 and 1447 that surveys of ships were required. A Low Countries Ordinance of 1549 required a survey before and after loading. A law was introduced in Spain in 1563 requiring both the builders and owners of ships to ensure seaworthiness, check the laden draft and securely lash the cargo. In 1569, Venice forbade particular cargo from being stowed in certain locations in the ship. King Henri III of France issued an edict in 1584 that required ports to monitor the abilities of ships' masters. A Genoese law from 1607 required surveys to be undertaken by 'magnificent curators of the sea'. A requirement for a dual survey of French ships, at the commencement of the outward voyage and upon return, was introduced through a Royal declaration in 1779 followed by an Act of 1791 which placed a strict obligation on captains of ships proceeding upon a long voyage to ensure that a survey was carried out before the ship was equipped and loaded. Surveys were carried out by certain navigators, ship-builders or carpenters holding the office of Huissier-visiteur, appointed by the Commercial Courts of local mayor.[3]

In England there were historically no such measures, and little enthusiasm for any departure from the age-old methods of designing and building wooden ships. In 1737 a practical chemist named Jackson promoted a process to improve the durability of wood used in ship-building. However, the outcry from ship-builders that it would poison their workers and reduce their profits if ships were more durable succeeded in stopping experiments until a report received from the Royal College of Physicians verified that the substance was not harmful to health. A Treatise on Shipbuilding and Navigation was published in 1754. Although this was recognized as being the only available source on the subject that could lay claim to any science, both the author, Murray, and the book were 'consigned to the same unmerited obscurity'.[4]

The first voluntary standards for the hull and rig of a ship evolved in the mid-eighteenth century through what came to be known as classification societies. These organisations developed out of a need for merchant ship owners to be able to provide evidence to their insurers and charterers that their ship had been built and rigged to a suitable standard. The first classification society was that of Lloyds, named after the London coffee house where merchants, marine underwriters and others connected with shipping gathered from the seventeenth century.[5] The owner of this establishment, Edward Lloyd, published a printed news-sheet, Lloyd's News, with information on foreign and war news, trials, executions and parliamentary proceedings, and marine news and gossip.[6] In 1760 a Register Society was incorporated, and, by 1764 a Register of Ships was published to give information on the condition of ships to merchants and marine underwriters.[7] The initial attempt to introduce a system of classifying ships by Lloyds, in 1798, met with widespread derision;

> Instead of classing the ships of which they gave an account [to the insurers and shipowner] according to the actual state and condition ascertained by a careful surveyor, they stamped the character of a ship wholly by her age and the port at which she was built, without any regard to the manner in which she was built, the wear or damage she might have sustained, or the repairs she might from time to time have received, or even being new built thereby lessening the inducement to build ships on principles of durability, obviating the necessity of surveying their hulls, and taking away the encouragement to keep them in the best state of repair.[8]

The ratings provided by classification societies became an essential tool for underwriters but were not popular with ship owners and shipbuilders as they discriminated against certain shipbuilding areas, and the information was confidential to insurers. A ship would be registered as First Class, regardless of her standard of construction, for between six and twelve years after which it was the view of the industry that she would be…'superannuated to be replaced by some hastily and cheaply built successor, expressly designed to last no longer than the allotted period of first class vessels… many of these frail barks foundered on their first voyage, few of the crews survived to give the melancholy account of their disaster, and of those who did survive not one in a thousand was capable of tracing it to its proper cause'.[9]

As a direct result of a Lloyds Register publication in 1797, which discriminated against any ship not built on the Thames, ship owners formed their own register. The two separate registers did not prove successful in the long term and merged in 1834 as the Lloyds Register of British and Foreign Shipping. The new organization, which included merchants, ship owners and underwriters, published rules in 1834 for the survey and classification of ships; hence the commonly known term 'Class'.[10] Even with the establishment of Class ship owners were still free to be built to whatever standard the shipbuilder deemed appropriate if the ship was uninsured, and to allow the Masters of their ships, who were often part owners, to operate and navigate entirely autonomously as 'Master under God'.[11]

At the turn of the century Ireland followed the example of Scotland in 1707 and, albeit reluctantly, entered into political union with England in 1800;[12] thus making Britain 'Great'. The population of Great Britain was unknown in 1800 but the first official census in 1801 indicated a total of ten million in England, Scotland and Wales and a further 5.2 million in Ireland[13]. Statistics at this time showed 126,774 seamen[14] crewing 15,734 British ships with a total tonnage of 1,699,000 net registered tons[15], giving an average sized ship of 107 ton crewed by 8 seamen. These ships and their crews were entirely unregulated in matters of safety and seaworthiness.

In 1803 the British Parliament brought into effect the first legislation to specifically deal with passengers aboard ships; the Passenger Vessels Act, 1803,[16] – *to regulate transportation of immigrants and to protect emigrants on board ship from exploitation by transportation companies, such as exorbitant rates and poor sanitary conditions.* The Act imposed better conditions relating to hygiene, food and comfort on passenger ships going to 'His Majesty's Plantations and Colonies in North America'. However, this law was not always rigorously applied by captains and the spread of contagious diseases accelerated.[17] Due to endemic overcrowding on emigrant ships, the Act introduced a relationship between tonnage and the maximum number of passengers and crew, including children, who could be carried. The ship was not to sail with more than one person, (including children and crew) to every two tons.[18] Although the Act was introduced to deal with humanitarian issues, an unintended consequence was a marked increase in the cost of passage, which acted as an impediment to emigration, possibly intentionally. Landlords feared the loss of their workers and tenants through emigration and lobbied extensively for this legislation. As a result, where it had previously been possible to emigrate to Canada for £3–4, the price for the same passage after introduction of the Act was, in some cases, more than £10. The ability to emigrate was consequently limited to a smaller and wealthier class of people.

The 1803 Act was amended a number of times in the following years to extend its coverage to Newfoundland,[19] Labrador,[20] the United States,[21] and to British Colonies in North America.[22] All of these Acts were repealed by The Passengers Vessels Act, 1823[23] – *An Act for Regulating the Carriage of Passengers from England to Foreign Parts,* which was in turn repealed by the Passenger Vessels Act, 1825.[24] These Statutes dealt solely with passenger welfare.

There was large loss of life in a number of shipwrecks during the early nineteenth century; many of them emigrant ships. It was estimated by Lloyds that a ship a day was lost in the year 1800 and an average of 1000 seamen were ultimately to be lost per year throughout the nineteenth century.[25] Many of these ships carried large numbers of crew and passengers although the average sailing ship was very small. Not all deaths were the direct result of unseaworthiness or overloading. Many were caused by navigational errors or simply force of weather. Seafaring, in the age of sail, was an inherently very dangerous occupation.

Almost 1000 persons were lost in one year alone, from the wrecks of four ships early in the century, many of them troops involved in the Napoleonic Wars. The East Indiaman ***Earl of Abergavenny,*** with about 400 persons on board, sailed from Portsmouth for the East Indies on 01 February 1805. On 15 February, when at anchor in the Portland roads, the ship struck the Shambles reef about two miles offshore. The decision was made to run the ship ashore and, despite the best endeavours of the crew, the ship became a total loss and 300 souls were lost.[26] The same year 340 persons were lost on the emigrant ship ***Ameas*** off Newfoundland and a further 300 were lost when the ***Aurora,*** carrying troops from Monktown, Ireland to Hanover to take part in the Napoleonic War, was wrecked on the Goodwin Sands.[27] Half the 26th Regiment of Foot were lost in the wrecks of both the ***Aurora*** and another ship in the convoy of three, the ***Maria,*** on the Haak Sands off Texel. All were lost on the ***Aurora*** and only 17 survived from the ***Maria***. In December 1805 a total of eight British troopships were lost along with their crews and 2000 troops on their way to Bremen.[28]

England, and her shifting cast of Continental allies, had been engaged in the Revolutionary Wars with France from 1793 until the uneasy, and short lived, peace brought about by the Amiens agreement in 1802. However, 'the Treaty of Amiens had nothing but mistrust'. Bonaparte taunted the British Government that 'in London there are two factions struggling for power; one of them has made peace, the other has sworn implacable hatred to France. While this partisan strife lasts, the Republic must take precautions. Half a million must be ready to defend and avenge her... Alone England can never resist her!'[29] By mid-May 1803, after protracted negotiations between Britain and France had failed, hostilities resumed and were to continue, with a brief respite during Bonaparte's incarceration on Elba, until his defeat at Waterloo in 1815. The scale of involvement of merchant ships as troop transports is demonstrated by the fleet gathered off Deal, Kent, in July 1809 readying for an expedition to destroy Antwerp. 40,000 men were embarked aboard nearly 400 transports, along with over two-hundred men-of-war, thirty-seven of which were temporarily fitted out to transport horses.[30]

Troop transports were often merchant ships of all sizes depending upon need, often carrying great numbers of troops, their equipment, arms and horses. Upon news of Bonaparte's escape from Elba and re-entry to France in 1815, troops were immediately dispatched to Europe aboard small transports of shallow draft, owing to sandbars at Ostend. The 16th Light Dragoons were carried aboard colliers that could carry between ten and thirty-five horses 'standing on a ballast of beach stones with their backs to the boats sides and a manger down the centre to which they were tied'. The 16th disembarked by throwing the horses overboard and them hauling them ashore by a long rope attached to their head-collars. Other ships discharged theirs by 'swing-pulleys' with the troops wading into the water to bring them ashore. Twenty to thirty of these small ships would discharge their cargoes and then return for another voyage.[31]

These long and seemingly unending hostilities had a profound effect upon merchant shipping and seafarers. Many thousands of merchant seamen answered the call to man the increasing number of warships being rapidly brought into service and impressment was enforced without stint. The requirement under the Navigation Acts for three quarters of the crew of a merchant ship to be English was relaxed, along with apprentices of fishing smacks and certain other crew being free from impressment for two years. It was common for East Indiamen, anchored in the Downs after a six month voyage to India, to be boarded and their seamen impressed into the Royal

Navy.[32] To compound the problem, both English and French ships were subject to capture during the wars resulting in many British seamen sailing under the American flag and British shipowners investing in American ships. The English Government, annoyed by this wholesale desertion to American ships, insisted upon their right of search for British subjects. British warships 'took out those sailors who could not make good their claim to American citizenship. This became a prominent cause of the war with America, declared in 1812'.[33]

Another significant factor in the fortunes of British shipping at this time was the outcome of the 1812 to 1815 war with America; a war largely fought for reasons of trade, with blockades of American ports to prevent trade with France, and 'recovery' by the Royal Navy of British seamen from American registered ships. America had previously, as a British colony, enjoyed the benefits of the Navigation Acts and their ships traded freely between British and American ports. After gaining their independence, when their ships were treated by the British as foreign vessels, the Americans retaliated in 1790 to 1792 with the introduction of their own version of the Navigation Act which prevented British ships from carrying British goods into the America.[34]

In 1814, six months before the Battle of Waterloo, a peace treaty[35] was signed between Britain and America, one of the provisions of which was that the Navigation Laws of both countries were mutually rescinded; the first approach to reciprocity of trade granted by the English Government in centuries. 'The war had been disastrous for American foreign trade with a reduction from fifty to four million tons in three years'.[36] With the end of the Napoleonic Wars in 1815 shipping in Great Britain entered a ten year long slump. Despite the wars the British merchant fleet had increased to 24,418 vessels with a capacity of 2,616,000 tons burthen.[37] However, many of the ships were old and chasing insufficient cargoes; the advent of peace reintroduced a large number of ships that had been employed in Government service, and British and American ships, under the Treaty of Ghent, could carry cargo both ways across the North Atlantic, rather than in ballast for one of the passages.[38]

> The effect of peace and of the American Treaty was to depress British shipping so that tonnage was absolutely at a standstill for many years.

> There were several reasons for this. 'In the first place, the accession of peace threw upon the market a large amount of tonnage which had been employed by the Government; and, in the next place, both British and American ships, which had been travelling the Atlantic in ballast, were now getting cargoes both ways; and the curious fact is seen that American tonnage was for years in the same position. On the other hand, the shipping of the British colonies, principally in Canada, doubled itself in twenty years'.[39] A separate and unrelated initiative affecting freedom of trade was when the Government, in 1813, had thrown open the centuries old right of the venerable East India Company to trade exclusively to the East coast of India, due to opposition from some of the principal ports in England to this long-standing monopoly.

At the turn of the century there was a significant development in efficiency of the steam engines that had been powering the industrial revolution during the eighteenth century. Until the end of the eighteenth century steam engines had been 'atmospheric', using very low pressure and large boilers. The challenge, to obtain more power, was to design a boiler of sufficient strength to withstand the forces involved with design of the high-pressure engines necessary for steam locomotion over land, and the sea. This challenge was met and solved by Richard Trevithick of Cornwall who presented his prototype publicly in late 1801 and was granted a patent; 'Steam engines – Improvements in the construction thereof and Application thereof for driving carriages' in March 1802. This was a landmark in the history of steam, as described by H.W. Dickinson in *A Short History of the Steam Engine*;[40] 'It is difficult at the present day to realize what fundamental changes were involved in introducing the high-pressure engine. The ponderous beam see-sawing in a massive engine house crowded with valve gear, air pump and condenser, costly to install and run, was replaced by a faster-running direct-acting engine with a simple valve gear, occupying little space, requiring hardly any foundation, cheap in first cost and easy to work'.[41] It was of even greater significance for the development of ever larger and more powerful steamships and resulted in rapid growth of steam ship services on coastwise voyages.

The steamship had arrived, and Scotland became the principal home of ship construction, engine design and building for the entire nineteenth century and beyond. The first commercial steamships were in a tiny minority with one steam vessel registered in Britain in 1814 and one more in the colonies,[42] increasing to 24 and 8 respectively in 1819. [43] As these small vessels operated mainly in local waters they had little or no impact upon the navigation of the thousands of trading sailing vessels, but their power and reliability made a great impression on the public who now began to appreciate the value of steamers. Prejudice vanished and travel by sea increased with such rapidity that, in 1816, it was not unusual for 500 or 600 passengers to enjoy, in the course of one day, water excursions on the Clyde'.[44] In 1815, the steam paddle wheeler ***Margery,*** built in Glasgow, was towed to London for service on the Thames. The ship was bought by a French company in 1816 for operation on the Seine and became the first steamer to cross the English Channel when proceeding from Newhaven to the mouth of the Seine on its delivery voyage.

As early as 1819 a small American 'side wheeler', the ***Savannah***; a converted sailing ship of 350 tons, took 25 days to complete a passage between New York and Liverpool, but, as it used its steam propulsion for only eighty hours[45] this could not be claimed as the first trans-Atlantic crossing solely under steam power. The voyage of the ***Savanah*** emphasised the Achilles heel of steam propulsion at this time. No vessel could undertake a long ocean passage due to inability to carry sufficient coal for the voyage. Steam power was, accordingly, confined to coastal voyages with ready access to fuel until vessels increased in size and fuel capacity, and steam engines became more efficient.

The first regular steamship service in Great Britain was inaugurated by the ***Comet*** in 1819 between Glasgow and the Western Highlands and only operated for one year before the little ship was wrecked off the coast of Argyll in December 1820.[46] The same year, the first steamship company was formed in England, the General Steam Navigation Company, with their first ship, the 401 ton ***City of Edinburgh,*** being built in 1821.[47] The first scheduled Cross Channel service was operated by the ***Rob Roy,*** of 90 tons with a 30 HP engine, and the ***Prince Coburg,*** a steam packet, commenced service to the Isle of Wight; a service extended to Le Havre in 1823.[48] By 1822 forty-eight steamers had been launched from the Clyde.[49] In 1823 the recorded numbers of steamships, in Britain and the colonies respectively, were 101 and 10 requiring an amendment to tonnage measurement law to allow for the non-earning space occupied by the steam propulsion machinery.[50] Steamships steadily grew in size, power and speed, with the ***United Kingdom*** of 1826 being 175 feet long and 500 tons with an engine of 200 horsepower.[51]

There was much interest at this time in extending the range of steamships, not least to severely test the reliability of steam machinery. In 1825 the East India Company chartered the 470-ton paddle steamer ***Enterprise*** to undertake a passage to India via Capetown, which the ship achieved in 113 days, 103 of which were solely under steam power. The passage time was similar to that achieved by the company's sailing ships. Keen observers of this increasing and expanding use of steam propulsion were the Admiralty who, after the Napoleonic wars, had become responsible for postal services to British possessions, delivering those services with small sailing packets. By 1830 their Lordships were confident enough of the benefits of steam propulsion to commence replacing their sailing vessels with steam ships, bringing about, for example, a reduction in a round voyage from the UK to Corfu from three months to one month.[52]

During this period of rapid developments in steam propulsion there were no scheduled passenger services across the stormy, fogbound and ice strewn North Atlantic. However, in 1815, with the end of the Napoleonic and North American conflicts, and the Ghent Treaty opening up trade between the United States and Great Britain, an opportunity arose for American designed and built ships to enter this challenging trade with sailing vessels far superior to their British counterparts in design, operation and crewing.

British ships and trades were still bound by the tonnage requirements of the Navigation Acts;[53] a regulatory regime focussed upon protection of trade to British colonies and possessions, which had, for two centuries, stifled any significant improvements in their design and performance. The mandatory tonnage rules had resulted in 'narrow, deep, flat-sided and full bottomed-ships – bad vessels in a seaway, slow, and often requiring a considerable quantity of ballast, even when loaded, to keep them from rolling over'.[54] An added factor in the lack of progress in ship design was the dominance over this same time frame of the Honourable East India Company ('The United Company of Merchant Venturers of England trading to the East Indies'), founded in 1600 under a Royal charter which gave the 'John Company' the exclusive right to trade to East India and China. The East Indiamen were designed and operated along the same lines as naval frigates, including two decks of guns and large crews, but were more full-bodied for cargo carrying. They were, however, slow and cumbersome and undertook cautious passages with safety and comfort for the passengers foremost. Their guaranteed trade stifled initiative and development, with the ships remaining essentially unaltered for more than two hundred years and having the same design and stability shortcomings as other British merchant ships.[55]

During the late eighteenth century the predominant nation for ship design and construction was France. The finest frigates in the Royal Navy were captured French ships. During the Revolutionary war a number of French luggers and frigates operated in American waters and, when in dock, their lines were taken off by American shipwrights and studied as to the reasons why the French ships were so much faster. This resulted in fast American styled frigates, and privateers; ships that outsailed their British opponents; both warships and merchantmen, during the war of 1812.

In the early nineteenth century sailing ships ran to no set schedule but sailed when they were fully loaded. In 1817 the American Black Ball line introduced a scheduled service between New York and Liverpool with four full rigged sailing ships carrying mail, passengers and cargo. Known as 'packet boats' as they were carrying packets of mail under a Government subsidy, the ships ranged initially from 300 to 500 registered tons and averaged passages during their first 10 years of operation of 23 days Eastbound, and 40 days Westbound into the prevailing westerlies;

> Their Captains were the finest men whose services money could secure, and to their care were entrusted the lives of eminent men and women, government despatches, the mails and specie. Rain or shine, blow high, blow low, one of the Black Ball liners sailed from New York for Liverpool on the first and sixteenth of each month, and for many years these were the European mail days throughout the United States.[56]

A number of other American owned lines entered the 'packet trade' with the size of the ships slowly increasing until, in the 1840s when they were competing with steamships, ships of 1400 tons were being built. 'By the late 1830s, twenty packet ships were running from New York to Liverpool, and sixteen to Le Havre. Every month a dozen packets left New York for Europe and a dozen more arrived; an average of one ship every thirty hours, all year long'[57]. The fastest passage recorded by a sailing packet was 14 days Eastbound and 16 days Westbound[58] but these were exceptional voyages. When the sailing packets were at their heyday the threat of competition from steam ships arose, as, with improved steam engines of greater power, and more economical fuel consumption, it became theoretically possible to traverse the 3000 miles from the United Kingdom to the United States in 15 days. This thinking was made possible by the development of the side-lever engine which lowered the weight, and centre of gravity, of the engine/s to reduce rolling and pitching at sea. Construction of the engine was in wrought iron, rather than cast iron, further reducing its weight. The engine was designed to be very strong and reliable for ocean crossings, and proved to so be. Boiler pressure was still limited due to inherent weaknesses in boiler construction, limiting pressure to a modest five pounds per square inch and increasing fuel consumption.

> An added complication to the undertaking of long voyages under steam was that of the necessity to mix cold seawater with steam in a condenser to cool the steam to condense it back to water and generate a vacuum. This saline feed water resulted in rapid scaling of the inside of the boiler plates, tubes and steam pipework as described by Colin Fleetney in an article published in *Paddle Wheels* in 1969.[59]
>
> On a voyage lasting more than two or three days the boilers became foul, and the feed water increasingly more saline. It then became necessary to shut down, blow down, empty and clean each boiler in turn. I have intentionally omitted 'cool' from this list. Long before the boilers had time to cool the black gang would be inside, attending to this terrible job. In fair weather, or foul, each boiler demanded the attention of these toiling half-naked men. Neglect of the job could result in burnt plates and the very real possibility of an explosion. In 1834 this problem was largely solved through the introduction of the surface condenser; an iron container with an array of internal thin brass tubes through which the cool seawater was pumped so that the spent steam condensed on the outside of the tubes.[60]
>
> In spite of these limitations, the first ship to complete an east-bound crossing of the North Atlantic, from Halifax, Nova Scotia to Cowes on

the Isle of Wight, almost entirely under steam power, was the Canadian built Royal William (1831); 160 feet long and 1370 gross tons, fitted with a paddle wheels and a 200 HP steam engine and rigged as a three-masted schooner. The Royal William had been built to operate on the difficult route between Halifax, Montreal and Quebec; a route which sailing ships, due to fog, ice and/or adverse currents would sometimes take five weeks to complete. The ship was placed into the management of a shipping agent in Halifax who'd been managing mail ships operating between Halifax, Boston and St. Johns, Newfoundland and as far afield as Bermuda for a number of years and who had earned a good reputation with British authorities. When asked in 1829 to become involved in a scheme for a steamship he'd stated 'We are entirely unacquainted with the cost of a Steam Boat and should not like to embark in a business of which we are quite ignorant and must therefore decline taking any part in the one you propose getting up'.[61]

This American, born into a Quaker family exiled to Nova Scotia after the American Revolution, was Samuel Cunard. Within a year of the above statement he had shrewdly obtained the power of general management and control of funds for a company which raised money to build a steamship for the Halifax, Montreal, Quebec route. After two unsuccessful years the Royal William was sold in 1833. After an abortive return trip to Boston under the new owners it was decided to send her to England to be sold again; a voyage conceived in financial desperation. She left Nova Scotia on 18 August 1833 with only seven intrepid passengers, 324 tons of coal and virtually no cargo and completed the voyage in nineteen days in spite of having to stop every four days to de-scale her boiler. Upon eventually proceeding to London from Cowes the ship was sold to the Portuguese Government.[62]

Although there was a complete void in legislation concerning the safety and seaworthiness of ships at this time, there was ongoing concern and interest from some individuals in these matters with attempts, usually unsuccessful, to bring them to the attention of Parliamentarians. In 1814, one Cadogan Williams had unsuccessfully attempted to submit a petition to Parliament through Lord Stanhope; a statesman and scientist, to increase the safety of merchant vessels by requiring four separate waterproof compartments, "so that if a leak were to spring in either of them it would not always endanger the safety of the ship, as her buoyancy would not be diminished one-third with some description of cargo". Stanhope agreed and told Williams that he had already submitted a similar plan to the Lords of the Admiralty for thirteen compartments. Undeterred, Williams presented the same petition in September 1831 to the House of Commons Committee on Steam Navigation, for the safety of steam vessels; again unsuccessfully.[63]

> A seaman at this time led a life of hardship and danger and had constant concerns regarding his employment, health, life, injury, living conditions and remuneration. 'Given a background of a general recession after the end of the Napoleonic War, government indifference, legislative quiescence and inferior vessels it is hardly surprising that the sailor's lot was unenviable. His wages had fallen 40% between the end of the Napoleonic wars in 1815 and 1833, and in the latter year the workforce was some 14% smaller than in the former'.[64]

Long hours were common in all walks of life, but seamen had the additional burden of broken and irregular rest periods due to the watch-and-watch system that gave them no more than three and a half hours of sleep at a time. Until the nineteenth-century was well advanced legislation relating to conditions for seamen centred chiefly on discipline and liability for naval service. Britain was at war for fifty of the seventy five years from 1740 to 1815, and with no long-service ratings in the Royal Navy the Imprest Service was more likely to be active than idle in those years. It was estimated that, during the 15 year Napoleonic wars, 30,000 merchant seamen were in naval service. [65] Many of these ended up begging on the streets in 1815 due to a severe downturn in merchant shipping.[66]

> The end of the French war also saw 200,000 disbanded soldiers and sailors flooding the labour market. Government spending fell, and recession set in, causing widespread disorder. At home post-war demobilization and the adjustment to a peace-time economy brought widespread unemployment, social hardship and a long and difficult Tory administration under Robert Jenkinson, second Earl of Liverpool. Even after Liverpool's fall in 1827 he was succeeded by Tories: Canning, Lord Rippon briefly, and the Duke of Wellington, so it was 1830 before the election of Charles, Earl Grey, a Whig, initiated the belated reform of Parliament and the much needed social improvements which, in Britain at least, characterized the later 19th Century.[67]

In spite of the relaxation of trade restrictions between Britain and America 'the 1815 Parliament, still representing the landed interest', introduced an Importation Act which imposed a tariff on imported wheat as a means of sustaining farm incomes. This 'Corn Law' increased the price of bread and led to riots in the cities, while in the factories so-called Luddites smashed labour-saving machinery. This unrest, which was widespread across the provinces, terrified the authorities, with their recent memories of the 'sans culottes' of Paris. After the 'Peterloo massacre' in 1819 Liverpool was shocked into passing six acts as draconian as those of Pitt, restricting freedom of speech, publication and assembly; meeting to promote reform was considered 'an overt act of treasonable conspiracy'.[68] The Corn Laws proved to be an additional barrier to free trade for the thirty years they were in effect until finally being repealed in 1846. In the next few years restrictions of trade under the Navigation Acts lessened, brought about by the so-called 'sole-market' theory; a doctrine that nations should restrict trade to ships under their flag and crewed by their nationals, thus confining all foreign imports to their own ships and refusing to receive the products of other countries in ships registered in their countries.

Seamen had been regulated since at least the Navigation Act, 1660, but not regarding matters of safety, welfare and living conditions. The Navigation Acts had nothing to do with navigation as in ensuring a ship was safely navigated from one place to another, but in protection of trade as stated in s.1 of the 1660 Act; *For the increase of shipping and encouragement of the navigation of this nation wherein, under the good providence and protection of God, the wealth, safety, and strength of this kingdom is so much concerned.* The original focus of the 1660 Act was upon ensuring that British ships carried British goods to British colonies as stipulated in s.7 and that they must be crewed with a defined proportion of British seamen; the Master and at least three quarters of the crew, except in times of war. This requirement largely survived until repeal of the Navigation Acts in 1849.

Further relaxation of the Navigation Acts came about in 1823 when Prussia, recalling the actions of the Americans in 1812, closed its ports to British ships. This directly led to enactment of the so-called Reciprocity Acts[69] in 1823 and 1824 whereby the King in Council was empowered to grant reciprocity to such nations as would place them on an equal footing in matters of trade to Britain. 'Thus the back of our navigation law was broken, although it survived for some years longer'.[70] The Acts also had the effect of rejuvenating trade and reversing the effects of the ten year long slump in shipping; the legacy of William Huskisson, President of the Board of Trade and an active proponent of free trade.

A series of Acts had dealt with the regulation and administration of seamen, dating from *An Act for the Increase of Seamen, and better Encouragement of Navigation and Security of the Coal Trade*[71] in 1703, to the Merchant Seamen Act 1833[72] – *An Act for Facilitating the Recovery of the Wages of Seamen in the Merchant Service.* These Acts covered such matters as prevention of desertion, seamen in the coasting trade, relief of seafaring men and boys, numbers of apprentices, and recovery of wages (in cases of desertion). The Acts also had a prime purpose of ensuring that there were sufficient merchant seamen available to crew Royal Naval vessels in time of war.

Meanwhile, at sea, loss of life continued. Another wreck causing large loss of life to the military was that of the transport ***Seahorse***, wrecked in Tramore Bay, Ireland on 30 January 1816. The ship was carrying 16 officers and 279 soldiers of the 2nd/59 Regiment along with 71 women and children, a crew of eighteen and a young Naval officer. Only 30 survived the wreck.[73] The same year a total of 371 British ships were wrecked with the entire crews of sixteen ships being lost along with another 940 souls.[74]

In 1820, Robert Seppings, later to become Surveyor of the Navy, unsuccessfully attempted to have the advanced methods of construction he'd introduced aboard naval ships while Master Shipwright at Chatham, to merchant ships. But no progress was made; 'overbuilt, capacious, burdensome vessels still continue in repute with British shipowners, which necessarily induces shipbuilders to build them of that description and form. They build them to answer the rules of classification laid down at Lloyd's, and if they were to build on a superior principle they would get no credit for their pains.'[75]

During the terrible Northern European winter of 1820, 2000 ships and 20,000 seafarers were lost in the North Sea,[76] and the carnage continued both in terms of ships and numbers of persons lost, throughout the 1820s and 1830s without any form of responsive safety regulation for ships. Clearly, not all of these losses were due to unseaworthy ships or overloading. Many were inevitably, in the age of sail, due to age old 'perils of the sea''; force of weather, ice, collision, embayment and stranding. Lloyd's List recorded that 677 British ships were lost in 1830.[77]

In 1828 the Passengers in Merchant Vessels Act[78] was introduced – An Act to Regulate the Carriage of Passengers in Merchant Vessels from the United Kingdom to the Continent and Islands of North America. The Act continued to deal solely with passenger welfare.

Conditions for seamen were primitive. W.S. Lindsay[79], who was at sea in a 420-ton timber and sugar carrier in 1834, has left the following vivid pen-picture of his life on board.

> The cook, ten seamen and three apprentices had their abode in the forecastle. This place, which was in the 'tween decks at the extremity of the bow, may have been about twenty-one feet in width at the after or widest part, tapering gradually away to a narrow point at the stem. The length in midships was somewhere about twenty feet, but much less as the sides of the vessel were approached. The height was five feet from deck to beam, or about five feet nine inches from deck to deck; the only approach to it being through a scuttle or hole in the main deck, about two and a half feet square. Beyond this hole there was no means of obtaining either ventilation or light, and in bad weather, when the sea washed over the deck, the crew had to do as best they could without either, or receive the air mixed with spray, and sometimes accompanied by the almost unbroken crest of a wave, which in defiance to all tarpaulin guards, too frequently found its way through the scuttle. Here fourteen persons slept in hammocks suspended from the beams and had their daily food. There was no room for tables, chairs or stools so the tops of their sea chests in which they kept their clothes and all their worldly possessions were substituted for those useful and necessary household articles. ... At all times it was a foulsome and suffocating abode, and in bad weather the water and filth which washed about the desk and among the chests and casks created the most intolerable and loathsome stench. Here, however, these fourteen sailors and apprentices slept, washed, dressed and had their food, except in fine weather, when they took their meals on deck, their food consisting almost entirely of inferior salted pork or beef, which was sometimes as hard and unpalatable as the kits in which it was served, and brown biscuits, too often mouldy and full of maggots.

> There were no sanitary arrangements for seamen in this period, and the 'heads' in the bows of vessels were a sea-washed area beneath the bowsprit without privacy or comfort. Inadequate clothing led to 'ship-fever' or typhus in cold climates, with the disease transmitted by body lice, while yellow fever, malaria and bubonic plague were picked up in the tropics. The diet of salt meat and long baked biscuit meant that scurvy was common on 'foreign'.
>
> The combination of poor food and living conditions, hard work, exposure to the elements and ship-borne diseases ensured that seamen were poor physical specimens. A study on sea medicine in the late eighteenth century noted that seamen were 'in general short, and have their constitutions worn out ten years before the rest of the laborious part of mankind. A seaman at the age of 45, if shewn to a person not accustomed to be among them, would be taken by his looks to be 55, or even on the borders of 60.[80]

The officers of these vessels were practical seamen, brought up in the school of hard knocks with no formal training or qualifications, who'd learnt their trade on deck and generally lacked both the competence and equipment for precise navigation. 'It was rare to meet with a scientific, efficient navigator, and not one ship in a hundred was furnished with a chronometer'.[81]

All of the extant Merchant Seamen Acts introduced since 1703 were repealed through the first major consolidation Act of the nineteenth century; the Merchant Seamen Act, 1835[82] – *An Act to amend and consolidate the Laws relating to Merchant Seamen of the United Kingdom, and for forming and maintaining a Register of all the Men engaged in that Service.* The requirement of s.19 of the Act; establishment of a General Register Office of Merchant Seamen, continued a form of registration of seamen first set up by the 1696 Navigation Act.[83]

The preamble to the 1835 Act made it clear that the prime purpose of the 'register of all the Men engaged in that Service' was to ensure the Royal Navy was adequately manned in times of war, and that the carriage of cargoes was a secondary consideration;

> Whereas the prosperity, Strength and Safety of this United Kingdom and of His Majesty's Dominions do principally depend on a large,

> constant and ready Supply of Seamen, as well for carrying the Commerce as for the Defence thereof; and it is therefore necessary to aid by all practicable Means the Increase in the Number of such Seamen, and to give them all due encouragement and Protection, and to this end to amend and consolidate the Laws relating to their Regulation and Government…

A significant provision, in the context of seaworthiness of ships, was Part IV of the Act that stated;

> And be it further enacted, That in case a Seaman shall at any time, after having signed an Agreement as herein-before mentioned, neglect or refuse to join the Ship on board of which he shall have engaged to serve, or shall refuse to proceed to sea in her, or shall himself therefrom without Leave, it shall be lawful for any Justice of the Peace in any of his Majesty's Dominions at Home or Abroad near to such place as the Ship shall happen to be, upon Complaint made upon Oath by the Master, Mate of Owner thereof, and such justice is hereby required, by his Warrant to cause such Seaman to be apprehended and brought before him; and in case such Seaman shall not give a Reason to the Satisfaction of Such Justice for his Neglect, Refusal or Absence as the Case may be, upon due Proof of such Neglect, Refusal, or Absence it shall be lawful for any such Justice to commit such Seaman to the House of correction, there to be kept to a period of hard Labour for a Period not exceeding Thirty Days; Provided always, that in case such Seaman, upon being apprehended and brought before a Justice, shall consent to join the Ship and proceed on the Voyage for which he shall have agreed, it shall be lawful for the said Justice, at the request of the Master, instead of committing such Seaman, to cause him to be conveyed aboard the said Ship or to be delivered to the Master for the purpose of proceeding on the Voyage, and also to award the Master such Costs incurred in the Apprehension of the Seaman as to such Justice shall deem reasonable.

This punitive provision, the severity of which was to be increased later in the century, became central to the vexed issue of seamen refusing to sail aboard overloaded or unseaworthy ships for the greater part of the nineteenth century.

The sailing ships of this era were comparatively small but, as many also carried emigrants, they carried disproportionately large numbers of people. The old and generally unseaworthy ships used to carry timber from the Canadian colony to the United Kingdom, were entirely unsuitable for their normal practice of carrying the emigrants on the otherwise empty return voyage. In his Treatise on the Law relative to Merchant Ships and Seaman, [84] Abbot states that;

> ...during 1834, no fewer than seventeen ships, with passengers on board, bound for Quebec, were wrecked on the passage, seven hundred and thirty-one emigrants losing their lives in consequence, while many more lost most part of their property, and were reduced to the greatest distress. Emigrants to Quebec are mostly taken out in ships engaged in the timber trade, and it is well known, that speaking generally, these are a very inferior class, it being the usual practice to turn worn-out ships unfit to carry dry cargoes into this department. Most part of the catastrophes alluded to may, we are assured, be ascribed to this circumstance, and to the misconduct of the master and crews.

Typical of these ships were the barque ***Lady Sherbrooke,*** 377 tons, which, whilst on passage from Londonderry to Quebec, carrying 285 passengers and 15 crew, was wrecked in a gale near Cape Ray, Newfoundland on 16 August 1831; 235 persons were lost.[85] In nearby waters, in 1833, the emigrant ship ***Lady of the Lake*** struck ice and sank within twenty minutes. Some of the crew and passengers escaped in the only two boats but 265 were lost[86]. In September 1834 the ***Sibylle***, an emigrant ship out of Cromarty, Ireland, was wrecked at St. Paul Island, Nova Scotia. 300 were lost.[87]

In 1835 the Passengers in Merchant Vessels Act, 1828 was repealed through introduction of the Merchant Vessels etc. Act, 1835[88] – *An Act to repeal an Act of the Ninth Year of His late Majesty, for regulating the Carriage of Passengers in Merchant Vessels from the United Kingdom to the British Possessions on the Continent and Islands of North America; and to make further Provision for regulating the Carriage of Passengers from the United Kingdom.* The Act remained primarily concerned with the welfare of passengers; largely emigrants, but introduced, in Part VII, a new word into British nineteenth century legislative language – 'sea-worthy';

> And be it further enacted, That if Doubts shall arise whether any Ship

> about to proceed with Passengers as aforesaid is Sea-worthy, so as to be fit for her intended voyage, and such Doubts shall not be removed to the Satisfaction of the Commissioner and Comptroller of Customs at the port from which such Vessel is to be cleared out, it shall be lawful for such Commissioner and Comptroller at any Time to cause such Ship to be surveyed by Two competent persons; and if it shall be reported by those Persons that such Ship is not in their Opinion Sea-worthy with reference to such Voyage, such Ship shall not be cleared out unless the Contents of such Report be disproved to the Satisfaction of the Commissioners of Customs, or until such Ship shall have been rendered Sea-worthy.

Excerpts from the introduction by William Gladstone of the Passengers Act Bill in March 1835, and the ensuing debate, shed some light on the reasons for inclusion of a requirement for seaworthy vessels in the emigrant trade;

> ……and, secondly, whether some mode of surveying vessels as to their sea-worthiness could not be adopted by the revenue officers? He should not refer to any documents, of which he possessed an abundance, to prove the necessity of the measure, as he should assume it would meet with no opposition; but he should merely allude to the returns of the total amount of emigration in each year since the passing of the Act (1828) to be repealed, for the purpose of disproving the arguments then generally adduced against all legislative interference with the subject:— (total passengers carried per year had steadily increased from 12,000 in 1828 to 51,000 in 1832).
>
> In 1833 and 1834, there was rather a diminution, but that was entirely attributable to the improved state of the country. These numbers proved that the passing of the Act had not decreased, as it was asserted it would, emigration from this country; but, on the contrary, materially increased it. He should also beg to refer the House, in support of the necessity of the measure he proposed to introduce to its notice, the Report of the Emigrants' Friend Society for the present year. The hon. Member concluded by making his Motion.
>
> Mr Hume MP replied that it was true he had opposed the Bill of 1828, because he believed that all minute legislative interference on such subjects was vicious as well as unnecessary. He thought that there were three duties which it was imperative upon the Government to

> perform. The first was to see that the vessels carrying emigrants were trustworthy, and not what was commonly called coffin ships; the second was to see that the emigrants were protected from imposition by fair contracts with those who conveyed them; and the third was to take care that the vessels had on board provisions adequate to the length of the voyage and to the number of passengers.
>
> Mr Baring MP...Last year seventeen vessels had been wrecked, and seven hundred lives of emigrants chiefly Irish, had been sacrificed, and the accidents had almost all arisen from improvidence and mismanagement. He thought it the duty of the House to interfere in behalf of those who were so helpless....
>
> Mr Patrick Stewart MP thought that the Bill would be useful in all its branches. He thought that the sea-worthiness of the ships ought to be ascertained by Government officers on their responsibility. He trusted that all the hon. Member's measures would be as useful as this promised to be.... Leave given to bring in the Bill.[89]

At this time there was no legislation ensuring the seaworthiness of ships, or safety of crew and passengers. The initiative to include a provision in a Bill on passenger welfare whereby seaworthiness could be determined by competent persons reveals the complete lack of an effective Government body with oversight of maritime safety. This situation; not to be remedied until 1850, may explain why maritime safety provisions started to be bolted on to longstanding passenger welfare statutes; a practice that was to continue even after development of maritime safety legislation, leading to ambiguity and misalignment of critical safety provisions such as carriage of lifeboats. It also reflects an ongoing dichotomy throughout the nineteenth century whereby the lives and welfare of passengers assumed a far greater importance in the minds of legislators than those of the crews of the ships they travelled aboard.

It is not clear what particular development or events prompted this initiative but the Parliamentary debate on introduction of the above Bill would indicate it may have been a result of the widely expressed concern at this time regarding shipwreck; particularly the large loss of life aboard emigrant ships to North America. Concern had been widespread for a considerable time at the large numbers of ships and seamen lost as recalled by an article in The Monthly Review of May 1838;

> The rapid increase in the number of shipwrecks between the years 1800 and 1836, created considerable excitement some short time since, and led to the inquiry of a parliamentary committee on the subject. It is an ascertained fact, and one which merits the deep consideration of the British public, that shipwrecks have been very much upon the increase during the last ten years. By returns from the books at Lloyd's, it appears that for a period of three years, from 1814 to 1818, the number of ships wrecked and missing amounted to 1,203, while the number lost from 1833 to 1835 amount to 1,702. The loss of property occasioned by these wrecks is estimated at £6,015,000 for the first period, being an average of £2,005,000 per annum: and for the second period £8,510,000, being an average of £2,836,666 per annum. The loss of life, which to the shipping interest seems a secondary consideration to the loss of property, has been estimated for the first period at 2,228 or 763 per annum; and for the second period 2,682 or 864 lives per annum. During a period of four years 272 vessels were lost from the port of Tyne alone, and assuming them to have been total losses, and the value of the whole to be £10 per ton, the loss of property from this single port would average £151,222 per annum. The number of lives lost in the above-mentioned period was 682, and the amount of money paid out of the Seamen's Association of Shields, for relief of members of that society, only amounted to £1935. 15s. 9d. The entries in Lloyd's books are far from embracing the whole extent of loss of property by shipwreck in the United Kingdom; but calculating from them, and allowing for the losses of which no record is preserved, it has been assumed that the annual loss of property in British shipping may be estimated at three millions sterling; while the annual loss of life has, on the same grounds, been very fairly estimated at one thousand souls.

It was clearly time for the Government to investigate the causes of shipwrecks and legislate to improve the safety of ships, their crews and passengers. 'The extent of the scrutiny and its subsequent agitation was widespread, fed by newspaper articles reporting shipwreck and the brutality of Masters and Mates; indeed, the whole of the British maritime world was in a state of complete unrest, and the minds of shipowners, mariners, and the benevolent public alike was exercised to find a remedy. Public meetings were held throughout the country, notably in Edinburgh, and Parliament was inundated with petitions to inquire into the causes of such increased loss of life. The seamen of Sunderland did the same, specially referring to badly constructed and worn-out ships; marine insurance and its abuse; and the incompetency of masters as to the prevailing causes [of loss of ships] and inter alia prayed the House of commons to 'appoint an experienced nautical committee to examine vessels, their story, the number of the crew and their berths, and into the ability of commanders and officers'.[90]

Chapter 2

Shipwreck and Cannibalism

Throughout the nineteenth century there were a series of reactive Government enquiries into the questions of shipwreck, seaworthiness, overloading, and safety appliances for ships ranging from 1836 to 1889.[91] The first of these was when the Government, no longer able to ignore statistics and public concern, was shamed into action through the regular publication of statistics and details of shipwrecks by the Nautical Magazine from 1832, and by Lloyds Weekly News.[92] Statistics published by the Nautical Magazine showed that in the first eight months of 1832 a total of 404 ships had been lost, with the number of ships lost per year being greater than the number of newly constructed ships.[93] When further publicity was given to this compelling issue by the Edinburgh Review[94] the Government yielded to public pressure and fifteen Members of Parliament were appointed to a Select Committee which undertook its work during 1836.

The Committee; chaired by Silk Buckingham MP, a reformer, and including Members of Parliament Aaron Young and George Fredericks of the shipowners lobby,[95] was charged with inquiring into and answering "such statements and complaints as were now made respecting our Mercantile Marine". Alarming and dramatic testimony was heard on these matters; that the wreckage of British ships was largely on the increase and, consequently, loss of life; that foreign ships were being preferred in foreign ports to British ships, and were commanding better freights; that the reason for this was that foreign ships were better built and that foreign shipmasters were better educated and more careful and their ships were better manned than our own. The Select Committee on Shipwrecks sought the views of a wide range of persons involved in the maritime industry including ships' masters, underwriters, dockmasters, shipowners, seamen's representatives and Lloyds surveyors. Enquiries were made across a wide scope of known issues including unseaworthiness, overloading, construction of ships, insurance, incompetency and sobriety. The new class Rules introduced by Lloyds in 1834 had, for the first time, taken into account the real state and condition of the ship and its age in assigning a Class notation for insurance purposes. Additionally, repaired ships could be reassigned A.1 class for a limited period providing a certain percentage of the timber in their frames was bolted rather than fastened, as was the age-old practice, with wooden dowels.

The committee heard that there would be increased costs of up to one-sixth of the whole cost if ships were bolted together as in the Navy (and as recommended by Spedding in 1820), which would prevent ships from competing successfully with foreign ships, and; '...moreover, if ships were generally filled in in this way, as the risk would be less the premiums of insurances would be reduced in proportion. So that it is neither the interest of the ship owner or underwriter that the principle of safety should be carried to the utmost'. However, in the opinion of one witness to the Committee; "These were very important improvements, and if rigorously carried into effect, would in a great measure have corrected the evil. But with the lax administration of Lloyd's committee they had the effect of lulling the disapprobation of the public, and promoting the system of insurance".[96] There was no compulsion for ships to be in class at this time.[97] Of the 12,000 British vessels in service above 50 tons in 1836, 7000 were in class. It was stated to the enquiry that it is "almost impossible to insure any ship that has not been so registered".

The evidence of Mr. Ballinghall, manager of a shipping company and a surveyor of shipping at Kirkaldy, in response to a question as to whether it was in the interest of the ship owner or underwriter that the principle of safety should be carried to the utmost in construction of a ship was described in the Report as 'curious and decisive';

> Do you think that the additional cost which this would incur, is the chief reason why the ship-owners do not adopt this plan? – "No, I do not. I apprehend if you put a safe ship and an unsafe ship in a ship owner's option at the same price, he will take the unsafe ship and insure it in preference to taking the safe ship and insuring it."
>
> What induces you to think so? – "A very plain reason. If I am proprietor of a vessel costing £1,000, and she is sent on a voyage — if she gets exposed to danger on a rock or sand bank, and if she goes to pieces, I call on the underwriters, and I get the £1,000, the sum she is insured for; but if, instead of going to pieces, she be got off in a damaged state, she must

be repaired, and the underwriter will only pay two-thirds of the amount of the repairs. So that if the repairs amount to £300, he will only pay £200 and the owner must pay the remaining £100 out of his own pocket. This is not all. During the time the vessel is undergoing repairs, the owner must pay the wages and provide the victuals of the master and crew, which may be reckoned at £50, making £150 which the owner will have to pay for his vessel being preserved instead of being lost".

He says this is a very simple abstract question. – "I am a shipowner for the purpose of making money; am I to make £150 or lose it? I have stated £100 and £1,000 in these proportions, but it will hold good with other sums in the same proportions".

For these reasons you think it is more the interest of a shipowner when his ship does get on shore that she should go to pieces and he should recover the whole value than that she should be saved, by which he is put to considerable expense ? – "Decidedly".

You think no ships are built sufficiently strong? – "Most decidedly, not one ship is built sufficiently strong in Britain".

The lack of experience, competence and training of ship's officers, including masters, was highlighted by the report of the committee with examples given of owners placing their sons, as young as 14, in command of their ship:

The next cause of calamities at sea which seems to us most deserving of attention is the incompetency of masters and officers, to which may be appended the drunkenness of officers and men. The greater number of ships in the outports are held by tradesmen in shares, who are totally incapable of judging of the competency of their commanders or the finding of their ships. The instances of the gross ignorance of masters are too numerous to mention. There is no board or office at which any person is required to give proof of his capacity. Even certificates of apprenticeships and fidelity of service are dispensed with. In many instances neither the captain nor any of his crew had served a regular apprenticeship.

The tradesmen who have become part-owners of ships send their sons to sea, and, after they have made a voyage or two, they give them charge of vessels as mates or captains. Mr. Woodroffe states it as a fact that a young man was taken from a butcher's shop to be put in command of a vessel, when neither he nor his mate could make out a common day's work in navigation. Ships with such incompetent commanders are insured to a large amount, very often beyond their actual value. No inquiry is made by the Insurance office as to the character of the commanders; no inquiry is made as to the cause of the loss of a ship by his ignorance or neglect. Some men have been known to lose three or four vessels in a short space of time.

The ignorance and mismanagement of officers leads to the insubordination and carelessness of sailors. They lose all respect for the commander because they know he is not a seaman, and instead of moving with alacrity to the order from the quarter-deck, they stand thunderstruck to see the orders coming promiscuously contrary to the rules of nautical science, and most unquestionably no men have a better right to express their indignation than they have ; for, in case of wreck, they lose either their lives or their property without having any legal claim for wages, after the loss, on the owner, who walks off with the full value of his unseaworthy or mismanaged ship in his pocket.

The Committee heard the following corroboration of these claims from a person referred to as "a highly intelligent witness";

To what do you attribute the appointment of persons of so early an age and so little experience? – "I know several persons who boast of having three or four young sons and nephews in command of ships, and stating that they were in command of ships at eighteen".

Are you acquainted with any case in which a still younger person than that had the command of a vessel? – "Yes: I can mention a lad named Storey, who commanded a ship named the *Headby's* of 270 tons sailing from Belfast to Quebec who was but 14 years of age".

He was nominally the commander, but the authority over the crew would be in some one inferior to himself? – "Yes; he could not manage them. I can only account for it by supposing, probably, his father might have been the owner ; that his father died, and he, coming to the property, possibly might say 'I'll be captain', and as it was his own property nobody could turn him out of it: that he actually did command the ship there is no doubt".

Is it mainly to the youth and incapacity of the commanders that you attribute these losses? – "There is no doubt about it in my mind, having witnessed several hundred instances during the last 18 years".

Witnesses were unanimous in their opinion that drunkenness was rife aboard British ships from the Captain down, due to the ready availability of duty free liquor, and that this led directly to inefficiency, insubordination and losses of ships. In the words of the Select Committee;

Turn we now to the pendant of disasters by ignorance, disasters by drunkenness. This is undoubtedly the greater and more general evil of the two, for even in cases where officers are competent seamen, they render themselves unfit for the exercise of their knowledge and the discharge of their duties by intemperance. This is the chief cause of disasters at sea, — the great impediment to improving the character of seamen.

With regard to the merchant vessels, whole crews are frequently shipped in a state of beastly intoxication, the vessel being worked out of port by substitutes technically termed 'riggers': many vessels have been run ashore by the mismanagement of these bad deputies of drunken seamen, and even on the voyage the actual strength of the ship's company, — so necessary in cases of emergency — is very much diminished in efficiency by the grogginess of a greater or less number of individuals.

A pilot whom he took on board at Dungeness, stated to Mr. Purnell, dock-master of Liverpool, that he frequently boarded ships in the Channel, near, or at the pilot stations, and the first sight that attracted his notice was the captain drunk and stretched on the quarter deck, or some other convenient place, and totally unable to command his ship.'

Are those details at all in accordance with your experience as to what you have either seen, or known, or heard of vessels sailing to and from Liverpool? – "Yes; I believe nine-tenths of all the losses which occur are caused directly or indirectly through intemperance".

Has this subject attracted very much attention at Liverpool among ship-owners and merchants and captains? – "It has; so much so, that some ship-owners have determined on sending their vessels to sea without ardent spirits on board".

> Have any vessels returned or completed their voyage, having gone out without any spirits on board? – "Several".
>
> What has been the impression on the minds of the merchants who tried this experiment, whether it was advantageous or otherwise? – "That it was advantageous".

W.S. Lindsay,[98] who had served aboard sailing ships and later become a shipowner and Member of Parliament, stated; "...although it can scarcely be said that the character of British seamen degenerated from the time of the Declaration of Independence by the American colonies towards the close of the first half of the present century, there is no doubt that those of other nations were making rapid strides in advance of them. Indeed, many causes had combined to raise alike the position of shipowners and seamen of foreign nations, not the least of these being the protection afforded to our shipowners by the Navigation Laws; as under that protective system, they felt it less necessary to exert themselves to contend with the foreigner as keenly as, under other circumstances they would surely have done".

Blackmore[99] disagreed with this view, claiming; "Protection had little or nothing whatever to do with the moral degradation of either shipowner or mariner, but, if a cause must be sought, it will be found in the low state of education then existing throughout England, and the fact that too many took to sea life to escape books and tutors, imposed by the sea that, for a sailor, book learning was unnecessary".

An American view of British seamen, by an American Master in sail and steam,[100] was that; "The 'skippers', 'maties' and 'jackies' alike belonged to the lowest stratum of British social classification, which, according to the chronicles of those days, was pretty low. They were coarse, vulgar, ignorant men, full of lurid oaths; their persons emitted an unpleasant odour of cheap rum and stale tobacco; they had a jargon of their own and were so illiterate as to be unable to speak or write their own language with any degree of correctness. In a certain sense the captains were good sailors, but their knowledge and ambition were limited to dead reckoning, the tar bucket and marlinspike, a wife in every port, and plenty of rum and tobacco with no desire or ability to master the higher branches of navigation and seamanship".

Testimony also agreed that, in contrast, American ships were largely 'dry', of far better construction, safer and more efficiently operated, with insurance companies increasingly offering discounts on premiums of five per cent if the ship was 'dry';

> Is this system of sailing without spirituous liquors extensively practised by the Americans? – "To a very great extent".
>
> Have you any idea of the number of ships that sail on what are called temperance principles? – "Some say three-fourths, others nine-tenths of the American vessels are now sailing on temperance principles; I know it is a very rare thing to meet with an American vessel in Liverpool with ardent spirits on board for the use of the officers and crew".
>
> Speaking generally, what is the estimation in which American ships and American officers are held in Liverpool, as compared with English? – "Generally speaking, the ships are esteemed as a class superior in construction and better governed than very many of our English ships, and consequently they have the preference of goods and passengers".
>
> Are goods shipped in American vessels more readily than in English vessels, supposing the tonnage and the voyage to be the same? – "1 have heard observations to this effect from American captains, 'I do not care how many English ships are put up in opposition to me, we only fear each other;' that is to say, they are only afraid of American ships opposing American ships, but are not apprehensive of loss from English ships being put in opposition to them, knowing a preference will be given to them both for passengers and goods".
>
> Is that consistent with your own experience? – "Yes, I believe it to be perfectly true".
>
> Do you think the superiority of the American ships, in their non-liability to accidents from fire and wreck, and running foul of each other from the drunkenness of the officers and men, is one of the elements in the consideration of the men who prefer it? – "I have no doubt of that, and I feel afraid that our commerce suffers considerably in consequence of it".

> Have you heard that assigned as a reason? – "I have frequently".
>
> In point of fact, is the loss of American ships, sailing between America and Liverpool, equal to the loss of English ships? – "I think not; it is a very rare occurrence; I seldom hear of the loss of an American ship on the coast of England".

The very comprehensive report[101] of the 1836 select committee concluded that, although the number of persons drowned at sea was about the same in 1833-35 as in 1816-18, the number of shipwrecks in which all hands had been drowned had risen from forty-nine to eighty-one, and estimated that the cost to the nation of these losses of ships and crew was 1,000 lives and £3m a year.[102]

The causes of shipwrecks were reported to be many and various and confirmed the parlous state of the unregulated shipping industry, highlighting; defective construction of ships, inadequacy of equipment, imperfect state of repair, improper or excessive loading, inappropriateness of form, incompetency of master and officers, drunkenness of officers and men, the nature and operation of marine insurance which contributed to risk, neglect and even deliberate destruction or abandonment of vessels, want of harbours of refuge and imperfection of charts. Other matters identified as needing Government control were the lighthouse authorities, and engineering, design of ships, and pilotage.

The proposed remedies included; formation of a Mercantile Board to regulate the affairs of the Mercantile Marine; formation of a standard of acquirement for officers by the establishment of examinations; savings banks for seamen; asylum for worn out seamen; registry offices at which seamen's characters shall be recorded and kept; nautical schools; courts of inquiry into shipwrecks with powers to censure and power to reward by money; medals or otherwise; tribunals for speedy settlement of disputes, and discouragement of drinking on board ship.

Attention was also called in the report to the vast superiority in officers, crews, and equipment, and consequent success and growth of American shipping;

> The American ships frequenting the ports of England are stated by several witnesses to be superior to those of a similar class amongst

> ships of Great Britain, the commodores and officers being generally considered to be more competent as seamen and navigators, and more uniformly persons of education, than the commanders and officers of British ships of a similar size and class trading from England to America, while the seamen of the United States are considered to be more carefully selected and more efficient.

A private Bill was introduced in 1837 by the Chairman of the Select Committee, Mr. Silk Buckingham, containing in detail all the recommendations of the committee. The Bill received strong support from Joseph Hume (son of a shipmaster) who was known as a 'financial reformer', along with 'the peoples friend' Admiral Sir Edward Codrington and many others. However, it was seen to be revolutionary in character and too cumbersome and expensive in its working clauses. There was strong opposition to the Bill from all the shipowning Members of the House, including the Member for Sunderland, notwithstanding a petition from the seamen of the port.

While the Bill was before the House shipowners held their annual general meeting where Aaron Young, one of the two ship owning members of Parliament on the Select Committee, spoke at great length to the effect that "compulsory regulations would be subversive to the best interests of maritime commerce".[103] Further views expressed in the debate were that examinations of Masters and Mates were not required because "a great many Masters would be found untrustworthy"; one MP opposed the Bill "as nothing was said in it as to the cause of shipwreck"', and a third declared the Bill to be a "legislative monstrosity".[104]

The President of the Board of Trade, Poulett Thompson, sympathized with much of the intention of the Bill but could not support it as it "was so badly drafted it would not survive its committal". He did, however, suggest that Trinity House should introduce voluntary examinations for shipmasters and officers. The Bill was defeated by 176 votes to 28. In spite of this Sunderland shipowners and masters took matters into their own hands, instituting examinations for themselves, and enforcing regulations which had been utterly opposed by their own Member of Parliament. It was also proven on evidence that private firms had instituted examination of masters and officers for themselves. One firm, Messrs. Daniel & Co., of Mincing Lane, whose ships had been remarkably free from casualties, having lost only one ship in twenty years, attributed their success to such a plan.[105]

Not daunted, Alexander Becher, an ex-Naval officer and the energetic editor of The Nautical Magazine, continued to give publicity to losses at sea throughout the 1830s, and in 1838 published an account of the wreck of the timber ship ***Caledonia*** during the previous year. The sole and compelling reason for the Government's unusually prompt investigation into this issue through the Select Committee on Shipwrecks of Timber Ships, 1839, was due to the mention of one word, cannibalism; a practice fascinatingly abhorrent to nineteenth century British society. "That a thousand men should drown was not particularly remarkable at this time, but that a seafarer adrift aboard a waterlogged timber ship should be so reduced by hunger as to eat another stirred Parliament to swift action".[106]

Becher gave the story of cannibalism aboard the ***Caledonia*** restrained treatment, but the eyewitness account of the wreck by the Master of the Whitby registered ship ***Earl of Moira*** printed in the Commercial Gazette for January 1839, and later reproduced in the 1839 Report, was most explicit;

> I am sorry to have to report a most melancholy spectacle I witnessed on board the Earl of Moira of Whitby, timber laden; we fell in with this vessel in lat. 45 deg. north, and longitude 21 deg. 54 mins west on the 19th of this month, water-logged and with only one mast standing; although there was a considerable sea at the time, we managed to get a boat alongside of her, and on going on board of her, found four men quite dead in a sail which they had hung up under the main-top to shelter themselves from the weather, Besides these, there was part of another cut up in pieces, and hung up just like meat in a butcher's stall. No doubt these poor fellows must have undergone the extremity of hunger before they were reduced to a necessity so revolting as to devour a fellow creature.

The story was later confirmed by the Master of the ***Sarah*** who told George Charles Smith, the secretary of the British and Foreign Seamen and Soldier's Friend Society, that he had sighted the ***Earl of Moira*** on the 30 November 1838 when;

> ...there were eight persons alive in the maintop; but the most horrible

> sight was one swinging and hung by the neck evidently as food for the rest. He had black whiskers, and his intestines had been taken out, and a piece of the shoulder was cut off. The crew of the Sarah had been unable to get alongside to rescue these survivors, and two of the eight had been drowned before their horrified gaze as they tried to swim to safety.[107]

Ships in the North and Central American timber trade tended to sail in waters not used by other vessels, with the result that, if they became water logged and semi-submerged; kept afloat only by the buoyancy of the timber cargo so that the crew had to take shelter in the rigging, it might be weeks or months before help came. All food and fresh drinking water would usually be contaminated or inaccessible in the semi-submerged hull, often bringing the starving crew, desperately clinging to the rigging, to cannibalism.

A Select Committee on Shipwrecks of Timber Ships was promptly appointed on 9 April 1839 to 'inquire into Shipwrecks of Timber Ships, and the loss of life attendant thereon'; and to report to The House 'whether any or what means can be adopted to reduce the Amount thereof in future'. The ensuing report's summary of losses of timber ships for the period 1834 – 1838 made for sombre reading;

> By the extracts from Lloyd's Lists, in the evidence given by Captain D. Sutton, it appears that in the year 1834, there is recorded in the list of that year the loss of four timber ships from America, wrecked on the shores of America or Europe ; and seventeen lost at sea; of six of which no account whatever of the crews had been obtained; and in the case of three of the remaining eleven, it had been ascertained that the sufferings of the crews had been very great indeed ; in one of those, the "Lucy," after nineteen days privation, only two of the crew having been found alive. In the year 1835, fifteen ships are reported wrecked on the shore, and thirty-four at sea; of seventeen of which no account of the crews had been obtained; and of the other seventeen, the sufferings of the crews of six had been very great; in one, the "Francis Spaight" reduced by having been without water or provisions to the necessity of sacrificing four of their number, by lot, for the preservation of the rest. In 1836, twenty-seven ships are reported wrecked on the shore, and forty-four at sea; of eighteen of which no accounts had been received of the crews; and of the other twenty-six, the sufferings of the crews

> of three had been very great; in the "Earl Kellie," the second mate and two men are reported to have been starved to death.
>
> In 1837, seven ships are reported wrecked on the shore, and twenty-five at sea; of nineteen of which no accounts had been received of the crews; and of the other six, the sufferings of the crews of three had been extreme; in one, the " Caledonia," two are reported, when near death, to have had their throats cut for the sake of their blood, and when fallen in with by the "Dryden," which saved the remainder of the crew, they were about to sacrifice a boy. In 1838, eighteen ships are reported as wrecked on the shore, and forty-eight at sea; of twenty-seven of which there had been no accounts of the crews; of the remaining twenty-one, the sufferings of the crews of two had been extreme ; in one, the "Earl Moira", four bodies only having been found under the main top, all dead, with part of one of their comrades hung up like butcher's meat in a stall ; and in the other, the " Anna Maria," five bodies were found dead, with part of the leg of a woman by the side of one of them, who had evidently been feeding upon it; and one-more, the "Frederick" of St. John's, fallen in with by the "Hope" with her crew lashed to the main-top, without the power of assisting them.[108] By the Custom-house Return.... it appears that the number of ships from British North America lost or missing in 1836 was 74-; in 1837, 51 ; and in 1838, 101 ; out of the whole number which cleared out from British North America in 1836, 1,942; in 1887, 1,815, and in 1888, 1,670.'[109]

The casualty rate for vessels loaded with timber clearing from North American ports was 4% per voyage in 1836, 3% in 1837 and 6% in 1838. An examination of the Lloyds' List statistics for the period shows that the timber ship casualty rate was more than double that for all British merchant vessels. The reasons for the high rate were that, as one shipowner stated to members of the select committee; "the ships that go in the timber trade are worn out in other trades", and that they were "under-ballasted, over-loaded, held together with chains and cranky at sea because of excessive deck loads. Many were old East and West Indiamen long past their prime. When timber deck cargoes were lashed down to ringbolts and made fast by ropes secured through the washports any heavy sea had the effect of lifting the planking and straining the bulwarks so that these vessels tended to leak inordinately in all weathers; kept afloat only by the buoyancy of the timber cargo underdeck, and incessant pumping".

From an economic point of view, a deck load was always a gamble on a North Atlantic passage; if it could be brought home there was up to 10% additional profit, if it had to be jettisoned to save the ship in a gale of wind the whole enterprise could fail.[110] Such ships carried emigrants on their otherwise empty return passages to North America. Issues with the seaworthiness of these ships also existed in the timber trade from North America to Central America.

The report of the Committee further summarized the numbers of ships and lives lost over the period 1834 – 1838, and some of the causative factors;

> In adverting to the above evidence and returns, Your Committee are concerned to observe, that the instances proved each year of great suffering of the crews of some ships, from their having been fallen in with, with two or three only left on board alive to tell the tale of their disasters, or the remains of dead bodies in others; equally proving the fact, can only be considered as an index of the suffering to a like extent in all those other vessels, the crews of which have never been heard of, and which appear in the return to a most frightful extent, being in the last three years no less than 64 ships, which together with the nine ships in which some remains of the crews were found, making a total of 78 ships by Lloyd's List alone, the crews of which amounted to 949 seamen ; this, without making any allowance for the additional number of ships reported as lost in the Custom House Returns. They also observe, from the characters of the ships lost in 1836 and 1838, the characters not having been named against those of 1837, there is as large a proportion of A.1, and good ships lost, as of old and inferior ones; thus proving beyond a doubt that the loss is occasioned by other causes than the frailty of the vessels themselves. The average tonnage of the ships lost is from 320 – 330 tons, old measurement; and the average number reported to have been lost in the last three years by the Custom House Return, and the account given in Lloyd's List in that period, appear to have been 196, or 68,800 tons, manned by 2,548 seamen, valued with their freight and cargoes at £5,100 each, or at the whole sum of £999,600.[111]

Apart from the ever present danger of foundering, living conditions for the crew of timber ships were severely compromised by the desire of the owner to carry deck cargo, which was not taxed under tonnage taxes, in every available space. Charles Walton, a shipowner, testified that a tier of timber was loaded into the fo'c's'les in some vessels so that the crew had to sleep on wet wood. Captain William Davis confirmed that this was the case;

> ...sailors do not like to go on a timber voyage if they can get a Mediterranean voyage on account of the wood coming into the bows of ship where the men lodge and their lying on wet timber'. Seamen had only four feet of headroom in the fo'c's'les of many timber carriers: they could not sling their hammocks, and to save space the ships' stores were often crammed into the fo'c's'le as well as spare rope and ships' gear. Deck loads reached to the top of the bulwarks so that men moving about had to hold onto ropes, or spars jammed into the cargo, to keep a foothold. Seamen in the trade received an extra fifteen shillings a month because of 'hardship and suffering'.[112]

The Committee recommended on 18 June 1839 that deck-loading should be forbidden on vessels in the North Atlantic timber trade during the winter (1 September – 1 May), and went beyond the scope of their enquiry in recommending that all merchant ships should be surveyed;

> After a full consideration of the evidence received, Your Committee give it as their decided opinion, that no deck-loads should be suffered to be carried on any timber-laden vessels from North America, and that every inducement should be given towards promoting a fair and efficient survey of every ship in the merchant service.[113]

The evident dangers of this trade and the seaworthiness of vessels employed in it was such that these recommendations could hardly have been avoided. Parliament moved with uncharacteristic haste on this emotive and tragic issue, introducing a Bill very soon after the publication of the Report. The Timber Ships British North American Act, 1839[114] was passed on 17 August, a mere eighteen weeks after the matter had been first raised in the House. The recommendations for compulsory and universal survey were ignored, as were any form of year-round ban on timber deck cargoes. The carriage of timber cargo on deck was forbidden on vessels; 'wholly or part laden with timber, and clearing from any British Port in North America" during the winter (1 September – 1 May)'. *The Captain was not permitted to clear port until a certificate had been procured from the clearing officer that all cargo was below the deck.* Penalties were introduced through the Act of one hundred pounds for the; *Captain, Owner or Supercargo or any other person having command of a ship or vessel... in breach of the requirements of the Act.*

In his treatise on Seamen and the Law, Dixon (1984) sums up the pervasive impediment to legislative reform during the first third of the nineteenth century as one of "benign neglect".

> Reform, when it came, was compelled by events which had the effect of shocking the early Victorians into an acceptance of government intervention in the interests of safety at sea, rather than in consequence of measured argument and leisurely debate. [During] the first third of the nineteenth-century the attitude of government towards the merchant service and its work force was one of benign neglect. Some of the factors creating this attitude were exogenous – a general recession and a surplus of tonnage worldwide – and some reflected the prevailing view of the relationship between master and man. The administration's interest in the lot of merchant seamen was at a low level because of split departmental responsibility and Parliamentary quiescence. On the surface, the Navigation Acts with their characteristically mercantilist flavour dominated the world of shipping, but the creed of free trade – a dogma with much appeal for the dominant class of the first industrial nation – was in the ascendant. Where there were exceptions to the non-interventionist spirit of the times these exceptions have the character of special cases rather than significant departures from a trend....and, although the 1836 Select Committee on Shipwrecks was a triumph for public opinion it was not possible to convert the good intentions it engendered into action.

Contrary to the stagnant state of trade under sail a lot of energy and innovation was being put into the development of ocean-going steamships. In April 1838 the Victorian engineer Isambard Kingdom Brunel was vying for the honour of achieving the first entirely steam-powered west-bound crossing of the North Atlantic in his ***Great Western,*** of 236 feet long and 1340 tons. Brunel was a minor director of the Great Western Railway and the engineer in charge of construction of the railway from London to Bristol. This massive project had scarcely begun when, in 1835, a director of the Great Western Railway commented that the railway was too long to ever be completed. "Brunel responded that, on the contrary, it should stretch all the way to New York by linking in with a dedicated steamship service";

resulting in formation of the Great Western Steamship Company.[115]

The prevailing view of steamships, including that of Brunel's father, a former Naval officer who had experience as an engineer in several steamship companies, was that "steam can do nothing for distant navigation" and that steam engines should be auxiliary, to power sailing vessels in calms, or as coastal vessels and ferries. Brunel disagreed and suggested that the problem of enough fuel capacity could be overcome by increasing the size of the ship. In what was to be a major breakthrough in development and design of steamships Brunel proved that doubling the size of the ship would not require a doubling of the power, or fuel, for propulsion, a theory that was to become a fundamental tenet of naval architecture.[116] Brunel's expert advisers in the planning of the ***Great Western;*** a semi-retired Naval officer, Christopher Claxton, and local shipbuilder, William Patterson, calculated that a "steamship of 1200 tons and 300 horsepower, loaded with 580 tons of coal, would average between six and nine knots across the Atlantic in less than twenty days to the west, and just thirteen days to the East; roughly half the average voyages by sail".[117]

London and Liverpool at once took up Bristol's challenge, laying down the much larger ***British Queen*** (1,800 tons), and the ***Liverpool*** (1,140 tons), respectively to stake their claim to a share of the New York route.[118] When the construction of the ***British Queen*** was delayed the company chartered the much smaller paddle-wheeler ***Sirius*** of 700 tons. In the resultant race the ***Great Western*** crossed the North Atlantic in 15 ½ days, two weeks faster than a crack sailing packet and four days faster than the ***Sirius,*** with 200 ton of coal to spare.[119] The ***Great Western,*** the first purpose built ocean liner, had, by another five scheduled and routine crossings of the North Atlantic in 1838, set the standard for a regular trans-Atlantic steamship service. Over the next eight years she completed sixty-seven crossings, including one east-bound run of twelve days six hours and had proven the viability of regular trans-oceanic steamship services.

The Admiralty announced in 1839 that subsidies would be available for steam navigation between England and North America for carriage of Royal Mail, to replace the Admiralty's slow and unreliable ten-gun mail brigs; known as 'coffin ships' as every year at least two to three hundred people were lost due to the ships' fine lines and instability. Cunard stated;

"I come home in these ships very frequently, and of course felt the danger and discomfort of coming in them and have lost a great many friends in them". In January 1839, as Cunard was crossing to England, the west-bound [mail] packet disappeared. "I lost five or six intimate friends. They were never heard from again".[120] The scene was set for establishment of the first steam ship company offering the frequency of scheduled sailings required by the very demanding Admiralty contract for the carriage of mails. Cunard caught the first available sailing packet to England to present the Admiralty with a completely different proposal to their required monthly mail service. His proposal was for four ships providing a weekly service, to offer very serious competition to the American sailing packets. Cunard and the Admiralty initially negotiated a fortnightly service to Halifax with the mail carried by more low powered steamers from there to Boston with an annual subsidy of £55,000 per year.

Needing an engine designer and a shipbuilder, Cunard selected Glaswegians Robert Napier, who had built the engine for the ***British Queen***, and shipbuilder John Wood to determine whether they could build two steamships of 800 tons and 300 horsepower within 12 months. They could, but after further discussions with the Admiralty, the final contract was for four steamships of 400 horsepower, 206 feet long and 1120 tons sailing twice each month between Halifax and Liverpool, and then Halifax and Boston, for a payment of £60,000 annually for seven years. The official name of the company to operate the contract was the British and North American Royal Mail Steam Packet Company, known from the start as Cunard's Line or the Cunard Line.[121] Cunard returned to Halifax as one of the 120 passengers on the maiden voyage of the ***British Queen***; taking a keen interest in the ship.

The ***Britannia, Acadia, Caledonia and Columbia***, of essentially identical size and design, although built by four separate shipyards, were designed with very little cargo capacity (225 tons) and an emphasis on the carriage of mail, high value cargoes and 115 cabin passengers. The engines were designed by Napier and continued a trend established with his engines for the ***Great Western*** of higher boiler pressures to achieve more power and lower fuel consumption. Boiler pressures for the Cunard ships were almost double that of the ***Great Western*** (from five to nine pounds per square inch) reducing daily coal consumption from forty-four to thirty-eight tons. Within a year of the commencement of Cunard's trans-Atlantic service his ships had beaten the ***Great Western's*** record and over the first two years of service averaged thirteen days and six hours to Halifax and eleven days five hours on the return passage to Liverpool.[122]

In spite of this remarkable reliability and regularity not all passengers enjoyed the experience of early steam passenger ships. In January 1842 Charles Dickens and his wife, impressed by Cunard's publicity material, booked passage from Liverpool to Boston aboard the ***Britannia*** to undertake a six week tour of America. His scathing account of the voyage, published in his *American Notes for General Circulation*, must have dismayed Cunard, but was more a by-product of undertaking a passage in mid-winter;

> The Atlantic crossing turned out to be one of the worst the ship's officers had ever known. There were gales and high seas for much of the time..."on the tenth day the smokestack had to be lashed with chains to stop it being blown over and setting fire to the decks. All the lifeboats were smashed by the bad weather".[123] 'The sounds of the ship – creaking, groaning, moaning – made him [Dickens] think, yet again, of death. The steam engine under his feet terrified him: "fire in hiding, ready to burst through any outlet, with its resistless power of death and ruin". One morning he awoke to find an inch of seawater sloshing around on the cabin floor and all his possessions soaked. Thinking the ship was going down, he stopped a steward in the passageway and demanded to know what was happening; "rather a heavy sea on, sir," came the laconic reply.[124]

Regardless of the severe adverse weather, and an overnight grounding at the entrance to Halifax harbour, the passage to Boston was completed in eighteen days. Dickens and his wife returned from North America aboard a German sailing ship. The ***George Washington*** (1821, 462 tons gross) carried them home to Liverpool in twenty-two days.

Chapter 3

Legislation, Lifeboats and Education

Parliament dipped its toes very cautiously into the troubled waters of legislating for the safety of ships. As the Timber Ships British North American Act, 1839, was passed in haste it only continued in force 'until the End of the next Session of Parliament'. The 1839 Act was continued, with a similar prohibition regarding British ships carrying timber deck cargoes extending to ships clearing out from Honduras; through passage of the Timber Ships, British North America Act, 1840.[125] Parliament continued its cautious approach with the 1840 Act staying in effect only until the first day of May, 1842.

The 1840 Act was continued until the first day of May 1845, through the Timber Ships Act, 1842[126] – *An Act for preventing, until the first day of May one thousand eight hundred and forty-five, ships clearing out from any Port in British North America, or in the Settlement of Honduras, from loading any Part of their Cargo of Timber on Deck*. There was significantly increased emphasis on penalties in the 1842 Act. The fine for non-compliance remained at one hundred pounds but a Schedule was attached to the Act in a Form of Warrant of Commitment for a Penalty whereby Justices of the Peace were empowered to imprison the offender.

A reason for the short duration of the Act could have been the pending enquiries of a Select Committee, appointed in early 1843, to enquire further into the shipwreck of British Vessels. Partially taking into account the summary and recommendations of this Committee, restrictions on the carriage of timber deck cargoes during the North Atlantic winter were continued in perpetuity through enactment of the Timber Ships Act, 1845.[127] A more liberal view was taken regarding penalties with the one hundred pound fine, and more draconian provisions of the 1842 Act, being deleted.

This legislation, which dealt with only one particular issue regarding seaworthiness, and was introduced very tentatively, was nevertheless significant as the first legislative initiative by Great Britain, outside of the Merchant Vessels Etc. Act, 1835, to address the longstanding issue of the safety of ships without a focus upon passengers, but upon the safety of seafarers. The application of the Merchant Vessels etc Act, 1835 was extended through the Passenger Ships Act, 1840[128] to include The Bahamas, Bermuda and South America. This was followed, in 1842 by enactment of the Passengers in Merchant Ships Act, 1842[129], – *an Act for Regulating the Carriage of Passengers in Merchant Vessels* – that repealed the 1835 Act. The Act prescribed that no more than three persons were to be carried to every five tons registered burden of the ship, and allotted space per passenger dependent upon the length of the voyage; for example, *One Passenger for every Ten such clear superficial feet, if such Ship is not to pass within the Tropics during such voyage*. Quantities per passenger of water and food were prescribed along with a proper supply of medicines.[130]

Emergence of passenger carrying steamships along with growing concern from the early 1840s about standards for carriage of emigrants to Australia, New Zealand and North America, brought about requirements in the 1842 Passenger Act for the carriage of a specific number of boats, dependent upon tonnage and passengers;

> No Ship shall carry Passengers on any such Voyage as aforesaid unless such Ship shall be provided with good sound Boats of suitable Size, and properly supplied with all Requisites for their Use, in the following proportion to the registered Tonnage of such Ship as aforesaid; that is to say, -
>
> Two Boats, if the Tonnage of such Ship be One hundred and fifty Tons and upwards, but under Two hundred and fifty Tons:
>
> Three Boats, if the Tonnage of such Ship be Two hundred and fifty Tons and upwards:
>
> Four Boats if the Tonnage of such Ship be Five hundred Tons and upwards, and the number of passengers exceed Two hundred:
>
> Nor unless One of such Boats be a long Boat of a Size duly proportional to the Tonnage of the Ship.

The Act was silent on the size, capacity and stowage of such boats. The Passengers in Merchant Ships Act, 1842, was the first Act to require ships to carry boats but was also the genesis of fatally flawed and confused legislation, limited to passenger ships, based upon the tonnage of the ship almost regardless of the total number of persons on board, throughout the nineteenth century and beyond. The option for a survey by two competent persons to attest to seaworthiness before departure, if necessary, was continued from the 1835 Act.

In 1843 Members of Parliament again turned their minds to the ongoing question of shipwreck, revisiting some of the recommendations of both the 1836 and 1839 Select Committee Reports, reviewing statistics on losses for the years 1836 to 1843, and considerably broadening the scope of those earlier inquiries. They were energetically encouraged by the newly elected Member for Durham, Captain Robert Fitzroy,[131] who organized a deputation of Members in 1842 to implore the President of the Board of Trade, the Earl of Rippon, to address the recommendation of the 1836 Report regarding the incompetence of ships' officers. The deputation was informed that further evidence would be required before the matter could be dealt with. Fitzroy persisted through the introduction of a Bill in July 1842 proposing a method he'd developed of examinations for ships' officers, only to be told by Gladstone, Vice-President of the Board of Trade, that shipowner Members of Parliament were divided on this matter. The draft Bill was simply printed and distributed as a circular. Undeterred, Fitzroy tabled a question in the House on 24 February 1843 enquiring if any legislation was planned on this matter, to be informed by Gladstone that a Select Committee established very recently could possibly consider it.[132] Unsatisfied with this response Fitzroy arranged for a friend at the Foreign Office, James Murray, to send a letter to all British Consuls seeking them to answer a somewhat leading question regarding their opinion of British shipmasters; "...I am particularly desirous of gaining information in regard to instances which have come under your observation of the incompetency of British shipmasters".

The subjective topic of the letters resulted in a largely unbalanced and damning view of shipmasters with egregious examples of drunkenness, incompetence, ignorance, illiteracy, lack of navigational skills, and even robbery. One Consul balanced his views by stating; "...sober navigators had lost four ships in the past four years while drunken incompetents had suffered no losses". Regardless, Murray had received the evidence Fitzroy needed to pursue his cause. A letter was sent to Charles Canning, Foreign

Secretary on New Year's Day 1844, and circulated amongst members of the Government, urging that a single regulatory body be established for the merchant service with a duty to examine officers. Although the Admiralty correctly considered the views expressed in the letter to be overly pessimistic Gladstone was persuaded to look into the question of legislation.

In August 1844 Lord Ingestre asked in the House of Lords whether a measure for examination of masters and mates would be included in legislation, to which the Admiralty replied that it would, immediately. The committee referred to by Gladstone was the '*Select Committee appointed to enquire into the shipwreck of British Vessels, and the Means of Preserving the Lives and Property of Shipwrecked Persons, and to whom the Reports of 1836 and 1839, and the several Petitions on the subject, were referred, and who were empowered to Report thereupon from time to time to the House*'. Key witnesses were Alexander Belcher of the Nautical Magazine and Captain John Washington, commander of a survey vessel. When Captain Washington was asked whether he had any suggestion to offer for the prevention of shipwrecks his brief and succinct response was "make masters and mates pass an examination".[133]

Murray's letter of 1844, summarizing the views of various British Consuls on British shipmasters, languished on the desks of the Foreign Office until being laid by them before Parliament in 1848. Murray's conclusions were;

1. That the character of British shipping has declined, and that of foreign shipping had improved

2. That there was not sufficient control over British ship-masters either at home or abroad, while foreign vessels were subject to considerable control

3. That there was no system of regular education for the merchant service of Great Britain, but that in certain foreign countries this matter was much attended to

4. That the sort of education which a British subject receives when training for the higher grades of the merchant service, does not qualify him to represent with advantage the merchant by whom he may be employed in that merchant's interest, and that he may often neglect those interests, and the merchant not be aware of the fact

What Murray wanted was "not merely a study of navigation and seamanship, but a thorough knowledge of ship's husbandry, and of the stowage of cargoes, of exchanges, and other commercial information which would qualify the master to act if necessary as the representative of his employer in the character of merchant; the commander of the ship being, in law, considered the representative of the owners of the property on board".[134]

Fitzroy's appeal for "a single regulating board for the merchant service with the duty of examining officers as to their competence"; a compulsory certification regime, had to wait until enactment of the Mercantile Marine Act, 1851 to finally be realised.

The First Report of the select committee, at 680 pages, was published in August 1843[135] with the preamble summarizing statistics of losses between 1836 and 1843;

> The select committee....have considered the Matters referred to them, and have agreed to the following, being their First Report: — Their enquiry has embraced two points: lst. The Loss of British vessels, and the means of diminishing that loss in future. 2nd The means of Preserving the Lives and Property of Shipwrecked Persons. Having obtained returns of the British ships lost during the years 1841-2-3, as regards the whole of the mercantile marine, from Lloyd's, and also of the loss of timber-laden ships from British America to Europe from September 1839, the date from which the Act took place prohibiting the deck-loading of these ships, they have been enabled to make a. comparison; 1st, of the general loss of ships in the years 1841-2, with those lost in 1833-4~5, in proportion to the registered tonnage; and, 2dly, of the loss of timber ships, in the years 1840-41 and 1842, with those lost in 1836-78. In both cases they have the satisfaction to find, that the loss has been much less in the later periods than in the earlier, more especially as regards timber-laden ships, and the lives of the crews employed on board of them, where there has been a reduction in loss of ships in each year from 56 to 23; and, as near as can be calculated, a saving of 200 lives of seamen. In no one instance during the last period do they find, in those ships to which the Act of Parliament alone applies, any of those horrible cases stated in the Report of the Committee of 1839, of the crews of several ships in each year having been reduced to the necessity of existing on the remains of their

> comrades. They feel, however, bound to report one of this description, which appears to have taken place but a short time ago;...reported from New York, 14th December 1842, in regard to the "Naiad" bound from Halifax to Demerara, where one man remaining only out of a crew of 17, was taken from the wreck 50 days after the 22nd September, when the ship had been upset. (see Evidence, No. 3699)'

The Select Committee's sole recommendation regarding seaworthiness was that;

> Your Committee consider that no ship can be sea-worthy, when her upper deck is lumbered with cargo of any kind, and they strongly recommend to the consideration of Her Majesty's Government, a still further extension of the prohibition clauses of the Act of Parliament against deck-loading of ships.

The first purpose of the committee's enquiry was to enquire into – *The Loss of British vessels, and the means of diminishing that loss in future*; a broad scope covering the loss of all types of British vessels, as did the 1836 report. The committee did undertake a comparison of the losses of timber ships against all types of ships but restricted its one recommendation to the question of deck cargoes, although the recommendation was aimed at an extension of the 1839 Act provisions to deck cargoes aboard all vessels. This recommendation was partially adopted through continuation of the Timber Ships Act, 1845, in perpetuity, but the amendment did not extend to deck cargoes aboard all vessels.

The second purpose was to 'enquire into those points which seemed to them more essentially to regard the security of Shipping'. (For "security" the word safety might better describe their intentions in a modern context.) These sections of the Report examined the issues of; The character of ships; The competency of masters and mates; The facility of obtaining good pilots; Harbours of Refuge; Lighthouses and beacons etc., and Charts and Compasses. In examining the ensuing recommendations, some of which are preventative and others reactive to shipwreck, it will be recalled that the 1836 Report made recommendations on the prevention of shipwreck generally, while the 1839 Report focused solely upon the wreck of timber ships in the North Atlantic trade.

The term 'character of ships' referred to the matter of construction standards of ships and surveys to ensure that ships were sound. There was a sea change in the attitudes of shipowners on the need for surveys with the report commenting that any objections to the system of surveys and classification by the Lloyds Register established in 1834 '... of having them classed in the Register-book in the first instance are now removed, and shipowners are generally ready to submit their ships and stores to the fair examination of the Surveyors of the Society, for the purpose of having them classed in the Register-book according to their real quality'[136] Such surveys were a private arrangement between the shipowner and Lloyds, for example, for insurance purposes. They were not a statutory survey by surveyors appointed by a Government administration such as the Board of Trade for the purpose of ensuring that the vessel met all legislative requirements; a requirement clearly not feasible at a time when there was no legislation for the safety or seaworthiness of ships and no effective Government administration.

The committee recalled the loss without trace between 1816 and 1843 of '11 warships of the class of 10-gun brigs, 6 of these having been employed in the [Mail] Packet Service'. On the basis of this evidence concerning somewhat irrelevant wooden sailing vessels they came to the totally unrelated conclusion that; 'Your Committee recommend to the consideration of the House the propriety of an enquiry being instituted as to the necessity of introducing an Act of Parliament, placing all Steam vessels carrying passengers under superintendence of competent persons, to be appointed by the Government'.

Although it is not clear what type of 'competent person' or 'superintendence' was intended, a provision in the Passengers in Merchant Ships Act, 1842[137], under the paragraph reference 'Seaworthiness of Ship may be ascertained by Survey' may have guided the Committee;

> And it be enacted, That if Doubts shall arise whether a Ship about to proceed with Passengers....is seaworthy so as to be fit for her intended Voyage, and such Doubts shall not be removed to the Satisfaction of the Collector and Comptroller of the Customs at the Port from which the Vessel is to be cleared out, or in case there shall be a Government Emigration Agent at such Port, then to the Satisfaction of such Emigra-

> tion Agent, it shall be lawful for such Collector and Comptroller, or for such Emigration Agent, (as the Case may be) at such Time to cause such Ship to be surveyed by Two competent Persons, and if it shall be reported by these Persons that such Ship is not in their Opinion seaworthy with reference to such Voyage, such ship shall not be cleared out, unless the Contents of such Report be disproved to the Satisfaction of the Commission of the Customs, or of the Colonial Land and Emigration Commissioners in those Cases in which the Report shall have been made at the Instance of a Government Emigration Agent, or such ship shall have been rendered seaworthy.

It is clear that the officials referred to in the Act would not have had the experience or technical expertise to determine whether a ship was 'seaworthy so as to be fit for her intended voyage'. The officials had been charged since 1803, under a series of Passenger Acts, with responsibility for ensuring compliance with the general requirements of these Acts such as provisions, water and accommodation space prescribed for each passenger. Their duties could also have included compliance with the new requirement for the ship to carry a number of boats based upon the tonnage of the ship as introduced by the Passenger Act, 1842. The competent persons referred to are not defined and could well have been Lloyds surveyors.

All of the matters addressed in both the 1836 and 1839 Reports concerned wooden sailing vessels; both passenger and non-passenger. It can only be presumed that the explicit emphasis on passenger carrying steam ships, to the detriment of the vast majority of sailing vessels at this time, was due to the introduction of scheduled, and almost entirely unregulated, passenger services by Cunard paddle-steamers in 1840.[138] The Committee may well also have had in mind the disappearance in March 1841 of the wooden paddle-steamer ***President*** (1840) of 2360 ton; the largest ship in the world at the time, certified to carry 154 passengers. At the time of her last sighting, one day out of New York at the beginning of a passage to Liverpool, she was carrying 136 souls, all of whom were lost after the vessel was believed to have foundered in heavy weather on the shallow Georges Bank between Cape Cod and Sable Island.

Captain Robert Fitzroy's crusade within Parliament regarding the competency of ships' officers and the need for examinations and certification would have been well known to his Parliamentary colleagues but his views were not formally considered by the Committee. The 1836 Report had clearly identified 'the lack of experience, competence and training of ship's officers, including masters', as one of the causes of shipwreck and recorded some alarming examples of incompetent masters in particular and had recommended that there be formation of a 'standard of acquirement for officers by the establishment of examination'.

The 1843 Committee heard contradictory evidence on this matter. Examples were given of foreign nations with established Boards for the Examination of Masters and Mates. The following extract from Blackmore[139] summarises the standards of qualifications and examinations required at this time by some European nations;

> As a comparison had been drawn between the British sailor and his foreign competitor, which appeared so much to our discredit, let us now take a glance at foreign countries, and see how matters stood with regard to their merchant officers – premising that nothing had ever been done in this country by the Government to educate our merchant sailors, or to improve their general intelligence in any way whatever; to bind him to serve an apprenticeship was the utmost stretch of our national wisdom.
>
> Long before we thought it necessary to institute and test of the capability of our officers, a most perfect system, not only of examination, had been in use in nearly all, if not all, the countries of Europe.
>
> In Denmark no seaman could undertake the command of a Danish vessel until he had made two foreign voyages as mate, or before he had passed an examination of the severest order. He had to prove himself an intelligent navigator by dead reckoning; by a knowledge of astronomy, and the motions of the sun, moon and stars, and how to find their positions; by a knowledge of tides and currents, and a perfect knowledge of general seamanship. In Norway and Sweden, they had to undergo a similar examination, and were required to have a general knowledge of ship's business, some knowledge of shipbuilding and the various parts of her construction, and an ability to measure the ship's capacity.
>
> In Russia and Prussia an equally severe examination was made; and

in addition to a competent knowledge of their own language, and the ability to write it with accuracy, there was required some knowledge of English and French. In the Dutch ships the qualification for both masters and mates was considerable. Gentlemen of good families and superior education entered the merchant service of that country, and masters and mates of long-voyage ships were subjected to a severe examination.

But France had gone well beyond all other countries in this respect. The combination of her naval and mercantile services is very complete, as the officers and masters of her foreign-going ships not only pass similar examinations as the lieutenants and sub-lieutenants of the government service, but they also acquire the same rank. In all these countries schools had been set up in all the larger seaports, where not merely the rudiments of navigation were taught, but considerable attention was also paid to moral and intellectual improvement,. In France, before one could obtain a certificate entitling the holder to command a foreign-going vessel, he had to attend a full course of study for at least six months at a naval College, and not until then might he become a "Capitaine de long cours".

In America, says Mr. Consul Peter, in a report made by him upon the American Marine, "a lad intended for the higher grade of the Merchant Service, after having acquired (in addition to the ordinary branches of school learning) a competent knowledge of mathematics, navigation, ship's husbandry, and generally French, is commonly apprenticed to some respectable merchant, in whose counting-house he remains a couple of years, or at least long enough to make him familiar with exchanges, and other commercial matters. He is then sent to sea as a junior mate, and gradually rises to the position of captain". He also adds: "An ignorant American native seaman was scarcely to be found"; and further "Cases of disputes between native born Americans and their Captains have ever been less frequent, both in this country and abroad, than between British masters and seamen, owing in great measure to the superior education, and the more vigorous discipline on board American ships".

In the face of such educational advantages, was it any wonder that the foreign merchant sailor was a better educated man than the British, who was dependent entirely upon his own resources, and left to pick

> up his knowledge as best he could, unless he, as sometimes happened, was a fairly well-educated young man before he ever thought of going to sea?' Regardless, vehement evidence was heard from shipowners who were 'decidedly hostile to the enforcement of examination by Act of Parliament, considering such compulsion examination an unnecessary interference with their interest in the selection of such persons as they may think most likely to serve them best in the various duties they have to perform'.

In addressing the committee Blackmore stated that incompetence was the principal cause of the losses of British ships;

> I think the principal cause of the losses of British ships has been the neglect or incompetency of those in command of them. It is very rarely that any vessel is lost except in consequence of neglect or mismanagement. In saying neglect, I mean not attending sufficiently to the position of the ship, to heaving the lead, to taking all those precautions, in short, which ought to be taken by a good seaman anxious for the safety of his ship, and knowing how to take care of her; and incompetency from not knowing how to make proper observations for ascertaining the ship's place, and not being practical seamen acquainted with their duty, having had sufficient experience either as masters or mates of merchant ships to entitle them to take under their charge, not only the ship and cargo, but the lives of all who are embarked on board, and to navigate from one part of the world to another. This I consider to be the principal cause of the loss of ships; for my opinion is decidedly, that ships which are not struck by lightning, nor disabled by fire, nor by any casualty which is not within man's power to control, are lost upon known coasts by the mismanagement of those in command of them.[140]

Faced with these widely divergent and conflicting opinions the Committee noted that all parties agreed to the 'propriety of encouraging the increase of scientific knowledge as much as possible in the Mercantile Marine' and came to the conclusion that;

> It would materially promote science, and prevent the loss of life and property, if a legislative enactment were introduced by the Government, establishing Boards for the purpose of examining the ability, conduct, and character of all who wish to qualify as Masters and Mates

> in the Merchant Service. And your Committee further recommend the establishment of Schools for the purpose of teaching Navigation in the different sea-ports, to be supported by a small tonnage duty, to be levied on the vessels belonging to the port.

The Government did not immediately take the opportunity to legislate on such measures and left all reference to the education and examination of Masters and Mates out of the Merchant Seaman Act, 1844. The Admiralty's promise to Lord Ingestre in August 1844 of immediate action was met through an Order in Council to introduce a voluntary regime for examinations, published in the London Gazette of 20th August 1845; *Notice is hereby given, that from and after the 1st day of November, 1845, the following arrangements and regulations for examining masters and mates in the merchant service, voluntarily offering themselves for examination, will take effect.*

With the entrenched negative views of many seafarers, and shipowners, regarding voluntary certificates it's not surprising that the system failed. By the end of 1846 fewer than 200 candidates had obtained their certificates, the majority in London; compulsion was clearly necessary. Early moves towards this emanated from the Admiralty who refused to permit the Transport Board from chartering vessels as troop or convict transports after 23 March 1847 "unless the master and mates have obtained the required certificates". This coercive ruling spread rapidly to cover all vessels carrying mails or in any way coming under state influence, so that in the following year 400 passed their certificates; thereafter the number steadily increased .[141] At the end of 1850 more than 3000 had passed including almost all of the officers holding the higher positions in the mail and other contract Government services.[142]

Another matter considered by the Committee to be of direct relevance to prevention of shipwreck was Charts and Compasses. The concerns expressed on compasses were 'great and unequal deviation of the Needle in different vessels and situations, from the local attraction on board, from 3° to 18° degrees, according to a report from the Admiralty, which may have been the cause of the loss of some vessels, from the master not being aware of it, and which can alone be guarded against by the closest attention'. The Committee correctly considered that 'the safety of ships, and the lives of all on board so much depending upon the correctness of charts, a general and constant revision of those most in use is well worthy of the continued attention of the Government, and would be a great boon to the Mercantile Marine'. The Committee also emphasized the responsibility of shipowners to supply the master with the latest authorized edition of charts. The remaining matters dealt with by the 1843 Committee were those services supplied to ships, such as pilotage, safe harbours, lighthouses and beacons and issues associated with the aftermath of shipwreck such as 'the means of preserving the life and property of shipwrecked persons'.

Other comments and recommendations pertinent to the safety and seaworthiness of ships in the Report included;

> ...water-tight divisions in steam-vessels are calculated to prevent total loss of vessel and machinery, and to ensure the preservation of life, by affording time for the preparation of boats for the reception of passengers and crew; Your Committee, however, are not prepared to point out what number of these water-tight divisions should be before and abaft the engine-room and machinery space; and...some better code of Maritime Law than that which now exists for the regulation of the duties of the Master and Seamen on board Merchant Vessels is much wanted, with a view of increasing the security [safety] of shipping, promoting the comfort and health of seamen, and of preventing desertion; and...your Committee have received various suggestions for life-boats, safety-capes and belts; and some drawings and models have been presented for their inspection; but not having sufficient means of testing their respective merits, they can only now recommend them to the consideration of Her Majesty's Government, in the event of any legislative enactment on that subject.

The Committee presented a brief Second Report in November 1843 to record their concerns and further recommendations resulting from reports of the losses, as they were nearing completion of their First Report, of two steamships; the coastal passenger steamer ***Pegasus*** (1835) of 130 ton, in August 1843 with the loss of 51 of the 57 souls aboard, and the grounding in thick fog, and total loss on Seal Island, Nova Scotia, of the Cunard passenger steamer ***Columbia*** (1840) of 1150 ton, in July 1843, without loss of life.

The loss of the ***Pegasus*** caused a great deal of concern and public comment regarding the safety of passengers aboard unregulated steamships, as in the *Spectator* of August 13, 1843, under the heading 'Preservation of Life at Sea';

> THAT the miserable wreck of the Pegasus continues to excite a regretful attention, is shown in the letters which we still receive on the subject. One correspondent calls upon us to do justice. He takes exception to so much of our remarks as was based upon the supposition that Mr. MILLER, the master of the vessel at the time of the wreck, had also been the master when some previous accidents occurred. Mr. MILLER, it appears, was mate of the Pegasus for four or five years, and master for two years and a half; and in all that time no mishap had occurred. All that we founded, therefore, upon the alleged continuance of a foolhardy man in so responsible an office, falls to the ground. Another correspondent remarks, that such disasters create a great sensation for a time, but the sensation passes of, and nothing is done to prevent loss for the future. The remark is one made in every case of the kind; but the reproach particularly applies to shipwrecks, because several aids to safety, that are easy to procure, are as much neglected as if they did not exist. There are various safety-jackets, that of Caoutchouc seeming the most convenient; yet they are used anywhere but at the worst need.... all the souls on board the Pegasus might have been so provided that it would have been impossible to them to drown. But people reserve these life-preservers for the perils of pleasure-bathing: those who go to sea and incur actual shipwreck take less precautions, or rather none.
>
> Who should begin? Undoubtedly, the Legislature should enter heartily upon the subject of passage-boats with a view to their effectual regulation. A little inconvenience incurred in cabs and omnibuses gives rise to the most stringent laws for controlling hackney-carriages; but danger and death are privileged occupants of steam-boats. The seaworthiness of the vessel, the safety of its boilers, the capacity of the commander, are all points to be secured by competent legislative control. Vessels should not be allowed to do as many do on the Thames—to go in perpetual danger of upsetting or foundering from being over-crowded. A proportion should be fixed between tonnage and passengers. And above all, steam-boats should be provided with the means of enabling all on board to float. But legislation is slow, and should if possible be anticipated. Passengers, indeed, cannot well be expected to furnish themselves with a floating-apparatus: the

> landsman, who takes a trip to Edinburgh, Boulogne, or Herne Bay, once in a year, if so often, would hardly buy a dress for the purpose. People would laugh at his cowardice. But steam-boat owners are no less bound in humanity than they would be justified in self-interest, to begin the practice of keeping a floating-apparatus for all their passengers. The individual passenger only goes to sea once or so; they have passengers always at sea. The more they diminish the perils of the ocean, the better for their profit. Why does not some company begin, and take steps to announce in its handbills—"Plenty of safety-jackets and other floating life-preservers for all the passengers on board?"[143]

The Select Committee summoned some of the survivors of the ***Pegasus*** and ***Columbia*** to give evidence before them and concluded that such evidence; "most strongly confirms them in everything they have recommended in their First report, especially the importance of all steamers being fitted with paddle-wheel boxes; irrespective of lifeboats and other boats; and that such steamers should be built with water-tight divisions". They also recommended, in spite of the fact that neither vessel was involved in a collision, that; " by international agreement with foreign powers, all steamers on meeting each other (to avoid collision) should be required to put their helms a-port". [at this time, the order would have had the effect of turning the vessel's bow to starboard].

It was not until 1846 that Parliament turned its attention to some of these recommendations through enactment of the first significant legislation with a focus upon the safety and seaworthiness of ships; compelled into action by the development of passenger carrying steamships, and largely limited to steamships; "which may more generally be considered passenger ships"; the Steam Navigation Act, 1846[144] – *an Act for the Regulation of Steam Navigation, and for requiring Sea-going vessels to carry Boats* which came into effect on the first day of January 1847. The preamble to the associated Bill declared it; *...to be expedient to make further provision for regulating the construction of seas-going steam-vessels, and for preventing the occurrence of accidents (as far as may be possible) in steam navigation*. After consideration by Parliament the 1846 Act extended these aims through its preamble to include a requirement for all vessels to carry specified boats; *Whereas it is expedient to make further provision for regulating the construction of Sea-going Steam Vessels, and for Preventing the Occurrence of Accidents (as far as may be possible in Steam*

Navigation), and for requiring Sea-going vessels to carry Boats...

The very different construction and layout of steam vessels, as compared to sailing vessels, and possibly the loss of the steam passenger vessel ***Columbia***, was recognized in the requirement of Part I of the Act that clearly differentiated between power driven and sailing vessels, to the detriment of the latter usually un-subdivided from end to end. The Act also did not apply to wooden steam ships built after 01 January 1847.

Part I – *Iron Steamers of 100 Tons and upwards to be divided by Water-tight Partitions* required that;

> ...all Steam Vessels built of Iron of One hundred Tons Burden or upwards, the Building of which shall have commenced after the passing of this Act, shall be divided by transverse Water-tight partitions, so that the fore Part of the Vessel shall be separated from the Engine Room by one of such Partitions, and so that the after Part of such Vessel shall be separated from the Engine Room by another of such Partitions.

The requirement of Part II – *Sea-going Vessels to be Provided with the Number of Boats and the dimensions herein mentioned* – harks back to the title of the Act and separation of 'steam navigation' and 'sea-going vessels'. For example, whereas Part I applies specifically *to all steam vessels built of iron* Part II applies to *all sea-going vessels* while Part IV requires *steamers* to carry extra boats.

Part II also required all seagoing vessels of 100 tons and upwards not to proceed to sea unless carrying boats specified for vessels of various tonnages up to '850 ton and upwards'. Two boats for vessels from 100 – 350 tons, 3 boats from 350 – 650 tons, and 4 boats from 650 tons upwards; tonnage divisions for numbers of boats that differed from those required by the 1842 Passenger Act. No account was taken of the number of passengers carried apart from a requirement for an extra boat *fitted up as a Life Boat, with all Requisites for its Use, together with Two Life Buoys.*

Rigorous survey and reporting provisions were enacted to ensure that steam vessels were in a seaworthy state with regard to condition of the hull and machinery under Part XIV of the Act;

> And it be enacted, That on or before the Thirtieth Day of April and the Thirty-first Day of October in every Year the Owners of every Steam Vessel shall transmit to the Lords of the Committee of the Privy Council for Trade the following Two Declarations in Writing, (that is to say);
>
> First, -A Declaration of the Sufficiency and Good Condition of the Hull of such Steamer under the hand of a Shipwright Surveyor, to be approved by the Lords of the said Committee
>
> Second – A Declaration of such Sufficiency and Good Condition of the Machinery of such Steam Vessel under the hand of an Engineer, to be approved in like Manner by the Lords of the said Committee; such declarations bearing Date of some Day in the said Months of April or October respectively

Upon satisfactory and timely receipt of such declarations the Board of Trade was to register the declaration and issue the ship with a Certificate of Registry. The ship was not to be cleared outwards by a Customs Officer unless valid a Certificates of Registry was available. These provisions did not apply to *Steam Vessels…employed in the Royal Mail Service, or the conveyance of the Royal Public Mails or Despatch under Contract with and under Superintendence of the Lord High Admiralty*. Such Admiralty contracts, under which generous Government grants to shipping companies for carriage of mail were provided, enabled many of the earliest scheduled trans-Atlantic steam ship companies to fund the construction of their ships and continue such services. Admiralty contracts were extremely detailed and onerous and, at this time, insisted on wooden hulled ships.

Other clauses in the Act provided for inspection of vessels, measurement of tonnage, reporting of accidents and for penalties. Some consideration to the safety of passengers aboard steamers, built after the commencement of the passing of the Act, was provided by Part IV which required steamers proceeding to sea with any number of passengers to;

> …in addition to the Boats specified in the foregoing Table, and in lieu of a Boat fitted up as a Life Boat, be provided with such Boats as are usually called Paddle Box Boats or with such other Boats as may be directed in lieu thereof by the Lord High Admiral or the Commissioners executing the Office of the Lord High Admiral for the time Being

However, in spite of the fact that Part XXXVII of the 1846 Act explicitly applied to *all sea-going vessels of 100 tons and upwards* (including passenger ships) the Act specifically saved the provisions of Part XIII of the Passengers in Merchant Vessels Act, 1842 – *Sufficient Boats to be carried* – that, with different tonnage brackets, required;

> Two boats, if the tonnage of such ship be 150 ton and upwards but under 250 ton
>
> Three boats, if the tonnage of such ship be 250 ton and upwards, and
>
> Four boats, if the tonnage of the ship be 500 ton and upwards and the number of passengers be more than 200,
>
> Nor unless any of such boats be a long boat of a size duly proportionate to the tonnage of the ship

Sentiments on this confusing and ambiguous legislation lingered on, well into the nineteenth century. The Journal of the Society of Arts 1866, (p. 242) poured scorn upon the complexities and perceived contradictions of the 1846 Act requirements for the carriage of boats and lifebuoys;

> ...a sailing ship of 210 tons carries on the average twelve hands all told; she is required to carry either three boats of 750 cubic feet, or two boats, one of which must be a launch twenty feet long and the other a lifeboat, and she must also carry two life-buoys. A steam-ship of 121 tons must carry similar boats to the sailing vessel of 210 tons, whether she is a passenger steamer or not. If she is a passenger steamer she will sometimes, according to the lists published by the Board of Trade, carry between 500 and 600 persons to the three boats and two life-buoys. If she is not a passenger steamer, but is, for example, a screw collier, she will have on board about twenty hands for the same life-boats and life-buoys. Again, a sailing vessel of 601 tons must carry five boats of 1,463 cubic feet; or if she does not carry five boats, she must carry four boats – one 16 feet long, two 24 feet long, and one launch 25 feet long; one of these boats must be a lifeboat and she must carry two lifebuoys. These four or five immense boats will, if the vessel is not a passenger ship, be provided for the safety of about twenty-five people, so that five persons could go in each boat, and each person could have the twelfth part of a life belt to himself. A steam ship of 361 tons must

> carry boats and life-buoys of the same number, size and description as the sailing vessel of 601 tons, and she may carry from 1,200 to 1,300 passengers, so that she will have from 250 to 300 people in each boat, and about the 700th part of a life-buoy per person.

The very real and longstanding threat of fire aboard ships was recognized by introduction of a minimal requirement in Part V that *No Steam Vessel of 100 Tons Burden or upwards shall proceed to Sea unless it shall be provided with a Hose for the purpose of extinguishing Fire capable of being connected with the Engines of the Vessel.*

The genesis of ultimately comprehensive regulation for the avoidance of collision was contained in Part IV of the Act which required – *steam vessels to pass port to port within the narrow confines of rivers and channels and to keep to the starboard side of the channel when passing.* Part X enabled regulations to be made for exhibition of lights by steam vessels, with Part XII requiring such lights to be exhibited at night …*in any River or narrow Channel in Great Britain or Ireland, or the adjacent Islands, or upon the Sea within Twenty Miles in any Part of the Coast of Great Britain or Ireland …whether under Weigh or at Anchor, between Sunset and Sunrise…'.*

To place the minimal effect of application of the Steam Navigation Act 1846 into perspective it is estimated that there were, at the time of its introduction on 1 January 1847, 24,167 sailing vessels of 131 average net tonnage and only 1,033 steam vessels of 400 average net tonnage[145]. This first attempt by the British Parliament to regulate the safety of ships was met with derision and defiance by the shipping industry and was seen to be an interference in the long standing right of ship owners to be the sole arbiters of the safety of their ships. The requirements were seen to be excessive for small sailing vessels with small crews and totally inadequate for larger vessels carrying passengers;

> The existing requirements respecting boats are evaded by the majority of coasters and home trade vessels because they are beyond reason and because there is no provision to secure compliance....on the one hand it will be seen that there are not enough hands on board a vessel to save to boats, whilst on the other hand there are not enough boats to save the passengers and crew; and that the lifebelts required by the Act are utterly inadequate. When this class of legislation is operative

> it is frequently vicious because the minimum of necessity must be adopted as the maximum of efficiency, and where it is inoperative it is mischievous and delusive, since it leads the public at large to believe that it provides for cases that it never reaches. [146]

There was considerable suspicion of what was seen to be over zealous supervision of ships by the Government that could increase costs and be an impediment to unrestricted free trade. It was widely believed that the ship owner, who had funded the purchase of his ships, would provide the best safeguard of their safety[147] in spite of statistics that indicated this wasn't entirely the case.

These views of prescriptive and unnecessary legislation for the safety of ships in 1846 were further reflected in the remarks of a commentator in 1866;

> The Steam Navigation Act of 1846, with its unpretentious title, is a very remarkable instance of the application of the thin edge of the wedge. When it was before Parliament it appears to have raised so little curiosity that no mention is made in "Hansard" of any remarks or debates respecting it during its passage through either House, and yet this Act was the germ of one of the most extensive and most thoroughly organised systems of Government interference and official superintendence now existing…the Act of 1846...was not well received, and it was evaded; and in 1848 it was found necessary to pass a further Act [the Steam Navigation Act, 1848] to "compel" owners of steamers to attend to the provisions of the former Act.[148]

By the 1840s the Industrial Revolution had moved beyond a reliance upon close access to sources of fuels such as coal and iron ore, and a need for fast flowing water power for mills. The introduction of a widespread network of railways during the 1840s supplemented the canal system and provided the means for manufacturing centres to spread across the midlands and the north. Transport transformed industry internally, but manufacturing relied upon cheap imports of raw materials for its export of products through ports, and cheap food for its workers.

Tariffs were the enemy of imports and exports.[149] The Tory Prime Minister, Robert Peel, who was a champion of free trade, welcomed the support of the radical industrialists Richard Cobden and John Bright who founded the Anti-Corn Law League to campaign for cheap food. When the price of food rose sharply in 1846 due to bad weather in England, causing a failure of the harvest, along with failure of the Irish potato crop, the spectre of famine in England arose. It was necessary to reduce the price of the staple diet of the working class, who ate an average of five pounds of bread a week, by removing the tariff upon imported wheat. Peel attempted to convince his Cabinet colleagues of the benefits of free trade and failed. He resigned on this issue but came back to power shortly afterwards when the Whigs could not form a Government. In February 1846 he successfully moved a package of measures abolishing duties on imported corn over three years. Average bread prices fell by half over the subsequent thirty years.[150]

The slow movement towards completely free trade that had come about through the Reciprocity Acts in 1825, and increasing numbers of free trade agreements with other nations, gathered a head of steam of appreciation amongst politicians and the public that culminated with repeal of the age old protectionist Navigation Acts in 1849.

With the advent of a scheduled and frequent North Atlantic steamship service in 1840 the sailing packets could not meet the increased expectations of passengers especially regarding shorter passage times and scheduled arrival dates. The packets could depart on schedule but were at the mercy of the wind and weather and arrival times could vary by weeks. But, over a more than thirty year period from 1816 until 1850 the sailing packets set a template and a standard for reliability and safety that would not be met by scheduled steamship services for many years; particularly regarding safety. In the thirty-four years that the sailing packets operated until 1850, in spite of the ships being hard-driven by their American masters and officers, and largely British/Irish/Scandinavian crews, only two ships were lost; the ***Albion*** off Ireland in 1822 with the loss of forty-four lives and the disappearance of the ***Crisis*** in 1826 with her crew and about a dozen passengers.[151]

Regardless of the competition from steamships the owners of sailing packets continued to refine the design and size of their vessels with the enormous ***Great Republic*** being designed and built by Donald MacKay in 1853; at 335 feet long and 4500 ton, larger than any steamship operating across the North Atlantic at that time. The ship never had the opportunity to demonstrate her potential; catching fire when fitting out before her maiden voyage. The ***Sovereign of the Seas***, another MacKay ship, was advertised as the fastest ship in the world. Her record passage of 13 days, 22 hours was achieved during a crossing from New York to Liverpool in 1853.[152]

The introduction of relatively large scheduled trans-Atlantic passenger liners, saw a sea change in the composition of ships' crew. The frustrations of voyaging under sail and total dependence upon the wind for propulsion were inexorably being replaced by increasingly efficient steam propulsion. The potential had arrived for ships to no longer be at the mercy of the weather, and the agony of being becalmed, as Conrad eloquently described at the opening of Chapter Three of 'The Nigger of the 'Narcissus' (1897);

> Meantime the *Narcissus*, with square yards, ran out of the fair monsoon. She drifted slowly, swinging round and round the compass, through a few days of baffling light airs. Under the patter of short warm showers, grumbling men whirled the heavy yards from side to side; they caught hold of the soaked ropes with groans and sighs, while their officers, sulky and dripping with rain water, unceasingly ordered them about in wearied voices. During the short respites they looked with disgust into the smarting palms of their stiff hands, and asked one another bitterly:—"Who would be a sailor if he could be a farmer?" All the tempers were spoilt, and no man cared what he said. One black night, when the watch, panting in the heat and half-drowned with the rain, had been through four mortal hours hunted from brace to brace, Belfast declared that he would "chuck the sea for ever and go in a steamer.

Over the course of the nineteenth century a new breed of seamen, the marine engineer, would slowly hold sway;

> 'From coupler-flange to spindle-guide I see Thy Hand O God,
> – Predestination in the stride o' yon connectin'-rod.'[153]

Steamships required firemen (stokers), greasers and coal-trimmers; collectively known as the 'black gang' or 'black watch', and supervised by marine engineers; the invisible men of the steam age.[154] One shipmaster gave a view from on deck of the work of a stoker;

> If you look down on the stokehold gratings, full forty feet, you may, as the glare from an open furnace door momentarily lights up the gloomy depths below, catch a glimpse of him. You have a birds-eye view of a man in a bent position deftly throwing one, two, three shovelfuls of coal into the centre of the glare; then comes the clatter of an iron door closing with a snap, and to you all is darkness. Then from another direction comes the creak of rusty hinges followed by another glare of light, and the process is repeated[155]

The very large quantities of coal necessary were stored in spaces to either side of the stokehold; essentially a double hull with hatches through the deck for loading the coal and watertight doors to give access from the engine room. The coal had to be shovelled into barrows and wheeled to the furnace doors for use of the stokers; difficult, dangerous and dirty work;

In darkness, only punctuated by the dim light of a safety-lamp, in an atmosphere composed of the exhalations from the coal and a modicum of dust-laden air; liable at any moment to be overwhelmed by the down-rushing masses of coal as the ship's motion displaces it, the grimy sweat-soaked man works on[156]

The third, and perhaps most dangerous task in the engine room was that of the Greaser, who, under the guidance of the engineer, monitored and lubricated the exposed steam machinery; 'feeling her over'. Less onerous than trimming or stoking, it was still physically demanding;

> Starting from the main shaft bearings, crankpins, and eccentric straps, you hastily run over the smaller gear in a temperature of 100 degrees [Fahrenheit]. You then mount to the middle platform with your oil-can and wad brush, touching lightly and oiling piston– rods, guides, sockets, lever bearings, all the multitudinous smaller oscillating and rotating parts. Here the temperature will probably be 115 degrees, but by the time you get close up under the cylinders, it will be 125 degrees at least. [157]

With the development of steam passenger ships came a need for ever increasing numbers of stewards to attend to the wellbeing of passengers and officers; creating a new department aboard steamships, alongside the deck and engine departments; the provedore or catering department, headed by the Chief Steward; derisively referred to by the rest of the crew as 'pot wallahs'. As passenger ships increased in size and power the engine and catering departments eventually grew to become far larger than the deck department. Aboard the largest passenger steamers, the Chief Steward headed the largest department; ranking alongside the Chief Officer and Chief Engineer but of far greater visibility to the passengers. The catering department also gave women an opportunity to work at sea as a small number of stewardesses were engaged to look after women passengers and children.

Sailing ship seaman who took up work in steamers considered that they were 'giving up the sea' and were looked upon by their late shipmates as having become 'half-landsmen' or, with allusion to the steam engines, 'coffee-pot sailors'. Author Frank Bullen, who spent twenty-five years at sea, wrote in 1900 that on steamships;

> ...you shall often find a man occupying an A.B's position [Able Bodied Seaman] who is really only an unskilled labourer. Placed on board a sailing ship he would be as helpless and useless as any landlubber, except that he would not be seasick[158]

The three departments tended to work in isolation from each other and relationships were not always harmonious, as reflected in the saying regarding the deck and engine departments, and still in use, that 'oil and water don't mix'. This was borne out by a passenger on a steamship in 1886 who asked a quartermaster [a seamen who worked on the bridge and steered the ship] if he had any news about a fireman who'd fallen ill. The reply was – "He knew nothing of the man for we don't mix with any of those fellows...we keep to ourselves, you see. Sir!"[159]

Sailing ships would continue to evolve and trade for the entire nineteenth century and beyond; manned as they had been for millennia by a complement of expert seamen working together to gain the maximum possible advantage from the wind, with almost the entire crew from the Captain down being able to hand (set the sails) reef (shorten sail) and steer, and to take soundings to determine the depth of water. By the 1860's their labours would be eased by the introduction of deck mounted steam donkey boilers driving winches and pumps but, the essential propulsion force remained as it always had been, the wind. These increases in efficiency reduced the labour intensive nature of sailing ships and enabled cost savings through reduced crew numbers. Sailing ships continued to be competitive through much lower construction costs than steamships and the carriage of non-perishable bulk cargoes where speed gave no advantage.

With the combination of efficient and reliable steamships and lucrative Admiralty mail contracts on the North Atlantic, the model was set for rapid expansion of steamship services worldwide. The Royal Mail Line obtained a ten year contract to carry mails to the West Indies in 'at least fourteen good substantial and efficient steamships' and soon expanded their service to the West coast of South America. The Pacific Steam Navigation Company received its charter in 1840 and served the Pacific coast of South America. Two of their ships built in 1840, the ***Chile*** (682 tons) and ***Peru***, (690 tons) were the first steam ships to pass through the Straits of Magellan. Also in 1840, the Peninsular and Oriental Steam Navigation Company (P & O) was incorporated by Royal Charter; a company which had started life in 1837 as the Peninsular Company operating a fleet of steam mail packets to the Iberian Peninsula under contract from the Admiralty who, by this time, had been operating thirty-seven ships. This service was extended to Malta and Alexandria in 1840 with the Company being renamed Peninsular and Oriental. Passengers and mail were transferred to Suez by a combination of the Mahmoudieh Canal to the Nile, to Cairo by steamer and thence overland on camels to Suez. In 1844 P & O undertook the mail service from England to Alexandria and then onwards from Suez to Ceylon, Calcutta and China using ships of the East India Company until 1854 when P & O took over this service; the same year that they started a service from Singapore to Australia.[160]

At this early stage in the evolution of ocean-going steamships, limiting factors were the increasing inability of wooden hulls to withstand the forces and stresses generated by increasing power of steam engines, and the inefficiency of paddle wheels. There was also a general reluctance to introduce iron construction, not least from the Admiralty which stipulated in its mail contracts that such ships must be constructed of wood, through a fear of piercing wooden hulls underwater with propeller shafts for screw propulsion.

Even before the ***Great Western*** had completed her second voyage Brunel was turning his creative and open mind to her much larger successor, originally designed as a wooden paddle steamer – the ***Great Britain***. However, the rapid pace of technological change benefited the final design of the ship. Before construction commenced, John Laird's channel packet ***Rainbow***, one year old and the largest iron hulled steamer yet built, called at Bristol. The Admiralty were familiar with this ship having carried out experiments aboard her to determine the effects of iron hulls upon the compasses. Brunel sent his advisers on a return passage to Antwerp aboard the ***Rainbow*** and they returned as enthusiastic converts to iron construction. Brunel successfully convinced his board of the benefits of iron hulls. This method of construction was very much the exception to the rule of all wooden construction which was to remain dominant throughout the 1850s.[161] Another U-turn took place when construction was well underway. Brunel was unhappy with the performance of paddle wheels and was considering a new type of paddle that would provide more speed with less fuel consumption.

At this very time the small propeller driven ***Archimedes*** visited Bristol. The 200 ton ***Archimedes*** was launched in the autumn of 1838, fitted with a 90 horsepower engine. After some initial problems, including a boiler explosion which killed the engineer, the vessel undertook successful trials with a much shortened 'helix' of only two blades and outran sailing packets at Dover. The little steamship, which glided along with no sails or paddles then undertook a triumphant tour of the main English ports, in the course of which she serendipitously called at Bristol.[162] Even though the ***Great Britain's*** paddle box frames had already been fitted, Brunel was so impressed by the performance of the small screw steamer that he wrote a long report to convince the Great Western directors of the benefits of screw propulsion;

> Taking up twenty-three pages of a letterbook, the report shows Brunel at the height of his persuasive powers. His tone was initially impartial, as though he were simple applying one of the finest engineering minds of the time to an interesting scientific question. He considered the problem of 'slip', of how much energy a screw or paddle wasted in moving a vessel through the water, and described tests of resistance and friction upon a hull. On these points screws and paddles were judged comparable, with slight advantages for screws. In apparent candour, Brunel noted that the Archimedes was actually a poor model of a screw powered vessel; limited by a faulty engine and gearing, the

> screw surface already roughened and made less efficient by corrosion, and the hull badly designed, and the ship generally 'uninhabitable' for passengers. With proper design and engineering, though, the screw offered compelling advantages. It would save weight, especially at the top of the vessel, where high paddle wheels and their machinery raised a vessel's centre of gravity and made her less stable in heavy seas. It allowed for a simpler, more compact ship structure, with more space below for cargo and passengers. By eliminating the bulky paddle boxes, it offered less resistance to head winds and waves. When a ship rolled from side to side, a screw would remain submerged and moving the ship forward, unlike side paddle wheels, which could roll out of the water, alternately racing and overloading the engine, harming machinery. Without paddle boxes, a ship would present less beam for tight manoeuvres in rivers and harbours. Paddles might start a voyage too deeply immersed under a full load of coal, then rise too far out of the water as fuel was burned; a screw stayed efficiently under water regardless. Screw machinery cost less initially, and – because it was less vulnerable to passing shocks – would be cheaper and less trouble to maintain.[163]

Construction was halted for nine months, with the half-finished paddle wheel boxes being discarded and the partially built hull redesigned for screw propulsion. Commercial success of the ship depended upon performance of an unproven propeller on an ocean-going ship and Brunel spent more time on this aspect of the design than any other. The Admiralty was, at the same time experimenting with screw propeller propulsion, as it would be less vulnerable to gunfire than paddlewheels. Brunel worked with the Admiralty on this project and also borrowed some of their ideas. The final design was for a propeller with six narrow blades; a prudent but flawed design which proved to be an unfortunate choice during her second voyage.

The development of a screw propeller had come from a most unlikely source. A patent had been taken out by Francis Pettit Smith, a grazing farmer interested in model boats, in 1836 for a steam powered vessel propelled by a screw at the stern. Upon obtaining financial backing a thirty-four foot screw steamer of ten tons and six horsepower was built with a propeller resembling an Archimedes helix that wound completely around its horizontal axis in two revolutions. During trials an obstruction was hit and caused the helix to break in half but, up until this misfortune it had surprisingly increased performance. The Admiralty showed interest and, after the vessel was demonstrated to them in March 1838, requested that the screw principle be proven aboard a larger ship.

Finally, after five years of planning, replanning, redesign, building, rebuilding and delays, the ***Great Britain*** was launched by the Prince Consort in 1843. After fitting out, she undertook her maiden voyage with 600 ton of cargo, sixty first class passengers, and steerage passengers, in 1845; the largest ship yet constructed, the first ocean-going ship with an iron hull, and the first such ship with a screw propeller. Of 332 feet in length and 3,270 gross tons, her engines produced 1,500 horsepower to achieve 12 knots. She was also fitted with six masts and a schooner rig that could be used as a back-up.[164]

Apart from excessive rolling due to her hull design and the lack of paddle boxes, her return maiden voyage was successful, albeit slower than the record holder ***Cambria*** – almost 15 days westbound and thirteen and a half eastbound. In an attempt to increase speed two additional inches of iron were riveted to each propeller blade in Liverpool before her second westbound voyage during which she lost her foremast in a squall five days out, and later lost three propeller blades on one side, leaving the propeller dangerously unbalanced, and arriving in New York after eighteen days. Passengers also complained of intolerable rolling. After repairs she departed for Liverpool with only 23 passengers aboard and 'the propellor again fell apart, piece by piece, until it was down to just the nubs of two arms'. The ship was laid up in Liverpool and underwent extensive repairs and modifications, including a far stronger four bladed cast iron propeller and bilge keels to reduce the rolling. Improvements were also made to her engines and boilers for more speed. Public opinion turned against the ship with the formerly enthusiastic *Mechanics Magazine* stating that the Great Britain had succumbed to a 'leviathanism which was wholly uncalled for' and 'manifestly beyond the reach of any engineering skill possessed by those who planned and built her'.[165]

Regardless of these criticisms Brunel and the ***Great Western*** had clearly and boldly set the template for the future design of ocean-going steamships; one that would eventually be followed as confidence and experience was gained in iron hulls and screw propulsion. Unfortunately, the lamentable experience of screw propulsion demonstrated by the ***Great Western***, and her unfortunate grounding on the Irish coast on her third voyage; put down to her compasses being affected by the iron hull, did nothing to alter the traditionally conservative views of shipowners. Wooden hulls and paddlewheels largely remained the stock standard design of ocean-going steamships throughout the 1840s with the only changes being those of steadily increasing size, horsepower and speed.

The Cunard Line had a virtual monopoly of the North-Atlantic trade throughout the 1840s and were well on their way to establishing an enduring and highly prized safety record. 'Nor can one over-estimate the importance, not only to the shipping industry, but to the world at large, of the services rendered by this undertaking. By method, skill and care, regularity, speed, dispatch and safety combined with an ever increasing comfort have been obtained. The greatness of the success of Mr. Cunard and his partners can only be grasped when a comparison of their work is made with that of some of their less fortunate competitors'.[166]

Cunard had built two more ships in the early 1840s; the ***Hibernia*** in 1843, to meet requirements of a renewed mail contract, and the ***Cambria*** (1844) to replace one of the original four steamers; the ***Columbia,*** which had sunk, with no loss of life, after striking a rock in fog off Nova Scotia. These ships were slightly larger and more powerful versions of their predecessors and, like them, were built in a style that was to become a hallmark of Cunard service; austere comfort. In 1846 Cunard became aware that the American Government was to make a grant of $400,000 to some New York businessmen to start a steamship mail service across the Atlantic. This spurred Cunard to use this information as leverage in his negotiations with the British Government and he was successful in gaining an increase of £65,000 to his existing mail contract. By 1848, Cunard had built four more steamers to meet the coming American competition; the ***America, Canada, Europe*** and ***Niagara*** all of 1820 tons, 1400 horsepower and capable of ten and a quarter knots. The new quartet, with more powerful engines and boiler pressures (18 pounds per square inch) double those of the original quartet, reduced passage times by almost one day Westbound and ten hours Eastbound. Two further ships were built in 1850; the ***Africa*** and ***Asia***; sister ships, at 2226 tons the largest yet Cunard ships, but slower than their American rivals.[167]

Chapter 4

Famine, Fire and Free Trade

The predominant cause of loss of life at sea during the years straddling the mid-nineteenth century from 1846, came from death through sickness, or loss of emigrant ships, during the mass exodus from the Irish famine to North America. Emigrant ships, predominantly sailing vessels, carried one and a half million people across the North Atlantic between 1846 and 1855; many desperately seeking a new life in the New World, principally the British colony of Canada.

Living conditions aboard these ships were very basic with large numbers of passengers carried aboard relatively small sailing vessels in very unhygienic conditions; often resulting in what was known as 'ship fever'; the extremely contagious diseases of Cholera, Typhus and Smallpox. Many emigrants died aboard these ships before reaching the Quarantine Station at Grosse Island in the St. Lawrence River. During 1846 an estimated 33,000 people of all nationalities landed at Grosse Island, with 84,500 landing the following year. Nearly 70% were Irish. About one-third of Irish passengers died during their voyage or immediately after landing. Little wonder that the emigrant ships from Great Britain to North America became known as 'coffin ships'.[168] A graphic account from the early twentieth century, when the experience of emigrants during the famine was still fresh in living memories, brings home many of the tragic issues surrounding this desperate time.

> A member of the New York Academy of Medicine went aboard the Ceylon from Liverpool in 1847. He found that many of the passengers had died on the voyage, and one hundred and fifty were still ill with typhus. "We passed through the steerage but the indescribable filth, the emaciated, half-nude figures, many with the eruption disfiguring their faces, crouching in the bunks or strewed over the decks and cumbering the gangways, broken utensils and debris of food spread recklessly about, presented a picture of which neither pen nor pencil can convey a full idea. Some were just rising from their berths for the first time since leaving Liverpool, having been suffered to lie there

during the entire voyage wallowing in their own filth". The lower deck of an immigrant vessel was often little better than that of a slave ship. According to Friedrich Kapp, chairman of the New York Board of Emigration Commissioners, a death-rate of 10 per cent was not uncommon, and it sometimes happened that a third of the passengers died before reaching land;

In the dreadful years of the Irish famine the mortality at sea was ghastly. In 1846, out of 98,105 Irish emigrants, 20,365 are known to have died. In the following year the mortality was 17.2 per cent of the embarkation. An old-fashioned sailing vessel once visited by typhus, cholera, or smallpox often carried the germs of contagion for years; and the hapless human beings in the crowded steerage, unclean, ill-fed, and weakened by confinement in an atmosphere foul beyond description, were frequently decimated by disease. The frightful mortality in the years of the Irish famine brought about the passage of a British Passenger Act which instituted a much needed reform in sailing regulations. The English ships had the evil distinction of the highest death-rate, partly because they were under less stringent regulations than others, and partly because they brought more Irish, who were the poorest and most helpless of all immigrants. In 1847 three-fourths of all the patients in the New York quarantine hospital were from English ships.

The New York Commissioners of Emigration reported that in 1847 and 1848 sick passengers averaged thirty in a thousand on British ships, nine and three-fifths on American ships, and eight and three-fifths on German ships. As soon as the pestilence accompanying the famine ended, sanitary conditions began to improve. From 1855 to 1860 the death-rate for all immigrants was only 6.1 per cent. In 1867 the death-rate was 11.67 in the thousand on sailing vessels and 1.03 on steamships. Five years later it had been reduced by more than 50 per cent on both classes of vessels.[169]

During the nineteenth century no material reduction was made in the length of the voyage from Great Britain to North America until the transition was effected from sail to steam. Much of course depended on the season of the year and weather conditions. Vessels were fortunate when they made the passage from Europe in less than a month; unfortunate, when it took them two months. In 1830 emigrants embarking

> from England were required to provide themselves with food for six weeks, and this was thought to be sufficient to allow for delays due to any ordinary causes. In 1867 the average length of the voyage by sail for all immigrants was about forty-four days and six hours, and five years later the time had been reduced by little more than an hour.
>
> In 1828 on a ship from Scotland so little room was available that six families lived during the many weeks of the voyage in the life boat on deck. It was customary for the captain to lease to an emigrant agent the space reserved for passengers, and to assume no responsibility himself for their comfort and well-being. Into this space the agent packed without regard to age, sex, or state of health as many human beings as the law permitted the ship to carry. The food, bedding, and other baggage they brought with them were very often filthy and unfit for a long voyage. The ventilation was wretched, the facilities for cooking altogether inadequate, cleanliness was impossible, and arrangements for proper treatment of the sick were lamentably insufficient. The passengers were completely at the mercy of the officers and crew, and brutal treatment was the rule rather than the exception.

The 'coffin ships' engaged in the North American emigrant trade were the same timber ships that were the catalyst for the Select Committee on Shipwrecks of Timber Ships, 1839 and resultant legislation to deal with the issue of the carriage of deck cargoes of timber in the North Atlantic winter. The Select Committee learnt of the generally old, unsound and unseaworthy condition of these ships, yet they were considered suitable for the carriage of large numbers of emigrants upon their otherwise empty return voyages, often under appalling conditions. Issues with these particular ships were to rumble on throughout the nineteenth century.

During the six years of the famine about fifty emigrant ships foundered in the North Atlantic.[170] The Cork Examiner of 6 February 1846 recorded the losses, from December to February alone, of nine sailing vessels involving the deaths of 80 people. In 1847 there were two losses of emigrant ships; one with great loss of life. In March the old and very small ***Carricks*** (1812), of 244 tons, departed Sligo for Quebec with 187 emigrants onboard. Six weeks later she was wrecked in a severe storm in the Gulf of St. Lawrence with 86 lost. All of the crew except one boy survived. The small sailing ship ***Exmouth***, (1813) of 320 tons, departed from Londonderry for Quebec on

25 April 1847 with an estimated 240 emigrants and 11 crew. The ***Exmouth*** was registered for 165 and a half persons but, as a large proportion of the passengers were children, two of whom counted as one adult, the ship carried a greater number of passengers. In a gale shortly after sailing the sails were blown out, and the longboat and lifeboat washed away. Shortly after midnight on 28 April the ***Exmouth*** was driven ashore on the coast of Islay and was completely broken up within ten minutes. Only three crew members managed to scramble ashore from the rigging. All remaining passengers and crew were lost.[171]

As they were carrying passengers, such ships were required to meet the standards of the Passengers in Merchant Ships Act, 1842[172], – *an Act for Regulating the Carriage of Passengers in Merchant Vessels* – that dealt predominantly with the welfare of passengers aboard all ships; sail and steam. The Act prescribed that no more than three persons were to be carried to every five tons registered burden of the ship, and allotted space per passenger dependent upon the length of the voyage; for example, "One Passenger for every Ten such clear superficial feet, if such Ship is not to pass within the Tropics during such voyage". Quantities per passenger of water and food were prescribed along with a proper supply of medicines.[173]

The emergence of passenger carrying steamships along with growing concern from the early 1840s about standards for carriage of emigrants to Australia and New Zealand and North America, brought about requirements in the Passengers in Merchant Ships Act, 1842 for the carriage of a specific number of boats, dependent upon tonnage and passengers, and for a survey by two competent persons before departure to attest to seaworthiness. The Act was silent on the size, capacity and stowage of such boats. The Passengers in Merchant Ships Act, 1842, was the genesis of flawed and confused legislation, initially limited to passenger ships, based upon the tonnage of the ship almost regardless of the total number of persons on board, throughout the nineteenth century and beyond.

An ever-present danger during the long era of wooden ships was due to reliance upon naked flames, and during carriage of cargoes subject to spontaneous combustion, was fire at sea. Joseph Conrad spoke in 1881 from personal experience as Second Mate of the 427-ton barque ***Palestine*** (1857)[174] of the perils of fire at sea. In his book entitled *Youth* he tells of the ordeal of the crew of the fictional sailing ship ***Judea*** which had to be abandoned off the coast of Sumatra after its cargo of coal caught fire, as narrated by the Second Mate;

> The smell down below was as unexpected as it was frightful. One would have thought that hundreds of paraffin-lamps had been flaring and smoking in that hole for days. I was glad to get out. The man with me coughed and said, "Funny smell, sir." I answered negligently, "It's good for the health, they say," and walked aft. The first thing I did was to put my head down the square of the midships ventilator. As I lifted the lid a visible breath, something like a thin fog, a puff of faint haze, rose from the opening. The ascending air was hot, and had a heavy, sooty, paraffiny smell. I gave one sniff and put the lid down gently. It was no use choking myself. The cargo was on fire.[175]

Conrad's crew were rescued from their boats but other crew and passengers during the nineteenth century were not, particularly those aboard emigrant ships with large numbers of passengers. The American registered sailing ship ***Ocean Monarch***[176], (1847) of 1301 tons, sailed from Liverpool for the United States on 24 August 1848, with a total of 398 persons onboard; the majority Irish emigrants. At midday the same day smoke was observed coming from a ventilator and within five minutes the ship was ablaze aft and amidships. The anchors were dropped to keep the bow into the wind and most people aboard congregated on the bowsprit to avoid the flames. Two boats were launched from the ***Ocean Monarch,*** but the other two boats were lost in the fire. Fortunately, there were a number of other vessels in the vicinity that launched boats and rescued a large number of passengers and crew. The ship burnt to the waterline and sank at 1330. In spite of the efforts of rescuers 178 were lost as reported graphically in the United Service Gazette of August 26 1848[177];

> Great was the anxiety to learn any tidings whatever of the vessel, but it was not till the arrival, about half-past five, of the Queen of the Ocean yacht, belonging to T. Littledale, Esq., that the extent of the calamity was known. Mr. Littledale, was returning in his yacht to Liverpool with a party of friends. About 12 o'clock, when near the Great Orms-head, they observed the Ocean Monarch about five or six miles to the eastward of the Ormshead, in Abergele Bay, between the Ormshead and Abergele. Mr. Littledale and his friends were admiring the beauty

> of the splendid ship as she was pursuing her course to the Atlantic. On a sudden the Ocean Monarch was observed to put up her helm as if returning to Liverpool. A flag of distress was immediately hoisted, and in a few seconds flames were observed to burst out abaft. The ship was lying right in the course of the yacht, and Mr. Littledale immediately bore away for her. On nearing her, although there was a stiff breeze blowing, with a heavy swell, the boat of the yacht was lowered, and proceeded to the ship for the purpose of rendering what assistance she could. Of course, with the swell on, it would have been next to certain destruction to the yacht had she been run alongside the ship, but the exertions of Mr. Littledale were of the noblest description, and he has the satisfaction of knowing that he has been the means of rescuing thirty-two persons from death…The flames were bursting with immense fury from the stern and centre of the vessel. So great was the heat in these parts that the passengers, male and female – men, women, and children – crowded to the fore part of the vessel. Their shrieks for aid were carried by the breeze across the waters. In their maddened despair, women jumped overboard with their children in their arms, and sunk, Men followed their wives in frenzy, and were lost. Groups of men, women, and children also precipitated themselves into the water, in the vain hope of self-preservation, but the waters closed over many of them forever. No pen can describe this scene. The flames continued to rage with increased fury. In a few minutes the mizenmast went overboard – a few minutes more, and the mainmast shared the same fate. There yet remained the foremast. As the fire was making its way to the forepart of the vessel, the passengers and crew, of course, crowded still further forward. To the jib-boom they clung in clusters, as thick as they could pack, even one lying over another.

Further large loss of life, caused by fire aboard a wooden emigrant ship, occurred aboard the American built Packet Ship ***Caleb Grimshaw*** (1848) of 987 tons. The ship caught fire and sank off the Azores on 6 November 1849 whilst on its sixth voyage carrying emigrants from Liverpool to New York. Ninety of the 425 passengers were lost. The toll would have been considerably higher if the small Nova Scotian barque ***Sarah*** had not continued to stand by the ***Caleb Grimshaw*** for five days during stormy weather until she had managed to rescue 399 persons with her boats. The Captain and the great majority of the crew of the ***Caleb Grimshaw*** had disgracefully ignored their responsibilities by taking to the ship's boats shortly after the fire was discovered, with the Captain's boat, including his wife and her bed, laying on a line astern of the ship for the five days that the few remaining crew and starving passengers fought the fire.[178]

At this time there were no requirements for vessels of any type to carry navigation lights to indicate their presence at night or in times of reduced visibility, and to assist with prevention of collision. It wasn't until July 1848, under Part X of the Steam Navigation Act, 1846, that steam vessels were required to exhibit navigation lights through regulations made pursuant to the Act by the Admiralty. This was not initially well received by some mariners;

> To the Editor of the Nautical Standard[179].
>
> Sir,-
>
> Is it not absurd to compel our steamships to carry three lights of different colours, without defining any particular object, when one light, of a different colour, can be made to demonstrate all that is necessary to warn vessels and prevent collisions? and can there be anything more unjust than compelling us, under the penalty of £20 or £40 a night, to carry these lights; -and our being liable to the penalty, even should the light go, out by accident? The three lights ordered by the Admiralty convey no meaning, and what is still more stupid, sailing vessels are not required to carry any light whatever; and, therefore, on a dark night, may become a trap for steamers to fall foul of. In fact, under the present system, collisions will increase. I am glad to see you have taken the matter up, for we captains of steam-ships know that we shall be much bothered to keep three lights constantly going, and besides the great expense, we risk being fined. Had the Admiralty adopted Mr. Rettie's signal, of showing a single lamp of a particular colour at the lookout station, we should at once show our true course to vessels coming upon us, and thus would be prevented a recurrence of those cases which we almost daily see in the papers, under the "Law Reports, "especially that of the Birkenhead and the schooner, where the former was most unjustly cast in heavy damages. I am convinced were a new trial of this case granted, the verdict would be different ; for, a jury would be made to understand the absurdity of sailing vessels not being compelled to carry any light, and that a plain

light gives no warning to a steamer, which can only be effected by the coloured light on Mr. Rettie's plan. I am, Sir, yours, &c.,

Captain of a Steam-ship'.

When regulations were drafted and published by the Admiralty it became clear that their intent, as reported by *The Economist* on 29 June 1848, was to require steamships to carry navigation lights of a character almost identical to those carried by ships today;

By the Commissioners for Executing the Office of the Lord High Admiral of the United Kingdom of Great Britain and Ireland, &c., &c. Whereas under, and by virtue of, the Act of Parliament, passed in the tenth year of the reign of her present Majesty, intituled an "Act for the Regulation of Steam Navigation," &c., we hereby require, in pursuance of the said act, that lights shall be exhibited by all British steam vessels, between sunset and sunrise, of such description and in such manner as hereinafter mentioned, that is to say-

When Under Weigh.– Bright white light at the foremast head :Green light on the starboard side ;Red light on the port side. When at Anchor.– A common bright light.* The following conditions to be observed, viz. :-

The mast-head light to be visible at a distance of at least five miles in a clear dark night, and the lantern to be so constructed as to show a uniform and unbroken light over an arc of the horizon of twenty points of the compass, viz., from right a-head to two points abaft the beam on each side of the ship.

The coloured side lights to be visible at a distance of at least two miles in a clear dark night, and the lanterns to be so constructed as to show a uniform and unbroken light over an arc of the horizon of ten points of the compass, viz., from right ahead to two points abaft the beam on their respective sides. :

The side lights to be moreover fitted with inboard screens, of at least three feet long, to prevent them from being seen across the bow. The screens to be placed in a fore and aft line with the inner edge of the side lights.

> The lantern used when at anchor to be so constructed as to show a good light all– round the horizon.
>
> 'It is understood to be the intention of the Lords of the Admiralty to issue regulations in accordance with the foregoing announcement, and to have them published in the London Gazette, so that they may he in force from the 21st of July next'.

One significant flaw in this regulations was the exclusion of the vast majority of vessels such as sailing and fishing vessels. The fishermen of the day would have taken little comfort from the introduction of such regulations for the steam ships they referred to as 'whispering death' due to the frequency with which they were run down, whether within twenty miles of the coast or further out to sea. However the steamships, ever increasing in size and speed, would have had little awareness of the close proximity at night of unlit sailing and fishing vessels, or of their course.

The rigorous requirements for surveys of steam vessels and regular declarations to the Board of Trade made by the 1846 Act were reiterated through the Steam Navigation Act, 1848[180] – *An Act for the further Regulation of Steam Navigation, and for limiting in certain Cases the Number of Passengers to be conveyed in Steam Vessels.* It was clear that there'd been little enthusiasm for these surveys and declarations so the Board of Trade fired a shot across the bows of owners of steam vessels with a further charge for non-compliance. The fine of one hundred pound, imposed by the 1846 Act, was retained with a further "Sum of Ten Shillings for every Day that the sending of such declarations is delayed…"

Part II the Act provided for the Board of Trade to insert in a certificate a notice of the number of passengers steam vessels are constructed to carry which was to be placed in a conspicuous position on the vessel. This provision was primarily introduced to deal with steam vessels navigating on rivers carrying excessive numbers of passengers, as raised in the House on 1 August 1848 by the newly appointed President of the Board of Trade. Henry Labouchere, who became President for the second time in July 1847, was a late convert to the doctrine of intervention, having come to appreciate that reform of the merchant service was a necessary adjunct to maintaining the nation's competitive edge in development of free trade;[181]

> Mr. Labouchere proposed a Resolution to enable him to bring in a Bill to make some alteration in the law as regarded steam navigation. The object which he had in view was simple. All steamboats going to sea were required to have their machinery inspected by surveyors, and penalties were imposed on boats going to sea without such inspection; but there were no penalties attached to steamboats navigating rivers, and it was almost as important that there should be an inspection of steamboats on rivers, as of steamboats going to sea. Some cases of great abuse having lately been brought under his notice, he thought it not right to leave the public exposed to such dangers. This was the principal object of the Bill; but there was another provision in the Bill, which he thought desirable. It was to give the Board of Trade a general power to fix the maximum of passengers to be carried by steamboats. Nothing could be more unadvisable than that the Board of Trade, or any other department, should exercise a vexatious interference with the number of persons carried by steamboats. It was not necessary to exercise this power as to sea-going vessels; but it was notorious that some of the steamboats which navigated the Thames, owing to the great competition which existed on the river, were occasionally crowded in a manner dangerous to the public. He therefore proposed to give power to the Board of Trade to fix a maximum to the number of passengers which steamboats should be allowed to carry, as a maximum was fixed to the number passengers which stage-coaches and omnibuses were allowed to carry.

Approaching mid-century there was a flurry of consolidation and reformation activity in Parliament through the introduction of three more Acts of significance to merchant shipping; one consolidating a number of Passenger Acts, with the other two heralding an abandonment of centuries of protection and an acceptance by Parliament of the virtues of almost unfettered trade.

The requirement for passenger ships to carry boats had been continued by the Passenger Ships Act, 1845[182], the Passenger Act, 1847[183] and, in 1848 by the Passengers to North America Act[184]. This series of Acts remained concerned primarily with standards for the carriage of passengers, particularly emigrants, with frequent amendments being a response to the horrors of the exodus from Ireland.

The Passenger Ships Act, 1849,[185] described as – *An Act for regulating the Carriage of Passengers in Merchant Vessels* – repealed all three of the above Acts, and continued to deal with many matters concerning numbers of passengers, their health, welfare and provisioning, along with carriage of boats, and surveys. The provisions of the 1835 and 1842 Acts for *a survey to attest to seaworthiness if required* was made mandatory for all passenger ships, to reflect, and expand to sailing vessels, the provisions of Part XIV solely to steam vessels in the Steam Navigation Act, 1846.

The Passenger Act, 1849, echoed the requirements of the Steam Navigation Act, 1846, for the carriage of boats and took into account the number of boats required for a lesser number of passengers carried. The Act made a distinction between 'passenger ships'; – *vessels carrying more than one passenger to every 25 tons of the ship's registered tonnage,* and ships carrying less than that number of passengers. All the provisions of the Act applied to the former, while only sections 8, 12, 13, 32, 33 and 35 to the latter. Accordingly, a ship of 350 ton would be able up to carry up to 14 passengers before the provisions of the Act were applicable. The Act required a similar scale of lifeboat carriage to that of the 1842 Passenger Act;-

> '...suitable and seaworthy boats are to be taken according to the tonnage of the ship and the number of passengers, on the following scale':
>
> For a ship of 100 to 199 tons – 2 boats;
>
> For a ship of 200 to 499 tons (if the passengers exceed 50) – 3 boats
>
> For a ship of 500 tons an upwards (if the passengers exceed 200) – 4 boats

The requirements of the Act regarding carriage of boats paid no heed to the very large numbers of passengers being carried aboard emigrant sailing ships. For a small ship of 100 to 200 tons with very few passengers two boats may have been enough to accommodate all on board but it is extremely doubtful that the prescribed number of boats would have been able to accommodate the large numbers of emigrants carried aboard many smaller vessels between 200 and 500 tons, or greater than 500 ton. The existing ratio of passengers to tonnage allowed a 500-ton ship to carry a total complement of 250 persons. It can be seen from accidents already referred to that small sailing vessels of the 1830s often carried well in excess of the maximum complement allowed by the Passenger Vessels Act, 1803; for example the ***Lady Sherbrooke***, 377 tons carrying 300 persons, the ***Exmouth***, 320 tons carrying 251, and the ***Carricks***, 244 tons carrying 187 passengers plus crew.

Towards the end of the first half-century there was a change in the view of Parliamentarians regarding protection of trade between England and her colonies through a growing awareness of the economic benefits of free trade. This protection dated back to the reign of King Richard the Second when a law was passed in 1381 to ensure that only English ships carried cargo to and from that country but, due to the small number of English ships, the law was never enforced.[186]

It was not until the 17th century, when England had gained colonies in North America and the West Indies that legislation was introduced which forbade foreign flagged ships from trading between England and her colonies, and required the Master and three quarters of the crew to be English.[187] The Navigation Act, 1660,[188] first required ships to be registered and also excluded foreign built ships unless the English owner could prove his nationality and could also declare how much he'd paid for the ship and from whom it was purchased. Upon compliance with these requests a certificate was issued. A register of all such certificates was maintained Customs in London. As well as protection of trade these requirements formed the basis of ship registration world-wide.

Over the next two centuries further Acts; *An Act for Prevention of Frauds and Regulating Abuses in the Plantation Trade*, 1696,[189] *An Act for Further Increase and Encouragement of Shipping and Navigation*, 1786,[190] *The Navigation Laws Act*, 1817,[191] and Acts of 1823,[192] 1825,[193] 1833,[194] and 1845[195] consolidated requirements under the so-called Navigation Laws and the associated matter of registration of ships. The requirements for registration encompassed ownership, transfer of ownership, proof of location of build, tonnage, record of identity of the master and provision of a unique registration number carved into the main beam to provide evidence of the identity of the ship in case of shipwreck. All of these requirements for registration underwent a major consolidation through the Mercantile Marine Act, 1850.[196]

The Navigation Laws were repealed through the Navigation Act, 1849[197] – *An Act to amend the Laws in force for the Encouragement of British Shipping and Navigation.* The original Bill was amended during the Parliamentary recess in 1848/1849 to largely include freedom for foreign flagged vessels to compete in the coasting trade as reported in the Nautical Magazine and Marine Journal;[198]

> The Ministerial measure of last session for the repeal of the Navigation Laws has been amended in one important particular during the recess. The measure of 1848 proposed that the coasting trade of Great Britain should be protected as before, but that any vessel might bring any cargo from any foreign or colonial port to any port of the United Kingdom. It was forbidden, however, that the foreign or colonial vessel, after unlading part of its cargo at the port of entry, should proceed to a second or third port to discharge the rest. The measure, as amended by Mr. Labouchere, and brought before the House of Commons on Wednesday last, carries out the principle of Free Trade to a full extent. It still preserves a portion of protection to the coasting trade, but allows the foreign or colonial vessel to deposit any portion of its cargo at the port of entry, and to proceed with the remainder to another port. As a waste of freight might occur by the sailing of a vessel with only a portion of cargo from one British port to another, foreign vessels may complete their cargoes at the first port, and dispose of them in the second, For the more effectual protection of the revenue against smugglers, the liberty of carriage granted under these conditions of foreign or colonial vessels will be restricted to vessels above a hundred tons burden. Such, in few words, is the measure for the repeal of the Navigation Laws which Government has brought forward; and upon which, if we may judge by present appearances, the old and obstinate battles of Free Trade against Protection will be fought with undiminished animosity by the respective champions of each case. A preparatory skirmish took on Wednesday, when Mr. Herries, as Protectionist leader, announced his intention to give the measure his most strenuous and determined opposition. By mutual consent, however, leave has been given to bring in the Bill, with the understanding that no further discussion shall take place until the second reading. In the meantime, the measure is left for the study of the honourable members, and for the consideration of the country generally.

Some shipowners saw this as the last straw but a spirit of competition prevailed and introduced a half century of competition and expansion of trade. The Americans also repealed laws on restraint of trade but retained their "coasting' trade, with a definition that considerably stretched the definition of 'coast' to include voyages from the Atlantic to Pacific ports and vice versa, although such ships were rounding Cape Horn and passing through foreign waters.[199] The eventual opening up of the United Kingdom coastal trade to foreign vessels was enacted through the Coasting Trade Act, 1854[200] – *An Act to Admit Foreign Ships to the Coasting Trade.*

Chapter 5

Collision and Consolidation

By mid-century the numbers and tonnages of steamships had increased but they were still a small minority. In 1850 the British fleet of merchant ships had grown to include 1,187 steam vessels with a total of 168,000 net tons, and 24,797 sailing vessels with a total of 3,397,000 tons.[201] British registered ships comprised 46.86% of world total tonnage and 42.7% of world steamship tonnage. There were still a lot of very small ships of both types on the register as can be seen by the average tonnages of 141.5 for steamships and 136.9 for sailing ships. The trans-Atlantic passenger steamers, such as the Collins Line's wooden paddle steamer ***Baltic***, were gargantuan by comparison.

The success of Cunard Line, and consequent demise of the American sailing packets, had not gone unnoticed in America, leading to the establishment of one of the 'less fortunate competitors'; the Collins Line in 1850. 'The United States Government determined to make a great effort to regain, by means of a subsidized line of steamers, the coveted supremacy on the North Atlantic'.[202] In 1850 the Collins Line entered the North Atlantic mail and passenger trade with four new purpose built sister ships; ***Atlantic, Arctic, Pacific*** and ***Baltic***; each of 2,800 tons and 814 horsepower. They were built with luxurious accommodation and were considerably larger and faster than the latest Cunard ships. Fierce competition ensued with passengers benefiting from a price war. Great interest was taken on both sides of the Atlantic, especially in passage times, with many wagers being placed. Collins Line steamers soon established successive records with the ***Pacific*** completing the first passage under ten days in 1851, averaging more than 13 knots. Three months later the ***Baltic*** completed a westbound passage in less than 10 days. Both records were soon bettered by the ***Arctic*** and ***Baltic***.

Although the rivalry between these two shipping companies did much for the technical improvement of hull and machinery design, the power required for the record breaking speeds by Collins Line ships came at a cost to the structure of the wooden hulls and reliability of the engines; the ships suffered many breakdowns and were often withdrawn from service for considerable periods without notice. Working expenses amounted to twice those predicted, and this, coupled with very low passenger fares and high interest repayments resulted in average losses of $17,000 per trip. By the end of 1851 the company was facing bankruptcy. The company went cap-in-hand to the American Government for an increase in the mail subsidy of $385,000 per year for forty voyages per year. Negotiations took place over a considerable period of time, with the Collins Line eventually achieving more than double the subsidy to $858,000 for fifty-two annual voyages.[203]

By the mid-1850s the Admiralty had accepted the concept of iron hulls and screw propellers and, in 1859, commenced construction of ***HMS Warrior***, a 40-gun steam-powered armoured frigate which incorporated technical developments used by ocean-going merchant ships for many years, including a screw propeller. The Admiralty also relaxed its outdated policy that all mail steamers must be wooden hulled. The ***Tubal Cain*** of 737 ton, built in Liverpool in 1859, was the first ship to be built of composite construction; iron framing with wooden planking. [204]

The second half of the nineteenth century started off quietly for steamships with 13 being lost in 1850, but 598 sailing vessels were lost in the same year for a combined lost tonnage of British ships of 111,976 tons. These high losses continued throughout the 1850s with a total of 5123 British ships and 4400 lives lost between 1853 and 1858. Many more ships and lives were lost in the great storm of 25 and 26 October 1859. To put these losses of ships and their crews into context, the United Kingdom had a total of 19,270 ships registered in 1856 totalling 4,156,077 tons, crewed by 173,918 seamen. This total comprised 18,419 sailing ships and 851 steam ships.[205] The average sailing ship in 1856 was of 207 tons, crewed by 8 men, with the average steamer being 389 tons with a crew of 27. In 1856 6.25% of ships and 2.56% of seamen were lost.

One of the vessels lost in 1851 was as the result of a collision in the Malacca Straits with another vessel belonging to the same shipping company. Both vessels displayed navigation lights but a great deal of confusion existed on the part of each vessel as to the other's intentions; not least by the sole mast-head light on one vessel which '… as customary, was lowered at half-past eleven for the purpose of being trimmed…' as explained in the following article from the Argus, Melbourne of 13 November 1851.[206] This misfortune was compounded by the lack of a requirement in the 1848 Regulation for navigation lights for steam vessels for larger vessels to carry a second mast-head light aft of the foremast light;

> The chief event which has occupied the public attention at Singapore for a week past, is the frightful collision which took place between the Peninsular and Oriental Company's steamers Erin (1846) of 797 GT, and Pacha (1842) of 548 GT, on the night of the 21st instant, and which resulted in the almost immediate sinking of the latter, and a serious loss of life. On the afternoon of the 22nd instant the Peninsular and Oriental Company's steamer Erin, Captain Tronson from Calcutta, arrived here, presenting a very disabled appearance, her bowsprit being gone, and her bows very much injured. It was soon ascertained that a collision had taken place on the preceding night between the Erin and the Peninsular and Oriental Company's steamer Pacha, Captain Miller, which left this [port] on the preceding afternoon, and that the latter was totally lost.
>
> It appears that on the night in question the Pacha was proceeding up the Straits, standing on the usual course, north-west by west; but as Captain Miller, who only joined the vessel at Hongkong, had been told that there was a variation in the compass of about five degrees, and as Horsburgh's Chart lays down a bank a good way out from the land off Mount Formosa, he felt rather anxious as to his position. About half-past eleven o'clock some lightning over Mount Formosa gave him a glimpse of it, and immediately afterwards he saw a light which he considered to be on shore or to proceed from some boat or other vessel close in with the land. This light, which it was afterwards ascertained was the light at the masthead of the Erin, and which as customary, was lowered at half-past eleven for the purpose of being trimmed, then disappeared; and as Captain Miller thought he was too close in to clear the Formosa bank on his present course, the helm was put starboard and the course was shaped west by north, and afterwards west to run out towards the middle of the Strait. The light was again seen, as well as a red light on the port side, and a blue light being burned in the Pacha, and answered from the other vessel, it was now known to be the steamer Erin coming in the opposite direction, but it was thought that by a still standing out the Pacha would give clear

> berth both to the shoal and the approaching steamer. The object of this movement on the part of the Pacha was not guessed at on board the Erin, and the latter therefore kept porting her helm so as to pass the approaching vessel on the larboard side, in accordance with the rule laid down by the Trinity Masters. Both steamers therefore went out towards the middle of the channel, approaching each other on two curves. The hulls of the steamers were not visible until they were close to each other and collision became inevitable.
>
> The Erin's engines were then ordered to be reversed, but too late to prevent them coming in contact, the Erin striking the Pacha a little before the starboard paddle-box. The Pacha's masts immediately fell over the side, and she went down within less than seven minutes after the accident, in about 25 fathoms water. Many of those on board the Pacha were asleep, and had barely time to rush up from below before she sank, and some it is probable never gained the deck... The Erin sustained considerable damage, and the water rushed in at her bows, but being built with water tight compartments only two filled, and as the pumps were got to work with the engines, it was found that the water could be kept sufficiently under to enable her to reach Singapore, whither her course was directed, after having remained near the spot where the collision took place about four hours to pick up the survivors.

In spite of ongoing accidents at sea, the dawn of the second half of the nineteenth century saw a positive change in governance of the maritime industry and regulation of ships. An era of consolidation and reformation of many existing Acts began along with the introduction of one of the principal merchant shipping and mercantile Acts of the nineteenth century; the Merchant Shipping Act, 1854.[207]

Efforts were also made to address a problem that had existed from the introduction of regulations for seaworthiness, safety and for the carriage of boats in the 1840s; the lack of an effective maritime administration charged with monitoring the maritime industry and enforcing compliance. For the first half of the century there were at least seven Government departments involved in shipping, ranging from the Admiralty to the Colonial Office who administered conditions aboard ships for emigrants through the various Passengers Ship Acts dating from 1803.

The Board of Trade had begun to take a greater interest in regulation of ships after a Statistics Department was established in 1832. The Steam Navigation Act, 1846, had started to address safety issues by providing for the Board of Trade to grant certificates of the sufficiency and good condition of steam vessels, requiring all accidents to be reported to the Board, and stating that the department may appoint inspectors to report thereon. Section 17 of the Passenger Act, 1849 required ships' boats to be approved by the emigration officer at the port of clearance and penalties were provided in the Act for non-compliance.

Parliament finally recognized the longstanding issue of fragmented Governmental oversight of ships and seafarers and, in 1850, enacted the Mercantile Marine Act – *An Act for improving the Conditions of Masters, Mates and Seamen, and maintaining Discipline in the Merchant Service.*[208] In order to have effective control of seafarers, and to have legislative processes in place for, amongst other matters, improving conditions and maintaining discipline, the 1850 Act removed responsibility for oversight of ships from the Admiralty and created, through s.6 of the Act, a Naval Department of the Board of Trade responsible for administration and qualifications of seafarers; – *And be it enacted, That the "Board of Trade" shall undertake the general Superintendence of Matters relating to the British Mercantile Marine, and shall be authorized to enforce by legal Proceedings or by such other lawful Means as may seem expedient the Provisions of this Act and Laws relating to the British Merchant Service…*

Section 7 provided for Local Marine Boards to be established at ports with a total of thirty thousand and upwards registered net tonnage of foreign-going ships for *…carrying into effect the Provisions of this Act, under the Superintendence of the "Board of Trade"…* The extent of previous lack of regulation of ships and seafarers can be gleaned from the scope of the Act which can be summarized as; compulsory examination of Masters and Mates of foreign-going ships, establishment of Shipping Offices to superintend contracts between seafarers and ship owner, and matters such as desertion, discipline, health, log-books, wages and seamen's discharges.

A critical recommendation of the 1836 Select Committee on Shipwreck, and failure of the 1845 Order in Council for voluntary examinations, was enacted through the provisions of section 24 of the 1850 Act *…that Examina-*

tions be instituted for Persons who intend to be Masters or Mates of "Foreign-going Ships" or wish to procure Certificates of Competency.... Provision was made through section 27 for the experience, before 1 January 1851, of persons in the merchant service, and certain naval officers, to be recognized through Certificates of Service.

A letter to the Editor of the Nautical Journal and Naval Chronicle, 1850, along with a comment to Parliament and reply from the Board of Trade may well have been the catalyst for an increase in the penalty provided in the Merchant Seamen Act, 1835, for refusal to join a ship, desertion, or to serve aboard her

> Ship "Barham", January 7th, 1850.
>
> Mr. EDITOR. —... I was induced to write again to Mr. Labouchere, on the 12th of January, and urge the necessity of inserting a clause in the Merchant Service Bill, for the purpose of effectually checking and controlling the very serious and frequent offence of seamen refusing to serve after they had bound themselves by subscribing to the Ship's Articles. From the information which I have obtained, it appears that this offence is of such common occurrence at other ports, that ships have been detained a considerable time, and a heavy expense has been incurred thereby; and that in most of the cases, the seamen themselves, had no just or reasonable grounds for the violations of their pledges. Moreover, I have been assured that the only redress commanders of ships could obtain, was the stoppage of a seaman's wages, whilst he persisted in his refusal to do his duty, and that, unless he declared that he would not proceed to sea, in the ship to which he was bound, summary measures were considered as beyond the jurisdiction of a magistrate. It is therefore, obvious, that a grievance so inadequately provided for in Act 7th and 8th of Victoria, demands revision, and a sure and certain remedy. Under this conviction, in my own mind, I suggested to Mr. Labouchere, that a clause should be inserted in the Merchant Service Bill, empowering Magistrates to issue a warrant for the immediate apprehension of every seaman, who may refuse to serve, and also afford those summary means of redress which the case would require... It is very evident, that good order and discipline, so essentially wanting to improve the condition of the Merchant Service, cannot be obtained unless a frivolous and vexatious refusal to serve

> is effectually eradicated. This evil prevails more in harbour than at sea, and is, in some in stances, owing to a laxity of discipline when the commander is on shore, and when officers fail in upholding their authority, and betray a want of due judgment and discretion; whilst other cases prove that a love of change, the hope of indulgence on shore, and the probability of obtaining a higher rate of wages in another ship, are the causes which lead to this dereliction of duty, and breach of trust. But I have no hesitation in saying, that the majority of cases of this nature, prove that the conduct of seamen is exceedingly reprehensible, and would occasionally bear the stamp of a decided spirit of conspiracy or combination; because there are many proofs of more than half a ship's company striking work without the slightest provocation, or any reasonable cause of complaint against either their ship or their officers; and it is very certain, that when once a seaman has refused to serve, and persists in that refusal, the penalty he incurs of the forfeiture of six days' pay for every day he is off duty, very soon exhausts the balance of his wages, and renders him callous to ulterior consequences. Some cases of this description (within my own knowledge) would warrant the commitment of seamen for a conspiracy, and send them before a higher tribunal ; but magistrates have been deterred from that alternative, because the detention of the ship, and serious losses would inevitably be the result of such a determination...
> (Signed) J. W. VAILE.

Captain Vaile received an encouraging reply from the Board of Trade;– 'SIR. — I am directed by Mr. Labouchere to acknowledge the receipt of your letter of the 12th ultimo. Mr. Labouchere desires me to thank you for your suggestion, that a clause should be introduced into the Merchant Service Bill, to enable a Justice to punish a seaman refusing to serve after having signed an agreement, and to say that he is disposed to introduce such a clause into the Bill'.

The resultant section 70 in Part XII of the Mercantile Marine Act, 1850 read, in part;

...And it be enacted, That if an "Seaman" after signing the Agreement as herein-before required, or any Apprentice, willfully neglects or refuses to join his ship, or deserts, and then or afterwords is found or arrives at any Place in which there is a Court of a Justice capable of exercising jurisdiction under this Act, he shall, on due proof of the Offence, and when practicable, of a proper entry in the Official Log Book, be summarily punished by Imprisonment for a period not exceeding Twelve Weeks, with or without hard Labour, at the discretion of the Court or Justice inflicting the same...

Penalties were also included for persons *...harbouring or secreting deserters,* and were extended through the Mercantile Marine Act Amendment Act, 1851[209] – *An Act to amend the Mercantile Marine Act, 1850* – , to include persons *...harbouring or secreting any Seaman who after duly signing the Agreement willfully neglects or refuses to join his Ship, or any Apprentice who so neglects or refuses.* These provisions were to be central to the clamour surrounding unseaworthy and/or overloaded ships that was to dominate maritime safety matters during the 1860s and 1870's and beyond. There were no provisions in the 1850 Act concerning oversight of the seaworthiness of ships; the Act was solely administrative.

There was a clear need for comprehensive legislation that included the safety of all vessels; sailing vessels and steamships, as demonstrated during the first year of the decade. In March 1850 the passenger steamer ***Royal Adelaide*** of about 450 tons, from Cork to London, was lost in a gale on the Tongue Sand off Margate. All 240 souls aboard were lost.[210] Three months later the 898 ton paddle steamer ***Orion*** with 38 crew and 212 passengers aboard went aground off Portpatrick with the loss of 41 souls.[211] On 15 November 1850 the 950 ton barque ***Edmond*** departed Limerick for Quebec with 195 emigrants aboard and a crew of 21. Four days later the ship was driven ashore in Kilkee Bay near Dublin with the loss of 98 souls.[212]

Safety and seaworthiness of ships, recognition of issues such as the lack of lifesaving appliances, inadequate means of signalling distress and increasing numbers of collisions arising from the rapid development of steamships, were addressed through the Steam Navigation Act, 1851[213] – *An Act to consolidate and amend the Laws relevant to the Regulation of Steam Navigation, and to the Boats and Lights to be carried by Sea-going Vessels;* more than ten years after the commencement of scheduled steamship services across the North Atlantic. The use of the word 'steamship' in the title of the Act, and that of 1846, recognised concerns that had steadily grown during the preceding decade concerning the growth in numbers, size and horsepower of steamships. In 1840 when there were 771 steamships, the first scheduled crossing of the North Atlantic to Halifax was completed in just over 14 days by Cunard's ***Brittania***, of 1156 tons and 440 HP. Of the 1,187 steamships operating in 1850 the largest were the Collins Lines sister ships, ***Atlantic***, ***Pacific***, ***Arctic*** and ***Baltic***, each of 2800 tons and 814 horsepower; providing 13 knots service speed and average passage times across the North Atlantic to New York of under 10 days. Freedom from the archaic tonnage regulations of the Navigation Acts allowed British shipbuilders to design swift and very competitive sailing ships, resulting in fierce competition between British and American shipping. Cunard and the American Collins line vied for supremacy in the 'Atlantic ferry' trade while crack British and American clippers competed for the fastest passages carrying high value cargoes such as tea. The competition for fastest passages on the North Atlantic, and the interest this caused, are captured in an article published in 1851;

> ... To the general reader at home, it is next to impossible to convey an adequate idea of the interest which the contests between the English and American mails excite in Boston, New York, and Philadelphia. Each run is carefully noted and compared, fears are excited, hopes raised by every voyage, and half a dozen hours in the length of a trip of three thousand miles is thought a considerable variation. The struggle for mastery at this moment lies between the English Mail Asia and the American Mail Atlantic; and the recent voyage of the Asia was the quickest ever yet performed. This passage from New York to Liverpool was made in ten days, four hours, and five minutes; being four hours and fifteen minutes less than the best voyage eastward made by the Atlantic. The New Yorkers are building still more powerful vessels for this line of Service. The prize is a great one. The fleetest vessels must carry out letters, orders, news, government despatches, and, having the prestige of scientific excellence and success, will generally command a choice of the passenger traffic.—Athenaurn.'[214]

The 1851 Act repealed, built upon and broadened the provisions of the 1846 Act; repealed the Steam Navigation Act, 1848; took account of the 1850 Act, and didn't repeal or alter any of the provisions of the Passenger Act, 1849. The provision under the Mercantile Marine Act, 1850, that ...*the Board of Trade shall undertake the general Superintendence of Matters relating to the British Mercantile Marine*, was still clearly 'general' as Part XXII of the 1851 Act stated that requirements of the s.9 of the Passenger Act, 1849 regarding boats was not to be affected and provided that ...*the Enactments with respect to boats and Lifebuoys herein contained shall not apply in any Case in which a Certificate has been duly obtained under the Ninth Section of the Passengers Act, 1849*. This provision perpetuated the different administration and carriage requirements for boats under the two Acts.

The 1851 Act also contained a detailed table for determination of numbers of lifeboats to be carried, based solely upon the vessel's registered tonnage and category; sailing vessel or steam vessel. There was no account taken of the total number of persons on board.

For the first time a distinction was made between boats required aboard steamers and sailing ships of similar tonnage; for example, a steamer of 500 tons was required to carry the same boats as a sailing ship of 800 tons and the largest ship was required to carry five boats. The maximum required lifeboat capacity on a steam vessel greater than 500 registered tons (5 boats of 22 foot length) was 150 persons, and there was no increase in numbers of boats required to be carried as tonnage increased above 500 registered tons.

Part XIII of the 1851 Act broadened and expanded upon requirements for firefighting and signals of distress for steam vessels, albeit allowing a bewildering variety of distress signals;

> No Steam Vessel, except Vessels used solely as Steam Tugs, shall proceed to Sea unless it shall be provided with a Hose adapted for the Purpose of extinguishing Fire in any Part of the Vessel, and capable of being connected with the Engines of the Vessel, nor if carrying Passengers, without being provided with the following Means of making Signals of Distress, that is to say Twelve Blue Lights, or Twelve Portfires, and one Cannon, with ammunition for at least Twelve Charges, or in the Discretion of the Master or Owner of such Vessel, with such other Means of making Signals as shall have been previously approved by the Lords of the Said Committee

The Admiralty still retained a role in the making of regulations for navigation lights and prevention of collision in spite of establishment of a Naval Department in the Board of Trade. The issue of vestigial navigation lights and collision rules for steam vessels, but none for sailing vessels, was addressed through Part XXVI and its chapeau; *And with respect to the Lights to be carried, and other Provisions to be made for guarding against Accidents from*

Collision, be it enacted as follows;

> The Lord High Admiral, or the Committee for executing the Office of the Lord High Admiral, shall from time to time make Regulations requiring the Exhibition of such lights, by such Classes of Vessel, whether Steam or Sailing Vessels, within such Places and under such Circumstances as they make fit...published in the London Gazette... copy to the owner or Master of a Vessel who applies for the same... existing Regulations to remain in force until revoked.

Part XXVII of the Act included sailing vessels in the rules to be observed by Steam Vessels passing each other; introduced through Part IX of the Steam Navigation Act, 1846.

Part XXXI took account of issues with increasing steam pressure in boilers by requiring every Steam Ship...*to be provided with a Safety-valve upon each Boiler, free of the care of the Engineer and out of his Control and Interference...*

The steady transition from sail to steam, along with increasing use of steam vessels for carriage of emigrants, resulted in it being deemed expedient by Parliament to enact the Passengers by Sea Act, 1851,[215] – *An Act to Amend the Passengers Act, 1849*. The Colonial Land and Emigration Commissioners were authorised to – *declare from time to time the length of voyage of passenger vessels;* a measure used under the various Passenger Acts to determine a wide range of provisions for the welfare of passengers, and to differentiate between average lengths of voyage of steam and sailing vessels. Account was also to be taken of ...*Vessels having Steam Engines to be used occasionally, or in the aid of their Sails, and Vessels having Engines of full Power for constant use...*

The following year the Passengers Act 1852[216]; *an Act to Amend and Consolidate the Laws Relating to the Carriage of Passengers by Sea,* repealed existing laws relating to the carriage of passengers by sea and, under Part XXIV, updated provisions for the carriage of boats to take account of the increasing size and carrying capacity of passenger ships;

> Every "Passenger Ship" shall carry a Number of Boats according to the following Scale (that is to say,) Two Boats – for every Ship of One hundred Tons and Upwards

> Three Boats – for every Ship of Two hundred Tons and Upwards, if the number of Statute Adults shall exceed fifty
>
> Four Boats – for every Ship of Five hundred Tons and Upwards, if the number of Statute Adults shall exceed Two hundred
>
> Five Boats – for every Ship of Eight hundred tons and Upwards, if the number of Statute Adult passengers shall exceed Three hundred
>
> Six Boats – for every Ship of Twelve hundred tons and upwards, if the number of Statute Adults shall exceed Five hundred and Fifty

A *Statute Adult* was defined by Part III as *...a Passenger of the Age of Fourteen Years and Upwards, or Two Passengers above the age of One Year and under that of Fourteen,* while the term *Passenger Ship;*

> ...shall signify every Description of such Ship carrying upon any Voyage to which the Provisions of this Act shall extend a greater number of Passengers when propelled by Sails, than in the Proportion of One Statute Adult to every Twenty-five Tons of the registered tonnage of such Ship, and when propelled by Steam than in the Proportion of One Statute Adult to every Ten Tons of the registered Tonnage of such Ship...

The year 1852 saw one of the most dramatic shipwrecks in maritime history; one that left a legacy of heroism and selflessness that still resonates through the phrase 'women and children first'. H.M.S. ***Birkenhead,*** (1846), an iron steam troopship of 1400 tons, struck an uncharted rock southeast from Capetown on 25 February 1852. The ship was carrying a total of about 643 persons from Simon's Bay to Algoa Bay, comprising mainly troops of the 76th Regiment of Foot along with a number of women and children. There were not enough boats for all on board and the soldiers stood firm in silence as the women and children took to the boats. 450 persons were lost. The soldiers' stoicism in the face of almost certain death became a symbol of courage in the face of impossible odds; known as the 'Birkenhead Drill', as immortalised in Rudyard Kipling's tribute to the Royal Marines in 'Soldier an' Sailor Too;[217]

> To take your chance in the thick of a rush, with firing all about,

Is nothing so bad when you've cover to 'and, an' leave an' likin' to shout;

But to stand an' be still to the Birken'ead drill is a damn tough bullet to chew,

An' they done it, the Jollies—'Er Majesty's Jollies—soldier an' sailor too!

Their work was done when it 'adn't begun; they was younger nor me an' you;

Their choice it was plain between drownin' in 'eaps an' bein' mopped by the screw,

So they stood an' was still to the Birken'ead drill, soldier an' sailor too

The Earl of Cardigan stated in the House of Lords on 28 June 1852 stated; "..never was there a more brilliant or a more beautiful exemplification of discipline than that exhibited by those gallant but unfortunate soldiers. Standing on the brink of death, they were steadily obedient to their officers to the last. They allowed themselves to be swept away into the tomb without a murmur, in order that they might secure a safe escape for the women and children on board the vessel from the common danger which they remained to brave".[218] This first well known example of women and children being given priority during an emergency evacuation of a ship gave rise to the expression 'women and children first'; an ethical and moral standard that has never been codified in law, and a custom often more honoured in the breach than the observance.

As with the Steam Navigation Act, 1851; the Passengers Act, 1852[219] contained requirements for other lifesaving appliances, albeit they were different. Ships that chose to meet the higher requirements of the latter Act regarding boats were exempt from those of the former;

> …there shall likewise be on board each "Passenger Ship" Two properly fitted Lifebuoys, kept ready at all Times for immediate Use, and some Adequate means, to be approved by the Emigration officer at the Port of Clearance, of making Signals by Night; also a Fire Engine, in Proper working Order, or other apparatus for extinguishing Fire,

> to be approved by such Officer; provided that the "passenger Ships" which comply with the Requirements of this Act as regards Boats shall be exempted from the Requirements respecting Boats contained in the Steam Navigation Act, 1851

Some notable maritime disasters contributed to the ongoing mournful toll in ships and lives lost that occurred between the Steam Navigation Act, 1851 and its successor, the Merchant Shipping Act, 1854. Ships and lives continued to be lost during 1853 for a wide variety of reasons. A total of 832 ships were lost within 10 miles of the British coastline in 1853 with the loss of 689 lives. Of these 832 ships, 369 were totally wrecked, 52 totally lost in collisions, 386 damaged seriously and had to discharge and 25 seriously damaged in collision.[220] These losses included a collision off the entrance to the Humber, in thick weather, between the German screw steamer ***Marshall*** (1846) of 307 tons and the barque ***Woodhouse*** resulting in the loss of the ***Marshall*** and all 48 persons on board, and the loss of one crew member of the ***Woodhouse***.[221] On May 3 1853 the American emigrant ship ***William and Mary,*** on passage from Liverpool to Australia, struck a rock near the Bahamas and sank with the loss of 170 persons.[222] Steamships were not impervious to the forces of weather as demonstrated by the loss of the iron paddle steamer ***Duke of Sutherland***, (1847) of 514 tons; wrecked on the breakwater at the entrance to Aberdeen harbour in April 1853 in a South-easterly gale with thick visibility. Thirty-six of the 52 people aboard were saved at the cost of the lives of five rescuers.[223] The sailing ship ***Dalhousie,*** of 800 tons, bound from London to Sydney with 10 cabin passengers and the Captain's wife and two children, capsized off Beachey Head with the loss of 50 persons. Only one crew member survived.[224]

The perils of seafaring, and the graphic effects of winter storms were summarised in an account, published in the Journal of the Society of Arts in 1854, for shipwrecks around the British coast;

> From the summary attached to the admiralty register of wrecks just published, we learn that the casualties in each month [for 1853] were as follows:– January, 126 : February, 77 : March, 32 : April, 44 : May, 41 : June, 29: July, 18 : August, 42 : September, 85 : October, 164 : November, 189 : December, 268 – total 1,115. Of these 464 occurred on the east coast of Great Britain, 158 on the south coast, and 235 on the west coast. 128 wrecks strewed the coasts of Ireland, 5 were cast

> on shore at Scilly, 9 at the Channel islands, 18 on the Orkneys and Shetland, and 18 at the Isle of Man; the remaining 80 occurred in the surrounding seas. The gales of January caused 126 casualties as shown above; they prevailed during the whole month and the early part of February; the spring, summer and autumn were moderate, but on the 26th October an easterly gale began that in six days strewed the coasts with 102 wrecks. Strong breezes, and a short lull of moderate weather, were followed by gales of ordinary force at this period of the year; but on the 24th December a heavy storm from the S.W. burst over the country, and continued to the end of the year, with such violence that by the 29th there was scarcely a vessel in the neighbourhood of the British Islands left at sea – some had found safety by running into port, while of others the returns show a list of 183 casualties, of which 103 were totally wrecked, making a daily average of 30 wrecks during this awful and destructive gale. The whole loss of life during the year, so far as has been ascertained, amounts to 920.[225]

In the last days of this calamitous year at sea there was further large loss of life when the American sailing packet ***Staffordshire*** (1851) of 1817 gross tons, sprung her rudder and lost steering on 24 December 1853 in a violent snowstorm off the coast of Nova Scotia. The ship was fifteen days into a fast and uneventful passage from Liverpool to Boston with a total of 214 people aboard; mostly emigrants. The following day the bowsprit and foremast were lost, the ship became unmanageable and eventually drifted onto a rock off Cape Sable, Nova Scotia on 29 December. There were not enough boats for all aboard and 175 souls, including the badly injured Captain, were lost;[226]

> Another instance of this fatal parsimony in not equipping ships with sufficient boats was the loss of the clipper Staffordshire on the rocks near Cape Sable in December 1854 (sic).....The boats were dropped into the water, and all the women and children were put in them, but when they were already dangerously overloaded many poor wretches in the water grasped the gunwales, begging to be saved. Those in the boats, to save themselves from being swamped, were forced to the inhuman necessity of pushing off those who so pitifully tried to be saved.[227]

Chapter 6

Prevention of collision

An ever-present peril of the sea, and one that increased considerably with the advent of steam propulsion and a dramatic increase in trade, tonnage and speed during the nineteenth century, is collision. The vulnerability of a vessel at anchor to collision had been identified during Byzantine times (600 – 800 A.D.) through the Rhodian Sea-Laws. Chapter 36 on collision stated that, in the case of a ship under full sail and a ship at anchor, the ship at anchor at night would be fully liable for damages from being run into by the ship under full sail if it did not give notice of its presence by a light.[228]

The first collision avoidance rules were laid down for warships. The Duke of York and Earl of Warwick, in 1640 and 1675 respectively, decreed that "no captain shall take the wind of the Admiral". A rule for ships on opposite tacks had been agreed towards the end of the eighteenth century and become established practice. Naval ships in the early 1780s observed Admiralty regulations which required '…a ship on the larboard [port] tack to bear up for another on the starboard tack'. In 1828 it was ruled that; 'The ship which has the wind at large may go to either leeward or windward but, as a general rule, she ought to expect that the ship which is close-hauled will keep to windward, and therefore she ought to go to leeward unless it is quite clear that she can go to windward with safety'.[229] Until the mid-1800s, 'no ships carried navigation lights, except warships travelling in squadron by night. Whenever two vessels approached each other, it was customary to show one's presence by hoisting a flag or lighting a flare'.[230]

The advent of relatively large steam vessels in the late 1830s led Trinity House[231] to decree, in 1840, that steam vessels at risk of collision, should '… each put her helm to port, so as to pass on the larboard side of the other'. Steam vessels in narrow channels were to always leave the other vessel to port. These standards had no statutory authority but were enforced by the Admiralty Court and formed the basis of subsequent collision avoidance regulations.

At this time the fishermen of the English Channel referred to the 'new-fangled and badly handled screw-driven steamers as 'silent deaths''[232] but it wasn't always the steamships who were at fault in collisions. The steamship ***Mercury*** 'sailed from Bordeaux for London on the 10th May 1855. The following evening she was run into by a large outward-bound barque, apparently French, which struck the ***Mercury*** amidships. Within 10 minutes the ***Mercury*** had lost power, and the ship sank within a half hour. The sailing vessel didn't stop to offer assistance. The ***Mercury's*** crew of 22, drifted in the Bay of Biscay for 20 hours without water until being rescued by the British barque ***Johanna***, which carried them to Gibraltar'.[233]

In 1846 Trinity House rules were the basis of a set of basic 'give way' rules for prevention of collision in narrow channels and fairways; applied only to steam vessels in such waters, along with 'meeting and passing' rules for steam vessels in all other waters, through Part IX of the Steam Navigation Act, 1846;

> IX. And be it enacted, That every Steam Vessel when meeting or passing any other Steam Vessel shall pass as far as may be safe on the Port Side of such other Vessel; and every Steam Vessel navigating any River or narrow Channel shall keep as far as is practicable to that Side of the Fairway or Mid-channel of such River or Channel which lies on the Starboard Side of such Vessel, due regard being had to the Tide and to the Position of each Vessel in such Tide; and the Master or other Person having the Charge of any such Steam Vessel, and neglecting to observe these Regulations, or either of them, shall for each and every Instance of Neglect forfeit and pay a Sum not exceeding Fifty Pounds

Pursuant to the 1846 Act, regulations were made by the Admiralty in 1848 requiring steamships to carry; ... *When under Weigh – a Bright white light at the foremast head; Green light on the starboard side; red light on the port side. When at Anchor – A common bright light*. It would not be until 1858 that sailing vessels were required to carry port and starboard navigation lights. [234]

There was unprecedented and explosive growth in Britain's overseas trade during the nineteenth century with exports growing at a greater rate than before or since between 1840 and 1850.[235] With this increase in trade came a steady increase in the number and size of vessels to carry it – sail and, increasingly, steam. The number of steamships registered in Britain more than doubled between 1849 and 1856 from 414 to 851 with their average tonnage increasing from 262 to 389 gross tons. Over the same period there was steady, if less spectacular, growth in sailing vessels from 17,807 to 18,419 with an average gross tonnage in 1856 of 208.[236] Greater numbers of vessels brought greater risks of collision and an urgent need for more comprehensive rules for prevention of collision, particularly between sailing vessels, encumbered to a greater extent in their ability to manoeuvre, and increasing numbers of steam vessels.

Part XXVII of The Steam Navigation Act, 1851 expanded upon the requirements of the 1846 Act and applied them to all vessels – steam and sail; taking into account the difficulties in some circumstances of manoeuvring sailing vessels;

> Whenever any Vessel proceeding in One Direction meets a vessel proceeding in another Direction, and the Master or Person having charge of either vessel perceives that if both vessels continue their respective Courses they will pass so near as to involve any Risk of a Collision, he shall put up the helm of his Vessel to Port, so as to pass on the Port Side of the other Vessel, due Regard being had to the Tides and to the Position of the other vessel with respect to the Dangers of the Channel, and, as regards Sailing Vessels, to the keeping of each vessel under Command, and the Master of any Steam vessel navigating any River of Narrow Channel shall keep as far as is practicable to the Fairway or Mid-channel thereof which lies on the Starboard Side of such Vessel; and if the Master or other Person having charge of any Steam Vessel neglects to observe these Regulations, or either of them, he shall for every such Offence be liable to a penalty not exceeding Fifty Pounds.

At this time the vast majority of ships were powered by sail, and not required to carry any form of navigation light, a matter that caused considerable concern amongst the owners of steamships who were held liable if in collision with an unlit sailing ship. The 1851 Act – *An Act to consolidate and amend the Laws relating to the Regulation of Steam Navigation, and to the Boats and lights to be carried by Sea-going vessels* – empowered the Admiralty to establish regulations relative to lights to prevent collision;

> XXVI. The Lord High Admiral, or the Commissioners for executing

> the Office of the Lord High Admiral, shall from Time to Time make Regulations requiring the Exhibition of such Lights, by such Classes of vessels, whether Steam or Sailing vessels, within such places and under such circumstances as they think fit, and may from Time to Time revoke, alter or vary the same and they shall cause such Regulations to be published in the London Gazette, and to be otherwise publicly made known…

The Admiralty established a committee on the 14th of February 1852 to examine the feasibility, desirability and practicality of sailing vessels carrying and exhibiting lights. The report of the committee to the Admiralty on the 22nd of March stated that as no agreement could be reached amongst the four vastly experienced mariners making up the committee; both naval and merchant service, opinions were gained from a wide cross section of the shipping industry to no avail. Their report made the ineffectual recommendation that;

> The Committee are of the opinion that the master of every sailing vessel on approaching, or being approached by another vessel, and whether such vessel is stated to have been seen or not, should be held responsible for showing a sufficient light in time to avoid collision; but it must be left to the discretion of the master to determine on his own responsibility whether such light is to be kept constantly displayed. It has been remarked by some of the witnesses… that a want of vigilance has been observed in vessels which have been in the habit of fixing a light.[237]

The crossing and narrow channel provisions of the 1851 Act were expanded upon and consolidated through the Merchant Shipping Act, 1854 which brought into effect minimal Lights and Fog Signals, and Meeting and Passing requirements. The Admiralty were further empowered under s.295 (2) to; *…if they think fit, make Regulations requiring the Use of such Fog Signals, by such Classes of Ships, whether Steam or Sailing Ships, within such Places and under such Circumstances as they think fit, and may from Time to Time revoke, alter, or vary the same.* Pending the implementation of regulations regarding the use of fog signals, a major British shipping company operating to the Far East wasted no time in reminding their ships of the need to sound such signals;

Fog Signals in Steam Vessels.

The Directors of the Peninsular and Oriental Steam Navigation Company have issued the following caution to the commanders of that company's vessels;

'Special Circular.-

The recent deplorable loss of life and property occasioned by the foundering of the steamship Arctic, as well as the other fatal accidents from collisions at sea during fogs, have induced the directors of the Peninsular and Oriental Steam Navigation Company to issue this special circular, in addition to the cautions enjoined in the 14th article of their existing printed 'instructions for the safe and efficient navigation of their ships';

When the weather sets in thick so that objects cannot be distinguished – say a-quarter of a mile distant – the vessels are to be slowed to half speed ; or, if the fog becomes more dense, the speed is to be still more reduced, or the ship stopped altogether, according to the discretion of the commander.

The steam-whistles are constantly sounded during fogs or thick weather. The diminution of speed and the fact of the steam-whistle having been sounded are to be recorded in the logbook. Any deviations from the important cautions contained in this circular will be visited with the dismissal from the company's service of all parties inculpated is such disobedience and neglect. By order of the board, C. W. Howell, Secretary.[238]

An Admiralty Notice – *Respecting Lights and Fog Signals to be Carried and used by Sea-going Vessels, to prevent Collision* – was published on the 24th February 1858; revoking a previous Notice published in 1852. Paragraph 5 of this Notice – Fog Signals – required that;

All Sea-going Steam Vessels, whether propelled by paddles or screws, when their steam is up, and when under way, shall in all cases of Fog use as a Fog Signal a Steam Whistle, placed before the funnel at not less than 8 feet from the deck, which shall be sounded at least once every five minutes; but when steam is not up, they shall use a Fog

Horn or Bell, as ordered for Sailing Ships

The ***Arctic/Vesta*** collision prompted an American shipowner to approach Lieutenant Matthew Maury, Superintendent of the U.S. Naval Observatory and Hydrographic Office, to see whether separate sea lanes could be developed for East and Westbound steamers in the vicinity of the Grand Banks so as to prevent collisions in restricted visibility without lengthening passages. Maury applied his experience in developing well proven pilot charts for the main routes taken by sailing ships to this problem and drew upon data supplied by shipmasters from the logs of ships covering forty-six thousand days of observations on these routes, and from this developed two twenty-five mile wide sea lanes for steamers. A northern route would serve westbound steamers, with an eastbound route between 60 and 600 miles to the south dependent upon the season. Sailing vessels would be warned to stay outside these lanes. The work was published in 1855 as *Lanes for the Steamers Crossing the Atlantic.* The lanes were not universally adopted with many shipmasters preferring to follow their customary and longstanding routes.[239]

Paragraph 6 of the 1858 Admiralty regulation required sailing vessels to carry red and green sidelights, and use fog signals on a Fog Horn when on the starboard tack, and to Ring a Bell when on the port tack, both at intervals of at least 5 minutes. All Sea-going Vessels, were required;

> ...when at Anchor in a Roadstead or Fairway shall between Sunset and Sunrise exhibit where it can best be seen, but at a height not exceeding 20 feet above the hull, a White Light in a Globular Lantern of 8 inches in diameter, and so constructed as to show a clear, uniform and unbroken light all around the horizon, at a distance of at least 1 mile.

The Admiralty Notice came into effect on 01 October 1858.

Rules as to Ships meeting each other, in Section 296 of the 1854 Act, remained substantially the same as in the 1851 Act with the addition of some guidance as to the action of sailing ships, outside of harbours and narrow channels rules, on the starboard tack *...and as regards Sailing Ships on the Starboard Tack close-hauled, to the keeping such Ships under Command;*

> 296. Whenever any Vessel proceeding in One Direction meets a vessel

> proceeding in another Direction, and the Master or Person having charge of either vessel perceives that if both vessels continue their respective Courses they will pass so near as to involve any Risk of a Collision, he shall put up the helm of his Vessel to Port, so as to pass on the Port Side of the other Vessel. ; and this rule shall be obeyed by all steam ships and by all sailing ships whether on the port or starboard tack, and whether close-hauled or not, unless the circumstances of the case are such as to render a departure from the rule necessary in order to avoid immediate danger, and subject also to the proviso that due regard shall be had to the dangers of navigation, and, as regards sailing ships on the starboard tack close-hauled, to the keeping such ships under command.

'Putting the helm to port' meant an alteration of course to starboard, from the days when ships were steered with a tiller.

The editor of a legal guide to the 1854 Act[240] commented on this rule; –

> It would be foreign to my purpose to enter into a discussion here upon the merits of the controversy as to whether the enactment of any express "rule of the sea" tends to lessen or to aggravate the evils it is designed to remedy or alleviate. That the most intelligent and practical sailors consider the present rule highly objectionable, especially as applied to sailing vessels, is notorious ; and the report of the Sunderland Ship owner's Society designates it as "likely to prove fruitful of accidents and embarrassing".

The need for clarity in collision rules regarding interaction of sailing vessels was emphasized by a collision in the English Channel, as reported by the *Times*, Sep 22, 1854;

> Intelligence was received at Lloyds in the course of yesterday of a most fearful collision having taken place in the Channel off the Start early on Tuesday morning, which resulted in the foundering of a large Norwegian bark called the Oceanus, Captain T. Norbeck, and the loss of one of her crew. The unfortunate ship was from Akyab, laden with upwards of 500 tons of rice, and was bound for Amsterdam. She had called at Cork for orders and was making her way up Channel. The weather on Monday night set in thick, hazy, and very dark, wind WSW. At 8'clock the Lizard light bore some 24 miles distant NW by

W. The bark continued her course, and at about half-past 2 o'clock on the following (Tuesday) morning a large full rigged ship, apparently of American build, painted black and in ballast, was observed by the look-out men close on the starboard bow, and in less than 2 minutes after she had been seen she came on and struck the Oceanus with tremendous force on the starboard side, just a little abaft the foremast, which gave way and went over the side, killing in its fall one of the crew, named Tobias Atkinson.

The strange ship almost immediately got clear of the barque and stood off. The captain of the Oceanus soon found his vessel had been cut down to the water's edge ; she was evidently filling fast, and he with his crew, hailed the American to keep by them for a short time, so as to pick them up, as they were going to take to the boats. After some difficulty they succeeded in lowering two of them. Captain Norbeck, mate and carpenter, and three of the men got into the gig, and the remaining 10 of the crew took to the quarter boat …. By this time the water had nearly reached up to the bark's deck, and the boats had just time to get clear of the eddy made by the ill-fated vessel, when she went down in deep water, the Start Point bearing ESE.

The men in the boats remained on their oars for some time, in the hopes that the American would make an attempt to pick them up, However, she went on, and was not seen afterwards, nor could anything more be learned as to her name and destination. The boats then parted company, and the unfortunate occupants suffered much from exposure. At length, after many hours' buffeting about, the gig, containing the captain and five others, was picked up by the fishing lugger Hero, of Brixham, where they were landed.

The quarter boat, with the ten men in it, was taken higher up the coast and at eleven o'clock on Tuesday night the craft was driven ashore in the vicinity of Lyme, near Gun Cliff. The poor fellows were much exhausted. The Coast Guard rendered them prompt relief. The Oceanus belonging to Christiansand. A ship answering the description given of the vessel which came in collision with the bark was seen off the coast early on Tuesday morning.[241]

Navigation lights for sailing vessels were finally required through an Admiralty Notice, issued on the 30th of September 1858. The Notice revoked the

1852 regulations, included *inter alia* lights and fog signals for sailing vessels and all vessels at anchor, and diagrams to aid mariners in their understanding of the lights to be carried, their sectors, and which lights could be expected to be seen in various crossing and meeting situations;

Sailing Vessels

- All Sea-going Sailing Vessels when under way or being towed shall between sunset and sunrise exhibit a Green Light on the Starboard side and a Red Light on the Port side of the Vessel, and such lights shall be constructed as to be visible on a dark night, with a clear atmosphere, at a distance of at least 2 miles, and shall show an uniform and unbroken light over an arc of the horizon of 10 points of the compass, from right ahead to 2 points abaft the beam on the Starboard and Port sides respectively.

- The Coloured Lights shall be fixed whenever it is practicable so to exhibit them; and shall be fitted with screens projecting at least 3 feet forward from the light, so as to prevent the Lights being seen across the bow.

- When Coloured Lights cannot be fixed (as in the case of small vessels in bad weather), they shall be kept on deck between sunset and sunrise, and on their proper sides of the vessel, ready for instant exhibition, and shall be exhibited in such a manner as can be best seen on the approach of, or to, any other vessels, in sufficient time to avoid collision, and so that the Green Light shall not be seen on the Port side, nor the Red Light on the Starboard side

Fog Signals. – All Sea-going Sailing Vessels, when under way, shall, in all cases of Fog, use when on the Starboard Tack a Fog Horn, and when on the Port Tack shall rind a bell. These signals shall be sounded once at least every five minutes.

Sailing Pilot Vessels are to carry only a White Light at the Masthead, and are to exhibit a Flare-up Light every 15 minutes, in accordance with Trinity House regulation.

Vessels at Anchor

> All Sea-going Vessels when at anchor in roadsteads or fairways, shall between sunset and sunrise exhibit where it can best be seen, but at a height not exceeding 20 feet above the hull, a White light in a Globular Lantern of 8 inches in diameter, and so constructed as to show a clear, uniform, and unbroken light all round the horizon, at a distance of at least 1 mile.

The 1854 Rules were significantly updated in the Merchant Shipping Amendment Act, 1862, after consultation with the French Government. In an effort to further assist mariners in their understanding of the Steering and Sailing Rules the Board of Trade and their French equivalent body, jointly updated and reproduced the diagrams published in the Admiralty Notice of 1858. In 1863 the Board of Trade published the Rules in French.

Upon introducing the second reading of the 1862 Merchant Shipping Bill, Lord Stanley of Alderley commented;

> It also established a fixed code in respect to what might be called the rule of the road and the showing of lights at sea. As that code had been adopted by the Government of this country in conjunction with the Government of France, he hoped that it would receive the concurrence of other nations, and that it would thus, in an important respect, facilitate the commercial intercourse of the world, by assimilating the law in this respect.[242]

Table 3 in the Schedule to the 1862 Act contained amended Regulations for Preventing Collisions at Sea. For collision prevention regulations to work satisfactorily in the matter of navigation in fog and the many other difficult meeting, crossing and overtaking circumstances vessels can find themselves in, they must be uniformly agreed and observed by ships of all nationalities in all waters. The two prime concerns amongst shipowners and seafarers were the steering and sailing rules in the 1854 regulations, and the lack of any uniform international standard for 'Rules of the Road at Sea'. Article III – *Lights for Steam Ships* – of the 1862 Rules required that;

Seagoing steam ships when under weigh shall carry:

> (a) At the for]emast head, a bright white light so fixed as to show

> a uniform and unbroken light over an arc of the horizon of twenty points of the compass [225 degrees], so fixed as to throw the light ten points on either side of the ship – viz., from right ahead to two points [22.5 degrees] abaft the beam on either side, and of such a character as to be visible on a dark night with a clear atmosphere at a distance of at least five miles.

A problem for steamships, most of which continued to carry sail until well into the nineteenth century, was the possibility of the solitary white mast-head being obscured by sails, causing confusion to other ships as to the nature of the vessel, and the action that should be taken to avoid collision, as explained by an experienced shipmaster of the day;

> ...But much stress is always laid on the masthead light as being capable of materially assisting their judgment, far more so in my opinion than is warranted by facts. For it is so likely to be obstructed from such a variety of causes, by its position under the top, as the head sails when set must interfere with its being seen (and this fact I do not think has ever been referred to at any court of enquiry on collisions, I certainly do not remember having seen it), besides the possibility of its being rendered useless when the foresail is hauled up. These with many others all tending to destroy its efficiency, and when combined, create very grave doubts on the ability of this particular light at all on which so much is made to depend.[243]

In commenting on placement of the masthead light and sidelights, one judgement stated that "The law does not appoint any particular place at which the lights should be fixed, but they must be placed so as to be perfectly visible".[244] Further, that "besides carrying the proper lights, a ship must not do anything that will render them ineffectual; thus it was held to be negligence on the part of a steamer to go at full speed under steam and sail before the wind, whilst her smoke was blown over the bows. This obscured the lights, and prevented her from seeing, and being seen, by other ships approaching from an opposite direction".[245]

It was unfortunate, in this era when all large seagoing ships, both steam and sail, were fitted with more than one mast for carriage of a large rig of sail, that thought was not given by either the Board of Trade or seafarers to the benefits to collision prevention of having two masthead lights on widely spaced masts, as was agreed, but only as an option, at the 1889 International Maritime Conference. This arrangement of lights gives the best and earliest indication of the aspect of an approaching ship, and risk of collision, even while the approaching ship is still 'hull down' over the horizon.

The obligations of an overtaking vessel were succinctly covered in Article 17 – *Vessels Overtaking other Vessels;*

> 17. Every vessel overtaking any other vessel shall keep out of the way of the said last-mentioned vessel

However, for this rule to be effective it relied upon the overtaking vessel being able to see the overtaken vessel ahead. This was not assisted by the fact that the Rules did not, at this time, require any vessel, sail or steam to carry a stern light. Thus, an arc of 135 degrees of the horizon astern of the ship was unlit, leading to the very clear danger of a ship being run down from astern; particularly in an era when the great majority of vessels were propelled by sail. As one commentator said at the time;

> Another point is the suggestion that a white light should be shewn over the stern of a ship when she is being overtaken by another ship. Such a regulation being an addition to the rule cannot of course be made compulsory in the international regulations, until it is discussed and agreed to by the parties to the regulations. In favour of it, it may be urged that a white light shewn at the stern, will often indicate to a steamer crossing the channel in a dark night the presence of a sailing vessel ahead of her whose lights are shut off by the screens. It may also be urged that the sailing ship ought to do something to contribute to her own safety. Against it however, must be borne in mind the fact that at present the obligation to get out of the way is thrown on the steamer and on her alone ; and this being so the steamer looks out, whilst the throwing of the responsibility on the sailing ship of showing a white light, would divide the responsibility with, and therefore lessen the responsibility of the steamer, and if by chance a steamer should, whilst neglecting to keep a good look-out, happen to run down a sailing vessel by overtaking her, the steamer would, if the light were not seen, plead that the sailing vessel did not show it and was therefore in fault. This suggestion however is a legitimate one for discussion and

arrangement, and will no doubt be settled satisfactorily.[246]

A contemporary judgement stated;

> It has long been doubtful whether the vessel ahead ought to exhibit a light to the vessel following her. These rules do not make any provision for lights in such cases, and there is no doubt that it is improper for a ship to carry a fixed stern light, since Article II prohibits the carriage of any lights but those prescribed in the other rules. But though there is no fixed and definite obligation in all cases to exhibit such a light to a ship astern, yet if a vessel sees another approaching and has reason to suppose that the approaching ship does not see her, the Privy Council have lately laid it down that it is then the duty of the ship ahead to give some warning to the other, not necessarily by exhibiting a light, but by some signal, such as firing a gun, showing a light, or otherwise. This would indicate her position, and call the attention of the approaching vessel to the danger of a collision'.[247]

It would not be until 1948 that stern lights became mandatory for nearly all vessels.[248]

One of the matters that 'the most intelligent and practical sailors found highly objectional' in s.296 of the 1854 Act, was that ships at risk of collision were required to follow the requirement to *...put up the helm of his Vessel to Port, so as to pass on the Port Side of the other Vessel,* regardless of the fact that, in certain circumstances, this would require them to cross ahead of the other vessel. The Merchant Shipping Act, 1862, addressed this issue through amended wording of the Steering and Sailing rules; allowing for a variety of meeting and crossing situations;

> Art. 12. When Two Sailing Ships are crossing so as to involve Risk of Collision, then if they have the Wind on different Sides, the Ship with the Wind on the Port Side shall keep out of the Way of the Ship with the Wind on the Starboard Side, except in the Case in which the Ship with the Wind on the Port Side is close hauled and the other Ship free, in which Case the latter Ship shall keep out of the Way ; but if they have the Wind on the same Side, or if One of them has the Wind aft, the Ship which is to windward shall keep out of the Way of the Ship which is to leeward.

Articles 11 and 13 were at the heart of seafarers' concern about the effectiveness of the Rules;

> Art. 11. If Two Sailing Ships are meeting End on, or nearly End on, so as to involve Risk of Collision, the Helms of both shall be put to Port, so that each may pass on the Port Side of the other.
>
> Art. 13. If Two Ships under Steam are meeting End on, or nearly End on, so as to involve Risk of Collision, the Helms of both shall be put to Port, so that each may pass on the Port Side of the other.

There were two major concerns; one with the interpretation of 'end-on or nearly end-on' and the other brought about by confusion amongst seafarers who did not have English as a first language about the intent of the requirement to 'port the helm'.

The first concern was brought about by the great difficulty in determining whether an approaching ship was 'end on or nearly end on' at night with either no masthead light, or a single light. Cleary, if both sidelights were visible the other vessel was 'end on' but this could also be the case if the other vessel was approaching from a fine angle on the bow. This was the situation in the collision, in the Red Sea in September 1866, of two ships owned by the Bombay and Bengal Steamship Company; a collision caused by uncertainty as to the heading of the other vessel, compounded by confusion and misinterpretation of a private company signal.

> The Bombay based company operated two screw steamships; the Bhima and the Nada on a feeder service to Suez to connect with ships operating between Alexandria and Liverpool. On a calm and clear night, with plenty of sea room, no other ships in the vicinity, and no sail up, the Bhima (Aden to Suez) and Nada (Suez to Aden) sighted each other twenty minutes before the collision. When Captain Hanscorn of the Nada came to the bridge he sighted the lights of the other ship one point on his starboard bow, put his helm to port until the Bima's lights were two points on his port bow, and then ordered the company's night time recognition signal to be burnt. It appeared that Captain Sproule of the Bhima took this signal to mean that the Nada wished to talk to him and he approached very closely. "Then he suddenly had his helm put a starboard, which brought his vessel directly under the

> bows of the Nada. He saw his danger, and shouted out an order to put the helm hard a port, but it was too late The Nada struck the Bhima on the forward part of the poop on the starboard side". The Bhima capsized and sank within five minutes with the loss of about ninety persons including the Captain, the Chief Officer, and the widow and daughter of another of the company's Masters. An inquiry, held when the Nada eventually arrived at Aden with 22 survivors, cleared the Master of the Bhima of all blame.[249]

The Vice President of the Board of Trade was defensive and overly optimistic in defending the current Steering and Sailing Rules in the House on the 6th of December 1867;

> ...No, Sir, no alterations are contemplated in the Rules of the Road at Sea. Collisions are not caused by observance, but by neglect or misconception of those rules. The Board of Trade has just completed a set of simple diagrams explaining in the clearest manner the way in which vessels should comply with the Rules of the Road under every circumstance. These diagrams are in accordance with the views of the Trinity House, and are now under the consideration of the Admiralty. We are only waiting for their official confirmation, to submit the Papers to the Judge of the Court of Admiralty and the Judicial Committee of the Privy Council, by whom questions relating thereto are eventually decided. When an authoritative interpretation of these rules is thus obtained, I believe that accidents resulting from misconception will be very rare.[250]

The diagrams did little but confirm that the arc of visibility of a single masthead light and sidelights made it very difficult for another vessel to determine both the heading of an approaching vessel displaying them, and the risk of collision.

The second concern regarding the intent of 'put the helm to port' was eventually addressed by a committee appointed by the Admiralty, the Board of Trade and Trinity House in 1876 which proposed that Art. 13 be amended to read;

> If two ships under steam are meeting end on, or nearly end on, so as to involve risk of collision, each shall put her helm to port, or in other words shall alter her course to starboard, so that each may pass on the port side of the other

It was clear from the Annual Wreck Returns, and informed articles in industry journals, that the 1862 Steering and Sailing Rules had done little to lessen the number of collisions. Articles 13 and 14 caused widespread and ongoing concern and controversy due to the impracticability of ascertaining risk of collision at night solely from the appearance of one sidelight and one masthead light; both of which covered an arc of the horizon of 115 degrees from right ahead to 25 degrees abaft the beam. The same situation applied to sailing vessels, which were not required to carry a masthead light. On the 30th of July 1868, an Order in Council was made clarifying Articles II and XIII;

> The two Articles numbered XI and XIII respectively only apply to cases where ships are meeting end on, or nearly end on, in such a manner as to involve risk of collision. They, consequently, do not apply to two ships which must, if both keep their respective courses, pass clear of each other.
>
> The only cases in which the said two Articles do apply are when each of the ships is end on, or nearly end on, to the other; in other words, to cases in which, by day, each ship sees the masts of the other in a line or nearly in a line with her own; and, by night, to cases in which each ship is in such a position as to see both the sidelights of the other.
>
> Article XIII – Two Ships under Steam meeting; there must be at least three points difference [33 and ¾ degrees] in the ships' courses to exclude them from the operation of this Article.

This 'end on or nearly end on' issue would later be largely resolved through echoing the words in the Order '…by day, each ship sees the masts of the other in a line or nearly in a line with her own; and, by night, to cases in which each ship is in such a position as to see both the sidelights of the other'.

Article 16 of the 1862 regulations emphasised the need to consider a reduction in speed, or stopping, to avoid collision and when navigating in fog;

> Art. 16. Every Steam Ship, when approaching another Ship so as to involve Risk of Collision, shall slacken her Speed, or, if necessary, stop and reverse; and every Steam Ship shall, when in a Fog, go at a moderate Speed.

Throughout this era of highly competitive steam passenger liners on the North Atlantic, and far beyond, there were masters who were driven more by commercial pressures, the perceived need to maintain timetable, and hubris, rather than the dictates of prudent seamanship when navigating in reduced visibility and areas of known and reported ice; as had been demonstrated by the fatal collision between the Collins Liner ***Arctic*** and the small French cargo ship ***Vesta*** (200 ton) in September 1854. Two years later Cunard's new passenger liner, the ***Persia*** (1856) of 3,300 tons, arrived in New York on her maiden voyage with her bows badly damaged after hitting an iceberg at full speed. Commentary at the time focussed upon the strength of her iron hull and safety of her many watertight compartments rather than the folly of trying to achieve a faster passage than the Collins Line passenger liner ***Pacific*** that had sailed from Liverpool three days earlier. The ***Pacific*** never arrived in New York and is assumed to have been lost after hitting an iceberg.[251]

A number of judgements were handed down, during the second half of the nineteenth century, regarding excessive speed in reduced visibility;

> A steamship in fog *shall* go at a moderate speed. It has been held in America that when a fog is very dense the steamer should proceed as slowly as possible consistent with maintaining steerage way[252]
>
> What is a moderate rate of speed must depend upon the locality, density of fog, state of weather, and the attendant circumstances[253]
>
> ...even in mid-ocean at about 200 miles east of Sandy Hook, but in the track of vessels going to New York, seven knots an hour has been held too fast for a steamer during thick fog[254]
>
> It is no excuse for an excessive speed that the steamer could not otherwise fulfil a contract for the carriage of the mail[255]

However, the casualties continued. In 1879 the almost new Guion Line passenger ship ***Arizona,*** a single crew iron ship of 5,164 tons, built for speed to gain the coveted Blue Riband, set a record for the fastest eastbound voyage of seven days and eight hours at 15.96 knots and soon established a new westbound record of seven days and ten hours at 17.73 knots. This quest for speed at all costs came to sudden stop in November 1879 when the ship, steaming at full speed in dense fog, ran head-on into a very large iceberg. She survived this impact due to her watertight bulkheads but incurred considerable damage, remarkably with no deaths or injuries. The Master was held to blame with his certificate of competency being suspended. 'Curiously enough the owners and the ***Arizona*** emerged with enhanced reputations; a perverse Atlantic travelling public decided that if a ship could collide with an iceberg and complete her voyage virtually unscathed she must indeed be the 'strongest and safest ship afloat'. As a result she was always well patronised'.[256]

Regardless of the possibility of collision, a graphic example of the dangers involved to passengers and crew in attempting to maintain a schedule through driving a powerful passenger steamer at full speed in adverse weather is that of the White Star liner ***Germanic*** when steaming into a gale and a heavy swell in 1885. The ship met 'brutal waves that knocked out the Captain, killed several people, and swept away the forward steering gear, pilothouse, and all the lifeboats. At half speed the ship might – perhaps – have nursed a better chance of escaping such death and destruction".[257]

The perils of steaming at full speed in thick fog were graphically illustrated when a sister ship to the ***Germanic***; the ***Britannic*** (1875) of 5004 ton, came into collision with another White Star liner, the ***Celtic*** (1872) of 3867 tons, 350 miles east of Sandy Hook on the 19th May 1887. The ***Celtic***, with 870 passengers, was inward bound from Liverpool to New York, while the ***Brittanic*** was on the second day of her passage from New York to Liverpool with 450 passengers. It was reported after the event that 'the Britannic's fog bell had been kept ringing all the afternoon, but her speed had been kept at a high rate. The ***Celtic*** was not sighted until the moment before the collision, although her bell had been heard'.[258] The ***Celtic*** struck the ***Brittanic*** aft of amidships on the port side causing a large hole, partly underwater, which flooded the steerage accommodation and the number five hold; killing six passengers outright and seriously injuring another twelve. The ***Celtic***, which had penetrated the other ships afterdeck by ten feet, suffered considerable damage to her bow, but her collision bulkhead held. The ***Brittanic*** successfully launched five lifeboats with passengers onto the calm sea but these were either recalled, or transferred passengers to the ***Celtic***, when it was realised that the ship would remain afloat. Both ships, escorted by other ships, slowly made their way to New York, arriving on the 22nd

May.[259]

The issue of excessive speed in reduced visibility continued in spite of these dramatic casualties, as highlighted through the trenchant criticism of Sir Charles Butt in 1889 in The ***Resolution***[260] when he stated that; "…I will not yield to what I know is the strong disinclination of the masters of these large vessels to stop their engines. They hate and abhor the very idea, but it is, to my mind, their duty to do so, if they cannot otherwise reduce their speed sufficiently" .

Article 16 – *Speed to be moderate on Fog* – was reiterated through the Merchant Shipping Act, 1894 and expanded to cover other forms of restricted visibility;

> Every vessel shall, in a fog, mist, falling snow, or heavy rainstorm, go at a moderate speed, having careful regard to the existing circumstances and conditions. A steam vessel hearing, apparently forward of her beam, the fog signal of another vessel the position of which is not ascertained, shall, so far as the circumstances of the case admit, stop her engines, and then navigate with caution until danger of collision is over.

Mr Justice Gorell Barnes[261] in his 1896 judgement in The ***Germanic***[262] stated;

> This is a most salutary rule, the safety of life and property in thick weather at sea, and especially in narrow and crowded waters, depends largely upon a strict compliance with its provision. If all vessels moving about in thick weather comply with the rule, their speeds will be so reduced that, although one may be seen from another only at a short distance, time will still be left for each to take proper steps to avoid the other. If the ordinary slow speed of fast steamers (whose engines, when working at slow, may give them nearly as much speed as less powerful vessels only make at full or half speed) will not produce safe navigation, the engines must be reduced to dead slow, and if that is not sufficient they must be stopped from time to time.

The matter of international uniformity in steering and sailing rules, at a time when there were no international safety standards for ships, was addressed for waters under British jurisdiction by the s.57 of the Merchant Shipping Acts Amendment Act, 1862.

> 57. Whenever foreign ships are within British jurisdiction, the regulations for preventing collision contained in Table C in the schedule to this Act, or such other regulations for preventing collisions as are for the time being in force under this Act, and all provisions of this Act relating to such regulations, or otherwise relating to collisions, shall apply to such foreign ships; and in any cases arising in any British court of justice concerning matters happening within British jurisdiction, foreign ships shall, so far as regards such regulations and provisions, be treated as if they were British ships.

Whilst s.57 of the Act dealt with interaction between British and foreign flagged ships within Britain's narrow territorial waters s.58; *Regulations when adopted by a Foreign Country, may be applied to its Ships on the High Seas,* went considerably further and made the bold move of extending this territorial requirement to ships of any other States willing to accept this standard in waters outside British jurisdiction. [263]

> 58. Whenever it is made to appear to His Majesty in Council that the Government of any foreign country is willing that the collision regulations, or the provisions of Part V. of this Act relating thereto or otherwise relating to collisions, or any of these regulations or provisions should apply to the ships of that country when beyond the limits of British jurisdiction, His Majesty may, by Order in Council, direct that those regulations and provisions shall, subject to any limitation of time conditions and qualifications contained in the Order, apply to the ships of the said foreign country, whether within British jurisdiction or not, and that such ships shall for the purpose of such regulations and provisions be treated as if they were British ships.

An increasingly large number of foreign countries [264] accepted this offer which was repeated in the Merchant Shipping Act, 1894,[265] and went on to make it sweepingly and abundantly clear in s.61 of that Act that extraterritorial jurisdiction would be exercised;

> 61. Whenever an Order in Council has been issued under this Act, applying any provisions of this Act or any regulation made by or in pursuance of this Act to the ships of any foreign country, such ships shall in all cases arising in any British court be deemed to be subject to such provisions or regulation, and shall for the purpose of such provi-

sion or regulation be treated as if they were British ships.

In spite of the sting in the tail, this proactive stance by Britain was a graphic illustration of its dominant and all pervasive influence in the development of maritime law throughout the shipping world of the nineteenth century, and of the ability to establish customary law through agreement amongst sovereign States in vital matters of safety at sea.[266] By the end of 1864 the British/French Regulations for Preventing Collisions at Sea, 1862, had been adopted as an international standard by more than thirty States;[267] a testament to the leadership of the world's largest maritime nation, the international goodwill of many countries in this critical matter of safety, and the acceptance, in an era where there was no representative international maritime body, of customary international law.

With increasing agreement, and reliance upon customary law, the United States of America convened the first International Maritime Conference in Washington during 1889 with the explicit purpose of considering international regulations for prevention of collisions at sea. Agreement was reached on the need for a stand-on vessel to keep her course and speed; for a giving-way vessel to avoid crossing ahead of the stand-on vessel, and larger steamships were given the option of carrying a second masthead light.[268]

A further International Maritime Conference was convened in Brussels in 1910 where agreement was reached on minor amendments to the collision regulations agreed at Washington in 1889,[269] and the collision regulations then remained fundamentally unchanged until 1954. At an international conference in 1929 a recommendation 'that helm and steering orders should be given in the direct sense, so that 'right rudder' or 'starboard' meant 'put the vessel's rudder to starboard', was accepted and came into force in 1933. At an international conference on Safety of Life at Sea in 1948, a second masthead light was made compulsory for power-driven vessels of 150 feet or upwards in length, a fixed stern light was made compulsory for almost all vessels under way, and the 'wake-up' signal of at least five short and rapid blasts was introduced as an optional signal for use by a stand-on vessel. The revised Rules came into force in 1954.[270]

Chapter 7

Merchant Shipping Act, 1854

The year 1854 saw the greatest number of ships and people lost between 1848 and 1878, including a total of 987 ships and 1549 persons lost within 10 miles of the British coast.[271] Further afield four wrecks alone counted for the loss of more than 1,381 people.[272] The year was also notable for enactment of one of the most comprehensive Acts of consolidation during the nineteenth century, the Merchant Shipping Act, 1854.

At the very beginning of this calamitous year there occurred one of the worst maritime disasters of the nineteenth century, a tragedy that could have well been avoided. The new iron emigrant ship ***Tayleur,*** (1,750 tons) on her maiden voyage from Liverpool to Melbourne with 581 emigrants, and a crew of 71, was wrecked on Lambay Island off the coast of Ireland near Dublin on 21 January 1854. The ***Tayleur*** was originally designed as a screw steamship but, due to the lack of a suitable engine, was lengthened and modified to a sailing ship. After her launching she was fully rigged, equipped and loaded. She had not undertaken any form of sea trials as a sailing ship. In her very short and tragic career she was found to be very difficult to handle due to a rudder that was alleged to be too small to be effective, and was reported after the accident to have taken up to one hour to tack, losing five miles in the process. The running rigging had not been properly stretched or set up and it took the crew three hours to reef the topsails. Her compasses were wildly inaccurate, and she had a very inexperienced and polyglot crew who could not effectively communicate.[273] More than 400 souls were lost. Only 3 women out of an estimated 200, and 3 of the fifty children aboard survived. The crew were all saved except for six.

Until the advent of reliable and powerful steam propulsion ships had always been at the mercy of the wind and weather, especially when close to the coast. Even with the advances in technology and speed of the hard driven packet and clipper ships of the nineteenth century a sailing ship still depended on the ability to sail as close to the wind as possible for survival when beset upon a lee shore. Many were lost due to a lack of weatherliness when embayed, and loss of their ultimate protection, anchors and cables. When ships were driven ashore in such dreadful circumstances it was often impossible to use the few boats carried and large loss of life ensued. A contemporary painting of the ***Tayleur*** showed four boats. It was reported at the time that 'A raft was constructed were (sic) great numbers embarked, but it drifted on the rocks and upset, all on it perished'.[274]

The cause of wreck was attributed primarily to a lack of proper sea trials. "Had such trials been conducted they would almost immediately have become aware of the inherent flaws of the ship, its masts placed too far aft, the improper state of the running and standing rigging, the unsuitability of the rudder and the compass errors".[275] The ***Tayleur*** was fitted with three compasses, supplied by John Grey 'compass maker to Her Majesty'. They were compensated for the combined magnetic influence of the ship and the earth's magnetic field two months before the sailing of the vessel, and before the cargo had been loaded. At the Coroner's inquest into the sinking of the ship it was stated that, whilst the ship was departing Liverpool, the pilot noticed a point (eleven and a quarter degrees) of difference between the compasses. Later in the tragically short journey further compass errors of up to 1½ points were recorded.

In the absence of a comprehensive understanding of magnetism aboard ships at the time of the loss of the ***Tayleur***, the problem of total error of the ship's compass (the combined effect of variation and deviation) could not be approached analytically, fully understood or corrected. It was not until the groundbreaking work of William Thomson (the later Lord Kelvin) in the 1870s that all influences upon a ship's compass were identified, including heeling error, means of identifying and compensating for these accumulative magnetic effects were established, and an efficient compass and binnacle with correctors was designed.

In these days of instant worldwide communication it is difficult to conceive the apprehension which attended the departure of every passenger ship for any destination in the nineteenth century, but particularly if the passage of indeterminate length was to another country. Shipwreck was common and evidence of the cause was usually available; whether through foundering, collision, fire, grounding or any other cause.

By 1854, millions of passengers had left Great Britain for new homes; mainly to North America but also as far distant as Australia and New Zealand. Many never arrived and the perils of travelling by sea were well known but unavoidable. The only comparison with the present day would be travel by air which, fortunately, has always been well regulated, but the shock of the loss of a large passenger aircraft and all aboard would be similar to the emotions felt by the families and friends of those embarked upon a missing ship in the nineteenth century. The main difference would be that the news would now be almost instantaneous and the cause would, almost always, be eventually determined.

Early in 1854 a large passenger ship disappeared. At this time there was no way to communicate between Europe and America; the trans-Atlantic cable was not laid until 1866. The only way for a ship's owners to know if a ship had arrived was to receive a report from another ship. On March 1, 1854, Inman Line's ***City of Glasgow***, (1609 gross tons), left Liverpool bound for Philadelphia with a total of 480 persons on board, including 293 emigrants. The iron ship, built in 1850 as one of the first ocean going passenger ships to utilise a screw propeller, had been refitted in 1852 to carry 400 emigrants. The vessel was the pioneer of a direct line of steam communication between Philadelphia and Liverpool and carried thousands of Irish emigrants to America in the four years she operated on the North Atlantic. But after leaving Liverpool on March 1, 1854 she was never seen again.

In early April, over five weeks after she sailed, there was still no word of her. The Liverpool office of Richardson Brothers even released a statement that they were not concerned about the ship and that she had provisions for up to seventy days if they were used prudently. They believed, or at least they said they thought, she was locked in the ice somewhere off Newfoundland. Many reports arrived at the office of William Inman but none of them could confirm the loss of the ***City if Glasgow.*** It was the first loss of a ship for the Inman Line and one of the worst disasters on the north Atlantic to date. It has never been determined what caused the ship to be lost although reports from other ships were received of possible sightings.[276] One such report might have shed some light on a possible cause of the total loss of the ship and all on board;

The Missing City Of Glasgow, Steamer.– The New York Herald says – At last, after months of painful suspense, indications of the probable fate of the steamship City of Glasgow, and of the hundreds of unfortunate beings who embarked in her, have come to light. Captain M'Leary, of the barque Mary Morris from Glasgow, arrived here yesterday, and reports that on the 18th August, in lat. 53° 26', lon. 16 ° 07', weather very thick at the time, and a heavy sea on, he fell in with the hull of a large iron vessel, apparently Clyde-built, painted black, with a bright red bottom. There were three or four compartments in the hull, and all the wood work was entirely burnt out of her. Some of the men who were sent aloft to look into her, perceived she had machinery in her. On the next day Captain M'Leary fell in with and took on board a full-length female figure head, about seven feet in height, with her hands extended, and a wreath upon her head, and green stripes in her dress. The figure can be seen on board the Mary Morris, at the foot of Pine-street. It was the impression of all on board the barque that the wreck was that of an iron propeller, supposed the City of Glasgow. From the circumstance that no other iron vessel has been reported lost, except the steamer Helen Sloman, some three years back, appearances favour the belief that the wreck was that of the City of Glasgow, and that the fate of the poor souls on board, though different from that hitherto supposed, was the most awful that can occur among the many disasters incidental to the ocean. Though the proofs are but small to identify the wreck as that of the City of Glasgow, the weather being too unfavourable to make a more thorough examination, still enough may have been seen to guide those to a decision who were acquainted with the unfortunate vessel. Our Philadelphia correspondent telegraphs that the City of Glasgow had no such figurehead as that picked up by the Mary Morris. We think he is mistaken. She had such an ornament when she left this port, but it may have been taken off. She had, however, a red bottom. The figure-head may have belonged to some other vessel.[277]

The cause of the loss of the City of Glasgow, as with the disappearance of the President in 1840, has never been positively determined.

Leading up to 1854 the British Parliament was drafting a major Act to improve safety at sea and to consolidate all existing maritime legislation, with the exception of Acts relating to Customs duties, harbours and emigrant ships;[278] the Merchant Shipping Act, 1854, effective 01 May 1855 – *an Act to amend and consolidate the Acts relating to Merchant Shipping*; a mammoth enactment occupying a fifth of the statute book for the year.[279] Mid-Victorians had come to the conclusion that merchant shipping law was very unsatisfactory. There was an 'urgent need to cut through a thicket of close-growing legislation by means of a single sharp and shining instrument of their own' for, as a back-bencher had proclaimed in 1850, they were tired of a 'mode of legislation by patches'.[280] Also, as demonstrated by repeal of the Navigation Acts, the philosophy of free trade was now more generally acceptable; in the words of the mid-nineteenth century, protectionism was a 'dead letter'.

Many of the deep-seated fears of shipowners regarding the Merchant Shipping Bill had been calmed by an explanatory pamphlet entitled 'Memorandum on the Merchant Shipping Law Consolidation Bill', written by Thomas Henry Farrer[281], the Assistant Secretary at the Board of Trade, and Henry Thring, a barrister at the Board of Trade, that reassured shipowners that their authority would not be eroded. There was a remarkably low level of debate on the Bill. Labouchére congratulated the House of Commons on the "absence of party spirit", and, while the Economist complained that the measure was 'disgraceful to the legislature', it did not meet with any serious opposition and passed through the Commons at a single sitting.[282] Labouchére, now out of office, had worked with Joseph Henley[283] on the consolidation of existing legislation, with Edward Cardwell[284] as President of the Board of Trade; supervising both of them. These two; an arch conservative and a champion of free trade, found themselves in almost complete agreement on the substance of the Act.[285]

The Merchant Shipping Act, 1854; the foundation upon which all subsequent shipping legislation was built, set standards in eleven parts, the great majority of which dealt with administrative and social rather than technical matters, but included many of the matters considered by previous Acts and Select Committees on Shipwreck;

> Part 1, Functions of the Board of Trade; Part II, Ownership, Measurement and Registration of British Ships; Part III, Masters and Seamen; Part IV, Safety and Prevention of Accidents; Part V, Pilotage; Part VI, Lighthouses; Part VII, Mercantile Marine Fund; Part VIII, Wrecks,

> Casualties and Salvage; Part IX, Liability of Shipowners; Parts X & XI, Legal Procedures, Punishment of Offences, Recovery of Fines and Penalties, and other Miscellaneous Matters such as Contracts, Expenses, and other Acts affected or otherwise by the Act.

Part III – *Masters and Seamen* – included and updated administrative matters contained in the repealed Mercantile Marine Act, 1851 such as Local Marine Boards, Shipping Offices, Examination of Masters and Mates, Apprentices, Engagement of Seamen, Allotment of Wages, Provisions, Health and Accommodation, Discipline, Protection of Seamen from Imposition, Naval Courts on the High Seas and Abroad, Crimes committed on the High Seas and Abroad, Repatriation and Returns respecting Seamen, and Official Log Books.

Section 230 required that '*every Foreign-going Ship having One hundred Passengers or upwards on Board shall carry as part of her Complement some Person duly authorized by Law to practice as Physician, Surgeon or Apothecary…*' However, in spite of Part I, s.6, of the 1854 Act stating that;

> The Board of Trade shall be the department to undertake the general Superintendence of matters relating to Merchant Ships and Seamen, and shall be Authorised to carry into execution the Provisions of the Act, and of all other Acts relating to Merchant Ships and Seamen in force for the Time being, other than such Acts as relate to the Revenue section 230 went on to defer to the Passengers Act, 1852, in that;

> …nothing herein contained shall in any way affect any Provision contained in the Passenger Act, 1852 concerning the Carriage of Medical Practitioners by Class of Ship…;

The Admiralty were empowered under s.295 (2) to; *…if they think fit, make Regulations requiring the Use of such Fog Signals, by such Classes of Ships, whether Steam or Sailing Ships, within such Places and under such Circumstances as they think fit, and may from Time to Time revoke, alter, or vary the same.*

An Admiralty Notice; *Respecting Lights and Fog Signals to be Carried and used by Sea-going Vessels, to prevent Collision,* was published on the 24th February 1858; revoking a previous Notice published in 1852.

Part IV; *Safety and Prevention of Accidents,* comprising less than four percent of the content of the Act, largely continued and updated the provisions of the repealed Steam Navigation Acts of 1846 and 1851. There was a focus upon the main causes of accidents at that turning point in the development of ships, albeit it with a focus upon only steamships: carriage of boats, prevention of collisions, build and equipment of steamships, surveys of passenger steamers and reporting of accidents. The application of Part IV was to; *...all British Ships; and all Foreign Steam Ships carrying Passengers between Places in the United Kingdom shall be subject to all Provisions contained in the Fourth Part of this Act and Likewise to the same provisions with respect to the certificates of Masters and mates thereof to which British Ships are subject.*

Section 300 continued the requirements of the 1846 Act regarding water-tight bulkheads and extended them from only passenger ships to *...every Steam Ship built of Iron*. Section 300(2) required that such ships, *...the building of which commences after the passing of this Act, shall be divided by such Partitions as aforesaid into not less than Three equal Parts, or as nearly as Circumstances permit,* and required under s.300(3) that *...In such last mentioned Ships each such Part as aforesaid shall be of equal Strength with the Side plates of the Ship with which it is in contact*. There was a nod to the introduction of screw propulsion in that all such ships built after the introduction of the 1854 Act were required by s.300 (4) *...to be fitted with a small Water-tight Compartment inclosing the After– extremity of the Shaft.*

There had clearly been issues of engineers 'controlling and interfering with' the safety valves required on steam boilers by the 1851 Act as this provision was significantly strengthened through s.302 of the 1854 Act;

> ...If any Person places an undue Weight on the Safety Valve of any Steam Ship or, in the Case of Steam Ships surveyed as herein-after mentioned, increases such Weight beyond the Limits fixed by such Engineer Surveyor as herein-after mentioned, he shall, in addition to any of the Liabilities he may incur by so doing, incur a Penalty not exceeding One hundred Pounds.

The 1854 Act increased the scale for carriage of boats to reflect increases in the size of steam ships. Two further categories of ship were added to the table under the 1851 Act; for steam ships from 800 to 1,000 tons and for those over 1,000 tons. Steam ships between 800 and 1,000 tons were required to carry the same number of boats (4 or 5) as those between 500 and 800 tons under the 1851 Act. Steam ships over 1,500 tons were required to carry seven boats, one of which was required to be a lifeboat. Detailed guidance to the Table was provided in footnotes to s. 292 of the Act; for example;

> In sailing ships carrying the number of boats above specified, and steamships carrying the larger of the two numbers above specified the boats are to be considered sufficient if the aggregate cubic contents are equal to the aggregate cubic contents of the boats specified. – In steamships carrying the smallest of the two numbers above specified, one of the boats must be a launch of the capacity specified in Column 2. – In sailing ships of 200 tons burthen and under, not carrying passengers, a dinghy may be substituted for the boat in Column 4. – In sailing ships of 150 tons burden and under, not carrying passengers, a substantial boat of capacity sufficient to carry the crew may be substituted for those above specified. – In all steamships, two paddle box boats may be substituted for any two of the boats in Column 3

It is of great significance that the amended requirement by the 1854 Act for the carriage of lifeboats, and the number of lifeboats to be carried, continued to relate to the registered tonnage of the ship and not to the total complement of crew and passengers. This ongoing flaw in the regulation of safety aboard British ships, combined with the influence and parsimony of shipowners, and neglect of politicians, was to be the direct cause of the loss of many lives during the second half of the nineteenth century and well into the twentieth.

Section 310(3) continued fire-fighting requirements largely unchanged from that of the 1846 Act in that; *Every sea-going Steam Ship (unless used solely as a Steam Tug) shall be provided with a Hose adapted for the purpose of extinguishing Fire in any Part of the Ship and capable of being connected with the Engines of the Ship*. The remaining Parts of the 1854 Act regulated a variety of administrative matters including registration of ships, pilotage and lighthouses. The Merchant Shipping Act, 1854, which came into effect on 01 May 1855, remained the mainstay of safety regulation of British ships until being repealed by the Merchant Shipping Act, 1894.

There were mixed views about the 1854 Act. Farrer referred to it as "a code of imperial statute law, relating to British Merchant Shipping" while Thring believed it was simply "a digest of maritime regulations". The editor of a publication on the Act (a politician and Barrister-at-Law) stated that, in his view, "it seems to me to less of the former and more of the latter; though not possessing the symmetry or exactness of a 'code', it embraces legal principles and contains substantive enactments which raise it above the rank of a 'digest'",[286] and went on to summarise and eulogise the Act;

> It is in fact a consolidating and amending act. It professes to reduce into the scope and compass of a single act, a number of acts passed from time to time, as the exigency of the state required, without any conformity of purpose, or any consistency of detail – acts, now partially repealing former acts – now conflicting with and not repealing them, mutually qualifying or restraining each other, and leading to doubtful interpretation and perpetual confusion. It was well observed by the Lords' Committee on Foreign Trade in 1820: -'Perhaps no service more valuable could be rendered to the trade of the empire, than an accurate version of the vast and confused mass of commercial legislation'
>
> To render this service, and effect this revision, so far as it relates to our merchant shipping and navigation laws – to regulate and harmonise what we before entangled and confused – to reduce a large and mystified bulk into a popular and portable shape – to condense a library into a volume – was the work which Mr. Cardwell professed to undertake, and which he has successfully accomplished....of this great work of Mr. Cardwell, it may be said as Lord Tenterdin did in allusion to the French Code of 1681, that it has been; Composed in the reign of a political Prince, under the auspices of an enlightened Minister, and in the matter, method and style, is one of the most finished Acts of legislation that was ever promulgated.

On the 20th of September 1854, the American Collins Line passenger ship ***Arctic*** sailed from Liverpool for New York with 281 passengers and 153 crew. Seven days later, when steaming at her full speed of 13 knots in dense fog on the Grand Banks, the ship collided with the small French steamer ***Vesta***. The Master of the ***Arctic*** immediately ordered the Chief Officer to launch a boat to assist the ***Vesta*** as she appeared to be severely damaged. He also instructed the Second Officer to inspect the starboard bow to determine the extent of the damage which proved to be extensive. The crew's efforts to block the ingress of water with sails, mattresses and pillows were ineffectual. At this time the Master decided to leave the ***Vesta***, and the Chief Officer's boat never to be seen again, and steam at full speed for Cape Race, about sixty miles away. In the course of leaving the scene of the collision the ***Arctic*** ran down and sank one of the ***Vesta's*** lifeboats killing all aboard except one crew member. The intake of water in the ***Arctic's*** engine room increased rapidly to the extent that boiler fires were progressively extinguished. After working for thirty minutes in increasingly desperate circumstances the engine room crew downed tools and rushed onto deck, some with drawn knives. "From this time", one passenger related, "all order and discipline ceased". Four and a half hours after the collision the ***Arctic*** sank amidst scenes of mutiny and panic by the great majority of the crew. [287]

As was typical of ships of the day the ***Arctic's*** lifeboats could only carry 40 percent of the total complement of 434. Only 23 passengers survived and all of the 109 women and children perished. The unimaginable horror of the tragedy is highlighted by the raw statistic that 61 of the 153 crew survived including 4 out of the 5 senior officers and half the firemen and trimmers. Among the passengers lost were the wife, son and daughter of Mr. Collins, founder of the Collins Line, and his brother's wife. "The ***Arctic*** disaster shattered high Victorian notions of how men were supposed to respond under duress. In this desperate crisis, the muffling, protecting layers of civilisation slipped away too easily, and human beings behaved like any other wild, self-preserving animals. It broke the social contract in alarming, revealing ways. Worse than shocking or tragic, it was shameful'.[288] Ironically, the ***Vesta*** survived the collision; a ship well placed to have rescued all of the crew and passengers of the ***Arctic***.

The Collins Line immediately voluntarily equipped its ships with watertight bulkheads and more lifeboats, but this was as much by way of a public relations exercise to restore confidence as it was to improve safety. The masters of the Collins Line ships, as did their competitors, continued to steam at full speed in fog, ice and heavy weather, pushing their vessels to the limit to maintain schedules. In spite of building an even more luxurious replacement for the ***Arctic***; the ***Adriatic***, the Collins Line collapsed suddenly in 1857 after it lost all confidence of the travelling public when the sister ship to the ***Arctic***, the ***Pacific***, with a crew of 141 and 45 passengers disappeared without trace in January 1856. In the words of a commentator in 1914; 'The probability is that she foundered after a collision with an iceberg – a victim perhaps of the insane desire for speed, which then, and now, was one of the unfortunate features of Trans-Atlantic voyages'.[289]

Another wreck in 1854, with very large loss of life, was that of the emigrant brig ***Annie Jane,*** (1853) of 1,295 tons, driven ashore at Barra Island in the Hebrides in October with the loss of 348 of the estimated 450 persons on board.[290] It was also reported that, in a three day storm from November 13th 1854 in the Black Sea during the Crimean War, eleven British transport ships were wrecked and a further six ships disabled. One of these ships, a new steamship the ***Princess,*** was lost with 144 lives, while the loss of life in the other shipwrecks was estimated at 340.[291]

Chapter 8

Continuing calamities

Only two days after the Merchant Shipping Act, 1854, came into force there was a graphic and tragic example of many of the issues the Act sought to address. On 3 May, 1855, the emigrant ship ***John*** of 465 tons was wrecked on the Manacles shortly after departing Plymouth for Quebec with 154 adult passengers, 98 children, 16 infants and 19 crew; a total of 287 souls aboard. The ship, built in 1810, was long out of Class, and had departed with more passengers than allowed and without being equipped with a signal gun, muskets, rockets, or blue lights as night signals.[292]

With a clear reference to the very recently introduced Merchant Shipping Act, 1854 the Court of Inquiry noted that –

> ...the boats on board the John were not stowed in their proper places, nor were they prepared for service if wanted. We may venture to add, as a fair deduction from the evidence, that even had they been properly stowed, and had they been prepared for service, there was not in them sufficient accommodation to secure the safety of the passengers...how is it that a master so incompetent to take the charge of a vessel is sent to sea at all? We had heard of a Merchant Seamen's Act, which was to bring about an entirely new order of things. Masters in the merchant service were to be submitted to the most stringent tests, and no one was to be placed in a position of authority who was not fitted for the post. In the very case before us, in addition to the shortcomings of the captain, the first mate held only a certificate of service, not one of competency. The only remedy is, that the Board of Trade should enforce to their utmost extent the penalties of the new Act against the owners of the John. If there be no regard for human life among the owners of emigrant ships, perhaps consideration for their own pockets may render them more careful in the selection of competent officers.'

One hundred and ninety-four souls were lost. In the first prosecution taken under the Merchant Shipping Act, 1854, the Captain was convicted of manslaughter. The Court of Enquiry issued the following damning findings;

That the ship was provided with four boats – three of which were inefficient, the other doubtful; that the lifeboat was neither stowed in the proper place nor prepared for immediate service as directed by the act; and to these circumstances probably the staving and loss of the lifeboat and the delay in endeavouring to get out the long boat are to be attributed.

That, with the exception of one single lantern, there were no means on board the ship of making a signal of distress by night. We think that, had there been adequate means of making such signals, and had they been shown when the ship first got on shore, while the weather was moderate, the boats would have come off at an earlier period, and thus have rescued a much larger proportion of passengers.

That with respect to the above deviations from the provision of the Passengers' Act, we consider that the Government emigration officers and owners of the ship are culpable.

That, either from the ignorance or gross and culpable negligence of the captain, the courses steered by his orders were the direct cause of bringing the vessel on the Manacle rocks.

That after the vessel struck, the conduct of the captain was most reprehensible in every respect; he appears to have taken no active means to save the lives of the passengers, did not assist them to leave the ship, quitted her himself while many of the passengers were still in the rigging and he and the mate were the only two persons who secured anything for themselves; the captain saving his cloak and the mate his quadrant.

That the chief mate appears to be ignorant of his duties and responsibilities and is culpable in not having personally rendered assistance to the passengers.

That the conduct of the crew, with the exception of Andrew Elder, and one or two others, appears to have been very bad, but would probably have been different had a better example been set them by their officers.

That the conduct of the chief boatman of the coastguard and his men,

> and of a fisherman named James Hill, and others associated with them, in going to and taking the passengers and crew off the wreck, was highly commendable.
>
> The circumstances of this case render it our duty to suggest to your lordships that in all passenger ships the first mate should be required to have a certificate of competency instead of one of services only, and that the number and nature of the night signals required to be provided by the owners of passenger ships should be specified.[293]

The Merchant Shipping Act, 1854, underwent a tidy-up through the Merchant Shipping Act Amendment Act, 1855,[294] – *An Act to facilitate the Erection and Maintenance of Colonial Lighthouses, and otherwise amend the Merchant Shipping Act, 1854*. Apart from colonial lighthouses, the amendment covered matters such as Registry of Ships, Destitute Seamen, Seamen's saving banks (extended to seamen serving in the Royal Navy and other sea services), Wrecks, Casualties and Salvage, and Legal Procedures.

The Passenger Act, 1855,[295] – *An Act Relating to the carriage of Passengers by Sea,* repealed the Passengers Act, 1852. The 1855 Act updated requirements for numbers of boats to reflect increasing tonnage of ships, extending the requirements to include ships of 1500 tons or upwards. Instead of having minimum numbers of passengers for each category of tonnage as in the 1852 Act, the 1855 Act included a general requirement for carriage of boats that; *...provided that no "Passenger Ship" shall be required to carry a greater Number of Boats than are sufficient in the Judgement of the Emigration Officer at the Port of Clearance to carry all the Persons on board of such Ship.*

This sensible, and long overdue provision, apart from reliance upon the judgement of the Emigration Officer, reflects the emphasis in the Act on carriage of passengers as had been the case since 1842. It will be recalled that the Passenger Act, 1842, was the first legislation, in the absence of any safety regulation for ships, to require passenger ships to carry boats. The disconnect between Passenger Acts and the various Merchant Shipping and Steam Navigation Acts regarding the number of boats to be carried, their tonnage divisions, capacities, distinction between sailing ships and steam ships, including the 1854 Act, was continued. The Merchant Ship Act, 1854 had taken no account at all of the number of persons on board; passengers or crew.

There were many issues with safety provisions in the various Passenger Acts. Drafting of the Acts by officials with no knowledge of, or access to, expert knowledge of ships; vagueness and inconsistency, variance with other Acts leading to confusion; reliance upon the judgement of an official with no demonstrable knowledge of ships and their operation to determine whether a passenger ship was in all respects seaworthy, and no penalty provisions if an Emigration Officer was to err in his judgement in any respect and allow an unseaworthy ship to proceed to sea.

Part XXVII of the 1855 Act summarised the increasing range and extent of matters upon which the Emigration Officer was required to exercise his judgement; –

> …one of such Boats shall in all cases be a Long Boat and one shall be a properly fitted Life Boat, which shall be carried in such Manner as to be, in the Opinion of the Emigration Officer, most available for immediate Service; Each of such Boats shall be of a Size and description to be approved by the Emigration Officer at the port of Clearance and shall be seaworthy, and properly supplied with all requisites and kept clear at all Times for immediate use at Sea; There shall likewise be on board each "Passenger Ship" if proceeding to the Southward of the Equator at least Two Chronometers, and if to any Place to the northward of the equator at least One Chronometer, and on board all "Passenger Ships" at least Three Steering Compasses and One Azimuth Compass, Four properly fitted Lifebuoys kept ready at all Times for Immediate use, and some adequate means to be approved by the Emigration Officer at the Port of Clearance, of making Signals by Night and in Fogs; also a Fire Engine, in proper working Order, and of such Description and power and either with or without such other apparatus for extinguishing Fire as such Officer may approve, and not less than Three Bower Anchors of such Weight, and with Cables of such Length, Size and Material, as in the Judgement of such Emigration Officer shall be sufficient for the Size of the Ship. In the case of Noncompliance with any of the Requirements of this Section, the Master of the Ship shall for each Offence be liable to a Penalty not exceeding Fifty Pounds nor less than Five pounds Sterling.

No provision was provided for exemption from the requirements of the Merchant Shipping Act, 1854, in respect of boats to be carried, if the requirements of the 1855 Act were followed, as had been the relationship between the Passengers Act, 1852, and the Steam Navigation Act, 1851.

Part XXV of the Passengers Act, 1852, stated that '*Every "Passenger Ship" shall be manned with an efficient Crew for her intended Voyage, to the Satisfaction of the Officer from whom a Clearance of such Ship may be demanded*'. Part XXVII of the 1855 Act expanded and clarified this requirement to state that the 'Officer' was the 'Emigration Officer' and went on to state that '*...the strength of the Crew shall not be diminished, nor any of the Men changed when once passed by such Emigration officer, without his Consent in Writing, or that of the Shipping Master of the Port of Clearance, as required by the Laws then in force regulating the shipping of Seamen on board Merchant Vessels...*'.

The '*laws in force regulating the shipping of Seamen*' in this situation were the provisions of Section 150 (4) of the 1854 Act – *Provision of Substitutes* – which amply provided for this situation without the involvement of an Emigration Officer; –

> In the Case of Substitutes engaged in the Place of Seamen who have duly signed the Agreement, and whose Services are lost within twenty-four Hours of the Ship's putting to Sea by Death, Desertion or other unforeseen Cause the Engagement shall, when practicable, be made before some Shipping Master duly appointed in the Manner herein-before specified; and whenever such last-minute Engagement cannot so be made, the Master shall, before the ship puts to Sea, if practicable, and if not, as soon afterwards as possible, cause the Agreement to be read over and explained to the Seaman; and the Seaman shall thereupon sign the same in the Presence of a Witness, who shall attest their Signature

If a substitute were required earlier than twenty-four before departure, the normal process of signing on would take place at the Shipping Office.

Provision was also made in Part XXVII of the 1855 Act to '*appoint Two other Emigration Officers, or Two competent Persons to examine the matter if the Owner or Charterer of the Ship should appeal in writing any judgement by the Emigration officer that the crew was inefficient*'. It is difficult to see how an Emigration officer, or anyone apart from the ship's officers, could determine the efficiency of the crew. No such provision was contained in the 1854 Act.

In light of all of the above it is worth repeating an opinion of the Court of Enquiry in to loss of the ***John***; 'That with respect to the above deviations from the provision of the Passengers' Act, we consider that the Government emigration officers and owners of the ship are culpable'.

Introduction of the Passengers Act, 1855, completed a remarkable few years of consolidation and reformation of merchant shipping law, during which the Mercantile Marine Act, 1850, had almost totally reformed the administration of merchant ships; the Merchant Shipping Act, 1854 had consolidated and repealed all or part of forty-nine Acts, and the Passengers Act, 1855 had repealed the Passengers Act, 1852. There was to be no further maritime legislation during this decade.

In spite of this comprehensive suite of maritime legislation introduced over a few short years, emergency equipment was still very limited and seafarers were often forced to rely upon their own resources to deal with dangerous incidents. The complete isolation of a sailing vessel on a long passage, and necessary resourcefulness of the crew, and passengers, to save the vessel from total loss by fire, is well illustrated in the account of an incident aboard the ***Ashburton*** (689 ton) in 1855 on a passage from Sydney to London.[296]

> The Ashburton, Captain King, arrived on Tuesday from London, having made the passage in 105 days; she brings no report of interest, not having seen any vessels since leaving the land. The following account of the narrow escape the vessel had on her homeward passage last voyage will be read with interest. She left Sydney with a cargo of wool, timber, &c., crew and passengers amounting to about eighty souls. After a moderate fine passage she reached latitude 43 ° 42 ' N., longitude 26° 56' W., up to which there was no appearance of heat from the cargo, nor yet of smoke, but a strong stench was experienced six or seven days previous, although no particular attention was paid to it beyond it being very disagreeable, and a survey taken of the hold, so far as possible. On the ninth day of July the stench became much worse and a light smoke was to be seen passing up out of the hatchways. On the following morning, Monday, we had a change of weather, the wind was N.N.E., strong, with rain; the stench became very strong, and after daylight the smoke became very thick, so much so that the passengers could no longer remain below deck. It was now

> very evident that the ship was on fire. The hatches were all battened down and every aperture whereby air could be conveyed to the hold was closed, the fire engine got ready, the boats all properly equipped and each person allotted to his boat, and everything prepared for the worst. It would be impossible to describe the awful scene of excitement that now took place – everyone on deck with their baggage ready to go (they knew not where) in the boats; but about noon it began to calm a little, and Captain King called all the gentlemen passengers and officers of the ship together and proposed breaking out the cargo in search of the fire, and called on all to assist and keep good order while the crew were at work. The courses were hauled up, the small sails stowed, and the mainyard laid to the mast, and the hatches opened, when all hands commenced working coolly and steadily, a number of empty water casks and some lumber were thrown overboard to make room for stowing the wool on deck as it came up. Whilst the men were working the stench and smoke was almost unsupportable, and after getting on deck about 200 bales of wool they reached the fire under the lower deck near the pump well, the bales were drawn out and hoisted on deck and overboard a solid mass of fire; further search was made, but, fortunately, all danger was removed, and before dark that night all the wool was stowed away below and everything in its place. The ship made all sail, steering her course, and everyone on board relieved from the dreadful thoughts of fire at sea.

After operating ever larger wooden paddle-steamers across the North Atlantic from 1840 Cunard finally built their first iron-hulled ship, the ***Persia*** of 3600 ton, in 1855, at this time the largest merchant ship,[297] but clung grimly to their long held view that paddle steamers were the only vessels suitable for the North Atlantic mail service even though, by this time, they operated a considerable number of screw driven steamship feeder cargo services. These cargo ships were smaller and slower than the mail ships, but were cheaper to operate with smaller engine rooms and far greater capacity for cargo.

With the ever present quest for size and speed across the North Atlantic naval architects became constrained by the limitations of side-lever engines, ideal for paddle steamers, and the need for superheated steam to achieve more power and speed, and reduce fuel consumption. In 1853, John Elder, who'd served his apprenticeship under Robert Napier, took out a patent for using a compound engine to drive a screw propeller. A patent for a compound steam engine had been granted to Jonathan Hornblower in 1781 but the technology did not exist at that time to construct a boiler of sufficient strength to contain the required superheated steam at high pressure. Superheating at a temperature higher than the boiling point of water, being only possible at high pressure, results in the absence of any water condensate in the cylinder. The compound, or double expansion, engine utilizes high pressure steam in the first and smaller cylinder which is then passed at lower pressure into the larger cylinder. Expanding the steam twice leads to a considerable saving in fuel, of the order of thirty to forty percent, and provides a smoother turning moment resulting in a more efficient propeller.[298] Around the same time "the old box-shaped tubular boiler yielded to James Howden's cylindrical or 'Scotch' boiler, smaller and lighter… yet stronger and safer at the higher pressures demand by compound engines. New machine tools, especially hydraulic riveters, allowed boilermakers to turn out tighter, more consistent products".[299] Construction of compound engines, operating at high speeds, was only possible through the development of some metal alloys, dating back to a patent granted in America in 1839; a tin alloy for large marine engine bearings and a phosphor bronze alloy about the same time for smaller bearings.

It was not until the 1860s that such engines attained the degree of reliability needed for ocean passages, with early adoption by both the Pacific Steam Navigation Company and P & O to benefit from the considerable reductions of fuel on their long voyages. The first compound engines on the North Atlantic were installed aboard the ***India*** of Anchor Line and the ***Holland*** of the National Line in the late 1860s. When their attributes became widely known they became the standard engine for new buildings almost overnight. In 1868 Cunard specified compound engines for his new builds; ***Batavia*** (2,550 tons) and ***Parthia*** (3,150 tons). By this time Cunard had also forsaken paddlewheels after the paddle wheeler ***Scotia*** had lost the Atlantic blue riband to the propeller driven ***City of Paris*** in 1867. By 1875 compound engines powered more than 2,000 vessels.[300] They were, however, not without their problems, one of which was misuse of pressure relief valves to gain more speed, an issue that'd been addressed through legislation as early as 1851.

The year 1856 started off disastrously at sea with the loss of one passenger ship and all except one of her complement, and the complete disappearance of four other ships; resulting in the deaths of 1069 crew and passengers, all in the space of the first two months of the year.

On the 27th of January 1856 the Collins Line passenger ship ***Pacific***; a sister ship to the ***Arctic*** and one of the original quartet of Collins Line ships, completely disappeared on her scheduled crossing from Liverpool to New York, with 45 passengers aboard for the mid-winter sailing, along with 141 officers and crew. The ship didn't arrive at New York when expected, and hadn't been reported by any other ships. Ice bergs and field ice had been reported earlier than usual on the great circle route from Liverpool to New York, and a passenger aboard another ship reported that he'd seen "broken ice and some floating cabin furniture on the Grand Banks". Collins Line continued to issue reassuring examples of the reasons for overdue ships; such as engine breakdowns or broken propeller shafts, but, after three months it had to be accepted by the company, and the public, that the ship was lost and the passengers and crew would never be seen again. Loss of the ***Pacific***, after the devastating loss of the ***Arctic*** eighteen months previously, dealt the death blow to the Collins line.[301]

On the 8th February the sailing ship ***Ocean Queen*** (1850) and 1,200 tons, departed London with 33 crew and ninety passengers, was spoken to off the Isle of Wight and then never seen again. The sailing ship ***Driver*** (1854) of 1,594 tons, sailed from Liverpool on the 15th February with a crew of 28 and 344 passengers, and was never sighted or heard of again.[302] The steamship ***Tempest*** (1854) of 866 tons of the Anchor Line, carrying a total of 150 crew and passengers departed New York for Glasgow on the 26th February 1857 and was never seen again.[303] The winter of 1855/56 was one of the worst on record for ice straddling the North Atlantic shipping lanes on and near the Grand Banks and may have been a cause of the complete disappearance of these four ships.

The ***Tempest*** was one of nineteen steamers carrying passengers and cargo that disappeared without trace on the North Atlantic; from the loss of the ***President*** in 1841 to that of the White Star cargo liner ***Naronic*** in 1890. Over this period of 59 years the accumulated loss of life was not far short of 2000 souls. Well known ships that disappeared over this period included the; ***United Kingdom*** (1857) of 1255 tons, also owned by the Anchor line that disappeared with 80 persons on board after leaving port on 17 April 1868; the ***City of Boston*** (1864) of 2778 tons, a square rigged iron steam-ship belonging to the Inman Line, that left Halifax on the 28th January 1870 never to be seen again, carrying 55 cabin passengers, 52 steerage and a crew of 84, and the ***Ismailia*** also of Anchor Line. The ***Ismailia*** (1870) of 1630 tons departed New York for Glasgow on 27 September 1873. The ship was built to carry 500 passengers but was carrying only a few on her last voyage. She was 'spoken to' by another ship on 2 October but then disappeared with the loss of all 52 souls aboard.[304]

C. L. Davy speculated in 1900[305] that these losses were probably due to one of three natural phenomena; "terrific Atlantic seas have overwhelmed these missing steam-ships, and others have gone down quickly and bodily after colliding with icebergs and [semi] submerged derelicts".[306] Another commentator, Thomas Wallace Cox, commented in 1886 that "the passenger steamers never heard from have been destroyed by icebergs, as in nearly every instance other steamers reported great quantities of ice directly in the track of the ill-fated vessel".[307] 'Out of the 120 steamers lost on the Atlantic between the years of 1840 and 1892 twenty-four disappeared as completely as if they had never existed before...over a period of fifty-two years, an average of one ship disappearance every two years.'[308]

Ice was definitely the cause of the loss of the American sailing ship ***John Rutledge*** (1851) of 1,100 tons, which departed Liverpool on the 10th January for New York with 120 steerage passengers and 20 crew. Two of her complement were lost during a stormy crossing before the ship reached the area of fog and ice in the Western North Atlantic; one crew member washed off the jibboom, and one passenger washed overboard. On the 19th February, navigating under sail in heavy ice the ship struck an iceberg heavily. Pumping and jettisoning cargo to lighten the ship were to no avail and the ship was abandoned. The sole survivor, a passenger, stated that the ship had five boats but they were not enough for all on board. Twenty-five to thirty were left onboard including the Mate and the carpenter. The survivor found himself in a boat with twelve others. The only supplies were a gallon of water and a few loaves of bread. After drifting for six days, when he was picked up by a passing ship, all others aboard had died through the intense cold and drinking seawater.[309]

Part XXVII of The Passenger Act, 1852, provided a scale which laid down the duration of voyage that either a sailing vessel or steam vessel had to be provisioned for upon departure on what was often a non-stop passage. For a voyage to the East coast of Australia the duration for a 'Ship Propelled by Sails alone' was 140 days; to New Zealand 150.[310] Emigrants to Australia and New Zealand made this daunting voyage in the 1850s aboard sailing ships; the great majority of which arrived safely. In her book *Life and Death in the Age of Sail: The Passage to Australia*[311], Robin Haines writes about her research into the safety of emigrant ships to Australia. She studied the annual returns of the Colonial Land and Emigration Commission, a British government agency that sent emigrants to the Australian colonies, and found that the Emigration Commission regulated its ships and provided a remarkably safe voyage;

> Some ships did run aground when they reached their destinations but no lives were lost. Until 1872, only two ships carrying assisted emigrants to Australia were sunk. They were the Cataraqui which sank near Port Phillip Bay in 1845 with the deaths of all its passengers and the Guiding Star which was lost without trace with all 543 emigrants in 1855. However, the remarkable statistic is that they were the only two wrecks of the Emigration Commission's 853 ships which carried 281,378 government-assisted emigrants to Australia, New Zealand and South Africa before 1872.'[312]

In September 1858 a tragic fire occurred resulting in one of the largest losses of life aboard a North Atlantic passenger ship. The iron steamship ***Austria***, 2,684 ton, launched in Scotland in June 1857 and operated by the Hamburg Amerika Line, departed Hamburg on 4 September 1858 bound for New York via Southampton. Upon departure from Southampton she had a total of 523 souls aboard; 420 passengers and 103 crew;

> The weather was very rough for the first eight days, with passengers confined to the accommodation. On the ninth day, with calmer seas and warmer weather, the passengers crowded upon deck to enjoy the fresh air as the accommodation had become 'intolerably fouled and fetid' In order to alleviate this state the Captain and the ship's Physician ordered that the passenger accommodation be fumigated. To accomplish this it was the custom to plunge a hot chain into a bucket of pine tar to produce a cleansing cloud of thick black smoke that it was believed

> would prevent sickness and the shipboard plagues of cholera and typhus. The Fourth Officer and Boatswain descended to the steerage accommodation to carry out this task, but, when the chain became too hot it was dropped onto the deck, overturning the bucket and setting the wooden deck on fire. The blazing tar spread across the deck with the fire fanned by open hatches and ventilators and swiftly took hold throughout the accommodation. By the time the Captain ordered the crew to their fire stations, the lead water pipes of the steam fire pump had already been melted and it was discovered that two groups of fire buckets had been chained in place. With the engine room crew all killed by smoke and flames the ship continued to steam into the light wind, feeding the fire. The ships magazine of guns and ammunition exploded. 'We are all lost!' screamed the Captain. 'My God! We are all lost''. The starboard boats were burnt out. Crew attempted to lower the port boats with the Captain, apparently unhinged, leaping into one of the boats to try and save himself. In the turmoil and confusion only one boat was safely launched. The propeller, still turning, chopped into boats and swimmers. A throng of passengers seeking safety on the poop were eventually forced to jump into the sea, many of them with their clothes afire. The Austria's unattended engines eventually lost steam pressure and the shipped stopped in the water, still burning from end to end. At five o'clock a French sailing ship, alerted by the smoke, picked up the survivors. The final toll was 471 dead, more than either of the recent Collins Line disasters, and almost as many as aboard the vanished Inman liner City of Glasgow in 1854. The Captain (who died) was criticized for deserting his ship, as were the surviving crew for not controlling the passengers.[313]

The minimal fire-fighting equipment carried aboard the ***Austria*** was most probably reflective of the standard for British ships introduced through the Steam Navigation Act, 1846, carried forward by the Steam Navigation Act, 1851, and echoed less explicitly by Part XXIV of the Passengers Act, 1852; *There shall likewise be on board each "Passenger Ship" …also a Fire Engine, in proper working order, or other Apparatus for extinguishing fire to be approved by such {Emigration] Officer…* Section 310(3) of the Merchant Shipping Act, 1854; "An Act to amend and consolidate the Acts relating to Merchant Shipping" required that; *Every sea-going Steam Ship (unless used solely as a Steam Tug) shall be provided with a Hose adapted for the purpose of extinguishing Fire in any Part of the Ship and capable of being connected with the Engines of the Ship*

In spite of the loss by fire of many ships and thousands of crew and passengers between 1846 and 1854, there had been no consideration given by the Board of Trade as to the effectiveness of such minimal fire-fighting requirements aboard passenger ships of ever increasing size and passenger capacity.

During 1859 a total of 1416 ships were lost within 10 miles of the British coastline resulting in the loss of 1645 lives.[314] In April 1859 the American registered emigrant ship ***Pomona*** (1400 tons) departed Liverpool bound for New York with 372 Irish emigrants on board. The following day, due to a navigational error, the ship was wrecked on the coast of Wexford, Ireland, with the loss of over 400 persons. Not a single woman or child survived.[315]

The perils of travel by sea, whether under sail or steam, throughout the nineteenth century were very real in the consciousness of the entire population;

Eternal Father, strong to save
Whose arm hath bound the restless wave.
Who bidd'st the mighty ocean deep
Its own appointed limits keep
Oh hear us when we cry to thee
For those in peril on the sea.

The words of this well-known hymn, written by the Reverend William Whiting in 1860, reflected the very real fear that had existed in the minds of people for millennia about the perils of the sea, but particularly during the nineteenth century due to the exponential increase in numbers of passengers carried. Whiting had survived a very rough passage in the mid-1850s and, upon being approached by a student terrified by an upcoming voyage to America, composed the hymn to "anchor the boy's faith". He may well have also in mind the recent wreck of the steam ship ***Royal Charter*** (1855) and 2,719 tons on the night of 25/26 October 1859;

> The ship, with 375 passengers and 112 crew, was as close to Liverpool as attempting to pick up a pilot when rapidly deteriorating weather made this impossible. The ship had made a brief stop at Queenstown in Ireland and was attempting to make the short passage from that port to Liverpool within 24 hours in order to achieve a passage of

> under 60 days from Australia. Battling under steam power into storm force Easterlies the ship became overwhelmed three miles off a lee shore by what came to be known as the "Royal Charter Gale' when the wind, with gusts of 100 mph, backed to the North. Both anchors were dropped off the coast of Anglesey but the cables parted in the Force 12 winds and the ship was driven ashore at Port Helaeth. A crew member swam a line ashore but the ship broke its back soon afterwards and only 21 passengers and 18 crew members survived. All women and children were lost. [316]

The 'Royal Charter Gale' was considered by the newly established Meteorological Office to be the most severe storm to hit the Irish Sea in the 19th century. The depression was first observed in the Bay of Biscay near Cape Finisterre on 24th – 25th October. The centre progressed northwards over Britain from Cornwall to the Yorkshire Coast with the strongest winds in the system developing as a narrow stream from the N or NNE over the Irish Sea. The winds reached hurricane force 12 on the Beaufort Scale and were estimated at well over 100mph. Wind speeds recorded in the Mersey were higher than any previously recorded. The storm claimed 800 lives and 133 ships with a further 90 badly damaged. Twice as many people were lost at sea around the British Isles than in the whole of 1858 including the ***Royal Charter,*** a tragedy that focussed attention in the press on the clear need for storm warnings.

Captain Robert FitzRoy; commander of ***HMS Beagle*** on Darwin's voyage, had established the first Meteorological Office in 1854 and believed that his department could provide such a service. He'd been collecting observations from around the British coastline since 1854 and, after analysing the storm produced a detailed report with charts to prove that it could have been tracked and its path predicted. Through his analyses of the ***Royal Charter*** and other storms FitzRoy demonstrated the validity of his models and proposed a national storm warning system. There was much doubt amongst the scientific establishment that the weather could be predicted in any meaningful way but the government permitted FitzRoy to test his new science of weather forecasting and to establish a Storm Warning service.[317]

In early 1860 Fitzroy received a letter from the American commander of the sailing ship ***William Cumming,*** William Johns, who had been within ten miles of the ***Royal Charter***. Johns used copies of Maury's wind charts and Fitzroy's publication 'Barometer and Weather Guide', and, correctly predicting the weather, shortened sail and tacked to seaward, stating that "I did not suffer *any damage whatever* more than usual in blows, only a little chafe and spray".

Speaking as a naval officer and very experienced commander of sailing ships; Fitzroy later stated, in 1863[318] that;

> ...with her [Royal Charter] power of steam, in addition to that of sails in perfect order, a few hours on the starboard tack, with but little way, would have saved her. So much, at such a time depends on individual judgement. Another ship but a few miles off, a wooden *sailing ship*, not a *steamer*, the Cumming, and several smaller vessels, acted thus – stood to the westwards – and not one was wrecked; nor even injured materially...'and that...'That ship [the Royal Charter] had excellent instruments on board when she left her last port – they *should* have given sufficient notice – but had they not been there, or had their indications been unheeded, those of the heavens should not have been disregarded – overlooked they *could* not have been from any ship – and *were* not by the Cumming, or by numerous coasters'

Chapter 9

Chain Cables, and Casualties

The decade commencing in 1860 was bookended by commencement of the American Civil War in early 1861 and opening of the Suez Canal in November 1869; both events having significant and long-lasting effects upon trade and the shipping industry. The first few years of the decade saw considerable legislative activity; amendments to the Merchant Shipping Act, 1854, considerable progress towards a customary international standard for the Rule of the Road at Sea, and continuing evidence of casualties resulting from poor seamanship in limited visibility. A matter very relevant to the seaworthiness of ships was addressed very early in this period. A ship, and a sailing ship in particular, is at its most vulnerable when forced to anchor on a lee shore in heavy weather to prevent being driven ashore. At such a time the seaworthiness of a ship is totally reliant upon the strength of its ground tackle; anchors and chain cables. In the cases of the Tayleur and Royal Charter their ground tackle proved to be tragically inadequate.

At the very beginning of the decade concern was expressed in the House of Commons as to the adequacy of the testing process for the anchors and chains of merchant vessels, as recorded in Hansard for 02 February 1860;[319]

> Sir James Elphinstone said, that it was in the knowledge of all who had considered the subject of which he had given notice, that imperfection in the cables and anchors which were manufactured for the mercantile service annually led to a very great loss of life and property… In 1859, Mr. Blake was deputed, by the operative chain makers, to address the directors of the Merchant Shipping Association and others on the subject. He stated, on behalf of the chain makers, that the inferiority of untested chains was very great, and caused an enormous annual loss of life. They therefore prayed that some remedy might be adopted, which should prevent the use of inferior chains… In 1857, Mr. McDonald, the superintendent of the chain cable testing machinery at Liverpool, reported to the corporation that a great many of the chains made and tested upon the hydraulic principle were defective, that innumerable cracks were discovered after the manufacturer's test. Mr.

> McDonald had, moreover, on the 13th of January, in the present year, made mention of the case of the Royal Charter as affording evidence of the necessity which existed for insisting upon an efficient public test of cables. He added that from 1855 to 1859 it was found at the testing-house that 82¼ per cent of chain cables sent to be tested were inferior…It was lamentable to see the ignorance of ship owners and surveyors in this respect, and it was very culpable on the part of Lloyd's to insure vessels which went to sea with untested cables…
>
> "He would give the House instances of three vessels which had been wrecked in consequence of the weakness of chain cables. It would be recollected that the Tayleur sailed from Liverpool, and in passing down the Irish Channel she could not be brought about. She dropped three anchors in succession, but in each instance the chain broke, and every soul on board was lost. The loss of the Prince at Balaclava had been attributed to the fouling of her screw, which prevented her from using her steam-power, while the loss of the Royal Charter was attributed to the surging of her cables consequent on the use of her steam; all the men-of-war rode out the Balaclava gale, and the probability is that the Prince would have done so too if her ground-tackle had been as good as theirs. It was, however, a moot point whether it was desirable to work a vessel under such circumstance up to her anchor. The Royal Charter had two chains, and the weather was moderating when her cable parted…" The motion was agreed to with, only one comment, for a select committee "to inquire into the manufacture of Anchors and Chain Cables for the Merchant Service".

The sole comment was from Mr. Milner-Gibson, President of the Board of Trade from 1859 – 1866 and an ardent supporter of free trade and laissez faire, who, while supporting the motion, included his view that; "… At the same time he must say, that the Government had no intention of appointing a department for the purpose of seeing that merchant vessels carried proper chain cables and anchors, for shipowners already considered that the Government interfered too much with them, by surveying their vessels, and taking care of the public interest…"

The very first days of the decade also saw yet another fatal accident to a North Atlantic passenger ship with the loss of the Allan Line steamer ***Hungarian*** (1859) of 2,200 tons, and all 237 souls aboard her, on the night of the 19th February 1860. The Allan Line released the following statement through the press on the 14th March;[320]

> It is with deep regret that I have to announce the loss of another of our Canadian steamers—the Hungarian having been wrecked on her last passage out, off Cape Sable, Nova Scotia, on the morning of Monday, 20th inst. It is to be feared that not a soul of her unfortunate crew or passengers has escaped to tell us the tale of her mishap. All that is known is that at three o'clock in the morning a steamer's lights were seen from the land, these shortly after became stationary, and that at daylight a large steamer was seen on the rocks of Cape Ledges, about half a mile from the land, with one mast and funnel standing, with people clinging to the former and the sea making a clean breach over all. At ten o'clock not a vestige had remained. The sea was running so high that no boat could live in it, to be despatched to the assistance of the doomed vessel. At low water part of the stern of the steamer is visible, and part of the mails, very much damaged, have been recovered. Portions of her cargo and two bodies have come ashore, that of a man and child. The mystery of her fate is still obscured, and probably will remain so until that day when the cruel sea will reveal its secrets. The anxiety felt here as to the fate of the many believed to be on board is intense, and cannot be relieved until we hear from England as to her passengers.

This loss occurred only three months after the Allan Line's ***Indian*** (1856) of 1,764 tons, was wrecked on Cape Race, Newfoundland, with the loss of 27 lives. This mournful toll of lost ships and seafarers continued throughout the 1860s with 5826 shipwrecks taking place on the British coast alone with the associated loss of 8105 souls.[321]

Competition increased in the North Atlantic passenger trade with an advertisement being placed in The Newfoundlander newspaper on Monday 1st August 1859 calling attention to monthly passages available between Galway and New York, via St. Johns, Newfoundland, aboard three steamers operated by the Atlantic Royal Mail Steam Navigation Company. Passages were offered for between 18 pounds sterling for First Class to seven pounds in Steerage.[322] The three ships were the ***Adelaide*** (1852) 1,400 ton, ***Circassian*** (1856) 1,387 ton, and ***Prince Albert*** (1857) 2,028 ton; all three of which were chartered for two, eight and fourteen voyages respectively.[323] The company, known as the Galway Line, had been formed in 1858 when it obtained a Royal Mail contract, which it subsequently lost in 1861 at which time sailings were suspended; not resuming until 1863 when a renewal of the mail contract managed to keep the company afloat until 1864.

During this brief period one of the only ships built specifically for the company, the ***Connaught***, was launched at Newcastle-upon-Tyne in April 1860. At 2,959 GRT and 110m long she was the largest and most luxuriant passenger paddle steamer yet built for the North Atlantic run. The ***Connaught*** successfully completed her maiden voyage on 20 September 1860, and, upon departing St. Johns on Saturday 06 October carried 50 Cabin passengers, 417 in steerage and a crew of 124. On the first night out of Boston disaster struck. The 9th of October edition of the New York Times[324] graphically recounts the ***Connaught's*** fate, through the eyes of a passenger, and the remarkable and heroic rescue in stormy weather of the entire complement of passengers and crew; a tribute to excellent seamanship and the good fortune in having a very small sailing vessel come to her assistance, despite having completely inadequate lifeboat capacity;

> Boston, Tuesday, Oct. 9 – P.M.
>
> The brig Minnie Schiffer arrived at 1 o'clock. She is about 300 tons burthen, and the standing room on her was completely covered by the rescued passengers of the Connaught. Mr. H. WHITTELL, of New-York, a passenger in the Connaught, furnishes the following statement as to the loss of that fine steamship.
>
> Passing the circumstances of the voyage from Galway, which port we left at 5 P.M. of the 25th ult., until about 8 P.M. of Saturday the 6th inst., he says: While heading westwardly, the wind blowing a northerly gale, the ship began to roll to the larboard with a singular motion, going far down, and keeping that way a long time, which caused some alarm. Meantime, the Captain was heard giving orders about steering, manning the pumps, &c. Firemen under the lee of the paddle-box were observed whispering, and there were other manifestations that something was not right. Considerable water was observed through the grating. The engine soon after stopped for a while. After strenuous exertions by Capt. LEITCH and crew, the ship righted, and the wheels commenced moving, when the passengers became more composed.

The sea was rough, the wind blowing what sailors call an ordinary full gale. Most of the passengers turned in, but passed a restless night.

SUNDAY, 8 A.M.—The ship began to roll again with that staggering motion similar to the evening previous. The Captain and crew could neither tack nor wear the ship. Soon after the engine stopped, and steam could not be raised in the boilers. The ship rolled frightfully to the starboard and the pumps were manned, and gangs of men commenced bailing with buckets. At 10 o'clock it was reported that the water was not gaining, but on the contrary that the pumps and bailers were gaining on the leak, and if the wind would stiffen we would reach Boston that night; but these hopes were soon changed to extreme terror when the word was passed around in low terms, "The ship is on fire" accompanied by the smell of burning wood. The fire appeared between the decks. Gangs were immediately formed, with pumps and buckets to extinguish the flames, taking the water from the sea, and passing it in buckets. As the fire gained, the bailers began to slacken work; all eyes staring around the horizon in hopes to see some means of safety. Several false reports of a vessel in sight were made, but at last we discovered a sail to the northward, and soon after another to the west ward—both very low down; but it became plain at 1 o'clock that both were nearing us, and the vessel steering north had three masts, and the one west only two We soon found out that the latter was passing, while the other still neared without showing any sign that she noticed us, which kept us in extreme anxiety and doubt until she bore directly for us, evidently showing that she observed the steamer's flags of distress, which had been hoisted since midday. We then commenced to steer away and launch boats, which was a very difficult job, the ship lying almost on her side in a trough of the sea. By this time the fire had cut off all communication with the saloons. The first quarter boat lowered was struck by the counter and lost, which caused hesitation about launching the others. But the worst of our fears was that supposing the boats should ride the sea which then showed signs of moderating, and that we could safely launch and fill them with passengers. There was no chance of remaining but a short time on board, the fire making such progress. The flames were momentarily expected to burst out and sweep the decks, the fire gangs having given up all hopes of extinguishing them, but continuing to apply wet blankets, &c. The side of the ship was then so hot that when she rolled it would hiss and make steam of the sea water.

> The gallant little Yankee brig sailed alongside, and hove to, seeing our deplorable condition, and showing every sign of anxiety for us, but we began to think it would be impossible to stow all our numbers on board, she looked so small. We have since ascertained that she was only 198 tons burden. Capt. LEITCH made all haste to get us into the boats, which was extremely difficult, being lowered one by one with ropes. Capt. LEITCH stood by all the time, commencing with the women and children, but, with all the exertions that could be made, when the sun went down only about 200 had been got on board the brig. Capt. WILSON, of the brig, said: "This is a horrible affair, to see the sun going down, and so many people yet on board; the wreck settling down and burning up. I will do all in my power to save them." Several of the boat's crew, on reaching the brig, refused to return, when Capt. WILSON said: "I will go almost alongside, and take a hawser from on board, and then you will be in little or no danger. I must get everyone from the wreck." This he did, which had the effect of giving confidence, and by great exertions all were got on board by 11 o'clock P.M. Capt. LEITCH and his first officer remained on board until almost surrounded with flames, and until every soul was saved. Capt. WILSON then went alongside to beg him to come away. The flames were shooting up the masts, throwing a strong and melancholy light over the sea. Capt. LEITCH reached the brig just at midnight. Scarcely a parcel of baggage was saved, the trunks and even money of the cabin passengers being left below during the confusion, and the alarm which called them on deck in the morning; after which Communication was cut off by the water and flames.'

Repeal of the Navigation Acts, provision of open access of foreign shipping to coastal trades and a wide acceptance of the benefits of free trade after centuries of protectionism had not met with approval by all participants in the shipping industry, or amongst some politicians, as voiced in the report of a Committee of the House of Commons sitting upon the subject of merchant shipping generally; published in July 1860.[325] The committee's broad brief was to consider defects in the Merchant Shipping Act, 1854. Commentators were, amongst many other things, not particularly happy with membership of the committee;

> The parliamentary committee, it appears, was composed of seventeen members, only one of whom had belonged to the maritime profession.

> It was, therefore, not to be expected that anything relating to the details of the management of ships could have been gone into. Still, there were in the committee some very able men, who were acquainted with the causes of the profit or loss on merchant ships, and they have certainly brought out a complete exposure of the sacrifices we have made for the benefit of foreign shipping, without the slightest advantage being derived by ours in return! It has been shown by their evidence that shipowners of moderate capital have been reduced to bankruptcy, and that no one but large capitalists can go on,—for these men are able to force on a monopoly of particular trades. Such has been the fatal injury done to the best interests of this country by following the favourite theories of men who have merely the powers of oratory without the slightest knowledge or experience of maritime affairs.[326]

There appeared to be a sound basis for these concerns, particularly in the widespread lack of reciprocity to the opening up of the British coastal trade from fifteen European maritime nations, and America. "Having thus opened our ports to the unrestricted competition of all nations, it appears that although many countries have, in return, thrown open their ports to English shipping, there are others that have hitherto refused to reciprocate. France, Spain, Portugal, and Belgium belong to the latter class; and the United States decline to allow British ships to participate in their extensive coasting trade, on both the Atlantic and Pacific seaboards."[327]

The committee addressed concerns regarding the shipowner's liability in cases of collision by recommending that – a clause be prepared, similar in principle to the 55th section of the Passenger Act of 1855, declaring, with reference to the liabilities recited in the 503rd and 504th sections of the Merchant Shipping Act, ...*that no policy of insurance shall be deemed invalid by reason of the nature of the risk*; and 2. ...*That an absolute sum of £15 per gross registered ton, whatever may be the actual value, shall be established as the definite valuation of the ship, and that all consideration of freight shall be "excluded".*

Of particular relevance to the safety of ships, their crews and passengers; great concern was expressed by the committee regarding the complete lack of any agreed international standard for navigation lights and for prevention of collision. 'The "Rule of the Road', as provided for by the 296th section of the Act of 1854, is considered in its operation " most unsatisfactory," and the Committee suggest that some understanding should, without delay, be arrived at with foreign Powers with a view to the establishing of an international system of lights at sea.'[328] Concerns were also expressed regarding the costs of light dues and compulsory pilotage.

This call by Parliamentarians, many of them shipowners, to relieve shipowners of the burdens placed upon them by various Acts was heeded with a Select Committee being formed 'To inquire into the state of Merchant Shipping, the operation of the burdens and restrictions especially affecting Merchant Shipping, and of the following Statutes: 9 & 10 *Vict.*, c. 93, an Act for compensating the families of Persons killed by Accidents; the Merchant Shipping Act (1854); the Merchant Shipping Amendment Act (1855); the Passenger Act (1855); and the Chinese Passenger Act (1855)'.[329] The particular burdens to be addressed included the liability of shipowners in the case of collision, the perceived onerous cost of compulsory pilotage, and certain liens upon cargo. The Bill also proposed a similar system of certification to that for Masters and Mates for senior marine engineers, and adoption of revised Regulations for Preventing Collisions at Sea.

In mid-1861 the toll of lives lost in the North Atlantic passenger trade increased by 35 when the Allan Line passenger steamer ***Canadian*** (1860) of 1,926 GRT, had the misfortune to strike ice whilst proceeding at a greatly reduced speed of 5 knots due to ice, through the Straits of Belle Isle north of Newfoundland. The shock was so gentle that passengers were unaware until they saw the boats being turned out. The iron hulled ship sank in 30 minutes with all passengers and crewed being saved by the ships lifeboats apart from 30 passengers lost through the capsize of one boat. Five crew members were also lost.[330]

The efforts of the Parliamentary committee on the merchant service and resultant select committee resulted in introduction of the Merchant Shipping Act Amendment Act, 1862.[331]*An Act to amend "The Merchant Shipping Act, 1854", the 'Merchant Shipping Act, Amendment Act, 1855" and "The Customs Consolidation Act, 1853"*. Part 1 of the Act made it clear that it was to be ...*construed with and as Part of "The Merchant Shipping Act, 1854, hereinafter termed the Principal Act.*' The Act dealt primarily with;

> *Registry and Measurement of Tonnage, Certificates for Engineers, Safety, Pilotage, Lighthouses, Wreck and Salvage, Liability of Shipowners, Lights,*

Sailing Rules, Salvage and Measurement of Tonnage in case of Foreign Ships and Legal Procedures

The requirement for *...engineers serving in steam vessels to be subject to the same system of examination that was established in the case of the masters and mates, and provided similar certificates of competency, to be forfeited in case of misconduct, and would subject to the discipline clauses of the Merchant Shipping Act* classes of vessels which were now exempted from their operation, brought about confused opposition from one Member of Parliament pursuing the fashionable mantra of conflating free trade and laissez faire.

Mr Aryton stated that; "...he must repeat his objection to the clause, that it introduced a new principle. It was the first time an Act of Parliament invested the Crown with the power of determining whether a man should be at liberty to carry on his own business. It was the greatest condemnation of the much-lauded principle of free trade that could be pronounced. There was no reason for requiring the proposed examination that would not equally apply to engineers of railways, mines, and engineers in general. If it was the opinion of shipowners that the engineers ought to be raised to the standard of a professional class, a clear explanation ought to be given of what was intended to be done. It was a startling fact that the shipowners could not manage their business for themselves, like the owners of mines and railways".

After more informed debate by other members, including the President of the Board of Trade, the draft clause was passed with a minor amendment unrelated to Ayrton's views. The provision applied to the two senior engineers aboard foreign going steamships of 100 nominal horsepower and upwards while the only engineer required to be carried aboard foreign going steam ships of lesser horsepower, or a Sea Going Home Trade passenger ship of any nominal horsepower, was required to hold either a Second Class Engineers Certificate or a Certificate of the higher grade. Examination and disciplinary processes were to be identical to those for Masters and Mates.

The Safety provisions contained in sections 13 – 28 dealt with matters associated with the introduction of amended Regulations for Preventing Collisions at Sea including *...'Owners and Masters to obey them', 'Breaches* *of Regulations to imply willful default of the Person in charge'*, *'If Collision ensues from Breach of the Regulations, Ship to be deemed in fault'*, *'Inspection for enforcing Regulations'*, *'Rules for Harbours under Local Acts to continue in force'*, *'In Harbours and Rivers where no such Rules exist they may be made'*. The regulations also addressed a long-standing issue where ships had not, on many occasions, rendered assistance to the Master, crew and passengers of the other ship after collision. The wording of section 33 made it abundantly clear that such conduct was unacceptable;

> In every Case of Collision between Two Ships it shall be the Duty of the Person in charge of each Ship, if and as far as he can do so without Danger to his own Ship and Crew, to render to the other Ship, her Master, Crew and Passengers (if any), such Assistance as may be necessary in order to save them from any Danger caused by the Collision. In case he fails so to do, and no reasonable Excuse for such Failure is shown, the Collision shall, in the Absence of Proof to the contrary, be deemed to have been caused by his wrongful Act, Neglect or Fault; and such Failure shall also, if proven upon any Investigation held under a Third or the Eighth Part of the principal Act, be deemed to be an Act of Misconduct or a Default for which his Certificate (if any) may be cancelled or suspended.

Lord Alderley in proposing, during the second reading of the Bill, the measures to be included in ss. 39 – 56 of the final Act, *Pilotage*, had stated;

> The measure effected some alterations in the law of pilotage; but it was not thought advisable that it should at once abolish the system of compulsory pilotage. It limited the compensation which could be recovered for accidents occurring at sea through the mismanagement of the crew to the sum of £15 for every ton in the case of personal injuries, and to £8 for every ton in the case of loss of property, so that the proprietors of the larger class of steamers should not be liable to ruinous damages. And it introduced some important Amendments in the law relating to lien upon freight.

Sections 57 – 64 of the Act updated *Lights, Sailing Rules, Salvage and Measurement of Tonnage in case of Foreign Ships*. A number of sections in Part IV of the 1854 Act on *Lights and Fog Signals, and Meeting and Passing* were repealed.; Sections 295 – Regulations as to *Lights and Fog Signals*; s.296 – Rules as to

Ships meeting each other; s.297 – Rule for *Steamers in Narrow Channels;* s.298 – *If Collision ensues from Breach of the above Rules, owner not entitled to Recover,* and s.299 – *Breaches of such Rules to imply willful Default, due to amended Regulations for Preventing Collisions at Sea;* were included in Table 3 of the Schedule to the Act.[332]

Table A of the Schedule to the Act – Enactments to be Repealed – included the *Customs Consolidation Act, 1853*[333]; *The last Proviso in Section 74, and Sections 170, 171, and 172, to be repealed immediately on the passing of this Act.* It is helpful to quote these provisions in full to understand the devastating effects their repeal could have for the ships, and their crews, carrying timber deck cargoes during the North Atlantic winter;

> s.170 – Before a Clearing Officer permits any Ship, wholly or in part laden with Timber or Wood Goods, to clear out from any British Port in North America or in the Settlement of Honduras for any port in the United Kingdom, at any Time after the First Day of September or before the First Day of May in any year, he shall ascertain that the whole of the Cargo of such Ship is below Deck, and shall give the Master of such a Certificate to that Effect; and no Master of any such Ship so laden shall sail from any of the Ports aforesaid for any Port of the United Kingdom, at any such Time as aforesaid, until he has obtained such certificate from the Clearing Officer.
>
> s.171 – No Master of any Ship in respect of which such certificate as aforesaid has been obtained shall place or cause to be placed or remain, upon or above the Deck of such Ship, any Part of the Cargo thereof, until such Ship has arrived at the port of her Destination; provided always that if the Master of any such Ship consider that it is necessary, in consequence of springing a leak or of other Damage received or apprehended during the Voyage, to remove or cause to be removed upon the Deck of such Ship so much of the Cargo, and may permit the same to remain there for such Time, as he considers expedient, provided also, that the Store Spars or other Articles necessary for the Ship's Use shall not be taken to be Cargo for the Purposes of this Act.

s.172 – *Penalty for default* – contained a penalty whereby the Master would … *forfeit and pay any Sum not exceeding One hundred Pounds* if in default of the provisions of ss. 170 and 171. These sections are virtually identical to those brought were brought into force in perpetuity through the Timber Ships Act, 1845 – *An Act to make perpetual and amend an Act of the Fifth and Sixth Years of Her present Majesty, for preventing Ships clearing out from and Port in British North America or in the Settlement of Honduras from loading any Part of their Cargo of Timber upon Deck.* Administration of this provision had been quietly devolved to Customs and included in the *Customs Consolidation Act, 1853.*

The Select Committee appointed in 1843 to enquire into the shipwreck of British Vessels, and the Means of Preserving the Lives and Property of Shipwrecked Persons, had obtained statistics from Lloyd's on the loss of timber-laden ships from British America to Europe from September 1839, the date from which the Act took effect prohibiting the deck-loading of these ships, and made a comparison between the loss of timber ships in the years 1840-41 and 1842, and those lost between 1836 and 1838. They had the satisfaction to find that "the loss has been much less in the later periods than in the earlier, more especially as regards timber-laden ships, and the lives of the crews employed on board of them, where there has been a reduction in loss of ships in each year from 56 to 23; and, as near as can be calculated, a saving of 200 lives of seamen". Clearly, thousands of seamen and hundreds of ships must have benefitted from the prohibition on deck cargoes during winter months, from 1839 to 1862.

Enforcement of the Act was through the process of clearing customs when departing Canada, but as the lucrative timber trade steadily increased British ships turned to evasion of the regulations, and the associated relaxation from import duty for deck cargoes, by stretching the definition of 'deck cargo'. Large quantities of timber began to be stowed within the poop and under the spar deck; a platform above the main deck for stowage spare masts and yards. As there was no seasonal prohibition on carriage of deck cargoes of timber aboard American ships, British ships would sometimes clear Customs from North America through an adjacent American port, such as Maine instead of nearby New Brunswick. The Board of Trade ordered Customs officers in Canada to forbid use of the poop, bringing angry complaints from shipowners and colonial interests whose argument was that the practice was long-standing, earned valuable freight returns, and didn't apply to foreign ships.[334]

The Board of Trade, after taking advice from its nautical experts, declared the practice to be illegal and instructed Customs to issue an order accordingly. Customs officers in Canada and other British possessions and territories were generally unwilling to enforce the order but in 1854 a prosecution was brought against the ship ***David G. Fleming*** which departed port with a large quantity of timber stowed under her poop, without obtaining a customs clearance. The prosecution failed, as did others, and by 1860 the Timber Ships Act, 1845, was unenforceable and inoperative – effectively a "dead letter". [335]

Finally, following a deputation from the St. Johns Chamber of Commerce headed by a leading shipowner, Mr. Milner-Gibson, President of the Board of Trade rose in the House on the 21 March 1862 to move for leave "to bring in a Bill to amend the *Merchant Shipping Act,* 1864, the *Merchant Shipping Act* Amendment Act, 1855, and the *Customs Consolidation Act, 1853."* The objective of the Bill was to – *give effect to some of the recommendations of the Merchant Shipping Committee, and to amend the Acts he had mentioned, so as to meet the various requirements of the shipping interest, and to remedy those defects which experience had shown existed in the Merchant Shipping Act* of 1854. Milner-Gibson also "proposed to repeal certain clauses in the *Customs Consolidation Act* prohibiting the carrying of deck loads in timber-ships, which were found "to be totally nugatory, and to interfere with the fair competition of the British with the foreign shipowner";[336] an egregious example of the laissez faire attitude of Parliamentarians, Board of Trade officials and shipowners during the major part of the nineteenth century.

Another requirement of the 1854 Act, critical to the seaworthiness of a ship and the safety of all aboard; s.300 *Iron Steamers to be divided by Water-tight Partitions,* was also quietly repealed by the 1862 Act. The matter of whether any ship should have watertight bulkheads would be left to the discretion of the shipowner as it was the view of such, along with Thomas Farrer, Permanent Secretary of the Maritime Department, Board of Trade, that "… the law concerning bulkheads in iron ships had proved mischievous".[337] Farrer was enthusiastically supported by his Assistant Secretary, Thomas Gray, a person described as "personifying the philosophy of administrative laissez faire"[338] who stated;

> There can be no question that Government interference is not only unnecessary but may really become vicious if it attempts to attain an

> end by official inspection and supervision that can be better attained by the development of free and healthy competition, and by self-interest and emulation of the trader'.[339]

In spite of safety legislation, and the lessons learnt from many maritime disasters in the North Atlantic passenger trade, ships and lives continued to be lost due to excessive speed in restricted visibility, failure to keep an accurate reckoning of the ship's position, to take soundings when approaching the land, and complete disregard for owner's instructions. The fundamental principles of watchkeeping have always been, and still are – 'log, lead and lookout'. That is; keep an up-to-date record of course, speed and position, take soundings when necessary and keep a good lookout. A German saying for 'good luck' from the days of the Hanseatic League – "Ich wuensche dir eine Handbreit Wasser unterm Kiel" – (I wish you a hands breadth of water under your keel) is self-evident. It is not possible to go aground if you have some water under your keel, and even better if you know how much.

A graphic example of such poor seamanship was the stranding, with great loss of life on 27 April 1863, of the British passenger steamer ***Anglo Saxon;*** (1854) of 1,713 ton, in which 237 lives were lost, including the Master. After departing Liverpool for Quebec on the 16th of April with a total of 446 aboard; made up of 48 cabin passengers, 322 in steerage and 86 crew, the ***Anglo-Saxon*** fell in with fog and ice approaching Newfoundland on the evening of the 25th of April. She reduced speed for a while and, when the fog and ice thickened, stopped engines from 10 o'clock that evening until 10 o'clock the following morning when, becoming clear of the ice although still foggy, she got underway building up to 12 knots, and with all sail set, made for Cape Race on the south-eastern corner of Newfoundland. Although a sight was taken at noon on the 26th followed by another at 4.00pm, there was still uncertainty about her actual position. At 8 o'clock on the 27th still in fog course was altered more to the south and speed reduced to half ahead, but the ship struck rocks three hours later. During the hour before the ship capsized and sank into deep water a total of 209 persons were saved by boats and by means of a spar which was thrown across to the nearest rock and a whip from the foreyard to which a basket was attached. The official report of the Board of Trade enquiry summarised their findings as;

> ...the speed at which the vessel was driven, during a thick fog and in the vicinity of land, was highly imprudent. I feel bound, therefore, acting under the advice of my nautical assessors, to pronounce that the Anglo Saxon was lost owing to a wrong estimate of the distance run; that there was a culpable omission to use the lead after 8 a.m., and that it was a most reprehensible act on the part of the commander to continue his course in a thick fog, even at half-speed, in such an uncertain position.[340]

The company owning the ***Anglo Saxon***, the Montreal Steamship Company known as the Allan Line, had a particularly unfortunate record in operating passenger steamers between Liverpool, Montreal and Quebec. A total of five of their ships, including the ***Anglo Saxon***, were lost between 1859 and 1863, with an accumulated loss of life of 503 souls. Additionally, the ***Canadian*** had run aground 50 miles below Quebec in 1857 and become a total loss, without the loss of any lives, and the ***Norwegian*** ran aground in dense fog and was wrecked on St. Paul Island in Cabot Strait only two months after the loss of the ***Anglo Saxon***. Fortunately, all were also saved on this occasion.[341]

The Passengers Act, 1855, was amended by the Passengers Act Amendment Act, 1863.[342] This was largely an administrative tidy-up with no implications for the seaworthiness of passenger ships. The provisions of the 1855 Act with regard to lifeboats remained unaltered. The definition of a 'passenger ship' in the 1855 Act was repealed and replaced with one which allowed more passengers to be carried aboard both sail and steam ships. The scope of voyages covered by the Act focused on longer passages where matters of health, hygiene and provisions were of greater significance, and continued to apply to British and foreign ships – *This Act shall extend to every "Passenger Ship" proceeding on any Voyage from the United Kingdom to any Place out of Europe, and not being within the Mediterranean sea, and on every Colonial voyage...*

Another measure of vital importance to the seaworthiness of ships was enacted in 1864, after discussion on a Bill in 1863 and work undertaken by the select committee 'to inquire into the manufacture of Anchors and Chain Cables for the Merchant Service'; appointed in 1860. The Chain, Cable and Anchor Act, 1864,[343] – *An Act for regulating and Proving the Sale of*

Chain Cables and Anchors – Whereas it is essential for the better Security of Lives and Property afloat in Sea-going Ships, to make Provision for the proper testing of Chain Cables and Anchors....

The Act, which continued in force to 01 July 1872, put in place a regulatory regime to give power to private businesses to provide proving establishments for testing chain cable and anchors, and power to the Board of Trade to grant, revoke or suspend licenses for proving chain cables and anchors, and to appoint inspectors on an annual basis. The tester was required to test all cables and anchors and impress them with an authorized proof mark and issue, if required, a test certificate. After 01 July 1865 it was unlawful under the Act for makers and dealers to sell unapproved chain cable and anchors.

Chapter 10

Loss of the London

When the American Civil War stuttered to an end on the 13th May 1865 one of its unintended consequences was destruction of the country's foreign shipping trade and any claims to supremacy by the American merchant service.

> ... the Civil War of 1861 took away any chance which remained to American ships of continuing as great sea-carriers. The American mind had to concentrate on fighting...while in Great Britain the accessibility of coal deposits, the cheapness of labour, the successful introduction of iron for shipbuilding, the great advances in ship construction, and especially the wonderful progress of the steamship, had been able to give back to Great Britain her supremacy as a mercantile marine. And when the Civil War was over, America was too interested internally to pay a maximum amount of attention to ocean trading.[344]

New England shipyards, formerly very competitive due to ready and abundant supplies of timber, lost the custom of shipowners to the Clyde with its nearby coalfields, necessary for producing steel and iron for shipbuilding. The four year period of the Civil War also brought about huge opportunities for expansion of British trade, not least to owners of the many British registered ships running the American blockade. Also, of necessity, alternative sources had to be found for cotton to feed the voracious appetites of the Lancashire textile industry resulting in new opportunities for the growth of shipping to Egypt and India, facilitated from 1869 by faster passages via the Suez Canal.

The British merchant service continued to grow and expand. In 1860 the proportion of world tonnage of the United Kingdom was 43.33%; United States of America, 39.51%. By 1870 British tonnage was 42.64% of world tonnage while American tonnage had fallen away to 25.02%. The tonnage of British shipping under sail still far outweighed that under steam by a factor of 9.25:1, but this changed considerably over the ten years from

1860 – 1870 to 4:1 as steam ships steadily increased in numbers and size.[345] By 1865 screw propulsion had largely replaced paddle wheels on ocean routes. Cunard's last paddle steamer was the 3,870 ton ***Scotia*** (1862) while P&O built no more paddle steamers after the ***Nyanza*** (1864).[346]

Public concern over seaworthiness of ships, and overloading, was very much to the fore in the minds of people from all walks of society at the beginning of 1866. Unseaworthiness cannot only be brought about by the dangerously deficient structural nature of the ship, or its equipment, but can also ensue from a perfectly sound ship being dangerously overloaded and being placed in a position where there is insufficient freeboard to provide adequate stability, particularly in adverse weather. An example of where this was probably the case was the total loss of the passenger ship ***London*** and all but 19 of her complement of 263 passengers and crew on the eleventh of January 1866.

The ***London***, a full rigged ship with auxiliary steam power of 200 HP, built in London in 1864, had already completed two return voyages to Australia when she departed London on the 13th December 1865 to load her passengers in Plymouth. An extract from an article in the Australian newspaper Argus, of 16 March 1866, mentions what might have been a critical design feature of the ***London***;

> She was modelled upon the favourite plan of the Blackwall clippers, which provides especially for a high rate of speed in smooth water and light winds, rather than for surpassing runs in heavier weather. How far this peculiarity of build had to do with her loss, and how far that dreadful misfortune was attributable to overloading, as the telegram suggests, will no doubt be brought fully out in the course of the inquiry into the causes of the wreck, which was proceeding when the mail left England.'[347]

The ship was 1,652 GRT with a beam of 35.9 feet and a length of 276.6 feet; an unusually high beam to length ratio of 1:7.7.

The amount of cargo carried by the ***London*** is uncertain but it has been claimed that the senior surveyor verified that her freeboard upon departure was three foot and six inches. When she sailed down the Thames one seaman who observed her pass near Purfleet remarked to his friend: "It'll be her last voyage...she is too low down in the water; she'll never rise to a stiff sea". One of the ship's officers wrote to his father from Gravesend saying he did not like his ship and feared she would be his coffin.[348] A similar opinion regarding the ship's draft from an expert witness was presented to the House by Sir John Pakington, First Lord of the Admiralty, on the 19th March 1866. "I will also read to the House a letter to which I attach great importance. It comes from a Captain Stewart, of the Royal Navy, who happened to be at Plymouth when the ***London*** passed that port. He says;"

> A sailor's eye can always detect whether a ship looks too deep in the water or not; and, notwithstanding the evidence adduced, and the endeavour to prove that everything was done for the safety of the passengers that human foresight could suggest, I maintain that the attention of spectators on the Hoe was called to the ship from her deepness of immersion while she lay at anchor in the Sound, and comments were freely passed upon the circumstance; and yet, anticipating bad weather, she is permitted to depart with fifty tons of coal on her upper deck, with her topgallant and royal masts on end, and topgallant yards across; the imprudence of which was subsequently shown in evidence by the coals choking the scuppers and the spars being carried away. In another place he writes—The shortcomings of some and the cupidity of others had far more to do with the loss of the ship than the elements. And again— The truth is, that the interests of the owners are paramount to every other consideration, and to this, and making a swift passage, the efforts of the captain are directed. It must be now obvious to all that such ships as the London, whose length is more than seven times their breadth, and fine at both ends, are not adapted for carrying heavy cargoes and passengers at the same time.'[349]

Pakington also informed the House of the stowage of 50 ton of bagged coal upon the ship's deck; an unseamanlike practice which contributed to the loss of the ***London***;

> While that ship lay at Plymouth fifty tons of coal were added to her stock. Those fifty tons were stowed on her deck in bags round the sides of her bulwarks, and there left entirely unsecured. The natural result was that as soon as she experienced the action of a heavy sea, those bags of coal broke adrift and burst. The coal covered the deck and

> stopped the scuppers. Captain Stoll [the Emigration Officer] himself stated in evidence that when he inspected and passed the ship at Plymouth the coal was stowed away in the manner I have described. Since I gave notice of my intention to bring forward this question I have received letters from various persons, chiefly seafaring men, all condemning in the strongest manner the way in which the coal was stowed on board the ship. This very morning I had a communication from a naval officer strongly impressing on me the impropriety of the emigration officer having allowed the ship to go to sea in that condition.'[350]

After many delays due to adverse weather the ***London*** departed Plymouth on the 6th January 1866, and struck heavy weather three days later in the Bay of Biscay. The cargo shifted, and the unsecured bags of coal burst and blocked the scuppers. Heavy sea swept the decks and flooded the engine room extinguishing the boiler fires. The Master decided to run before the weather under sail and return to Plymouth but was criticized in this action by the ensuing Official Enquiry as it took the ship back into the centre of the storm. Eventually, on 12th January, the ship succumbed to the sea through ingress of water through hatches, smashed poop deck windows and the engine room skylight, and foundered. One small boat was got away with 19 people, including three passengers, who had the good fortune to be rescued the following day by a passing sailing ship. Some passengers, realizing the end was near, wrote last messages to loved ones and cast them into the sea in bottles. These were later found on the Brittany coast and one of them poignantly corroborated the cause of the tragedy.[351]

> Mr. Gilbert Highton has just received the identical message sent by Mr. Denis, who was drowned in the London, to his brother, and finds that, owing, as he supposes, to the mistakes of the French copyist, its wording differs somewhat from the version hitherto given to the public. Though dated only two hours before the vessel went down, and when all hope was lost, it is nevertheless written in firm, clear characters, not distinguishable from Mr. Denis's ordinary handwriting, and he even displays a little peculiarity he had of spelling his name with one "n." "H. J. Denis to Jno. Dennis, Esq., Great Shelford, nr Cambridge. —Thursday, 10th January. Farewell, father, brothers, sisters, and my Edith," (his little daughter, now entirely an orphan.) "Ship London, Bay of Biscay, Thursday, 12 o'c. noon. Reason —Ship over weighted

> with cargo, and too slight a house over engine-room : all washed away from deck. Bad poop-windows. Water broken in. God bless my little orphan — . . . Storm ; but not too (violent ?) for a well-ordered ship." [352]

The official inquiry by the Board of Trade cited the Masters decision to return to Plymouth, the fact that the ship carried 345 ton of railway iron, and the stowage of 50 ton of bagged coal on deck which blocked the scuppers and prevented water shipped on deck to drain as the main causes of loss of the ship. A recommendation was also made that "the deep load line should be permanently marked on all vessels carrying passengers and merchandise".[353]

In spite of the fact that the ***London*** had lost some of her boats in the storm and had only one small boat remaining, the very fact that the Merchant Shipping Act, 1854, had required ships to carry lifeboats still rankled in some quarters and was still receiving trenchant criticism during this period as evinced by a contradictory statement made in 1866 that reflected both the major issue with extant legislation and the laissez-faire views of the time;

> It is admitted that, as regards boats, the Act [1854] is, to a great extent, a dead letter. It generally happens that in the greatest emergencies the boats, with all the statutory inspection, fail. Something must be done – one of two courses is open. First, for the legislature to pass a short Act containing an amended scale, in which the boats and life buoys shall be proportioned to the number of passengers on board, and in which provision shall be made for extended inspection and surveillance; or, secondly, that the boat scale shall be repealed entirely, and that the owners of a ship shall be held responsible for providing sufficient boats and lifebuoys, according to the exigencies of the case, and for keeping them efficient and ready for use. [354]

In February 1866 it was resolved in the House of Commons "That the Chairman be directed to move the House that leave be given to bring in a Bill to amend The Merchant Shipping Act, 1854." The Bill was *ordered* to be brought in by Mr. Milner-Gibson and Lord Clarence Page.[355] The Merchant Shipping Act (1854) Amendment Bill was presented to the House and read for the first time on the 9th March. The Bill proposed to deal mainly with matters of accommodation, health and welfare. In particular the scourge of scurvy in merchant ships, an age old problem that had long been identified, and been eliminated aboard ships of the Royal Navy. However, this Bill failed due to the dissolution of Parliament when the Liberal Party Reform Bill, put forward by Gladstone and Russell in mid-1866 to extend voting rights to 'respectable' working classes, failed due to divided support and led to the break-up of the Government through loss of a ruling majority.[356]

On the 17th July 1866 Mr. Graves MP proposed a motion;

> That an humble Address be presented to Her Majesty, praying that She will be graciously pleased to issue a Royal Commission to inquire into the present condition of the Seamen of the Mercantile Marine, with the view of ascertaining whether, within the last twenty years, the supply of British Seamen has or has not fallen off either in point of numbers or of efficiency; and, if in either a continuous decline should be apparent, then to ascertain further what are the causes which have led to such decline, and whether any remedy can be suggested."[357]

This motion arose more from concerns about there being adequate numbers of merchant seamen to man ships of the Royal Navy during hostilities than about the conditions they had to live and work under. The motion failed. Two days later the President of the Board of Trade, Sir Stafford Northcote, when asked in the House 'If he intends to proceed further with the Merchant Shipping Act (1854) Amendment Bill this Session?' replied that "it would not be possible to proceed this Session with that Bill or with the Waterworks Bill, and he therefore proposed that the Orders relating to them both should be read and discharged".[358]

Concern existed at this time that the amount and complexity of wider mercantile marine legislation made it very difficult to find, or understand, applicable law. At the second sitting of the new Government on the 7th February 1867, the President of the Board of Trade was asked whether it was his intention to 'introduce a measure to consolidate and amend the Laws regulating our Mercantile Marine?' to which Sir Stafford Northcote replied;

> I am aware that it is an object of considerable importance to consolidate and amend the laws relating to our Mercantile Marine. I am afraid, however, the task is one of great difficulty and labour. That,

> however, would not be any reason for our declining to undertake it. The reason why we are not now prepared with a measure of the kind is this:— It is our intention to introduce a Bill containing several important Amendments of the present law, and I think it will be much more satisfactory to discuss these Amendments by themselves. The Bill will be introduced into the House as early as the state of public business will allow. If we shall be able within a reasonable time to pass it, I hope we shall have time to prepare a Consolidation Bill and to lay it on the table of the House before the end of the Session, so that it may be well considered before the discussion be taken on it in the following Session.'[359]

Through the passing of the Reform Act, 1867, the new minority Conservative Government under Derby/Disraeli succeeded in achieving a more expansive franchise than that proposed the previous year. They revisited the Merchant Shipping Act (1854) Amendment Bill and enacted the Merchant Shipping Act, 1867[360] which amongst other matters provided for significantly improved, albeit it still woefully inadequate, living conditions for seamen and apprentices. 'In moving the Second Reading in the Lords the Duke of Richmond made an emphatic reference to the new principle that crew spaces were to be exempted from tonnage dues – a matter of some importance in the immediate future for the advantage it gave Board of Trade officials when dealing with shipowners'.[361]

Seamen aboard sail and steam ships lived in the very forepart of the ship, in the bow or forecastle, referred to as the 'focsle'. This triangular space had the hawsepipes for the anchor cables passing through it, and was also used to store mooring lines and maintenance equipment. Section 231 of the Merchant Shipping Act, 1854, – *Place appropriated to Seamen to have a certain Space for each Man; and to be properly constructed and kept clear;* allocated every seaman and apprentice nine superficial feet if sleeping in a hammock and twelve superficial feet if sleeping in a bunk. There was to be six feet of headroom, in well-constructed and ventilated sleeping places, which were to be kept free from stores and 'properly caulked'. Each seaman was to have six-foot headroom and fifty-four cubic feet of space if sleeping in a hammock and seventy-two cubic feet if sleeping in a bunk. This appeared to be a significant increase from the nine superficial feet provided by s.63 of the Mercantile Marine Act, 1850[362] but, taking into account the dimensions of a bunk at six feet by two, it is evident that no deck space outside of the bunk was allowed; a problem exacerbated by the fitting of bunks two to three tiers high to provide sufficient berths. There was, accordingly, no common area of deck at all, in a very limited space.

> It is difficult for twentieth-century man to appreciate how minimal these revised standards were, although a comparison with eighteenth-century prison conditions may be helpful. In 1773 the great prison reformer, John Howard, fired public indignation with his description of conditions in York Prison, A cell – described as 'horribly small' – had a space of 414 cubic feet, about six times greater than the minimum space granted to seamen by the 1867 Act.[363]

A high rate of scurvy aboard merchant ships had been caused by shipowners supplying sub-standard lime juice which became undrinkable. This was remedied through s.4 of the Act which required lime juice to be in glass bottles with 15 percent alcohol added, and to only be obtained from bonded warehouses. Medical stores and instructions were to be carried, along with medical inspections of crew, and privies (toilets) constructed for use at sea instead of the age-old 'heads' whereby crew had to hang over the bow for their toilet. However, this provision did not apply to existing vessels, only to new buildings, and although conscientious surveyors toured the shipyards chalking diagrams on bulkheads in order to instruct foreman shipwrights as to the fitting of privies... in at least one instance 'the delay in diffusion can be put at twenty years'.[364]

Resurfacing concerns about seaworthiness, of sailing ships in particular, arose from a number of sources. A decline in the total tonnage of sailing vessels commenced in the mid-1860s, put down according to one commentator to 'the re-introduction of the compound engine adapted for driving a screw propeller'. This technology saved between 30% and 40% of the fuel costs incurred by a single expansion engine of the same power.[365] Although sailing ships were still very much in the majority numerically, they were aging and tended to carry lower value bulk cargo with small profit margins allowing less money for maintenance. Sailing ship losses peaked numerically in the two decades between 1861 and 1880, with steamship losses highest in the 1880s.[366]

Concerns by seamen about unseaworthy and overloaded ships were long standing. On the 30th July 1835, the Merchant Seaman Act, 1835;[367] Part II of which had required that no Master should take persons to sea as crew without a written agreement specifying wages, capacity, and nature and length of the voyage, also provided, in Part VI, a penalty for – *Seaman refusing to join or to proceed in the Ship, or absenting themselves therefrom, may be committed to Gaol;*

> And be it further enacted That in case a Seaman shall at any Time, after having signed an Agreement as here-in-before mentioned, neglect or refuse to join a Ship on which he shall have been engaged to serve, or shall refuse to proceed to Sea in her, or shall absent himself therefrom without Leave, it shall be lawful for any Justice of the Peace in any of His Majesty's Dominions at Home or Abroad near to the place where such Ship shall happen to be, upon Complaint of the Fact made upon Oath by the Master, Mate, or Owner thereof, and such Justice is hereby required, by his Warrant, to cause such Seaman to be apprehended and brought before him; and in case such Seaman shall not give a Reason to the Satisfaction of such Justice for his Neglect, Refusal, or Absence it shall be lawful for any such Justice to commit such Seaman to the House of Correction, there to be kept to hard Labour for a Period not exceeding Thirty Days…

If the seaman had signed the Agreement without having seen the ship, as was often the case, and upon sighting or boarding the ship considered it to be unsafe, unseaworthy or overloaded and refused to proceed to sea in her, any of these reasons would not usually satisfy a Justice of the Peace. Part Ten of the Act – *Penalty for harbouring Deserters* included a penalty of ten pounds for any person harbouring or secreting a seaman who had signed an Agreement and who had deserted, or absented himself without leave from, the ship.

The 1835 Act was repealed by the Merchant Seaman Act, 1844,[368]– *An Act to amend and consolidate the Laws relating to Merchant Seamen; and for keeping a Register of Seamen.* Part VI continued the thirty day penalty in the 1835 Act, but also gave the option;

> *'… it shall be lawful for the said Justice, if he shall so think fit, at the request of the Master, Mate, or Owner, or his Agent, instead of committing such Seaman, to cause him to be conveyed on board the said Ship, or, to delivered*

> *to the Master, Mate, or the Owner, or his Agent, for the purpose of being so conveyed and proceeding on the Voyage...'* Part X continued the penalty for harbouring deserters.

The term 'sea-worthy' had been enshrined in legislation on the 31st August 1835, when the Merchant Vessels etc. Act, 1835[369], made provision for a passenger vessel to be surveyed by two competent persons if any doubt should have arisen whether *'any ship about to proceed with passengers...is sea-worthy'*. If found to be unseaworthy, the ship was not to be cleared out by Customs *'until such ship shall have been rendered sea-worthy'*. Section 70 of the Mercantile Marine Act Amendment Act, 1851[370], extended the punishment for any seaman who *'...willfully neglects or refuses to join his ship, or deserts...'* from thirty days to twelve weeks.

After enactment of the Merchant Shipping Act, 1854, the Merchant Shipping Repeal Act, 1854 under s.243,[371] repealed all provisions in previous Acts dealing with these matters and continued the offence of *neglecting or refusing to join and proceed to Sea*; slightly reducing the length of imprisonment but adding financial penalties;

> For neglecting or refusing, without reasonable Cause, to join his ship, or to proceed to Sea in his Ship, or for Absence without Leave at any Time within Twenty-four Hours of the Ship's sailing from any Port, either at the Commencement or during the Progress of any Voyage, or for Absence at any Time without Leave and without sufficient Reason from his Ship, or from his Duty not amounting to Desertion or not treated as such by the Master, he shall be liable to Imprisonment for any Period not exceeding Ten Weeks, with or without Hard Labour, and also at the Discretion of the out, to forfeit out of his Wages a Sum not exceeding the amount of Two Days Pay, and in addition for every Twenty-four Hours of Absence either a Sum not exceeding Six Days Pay. Or any expenses which have been incurred in hiring a Substitute

The severity of this penalty of up to twelve weeks imprisonment with hard labour, which could be, and was applied in many cases of refusing to join a ship due to concerns about safety and seaworthiness, including overloading, is highlighted by comparison with the other penalties for serious offences aboard ships. Section 243 provided for up to ten weeks imprisonment and financial penalties, for *"willful disobedience to lawful commands"*, *"assaulting the Master or Mate", "combining with other crew member(s) to disobey lawful commands"* or to " *neglect duty or to impeded the navigation of the ship or the progress of the voyage"*. A petition to Queen Victoria in 1855 complained that seamen were being compelled to sail in unseaworthy ships under threat of imprisonment. The Board of Trade obtained a legal opinion to the effect that seaworthiness was implied when a man signed-on, but that proof of unseaworthiness lies with the man who refuses duty.[372]

In reply to a question in the House on the 7th June 1867 in reference to the Copies of Memorials [petitions] 'on the subject of disasters at sea and their prevention', the Vice President of the Board of Trade replied;

> ...it was worthy of consideration whether any safe steps could be taken in this direction by ordering a survey in cases where there was ground for suspicion, and where complaint was made. Except in the case of passengers and crews, even this was more for parties interested than for the Government. As regarded passengers, they were already cared for; as regarded the crew, they were not obliged to proceed to sea if the ship were unseaworthy. But this was often a question difficult to determine; and the Justices who were called on to decide were often very much at sea themselves. It was under the consideration of the Board of Trade whether, in case of allegation of unseaworthiness, the Justices should not have the assistance of the Board of Trade Surveyor, to enable them to decide whether the crew should or should not be compelled to go to sea.[373]

Chapter 11

Overladen and Unseaworthy

The loss of the ***London***; a large modern iron hulled auxiliary powered sailing ship, with great loss of life, and associated allegations of overloading and unseaworthiness, further raised public awareness of the issue of overloading which had long plagued merchant ships, not only older, and smaller, wooden sailing vessels, but also well-found vessels purposely overloaded and possibly over insured. A revealing example of a shipowner with an irresponsible and overbearing attitude to the risks to his ship caused by overloading, in spite of the serious concerns of a number of expert mariners, occurred in March 1867. The following article is worth repeating at some length, in the language of the day, from an edited version of an article in an influential nautical journal;[374]

> The Utopia was built in 1853, and in 1862 she was registered A1, at Lloyd's, for five years. She had recently changed ownership, and was now the property of a shipowner resident in London. When loading in the Brunswick Dock at Liverpool for the present voyage to Bombay, it appears that she took the ground, and evidently thereby sustained serious damage by straining, as previously she had scarcely made any water, whilst immediately after that event twenty-eight inches was found in her, and on two subsequent occasions as much as forty inches. By the direction of the owners, she was pumped out by the men employed in stowing her cargo, usually at the expiration of each day's work. During the process of loading she was visited by the agent of Lloyd's Salvage Association at Liverpool, and by one of the surveyors of the Mersey Dock and Harbour Board, which latter gentleman offered his advice and assistance to the owner in the stowage of the cargo, mentioned the limits to which she might be safely immersed —viz., 20 feet 6 inches to 21 feet—and marked the side at the midship section to show the same, leaving a clear side of 6 feet 6 inches; little enough, we should say, for a voyage to India, looking to the gales of wind and heavy seas which in voyages of such a distance are sure to be encountered.

> Nevertheless, before leaving the Brunswick Dock, on the 7th March, she was loaded until she was immersed six inches deeper than had been marked as her safe load line, and afterwards, in the Wellington Dock, had 120 tons of coke put on board. On the same day she had been surveyed by the Surveyor to the Liverpool Underwriters' Association, who found she had only five feet of her sides above the water, and was still taking in cargo. He in consequence called in another surveyor, who agreed with him in considering her much overladen, and they so informed Captain Lean. The master then, not liking the position of affairs, and finding that his remonstrances with the owner in regard to the equipment of the vessel for so long a voyage were unattended to, threw up his appointment. The surveyor visited her on the 9th, when she appeared to him not to have more than four feet of clear side, and his final report was that she was scarcely seaworthy, and that he would not like even to cross to Dublin in her in a strong S.W. gale.

On the recommendation of a Liverpool agent, Captain J. Dickie was now appointed to the command; but on proceeding on board on the 9th, he naturally enough did not like the appearance of things any more than his predecessor; but in the words of the Nautical Assessors in their Report, "An extraordinary and most unwarrantable pressure was then put upon him to compel him to go to sea, in the shape of a letter written by a ship-broker at Liverpool, and signed by the agent" as follows;

> Dear Sir,—I am very much surprised to hear that you are making difficulties about going in the Utopia; and I must inform you that, if after I have recommended you to the owner, you do not go in the vessel, I will take care you never get any employment in a ship out of Liverpool, if I have any power to prevent you, as I will not put up with this sort of work.

> On the following morning, the 10th March, the pilot expressed his opinion that the vessel was overladen but the Utopia, overladen, undermanned, leaky, and ill-found in her equipment, was towed to sea to pursue her hopeless voyage. Upon the tug leaving, sail was made, the wind being fair, and weather moderate; but so ill-found was the cordage and rope generally, that the topsail halliards had to be unrove to cat and fish the anchor. Scarcely had they shaped their course when the well was sounded, when three feet three inches of water was

> found in the hold; some hands were therefore at once placed at the pumps, which from that time were more or less continuously worked. Nevertheless, the water gradually increased, there being on the 11th at eight a.m. four feet ten inches, which was the last correct sounding that could be got, as the pumps became then choked with sand.
>
> During the 12th and 13th the ship was observed to be settling gradually and the wind and sea increasing, the master thought it best to run for Cork, but she had now become unmanageable; and at four p.m. on the 13th, there being then only four or five inches from the covering board to the water's edge, and the ship settling down rapidly, the long boat was hoisted out. All hands were speedily got into it— the master being the last to leave the ship; and scarcely had they got clear of her, when she gave a plunge, and went down head foremost. Happily the weather was fine, and not having proceeded so far to sea as to be beyond the beaten track of ships, they were picked up on the same evening by a barque, and were all safely landed on the 16th at Crookhaven.

Although reports from the Board of Trade on casualties to merchant ships were routinely tabled in Parliament, the report on loss the ***Utopia*** occasioned no questions in the House, presumably because no passengers were carried, and no lives were lost. However, some Members of Parliament were concerned and a ground swell of dissatisfaction was building up with the status, content and effectiveness of the many laws regulating the safety of British merchant ships and their crews, with calls for review, amendment and consolidation, as reflected in concerns raised in the House in August 1867. The Vice President of the Board of Trade was asked 'if it was his intention to bring in a Bill early next Session to consolidate and amend the Acts which govern our Mercantile Marine?'

> Mr Stephen Cave replied that these laws would certainly have careful consideration during the recess. Amendments were required as well as consolidation; and it might be a question whether the consolidation ought not to be postponed until the Amendments were concluded, or whether it would be more advisable to combine amendment and consolidation in the same measure.[375]

The following day another Member of Parliament, Mr O'Beirne succinctly summarized the matters in urgent need of Parliamentary scrutiny;

,... in calling attention to the unsatisfactory state of the Merchant Shipping Laws, said, that his task would be an easy one, as he gathered from an answer given by the President of the Board of Trade to a Question put to him yesterday, that it was the intention of the Government to consider the subject, if not of the consolidation, at least of the amendment of the Merchant Shipping Laws.... There was a general feeling abroad that the remedies proposed by the Act of 1859 [sic] [1854] and subsequent Acts did not take within their purview the safety of the public sufficiently....Many issues were raised including the number of Acts (14) containing 700 sections, the role and value of Local Marine Boards, payment of seamen, the fragmented nature of pilotage, issues with salvage, and inadequate surveys of vessels, particularly passenger ships. Great concern was expressed regarding seaworthiness and adequacy of lifeboats; a great improvement would be effected if in all cases it was provided that there should be a final inspection before the ship left port. At present many seamen were brought before the magistrates of Chester and elsewhere for deserting, and the defence of the men often was that their ship was not seaworthy. If the principle of a final survey were enforced, many casualties arising from bad stowage and what was called deck hamper would be prevented. Again, the number of boats which the Act directed should be carried was entirely inadequate to the number of passengers which ships were entitled to take. It might be said that it was impossible to carry sufficient boats for taking all the passengers ashore; but the proportion of boats to passengers which the Act directed to be kept was not at all reasonable, and some larger reform was necessary on this point. 'A ship authorized to carry some 1,600 persons was not now obliged to take more boats than were capable of saving about 500, exclusive of the crew.'... He then moved; "That in the opinion of this House, it is necessary that the Laws with reference to Merchant Shipping should be revised and consolidated, and that such Amendments should be made therein as will better protect the interests of the public and the mercantile marine of this Country".

In reply, the Vice President of the Board of Trade summarized all of the merchant shipping legislation that had been enacted since 1851. Referring to the pending Merchant Shipping Act, 1867, he specifically mentioned that;

> Fragmentary as it was at best, it had been still more curtailed, and some valuable clauses it had been intended to include had had to be abandoned in order to secure its passage through this House, one of which was for the survey of ships alleged to be unseaworthy. They had it also in contemplation to alter the boat scale of steamers to which the Hon. Member had alluded, and to provide that they should carry boats more in proportion to their passengers and voyages than simply in relation to their tonnage. Mr. Cave stated that 'the hon. Member had attacked the system of inspection, and said the Government surveyors were not equal to their work. He admitted that this was sometimes the case, but this was hardly the fault of the Department; it was caused by the rapid transition from sailing vessels to steamers, from wood to iron. They proposed by degrees to appoint surveyors who had served an apprenticeship in the working of iron, and had likewise served at sea, so that the inspection to which he had alluded might be more effectual... He could assure the House that the Board were most desirous to put an end to the acknowledged evils which still existed, and that want of time only had prevented more being done in the present Session of Parliament.'[376] The Motion was, by leave, withdrawn.

Tragically, while politicians continued to delay, obfuscate, and support the laissez faire view that legislation on such matters would absolve the shipowner of responsibility, no fewer than 5987 passengers were to be drowned at sea between 1867 and 1882. Overloading was considered the significant cause.[377] The annual wreck return to the Board of Trade, was analysed by the Nautical Magazine and Naval Chronicle[378] for the year 1867. Commenting on the causes of wrecks off the coast of Great Britain, it was noted that;

> ...notwithstanding the attention this great and national subject has received in the last eighteen years, we are grieved to add that this number is 224 in excess of that in 1866; and, indeed, the total number (2,513) is larger than any number of shipwrecks on our coasts in one year hitherto published in this country... It is a noteworthy and lamentable fact that, according to this register, no less than 411 vessels appear to have foundered, or to have been otherwise totally lost on our coasts from absolute unseaworthiness, unsound gear, etc., during the last nine years; and the number of casualties arising from the same causes during the same period, and resulting in partial damage, is 449.

> Over half of the vessels lost were colliers; 188 laden and 713 in ballast. 1,333 lives were lost from these wrecks; 637 in vessels that foundered, 160 on board vessels in collision, and 445 in vessels stranded or cast ashore. This is in excess of the number lost in any year except 1859 [the Royal Charter year], when the number reached 1,647… 1,086 more crew would have been lost if not for the efforts of lifeboats of the Nation Lifeboat Institution. 729 vessels were wrecked when the wind was at force 6 or under —that is to say, when the force of the wind did not exceed a strong breeze, in which the ship could carry single reefs and topsails. 'Thus it is seen that in a large number of cases a shipwreck means not a tempest-torn craft, riven after a noble contention with the elements, but the wretched collapse of a rotten vessel which ought never to have been sent to sea, and the destruction of which hardly causes a pang to its owner! These are startling facts reflecting no credit on us as a people, and eminently deserving that public attention should prominently and continuously be drawn to them.[379]

At the heart of these concerns was a belief that existing merchant shipping legislation was inadequate in not addressing the obvious issues of overloading and seaworthiness, including the well-proven matter of inadequate legislative requirements for lifeboats aboard increasingly large passenger vessels. Questions were asked regularly in the House during the first half of 1868 regarding the status of work being undertaken to address these issues and to consolidate merchant shipping laws. The replies by the Vice President of the Board of Trade referred to delays in the drafting of amendments, drafters being engaged in more important tasks, the pressures of work in the House, or, on one occasion when Mr. Cave's patience with such questions was clearly wearing thin; "…he thought that the state of Public Business for some time past and at the present moment was a sufficient Answer to the hon. Gentleman's Question".[380] Widespread concern also existed about the high number of collisions at sea, as demonstrated by the Annual Wreck Registers, given wide publicity, leading to questions in the House… 'When the Papers having reference to the Rule of Road at Sea, and laid upon the Table in December last (but the issue of which has been delayed in consequence of some important Correspondence with the French Government on the subject), will be placed in the hands of Members?'[381] The Member was advised that the French Government completely agreed with the diagrams designed to assist mariners in their understanding of the rule of the road at sea, which would be published the following week.

The wreck returns for 1868 did not provide a lot of assurance that the status quo in matters of safety at sea was acceptable, even though losses of vessels and lives was lower than in 1867; a fact attributed to;

> ... no gales of remarkable duration and violence occurred during the past year, such as took place in 1866 and 1867; and that the number of wrecks is accordingly less than in those years.'[382] 1,747 ships of a total tonnage of 427,000 tons were lost along with the loss of 824 lives; 262 were lost in vessels that foundered, 86 lives were lost on board vessels in collision, and 409 in vessels stranded or cast ashore. 379 ships were lost through collisions, 527 were wrecks resulting in total loss, and 841 were casualties resulting in partial damage more or less serious. 'Of the 527 wrecks—i.e., total losses from causes other than collisions—265 happened when the wind was at force 9 or upward (a strong gale), 71 arose from defects in the ship or in her equipments (and of the 71, no less than 46 appear to have foundered from un seaworthiness), — 87 appear, from the reports made by the officers on the coasts, to have been caused by inattention, carelessness, or neglect; and the remainder appear to have arisen from various other causes.'[383] Seven percent of the total vessels lost in 1868 through wreck and collision were steamships (5.6% in 1867).
>
> 'Thus, excluding collisions, 158 total wrecks last year are clearly and directly traceable to the carelessness and indifference of man. It is also a remarkable fact, that from these very casualties the greatest loss of life takes place, inasmuch as the wreck is sometimes instantaneous, arising from the rottenness of the ship, bad anchoring gear, and other prolific sources of mischief, rendering it hardly possible for any succour from the shore to arrive in time to save the lives of the crews. It is really a disgrace to us as a nation, to learn from this authentic record that the total number of ships that foundered, or were otherwise totally lost on our coasts from unseaworthiness, unsound gear, etc., in the last ten years, is 482; and the number of casualties arising from the same causes, during the same period, and resulting in partial damage, was 531. We have no record of the loss of life from these wrecks, but it must have been frightful.'[384]

The 1868 Wreck Report included a statistical summary of all wrecks for the years from 1850 to 1868; a period in which a considerable volume of maritime legislation was enacted to, amongst other matters, improve safety at sea, Over these nineteen years a total 28,689 ships were wrecked on or near the British coast for an average of 1510 per year, the great majority of which were sailing vessels. Average losses per five year period from 1850 to 1868 increased by 180%. Over this same period the number of sailing vessels increased only marginally from 24,797 to 25,500, while the number of steamships more than doubled from 1,187 to 2944.[385]

Towards the very end of the 1869 session of Parliament, on the 9th August, the Government, met the pledge given at the beginning of the year by the President of the Board of Trade that before the House closed he would lay on the table of the House the long promised Merchant Shipping Bill. The aim of the draft Merchant Shipping and Navigation Bill was an Act which would consolidate all seventeen of the Merchant Shipping laws passed since, and including, the Merchant Shipping Act, 1854. As the draft Bill was not quite ready to be tabled, the President of the Board of Trade asked the Clerk of the Parliament, Mr. Shawn Lefevre, to explain the changes proposed "as it would be waste of labour for anyone without some guide to travel through the 800 clauses of the Bill, and, by comparison with the existing law, to ascertain those changes."[386]

Before doing so Lefevre took the opportunity to update the House on the significant changes that had taken place in the British shipping industry since the 1854 Act. The registered tonnage of Great Britain and her possessions had increased by 50% from 5,155,000 to 7,232,000 tons, of which 5,700,000 belonged to the United Kingdom. This tonnage, 50% of the world total, confirmed Britain's place as the leading maritime nation and the benefits of free trade. "In 1854, of an aggregate of 18,669,000 tons entering and clearing our ports for foreign trade, 10,744,000 tons were British, 7,924,000 under foreign flags—a proportion of 57 per cent British to 43 per cent foreign. In 1868, out of 33,680,000 tons, 22,660,000 were British, and 11,020,000 foreign, showing an increase of 120 per cent for British against 37 per cent foreign, the new proportion being 67 per cent British to 33 per cent foreign".[387]

Although the tonnage of the United Kingdom had increased 50 per cent, the number of seamen had increased since 1854 from 162,400 to 197,500, or 21 per cent. The proportion of crew to tonnage in the coastal trade had remained about the same; but in sailing vessels employed in the foreign trade the proportion of crew had fallen from 3.97 per 100 tons in 1854 to 2.90 in 1868, and for steamers from 7.69 to 5 men per 100 tons. Over the whole fleet of merchant vessels there had been a reduction of one man for every 100 tons. This reduction was mainly due to the increased average size of vessels, and also to greater efficiency of all kinds in working them; to the use of machinery, the adoption of double topsails, patent blocks, steam windlasses, and other means of economizing labour, particularly aboard larger sailing vessels employed in the foreign trade.[388]

Lefevre went on to provide a summary of the legislative activities between 1850 and 1869;

> He had quoted these figures in no spirit of boasting, but with the view of showing how vast were the interests affected by the Bill he proposed. They showed how idle were the fears of those who dreaded the repeal of the Navigation Laws, and they were also, on the whole, testimony to the general well working of modern legislation affecting shipping. That legislation might be said to have commenced in 1850, when the late Lord Taunton, then Mr. Labouchere, first provided for the examination of masters and mates of foreign-going vessels, established shipping offices for the protection of seamen, and provided for inquiries into wrecks. The next great change was in 1853–4, when his right hon. Friend the Secretary of State for War, then at the Board of Trade, placed the Trinity House under the control of the Board of Trade, and threw open our coasting trade to foreign vessels, and, lastly, consolidated all previous legislation in the great Act of 1854, which had since been the groundwork of our shipping laws. In the course of this he provided for a complete revision of the ship registry, for a new system of measuring tonnage, and for a limitation of the liability of owners in cases of collision. Since that time not a year had passed without additions or amendments to that Act. In 1856 seamen's savings-banks and money orders were established. In 1862 Mr. Milner Gibson extended examinations to engineers, laid down rules as to lights, and provided summary proceedings in salvage cases. In 1864, the Anchors and Chain Cables Act was passed. In 1868, Admiralty jurisdiction was given to County Courts, and this year an important Act was passed with reference to colonial merchant shipping. In the

> same time shipping had been relieved from a variety of local charges, passing dues and charitable charges; exemptions in favour of particular vessels and differential dues against foreign vessels had been disposed of. He had mentioned but a few of the changes, but, in fact, seventeen or eighteen Acts had been passed since 1854 regulating the business of shipowners, and interlacing one with the other in such a manner that on a subject in which, above all others, it was important there should be clearness and certainty, so that he who sailed might read, there was so much complexity and uncertainty that only experts could say what was the law. Consolidation, in fact, was almost as much needed now as it was in 1854, and although there was not so much field for improvement, there was still much to be done in detail. It was proposed, then, in the Bill which he should ask leave to introduce, to consolidate all these Acts, and include one great branch which was omitted in 1854 – namely, the Acts relating to harbours and the protection of navigation, the working of which had since been placed under the Board of Trade.' Homage was paid by Lefevre to the efforts of Mr. Farrer, the Permanent Secretary of the Board of Trade, and Mr. Thring, who were architects of the Merchant Shipping Act,1854, and all subsequent Acts, and who had subsequently been involved in administration of all of the Merchant Shipping Acts under consideration for consolidation. [Finally, he kept the waning fires of laissez faire flickering with his statement that] 'The House would perceive that the tendency of the amendments proposed was not in the direction of more minute regulations or further inspection. The experience of the Board of Trade was not favourable to such legislation. It tended to shift the responsibility from the shipbuilder or shipowner to some inspecting officer, and in some cases had certainly retarded, improvements.'[389]

A cursory summary was given to Members of the safety provisions proposed in Part III of the Bill; – "The next part of the Act had relation to safety and provision against accidents at sea. The present law contained numerous minute regulations as to the number of boats, the use of lifebelts, the safety valves of engines, compasses, and other such like matters. It was proposed to simplify these and to leave it to the Board of Trade to decide what in the case of passenger ships should be the actual requirements."[390] The major portion of the address, and the ensuing debate, was taken up with "the vexed question of pilotage"; the question of whether pilotage should be compulsory or voluntary, and the liabilities of a shipmaster in the event of a collision when his vessel was under pilotage. One significant question was raised by the Member for Oxford, Mr Henley, who said "he hoped that next Session a continuous Return would be published showing the proportion of wrecks to voyages during the last three or four years, that they might see whether their lodging the management of shipping to so large an extent in the hands of the Government had resulted in more or fewer wrecks". It was necessary for Members to turn to commentary in maritime journals to gain a more detailed understanding, and commentary on, the proposed Bill during the long summer break before Parliament resumed in February 1970.

Part III of the draft Merchant Shipping Bill; *Safety and Prevention of Accidents* contained 58 clauses. The Rules for Preventing Collision were to be contained in the Twelfth Schedule to the Act and were the same as those which came into effect in 1863. Commentary in the Nautical Magazine and Naval Journal, 1869, grudgingly stated that 'They appear to be sufficient and judicious but do not seem sufficient to prevent collision'. Concern was expressed about clause 330 of the Collision Rules which required …*the person in charge of any vessel coming into collision with another to use his utmost endeavor, so far as the safety of his own vessel will allow him to do so, to save those on board the other vessel from any danger caused by the collision….* The nature of the rule was not the issue, but the proposed offence provisions which were seen to be inadequate. 'We think that this clause might, without injustice, have been made still more stringent and have the master of a vessel guilty of willful neglect in this particular, liable to imprisonment. For, to desert a sinking ship, and deliberately leave those on board to perish, which has often been done, can be characterised as nothing less than willful homicide of the most dastardly and hard-hearted kind'.[391]

Proposed clause 332 – *Seaworthiness and Equipments* – contained nine parts which the Journal summarized;

> 1st. Requires that every seagoing ship to be provided with lights and the means of making fog– signals.
>
> 2nd That she shall have a scale of feet showing her draught of feet accurately, cut or painted on her stem and stern.
>
> 3rd That she shall be provided with efficient boats, rafts or other

appliances for saving life, kept at all times fit and ready for use, and supplied with all requisites for use, sufficient in numbers and of the size and description proper for the service, the size of the ship and the nature and deviation of the voyage, and like circumstances, and with a sufficient number of life-buoys and life-jackets for use in emergency.

4th. That, if carrying more than ten passengers, she shall, besides the above, be provided with a lifeboat, or sufficient numbers of lifeboats, kept at all times fit and ready for use.

5th.That, if built wholly or partly of iron, she shall have her compasses adjusted from time to time.

6th. That, if a steam-ship, she shall be provided with a safety-valve on each boiler, so constructed that the weight thereon cannot be increased when the steam is up, and that the pressure of steam in the boiler cannot be increased beyond a safe and proper amount.

7th. That, every ship shall be provided with proper pumps, with a hose capable of being connected with the engines of the ship, and adapted for extinguishing fire in any part of the ship.

8th. That every such ship employed to carry passengers shall be provided with twelve blue lights or twelve port-fires, and a cannon with not less than twelve charges of powder for making signals of distress.

9th. That every coasting steam-ship carrying passengers shall be provided with such shelter for their protection as shall be required by the Board of Trade

Although these summaries would clearly not reflect the full wording, and/or intent, of the final Act they were cause for concern in the Journal in a number of areas. It was considered that the requirement for draught marks fore and aft would have been much enhanced by a continuous load-water-line, cut and marked for the entire length of the vessel, and that suitable authorities be authorized to detain the vessel if overloaded. 'The loss of the ***London*** may be attributed to the lack of this law'. The requirements for boats, life-buoys and life-jackets were seen as a significant improvement upon the 1854 Act; 'but they nevertheless have the same fatal defect of vagueness which neutralized, to so great an extent the value of the latter, as they contain no definition of what are efficient life-boats, life-jackets, or life-buoys…[none] will be provided on merchant vessels unless some definition be made of their character'. It was believed that efficient lifeboats would never be fitted to passenger ships as 'the ship-owner will not incur any expense that they can avoid in the equipment of their ships'.[392]

Part XIV of the proposed Act summarized the functions of the Board of Trade. Clause 673 empowered the Board to appoint Inspectors to report to them on the nature and causes of any accident or damage a ship has sustained or caused to be sustained, whether the Act and its regulations have been complied with, and, whether the hull and machinery of any steam-ship are sufficient and in good condition.

The Journal had its serious doubts as to the efficacy of such measures; 'It will be readily conceived how much the success of an efficient supervision of our Mercantile Marine must depend on those officers. A board in London cannot be ubiquitous, and if those persons to whom it intrusted the duty of carrying its behest into execution are deficient either in capacity or honesty, all the most wisely-conceived regulations must be utterly useless. Thus a leaky, unseaworthy, ill-found or overladen ship might be suffered to go to sea through the incapacity of an inefficient Inspector, through the carelessness of a neglectful one, or through the venality of a dishonest one who directly or indirectly might think it is to his interest to avoid giving offence to a wealthy and influential shipowner, and lamentable loss of life might thereby ensue, as, it is patent to everyone, has times out of number happened through such ships being permitted to leave out ports'.[393] It was expected that the Bill would pass through Parliament in the next Session and come into operation on the 1st May 1870.

While Parliament was in recess until the New Year, seafarers continued to die on or near the British coast in increasing numbers. The Wreck Register for 1869 recorded the loss of 2,114 vessels with the associated loss of 933 lives. The death toll would have been much greater if it had not been for the efforts of the National Lifeboat Institution whose boats saved 933 lives. Taking into account the two vessels involved in every collision, the total number of vessels lost or damaged was 2,594; the highest number of casualties since records commenced twenty years previously. Lost ships totalled

537,605 ton; employing 22,579 crew. The statistics include 461 collisions which the report breaks down;

> ...The nature of the collisions is thus given: -17 occurred between steamers, and 193 between sailing vessels while both were under way; 76 collisions also happened between sailing vessels, one being at anchor and the other under way ; 66 between steamers and sailing vessels, both being under way ; and only 13 were– caused by steamers running into sailing vessels at anchor; 4 by sailing vessel under way running into steamers at anchor; and none by one steamer coming into collision with another at anchor; 92 collisions also occurred through vessels breaking from their anchors or moorings.'[394] The worst month for losses was October, with 333; many caused by the very strong Northerly gale of the 19th of October.

On the 13th of May 1869 a short Act came into effect, the principles of which proved to be of benefit to the author almost 100 years later in 1963 when joining a British ship holding a New Zealand Second Mates Certificate of Competency and later, in 1968, when holding a New Zealand Certificate of Competency as Master of a Foreign Going Steamship; the *Merchant Shipping (Colonial) Act, 1869*[395] *– An Act for amending the Law relating to the Coasting Trade and Merchant Shipping in British Possessions*.

Section 4, gave the Governments of British possessions the authority to regulate the coasting trade, subject to ...*publicly signifying Her Majesty's pleasure thereon*; treating all British ships in exactly the same manner as Ships of the British possession, and continuing and existing rights, as agreed by Her Majesty, were given to foreign Ships in the coasting trade of the British possession. Section 6 enabled registrars in British possessions to register ships, as provided for by s.30 of the Merchant Shipping Act, 1854, with s.8 providing that colonial certificates of competency would have the same weight and force as British certificates;

> Section 8 – Colonial certificates to master, mates and engineers; -
>
> Where the legislature of any British possession provides for the examination of, and grant of certificates to act as master, mate, or engineer on board British Ships, and the Board of Trade reports to Her Majesty that they are satisfied that the examinations are so conducted as to be equally efficient as the examinations for the same purpose in the

> United Kingdom under the Acts relating to Merchant Shipping, and that the certificates are granted on such principles as to show the like qualifications and competencies as those granted under the Acts, and are liable to be forfeited for the like reasons and in the like manner, it shall be lawful for Her Majesty, by Order in Council,
>
> (1) To declare that the said certificates shall be the same force as if they had been granted under the said Acts…

It was not until the 1860s that compound engines attained the degree of reliability needed for ocean passages, with early adoption by both the Pacific Steam Navigation Company and P & O to benefit from the considerable reductions of fuel on their long voyages. The first compound engines on the North Atlantic were installed aboard the ***India*** of Anchor Line and the ***Holland*** of the National Line in the late 1860s. When their attributes became widely known they became the standard engine for new buildings almost overnight. In 1868 Cunard specified compound engines for his new buildings; ***Batavia*** (2,550 tons) and ***Parthia*** (3,150 tons). By this time Cunard had also forsaken paddlewheels after the paddle wheeler, ***Scotia,*** had lost the Atlantic blue riband to the propeller driven ***City of Paris*** in 1867. By 1875 compound engines powered more than 2,000 vessels.[396] They were, however, not without their problems, one of which was ongoing misuse of pressure relief valves to gain more speed, an issue that'd been addressed through legislation as early as 1851.

The decade closed with an unprecedented event that changed forever the nature of shipping between the Western and Eastern hemispheres, the opening on November 17th after ten years work, of the Suez Canal. The dramatic decrease in passage times between e.g. London and the East coast of India; from 90 days for a sailing ship to 30 days for a steamer, caught the shipping industry by surprise. Initially shippers preferred the certainty of long passages by sailing ships around the Cape of Good Hope and the associated higher freight rates, but soon came to appreciate the benefits of steamships through the canal. However, it was soon demonstrated that the steamships that had been suitable for routes to the Mediterranean and North America proved to be unsuitable for the tropics, resulting in a boom in shipbuilding and an unprecedented increase in wages and the cost of shipbuilding materials for a few years.[397]

Chapter 12

The Seaman's Friend

The first few years of the 1870s were to be the busiest time for the shipping industry and Parliamentarians since the early 1850s, with the contentious matter of unseaworthy and overloaded ships finally being addressed by politicians under great pressure from the public and some in the shipping industry; a further Passenger Act in 1870; a second Chain, Cables and Anchors Act; introduction of a Merchant Shipping Act in 1871; a further Merchant Shipping Act in 1872; yet another Wreck Enquiry in 1873, and Merchant Shipping Acts in 1875 and 1876.

Parliament's merchant shipping business commenced on the 14th of February 1870 with a continuation of the debate on the first reading of the Merchant Shipping and Navigation Bill. Lefevre reported that during the long Parliamentary recess much work had been done on the Bill, taking into account suggestions made and feedback from personal enquiries he had made at various seaports. He proposed that;

> The Bill itself would be somewhat altered in form; instead of being one continuous measure, it would be divided into fourteen separate parts, each of which would be a complete Act in itself, but they would all form portions of one statute, and would be bound together; but it would be possible to obtain each separately for purpose of use and reference.'… 'The proposed Act would be 'a complete code of all the existing statute law affecting ships, with one exception,—namely, the regulations affecting passenger vessels. There were now pending negotiations with the United States for a common system of rules for emigrants, and in the meantime the Emigration Commissioners were unwilling to include their provisions in this measure.'….'[398] A fundamental principle of the Bill was for the Government not to interfere with matters such as loading, manning and operation but, it was wiser to place these responsibilities upon shipowners subject to legal sanctions if they caused injury or wrong to others. Accordingly, amendments proposed had not multiplied regulations, existing regulations would be simplified and made more general, and the liability of shipowners

would be made clearer. For example, to send an unseaworthy vessel to sea, so as to endanger life, would be defined as a misdemeanour. Again, in the not unfrequent cases where seamen refused to proceed, alleging that the vessel was unseaworthy, or, where having put to sea, vessels put back, or where seamen were summoned as offenders, it was provided that they should have the right to call in a Board of Trade surveyor to report upon the condition of the vessel; and as the issue was, in fact, one arising out of breach of civil contract, they thought the evidence of the men themselves should be taken.'…'It was also proposed to improve Courts of Inquiry so as better to elicit the cause of losses, and to provide the power to note the draught of water of vessels leaving ports'.[399]

Due to concerns expressed to him by Master Mariners in Liverpool, supported by two local members of Parliament, about Masters having their certificate of competency suspended or cancelled inequitably for moral judgements, Lefevre proposed;

…that the inquiry into the loss of the vessel should be kept quite separate from that into the conduct of the officers. The inquiry into the loss of the vessel would be in the nature of an inquest, and although the Court would have no power to suspend the master's certificate, it would have power to express an opinion as to the cause of loss. Subsequently, or, indeed, at any time, proceedings might be taken against the master or other certificated officers for the suspension of their certificates, if it appeared to the Board of Trade that the officers had been guilty of misconduct; but it would be proposed that there should be a strict definition of the powers of such court, and that suspension should be limited to those cases where incompetency, gross negligence, tyranny, or drunkenness were proved against the officer.' It was thought better to deal with the thorny question of compulsory or voluntary pilotage through a separate Bill in order that adequate consideration could be given to the matter.[400]

During the following debate Mr. Steven Cave stressed that;

…the power of seamen to give evidence in cases where ships were unseaworthy is exceedingly necessary, because, although it is quite true that in many instances seamen refuse to go to sea on the most frivolous and vexatious pleas, yet in other instances, where refusal is

> really based on justifiable grounds, it is impossible for the men to give evidence, and in fact no man has a right to go on board and receive the evidence however unseaworthy the ship may be.'[401]

The remainder of the debate focused in great detail, as in the previous August, upon the compulsory/voluntary pilotage conundrum. While this debate was underway there was increasing public concern over the fate of the Inman Line passenger ship ***City of Boston*** (1864) of 2,278 tons, which had sailed from Halifax for Liverpool on the 28th of January, since when the ship had not been sighted and was now considerably overdue. Other ships reported heavy ice and very strong Easterly headwinds for the duration of their voyage to the United Kingdom. She had a total of 191 people on board, made up of 55 cabin passengers, 52 steerage passengers and a crew of 84. The ship was never seen again. Amongst the many theories aired as to her loss the subsequent Court of Inquiry ruled out the rumour that the ship had been grossly overloaded.[402]

However, overloading would appear from evidence at the Inquiry to be causative into the loss with all nineteen crew of the steamship ***Sea Queen*** (1859) of 457 tons, which foundered off Yarmouth after departing Newcastle for Spain with a full load of coal on the 13th of February 1870. The Court of Inquiry were told that the ship's freeboard upon departure was only eight to twelve inches. Evidence was given by the widow of the Master that the Second Mate admitted overloading the ship and that she had to step up from the weather deck into the boat that took her off. The owner was present at this time and dismissed her comments regarding overloading stating that 'she was no deeper than when she left London last time'. The steward had told his wife, when he expressed concerns about sailing on the ship, that '…if he didn't sail he would get two months imprisonment'. A similar answer was given to the sister of one of seamen; he had signed articles, would be disgraced if he didn't sail, would lose his Second Mates certificate and face three months imprisonment.[403]

Seamen had been subject to imprisonment for what was treated as desertion when refusing to sail on an unseaworthy ship since 1854 but over time opinion changed and the application of s.234 of the Merchant Shipping Act, 1854, in such cases came to be seen as excessive, as refusal to sail might have been justified. Seamen refusing to sail were dealt with in exactly the same way as deserters or drunkards who had missed their ships, and a steady stream of complaints reached the Home Office and the Board of Trade from fellow seamen, prison chaplains and those concerned with the welfare of seamen ashore. The Board of Trade started keeping records of such imprisonments. In 1870, 467 seamen were jailed for refusing to proceed to sea. Unseaworthiness, insufficient accommodation, defective equipment, overloading and under manning were alleged in 132 cases and only one complaint was dismissed in that year as proof of unseaworthiness was readily available. The Report of the Inspector of Prisons for Southern and Western Districts in 1854 had revealed that in Plymouth Gaol fifty-three out of 239 male prisoners confined during that year had been seamen who had refused to sail because of unseaworthiness or undermanning.[404]

On the last day of March the Secretary of the Board of Trade was asked in the House for information on nine steam vessels lost at sea since the beginning of the year; whether the Secretary was aware that the Shields Gazette had reported that, in the last sixth months of 1869, twenty-eight steam vessels were lost at sea, and, how many courts of enquiry had been carried out into these losses. He replied that;

> ...the Board of Trade had received reports respecting eight of the casualties referred to by the right hon. Member. Of these, two were collisions, resulting in the total loss of two vessels, and in partial damage to two others. Of the six other vessels, three were reported as having foundered; two were stranded; and one was supposed to have foundered. Inquiries were held by the Board of Trade in three of these cases. In two the officers and crew were acquitted of blame; in another, that of collision, the court of inquiry held the officers of the Black Swan to blame. In reply to the question of losses in 1869 he fell back upon the Annual Wreck Register for that year, available later in the year, but did explain that 'the Board did not direct inquiry into any loss of life, but only into those where the facts tended to show that there was misconduct of officers, or that the vessels were sent to sea in an unseaworthy state, or overloaded.'[405]

Unseaworthiness and overloading were a significant cause for the loss of ships, especially smaller sailing ships as evidenced by the Annual Wreck Registers. Pressure was building upon Parliament to respond to its public duty to safeguard the lives of its citizens – seafarers employed aboard coffin ships. The term 'coffin ship' had been coined, by seamen, in the 1830s to describe the unseaworthy ships carrying timber deck cargoes from North America to Great Britain. It was resurrected during the great Irish famines of the 1830s and late 1840s to reflect the significant loss of emigrant ships, and also their very unhygienic conditions that resulted in the death of tens of thousands of emigrants through 'ship fever'. Due to the weight of public concern about losses of ships, officials had conducted inquiries into the causes of shipwreck from as early as 1836 without any proactive moves to ascertain the seaworthiness of all ships or deal with the dangers of overloading. The fates of the ***London*** and ***Utopia*** caused a great deal of public concern and prompted the magazine of the Royal National Life-boat Institution, in July 1867, to recommend that ships should be inspected independently and show a thin white line on the hull to show the legal maximum draft beyond which they could not be loaded, to remedy the 'discreditable state of things'.[406]

Some responsible and farsighted people in the shipping industry were also concerned about the dangers of overloading ships, such as James Hall, a wealthy and successful shipowner of Newcastle and director of two marine insurance companies. In November 1867 Hall wrote to the Shipping Gazette stating the urgent need to legislate to remedy "the unseaworthy condition in which many vessels, frequently overladen besides, are sent on their voyages". He recommended that a position of Government Inspector of Shipping be established at major ports to issue or withhold a certificate of seaworthiness and further suggested that Local Marine Boards should enquire into any unaccounted losses of ships. Although the article was repeated in the Newcastle Daily Chronicle nothing came of it.[407] In 1868 Hall wrote to The Times further stating his case through an example of where a patently unseaworthy ship had sailed and had to be abandoned in a sinking state three days later. In December that year again wrote to The Times stating that although there had been an increase in insurance claims in the north-east "some of which were directly traceable to the effects of overloading" he could see no evidence of any disposition to stop such happenings. He further stated that;

> Every practical authority I have consulted admits that a vessel should have a certain 'side' or 'freeboard', and yet we have spar-decked ships [those with a light deck built above the main deck]...sent to

> sea immersed some feet above the main deck and foundering on the voyage. Underwriters and marine insurance companies are charging increased premiums to meet the increased risk, and thus the merchant who ships his cargo and the shipowner who does not overload his vessel are paying for those who do...The first duty of a Government is to protect the lives of its subjects, and to every other class or workman, excepting sailors, this duty is discharged. A load line marking the extreme limit of flotation was the answer, and it was 'in the interest of humanity, not less than the duty of the Government' to establish one'.[408]

Hall and his fellow petitioners, and the seamen of the Merchant Service needed the support of a staunch advocate in Parliament to have their concerns heard at the highest level in the hope that the Government would carry out its duty to protect the lives of its subjects; the seamen and the passengers their ships carried.

The compelling, long-standing and well-proven risks faced by all who went to sea from unseaworthy and/or overloaded ships were finally to become the relentless, and almost fanatical, focus of one man from 1870; a man who became known as the 'seaman's friend'. Samuel Plimsoll was to remind yet another generation of the pejorative term 'coffin ship'; the result of what he deemed to be;

...the mercenary and murderous greed of the shipowner in sending overladen and rotten ships to sea and thereby causing a criminal loss of life'.[409] Plimsoll was to later take note of Hall's knowledge and expertise in shipowning and marine insurance, and promotion of mandatory load lines for ships, a few years after he entered Parliament. He first stood for Parliament, unsuccessfully, in the 1865 election as the Liberal candidate for the seat of Derby. His manifesto did not include any mention of the plight of seamen, although his main focus at this time was the rights of workers, particularly miners, but did include a wide extension of the electoral franchise which came about through the *Representation of the People Act, 1867;*[410] doubling the size of the franchise. This favoured the Liberals and enabled Plimsoll to gain the Derby seat in 1868 with a majority of two thousand.

In December 1868, possibly after reading Hall's article in The Times Plimsoll found his cause celebre and stated publicly that "I have just been elected to

Parliament. This is my opportunity to help those in peril on the sea. I shall do all in my power to put an end to the unseaworthy ships owned by the greedy and the unscrupulous".[411] However, he did not speak in support of a Merchant Shipping Bill, introduced in August 1869, which proposed that seamen be entitled to a survey if they considered a ship to be unseaworthy. It was not until March 1870, when Plimsoll heard Hall present a petition to Parliament on behalf of the Associated Chambers of Shipping for fourteen ports in the north-east, recommending inspections of ships, load lines, training of seamen and surveys of unseaworthy ships that he began his crusade on behalf of seamen, with the full support of Hall who finally had a voice and a champion in Parliament.

Another significant influence upon Plimsoll was the newspaper editor William Leng who, as long ago as 1856, had written an article for the Hull Free Press on the condition of some ships seen departing the port;

> ...If you have ever stood at the Humber dock-gate and seen a long, low steam boat, narrow as a racing gig, deep as a sand barge and wall-sided as a house, waddle up with a rocking stagger on her way out, you will have wondered whether it was possible that that cranky, rolling, deck-piled, half-handed vessel could possibly be expected to go to sea in that condition.

Leng was particularly concerned about loss of life at sea and, upon becoming aware of a report he wrote in November 1869 as editor of the Sheffield Daily Telegraph, Plimsoll contacted him, much to Leng's rather breathless delight;

> I felt like one who was groping in the dark for the hearts of mankind's humaner souls. No response. My voice had been as the voice of one crying in the wilderness. But at last it fell upon the pained ear of one who united a keen sympathy, a quick intelligence, abundant leisure, a loving spirit, a position of absolute independence and immense moral courage[412]

Thanks to Hall and Leng, Plimsoll now had the knowledge, understanding, confidence and position to begin his Parliamentary crusade. In April 1870 he moved that three additional clauses be inserted in the Merchant Shipping Bill to provide for inspections of all ships, a maximum load line and a prohibition on insuring any ship for more than two thirds of its value.[413] Sir John Pakington rose in the House on the 20th of May to propose that; – 'An humble Address be presented to Her Majesty praying that Her Majesty will be pleased to issue a Commission to inquire into the causes of the great loss of life and property at sea during the last few years, and to consider whether any and what changes can be made in existing Laws and Regulations with respect to collisions, over-lading, stowage of cargo, and other matters, with the view of giving increased safety to Passengers and Merchant Ships..' Pakington supported his Motion with statistics showing that;

> 16 Baltic steamers had been lost in the autumn of 1868, and 18 in the autumn of 1869. Further, that between the 1st of July and the beginning of November, 1869, 28 steamers [in total] were lost. As to December he had no information; but from the 1st of January to the beginning of March, 1870, to say nothing of those vessels which were stranded, nine steamers were lost, two of them by collision and seven by foundering at sea… It thus appeared that no less than 37 steam ships had been lost in the course of six months, or at the rate of six per month, or one and a-half per week'. Comparing the statistics for 1858 and 1868 'it was shown that in 1858 there were belonging to the United Kingdom 25,000 sailing ships and 1,900 steamers; in 1868 the sailing vessels had increased to 26,000, and the steam ships to 3,000, there being thus a total increase of somewhat less than 8 per cent. In 1858 1,107 losses and casualties happened; in 1868 the number had increased to 1,747—an increase of 50 per cent; though, had he taken the year 1867, the comparison would have been still more startling, for in that year the losses were more numerous than in the following one…. The number of lives lost had increased from 349 in 1858 to 854 in 1868… He asked the House to look to the fact that the increase of casualties was in proportion to the increase of steam ships, as compared with sailing vessels. There must be a cause for that increase, and what was the cause? Out of the House there was but one opinion—that the great increase of casualties was owing to the too prevalent custom of over-loading ships.[414]

Neither of these initiatives were initially successful. The Government refused to accede to Pakington's Motion on the ground that a Bill relating to the subject was already before the House. However, on the 13th of May, 1870, Parliament had agreed; '*On Motion of Mr. Plimsoll, Bill to provide for the greater security of Life at Sea, ordered to be brought in by Mr. Plimsoll and [the appropriately named] Mr. Wheelhouse.'*[415]

Leng took the opportunity to support and publicise Plimsoll's proposal, leading to long and widespread criticism in the Press for a number of months over what was seen to be delays by Parliament and lack of support for both Plimsoll and Pakington. On the 5th May the Pall Mall Gazette stated that '...it would seem that in the desperate struggle for life the weaker are sacrificed to the necessities of the stronger, and the seaman, who has to accept terms, dies for the sustenance of the capitalist who imposes them'.[416]

Before Plimsoll's Resolution could be presented, the second reading of the Merchant Shipping Bill took place on the 13th June 1870. The debate opened with a request for a debate on the opportunity for debating the measure by going into committee, along with acknowledgement that "the shipping interest had for many years urged upon the Board of Trade the necessity for amendment and for consolidation of the laws affecting shipping, and he admitted that the second demand was very largely though not entirely complied with in the present Bill"...He cheerfully admitted that most of the alterations proposed by the Bill were improvements, and would bring the law more in accordance with the circumstances of the present time. Sir John Pakington commented that "...This Bill was of the highest moment. It affected the whole of our vast shipping trade and the lives of our 200,000 seamen..."[417]

The Bill received general support, but with concern from some Members as to its size, at 700 clauses, and the difficulty of giving it satisfactorily consideration in the short time left in the Parliamentary year. This view was countered by others who pointed out that the prime purpose of the Bill was a consolidation of existing law, which made up ninety percent of the content. Calls were made for certain contentious parts of the Bill to be referred to a select committee but these were not generally supported due to the urgency of the measures, such as the new proposed clauses regarding inspections, draft marks, and removal of extant penalty provisions for seamen leaving an unseaworthy ship, and widespread public interest in these matters. Plimsoll did not contribute to the debate. It was finally agreed that the Bill would be "committed to a Committee of the Whole House for Monday next"; the 20th of June.

On the 4th of July Mr. Shaw Lefevre stated; – "he would suggest that the Committee should be postponed to the 1st of August, and that the Bill should be reprinted, with a view to its early introduction next Session."[418] When questioned by Pakington as to the intent of his statement it was clarified that the Bill "would be withdrawn for this Session" (i.e. until early 1871)

Plimsoll re-entered the debate on the 28th of July in moving;

> ...to call the attention of the House to the state of a portion of the Mercantile Marine of this Country, and to certain practices connected therewith, as...Parliament had extended its protection to the workers in mines and factories, and the safety of the people was one of its first considerations. He thought Parliament might interfere in the case which he was now considering, by providing that vessels should not be loaded beyond their maximum capacity, and that there should be a compulsory survey of unclassed ships.' [Plimsoll supported a need for such measures with a well-constructed presentation, and irrefutable facts and statistics, which included one pointed example of a shipowner]; a 'Member of this House', who had lost seven ships in a short space of time due to his 'inveterate habit of overloading'. [The worst case that had come under his notice] '...was that of a firm on the Clyde, who, out of 21 ocean-going steamers, had lost no less than 11 since 1867, five of them being so totally lost that the only record against their names was that they had never been heard of more. The owners in that case kept their vessels constantly under weigh, not even them to stop for necessary repairs, and never allowing an authorized surveyor to go on board to see their condition. [419]

He refuted the argument of excessive cost often presented against compulsory inspections of ships by explaining that of the 27,635 ships registered in British ports, 12,656 were surveyed by Lloyd's surveyors and 6,182 of the remainder had been built within the last five years. If all the ships belonging to Cunard, P&O, Inman, and General Steam Navigation were deducted, a force of 19 surveyors would be quite sufficient to do all the work required. By making the charges for surveys no higher than they were are at present, a handsome yearly surplus might be handed over to the Treasury. He concluded his introduction by stating that "...every ship which needed repair should be repaired, and that no ship should go to sea overladen. And what would be the result? That half of the lives lost every winter would be saved. No fewer than 500 lives per annum would be saved. If the Government would only bring in a short Bill this Session the whole thing might be done by October. If they refused, then these men must die." He then proposed an amendment after the word 'that' to the end of the question stating ... "in the opinion of this House, the statement in the Report of the Board of Trade that more than half of the losses at sea for the six years ending in 1868 are owing to overladen and unseaworthy ships of the collier class, requires immediate legislation, with a view to the diminution of such losses'.[420]

Plimsoll's logic regarding the insurance argument was questioned and more than one member still referred to the "army of inspectors required". Further, the current provisions in the bill "...to make it a misdemeanour on the part of the shipowner to send a ship to sea in an inefficient and unseaworthy state, and the further proposal to allow sailors to refuse to proceed to sea in unseaworthy ships, when discovered to be so, would also be a valuable security to the public".

The President of the Board of Trade (Lefevre) replied that;

> ...he deeply sympathized with the motives which actuated the hon. Member for Derby (Mr. Plimsoll), and he fully admitted the importance of the subject he had so ably brought forward...He regretted that he had been unable to proceed with the Merchant Shipping Code Bill, owing to the exigency of questions of greater magnitude. The time devoted to that measure, however, had not, he trusted, been altogether lost, as it had received much consideration from an informal Committee of Members interested in the question, which had met at the Board of Trade, and was in such a forward state that he believed the House would be able to deal with the question at a very early period next Session. Plimsoll's proposal for an official load line was 'worthy of great consideration' but was one of extreme difficulty as he'd never met anyone who agreed as to what it should be. The problem with the condition of colliers on the East coast would be solved over time by their increasing replacement by steamers but, it was not possible to deal with the motion in the very limited time remaining in the current session and he would not support it.

A firm view was also expressed that the proposed surveys would not be of any benefit, with such a system in France being held up as an example;

> That these Government surveys did not prevent the loss of lives and ships belonging to France was proved by statistics. In the year 1869 the number of English vessels that were lost was 1,172, being 4.40 per cent of the whole; German, 201, being 4.50 per cent; Norwegian, 105, being 3 per cent; and Swedish, 25, being 2.50 per cent. Government surveys prevailed in none of these countries; whereas the number of French vessels lost during the same year was no less than 279, or 5.30 per cent of the whole. He thought from these facts he was justified in saying that the Government survey in France had not proved a protection either to life or property.'[421]

Another Member stated vessels were not lost through any fault of the owner or master of vessels but by improper stowage of cargo by waterside workers. Also, "when vessels left port no one could tell the dangers with which the seamen would have to contend, and, looking to the number of ships which formed the Mercantile Marine of this country, he submitted that the loss of life in them was comparatively very small. He urged the House to be very cautious in legislating for the Mercantile Marine, because, in his opinion, the shipping interests of the country already suffered from too much legislation." It was also considered that "many of the statements by which it [the Bill] had been supported were exaggerated, and some of them quite untrue." Plimsoll did not re-enter the debate. The amendment, by leave, was withdrawn. [422] On the 9th of August, the final sitting day for 1870, an amendment to the Passengers Act, 1855, was given Royal assent through enactment of the *Passengers Act, Amendment Act,1870; An Act to authorise the carriage of Naval and Military Stores in Passenger Ships"*[423] an amendment with serious implications for the potential safety of not only passengers but also the crews of passenger ships.

The provision to be amended; Section 29 of the 1855 Act, required that;

> No passenger ship shall clear out or proceed to sea if there shall be on board as cargo, horses, cattle, gunpowder, vitriol, Lucifer matches, guano, or green hides, nor if there shall be on board any other article or number of articles, whether as cargo or ballast , which by reason of the nature or quantity or mode of stowage thereof, shall, either singly or collectively, be deemed by the emigration officer at the port of clear-

> ance likely to endanger the health or lives of the passengers, or safety of the ship

The preamble to the 1870 amendment to the principal Act, and the 1863 Act, did not give any specific reason for the amendment but stated;

> And whereas it is expedient that any of Her Majesty's Principal Secretaries of State should be empowered to authorize the carriage in passenger ships of naval and military stores whenever requisite for the public service...

The Annual Wreck Register for 1870 showed a significant improvement over previous years but ships lost or seriously damaged still totalled 1502; 1,865 when collisions are taken into account. The crew involved totalled 16,348 aboard ships of 404,000 total tonnage. Out of the 411 total losses, other than by through collision, 160 were due to weather related incidents with all of the rest being traced to defects aboard the ship or its equipment along with neglect and inattention. More than half of the ships were colliers in the East coast trade, of a great range of ages; some comparatively new. Curiously, the return did not specify total loss of life in these events, but the fact that the National Lifeboat Institution saved 4,654 lives would indicate that there were many crew who weren't saved. Boats of this organization had, by 1870, saved 20,000 seafarers since commencement of operations in 1824.[424]

One of the wrecks in 1870 where lifeboats of the National Lifeboat Institution were not used was that of the Anchor Line passenger ship ***Cambria*** (1869) of 1,997 tons, wrecked on the coast of Derry, Ireland, on the night of 19th October, with the loss of all but one person out of her complement of 179 people. The ***Cambria*** entered service the previous year and had completed twelve crossings between Glasgow and New York. She departed from New York on the 9th September with 104 passengers and 75 crew and had an uneventful passage until the evening of the 8th of October. Running before a fresh Westerly under full sail and power, she struck violently upon Tor Beg Rock, the most northerly landfall on Ireland; a half mile north-west of Inishtrahull Island, and about six miles north-east of Malin Head. There was a lighthouse on Inishtrahull Island. It became immediately clear that the ship was making a great deal of water; the stokehold fires were extinguished and the order given to abandon ship. The ship's five boats were launched, four of which were later found ashore, empty, on the Giant's Causeway. The fifth boat, with fifteen passengers aboard, capsized almost immediately and the sole survivor, upon regaining consciousness, found himself clinging to the gunwale. There was only one other person in the boat; the body of a dead woman. The sole survivor was rescued the following day by a passing ship.[425]

Chapter 13

A Contemporary View

The following verbatim extract from a prominent maritime journal in 1871[426] illustrates the entrenched views of many in the shipping industry regarding the perceived exclusive right of a shipowner to manage his ship without any interference by the Government. The commentary on the matter of insurance though, which was central to the ability of unscrupulous shipowners to over-insure their 'coffin ships' presents a more enlightened and in-depth view. Attempts were to be made to deal with this matter through legislation.

MERCHANT SHIPPING LEGISLATION.—IV.
INQUIRIES INTO WRECKS AND MISCONDUCT AT SEA.

"It is not the practice with destroyers of vermin to allow the little victims a veto upon the weapons used against them. If this were otherwise, we should have one set of vermin banishing small-tooth combs; another protesting against mouse-traps; a third prohibiting the finger and thumb; a fourth exclaiming against the intolerable infamy of using soap and water. It is impossible, however, to listen to such pleas. They must all be caught, – killed, and cracked, in the manner and by the instruments which are found most efficacious to their destruction; and the more they cry out, the greater plainly is the skill used against them." *Rev. Sydney Smith, "Edinburgh Review, 1808.*

The running of mankind to and fro on the face of the earth, and the consequent increase in knowledge and riches, are, if not mainly, at all events to a very great extent, due to the mercantile navies of the world; and pre-eminent amongst these navies stands the mercantile navy, or—as we now always call it—the mercantile marine of Great Britain. This pre-eminence is due in a great measure to the causes referred to in our former article; but working with these causes are others as great and as certain in their effects; causes which no statutes can affect, and no excess of prosperity on the one hand, or of adversity on the other hand, can interfere with, viz., energy and honesty. To impeach the honesty of the British shipowner, would be as great an act of folly as to question his energy. The happy combination of these two qualities has placed him at the head of all civilizers. But the pre-eminence of this great body for integrity has, unfortunately, often served as a cloak under which the dishonest have worked out many evil designs. A scoundrel obtaining admittance amongst a respectable body will, under the protection afforded by the fair name of the whole body, necessarily have endless opportunities of practising his scoundrelisms; and the more his professions and outward behaviour accord with the professions and outward behaviour of the general body, the less will he be suspected and the more likely will he be to escape detection.

The commonest illustration of this is to be found in cases where a pre-eminent rascal is also pre-eminent as a professing Churchman. He may obtain many social and other temporal advantages by his connection with a Church, and he may never be detected; but his presence in the flock is no element of strength to them, and his personal evil-doings are no evidence of evil in the other members of the flock. When the impostor is detected, the general body of the community to which he belongs not only does not suffer, but is actually benefited by his removal. The truths professed, the fundamental principles holding the members together, are vindicated and remain unimpeachable, and the society is altogether comforted and strengthened by the purging; it moreover, escapes the danger arising from contamination. This is true as regards black sheep in all other bodies and communities. We are about to bring forward in a part of our remarks some curious modern instances of dishonesty on the part of shipowners and shipmasters, but we do not bring these cases forward with a view to charging shipowners as a class with dishonesty, nor with the view to proving that they require special looking after in the way of State inspection and Government interference. On the contrary, we intend to refer to these modern instances with the special object of showing that no State inspection can possibly affect them. If a scoundrel is anything but an out and out fool, his first care when he wants to commit a fraud on underwriters, will be to comply in every possible way with statutory regulations as to surveys, inspections, and classifications. The honest and general body of respectable shipowners comply with all statutory requirements with honesty of purpose and singleness of heart, out of regard for the general good; the rogue will comply with them with a view to removing suspicion, but not even with this view alone, for he will have the further object of obtaining the evidence of the whole staff of Government officials in his favour in the event of suspicion afterwards arising. The more rigid the forms, the more strict the survey, the more minute and maternal the interference, the more will he like it. What such a scoundrel would object to is, not surveys and inspections, but inquiry. His fervent prayer would be that, whilst he might have to comply with endless forms and ceremonies and inspections and other outward manifestations, he might be preserved from subsequent investigation. A fairly good ship, a decent crew, good wages, good insurance, an "eccentric" master or mate, and a prompt settlement, but no inquiry. Inquiry is the instrument "efficacious to his destruction," and is in fact to the rogue in such a case exactly what the Rev. Sidney Smith's "small-tooth comb" is to the set of vermin who would "banish" it.

To proceed then with the matter in hand—

1. A ship may be lost without any act of omission or commission on the part of her owner or master—

(a) By the act of God—i.e., perils of the sea, of the elements, etc.

(b) By the hands of the Queen's enemies.

(c) By wreckers, pirates, and others outside the ship compassing her loss.

(d) By collision with another ship.

(e) By error of judgment.

(f) By the bursting of boilers, the breaking down of machinery, and other circumstances arising within the ship.

(g) By the unavoidable removal of buoys, beacons, etc.

2. A ship may be lost by an act of omission or commission on the part of the owner or master—

(a) By direct and wilful casting away,

(b) By inattention to necessary repairs.

(c) By not providing proper apparel and equipments, or officers and crew.

(d) By overloading, or improper loading or stowage.

(e) By employing her in a trade for which she is unfit.

3. It is not to the interest of the shipowner to keep his ship afloat if she does not pay, or if by her loss he will be paid better than by employing her in trade.

4. If a ship is to be lost, it can generally be so arranged that her loss or abandonment shall be brought about in such a manner as to evade detection of fraud and escape punishment.

5. Ships lost are generally replaced by a better class of ship, nevertheless shipwrecks are a positive evil, inasmuch as that they are attended with loss of life, and with waste of valuable material and labour. A reference to the Board of Trade Wreck Register results in the important revelation that in ten years 16,882 wrecks and other casualties happened to ships on and near the coasts of the United 'Kingdom. The annual average for the last five years (1869) is 1893. The number of lives lost on our coasts in ten years is 8056. The number lost last year was 662. In addition to the disasters and loss of life happening to ships on and near our coasts, we have to bear in mind casualties and losses abroad and on the high seas.

If we turn to the records of Insurance we shall find that in the last five years 9999 sailing ships and 589 steamers have been entered in the lists as totally lost, in addition to 1093 ships and thirty-seven steamers constructively lost. This record refers to losses over the whole world of ships chiefly insured in the United Kingdom.

In addition to the losses on our coasts, of which the numbers are given above but included in the 9999 and 589, there are 846 ships and crews whose end is utterly unknown, 149 steamers out of the whole number of steamers lost, having been lost on voyages to and from ports on the east coast of Great Britain. All we know of the 846 "missing" ships is, that they left their last ports of departure, and that they have never since been heard of. All the owners know of them is, that if they were insured, the sum for which they were insured has been duly received. All the underwriters know is, that the ships were almost wholly underwritten as "staunch, tight, strong, and well found," and as "good ships," and that the insurance has been promptly settled. The ships are posted up as missing—the crews are missing, but are not posted up—the crews, the passengers, the widows and orphans left—but we must not enter into speculations. To treat this matter in the manner commonly known as " feeling" would be to travel altogether away from the object of the present paper. It is not our present intention to enlarge upon shipwrecks from a sentimental point of view, nor to "improve the occasion" by introducing a sermon. On the contrary, we are about to proceed altogether in cold blood, and in the most hard-hearted business-like manner possible. To accomplish the object we have in view, we must speak of the loss of a ship with no more apparent concern than of the loss of a tea-spoon. It is better for a surgeon to sew up a gash effectually and coolly, and without any display of feeling, rather than to enlarge and weep upon the enormities of vices in general, and of combative drunkenness in particular, while the wound remains unattended. There are plenty of people who can write sentimentally about shipwrecks and preach and weep (*teste* Mr. Plimsoll at Manchester). Let them indulge by all means; but although we shall be willing to appreciate the views of the sentimentalists and preachers and weepers, at some fitting opportunity, for the present we must treat dry facts in a dry and clear manner. Such is the sentiment attaching to ships and sailors and perils of the sea, that but few people are to be found who write and talk about them as reasonably as about anything else. Wrecks and casualties looked on in a matter-of-fact light and treated in a business manner' will at least possess the claim of novelty. Our only regret is, that owing to want of time and want of space, we cannot treat the subject so completely as we could wish. As regards time we can only write these articles in moments snatched from rest after a heavy day's work; and as regards space, the *Nautical Magazine* would have little room for more entertaining matter if we were to trespass beyond our present bounds. We hope that someone with more leisure and better opportunities will at some future time take up the whole subject of marine disasters, and investigate it as fully and minutely as its importance deserves.

We shall now take a glance at wrecks both wilful and accidental, and consider how far they are likely to be affected by Inquiries, Surveys, Certificates, and Insurance.

Accidental Wrecks, Strandings, etc .

We begin with these marine disasters in which there can be no allegation that the loss arises from acts of omission or commission on the part of the owner, master, or crew; and the question for consideration is whether preliminary inspection can prevent such losses; and if not whether they should be followed by inquiry. If there is no allegation of fraud or inadvertence on the part of the owner or his servants, the question that naturally suggests itself is, why there should be inquiry? The answer is obvious. Let us take the case of the London. This is a case in which no suspicion of any improper act ever has existed or over will exist. The ship was as fine a ship of her class and as strong a ship as ever went to sea; the owners, men of known respectability. There is no allegation of unseaworthiness and no suspicion of foul play. If anything has ever been placed beyond a doubt it is the fact that the owners acted honestly and in bond fides; and, moreover, in the opinion of every official who had to do with her the London was seaworthy and fit for her voyage, and yet she foundered. The same may be said of the City of Boston, and yet she disappeared. Here we have two ships eminent for their soundness and fitness for the voyage. Both had been surveyed by Government surveyors over and over again, and by other surveyors besides; both belonged to owners whose respectability and honesty are beyond question; both had been declared to and certified, and both were lost with an immense sacrifice of life. The surveying and inspecting by Government officers did not prevent these losses for the reason that they were owing to circumstances altogether beyond anything that can be met or prevented by Government inspecting and surveying. But because these losses were not and could not have been prevented by Government surveys, that is no reason why there should not be inquiry (an inquest) afterwards. In the case of the City of Boston there was a full and searching inquiry ("Inman v. Jenkins") at which we were present, and it was then established to demonstration that the ship was in perfect order when she left port, that she was underladen rather than overladen, and that she ought to have made the voyage in safety. In the case of the London there was also an inquiry, with a similar result. But the immediate effect of the London inquiry was to set everyone thinking about improved coverings for hatchways, and ever since then improvement has been steadily going on in that direction. We could, had we space, give a score of cases in which a surveyed and certified ship has been stranded, or wrecked, or has foundered, or has met with a casualty to her machinery, utterly beyond and beside anything that could be met by surveys and certificates, and entirely without any fault whatever on the part of her owners, in which subsequent inquiry has been the means of bringing about some important improvement, or of effecting good directly or indirectly. For instance, inquiry has led to the establishment of lifeboats or rocket apparatus, to the use of lifebelts, to the establishment of a lighthouse or light-vessel, to the correcting of charts and sailing directions, to the alteration in the character of a light, and to improved arrangements in steamships as regards valves, pumps, etc.; to the prosecution of wreckers, to the removal of coastguard-men, to the removal of obstructions to navigation, etc., etc. All emigrant ships and all passenger ships are surveyed, inspected, etc; and all their officers have certificates, and notwithstanding this surveying, and certificating, and inspecting, losses happen. The following cases prove this :—Royal Charter, 446 lives; Cambria, 180 lives; City of Boston, 191 lives; London, 233 lives; Pomona, 424 lives; Amazon, 100 lives; Annie Jane, 360 lives. Seven ships, with a total of 1,934 lives. All surveyed, all certificated, and all lost. On what grounds then can it be urged that certificating and surveying will materially lessen loss of life? Why did it not prevent the losses we have named? Simply because these large losses arise from circumstances altogether above and beyond anything that can be affected by certificates and surveys.

Casting Away.

This part of our subject is decidedly unpleasant, but its un-pleasantness must not hinder us from looking into it. We have often in discussions met with good and able men who profess not to believe that a shipowner can be found in Great Britain who would wilfully cast away a ship. The possession of such a belief always bespeaks a manly heart, a just appreciation of right and wrong, a fine sense of moral duty; but inasmuch as such a belief is utterly opposed to fact, no one holding it can grapple with the present subject. Many of our readers judging other men by their own honest selves will at once say that if we intend to assert that there are shipowners in this country, in the reign of Victoria, with a free Church, free education, and almost manhood suffrage, a liberal Government, and heaven knows what blessings and advantages besides, who will deliberately and intentionally send a ship to sea to be lost, we shall utter a monstrous libel on the British shipowner. We can only proceed to proofs. "'Tis true, 'tis pity; pity 'tis, 'tis true." In the early part of this paper we have stated honestly our opinion of the character of British shipowners as a class; we must now refer to the social vermin that exist in that class. It is not with a view to leading the reader to form a bad opinion of his fellow-man that we are compelled to be plain at this point. Nor is it with a view to shewing that extra special precautionary legislation is needed. Our object here as before is precisely the reverse, viz., to shew that surveys will not meet these cases, and that the present law with a little care or system on the part of underwriters is sufficient. Our statement is that ships are sometimes deliberately sent to sea to be lost; and that in such cases when the loss is well managed, the profits to the parties implicated are large and quite sufficient to compensate them for the risk incurred. The case of the Severn may be given as an illustration.

The following statement is abridged from the opening speech of Sir RICHARD KARSLAKE, Solicitor General.

The prisoners, CHARLES WILLIAM LEE WEBB, aged 29, sailor; THOMAS BERWICK, aged 42, sailor; LIONEL HOLDSWORTH, aged 41, broker; and JOSEPH STANSFIELD DEAN, aged 42, agent, stood indicted. * * * Substantially the charge resolved itself into this:— That the prisoners HOLDSWORTH and BERWICK, being interested in a vessel called the Severn, with the assistance of DEAN, who sometimes appears as a partner of HOLDSWORTH, sometimes as a clerk at HOLDSWORTH'S, and sometimes as a' firm carrying on business in the name of Allsopp and Co., assisted and aided in procuring the prisoner WEBB to cast away this vessel at the time she was on the high seas, for the purpose of defrauding certain insurance companies to an enormous extent, and reckless of the peril to the lives of the crew that might he entailed by this most wicked act. The four prisoners, Webb, Berwick, Holdsworth, and Dean began to be associated together in this particular transaction early in the year 1866. Berwick was a master mariner, who resided near Liverpool, and in the year 1865 he was the owner of a vessel called the Jane Broun. Of that vessel, Webb was the carpenter in the last voyage she ever made. That vessel was lost at sea.

The prisoner Holdsworth was, or professed to be, a ship insurance broker. He was intimately connected with Berwick. Dean was also at one time a Liverpool man. During the transactions which led to the purchase of the Severn, Dean acted as clerk apparently, although sometimes he said he was the partner of Holdsworth. At other times, later in the year, he appears to have acted as Allsopp and Co.

In the beginning of that year (1866) Holdsworth interested himself in looking out for a vessel which would suit the purposes that the parties had in view. The object of the prisoners Holdsworth and Berwick was, beyond all doubt, to get the ship into their possession without having to find cash to pay for her.

The result was that for no cash payment at all the Severn found her way, nominally, into the hands of A. B., and actually, into the hands of Holdsworth and Berwick. That transaction having been completed, the vessel which is represented by Holdsworth in a letter to be in perfectly good order and condition, was to be sent round to Newport for the purpose of being loaded with coals. A question arose as to who should be the officers of the ship. Berwick said that the mate of the vessel was to be Webb, the prisoner, who had been the carpenter on board a vessel the Jane Brown, in which Berwick was unquestionably interested, and in which Holdsworth appears to have been interested also. This vessel was lost at sea, and with regard to her Webb made a statement that he had himself sunk the vessel by boring heles in her, as he afterwards did in the Severn. Webb was the person selected to be the mate. Holdsworth was to select a captain, and he chose a man under whom Webb was to serve as mate, a man who had been commander of a vessel called the Thomas, which, as a matter of fact, also foundered at sea. Berwick and Holdsworth represented Webb as an eccentric sort of man, from whom the master had better keep to some extent aloof, and not watch too narrowly his eccentricities. There were other conversations coming nearer and nearer the point to be achieved; and eventually the master was told that the Severn would never reach Shanghae. Then Berwick and Holdsworth getting bolder, the master was told that he was to connive at the act of Webb in casting the vessel away, and that what was in contemplation would put £700 in his pocket. Webb was found to be, as he had been described, somewhat eccentric; but the master was told by Holdsworth that he must put up with him as well as he could. The Severn was coppered higher than was usual; and she was tight and staunch in every respect.

Insurances amounted to some fourteen or fifteen thousand pounds, the freight alone being insured for a sum of £3,300. But not content with their insuring the vessel above its value, the Captain was offered £10 by another party if he would allow certain packages to be carried into his cabin; and he agreed to do so for that sum. He did take them into his cabin, and the £10 was actually paid to him. Upon these cases, said to contain arms, an insurance for £1,500 was effected. The arms wore said to consist of carbines, revolvers, and swords. But what were the actual contents of these cases which had been insured for £1,500?: These packages actually contained nothing but about £4 worth of salt.

After the trial, Inspector COZENS stepped into the witness-box and handed a document to Mr. Justice BLACKBURN. His Lordship said: I see that this is a warrant for the apprehension of Berwick, granted by the Liverpool magistrates, and charging him with scuttling the Kate Kearney. It has not been executed, has it?

Inspector COZENS: No, my Lord; the Captain went abroad for some considerable time, and the warrant could not be executed in consequence of his absence.

Mr. LEWIS: There is also, my Lord, a list of ships belonging to Berwick and Holdsworth, which I will hand up to you. Extract from the list, referred to by Mr. Lewis, of ships belonging to Berwick and Holdsworth.[427]

Mr. Justice BLACKBURN, in passing sentence, said: Prisoners,—After a very long and protracted trial, on evidence which is to my mind perfectly satisfactory, the jury have convicted each of you, and I think they came to a perfectly right decision. What you have urged, Holdsworth, is that in this case there has been perjured evidence against you.

I cannot bring my mind to believe that it is in any way consistent with the evidence to suppose that you could have honestly made these insurances, and endeavoured to collect them when the ship was, as I am thoroughly convinced, intended to be scuttled from the first, and was so scuttled.

You were acting for persons who sent out the ship that it might be lost. It was a part of the trade, which I am sorry to hear is carried on to a considerable extent. The ship was sent out to be lost; and you, acting as a broker, were quite aware of that. As for you, Berwick, the evidence in your case leads me very clearly to the conclusion that you were the person who sent out the ship as part of that trade. Moreover, the prosecuting counsel inform me that there are other cases, in several of which you were concerned, of ships having been lost, and certainly there is evidence in this very case that your name and repute were such among the underwriters that you could not insure the ship in your own name, and consequently it was necessary for you to register the ship in another name, or otherwise you could not have insured it.

It is a dangerous crime which you have com-mitted, for a ship cannot be cast away so as to lead the underwriters to suppose it perished by the perils of the sea, without exposing the lives of all who are on board.

The sentence which I shall pass upon you—and I can pass no lighter one—is that you, BERWICK and HOLDSWORTH, be each kept in penal servitude for the term of twenty years. You, WEBB, have committed a very bad offence.

It was actually your hand which executed the boring of the holes. I must pass upon you a sentence of ten years' penal servitude. As for you, DEAN, I shall take into consideration that the jury recommended you to mercy as being under the influence of Holdsworth. I cannot, however, believe that you could possibly have done innocently what you did as to the bill of lading, and as to the insurance of the £1,500 on the cases, I consider it to be an utter impossibility that you could have done that honestly.

I feel myself bound to pass upon you a sentence of penal servitude, but it will be the lightest sentence which the law allows me to pass. It is that you be kept in penal servitude for the term of five years.

The case of the Severn affords a splendid illustration of the demoralization that attends systematic wrecking; but it does not, strange as it is, convey any idea of the whole of that demoralization. The whole facts can only be appreciated by also including the proceedings of salvors and wreckers. Where a ship is sent down at sea it is bad enough, but when she is, by preconcerted agreement, taken to some convenient rock, or reef, or sandbank, and there wrecked, after due understanding between the master of the ship and the wreckers or salvors as to the division of the plunder, the case becomes infinitely worse. It has not been an uncommon circumstance in the history of wrecking for a master or owner of a ship to pre-arrange with wreckers hundreds of miles away that his ship shall get ashore at a particular place, on a particular voyage, on the understanding that he (the master or owner) shall have a stipulated sum for his part in the transaction. No amount of State inspection will prevent losses of this sort: but subsequent inquiry brings out the facts and leads to punishment. Is not opposition to inquiry, by such persons as Holdsworth, Webb, Berwick, and Dean, in the case of the Severn, an exact parallel to the case given by the Rev. Sydney Smith, of a certain class of vermin objecting to the "small-tooth comb "?

Inquiries into Minor Acts of Misconduct

We now have to consider cases of misconduct. Acts not arising from a determined intention to act dishonestly, but still serious and prejudicial: such cases as drunkenness, negligence, foolhardiness, error of judgment, etc., etc. Here again inquiry is necessary, but there are many persons who object to inquiry altogether, and many others who think that the tribunals before which these cases are at present tried, are not proper tribunals for the purpose. With the latter of these, to a great extent we cordially agree; with the former, we have no agreement whatever.

As regards the value of the present tribunal, let us take the case of a master or other officer charged with drunkenness. An inquiry is certainly necessary, but the nature of the charge seems to us to place it among those which should be investigated by a Police Magistrate. Such cases are now often tried by a Local Marine Board. Now a Local Marine Board is elected by shipowners, and consists wholly and solely of representatives of ship-owners. The only qualification of an elector is, that he shall be a shipowner of the port where the Local Marine Board is to be established. A Local Marine Board trying a master or a seaman, is simply a tribunal of employers trying the employed. We do not assert that the employers in these cases have been unjust in their decisions, but we do most emphatically assert that such a tribunal is opposed to all sense of justice, and that in no other case would it be tolerated; and we can only hope that some other tribunal may be found.

There is at present also a tribunal to which graver cases are referred, such as strandings, abandonment, etc., etc.—viz., two Justices of the Peace or a Police Magistrate, assisted by two nautical assessors. This tribunal is a very good one for many cases, but as regards others its associations are against it. It is manifestly degrading to a nautical man to find himself in a police court (in which brawlers and low people of all sorts are constantly tried), to be tried on some professional or technical point involving a question of scientific skill or of alleged professional negligence. Here again, whilst we feel bound to object to the tribunal, we feel equally bound to bear testimony to the fact that the cases have been conducted with skill and care, and that substantial justice has always been done. We also think it right to declare emphatically that although the decisions have often been objected to, they have never once been proved to be wrong. The patience of the magistrates, and the professional skill of the assessors are beyond question. One point is strongly in favour of this system, viz., that the extent to which their righteous decisions have caused certain classes to cry out, shews that the work has been well and effectively done. Still our objection to the tribunal remains, and we would say, by all means continue the system of inquiry, but let us, if possible, get rid of the police court associations.

We hope that British shipmasters will not cry out against inquiries, lest the cause of their cries be mistaken.

Inquiries on the High Seas and Abroad

By the 260th Section of the Merchant Shipping Act, 1854—

Any officer in command of any ship of Her Majesty on any foreign station, or, in the absence of such officer, any consular officer may summon a court, to be termed a naval court, in the following cases, i.e.:—

(1) Whenever a complaint which appears to such officer to require immediate investigation is made to him by the master of any British ship, or by any certificated mate, or by one or more of the seamen belonging to any such ship.

(2) Whenever the interest of the owner of any British ship, or of the cargo of any such ship, appears to such officer to require it.

(3) Whenever any British ship is wrecked, or abandoned, or otherwise lost, at or near the place where such officer may be; or whenever the crew, or part of the crew of any British ship, which has been wrecked, abandoned, or lost abroad arrives at such place.

A naval court consists of not less than three and not more than five members, of whom, generally, one is a consular officer, one a naval officer, not below the rank of lieutenant, one the master of a British merchant ship, and the other persons eligible as members are naval officers, British masters, and British merchants. These naval courts have large powers. They may supersede the master, may discharge seamen, may settle questions of wages, fines, and forfeiture, may make orders as to the costs of the court, may send officers home for trial, and may cancel or suspend the certificates of masters, mates, and engineers. These courts have been of immense benefit to commercial interests. It can be readily understood that a body of men like seamen, away from the tribunals of their own country, may get impatient of discipline; and that masters away from the check of the owners, and from the jurisdiction of the ordinary courts of law, are likely occasionally to commit acts requiring investigation; or to get into quarrels that can only be settled by someone outside the ship. The naval court exactly meets these cases. There is, probably, no tribunal better fitted for investigating the ordinary questions concerning the safety of a ship, the competency of her officers, and her discipline, than these courts. They are free from the objections taken to Local Marine Board investigations, and to enquiries in police courts. There is not, so far as we are aware, any valid objection to them.

Preliminary Inquiries or Inquests

Under the Merchant Shipping Act, 1854, sections 432 to 448, inquiry is to be instituted—

Whenever any ship is lost, abandoned, or materially damaged on or near the coasts of the United Kingdom.

Whenever any ship causes loss or material damage to any other ship on or near such coasts.

Whenever by reason of any casualty happening to or on board of any ship on or near such coasts, loss of life ensues.

Whenever any such loss, abandonment, damage, or casualty happens else-where, and any competent witnesses thereof arrive or are found at any place in the United Kingdom.

And whenever any ship has been in distress on the coasts of the United Kingdom.

These preliminary inquiries or inquests are held by receivers of wreck, with the assistance of officers of coastguard, or other professional seamen as assessors. The instructions issued by the Board of Trade to officers making these inquiries are as follows :—

In cases where a casualty happens on the coast, and the ship or any of her crew are still there, the officers named above will proceed to the spot as soon as possible, and make the inquiry before any of the necessary witnesses leave.

In cases where the casualty happens at sea, or off the coasts, and any of the crew or other witnesses arrive at any place within the officer's district, he will make the inquiry in like manner. In cases where he thinks it probable that other important witnesses can be found elsewhere, he will give notice to the officer of the district in which they are to be found, in order that the latter officer may make inquiry.

In making the inquiry, the attention of the officer is specially directed to the question whether the casualty happened from avoidable or unavoidable causes. Amongst the former his attention is particularly directed to the following:

Unseaworthiness or insufficient equipment of the ship. In-sufficient or improper manning. Improper loading, over-loading, and bad stowage. Explosions arising from the insufficiency of boilers and machinery. Misconduct, incompetency, or neglect on the part of the master, officers, or crew. Neglect of the regulations for preventing collisions at sea. Ignorance of lights or other sea– marks, or of the navigation of the sea or coast. Neglect of heaving the lead. Too great speed under the circumstances. Non-employment of qualified pilots. Ignorance, incompetency, or misconduct of pilots. Defective charts. Defective or improperly adjusted compasses. Deficiencies in the lights, leading marks or buoys on the coast. Want of harbours of refuge or other means of safety.

In making inquiry on the subject of harbours of refuge, the officer is directed to ascertain and state as accurately as he can, whether one of the harbours of refuge recommended by the Royal Commissioners would have probably saved the ship, and if so, which of them. In all cases where there is any point which it is important to establish, or any question of fact in dispute or in doubt, he takes the evidence in writing.

It is out of these preliminary inquiries that most of the formal investigations have arisen. There is not a wreck or a casualty of any magnitude on the coasts of the United Kingdom, nor of any British ship on the coasts of our Colonies that is not followed by a preliminary inquiry, and the evidence taken is always used in subsequent proceedings, whether by owners, salvors, or underwriters. Looking to the fact that the evidence is obtained on the spot, while the facts are fresh, and before a garbled statement can be prepared, they are undoubtedly of more value than evidence taken elsewhere. They supersede the formal notarial protests, in some cases a mere ingenious tissue of lies, or a tissue of lies without even the merit of ingenuity. The evidence obtained in these inquiries is always referred to in the Admiralty court, and is held to be of most vital importance by underwriters, salvors, owners, etc.; but naturally enough the inquiries are stoutly objected to by the persons whose conduct is called in question. The fact that these persons cry out so piteously tends to prove that the inquests are probing the wound, and are doing their work.

Compulsory Surveys

The hull, machinery, and equipments of all passenger steamers arc surveyed and certificated every six months, and all emigrant ships are surveyed every voyage; but notwithstanding these inspections and certificates, and notwithstanding the various means for inquiry to which we have referred, there are innumerable preventible losses on our coasts and at sea. The life lost is chiefly out of surveyed and certificated ships; but a great number of preventible losses happen to ships unsurveyed and unclassed, and the question is how shall the casualties be lessened. Some people think that the present law is sufficient if it is only carried into effect, and others think that inspection of every ship in the mercantile marine is necessary, practicable, and desirable. It is not enough to shew these latter people that the greatest loss of life happens in wrecks of ships actually inspected. It is not enough to shew them that the mere fact of a hull and her equipment being certificated, and of her officers being certificated, does not and cannot affect most of the causes leading to the loss of life at sea. It is enough for them to know that a great number of wrecks happen, and that some ships are old and unseaworthy: and the remedy immediately suggested is a wholesale periodical survey of every ship afloat, with extra surveys on change of cargoes. Argument is useless with such people, reason is thrown away. The system they propose would however simply be madness and would end in legal and certified losses, instead of as now leaving the question of the cause of loss open for inquiry. The advocates of wholesale inspection are running in the dark, they will not be warned by figures like these we have given above, nor will they learn wisdom from the practice in the United States. There the machinery and boilers of every steamship are built under inspection, the very plates of the boilers are certified before they are put in; repairs may only be made where, and when, and how the Government Surveyor directs; there are minute regulations as to the working boilers, the height of water, the pressure of the steam, the safety valves, etc., and yet explosions on board United States steamers are more numerous and more terrible than explosions on board any other steamships. The reason is obvious, for with all the minute statutory regulations, interfering with the business of the shipowner, it would be unreasonable to held him responsible. If he complies with the law and gets his certificate, his responsibility practically ends, and he himself is not actuated by any fear of loss for the consequences of blowing up his passengers. There is no use in blinking the matter any longer, if we are to go on meddling and muddling, and certifying, we must in common honesty remove responsibility from the owners. Let anyone contemplate such a state of things applied in other cases; let him imagine every Railway Board relieved of all responsibility for the lives of passengers, so long as certain regulations are complied with and certified to. Does any sane man think that fewer lives would be lost under such a system than are lost at present? And yet this is precisely what these persons who agitate for wholesale inspection and certificates are driving us to. Every compulsory survey followed by certificate, tends to lessen the owner's responsibility; and every step by which that responsibility is lessened, endangers life to that extent.

Still after all said and done it must be admitted that some rotten ships are knowingly sent to sea. It is a scandal that can and ought to be stopped. The "finger and thumb" must be ruthlessly plied, regardless of the cries of the little victims, who make their livelihood by owning "floating coffins." It is a well-known fact that seamen over and over again go to prison rather than to sea, and it is equally well-known that they have now no power of appeal to open inquiry. We have reason to hope that under Mr. Fortescue's Bill means will be adopted to discover whether the seamen are right or wrong in their objections to a ship, and that measures will be taken which will lead to the breaking up of an unseaworthy ship quietly ashore, instead of on some rock in the Bahamas or the Baltic, or instead of her finding a grave in mid-ocean.

By all means let some department of the State investigate allegations of rottenness and unseaworthiness; let the seamen have fair play in such cases; and when a ship is rotten let her be condemned and broken up. But such measures need not worry and delay the business of every shipowner in the United Kingdom. It may possibly be necessary to break up by the strong hand of the law many ships that ought to have been broken up before, but because this is so, it does not follow that every ship afloat should be surveyed and certified. If the law lays it down clearly that the owner is bound to send his ship to sea in a seaworthy condition and properly manned, the seamen and their friends will very soon do what is necessary to enforce the law.

Our paper would hardly be complete without a reference to the subject of -

Insurance

By the English law the assured may by previous agreement with the underwriter determine the amount to be paid by the latter to the former in case of total loss. It is obviously to the advantage of insurer and insured that value should be agreed upon by both parties before insurance is effected: and it is only in cases in which over valuation is found to be fraudulent that the underwriter can escape payment. Excessive valuation is not in itself sufficient to render the contract invalid. Excess may point towards fraud; but fraud alone opens a valuation.

As between the assured and the underwriter no harm is done by allowing a previous statement and agreement of value; but as regards the public, the system of valued policies opens the door to immorality. It renders possible, and directly encourages deviation from commercial rectitude. Of such deviation, the case of the Severn, already referred to, may be taken as an example. Seeing that the system of valued policies opens the door to fraud, many remedies have been attempted, and many suggested with a view to placing a limit on agreed value as between underwriter and assured. Wagering policies are forbidden by law, but who is to say where legitimate valuation ends and wagering begins?

We have already stated that it is not to the interest of a ship-owner to keep his ship afloat, if by losing her he can make more than by employing her. The fact that losses are more numerous in seasons when freight is low, would appear to shew that this is fully appreciated. What we have always felt in discussing questions concerning ships, is that very many points are simple and straightforward in themselves, but the moment the element of insurance is introduced they become complicated, and to a great extent immoral.

It is a remarkable fact that uninsured ships are, as a rule, safer and longer-lived than these insured. We are acquainted with a shipowner who has had but two losses in about forty years, who never insures, and who, in times of depression, has been able to work his ships at a profit when other owners were doing badly: this gentleman would make nothing by losing a ship, and would probably save about £15,000 to £18,000 a year by not insuring. To illustrate the comparative danger of insured ships we shall now refer to certain losses in which there exists no allegation of fraud, or wagering, or over-valuation. In the cases we are about to quote everything appears to have been fair and above board, strictly legal, and we may add, as we conscientiously believe, strictly honest. The comparison we are about to make is between the losses of British certified steamships, and Swedish certified steamships. The facts will be found in the parliamentary papers, and are striking. It appears that in 1868 there were 220 sea going steamships in Sweden. In the year 1867 there were 215 sea going coasting steamers in Great Britain. The numbers are peculiarly close, 220 Swedish to 215 British. The ships in both cases were steam coasters, they were in both cases certified and inspected, and in both eases commanded by certificated officers. In the ten years ended 1867 seventeen of the British coasters were lost under circumstances calling for inquiry. In the ten years ended 1867 three only of the Swedish steamers were lost; and the losses of British ships in the Baltic, as compared with Swedish ships there, in the ten years ended 1868, were ten British as against three Swedish. The Swedish ships were totally uninsured. They could have been insured, but owing to the character of their officers and crews, the owners did not think it necessary. It must not be forgotten, that what is possible in Sweden and in other countries with a small mercantile marine, is utterly impossible in a country like ours with an enormous mercantile marine. In Sweden the people are cautious, diligent, and attentive to small points, whereby it happens that their ships are navigated and that goods are carried in them with more care and with greater attention to details of safety, etc., and that cargoes of Swedish ships are, as a rule, delivered in better order than cargoes of English vessels. Our seamen, reckless, brave, riotous, do not shun danger like other seamen. The characteristics of our people render impossible the same methods of procedure as those adopted by others less adventurous and more careful. There can be no doubt that of a certain given number of ships belonging to the various maritime countries and states, the highest percentage of losses will be in the British or American ships, and this is owing to the "go ahead" character of their masters, officers, and crews, as compared with the masters, officers, and crews of ships of other countries and states. Our legitimate losses will always be higher because we run more (legitimate) risks. To lessen losses from these (legitimate) risks we must change the characteristics of the Anglo Saxon race. Our illegitimate or fraudulent losses will also always be higher, because, owing to the vastness of our business in connection with ships, frauds are more easily concocted and less easily detected with us than with our more easy going and less occupied neighbours. To lessen the fraudulent losses has ever been the desire of thinking men. Fraudulent losses would cease to pay if over insurances were rendered impossible. Many thinkers have therefore attempted or suggested a remedy in the direction of limiting insurance.

A suggestion having this object in view has been made that every ship, besides having an official registered name and number, shall have a declared and registered value, which may be called her official value; and that this official value shall be that on which dock dues and light dues shall be levied, and liability, etc., be calculated and paid. This official value it is proposed shall be stated and declared at the commencement of every voyage, and shall be binding for the voyage, and for all results of the voyage, both for and against the owner. It is then further proposed that to insure a ship for the whole of her declared or official value, shall be rendered absolutely illegal. A gentleman eminently qualified to give an opinion on the subject writes as follows:

"I would propose that instead of a liability of £8 per ton for property, and £15 per ton for life and property together, as now, it should be a proportion of the value of the ship, say for example, half for property, and three-fourths for life and property together, or any other proportion of value thought to be more equitable.

"That for the purpose of ascertaining such value, the owner, agent, or captain be required to declare the same at the Custom House on entering the vessel outwards upon any intended voyage, such valuation to be perfectly voluntary as to amount, but when once made, to be binding for that voyage, and for all results of the same, both for and against the owner of the vessel.

"That should the owner, agent, or captain omit or refuse to so declare the value, the customs shall assess it prior to permitting the ship to be cleared outwards, and such assessment shall be taken as the value both for and against the owner for such intended voyage, and for all results of the same, and shall remain in force until the owner or his agent shall give his own valuation; such new valuation, if given, to apply to any subsequent voyage, so soon as the vessel shall have completed the one already commenced, and have been moored for twenty-four hours in good safety.

The principle of liability, proportionate to value, I venture to think, would be more equitable as relating alike to steamers,—of which the average value is much more than £15 per ton, —and to sailing vessels,—many of which, of course fall far below that value,—than the one at present in use by which both are liable for an equal amount per ton, although their values are so exceedingly different."

"The voluntary valuation of his ship by the owner for all purposes before commencing a voyage, and so prior to any accident occurring thereout, would greatly tend to prevent disputes in subsequent events, and, if it were thought desirable, a power of appeal to an authoritative assessment of value might still be retained in favour of any parties aggrieved, excepting the owner who had voluntarily given his own valuation; although, judging from the very rare instances of 'opening the valuation' occurring in the case of goods valued in a policy, it would in practice seldom be required in reference to ships."

In some countries by express law, and in others by custom, insurance is limited to a proportion (say three-fourths) of the value of the property. The Right Hon. Stephen Cave, M.P., in speaking of this subject, stated—

"When these questions were laid before me in former days, three remedies were constantly pressed upon me. One was to limit the insurance, and the, other was to declare the sending of a ship to sea in an unseaworthy condition to be a misdemeanour; and the third was to have a loading line. I have always been in favour of the limitation of the insurance, but an opposite opinion prevailed among some members, and perhaps that opinion was right."

In the United Kingdom the principle of limited insurance is acted on in many of the country clubs, especially in Wales; but these clubs all have surveyors, by whom the ships are surveyed and valued before insurance is effected. They know each other's ships, and this knowledge and the usual jealousies, prevent concealment of defects. Such a system, although workable in country clubs, where weeks can be taken over one transaction, is deemed to be impossible in large communities, where business to the extent of £1,000,000 may be done in six hours. Underwriting, to be carried on as at present in such places as London and Liverpool and other great commercial centres, must be carried on with facility and despatch. To keep premiums up, the element of competition should be excluded, and large companies, or very respectable persons alone should be allowed to underwrite. But to keep premiums down, every company should be allowed to compete with every other company, and every member of a company with any member of the same or any other company. Premiums are lower now than ever. A London underwriter does not enter into minute details of particular defects; he calculates and takes his risks by actuarial rules, the result of general deductions from broad premises. An underwriter who, before under-writing any risk, would make inquiries into every minute detail of the build and equipment of the ship, the character and antecedents of her master, owner, etc., would never be able to do any business in London. An insurer, as a rule, seldom sees a ship and never sees a cargo he insures. An underwriter, sitting in his room in London, insures property in ships at Hamburgh, New York, Bombay, Calcutta, Sydney, etc., etc., as well as in ships in various places in the United Kingdom; he cannot, therefore, by any possibility make personal inspection or even personal inquiry. It may be asked, Why then should he underwrite in such cases? This is a very proper question for anyone to put who is not acquainted with the business of underwriting, but to anyone who is acquainted with that business the question is ridiculous. A merchant having to send home £100,000 worth of goods from the East, insures the whole to be sent home by a ship or ships. He insures partly in London, and at the time he insures, even the ships by which the goods are to be sent home may not yet have arrived in the East, and are not known to him. Underwriting is a business done on trust and mutual understanding—it is essentially a traffic of confidence. To prevent underwriting would really be to stop commerce. Facilities for underwriting are a commercial necessity; to interfere with those facilities would be to hamper commerce by delays and to raise premiums. To raise premiums is to put a heavy burden on shipping. Underwriting is an absolute necessity, and its accompanying frauds are, we fear, an inevitable part of it. Admiral Halstead, the late Secretary of Lloyd's, in speaking on this subject at the United Service Institution, said:—

"The remedy for shipwrecks?" I do not pretend for one instant to be able to provide a remedy, and I do not know anybody who can undertake to say what is the remedy for shipwrecks; but I will tell you this. If I could go on the Stock Exchange to-morrow morning, and by holding-up my hand could put a stop to all future shipwrecks upon the coast—(I am now speaking advisedly)— It would be a question how I should get safe with life off that Exchange. I do not know whether there be present or not a party more interested probably than most of us, who I may term a representative underwriter of Lloyd's, and with whom upon this very subject I had a very interesting communication of some hours not more than a week or ten days ago. When I put that position to him, he said, "It is perfectly true; you would stop our bread." I may say that this is not at all an individual case. There is the statement which was made to me the other day openly; it was not in secret; it was said openly and publicly at Lloyd's, that the whole question of our insurance did involve more or less of fraud, and that ships are purposely wrecked."

The rapidity and facility with which insurances are, and must necessarily be, effected, must, of course, directly open the door to fraud; and it so happens that ships and cargoes that have never existed have been insured, and it is not until a heavy claim is made for a fraudulent loss, or accident discloses the particulars, that the fraud is found out. As examples we may mention the cases of the Poseidon and the James. One of her Majesty's consular officers invented a ship which, in his capacity as Godfather, he called the Poseidon; and he then invented a cargo of oil, which, in his exceedingly fertile imagination, he shipped at Adramytti. He then issued "a clean bill of health" for the ship, which is in effect the same as a Custom House clearance, and it was said that she sailed from Adramytti. Insurances were duly effected in London on the mythical ship and cargo to the extent of £12,000. He subsequently caused a report to be sent to Lloyd's that a vessel had been seen burning at sea off the Isle of Lemnos. To the astonishment of everyone but the consular officer, the Poseidon did not arrive in England: and in due course he produced a certificate of a Greek consular agent that the Poseidon belonged to Tenedos, that she left Tenedos to load oil, and that no news had been heard of her. He also produced a certificate to the effect that burnt ship timber had been seen at sea, as well as certificates as to the clean bill of health, that the ship did load oil at Adramytti, and that she did actually sail for England. And yet the whole was a pure invention from beginning to end. The consul was unfortunate in being detected and adequately punished, but compared with real cases like the Severn, in which life is often sacrificed to obtain premiums, the Poseidon was a practical joke, improper and fraudulent, but playful and harmless.

So also was the case of the mythical smack James, and her equally mythical cargo of bloaters. This is the next case we mention, but it is not by upwards of a score the next in rotation. In the case of the James, one Brown, describing himself as a fish curer at Gravesend, called at the offices of the Monarch Insurance Company, and effected a policy of insurance on the smack James and 100 barrels of herrings for £200 on a voyage from London to Fecamp. A week afterwards he called again at the same office, accompanied by a boy named Terry, and told a pitiful story to the effect that the vessel sailed from the Thames on a certain day with the master, Thomas Moore, the mate, another man, himself and Terry on board; that on the following day (Sunday) about noon she struck upon a piece of floating wreck about two miles off the North Foreland, and almost immediately afterwards sank; that the master, mate, and another man went down with her; that he and the boy Terry, who were in the cabin at the time of the collision, barely escaped with their lives in the boat of the smack, and were afterwards picked up by a French lugger and landed at Margate on the same (Sunday) evening, whence they were sent to London by the agent of the Shipwrecked Mariners' Society. The circumstances so stated were afterwards embodied at the instance of the prisoner Brown in a formal protest, the truth of which both prisoners declared before Mr. George Matthew Arnold, a notary at Gravesend, and upon the production of that and the observance of other formalities the insurance company handed the prisoner a cheque for £200, the amount of the policy. It was afterwards proved that the boy Terry was at home at Gravesend on the Sunday until after the time at which the smack was alleged to have sunk, and that about three o'clock that afternoon the prisoner Brown and he took train at Gravesend and proceeded to Margate, where they arrived about five o'clock. They then proceeded to the jetty, where they were seen about six o'clock, and about eight the same evening they called there upon Mr. Strauack, of the Shipwrecked Mariners' Society, and having told him the story of having been shipwrecked and landed that evening at the jetty by a French lugger by which they had been picked up, he gave them money to buy provisions and a free passage to London. There was evidence to show that there was no such smack as the James, that no cargo of herrings had been shipped by the prisoner Brown from London to Fecamp, and that in short the whole story told by him and on which he obtained the £200 from the Insurance Company was a fabrication from beginning to end. It transpired also that the prisoner Brown had previously effected policies in five different offices for £1,330 altogether, and received the whole of the money.

Mr. Justice BYLES, in passing sentence, said: The case against Brown was very serious, and an offence which it was necessary to put down by a severe sentence, especially now that the charges for insurance were so very low, and insurance companies were entirely at the mercy of persons who were not more restrained by principle than the prisoner. The sentence was that he be kept in penal servitude for fifteen years.

So long as underwriters do their business in such a rapid manner as at present, taking no means, or at all events, no adequate means to ascertain the state or even the existence of property they are insuring, it is indeed a hard case if a designing man cannot sometimes make them suffer; and were it not that life is often lost in the transaction, our sympathies would be with the sharp defrauders rather than the underwriters, because their business encourages attempts at fraud. In Italy, France, and Spain, where the mercantile marines are small, and where all sorts of formal pre-cautions are taken, frauds are not uncommon. For instance, it is not long ago that some speculators obtained possession of certain ships, seven in all, comparatively worthless, insured them, lost them, and recovered insurance. One of the ships was partly insured in London, about £12,000 was the London risk, and she was wrecked near our coasts. Her reputed cargo was wines, liqueurs, etc., but was in reality rubbish, brown paper, etc. The outside value was not more than £500. We refer to these instances of fraudulent wrecks of foreign-owned ships to shew that all the care of a continental system does not prevent them, and we could give many similar cases of Spanish, French, Italian, American, and other ships.

Whatever our legislature may do in the matter of unseaworthy ships will be a step towards assisting the underwriters, and the underwriters on their part ought to set on foot some organization or system whereby certain men will forever be placed in their black books; they ought also to look out lest "for a consideration" some old Trapbois allows his name to be used to cover the designs of an owner on the black book.

Seeing that ships and cargoes must continue to be insured, the next question for consideration is, whether insurance cannot be limited to say three-fourths of value. We can only now glance at it, but it is to be hoped that someone may be found to go to the bottom of the subject at an early day.

If ships are over-valued for the sake of recovering a good round sum in case of loss, we must not forget that the premiums paid are on the assured value. An over insurance of £5000 imposes a burthen of £600 a year. If instead of assuring to the whole four-fourths of value, an owner could insure only to three-fourths, he would pay only three-fourths of the premiums. Assuming that at present an owner can overvalue a whole ship, he could of course also grossly overvalue three-fourths or four-fifths of her. The only difference would be that in one case, the latter, he would perhaps practise on a lesser sum, whilst he would pay less premiums than in the other case. In Spain, where the limit is two-thirds, the owner always overvalues so as to cover the whole interest. If it were only possible that the value of a ship could be put down at a certain sum per ton for all purposes both for and against the owner as proposed, then the proposed limitation of assurance would be easy, but would still, we think, be unjust. We shall, however, shew that a ship cannot be of one and the same value for all purposes, and that, therefore, she cannot be declared to be so. Valuation necessarily divides itself into four heads:— (1) Valuation between underwriters and assured. This is almost the only means of fraud, and yet it can never be done away with. (2) Valuation for general contribution. This has nothing whatever to do with value for insurance. (3) Admiralty court value for salvage. (4) Statutory value for cases of collision, etc. These values are all independent of each other, and must remain so. If A, one ship– owner, were to be liable to B, another ship-owner, according to the value fixed by A and B together, it would be to A's advantage to fix the value no higher than the market value, and it would not be to B's detriment, because B could get no more than that sum in the market; but in a matter of insurance between A, a shipowner, and C, an underwriter, such a value might be obviously unjust to A.

By the present law an owner is by no means required in a valued policy to fix the value of his ship, at what she will sell for at the moment in the market at the place where the insurance is effected. It would be most unfair to compel him to do so. A ship specially built and fitted up for a special trade, say for laying a telegraph cable, for summer traffic with holiday-makers in the Highlands, for raising heavy weights and wrecks, for docking ships and vessels (the Bermuda Dock) for a special intercolonial or foreign trade, any one of such vessels might and probably would fetch in the ordinary market almost nothing,—but for her owner's purposes she would be especially valuable, and may actually have cost more than any ordinary ship of similar tonnage. She may be sent to her destination by a special crew in a special manner at great cost. On the one hand the owner of the ship who has been at special expense not only in fitting her out but in sending her specially to her work, would be hardly dealt by if he could only insure her for what she would fetch at a certain place at a particular time; but on the other hand because he has insured her for a sum that really represents her lowest value to him, it would not be just to say that as regards damage done to another ship or to life, such a special ship should also be assessed at the high value for which she is insured. Take the case of collision between two ships of similar size. If A the ordinary and less expensive one were in fault, her owner would be liable to B to the extent of say £20,000, whereas if B were in fault, he would be liable to A under precisely similar circumstances for say £40,000, this not because she was in any way for sea-going purposes or trade a better ship than A's ship, but either because she had cost more, or because her loss would involve her owner in greater pecuniary losses than the loss of an ordinary ship, and he had insured her for more.

Again, in the case of a ship built and sent out for a special purpose, or as in the case of wreck raising or telegraph cable laying ships kept idle half the year. If value is to be taken as a basis on which to pay dues, these dues could only equitably be levied on the stated value whilst the ship is employed on her special work. This would give rise to all sorts of complications, and as regards dock owners, it is not easy to understand why they should charge one of two ships A twice as much as B if A and B are both of the same tonnage and size and occupy a like amount of dock space, merely because owing to the special purposes for which A is required, her owner has had to lay out on her and insure her for twice as much as has been laid out on B. If however, the proposed official valuation is not intended to apply to ships in dock we should have two values, one for voyages and one for port purposes.

Again, supposing that A wants to sell his ship, is the declaration of value to nullify the sale or prevent the sale if he cannot get the fixed value for her? Probably that is not the intention of the proposer, but considering that a ship can be and often is sold during her voyage, and considering that the official value shall be the value for all purposes for and against the owner, it might have this effect; and if it is not intended to have the effect of preventing a sale for less than the declared value, then a fraudulent or colourable sale for a small sum would interfere with the whole arrangement.

And again, supposing that A were to run into dock gates or through a jetty, the stoppage of the whole business of that dock or of that jetty might result, and the actual loss inflicted on the owner might be much more than the official value of the ship, and life might be lost besides. It is surely better to leave the liability of the owner unlimited in such a case (as at present), than by limiting it in one case and for one purpose to inflict positive injustice in other cases. The proposed scheme of official value necessarily provides that it shall be perfectly optional with the owner to fix or declare the value at what figure he pleases, but the value declared, shall it is proposed, be the value for all purposes. But suppose that the declared value, which is to be optional, is only to be declared for purposes of insurance, who may be sure that if the owner is about to lose his ship he will not declare that value at too low a figure. And if this is the case it appears to us that not only will the remedy fail even in the special case of insurance, but that so far from the proposal having a tendency to check over valuation where a check is required, it would really give an official sanction to dishonest over valuation.

And again, let us assume without admitting that the scheme of declared valuation of ships and limited insurance of ships could be carried into effect. It would utterly fail to realize the intention of its framers unless the rules were also applied to goods carried in the ship, as well as to the ship itself; and it would fail even then unless power were given to inspectors to open every package to ascertain its contents. Such powers and proceedings would simply mean the entire stoppage of trade. If a man wished to recover money by fraudulent over-valuation under the proposed system he could still do so. The only change of practice necessary on his part would be that his jugglery would he especially directed to the cargo rather than to the ship. He would have to ship rubbish in packages, as in the case of the Severn; and the question is whether in doing so he would not gain more money and suffer less risk of detection under the proposed system than at present.

We think we have shewn that to attempt to fix one value for all purposes would be to attempt to do what as a matter of fact is untrue. It is better to leave liability as it is and to leave declared value as it is. As regards insurance if it is to be limited, which to us seems impolitic, it must either be limited by market value which must be manifestly unjust, because market value may be as we have shown by no means the real value to the owner; or it must be limited by the estimated value to the owners, a value that can only be stated by the owner for acceptance by the underwriter, a valuation that although offering facilities for fraud, affords more facilities for honest business than any other valuation. Perfect freedom is the safest principle in this as in all other commercial transactions. We think it will be clear that insurance can be no more limited than it can be destroyed.

Chapter 14

Mr. Fortescue's Act

Frustrated in his attempts during 1870 to gain any support in the House for a quick legislative remedy to the issues of overladen and unseaworthy ships, Plimsoll decided to take his crusade to the people in January 1871, with a series of three public meetings at Manchester. He was measured and moderate in this first appeal to public opinion on the issues; being careful not to overly criticize all shipowners;

> ...in the year 1866 the number of wrecks on our own coasts alone amounted to 2,131; and if this number was subdivided, it would be found that about half of it was represented by unseaworthy, overladen, and ill-found vessels of the collier class engaged in the coasting trade. The number of lives lost in the three years preceding that time was 3,053, and the loss therefore annually was 1,018. The Government, in their Report, stated these facts calmly and quietly, as if it were no concern of theirs, and yet he ventured to say that more than one-half of this loss of life might easily be prevented. Only some few years ago such a thing as insuring ships was unknown, but when ships came to be insured there was soon a great change. The result was that a large number of ships were going to sea at the present time which were utterly unseaworthy, and the large amount of ship wrecks which occurred every year was appalling. He was very glad to say that the shipowners, as a class, had done their duty nobly, for, whilst society and the Legislature had left them exposed to dreadful temptation to wrong-doing, they had loaded and maintained their ships with regard to human life. It was only a miserable minority of the shipowners who were guilty of the practice of sending unseaworthy ships to sea. Their names were well known in the ports in which they lived ; and there were in Liverpool at the present time a few men who went on Change, wearing broadcloth and fine linen, who more deserved to be hanged than any poor wretch who had suffered the extreme penalty of the law for the last ten years. In the last session of Parliament he had brought forward a measure with the view to compel unseaworthy ships to be inspected, repaired, and not allowed to go to sea over loaded. These

> were very simple demands, and he trusted in the next session of Parliament his measure would be carried. It would scarcely be believed that at the present time there was no legal power existing to stop a ship from going to sea however unseaworthy it might be. The people of the seaports had done their duty, and they now expected the inland towns to help them in putting down this damnable, manslaughtering, and widows-and-orphans-manufacturing system. Manchester was always foremost in endeavouring to improve the condition of the working classes, and he trusted it would also be foremost in seeking to improve the condition of our merchant seamen. .[428]

Plimsoll's speeches were given sympathetic coverage in the press, with the Sheffield Daily Telegraph printing a special edition, published on the 14th of February, devoted entirely to a word-for-word account of the events.[429] Before the public could read this verbatim account, Plimsoll's major concern about the seaworthiness of colliers in the North Sea trade, reported in successive Wreck Returns over a number of years, was tragically borne out when, on the 10th of February, a destructive storm wrecked a large number of colliers at Bridlington on the Yorkshire coast.

The winter of 1870/1871 had been particularly severe and there was an urgent need for supplies of coal in London, and also in Paris to assist the population after a four month long siege in the Franco-Prussian war. A very large fleet of weather-bound colliers, estimated to be as many as 400, departed the Tyne on the 9th of February but, when the wind dropped, anchored in the shelter of Bridlington Bay, a known safe haven. A Northwest wind set in later and the ships proceeded to sea. However, at 4.00am on the 10th the wind suddenly changed to a hurricane force South-easterly with blinding sleet and snow and the ships found themselves on a lee-shore. Thirty colliers were wrecked, some of them purposely beached, and six of the crew of one of the two shore lifeboats were lost. Many of the ships, either beached or driven ashore, broke up completely immediately upon touching the gently shelving sandy bottom. It was estimated that seventy seamen were lost.[430] However, it is remarkable that, given the severity of the weather and the grave situation the ships found themselves in, the great majority of ships managed to weather the storm and survive.

This disaster caused widespread public concern; fuelled by newspaper articles calling attention to the '...utter worthlessness of a large portion of the fleet by which the northern coasting trade is carried...they were simply fair weather ships...at the first shock on the beach, they swamped like old tubs, or tumbled to pieces like rotten timber'. A member of the Coastguard was quoted as stating that the ships were "...nothing but graves for the seamen, and we shall always have wrecked colliers so long as such vessels are allowed to leave port". More than one paper linked the disaster to Plimsoll's campaign with the Newcastle Daily Chronicle of 11 February stating that 'We can scarcely believe it possible that another session of Parliament will be allowed to pass without such stringent legislation as shall have the effect of sweeping these lumps of painted touchwood from the sea without previously freighting them with precious human lives'. The Leeds Mercury of the 14th of February believed that '... Mr. Plimsoll will find his hands strengthened in a way which cannot well be resisted'.[431]

At the very beginning of the 1871 Session of Parliament two parallel Bills were introduced that were to lead to a clash of legislative imperatives resulting in a great deal of frustration and disappointment for both Plimsoll and the Board of Trade. Plimsoll's concerns about overladen and unseaworthy ships, presented to Parliament in 1870, had not been ignored. An informal Committee of Members interested in the question, had met at the Board of Trade during the Parliamentary recess. The day after Parliament resumed on the 9th of February, on the very day of the Great Gale of 1871, the Chairman of this committee moved a resolution that "leave be given to bring in a Bill to provide for the compulsory Survey of certain Merchant Ships, and for the adoption of a maximum load line". *A* Bill was *ordered* to be brought in by Mr. Plimsoll, Mr. Wheelhouse, and Mr. Lambert; the Merchant Ship Survey Bill.[432]

On the very next sitting day, the 13th of February, Mr Chichester Fortescue, President of the Board of Trade from 1871 to 1874, rose and presented a motion on the major consolidation of Merchant Shipping laws; – "...to move the House, that leave be given to bring in a Bill to consolidate and amend the Laws relating to Merchant Shipping and Navigation, ...he did not propose to trouble the House with any statement upon the merits of a Bill of that magnitude, and containing such a mass of details; but he had been anxious to introduce the Bill at a very early period, in order that a measure which must require so much time for examination even by those who were best acquainted with the subject should be as soon as possible in the hands of hon. Members. He intended to accompany the print of the Bill with a memorandum, which he hoped would be distributed in a few days, explaining the points in which the Bill would effect a change in the present law, and also the points in which, it differed from the Bill introduced last year. ...No pains should be wanting on his part or on that of his Colleague, the Secretary of the Board of Trade, to facilitate the passing of the measure. He should be happy to confer with hon. Members upon any part of this Bill, which they might feel inclined to criticize or object to, and to meet them as far as his duty allowed. In that spirit, he trusted, it might be possible this year to pass the measure into law".[433]

It was moved that leave be given to bring in a Bill to consolidate and amend the Laws relating to Merchant Shipping and Navigation. Leave was given and the Bill ordered to be brought in by Mr. Chichester Fortescue and Mr. Arthur Peel.

Seven sitting days later, on the 22nd of February, Plimsoll rose in the House to present the second reading off his Merchant Ship Survey Bill. His main concerns were with seaworthiness, overloading and marine insurance. The unseaworthy conditions of some ships, such as the "...great number of vessels lost every year simply from rot...sails might be taken, doubled in the hands, and rent.."; "...a mast of 16 inches diameter, which, when sawn asunder, was found to contain only four inches of sound wood" and "ships where they had great difficulty in preventing the men from shoveling up the bilge planks when they shoveled the coal"; "...Surely, with such facts as these in its possession, the House was competent to decide whether such vessels should be allowed to go to sea in a laden state without being repaired? The House could have no hesitation in at once pronouncing upon that issue."

He was also "prepared to say that several vessels were overladen with the positive design that they should sink in the course of their voyages;" a charge that drew exclamations of amazement in the House. He claimed that; "It was quite true, and he could substantiate the statement. Where this design did not exist the overloading was carried on to such an extent as to render the vessel practically unseaworthy. The House would, therefore, experience no difficulty in arriving at a decision on that issue also."

With regard to excessive insurance, Plimsoll stated that he was aware of several cases in which vessels, insured for sums far beyond their actual value, were lost, bringing financial advantage to the owners. He claimed that in one case the owner of a ship confessed he had only paid £300 for a ship but had actually insured it for £1,000. "Was it not an insult to common sense to suppose that the owner of that ship wished it to make its voyage in safety?"

Plimsoll also gave examples of the risk of vessels being lost through improper stowage of the cargo, inadequate manning, and deficient engine power. Evidence was given of widespread support from the shipping industry for his proposal for a load line;

> The Chambers of Commerce in nearly all the great towns had adopted similar resolutions, and all of them asked the Government to do that which he now asked the Government and the House to do. But the most signal confirmation of the justice and the propriety of the proposals which he submitted to the House was contained in a communication to *The Shipping Gazette,* from Mr. W. C. Rundell, a man of considerable experience and knowledge in the port of Liverpool. He said — "Mr. Plimsoll's proposal has met with a large amount of the support of the shipowners of this town. The committee of the Shipowners' Association have unanimously supported this—the enforcement of a load-line— as part of the Bill, as they consider that while this restriction on the loading of shipping will not affect those who load their vessels properly, it will act as a check on others who do not, and will considerably reduce the amount of insurance."

He further claimed to have received copies of thirty-one newspaper articles covering his speeches in Manchester, only two of which were not in agreement with his proposals. What he wanted to do was not to hamper the honest shipowner who wished to load his ships so that they might make their voyages in safety, but to meet the case of those—not so few in number, he was sorry to say, as some hon. Gentlemen supposed—who loaded a ship with the definite purpose that the load should sink the ship. The real practical difficulty was not in fixing upon a proper load-line so much as that those men were resolutely bent on shirking any such line at all, with the view of loading their ships just as they pleased… The remedy he proposed was a compulsory survey of unclassed ships. He insisted on; "the imperative necessity of having ships that had run out all their various grades of classification [after five years] being properly surveyed before they were allowed to go to sea with valuable lives on board, and also of putting some restraint on the homicidal cupidity of those who overloaded ships". He was careful not to tar all shipowners with the same brush; "All shipowners were not guilty of those practices; the great majority, indeed, loaded their ships with due regard to safety, and did their best to keep them afloat."

He then moved on to counter the main objections that'd been made in the House to his proposals; that such regulation would remove the shipowner's responsibility for his ships;

> He would reply that at the present moment no such responsibility existed; that through only requiring surveys of ships in class, the government would be recognizing the work of a private organization; "...it seemed to him that the State ought to be glad to recognize it wherever it was of so beneficial a character, and ought to rejoice to know that half the task of providing for the safety of our sailors was already accomplished;" that such a number of inspections would require an army of surveyors; "...Now, 27,000 vessels were registered in English ports, of which 13,000 were in Lloyd's book, and were annually surveyed, the work being done by 39 surveyors, who gave the whole of their time to it, assisted by 16 who were partially employed", and that such inspections would be too expensive; "...his system, he believed [from details tabled of expenditure and income by Lloyds], could be made not only to pay for itself, but to yield a large balance to be handed over to the Chancellor of the Exchequer." [434]

In seconding the Bill, Mr. Wheelhouse emphasized that "...he did so on perhaps even broader grounds than those urged by the hon. Member for Derby who brought it forward. He maintained the necessity of saving human life whenever and wherever it was in danger. If mines, buildings, and even cabs required competent supervision, it was ten times as necessary in a case like the present."

The majority of other MPs who spoke damned the Bill with faint praise and then proceeded to cruelly criticize it; "...the shipping interest would be saved from being made the victims of crude amateur legislation;" "... on looking at the back of the Bill it would be found to bear the names of three hon. Members representing inland constituencies, which fully accounted for the ignorance it displayed of the practical working of maritime affairs;" an ignorance well portrayed by another member in stating that… "the proposed regulations respecting coal were absurd, because it was well known that a ship of 1,000 tons was safer with 1,250 tons of coal on board than she would be if she carried 1,000 tons of iron." These statements were offset by some more moderate views and suggestions as to how there might be some progress in a matter that had clearly caused a degree of rancor and bitterness; "…He thought it a great pity that any element of bitterness should be imported into this subject, which was one of great importance, and one that concerned the lives of thousands of our best seamen. The House ought to consider it with as much calmness and deliberation as possible, for he was quite certain if a Commission of naval men and shipowners were appointed they would find means by which the problem might be solved…"

There were generally agreed views running through the debate that the clauses already in the Merchant Shipping Consolidation Bill would amply suffice in the matters of seaworthiness and overloading of ships; "…there was no doubt that many ships were lost through their unseaworthiness. He thought that any man who sent a ship to sea in an unseaworthy state for the purpose of obtaining the insurance on that ship was more guilty of cold-blooded murder than most of the criminals who were sent to the gallows; and he wondered how a shipowner who made sailors run even the smallest risk of that sort could sleep quietly in his bed when a gale of wind was blowing," but there was no support for compulsory surveys of all unclassed ships or for Government interference in the matter of insurance of ships; "…for instance, the hon. Gentleman spoke [in Manchester] of—"Some black-hearted villains who bought and owned ships and insured them not for three-fourths of their value, which was generally considered the proper thing, but for twice and even three times their value" and who then "set their wicked arts to work to accomplish the wreck of their ships in order to get the insurance money". The hon. Gentleman went on at the same meeting to say that; "that kind of thing happened every day. His statements of fact were equally extravagant."

Fortescue recalled draft provisions in the Merchant Shipping Consolidation Bill which he considered would address Plimsoll's primary concerns of overloading and seaworthiness;

> ... it provided that before a ship left port her draught of water should be carefully ascertained, in order that facility might be afforded in case of subsequent casualty, for judging as to whether she was or was not overloaded. In the next place, it made the sending of a ship to sea in an unseaworthy state a misdemeanour, thus imposing a serious responsibility upon the shipowner. The Bill would also enable any sailor to refuse to proceed with a ship in an un-seaworthy condition, and to demand an official investigation by the surveyor of the Board of Trade. Lastly, the Government Bill would provide that any person having or supposing he had, knowledge of a ship being unseaworthy, might demand and procure a Board of Trade survey.

Qualified support was given by some MPs involved in previous debates as ex-Presidents of the Board of Trade, such as Steven Cave, who thought the proper principle to act upon was to leave the fullest freedom to all parties, and then, judging by results, to punish with the severest penalties those who were guilty of the offences in question and; "he thought it would be for the convenience of the House if the hon. Member withdrew his Bill, and moved Amendments or additions to the Bill of the Government on those points which he considered defective". Sir John Pakington expressed his deep regret at the sacrifices of life that had resulted from the shameful manner in which ships were overloaded, and stated that he would support every part of the Bill as an effective remedy must be achieved. If Fortescue would not support the Bill he would repeat his proposal of 1870 for a Royal Commission of Inquiry.

In summarizing the debate it is useful to quote exact statements made, as recorded by Hansard, as these would be the source of considerable frustration and unhappiness in the future on the part of Plimsoll. Fortescue stated that; "A great many arguments had been put forward in favour of legislation, but not in favour of the measure now proposed, which he believed to be one of the most unworkable and impracticable propositions that had been brought before that House since he entered it." However, "... he said he was quite ready to bring in as a separate Bill such of the clauses of the Merchant Shipping [Consolidation] Bill as had been referred to, if the latter measure [the "Consolidation Bill"] should not receive the sanction of the House." The MP who seconded Plimsoll's motion attempted to clarify Fortescue's statement by saying; "...his right hon. Friend (Mr. C.

Fortescue) had been desirous to explain that he was perfectly ready to deal with this question this Session. If the whole of the large measure which had been alluded to could not be passed, his right hon. Friend would be prepared to eliminate those clauses of the Bill which referred specially to this subject, and to embody them in a separate Bill'. Plimsoll replied; "after the assurance just given, he would not press the Motion" which, along with a proposed amendment was, by leave, *withdrawn. The* Bill was also *withdrawn.*

Plimsoll was to raise only one further matter in the House during 1871, asking the Secretary of State for the Home Department on the 14th of March why ten crew members of the ship ***Epaminondas*** had been jailed for three months for refusing to sail on the grounds of unseaworthiness. They had claimed that the ship was making two and a half inches of water per hour.[435] The Secretary asked for leave to find more information and replied on the 28th of March that;

> ...the ship, of 1,072 tons and carrying 22 crew had departed South Shields of the 28th of February. After experiencing strong winds and heavy seas the ship anchored at Yarmouth Roads on the 6th of March, at which time nine seamen refused to go any further and insisted that the Master entered the nearest port and had the ship overhauled. The Master refused as he considered the ship to be perfectly seaworthy and only light pumping had been required, however, he eventually agreed to return to South Shields where a master surveyor declared the ship seaworthy. The evidence of the Master and Mate stated that the ship had not made an undue amount of water and was seaworthy; evidence supported by the pilot and the surveyor who stated that "...she was seaworthy, and that a nicer, more wholesome, and more seaworthy vessel he'd never seen anywhere." The ship had just been repaired at a cost of £500. The ship's carpenter agreed with these views and believed that the defendants had; "...no reasonable excuse for their conduct in refusing to proceed in her"' The Secretary went on to say that he could not direct a re-hearing of the case, as demanded by the seamen, but could only reduce the sentence if the facts did not warrant the punishment, and then only with the agreement of the Magistrates, who, in this case considered the sentences warranted.[436]

Fortescue was still hopeful of passing the Merchant Shipping Consolidation

Bill in the current Session as indicated in a reply to a question in the House on the 21st of April as to whether he would fulfil the promise made earlier to bring in the clauses of the Merchant Shipping Bill, relating to safety of life and property at sea, as separate measures in the event that there would be insufficient time for proper discussion of the entire Bill. He stated that he; "was still in hopes that he might be enabled to proceed with the whole Bill. Certainly that period of the Session had not yet arrived which would make it necessary for him to separate the clauses relating to the safety of life and property at sea from the general Bill."[437] However, by the 3rd of July time had run out and it was resolved; 'that leave be given to bring in a Bill to amend the Merchant Shipping Acts.' The Merchant Shipping Acts Amendment Bill was *ordered* to be brought in by Mr. Chichester Fortescue and Mr. Arthur Peel. The Bill was *presented* and read the first time. [438]

> On the 7th of August, after being considered in committee, the draft Merchant Shipping Act Amendments Bill was debated in the House. The committee had agreed that the draft of water was to be recorded and that a copy of the record left ashore should be provided to the Master and Chief Officer of the ship. Much of the debate in the House centred around draft Clause 7 of the Bill – *Survey of ships alleged by seamen to be unseaworthy,* with Fortescue eventually proposing; "he would accept the Amendment if the proportion [of seamen alleging the ship to be unseaworthy] were limited to one-fourth of the seamen belonging to the ship, or if the number of such seamen exceeded 20, then by not fewer than five of such seamen." This was agreed and the Bill, as amended, was; 'to be considered *To-morrow,* at Two of the clock.'[439] The Bill was considered the following day with no recorded changes, and was passed after its third reading on the 9th of August.[440] The Bill passed quickly through the House of Lords between the 10th and 11th of August and was reported back to the House of Commons on the 16th of August with some proposed amendments. These were considered on the 17th of August, and some agreed to, with Royal Assent being given to this Bill and twenty-eight others on the 21st of August; the last day of the 1871 Session.[441]

The Merchant Shipping Act, 1871, – *An Act to amend the Merchant Shipping Acts* – was an extremely abbreviated version of the monumental, but dormant, Merchant Shipping Consolidation Bill, including some new provisions of relevance to the vexed issues of how to deal with unseaworthy and overloaded ships, and reports of such ships by crews. The short Act was divided into three main Parts; *Registry* (Part II of the Merchant Shipping Act, 1854), *Masters and Seamen* (Part III of the Merchant Shipping Act, 1854), *and Safety* (Part IV of the Merchant Shipping Act, 1854).

The issue of ships being run down by unmarked ships, and that of Plimsoll's concerns regarding overloading had been heard and were addressed through new provisions under section 4 of *Registry*, albeit somewhat unsatisfactorily regarding the prevention of overloading;

> Every British ship shall, before registry, be permanently and conspicuously marked, to the satisfaction of the Commissioners of Customs, as follows; that is to say –
>
> Her name shall be marked at each of her bows, and her name and port of registry, shall be marked on her stern, on a dark background in white or yellow letters, of a length not less than four inches, and of proportionate breadth.
>
> Her official number and the number denoting her register tonnage shall be marked on her main beam.
>
> A scale of feet shall be marked on her stem and on her stern post, in Roman capitals or figures, six inches in length, the lower line of such letters or figures to coincide with the draught line denoted thereby.
>
> The Board of Trade may, however, exempt any class of ship from of this section, or any part of them.
>
> If the said scale of feet is in any respect inaccurate, so as to be likely mislead, the owner of the ship shall incur a penalty not exceeding one hundred pounds.
>
> The Board of Trade may, in any case or classes of cases in which they think it expedient so to do, direct any person appointed by them for the purpose to record, in such manner and with such particulars as the Board of Trade direct, the draught of water of any sea-going ship, as shown on the scale of feet on her stern and her stern post, upon her leaving any dock, wharf, port or harbour for the purpose of proceeding to sea; and such person shall thereupon keep such record,

> and shall from time to time forward the same, or a copy thereof, to the Board of Trade; and such record of copy thereof, if produced by or out of the custody of the Board of Trade, shall be admissible in evidence of the draught of water of the ship at the time specified in the record.
>
> The master of every British sea-going ship shall, upon her leaving any dock, wharf port or harbour for the purpose of proceeding to sea; record her draught of water in the official logbook (if any), and shall produce such record to any principal officer of Customs whenever required by him so to do, or in default of such production shall incur a penalty not exceeding twenty pounds.
>
> ...any principal officer of Customs may detain the ship until the provisions of this section are complied with.

Regarding overloading, Plimsoll's plea through his Merchant Shipping Survey Bill had been for a load line to indicate the maximum depth (and corresponding minimum freeboard) to which a ship could be safely loaded. The provisions of the 1871 Act did not achieve these ends. Whilst useful as an indication of how deeply a ship may have been laden, without an indication of the maximum safe draught the required draft marks did little but provide questionable evidence after the event if, or when, the shipowner was being prosecuted for the loss of his ship and possibly her entire crew.

The longstanding matter of unfair imprisonment of seamen for refusing to sail on, what they deemed to be, an unseaworthy ship was addressed through clause seven of the Act in the section covering *Masters and Seamen;*

> Whenever in any proceeding against any seamen or apprentice belonging to any ship for desertion, or for neglecting or refusing to join or proceed to sea in his ship, or for being absent without leave, and it is alleged by one fourth of the seamen belonging to such ship, or, if the number of such seamen exceed twenty, by not less than five such seamen, that such ship is by reason of unseaworthiness, overloading, improper loading, defective equipment, or for any other reason, not in a fit condition to proceed to sea, or that the accommodation on such ship is insufficient, the court having cognizance of the case shall take such means as may be in their power to satisfy themselves concerning the truth or untruth of such allegations, and shall for that purpose receive the evidence of the person or persons making the same, and

> shall have the power to summon any other witnesses whose evidence they may think it desirable to hear; the court shall thereupon, if satisfied that the allegation is groundless, proceed to adjudicate, but if not satisfied shall cause such ship to be surveyed.
>
> Provided that no seaman or apprentice charged with desertion, or with quitting his ship without leave, shall have any right to apply for a survey under this section unless previously to his quitting his ship he has complained to the master of the circumstances so alleged in justification.
>
> For the purpose of this section, the court shall require any of the surveyors appointed by the Board of Trade, under the Merchant Shipping Act, 1854, or any person appointed for the purpose by the Board of trade, or if such surveyor or person cannot be obtained without unreasonable expense or delay, or is not, in the opinion of the court, competent to deal with the special circumstances of the case, then any other impartial surveyor appointed by the court, and having no interest in the ship, her freight or cargo, to survey the ship, and to answer any questions concerning her which the court may think fit to put. Such surveyor or other person shall survey the ship, and make his report in writing to the court, including an answer to every question put to him by the court. The court shall cause such report to be communicated to the parties and unless it is proved to the satisfaction of the court that the opinions expressed in the report are erroneous, the court shall determine the questions before them in accordance with those opinions.

An example of an impartial surveyor appointed by the court was a complaint by crew regarding the seaworthiness of their vessel, the ***Petrel***, in September 1871. The steamship, enroute from London to Singapore, called into Poole when seven of the crew refused to go further, alleging that the ship was unseaworthy. The seamen were apprehended under warrant, but freed on bail, pending a survey in Southampton, ordered by the Magistrate. The Southampton Mayor read the report of the surveyor who had determined that the vessel was too deeply laden, the deck insufficiently protected, the deckhouse too large and insecure and the forecastle too small for the crew. The prisoners were released, with the Master being ordered to pay for the cost of the survey and Court costs.[442]

In conjunction with the requirement for the ships name to be clearly marked on the bows and stern, s. 9 of the Act required, in the event of collision;

> ...the master of each vessel to give to the master of the other vessel the name of his vessel, and of her port of registry, or the port or place to which she belongs, and also to the names of the ports or places from which and to which she is bound. Any failure to do so incurred the same consequence as that provided by the Merchant Shipping Act, 1862, for failure to render assistance to the other vessel, or to the master, crew or passengers thereof as required by s.33.
>
> In spite of the sometimes strong views expressed in Parliament about shipowners knowingly sending unseaworthy ships to sea, section 11 of the Act held the owner, or any other person in authority, liable but enacted a timid penalty;

Every person who, having authority as owner or otherwise to send a ship to sea, sends her to sea in an unseaworthy state so as to endanger the life of any person belonging or on board the same, shall be guilty of a misdemeanor, unless he proves that he used all reasonable means to make and keep the ship seaworthy, and was ignorant of such unseaworthiness, or that her going to sea in an unseaworthy state was, under the circumstances, reasonable and unavoidable, and for this purpose he may give evidence in the same manner as any other witness. A misdemeanor under this section shall not be punishable on summary conviction.

Section 12 repealed s.25; *Tonnage and Number of Certificate to be carved on the Main Beam,* s.34; *Name of Ship* (only required on the stern) of the Merchant Shipping Act, 1854. and s.13; *Exemption of certain Ships from having Name painted on Stern* of the Merchant Shipping Amendment Act, 1855. The 1871 Act repealed, as from the 1st of January 1872, s.25 (*Tonnage and certificate to be carved in main beam*) and s.34 (*Name of ship and port of registry on stern*) of the Merchant Shipping Act, 1854, and s.13 (*Exemption of certain ships* [pleasure yachts] *from having name painted on stern*) of the Merchant Shipping Act Amendment Act, 1855.

Plimsoll felt betrayed by 'Fortescue's Act'. Of the principal elements of his Bill; overloading, unseaworthiness, compulsory surveys for unclassed ships, and limitations on insurance, only the first two had been addressed, virtually unaltered from the way they'd been drafted for the Merchant Shipping Consolidation Bill before Plimsoll presented his Bill. The rest had been quietly ignored.

Parliament also turned its attention, at this time, to the question of adequate testing of anchor chain when, in mid-June 1871, a motion was approved to bring in a Bill to; 'amend the law respecting the proving and sale of chain cable and anchors'.[443] A committee worked on amendments to the Chain Cables and Anchors Act, 1864 and reported back to the House on the 10th of July. With the end of the 1871 Session firmly in sight work proceeded apace with a further report to the House of Commons on the 16th of August and consideration of the Bill by the House of Lords on the 18th and 19th of August. On the 21st day of August; the last day of the 1871 Session, the *Chain Cables and Anchor Act, 1871,*[444] was passed; coming into force on the 1st of July 1872.

The main objective of the Chain Cable and Anchors Act was to ensure the continuation, and reinforcement, of testing of chain cables and anchors, as the term of the 1864 Act was stated by clause 15 to be until; 'the First Day of July One thousand eight hundred and seventy-two, and no longer'. From their experience of the 1864 Act, the Board of Trade wished to ensure that testing remain in 'public hands' and had arranged for Lloyds to be responsible for testing and management of public testing machines in cases where no local body was prepared to take them over from the stock companies established to set them up under the 1864 Act. A table to the 1871 Act listed those public bodies in the main ports such as Liverpool, Newcastle, Sunderland, Glasgow, Bristol, Cardiff, Greenock, Hull, Middlesborough and Swansea.

The 1864 Act (s.7) had based the testing for merchant ships upon; '…the same Tensile Strain as that which Chain Cables and Anchors respectively of similar Size, Weight, or Description, are or shall be subject to before received for the Use of her Majesty's Naval Service…' There had been no requirement for a breaking strain test. Section 5 of the 1871 Act required the tester to remove three links from a fifteen fathom (90 foot) section of the chain cable and test them to a standard laid down in a Schedule to the Act of tensile strengths and breaking strains. If the first three links failed the breaking strain test, a further three links from this section of chain were to be tested. If the first or second three links withstood the breaking strain the full length of fifteen fathoms was to be subject to the tensile strength test laid down in the schedule. The Act provided for alterations, with six months notice, in tensile strengths and breaking strains through an Order in Council.

The protracted saga concerning the Merchant Shipping Consolidation Bill, was summarized in an article published in December 1871;[445]

> IT is a remarkable circumstance that in the British Empire the subject almost least understood and universally shunted by our Legislators is legislation affecting Merchant Shipping. For many years, as our readers are aware, has an enormous Bill been ready at the Board of Trade, and many times has it been submitted to Parliament. At the time when Sir Stafford Northcote was President of the Board of Trade, there were evident signs of the birth of this Bill. When the Duke of Richmond succeeded Sir Stafford a Bill was ready—was introduced in the House of Commons, and it was reviewed, part by part, in these columns ; but owing to circumstances, a small part of the scheme only was pressed on the Legislature and passed. After the Duke came Mr. Bright, and after Mr. Bright, Mr. Lefevre, but still nothing was done. Following Mr. Bright, we have Mr. Chichester Fortescue and Mr. Arthur Peel, but all they have been able to effect was the passing, last Session, of a few sections of the great measure, and they were only able to do this small piece of patchwork at the end of the Session, when members had been wholly worked out, by the interminable Ballot Bill and the Army Regulation Bill. It was not to be wondered at that, under these circumstances, it taxed the energies of Mr. Arthur Peel to get through with even the remnant he had under taken, in the absence of Mr. Chichester Fortescue, to press it forward in the Commons. Indeed, there are many persons who believe that had it not been for the persistence of Mr. Plimsoll (who, by the way, knows nothing of the wants of the Shipping Interest) in obtaining a pledge from Mr. Fortescue early in the Session, even the infinitessimal Act pulled through by Mr. Peel would never have been passed. How is it, then, that Mercantile Marine Legislation is so neglected in this essentially Maritime and Commercial State? It is not, as we have shown, that the subject is not ready for the consideration of the Legislature: we know that it has been ready for years, and that the Board of Trade, had, as a matter of fact, previously spent

> most of their time and energy on the measure. The fact is—and we think the sooner we make the statement the better—that shipowners are not so much concerned and as unanimous as they ought to be on the subject. The majority of the members of the Legislature look on the whole thing as a bore, and many of the Outport members, we regret to say, evince but little interest in it, and last, but not least, the head of the Board of Trade has refused to grant a Select Committee for its practical consideration... We do not hesitate, therefore, to press for a Select Committee of the House of Commons on the Merchant Shipping Bill, in the hope that it will be the means of producing and perfecting a substantial piece of legislation; and in order that we may be spared the further infliction of spasmodic, though well meant, attempts, and crude, insignificant, and incomplete measures —like the attempts made last Session, or like the measure passed in an almost empty House at its close.

The serious and immediate danger in going to sea; succinctly summarized through data provided by the Board of Trade for the period between 1855 and 1871, confirmed the usefulness of boats of any type aboard ships for saving life, regardless of whatever may be said about the inefficiency of ship's boats and the parsimony of ship owners. During this period, out of 56,111 lives saved, 65 percent were saved by ships' boats; 22,615 by ships' own boats and a further 13,874 lives by sailing and steam ships; invariably using their own boats. A further 8,765 were rescued by fishing boats, small craft and coastguard lifeboats, and 5,287 by rocket apparatus on the coast. The remaining 5,570 were saved by other unspecified means.[446]

Chapter 15

Procrastination, Plimsoll and Passengers

Eighteen hundred and seventy-two was to be yet another year with a dismal toll of ships and lives lost at sea, not only on or near the British coast but worldwide. Statistics for the year included foreign ships in waters under British jurisdiction. Six hundred and eight lives were lost on or near the British coast from the total loss of 501 ships through wreck, casualty and collision. A further 1,457 ships were partially damaged through the same causes. Eight hundred and sixty four British ships trading worldwide suffered total loss with a further 1,616 suffering partial damage through wreck, casualty and collision; events which, in total caused the loss of 1,980 lives.[447]

Parliament was silent on the pressing issues of unseaworthy and overladen ships during 1872. Plimsoll made no contributions to debates on the two merchant shipping Bills before Parliament; the Chain Cables and Anchors Act, 1871, Suspension Bill and the Merchant Shipping and Passengers Acts Amendment Bill, nor to the Steam Boilers Explosions Bill which dealt with industry wide issues common to those aboard steamships.[448] He did however contribute to a debate on a Mines Regulations Bill which dealt with similar safety and management issues to merchant shipping, and was a subject close to Plimsoll's heart; the safety of miners. He had made his fortune in the coal industry but had also campaigned tirelessly on behalf of the safety of miners and had come to be known as 'the miner's friend'.[449]

In his introduction of the Mines Regulations Bill, Mr. Secretary Bruce included some statements with direct parallels in the mining industry to issues regarding the safety of seafarers and management of ships, and to the reluctance of Parliament to interfere with the perceived rights of owners/managers in matters of safety;

> ...Every year the average of deaths [in mines] in the year amounted to 1,000, besides casualties of more or less gravity, which were four or five times that number.... These [mine] explosions led, no doubt, to very fatal consequences, but the average of deaths produced in that

> way was only about one-fourth of the whole that occurred in collieries. In 1870 the number of deaths from all causes was 991, and of these only 185 were due to the effect of explosions...It might be said that the only protection from those accidents must be found in the care and discretion of the colliers themselves; but that was not so, for if the colliery were properly overlooked by those who had the management of it, the colliers would be forced to take precautions for their own preservation. It was the opinion of the Inspectors, moreover, that if a greater degree of responsibility were thrown on those who had the management of the collieries, a great saving of life would be effected. He would ask hon. Members to reflect what was the ground for the interference of Parliament with the question? As a general fact Parliament was very loth to interfere with the mode in which any trader conducted his business; but when there was a business which necessarily involved great danger from loss of life, then Parliament thought proper—and he thought it was justified in so doing—to step in and see that proper precautions were adopted. ...If charges of a serious nature were brought against a manager, it might be in the power of the Secretary of State, as in the case of the misconduct of the captain of a vessel or a railway official it was in the power of the President of the Board of Trade, to order an inquiry to be conducted by competent persons....It seemed to him that colliers [coalminers] had the same right to protection as travellers by railway or by ships. [450]

Plimsoll did not make comparisons between miners and seamen, or refer to shipowners, surveyors, the safety of seamen and comparable annual death rates in his contribution to the debate, in spite of the obvious parallels. He;

> ... hoped that the responsibility of the mine owner would not be diminished in any way. No doubt there were some owners who would spare no expense to secure safety, but there were others whose responsibility rested on them so lightly that to save themselves from a small and necessary outlay they would expose the lives of a couple of hundred men to imminent peril...He quite admitted it would require a large staff of surveyors to go into every pit, but ...it should be the duty of the district surveyor to make an inspection of the mine. He hoped a power would be reserved to the miners to apply to the Government Inspector to have their mine surveyed whenever they believed it to be in a dangerous condition. [451]:

A longstanding safety issue with all mines, particularly coal mines, was explosions of the steam boilers providing power for the 'windings' [lifts] and for pumping. In May 1870 Parliament agreed to appoint a Select Committee, 'to inquire into the cause of Steam Boiler Explosions, and as to the best means of preventing them.'[452] Between June 1866 and June 1870 there were 219 boiler explosions, twelve of which were marine boilers, causing 315 deaths and injuring 450 people. One thousand and forty six steam boiler explosions across all industries had been recorded between 1800 and 1870, resulting in 4076 fatalities and 2093 injuries. Of these, 320 were marine boilers of various forms. The predominant causes were summarised as; faults of construction or repair – 95; faults to be determined by periodical examination – 62; faults which should be prevented by careful attendants – 54; extraneous or uncertain causes – 8. Undue pressure, overloaded valves, intentional or carelessness, caused 25 deaths. Of the 37 deaths and 23 injuries caused by explosion of marine boilers; 15 deaths and nine injuries were caused through weak flues or ends, or bad materials; 11 deaths and 7 injuries as a result of internal or external corrosion, and 11 deaths and 7 injuries through shortness of water.[453] [454]

In 1851, when a Steam Navigation Bill was being considered, a debate was held in Parliament on accidents to steam vessels and railways. The President of the Board of Trade, who had oversight of steam vessels, factories, mines and railways, was asked;

> ... whether it was the intention of the Government to propose any measure during the present Session for the more efficient protection of persons travelling by steam vessels or railroads, or of those employed in working steam machinery?...[as] during the last few months a number of fatal accidents had occurred, connected with steamboats, steam machinery, and railways; and, as it appeared, particularly at Glasgow, Lewes, Chester, and Bristol, that they had resulted from the gross and culpable negligence of the persons engaged in working the machinery.[455]

In his reply Mr Labouchere alluded to, what was to become, Part XXXI of the *Steam Navigation Act, 1851 – Every Steam Ship…to be provided with a Safety-valve upon each Boiler, free of the care of the Engineer and out of his control and interference;* – a strengthening of the requirements of the Steam Navigation

Act, 1846, Part XIV of which had required inter alia that – *A declaration of such Sufficiency and Good Condition of the Machinery of such Steam Vessel under the hand of an Engineer, be approved ..by the Lords of…the Committee of the Privy Council for Trade.* The provision re safety valves in the 1851 Act was strengthened through s.302 of the Merchant Shipping Act, 1854. The Merchant Shipping Consolidation Bill; in gestation from February 1866, included a draft provision; 'If a steam-ship, she shall be provided with a safety valve on each boiler, so constructed that the weight thereon cannot be increased when the steam is up, and that the pressure of steam in the boiler cannot be increased beyond a safe and proper amount'. Fresh in the minds of the Board of Trade officials drafting this Bill would have been the catastrophic loss of life through boiler explosions aboard an American paddle steamer on the Mississippi River.

Shortly after cessation of hostilities in the American Civil War, the large paddle steamer ***Sultana*** (1863) of 1,719 tons departed Vicksburg grossly overloaded. The ship was licensed to carry 376 passengers and 85 crew. There was an urgent need to repatriate thousands of Union soldiers held in Confederate prison camps and, when the ***Sultana*** departed Vicksburg to head up river it was estimated that there were a total of at least 2,137 persons aboard; made up of 1,960 paroled prisoners, 22 guards, 70 paying cabin passengers, and 85 crew members, plus an unknown number of stowaways. A faulty boiler had undergone a hurried repair at Vicksburg and, on the 27th of April, about eight miles north of Memphis, with the river in flood and steaming into a very strong current, the faulty boiler exploded, triggering the immediate explosions of two of the other four boilers and setting fire to the ship.[456] It was believed that the explosion was caused by low water and too much pressure in the boilers. Estimates vary as to the total death toll, but it was believed to be at least 1,800; the fourth worst death toll aboard a ship during peacetime in recorded history.

Dealing with the particular question of the role of the Board of Trade in ensuring the safety of passengers aboard ships and railways, Labouchere reiterated a view that permeated Parliament and the Board of Trade for most of the nineteenth century when stating;

> …He had come to the conclusion that any measure of a general description or application that might be introduced to diminish the

> responsibility of the directors, would be attended with more harm than good. As regarded security to passengers, he had carefully considered the various suggestions and propositions that had been made; but he could find no regulation of such general and universal application as that they could be laid down by Parliament as applicable, under all circumstances, to all railways. Therefore, he should object to giving any department of the Government that which they could not exercise properly, but which the directors could, namely, the superintendence of the details of railways, upon which, after all, the security of the public depended. Therefore, in the present Session, he was not prepared to introduce a Bill to increase the power of Government in this regard for the public safety.[457]

Plimsoll's longstanding concern for the welfare of workers was evident in two brief interventions made during the 1871 Parliamentary session, the first of which, in February, was a proposed clause in the Royal Parks and Gardens Bill whereby; 'a Park-keeper may apprehend any offender whose name and residence is not known.' Plimsoll "feared that if the Bill passed, the enjoyment of the Parks by the respectable working men would be interfered with."[458] The second occasion was in July 1872 when a Bill was being discussed to deal with the very real issue of detection of dangerous gases in mines.

> ...Where a mine subject to Clause 19 of this Act is known to give off dangerous gas, a barometer and thermometer shall be placed at the mine above or below ground, under charge of, and as directed by, the manager. The object of the Amendment was to enable the managers of mines, by reference to the barometer and thermometer, in the course of their daily occupations, to ascertain when great danger of explosion was likely to arise. According to a statement made before the Royal Society, it appeared that out of 525 explosions in mines in the years 1868, 1869, and 1872, 49 per cent occurred at times when there was great barometrical change, and 22 per cent when there were great changes of temperature. Plimsoll recommended; "the Committee adopt the clause without alteration, as providing a valuable protection for the men, while not inflicting any hardship on the owners'. [459]

During the debate on an Intoxicating Liqour Licensing Bill in July and August 1872 Plimsoll proposed a number of unsuccessful amendments to the Bill. It would appear that, during 1872, he was primarily occupied in the writing of a booklet on the plight of seamen.

Early in the 1872 Parliamentary session a question was asked of the President of the Board of Trade whether it was 'his intention this Session to re-introduce the Merchant Shipping [Consolidation] Bill; and, if so, whether he purposes afterwards to refer it, or any portion thereof, to a Select Committee…?' This question referred to what was becoming a hardy perennial; the long-standing desire of the Board of Trade, and the shipping industry, to consolidate the plethora of merchant and mercantile shipping law into one up-to-date Act. Mr Chichester Fortescue cautiously replied;

> …that there still remained an immense mass of legislation to be consolidated and amended relating to the various interests of the mercantile body, and he was quite willing that the subject should be referred to a Select Committee; but as he feared that, on account of other Committees sitting, it would be impossible for him, and also for other hon. Members whom it might be desirable to appoint, to take part at present in such a Committee, he refrained for the moment from giving a positive answer to the Question.[460]

Before the question of whether Fortescue's Bill would pass through Parliament and be enacted, attention was turned to the Chain Cable and Anchor Act, enacted in 1864 but which had continued in force only until the 1st July 1872. The Act had been amended in 1871 (Vict.34 & 35 c.101) to put in place a regulatory regime to give power to businesses to provide proving establishments for testing chain cable and anchors, and power to the Board of Trade to grant, revoke or suspend licenses for proving chain cables and anchors and to appoint inspectors on an annual basis. The compulsory nature of these requirements had rankled within the maritime industry since introduction of the 1864 Act, and more so with its continuance through the 1871 Act, as expressed in the editorial for June 1872 in the Nautical Magazine;[461]

> …The Act of 1864 never has found favour with the Government, because it is conceived and founded on compulsion. When Mr. Milner Gibson, the then President of the Board of Trade, relieved Mr. Laird of the charge of the Bill, the former gentleman did what he could to obtain the adoption of a voluntary scheme which would have estab-

lished trustworthy and independent proving houses to which persons wishing to prove chain cables might have sent them, in the spirit suggested in the paragraph number 5 below. The House of Commons, however, and as we think, and as we endeavoured to show in another case, in our leader on personal responsibility last month, took a wrong view of the subject and of the principles that ought to be observed in dealing with questions affecting trade, and went in wholly for compulsion. ...Although the Act never found favour with the Board of Trade, we are bound to say when they once had charge of it they administered it in such a manner as to make it really of use, and to command not only the approval but the respect of all persons interested. The Act is defective, as we shall point out below, its principle is bad, as we have pointed out above; but, on the whole, and in a rough and ready way, it has been of use. It was amended and perpetuated last year... The President of the Board of Trade (the Right Hon. Chichester P. Fortescue) has informed gentlemen interested in the subject, that he proposes to bring in a Bill to defer the operation of the Act of 1871... This action has been asked for on many grounds, two of which only are pertinent—viz., 1, that the Act ought not to apply to cables for export ; and 2, that there are not now, and are not likely to be for some time, enough public machines in existence to apply the tests... It may not be devoid of interest if, for a few moments, we consider some of the expedients by which the present circumstances can be met. The most obvious appear to be the following, viz;-

1. To sweep away both the old and the new Act ; but this would be sweeping away that which many people regard as a highly useful piece of legislation ; would be running counter to the views of the House of Commons, as embodied in the two Acts ; and would be to stultify altogether the recent action of the Government who carried the Act of 1871..

2. To suspend the operation of the new Act for a time (say twelve months) and to extend the operation of the old Act for the same time...

3. To make the public "proof" strain compulsory on all cables, whether for export or not, and to leave the test to the "breaking" strain to be applied voluntarily, as may be agreed between the parties...

4. To extend the old Act for a year, and to leave the breaking strain to be applied voluntarily, or unless by written contract the parties agree to forego the breaking strain…, or

5. To leave the application of both the "proof" strain and the "breaking" strain by a public machine, to the option of the parties buying and selling

Fortescue's amendment took account of the second and fifth options and the 1871 Act was amended accordingly by enactment on the 18 July 1872 of the *Chain, Cables and Anchors Act, 1872 – An Act to suspend the compulsory Operation of the Chain Cable and Anchors Act 1871.* The date of commencement of the 1871 Act, and continuation of the principle 1864 Act, was postponed from the 1st of July 1872 until the 1st of January 1873. During this period the compulsory nature of proving required by section five of the 1871 Act was suspended by the use of the word "may" rather than "shall";

> Provided also, that if, before the said first day of January one thousand eight hundred and seventy-three, any chain is brought to a tester for the purpose of being proved, he **may**, with the consent of the person bringing the same, test it in a manner provided by the fifth section of the said first mentioned Act [1871 Act] and **may** grant to such person a certificate of such testing.

Through replacement of the word 'shall' with 'may', the intent of the principal Act, that; – *…it is essential for the better Security of Lives and property afloat in Sea-going Ships, to make Provision for the proper testing of Chain Cables and Anchors…*; was replaced in 1872 by – *…it is expedient to Suspend the compulsory operation of the Act…*; a decision made by an ideologically driven President of the Board of Trade without any recorded debate during the rapid passage of the Bill through Parliament, resulting in the watering down of a critically uniform safety regime for all ships.

A more positive legislative initiative in 1872 was the passage through Parliament of a Bill which almost achieved the long overdue consolidation of responsibility for the administration of merchant ships into one Government department; the Board of Trade. On the 27th of June, after consideration of a committee report it was; '*Resolved,* That the Chairman be directed to move the House, that leave be given to bring in a Bill to amend the Merchant Shipping Acts and the Passenger Acts…' The Merchant Shipping and Passenger Acts Amendment Bill, *ordered* to be brought in by Mr. Chichester Fortescue and Mr. Arthur Peel, was presented and read for the first time.[462] The Bill, which received Royal Assent on the 10th of August,[463] came into operation on the 1st of January 1873 as *the Merchant Shipping Act, 1872* [464] – *An Act to Amend the Merchant Shipping and Passengers Acts.* The many Government departments with responsibilities for regulation of ships at this time, and the sweeping changes introduced, are evident in the following provisions of the Act.

The duties of Commissioners of Customs with respect to measurement and registry of ships were transferred by ss. 3 & 4 of the Act respectively to the Board of Trade and the Registrar General of Ships. Sections 5 – 7 dealt with transfer to the Board of Trade of the powers and duties of Emigration Commissioners; extensions of penalties for offences connected with applications for assistance in emigration, and transfer to the Board of Trade of the powers, under the Passenger Acts, of the Secretary of State. Primacy of the Merchant Shipping Act, 1854 was established under s.8 which required that passenger steamers be surveyed once in every year in accordance with the requirements of that Act. Sections 9 – 11 dealt with Pilotage; giving Trinity House the ability to modify rues as to pilotage rates, providing for alteration of payments made to the Trinity House Pilotage Fund by Cinque Port pilots, and allowing pilotage authorities to grant special sea licences. Section 12 ensured that any work undertaken by Trinity House in testing anchor chain and would be cost neutral by providing that;

> In the event of a license for testing of chain cables and anchors being granted to Trinity House under the Chain Cable and Anchor Act, 1871, all fees and other sums received by Trinity House in respect of such testing shall be carried to the mercantile marine fund, and all expenses incurred by the Trinity House in respect of such testing shall be chargeable on the mercantile marine fund.

Responsibility for survey and measurement of ships was firmly sheeted home to the Merchant Shipping Act, 1854 through s.13;

> All duties in relation to the survey and measurement of ships under this Act, or the Acts amended hereby, shall be performed by the surveyors appointed under the fourth part of the Merchant Shipping

> Act, 1854, in accordance with such regulations as may be from time to time made by the Board of Trade.

Under s. 14, all fees for surveys and measurements, whether undertaken by surveyors under the Merchant Shipping Act, 1872, or the Passengers Act, 1855, were to be paid to the superintendent of mercantile marine at the time and from there to the mercantile marine fund. All salaries and expenses were to be drawn from the same fund. A reference to the requirements of s.14, and to possible practices involving emigration officers appointed under the Passenger Act, 1855, was contained in s.15 which provided penalties for payments made directly to such persons.

The opportunity was missed in this broad devolution of responsibilities for safety of passenger ships to define which of the respective provisions for lifeboats in the Merchant Shipping Act, 1854, and the Passengers Act, 1855, had primacy in law.

Chapter 16

Load Line, Libel and Shipwreck Commission

On the clear night of 22 January 1873 the sailing ship ***Northfleet*** (1853), of 951 tons, was anchored off Dungeness with her anchor light burning brightly. She carried 379 persons, comprising 34 crew, the pilot and 345 emigrants, mostly railway workers bound for Tasmania, including 42 women and 52 children. She was loaded with a cargo of mainly railway iron. About 10.30pm, when most on board were asleep, she was run into amidships by an unknown steamer, and cut through to below the waterline. The steamship went astern and disappeared into the darkness, unidentified. A nearby fishing lugger and the pilot boat rescued a number of people but remaining ships in the anchorage were unaware of the impending disaster as no distress signals were fired from the ***Northfleet*** until 15 minutes after the collision. Two hundred and ninety-three people, including the Captain, were lost. Of the women on board only the captain's wife and one emigrant survived, along with just two of the children.[465] The steamer was identified in Cadiz shortly afterwards, with damage to its bows which had been freshly painted, as the Spanish registered ***Murillo*** of 300 GT.

The ***Northfleet*** disaster prompted a question in the House of Lords on the first sitting day of the 1873 Session, as to the situation with a number of extradition treaties currently being negotiated; one of which was with Spain;

> Assuming that version of the disaster to be correct, the act of the *Murillo* in deserting the *Northfleet* under such circumstances was one of the greatest iniquity and inhumanity that it is possible to conceive; but, apart from this particular instance, I think it desirable that we should understand the bearings of the case. I apprehend that if an English subject commanding a vessel acted in such a manner he would be answerable first of all civilly in the Court of Admiralty, and next criminally by an indictment for manslaughter— the fact of his making away after the collision without having given any assistance being probably taken as evidence of wrong intention on his part. It appears to me that in the same way a foreigner who has escaped to

> his own country could be made answerable in the English Courts, supposing always that there was an Extradition Treaty with the country to which he belonged; and I conclude that even where no Extradition Treaty existed, such a foreigner would be at once made amenable in the Courts of this country if he ventured to come here… Well, then, I want further to ask whether or not, in such a case as that of this collision—assuming the master of the *Murillo* to have acted as alleged—such a case would be covered by an Extradition Treaty? In three out of the four Treaties, while murder and attempt to murder are included among the offences for which Extradition will be granted, manslaughter is not. It is only in the case of the last of these Treaties—that with Germany—that manslaughter is provided for; and in this Treaty with Germany alone, which seems to have been prepared with unusual care, the case of sinking a ship at sea is provided for…[466]

The member was advised that '…We have no Extradition Treaty with Spain; but we are actively negotiating at the present moment with the view of having one completed'. Regardless, in September 1873 the ***Murillo*** was sighted on passage in British waters off Dover, arrested, and sold by order of an Admiralty court to meet the compensation claim filed by the owner of the ***Northfleet***. Her officers were severely censured. In the meantime there had been an amendment on the 7th August 1873; through the Merchant Shipping Act, 1873, to Part II of the Merchant Shipping Act, 1854, to include the following requirement;

> Every British ship registered after the passing of this Act shall before registry, and every British ship registered before the passing of this Act shall, on or before the first day of January one thousand eight hundred and seventy-four, be permanently and conspicuously marked to the satisfaction of the Board of Trade, as follows; Her name shall be marked on each of her bows, and her name and port of registry shall be marked on her stern, on a dark background in white or yellow letters, or on a light ground in black letters, such letters to be of a length of not less than four inches, and of proportionate length.

In November 1873 a suit claiming £24,000 was brought by the owners of the ***Northfleet*** and her cargo, for the loss of both by the collision. The Judge (Sir R. Phillimore) said, the only question in the case was that of identity, and he thought that it was clearly proved. His Lordship gave the following judgement;

> I grant the prayer of the motion; but I do not think I ought to be content myself with that mere part of my judicial duty. I find it difficult to express, in adequate terms, the indignation which the brutality and meanness of conduct of those who had the charge of the Murillo must excite in the bosom of every man not devoid of humanity. This case, indeed, represents all the cruelty, without the courage, of the pirate. – Court of Admiralty, Nov.4.[467]

Pressure was increasingly coming to bear upon politicians to look into the reason why loss of life at sea was continuing to increase in spite of comprehensive safety legislation introduced since 1846; a pressure which, through a combination of Plimsoll's crusade and public opinion, was to result in further legislation and the beginnings of yet another enquiry into the causes of loss of life at sea.

Frustrated and impatient with the slow machinations of Parliament, betrayed by 'Fortescue's Act' and disappointed with the lack of any meaningful legislative measure to address his primary concerns of seaworthiness, overloading and insurance, Plimsoll had taken stock during 1872 and decided on another approach. He'd laid the groundwork in March 1871 by gaining unqualified support from the Trade Union Congress for a campaign on behalf of sailors; support that was reiterated in January 1872. Plimsoll was well aware of the power of public opinion, having seen the Chartist movement in action in his youth, and had also noted that its leaders, Cobden and Bright, adopted a strategy of country-wide speech-making coupled with vociferous campaigning as Members of Parliament; a model he consciously decided to emulate.

Plimsoll decided to build upon the enthusiastic response to his limited campaign through public meetings and by appealing directly to the increasingly literate public. He wrote a 'pamphlet' for very wide distribution; a 128 page book entitled 'Our Seamen: An Appeal'. This was completed during 1872, drawing heavily upon James Hall's writings including his petitions to Parliament on load lines. Plimsoll personally funded the printing and distribution of 600,000 copies in January 1873;

"both fine and cheap editions, with a smaller pamphlet distilling its main points circulated to trade unions. Copies were sent to newspapers, with a note encouraging editors to use as much of the text as they wished".[468]

'Our Seamen – An Appeal' contained a preliminary section with detailed wreck statistics based upon reports from the National Lifeboat Institution and annual Wreck Reports compiled by the Board of Trade. A section on Underwriters propounded Plimsoll's view, with examples, that there is no risk to underwriters from over-insuring unseaworthy ships as the loss is spread amongst so many of them that the loss to any individual underwriter is negligible. He then went on to briefly discuss the major issue affecting the party closest to his heart; the Sailors;

> Seamen, too, are far more unprotected than other men, and this is especially so in the case of overloading (so great a cause of disaster), for their articles are signed before-hand, they have no voice in the matter of loading; and, if they refuse to sail for any cause, they can be, as they are, sent to gaol for periods of three weeks to three months; and men have gone to sea and to death in spite of terrible entreaties of wife and sister , driven by this cause alone, owing to the almost invincible repugnance of respectable men (the men I had in mind were engineers) to the contamination, the degradation, of a common goal.[469]

Plimsoll then moved on to shipowners asking the question; "Can we then look to the ship-owner, to his sense of justice, to his self-interest, to put a stop to this deplorable state of things?" He went on to compare the situation before ships were insured when the shipowner would take care after every long voyage to carefully overhaul his ship and, " if her cordage or rigging was getting tender, it was replaced with rigging new and strong – nothing was neglected to [e]nsure her safety; her return home was watched with utmost solicitude and anxiety" and claimed that over time this standard dropped and care was relaxed as, now that the ship was insured; "the owner's property was safe in any event". He addressed the detrimental effect of insurance on the loading of a ship by stating;

> I will now show how its effect in relaxing the good old rule of loading, viz, – that for every foot of depth of hold (measuring from the underside of the main-deck to the keel) 3 inches should be left above the water line, summarised as '3 inches of [ships] side to the foot of hold'. When you consider how small an addition to the fair load of a ship will augment the profits of a trip 25, and even 50, per cent, you will easily see how great was the temptation, especially in settled weather,

> to add the extra weight…when freights run low, the margin for profit over expenses is small; it may take nine-tenths of the cargo to pay the costs; an addition, then, of only 10 percent to the weight of the cargo will double the profit…[470] Lloyd's rules for spar-decked ships; where the side plating is carried up above the main deck as a lighter structure and is decked in with a "spar-deck" – a light deck traditionally built for sailing ships to carry spare spars and boats – decreed that one and a half inches of freeboard, instead of three inches per foot of hold was adequate due to the extra buoyancy provided by the higher side of the ship's plating.[471]

Plimsoll, fairly, did not tar all shipowners with the same brush and was thankful that affairs were not worse; "for it is well known in seaport towns that the great majority of our ship-owners do keep up repairs and do not overload…to put the case shortly, – before insurance was practiced, legislation was not needed; a new state of affairs has now arisen, which Parliament has not yet given attention to…"

> Clearly, then, we can no more look to ship-owners to remedy these evils (they having, as a class, done what they could), than we can to the seamen, nor to the underwriters, – and are, therefore, as clearly driven to this conclusion; That it is the duty of society generally to interfere, through the State, to extend to seamen the same degree of care as is bestowed on so many classes of our fellow-subjects. I say society instead of Government, because no Government can well move on the matter until public opinion requires it. Society means the individuals comprising it – therefore it is on you, who read these lines, that this great, this life-giving now devolves – you personally – not Parliament only merely, but *you*.[472]

He went on to give examples of many convincing precedents where Parliament had regulated industries, in particular mining, and appointed inspectors to ensure that these regulations were being complied with, and made the telling observation that;

> A still stronger precedent, however, may be cited. It is this:– that whilst it is all true which I have stated of merchant ships, every word of it, it is not the case with passenger ships. They are, and have been for years, surveyed by officers appointed by the Board of Trade at the cost of the

> Government. They are so surveyed twice in every year. What I want, and what I greatly wonder the working classes have not long ago demanded, is that the same measures of safety be employed when members of their order are concerned, as deemed needful, and employed, in the case of those who are above them. Clearly there is no lack of precedent.[473]

The sources of disaster were then summarized, with examples, of under-manning, bad stowage, deck-loading, deficient engine power, over-insurance, defective construction, improper lengthening, overloading and want of repair. He summarised remedies to these issues; one of which, over-loading, he demonstrated to be supported by the majority of Chambers of Commerce in the United Kingdom who, when considering a Merchant Shipping Bill in February 1870, made a proposal; 'That a periodical inspection of all sailing and steam ships not carrying passengers, unclassed at Lloyds, or by the Liverpool Underwriters' Association, should be compulsory." The meeting came to unanimous agreement;

> That, in consequence of the frequent losses of sailing and steam ships from the practice of *overloading*, the Association of Chambers are of the opinion that the attention of the Government should be drawn to this subject, and that it should be invited to take consideration whether the Bill should not contain provisions for determining the maximum load-line of sailing and steam ships.[474]

In discussing his proposed way forward Plimsoll stated that, in the coming (1873) Session he would; "...bring in a Bill providing for the compulsory survey of all merchant ships...and providing also that no ship shall be allowed to proceed to sea overloaded, giving the ship-owner the choice of all existing scales, subject to approval by the Board of Trade. He proposed a more cautious approach on the question of over-insurance and planned to "seek the advice of practical men in the meantime". If there was not time to include it "...my Bill will only deal with overloading and rottenness...." He also proposed to "move an address to the Crown praying Her Majesty to issue a Royal Commission to inquire into the other sources of loss I have referred to, and into the general subject;"

> ...but we must not allow even the issue of such a commission to delay legislation if we can help it on these two points, on which we are as able to pronounce as any commission, namely, – *That* ships unsea-

worthy by reason of want of repair shall not be allowed to go to sea unrepaired; and that ships shall not be overloaded'.[475]

At the end of the booklet, after presenting considerable irrefutable evidence, statistics and reasoned argument, Plimsoll rather overplayed his hand by including some heart-rending comments from the widows of seamen lost in overloaded ships, and then, in an apparent desperate attempt to gain support, thundering;

> Oh! my God! My God! what can I say, what can I write, to make people take thought on this terrible wrong? I tell you, you who read these lines, if you are a man, you deserve to perish suddenly, lacking sympathy and succor in your hour of utmost need, and leaving your nearest and dearest only the cold charity of the world to depend upon – for this is how sailors die – if you don't help. If you are a wife, you deserve that your husband should be taken from you without warning, and that to the anguish of bereavement should be added the material miseries of hunger and destitution – for this is how sailors' wives suffer – if you do not help. If you are a father, descending it may be into a vale of years, with sons strong and brave, the pride and support of your age, you deserve that they should perish with no hand to help them, leaving your remaining years uncheered by one filial greeting – for so the fathers of sailors are bereaved – if you do not help. If you are a mother, you deserve that your son should be taken from you in the pride of his young manhood, if you don't help stop this homicidal, this manslaughtering, this widow-and-orphan manufacturing system.[476]

Following pleas to fellow Christians, fellow Loyalists, working men and the gentlemen of the press, to support his cause, his final, more moderate plea was to;

> Whoever you are who read this…help the poor sailors, for the love of God. If you are a man of influence, call a meeting and confer on this Appeal; if you are not, and will write to me, I shall try to show you how to help. If you refuse – but this I cannot think – but if you refuse or neglect to use your influence, before another year has run its course at least five hundred – five hundred men! – now in life, will strew the bottom of the sea with their dead, unburied, unresting bodies, and desolation and woe will have entered many and many a now happy home…[477]

'Our Seamen – An Appeal' was launched at the Trade Union Congress on the 14th of January 1873 with a copy being given to each of the 130 members present. Copies were also sent to all major newspapers who immediately provided dramatic and ongoing support to Plimsoll's cause; The Time's stating that – "Mr. Plimsoll's 'Appeal' has excited a storm of indignation throughout the mercantile community."[478] One commentator's prediction; "...the libelous nature of some of the statements and references were calculated to produce great sensation and a great sensation was produced" was soon borne out with two ship owning MPs immediately suing Plimsoll for libel. Shipowners throughout the country dissociated themselves from the accusations in the publication. [479]

Upon returning to Parliament for the 1873 Session, Plimsoll lost no time in rising on the 10th of February; the third sitting day, to;

> ...move that the Chairman be directed to move the House, that leave be given to bring in a Bill for the Survey of certain Shipping and to prevent overloading, [and] said, that since he had circulated a book amongst the Members of the House on this subject he had had upwards of 300 letters from as many Members of the House, and of that number 97 had authorized him to put their names on the back of the Bill. That could not be done without great inconvenience, and therefore he had determined to take the first 10 names, and he asked the others to accept that as an explanation. [480]

Plimsoll had, provocatively, given copies of 'Our Seamen – An Appeal' to all MPs except those who owned ships. The only response in the House to his proposal was from Mr. Norwood, a ship owning MP from Hull, who stated; "he had no wish to oppose the Motion; but he expressed a hope that hon. Members who had received the book referred to would suspend their judgment on the ground that it was an *ex parte* statement capable of being satisfactorily answered;" a warning shot across the bow for one of the pending libel suits. The Motion was agreed to with the Bill being read for the first time.

A week later, presumably to assist with preparation of his Bill, Plimsoll asked Fortescue whether; "in the table of loss of life at sea published by the Board, any account is taken of the losses of the men who are washed or fall overboard during a voyage in ones or twos, or of those who are accidentally killed during a voyage by rough weather or other causes, as in boarding a vessel or landing in boats, &c.?" to which Fortescue replied; "it was impossible to add anything to the Returns annually laid on the Table. If the hon. Member looked at the Return presented last year he would find that all the deaths of British merchant seamen, whether occurring from disease or accident, were enumerated and analyzed."[481]

On the 20th February, by which time the ship owning members had seen copies of Plimsoll's book and digested the contents, a motion was proposed by Mr. Eustace Smith, a shipowner, on a matter of Breach of Privilege that; "to accuse, in a printed book, Members of this House of grevious offences, and to threaten them with further exposure if they take part in its Debates, is conduct highly reprehensible, and injurious to the honour and dignity of this House." Before making this motion Smith had asked the Clerk of the House to read a number of extracts from Plimsoll's book which referred to the purported activities of unnamed ship owning MPs. One of these extracts of particular concern referred to two or three unnamed ship owning MPs being; "what they call in the North 'the greatest sinners in the trade' having got into the House, it is there, and there only, that opposition to reform is to be expected, or is found."

At the heart of Smith's concerns was a comment in the book by Plimsoll regarding a debate in 1871;

> In 1871, when I brought in my Bill a second time, it was most anxiously debated by me with myself whether or not I should allude to those cases. Hoping to succeed without doing so, I did not allude to them in my opening speech, and, of course, was then precluded from doing so in my reply; and these two men actually took advantage of this omission to speak against the Bill, and put up another Member, who would, I am afraid, find it very embarrassing to answer some questions that might be put to him. (I recommend those gentlemen to be more discreet next Session, if they wish to preserve their incognito.)
>
> Smith asked the House; "...Now, what is the meaning of this 'incognito?" It cannot be the incognito of these gentlemen as Members of this House, or as shipowners, because their names can be discovered by the register of every ship belonging to them in the country. But the incognito he threatens to drop is the fact of their being the men

> against whom he has brought serious and grave charges; and he threatens them that if they speak against his Motion he will expose them still further. If that is not a distinct threat against Members of this House, and a distinct interference with the liberty of debate, for one, confess that I am ignorant of the meaning of the English language. The crimes with which the hon. Member charges other hon. Members are too serious for any of us to hesitate to speak respecting them. We all feel that these crimes are most outrageous; that if they be true—if the hon. Member has the facts to justify these statements, he ought to have brought forward at once the names of the persons he accuses, and have taken the consequences. That would have been the honourable, courageous, and more manly course. But if he had not sufficient evidence upon which to make the charges, he should not say that very strong language might be used with regard to them…"

Plimsoll was profoundly shocked by these accusations of stifling debate, threatening members of Parliament, and of breach of parliamentary privilege. In his haste while writing the book, and his naivety and lack of understanding of Parliamentary process, he had clearly not foreseen the potentially serious consquences of his actions. He made, what was accepted by other members, as a very ample and sincere apology and then withdrew from the House;

> Mr Speaker…having consulted the highest authority, I am advised that I have committed an inadvertent offence against the House. Sir, I am deeply concerned that such should be the case—that any language of mine could possibly convey any meaning which could be deemed lacking in that high respect for the House to which alike its honourable traditions and its high character give it so just a title. I beg to assure you, Sir, and every hon. Member of this House, that nothing whatever could possibly have been further from my intention. As, however, it does appear possible that my meaning and intention may have been so far misunderstood, I have to offer to you and to the House the sincere expression of my regret that, in the earnestness with which I sought help for the helpless, coupled with my inexperience as a Member, I should have left anyone room to doubt that for the House I entertain, and ever have entertained, feelings of the very highest respect. For my most unintentional fault, I offer to you, Sir, and to the House, the most ample apology it is in my power to make; and I assure the House that

> to have become one of its Members I esteem, and ever shall esteem, to be the greatest honour and the highest distinction of my life.[482]

Smith withdrew his Motion.

While being humbled in Parliament, Plimsoll was being lauded without question by the press and the public; his main audiences. The Times quoted two cases where Courts of Inquiry had been held into the loss of clearly unseaworthy ships in 1869 and condemned the Governments apparent inaction in preventing such ships from sailing; 'a trader may leave port in mid-winter with her main deck sunk below the water with railway iron, with her plates rusted through, her timbers rotten or parting, or her machinery out of order, without violating one jot or title of the law. Such an anomaly is wicked and ridiculous and must not be allowed to exist anymore.' The Thunderer identified another long-standing anomaly with the legislative status quo; 'it is a foolish and wicked distinction which has been drawn between passenger and trading vessels; it is not a law worthy to be called a law at all which minutely inspects an emigrant or store ship, but lets a mere merchantman go to sea and founder at the sweet will of weather and its owner'.[483]

Not all of the press were uncritical. The Nautical Magazine weighed into the debate in March 1873 with a pointed comment about Mr. Plimsoll's Book;

> We had proposed to publish this month an article criticising this remarkable effusion, and placing certain facts of our own knowledge in juxtaposition with Mr. Plimsoll's daring and alarming statements. The article is still in type, but we have advisedly abstained from inserting it, pending actions or proceedings taken, or about to be taken, against the honourable member for Derby.

One of the pending actions was a libel suit by Charles Norwood, Liberal MP for Hull, whose ship, the ***Livonia*** had sunk, without loss of life, shortly after departing Newcastle. Plimsoll's book contained a scathing account of the attitude of the unnamed shipowner, extreme overloading of the ship, and receipt of an insurance payment, without identifying the particular ship or the owner. Norwood had always been an avowed opponent of Government regulation of shipping as reflected in a remark; "I can assure you that we require on board our large ships a barrister even more than we require a doctor. There are so many acts under which we conduct our business that it is impossible for a ship's captain to know how to act to keep within the four corners of the law" and had opposed any regulation bringing in load lines.[484] Norwood lost his case and, for reasons given in the Judge's decision in June, the court decided that Plimsoll should not have inferred from the loss of the ***Livonia*** that Norwood was 'one of the greatest sinners in the trade;'

> Mr Plimsoll's reasoning seemed to be that so long as he had a laudable object in view he was entitled to say anything he pleased, and to make any accusation against whomsoever he chose...Mr Plimsoll believed his bill to be a good one, and perhaps it was, but...when members who were conversant with the subject got up and pointed out the discrepancies he was unable to substantiate them, and, in consequence he launched these libels at their heads in order to discredit their explanations, to shut their mouths and to put an end to their opposition to what he considered his good ends.

The ***Livonia,*** which was not insured, was the only ship belonging to Norwood to have been lost, and Norwood demonstrated to the court that he was not an owner who operated 'coffin ships'. Consequently, Plimsoll was ordered to pay his own costs. Experts in the shipping industry agreed, though, that the ship had sunk as a result of overloading.[485]

One of the other alleged 'great sinners' in Plimsoll's book was Edward Gourley, the MP for Sunderland who was anonymously described as a "... shipowner whose name was often mentioned to me in the course of the years 1869 and 1870. During my inquiries in the north and east, I heard his name wherever I went as that of a shipowner who was notorious for the practice of overloading, and for a reckless disregard of human life... it is really awful to contemplate the loss of precious human life from the operations of this one man alone". Plimsoll, foolishly, included a list of the vessels owned by this person which were lost, referring only to the first and last letters of each ship's names, and including the lives lost, if any, on each occasion; a total of 105 from the loss of twelve ships between 1867 and 1869. It was a simple matter for anyone in the shipping industry to identify the fleet, fill in the missing letters in each ship's name, and identify the owner.

Gourlay; three times Mayor of Sunderland, an ex-Alderman, magistrate and staunch member of the Baptist church issued libel proceedings against Plimsoll, an action that his lawyers imparted to The Times in a letter on the 15th February 1873. The case was still pending in June when Norwood failed in his libel action. Gourlay then withdrew his action due to a perception that Judges were sympathetic to Plimsoll's cause.[486]

The very wide distribution of Our Seamen, along with supportive articles in the press, brought about a great deal of support for Plimsoll, who quickly became a household name throughout the country, and particularly in the major ports where many families had suffered the loss of loved ones through the causes expounded by Plimsoll. He addressed public meetings in North Shields, Derby, Liverpool and Sunderland where there was also a meeting of shipowners whom, although deploring Plimsoll's accusations against their MP, and holding that corrosion in ships was caused by bulk cargoes of sugar, still supported the concept of a load line and a Royal Commission. The ground swell of support for Plimsoll's call for a Royal Commission had also reached Parliament and affected the views of many of its members. Independent financial support was given to Plimsoll through the establishment in March of the Plimsoll and Seamen's Defence Fund; initially to help defray his legal costs and publications but, as his campaign became increasingly busy and complex, to assist with costs of an administrative committee. Contributions were received from across all sections of society with Plimsoll's one condition that any money left over from immediate expenses be given to the dependents of lost seafarers.

On the 4th of March Plimsoll rose in the House to move that; "…an humble Address be presented to Her Majesty, praying that She will be pleased to issue a Royal Commission to inquire into the condition of, and certain practices connected with, the Commercial Marine of the United Kingdom". He supported his motion firstly by summarizing the deficiencies he had identified in existing legislation, stating that;

> …the law will not prevent me nor anyone else from building a ship of any dimensions which fancy or caprice may dictate; from using timber altogether insufficient in scantling and unsuitable in quality in building that ship; …from building an iron ship in any way I please, and of so-called steel plates of such a quality that a strong man with

a heavy hammer could knock a hole in them—plates, in point of fact, little better than cast metal; ...will not prevent me, having selected a design for a flush-deck iron steamer, and having had the ship so constructed, from building upon her, after she is launched, a poop 120 feet long, then adding a top-gallant forecastle 50 feet long, then uniting the two roofs and calling it a hurricane-deck, and then putting upon the latter donkey-engines, steam-cranes, and other gear, in such a way as to provoke the strongest representations that I had simply built one ship upon another, and that the whole must certainly founder the first time she encounters half a gale of wind and a beam sea. ...the law will not prevent me, urged by competition, from cutting a vessel in two, adding 50 or 70 or any other number of feet to her length amidships, without any diagonal bracing, any doubling of plates, any additional bulkheads, or any of those appliances which a competent naval architect would think necessary; ...will not prevent me from keeping my ships at sea in a state of unrepair, fraught with the highest peril to those on board—keeping her at sea until she is 70, 80, 90, 100, or even more years old—from keeping her at sea in fact, when she is so utterly rotten that if she takes the ground or touches a rock she must inevitably go to pieces with quick and sudden destruction; ...will not interfere to prevent my loading a ship, no matter of what class or kind, with an amount of cargo that shall sink her deck within a couple of feet of the water, and sending her to sea in a condition which not merely excites the forebodings of all on board, but gives rise to many condemnatory remarks on the part of those who see her set forth;...will not interfere to prevent me, having built steamers for what is called canal and general cargo traffic, from sending them across the Atlantic and loading them with grain in bulk, a most dangerous cargo, and requiring ships of extraordinary tightness and strength to carry in safety; ...will not prevent me from so overtasking the engine-power of my vessel as to load from 17 to 19 tons cargo per horsepower, a fair load per horsepower not being more than from 12 to 13 tons, and so overtasking the human power on board as to sail a steam-vessel of over 2,000 tons from a foreign port for England with only eight deck-hands on board, three only of whom were able seamen and competent to understand the orders which were given to them. And, lastly, that the law provides for the measurement of ships in such a way as distinctly to encourage the building of ships of an unsafe character, inasmuch as, if you cover your ship from end to end with a hurricane-deck, which will enable

> the vessel to throw off the seas, you make her liable to considerably increased charges—as tonnages, dues, &c.; which additional charges you altogether escape if you build merely a long poop and a forecastle, thus leaving the engine-hatches and apertures leading to the fire-hole open like a funnel to receive every sea which washes on board.

He went on to; "...ask the House to consider with me for a moment the extent of the mischief which has resulted from the state of things which I have endeavoured to describe...I am able to assure the House that the total annual loss for the ...four years is not less than I now give the figures for:—In 1868, the lives lost were 2,488; in 1869, 2,821; in 1870, 3,411; and in 1871, 2,296. In all, 11,016, or 2,754 per annum on the average...and proceed[ed] to consider the steps necessary to give effect to that will. We must first—and I trust that will be some time before we sleep—appoint a Commission which shall make a thorough and searching inquiry into the whole subject, including undermanning, bad stowage, deck loading, deficient engine power, over insurance, defective construction, improper lengthening, overloading, want of repair, necessity for certificated masters between Brest and the Elbe, rate of speed lawful in fogs, rule of road, and code of signals.

Plimsoll's motion was strongly supported by Sir John Pakington who had unsuccessfully called for a Royal Commission in 1870. In seconding the Motion; Pakington drew the attention of Members to some damning statistics;

> Members of that House and the public in general had very little idea of the immense extent of the loss of life and property at sea. In the year 1871, according to *Lloyd's Lists,* which he believed was the highest authority that could be referred to on the subject, more than 13,000 wrecks and casualties occurred, and the lives lost in the course of that year amounted to 2,040. In the year 1872, the autumn of which, as they must all remember, was very severe, the loss was above the average of former years. Of sailing ships the number absolutely lost was 2,682, of which 1,310 were British ships. He would now call attention to the distinction between wrecks and. casualties, and those ships that were either abandoned or foundered at sea, or were what was called "missing." The number of ships that foundered in 1872 was 637, and the number missing was 135—the meaning of "missing" being ships that went to sea, of which nothing was ever heard afterwards, and. the

> fair inference was that they had gone down to the bottom of the sea with every soul on board. The number of steamers lost during that period was 244 of over 100 tons, of which 142 were British ships. From the 1st January in the present year up to this time no less than 50 vessels were missing, many of them being fine iron steamers, and in all probability they had gone to the bottom. Under these circumstances, he considered it the duty of the House to inquire into the probable causes of the terrible loss of life and. property.

Mr Joseph Samuda, MP for Tower Hamlets, and a naval architect, strongly supported the motion, noting that;

> It appeared from the records published by the Board of Trade that the losses for the consecutive periods of the five years ending in 1853, 1858, 1863, and 1868 were respectively 969 ships, 1,118 ships, 1,488 ships, and 1,744 ships—which showed that there was a continually increasing loss of ships. He had had an opportunity of taking the average up to 1871, and making a similar division for the averages for 15 years, ending at the respective periods of five years before 1871, it appeared that the losses were 1,045 ships, 1,320 ships, 1,611 ships, and 1,805 ships, from which the House would perceive, as he had remarked, that there was a continually augmenting loss of ships. But then it might be said that our trade was now considerably greater, and that the increase in the number of our vessels would account for the increased number of losses. He would, however, be able to show that the House could not rely on any such explanation; for in 1858 the number of ships of all sorts on the books belonging to the United Kingdom was within 100 of 27,000, while in 1868 they were only 29,000; so that while the increase in the number of ships during these 10 years was only 8 per cent, the increase in the number of losses was at the rate of 50 per cent... in 1871, the 1,575 wrecks and casualties among vessels trading within the narrow seas represented 458,000 tons of shipping, or about £5,000,000 sterling a year... it stated in the official Report of the Board of Trade that the wrecks and casualties for the 10 years ending 1871 amounted to a grand total of 13,300, of which those resulting from stress of weather in a total loss numbered 7,300; those resulting in wreck from various other causes, or from causes unknown, numbered 2,500; while not less than 3,400 were set down as being lost from inattention, carelessness, neglect, and defective equipment; that, put in plain language, meant that nearly one-half of the losses arose from preventible causes...

At this point in the debate an amendment was proposed; "To leave out the words 'an humble Address be presented to Her Majesty, praying that She will be pleased to issue a Royal Commission to inquire into' in order to insert the words 'it is desirable that a Bill be forthwith introduced into this House by Her Majesty's Government for the purpose of constituting a Commission to inquire into upon oath and report upon.'

In replying to the proposal for a further amendment, the President of the Board of Trade made it clear that; "...he should state, without further delay, the intention of the Government with respect to this Motion, and that intention was to accept in substance the proposal of the hon. Member for Derby, though they would not be able to accept the exact words, for reasons which he would give presently... He went on to praise Plimsoll's book, but disagreed in detail with some of the statistics and content, and suggested the alteration of the Motion, so that it should "run in something like the following form":

> That a Royal Commission be issued to inquire into the condition of the Mercantile Marine, so far as regards the overloading of vessels; the unseaworthiness of vessels, whether owing to defective construction, condition, and equipment, or stowage, deck loading, under-manning; and the present system of marine insurance; and to report, if any, and what measures can be adopted to remedy the evils which may be found to exist.

There followed unanimous support for a Commission but considerable debate as to whether this inquiry should be instituted by a Royal Commission or by a Parliamentary Commission with power to administer an oath and to compel witnesses to attend. Plimsoll stated that he would thankfully accept the Commission offered by the Government. He trusted that the Government, while undertaking the responsibility of appointing the Commission, would take care that it had all the necessary powers conferred upon it. He was astute enough to realise that establishment of a Royal Commission could considerably delay his proposed Bill and made it clear that, regardless, he intended to introduce this Bill dealing with over-loading, deck-loading, and other similar matters, during the current session. Accordingly, he would withdraw his Motion. This approach was supported by the Prime Minister, Gladstone, who, in concluding the debate, assured members that;

> …The Government thought that without the smallest delay the Commission should be set to work. When the Commission was properly constituted, it would feel its own ground. The object of all of them was to have a very searching inquiry, and the Government would be most ready to ask either that witnesses should be examined on oath, or, if necessary, to go further. But it certainly would not be desirable that at the commencement the Commission, which would inquire into matters affecting the whole maritime population of the country, should be vested with powers such as were given to the Commission which inquired into the outrages at Sheffield. Such powers would impart to this inquiry a criminal character. No one was desirous of casting such an imputation upon the shipowners. On these grounds, he hoped his hon. Friend would be disposed to withdraw his Amendment.[487]

The amendment and motion were, by leave, withdrawn.

Chapter 17

Merchant Shipping Act, 1873

While parliamentarians were earnestly debating the reliability of wreck statistics and loss of life at sea a well-found, lightly loaded and seaworthy passenger paddle-steamer was preparing to depart from Liverpool for New York on her nineteenth voyage across the North Atlantic. Named after that very ocean; the ***Atlantic*** (1871) of 3,707 tons, was the second of four revolutionary passenger steamers built by the Oceanic Steam Navigation Company (White Star Line), founded by Thomas Ismay in 1869. The four masted iron hulled steamers were 420 feet long, with a beam of only 40.9 feet. The long slender hulls were powered by a compound engine of 600 horsepower driving a single screw, to achieve record breaking speeds of 14.5 knots.[488] The White Star line ships immediately achieved faster crossings than their Cunard and Inman rivals, averaging nine days nineteen hours westward and eight days twenty-one hours east bound, burning an average of 670 ton of Welsh coal into the prevailing weather on the longer west bound crossings. On the occasion of her nineteenth voyage the ***Atlantic*** carried 927 ton of coal; a mixture of high quality Welsh coal and lesser quality coal from Lancashire. On her previous westbound voyage she had consumed 810 ton of mixed quality coal and average consumption for the previous eighteen crossings had been 744 ton of Welsh coal.[489]

The ***Atlantic*** departed Liverpool on the 20th of March, lightly loaded with cargo and with only 33 cabin class passengers and 146 crew aboard. After stopping at Queenstown, Ireland, to embark 800 emigrants and load mail she departed for New York carrying a total of almost 1000 people; the passenger count being uncertain due to at least twelve stowaways who boarded at Queenstown. [490] The ship made good 938 miles over the first three days but then encountered a strong West to Southwest gale for the following four days during which time she made good only 747 miles. On Friday the 28th of March the Chief Engineer informed the Captain that the fuel consumption was higher than usual and he estimated that there was only 319 ton of coal remaining. Speed was reduced from twelve to eight knots to conserve fuel and steam heating of the accommodation was turned off. At noon on Monday the 30th there was only 127 ton of fuel remaining for the 460 mile passage to New York, the barometer was falling, and there were still headwinds. Halifax was estimated to be about 170 miles away to the north and it was decided to divert to that port to obtain sufficient coal to reach New York. All boilers were fired up and speed increased to twelve knots to reach Halifax as soon as possible in an attempt to still arrive at New York in time to fulfil the company's obligations under its mail contract.[491]

Of the ship's officers, only the Third Officer had previously been to Halifax but that need not, with careful and prudent navigation, have been an issue. The log was streamed occasionally, indicating twelve knots, but no soundings were taken. Shortly before midnight, when it was thought that Sambro Lighthouse, near Halifax, was forty to fifty miles away, the Captain went to the chartroom to get some rest, instructing the Second Officer to wake him at 0240 hours. When a quartermaster, Robert Thomas, came on duty at 0200 he immediately felt uneasy about the ship's location, believing it to be too close to the coast, and that Sambro Light should be in sight. When his concerns were abruptly dismissed by the Second Officer, Thomas raised them with the Fourth Officer, also on watch, and asked permission to keep a lookout from the main yard. This was refused and Thomas was ordered to take the wheel. At 0230 the Second Officer advised the Captain that visibility was worsening. When the steward arrived to call the Captain as requested at 0240 the Second officer told him not to do so as "there was no need to call him yet". When the log was streamed again at 0320 it was indicating more than twelve knots; with the alteration of course at noon the wind had become favourable. Very soon afterwards the lookout shouted "Ice dead ahead" and in spite of the Second Officer's orders for full astern and hard a starboard, the ship struck at full speed, about twenty-two miles to the west of Halifax harbour.[492]

The *Atlantic* pounded on the rocks at least five times "utterly destroying her hull", and all the port lifeboats were immediately swept away. The Captain and officers tried to launch other boats but all were smashed, and all persons aboard them lost, when the ship was suddenly set on to its beam ends by the large breaking seas. The after end of the accommodation rapidly flooded before breaking off, drowning many of the steerage passengers in their bunks. The Third Officer, quartermaster Thomas and two other quartermasters managed to swim a line to a large rock midway to the shore by means of which people were hauled to the rock. Thomas swam another line the remaining distance from the rock to the shore and raised the alarm with local residents who came to assist at first light with their fishing boats. Over the following few hours more than two hundred people were taken off the ship although two to three hundred women and children were swept out of the sunken stern section and out to sea to their deaths. Estimates of those lost vary but the total was at least 535, including all of the women and children, except for one young boy; the worst loss of life in a merchant ship between 1800 and 1898.

The Captain was reported as stating; "To think that while hundreds of men were saved, every woman should have perished. It is horrible. If I had been able to save even one woman I could bear the disaster; but to lose all! It's terrible! Terrible!" The seamanship and navigation displayed by the Captain was summed up by an experienced sea captain at the time;

> The position of the vessel on that fateful night demanded the utmost care and attention. Any prudent man would have doubled his look-outs, sent a man to the mast-head to keep a bright lookout for land or lights, and slowed his ship down until he saw something from which to take a sure departure; and he should have taken the further precaution of taking an occasional toss of the lead, and even stopped the ship 'dead' to do it. None of these precautions seem to have been taken, and the Atlantic went along at a 'happy-go-lucky' gait until she brought up all standing, pounded on the bottom two or three times, and then rolled over. [493]

A Court of Inquiry in Halifax found fault that the White Star Line had not provided sufficient coal for the voyage, and also questioned the quality of the coal. The shipping company, fearful for its reputation, went to great lengths through two further enquiries in England to eventually disprove this allegation. The Court also ruled that the Captain had been "glaringly defective" in resting while his command approached an unknown and dangerous shore. The Court of Inquiry suspended the Captain's certificate for two years, but White Star line re-employed him once it was reinstated. The Second Officer's certificate was suspended for three months.[494]

Keeping the pressure on the Board of Trade in Parliament, Plimsoll asked a question of Fortescue on the 24th of March 1873 concerning two alleged unseaworthy ships; the new build ***Hindoo*** and a ship berthed in London; the ***Parga***. The system for classifying and surveying newly built ships had clearly failed in the case of the ***Hindoo***. The President of the Board of Trade confirmed that, when built, the ***Hindoo*** had been classed A1 for twenty years by the Liverpool Underwriters Association and surveyed by Board of Trade surveyors at Glasgow, who issued a passenger ship certificate, then surveyed again in London before departing on its maiden voyage from London to Calcutta. The ***Hindoo*** experienced bad weather down Channel and put in to Plymouth, where she was to embark passengers, 'considerably damaged', with her steam-pipe valve damaged, her steering gear out-of-action, and making water. Her underwriters re-surveyed and passed her, but a Board of Trade surveyor cancelled her certificate and she was sent back to London to discharge all cargo and undergo extensive, and expensive, repairs to strengthen the ship. She then resumed her voyage.

Plimsoll claimed that the ***Parga*** was declared unseaworthy by a Board of Trade surveyor in London and; "steps have been taken to prevent her going to sea, under the recent Act of 1871." The facts of the matter, as reported at the time, appear to be somewhat different. Plimsoll, upon receiving a letter from a rigger about the alleged condition of the ***Parga***, had laid a complaint with the Board of Trade who had detained the ship as being suspected of being unseaworthy. The owner, who was also the Master, instructed his solicitors on the 22st of March to demand the source of Plimsoll's information, and an apology and compensation. Plimsoll's solicitors forwarded to the owner his intemperate reply;

> Sirs,
>
> Yours of the 22nd inst to hand.
>
> I will not give the name of my informant. I will make no apology, and as to compensation, the only compensation due to your clients and all other ship owners who load unseaworthy vessels to sea with men a thousand times better than themselves on board is, in my opinion a halter piece and the offices of the hangman.
>
> Do your worst.
>
> Samuel Plimsoll

This was not the end of the matter. The owner of the ***Parga*** appealed to the City of London Court who appointed a Lloyds surveyor and two other surveyors who inspected the ship on the 28th of March. The Lloyds surveyor and one other reported minor defects but both stated that they could not fully report on the ship's condition as she was fully loaded. The third surveyor declared her to be seaworthy. On the 5th of April a motion to release the ship was heard by the City of London Admiralty Court. Commissioner Kerr stated; "as he was informed that a full survey could not be made without the discharge of the cargo, he thought it only reasonable that it should be done....he would therefore make on order for the cargo, or so much of it as might be required to be removed, be discharged in order that the full and complete survey might be made." After this survey the three appointed surveyors reported that the vessel was seaworthy. There was no further survey by Board of Trade surveyors as the Master would not agree that they pierce some of the timbers, as was usual with older wooden vessels. The ***Parga*** successfully completed her voyage to Buenos Aries and return.[495]

Fortescue, tongue in cheek, thanked Plimsoll for passing on this information noting, pointedly; "...This is the first time the hon. Gentleman has given me information of unseaworthy ships that have come to his knowledge, and I am glad that in this instance information was given which may prevent an unseaworthy ship going to sea."[496]

A question the following day also didn't go well for Plimsoll when a Member asked the President of the Board of Trade whether he was aware of a statement made in a speech by Plimsoll; "...As to the animus of the Board of Trade, the Honourable Gentleman cited the case of an inquiry ordered by the House of Commons into the loss of the ***Sea Queen,*** with twenty lives, in which the damning evidence of the Custom House officers and the lumpers [stevedores] as to the unseaworthy state of the ship had, he said, been deliberately suppressed, and a surveyor's report printed in the Blue Book, trying to exculpate the owners from their responsibility, they having, he declared, pocketed £25,000, as the profit of sinking, the owner, too, having superintended the loading; and, whether such statement is correct?" Fortescue, in referring to; "...the very extraordinary statements in the speech of the hon. Member for Derby... demonstrated that were all completely unfounded."[497]

In reply to a further question from Plimsoll on the 28th of March as to the terms of reference and membership of the Royal Commission, the President of the Board of Trade stated;

> ...That a Commission should forthwith issue to make inquiry with regard to the alleged unseaworthiness of British ships arising from overloading, deck-loading, defective construction, condition, equipment, form, or machinery, age, or improper stowage; and also to inquire into the present system of Marine Insurance, and the state of the law on the liability of shipowners for injury to those whom they employ, and the effects of under-manning ships; and to suggest the best remedy for the removal of such evils as may have arisen from the matters aforesaid... With respect to the names which had been selected, and had received the approval of Her Majesty, they are as follows:—The Duke of Somerset (Chairman), His Royal Highness the Duke of Edinburgh, the right hon. T. Milner Gibson, Admiral Sir James Hope, the hon. Henry George Liddell, M.P., Mr. Thomas Brassey, M.P., Mr. Henry Cadogan Rothery, Registrar of the High Court of Admiralty; Mr. Arthur Cohen, Barrister-at-law; Mr. Peter Denny, of an eminent shipbuilding firm at Dumbarton; Mr. George Duncan, member of the committee of Lloyd's Register; Captain Edward Dover Edgell, head of the Survey Staff of Lloyd's Salvage Association; and Mr. Charles Watkin Merrifield, Principal of the Royal School of Naval Architecture and Engineering. Instructions are contained in the Warrant, to the effect that the Commission shall first and separately report to Her Majesty upon the question of overloading; and shall secondly and separately report upon the question of unseaworthiness and defective construction.[498] None of the proposed Commissioners were shipowners.

Although Plimsoll relied heavily upon the press to publicise 'Our Seamen' and to report his speeches, the risks associated with this caused a heated exchange in the House between him and Fortescue on the 7th of April. The latter claimed that the integrity of his staff had been seriously called into question by a statement reportedly made by Plimsoll in a speech before a 'huge assembly' at Exeter Hall in London, on Saturday the 21st of March; "...There are people who represent us, or who ought to represent us, on the Board of Trade, who are wholly unsuspected, who would give half their fortune to promote wrecks. There is one man who has busied himself considerably in this way, but I will not mention names". Plimsoll strongly refuted this claim, calling as his witness to the fact that he'd been misreported, the 20 to 25 Members of Parliament who had been at the meeting, and stating that he'd immediately contacted the offending newspaper which had published a correction the following day. He rounded off his rebuttal with the testy comment; "...It appears to me that was amply sufficient for all purposes of explanation; because, if every error which appears in a provincial newspaper is to be made a reason for putting an hon. Member *in loco pentitentiœ* to explain, we shall have nothing else to attend to, and no time for any other business."[499] The meeting at Exeter Hall in London, known as the 'great Plimsoll meeting', chaired by the eminent elder statesman the Earl of Shaftesbury, ended with a unanimous resolution to establish a committee of support, whose first members included six members of the House of Lords and eleven of the Commons, two Admirals and four shipmasters. On the 26 of March the Plimsoll and Seamen's Defence Fund was officially established by the Lord Mayor of London, who had joined the Committee along with twenty-five peers of the realm.[500]

After the Royal Commission was established on the 29th of March, 1873, there was a great deal of concern and dismay, amongst shipowners and in the maritime press, that Parliament had agreed in February to Plimsoll's motion to bring in a Bill to deal with certain matters that were part of the remit of the Royal Commission. A petition was presented to Parliament from the Liverpool Shipowners' Association, representing a total of seven hundred thousand ton of steamships owned in, or trading to, Liverpool. They believed that Plimsoll's proposed Bill would require almost every ship to be surveyed before going to sea and require a load line to be marked. '... These provisions, if carried into effect, would, in many cases, grievously hamper honest shipowners, and interfere with legitimate trade...' and;

> ...although, there can be little doubt that vessels have, in many instances, been sent to sea in an unseaworthy state, and that a case for public investigation by Royal Commission has been fully made out, yet it is almost as certain that in the course of recent public agitation on the subject many exaggerated statements have been made, and that the practical difficulties of the subject, and the best mode of remedying the evils which exist, have not been sufficiently considered. Your petitioners, therefore, humbly consider that the matter is not yet ripe for legislation.[501]

Plimsoll would not entertain any suggestion that his Bill should be postponed and reacted strongly, publicly, and without support, at a meeting in Sheffield to a letter he had received in which Gladstone pointed out; "that it would be disrespectful to the Commission to bring in a Bill for the protection of sailors before they completed their task." This letter was characterized by Plimsoll as "cruel, cold-blooded, murderous and infamous". He hinted that the Government did not dare bring in a Bill, lest they should lose the vote of the ship owners in the house, and appealed to the people of Sheffield to send Mr. Roebuck (their MP) to Parliament again, that he might have the support of "at least one honest man". Both the attack and the suggestion were reported as being 'resented by the audience'... [502]

However, Plimsoll's concerns regarding unseaworthy ships were gaining considerable Parliamentary traction and, on the 13th of May, the President of the Board of Trade proposed a Motion;

> ... that leave be given to bring in a Bill to amend the Merchant Shipping Acts, [explaining] that the object of the Bill was to strengthen the power and increase the responsibility of the Board of Trade in exercising the functions conferred on them by the Act of 1871 for the purpose of' preventing unseaworthy ships from proceeding to sea. In bringing in the Bill, he had not done it without communicating with the Royal Commission on the whole subject. The Commission was satisfied that this Bill would not anticipate their recommendations. The Bill also contained provisions relating to collisions at sea, the improvement of signals of distress, and other matters.[503]

Plimsoll rose in the House on the 14th May to seek support for the second reading of his Shipping, Survey &c Bill. He offered as evidence to refute claims that he had repeatedly exaggerated that Liverpool insurance underwriters might be expected to know what they were talking about; that they had claimed to occasionally have to do business with men; "who cared little about the profits of the carrying trade; men whose whole commercial history was made up of accommodation bills, average statements, liquidations, and composition deeds; who were always on the lookout for some crazy craft to insure... who pursued their nefarious calling under an honourable garb, and sometimes under the cloak of religion; and it was such men who were responsible for the heavy losses which underwriters had to sustain." As an example, he referred to a well-known shipowner of Shields, who had made over £100,000 by such practices. Plimsoll stated in a conciliatory tone that he believed these were the practices of a very small number of men, and; "he thought it wonderful that in the absence of all legislation on the subject, things were no worse than they were, and that the great majority of those who were connected with our shipping trade had so much care for the lives of their seamen.". He fended off criticism of his Bill viz-a-viz the Royal Commission by stating that he sincerely hoped and believed the Commission would do much good; ... but it could not have all the time required, unless some temporary measure was passed, claiming that if that were not done;; "we should incur all the danger of an ill-considered and hasty Report. It was perfectly competent by the forms of the House to pass a temporary Bill, and move for a Royal Commission." Concerning the load line ...what he desired to arrive at was such a degree of immersion as, in the opinion of the most experienced men, a ship might safely put to sea with. "The principle he had in view was this, that ships needing repairs should not be allowed to go to sea until they had been repaired, nor should ships be overloaded to a degree that would endanger their safety." With regard to deck-loading; "the law prohibiting the practice altogether had been swept away in 1862, as it was said, in the interests of trade, and with the most mischievous results. He proposed that it should be revived under certain regulations." During his conclusion he stated, "It might, therefore, be put down as a mathematical certainty that, in the absence of survey and of the load-line, many hundreds of men now living would not be living next year; and under these circumstances, forsooth, the House was asked to let things alone in order to save the dignity of the Royal Commission..." He begged, he entreated, he implored the House to read the Bill a second time. Plimsoll then proposed that that the Bill be read a second time.

The motion was opposed by the ship owning Member, Eustace Smith, and that was the end of the matter. Plimsoll had been 'talked out'; a ploy by which Members loaded the agenda in order to allow little insufficient time for a debate; 'And it being a quarter of an hour before Six of the clock, the Debate stood adjourned till To-morrow.' Tomorrow never came for Plimsoll's Bill. In the course of his response Smith referred to Fortescue's Bill of the previous day stating; "the Government had decided to bring in a Bill on this subject; but that Bill involved no new principle, and was only intended to extend the power already possessed by the Board of Trade under an old Act; and when it came on for a second reading it would be time enough to deal with it." [504] On the following day a meeting was held between Plimsoll, and MPs Smith, Candlish and Gourlay at which Plimsoll yielded to their objections to fixed load lines; agreed to let the location of a load line be determined by either Lloyds Register or the Royal Commission, and accepted that ships less than five years old should not be required to have a compulsory survey. Agreement was also reached to postpone further discussion for six weeks, pending an expected interim report from the commission.[505]

In response to a question from Plimsoll in the House on the 20th of May regarding the powers of the Royal Commission, the President of the Board of Trade took the opportunity to read a letter received from the Chairman of the Commission regarding Plimsoll's participation, and the lack of shipowner representation;

> …It appears that objection has been taken to the course pursued by the Commission in excluding the public and the reporters from our room while we admit Mr. Plimsoll or his solicitor. The Committee were desirous to give Mr. Plimsoll full opportunity to make out his case and to bring before them such evidence as he could collect … the Commissioners decided that where the conduct of any shipowner was impugned he should at once be written to, and have a Copy of the Evidence, so far as it concerned him, forwarded to him. Inasmuch, however, as some statements might be made indirectly affecting the character of shipowners, the Commissioners have decided to communicate with the Associated Shipowners, asking them to appoint a solicitor or other person in whom they have confidence, who might watch the evidence from day to day and prepare any witnesses for a reply.[506]

Following public criticism of the Royal Commission by Plimsoll, at a meeting at Grimsby, of the pace of work of the Commission and a claim that it met behind closed doors, he was banned from the hearings.[507]

On the 5th of June a question was asked by another Member regarding the urgent need for re-introduction of legislation to deal with the long-standing issue of timber deck cargoes. Fortescue explained; "the Merchant Shipping Acts Amendment Bill which he had introduced dealt to a certain extent

– to as large an extent as he thought it proper to attempt to deal under present circumstances – with the question of overloading; but the special question of deck-loading with timber from America and other countries was not embraced in that measure. That question [of overloading, and deck-loading] formed part of the reference to the Royal Commission on merchant ships."[508] The Commission heard evidence on the history of the timber deck cargoes legislation from the permanent secretary to the Board of Trade, Thomas Farrer, whose argument was that the deck loading ban was withdrawn in 1862 as it was; "too difficult to enforce." When Farrer was questioned about a Board of Trade official who knew of fifteen ships that left port overloaded, his reply was; "they all reached their destination". Plimsoll was moved to comment; "this ...monstrous indifference to safety demonstrated that the Board of Trade was the stronghold of the worst men in the shipping interest".[509]

Plimsoll received complaints from all quarters about alleged overloading and under-manning and, throughout June and July, either raised these issues in the House or arranged for one of his supporting MPs to do so if he was engaged elsewhere on his very hectic campaign of public meetings throughout the country. Questions were also addressed by him to the Board of Trade on numbers of jailed seamen, and the status of British seamen remaining aboard a ship after it had changed flag to a foreign owner. At this time Board of Trade officials were busy drafting a Bill which was to become the Merchant Shipping Act, 1873; an Act which would not entirely meet Plimsoll's expectations of an Act; "...providing for the compulsory survey of all merchant ships...and providing also that no ship shall be allowed to proceed to sea overloaded..." The resultant Merchant Shipping Acts Amendment Bill, which principally amended the 1854 and 1871 Merchant Shipping Acts, was introduced and had its first reading on the 23rd of June. The Bill was back in the House on the 21st of July for its second reading, a committee report was debated on the 25th and the third and final reading of the bill was held on the 28th of July. It was then considered by the House of Lords, with Royal Assent being given on the last day of the Session; the 5th of August 1873.

In the *Merchant Shipping Act, 1873*[510] – *An Act to Amend the Merchant Shipping Acts* – section two made it clear that;

> This Act shall be construed as one with the Merchant Shipping Act, 1854 and the Acts amending the same, and the said Acts and this Act may be cited collectively as the Merchant Shipping Acts, 1854 to 1873

As with the 1871 Act, the 1873 Act was divided into three main parts; *Registry* (Part II, MSA, 1854), *Masters and Seamen* (Part III MSA, 1854) and *Safety and Prevention of Accidents* (Part IV MSA, 1854). Part IV included *Miscellaneous and Appeal matters*. Three Schedules covered – *Signals of Distress, Signals to be made by ships wanting a pilot*, and a *Table of maximum fees to be paid for the measurement, survey and inspection of merchant ships.*

Amongst other amendments, the most significant under *Registry* was the addition, in section 4 – *Particulars to be entered in record of draught of ship*, of a requirement for minimum freeboard to be measured and recorded; the precursor of a marked load line, which officially recognized the importance of freeboard to prevention of overloading, stability and unseaworthiness;

> The record of the draught of water of any sea-going ship required under section five of the Merchant Shipping Act, 1871, shall, in addition to the particulars thereby required, specify the extent of her clear side in feet and inches.
>
> The term "clear side" means the height from the water to the upper side of the plank of the deck from which the depth of hold as stated in the register is measured, and the measurement of the clear side is to be taken at the lowest part of the side.

Under a new section nine; *Masters and Seamen*, a more just and humane provision was enacted for compensation to seaman for unnecessary detention on charge of desertion;

> If a seaman or apprentice belonging to a ship is detained on a charge of desertion or any kindred offence, and if upon survey of the ship being made under section seven of the Merchant Shipping Act, 1871, it is proved that she is not in a fit condition to proceed to sea, or that her accommodation is insufficient, the owner or master of the ship shall be liable to pay to such seaman or apprentice such compensation for his detention as the court having cognizance of the proceedings may award.

Part III of the *Merchant Shipping Act, 1871, Safety,* had broadly covered, in four sections – *Exchange of information in cases of collision, Complaints of seaworthiness* and *Owners liability for sending a ship to sea in an unseaworthy state.* Part III of the 1873 Act was more comprehensive and detailed, covering, in sixteen sections, new or updated provisions for – *Survey of ships suspected of being unseaworthy, Power of the Board of Trade to vary requirements as to boats, Liability for infringement of regulations in cases of collisions, Signals of distress, Signals for pilots, Private signals, Notice to be given of apprehended loss of ship,* and *Carriage of dangerous goods.*

Notable, among these amendments, was section twelve; *Survey of ships suspected of being unseaworthy,* clearly a result of the many complaints the Board of Trade were receiving about unseaworthy ships as a direct result of Plimsoll's crusade, and possibly, the Board's experience with the ***Parga***:

> Where the Board of Trade have received a complaint or have reason to believe that any British ship is by reason of defective condition of the hull, equipment, or machinery, or by reason of overloading or improper loading, unfit to proceed to sea without serious danger to human life, they may, if they think fit, appoint some competent person or persons to survey the ship, and the equipments, machinery, and cargo thereof, and to report thereon to the Board.
>
> Any person so appointed may, for the purposes of such survey, require the unloading or removal of any cargo, ballast, or tackle and shall have the powers of an inspector appointed under the Merchant Shipping Act, 1854.
>
> The Board of Trade may, if they think fit, order that any ship be detained for the purpose of being surveyed under this section, and thereupon any officer of customs may detain such ship until her release be ordered either by the Board of Trade or by any court to which an appeal is given under this Act...

Questions had been asked in the House in May regarding the desirability of being able to replace boats with rafts, and also on the need to provide boats for all persons on board. During the debate a motion was put forward; 'certificates should not be granted to passenger ships unless they were provided with lifeboats and deck rafts sufficient to save all on board in case of disaster or shipwreck.' The first speaker, Sir Charles Adderly, replied;

> ...In the great disasters which had occurred lately all the boats on board had not been used. In very rare cases had the boats been of any use. But suppose a ship wrecked in the middle of the Atlantic, with all the lifeboats and deck rafts proposed by the clause on board, and that all the passengers were lowered safely into them, what would become of them? They would simply be starved and die by inches instead of being drowned in the ship. Boats and rafts were useful to take passengers to any near shore, or ship, by relays such as there were seamen enough to manage: but more boats than there were men to manage were useless. A great number of boats and rafts would be the worst kind of deck-loading, and would impede the working and navigation of the ship. He considered that the existing law and the powers possessed by the Board of Trade were sufficient to effect the purpose in view. One Act stated a proportion of boats to tonnage very ample, if not excessive; and another Act enabled the Board of Trade to alter the scale, or to substitute rafts or life-boats.

In response to this bleak opinion Plimsoll presented a more compassionate view when stating;

> ...perhaps in 99 cases out of 100—boats proved useless, but rafts would not be open to the same objections, and would not be liable to be stove in as boats were in being lowered. There were rafts which could be easily stowed that were fitted up in the centre so as to carry preserved meats whereby people might be kept alive for a long time. Of course, there was no necessity for any alteration if the argument of the right hon. Gentleman were sound, and if it were better for the passengers to be drowned at once instead of dying a lingering death in the boats.

These and other opinions, before the motion was defeated, may have affected the Board of Trade's thinking in the inclusion of a new section 15 of the 1873 Act – *Power for the Board of Trade to vary requirements as to boats;*

> In the case of any ship surveyed under the fourth part of the Merchant Shipping Act, 1854, the Board of Trade may at the request of the owner authorise the reduction of the number and the variation of the dimensions of the required boats for the ship by section two hundred and ninety-two of that Act and also the substitution of rafts or other appli-

ances for saving life for any such boats, so nevertheless that the boats so reduced or varied and the rafts or other appliances so substituted be sufficient for the persons carried on board the ship.

A further outcome of the ***Northfleet*** collision was the introduction through section 15 of the *Merchant Shipping Act, 1873,* of a clause concerning the Master's responsibility in a case of collision;

> In every case of collision between two vessels it shall be the duty of the master or person in charge of each vessel; if and so far as he can do so without danger to his own vessel, crew, and passengers (if any), to stay with the other vessel until he has ascertained the she has no need of further assistance, and to render to the other vessel, her master, crew, and passengers (if any), such assistance as may be practicable and as may be necessary in order to save them from and danger caused by the collision; and also to give to the master, or person in charge of the other vessel the name of his own vessel, and of her port of registry, or of the port or place to which she belongs, and also the names of the ports and places from which and to which she is bound.
>
> If he fails so to do, and no reasonable cause for such failure is shown the collision shall, in the absence of proof to the contrary, be deemed to have been caused by his wrongful act, neglect or default...

Sections 18 and 19 referred to Tables in the Schedule for updated and simplified *Signals of Distress* and *Signals for a Pilot,* with s.20 providing for changes of updates through Orders in Council. Section 21 provided for *Private Signals;*

> Any shipowner who is desirous of using, for the purposes of a private code, any rockets, lights or similar signals, may register such signals with the Board of Trade, and the Board shall give public notice of the signals so registered in such manner as they may think requisite for preventing such signals from being mistaken for signals of distress or signals for pilots

Section 22 required the managing owner, or ship's husband, to notify the Board of Trade in writing; *if they have reason owing to the non-appearance of such ship, or to any other circumstance, to apprehend that such ship has been wholly lost....* Sections 23 – 28 covered the carriage of dangerous goods, including *Restrictions on carriage; Penalties for misdescription, Power to refuse to carry goods suspected of being dangerous; Power to throw dangerous goods overboard* and *Forfeiture of dangerous goods improperly sent.*

All sections under *Registry and Masters and Seaman* came into effect immediately, along with s.12, *Survey of ships being suspected of being unseaworthy,* s.13, *Costs of survey.* S.14, *Appeal from decision of Board of Trade;* s.15, *Power for Board of Trade to vary requirements as to boats;* s.17, *Liability for infringement of regulations in cases of collision* and ss. 28 – 33, *Miscellaneous and Appeal.*

The 1873 Act immediately repealed s.29 of the 1862 Act; *Regulations to be published* along with s.4, *Name on bows and stern, and draught marks* and s.10, *Survey of ships suspected of being unseaworthy* of the 1871 Act. Sections 327, *Notice to be given of apprehended loss of Steam Ships* and 329, *Collison to be entered in Official Log Book* of the 1854 Act; along with s.34, *Periodical Surveys of Passenger Steamers;* s.38, *The Provisions of the 329th Section of the Principal Act shall extend to Foreign Ships* [carrying dangerous goods] *when within the Limits of the United Kingdom* and s.9, of the 1871 Act, *Exchange of identity etc in case of collision,* came into effect on the 1st of November 1873.

Although the 1873 Act encroached upon the brief of the Royal Commission with introduction of a requirement to record freeboard, along with proactive rather than reactive powers regarding complaints of unseaworthy vessels and detention, it came in for none of the criticism aimed at Plimsoll's Survey, Shipping &c Bill; the prescriptive nature of which had been seen to remove responsibility from the shipowner to the Government. The Nautical Magazine pulled no punches in its satisfaction over the substance of the Act, and in its criticism of Plimsoll:

> We rejoice to see that Her Majesty's Government have rejected the proposals put forward by the humanitarians and doctrinaires who have supplied the froth and wind for the recent seasonal agitation, and that the management and supervision of Great Britain's vast mercantile fleet are not to be handed over to any Government Department, or any Registry Society. Everyone admits, as has been repeatedly stated and provided in the *Nautical Magazine,* that ships are sent to sea which ought not to be sent, and that lives are lost which ought not to be lost...But because these things are so, it is not right that susceptible and impulsive persons, who notably know nothing about ships and seamen, should

> propose all kinds of absurd measures, and carry them through on a wave of popular enthusiasm…the new Act commends itself to people... because there is nothing subversive of reason or principle, and everything to fix responsibility upon those who ought in justice to bear it.[511]

Plimsoll had shown little interest in the passage of the Merchant Shipping Act Bill through the House, probably due to the fact that he had taken leave from Parliament at this time due to exhaustion from his demanding round of public speaking engagements. He was pinning his hopes for significant reform on the deliberations of the Royal Commission.

In June 1873 there was a dramatic collision between a British sailing ship and a French passenger ship resulting in the loss of both ships and a great many lives. The French ship; ***Ville de Havre*** of 3,950 ton, had been built in Great Britain in 1863 for the Compagnie General Transatlantique as the ***Napolean III*** of 3,337 ton. In 1873 she was lengthened from 366 to 422 feet and converted from a paddle steamer to single screw propulsion along with a new compound engine. On her first arrival in New York after her conversion, on the 9th of April, the ***Ville de Havre*** was feted as the second largest passenger ship; behind the ***Great Eastern,*** to ever enter the harbor. On a later voyage that year she departed New York on the 15th of November with 176 passengers and 137 crew.

At two o'clock in the morning of the 22th of June, in heavy seas, she suddenly sighted a sailing ship. The ***Loch Earn,*** a three– masted iron sailing ship of 1,200 ton; built in Glasgow for the Glasgow Shipping Company Limited in 1869, was on a voyage in ballast from Glasgow to New York. The ships were in such close quarters that, in spite of the ***Loch Earn,*** the stand-on vessel, putting her helm hard to port and sounding her bell when collision seemed imminent, the ***Ville de Havre*** crossed her bow and was rammed amidships on the starboard side in way of the engine room. Two lifeboats were filled with passengers and preparing to launch when the ship's main and mizzen masts, spars and rigging fell across them killing many of those aboard. There was only time to launch two small boats, a whaleboat and the Captain's gig, before the ship sank only twelve minutes after the collision. The ***Loch Earn*** launched a boat to pick up survivors and the Second Officer of the ***Ville de Havre*** managed to reach the sailing ship in the whaleboat and transfer some survivors before rowing a mile back to the scene of the collision to rescue others, after 45 minutes in very cold water, including the Captain. Due to her badly damaged bow the ***Loch Earn*** put about and made for Queenstown in Ireland but had to abandon ship on the 28th November with all aboard being rescued by an American sailing ship, the ***Trimountain***, outward bound from New York. The ***Loch Earn*** sank shortly afterwards. Of the 331 souls aboard the ***Ville de Havre*** only 87 survived; twenty-four male and ten female passengers, along with fifty-three crew.[512]

Meanwhile, the Royal Commission, had met every few days from the 22nd of April to the 29th of July; a total of twenty-four sitting days, and heard evidence from forty-eight witnesses, some of whom appeared many times. Plimsoll attended the hearings three times.[513] Upon release of the Commission's preliminary report on the 23rd of September, after giving Plimsoll credit for his energetic labours, the Nautical Magazine stated that the 'Plimsoll Commission' '…has already done good work in standing between him and his Quixotic ideas, and commercial interests generally, and in dispelling some of his illusions.' The Commission's introduction to the Interim report included statistics obtained from the Registrar General of Ships and Seamen showing the total number of registered ships belonging to the British Empire to be 86,804 with a total registered tonnage of 7,213,829. It was estimated that these ships were crewed by 392,000 persons. The Commission then summarized its interim findings which were presented to both Houses of Parliament.[514]

On the first matter of Overloading the Commission firmly nailed its establishment colours to the masthead in refuting the contention of some witnesses that overloading prevails to a serious extent; 'The large numbers of ships in ballast being lost annually and losses from collisions show that the mismanagement and negligence of sailors are no less disastrous than the carelessness shipowners.' The Secretary of Lloyds observed; "I do not believe that overloading began suddenly in 1872, and yet the loss of ships in the winter of 1872 and the first months of 1873, was far greater than in any former year." The Commission did, however, acknowledge the dangers associated with overloading, but identified a difficulty in establishing criteria by which to judge whether or not a ship is overloaded.[515]

Plimsoll's heart must have sunk when he first read, what appeared to be, the Commission's final view on Loadlines;

> Some witnesses recommend that the Government should interfere for the protection of life, by the adoption of a compulsory loadline for all seagoing ships. This summary form of expression includes several divergent questions. 1st. The expediency of prescribing to what extent ships may be loaded. 2nd. The rule or principle on which this extent of loading shall be determined and indicated. 3rd. The expediency of marking a loadline amidships. 4th. The use to made of a loadline if marked.

Having said this, the long-established ratio of three inches of freeboard to every one foot depth of hold was referred to and; 'a computation found to have been practically convenient might, it is said, be legally enforced.' Another example given in the report was; 'a principle which was in use as a scale for a proportion of freeboard to depth of hold which varied with the size of ship.' Opposing these models were; 'experienced witnesses who contended that the use of such principles 'would inevitably lead to the building of light and weak ships, which would, under this scale, have an advantage over ships constructed with heavier scantlings and strong fastenings,' and came to the conclusion that 'A law prescribing such a rule would therefore enhance the perils of a seafaring life.' Although having included on the matter of Loadlines a statement; 'We have devoted much time and attention to this part of the subject, and we have taken evidence on the possibility, and expediency of, adopting such rules,' the Commission came to the surprisingly early and final conclusion that;

> Taking all of this into account…'we cannot recommend any enactment for establishing a fixed loadline, founded on the proportion of freeboard to the depth of hold of the vessel.'[516]

The Commission's brief also included Deck-loading; specifically alluding to the prohibition; enacted by the various Timber Ships Acts between 1839 and 1862, on the carriage of timber deck cargoes from Canada and other British colonies during the winter. The commission made reference to statistics on the numbers of lives lost before and after these Acts as being 'imperfect and untrustworthy,' recalling that 'the Committee of 1848, pointing to the benefit of the deck law state that the average loss of life in the years 1840, 1841 and 1842 was only 106, and they mention this as a satisfactory result of the law. Later returns show that, in the year of 1871, when there was no deck law, the loss of life in the same trade was only 16. The number of lives lost in the North American timber trade during the disastrous year of 1872 was 105'. The Commission did, however, propose to deal with this matter more fully at some future time.[517]

On the subject of Survey of all British ships; Plimsoll, in his 'Our Seamen', had used as an example of the merits of surveys a charterer of sailing ships loading guano in Chile who had stipulated that all such ships must undergo a survey before being chartered to; "prevent old coffins' or unseaworthy ships being employed in this trade. After this practice was adopted it was claimed by Plimsoll that no guano ships foundered; a claim reportedly supported by a surveyor from Chile. This claim was disproved by records obtained from the company of chartered vessels lost, abandoned or foundering, both before and after surveys were introduced. The surveys had made no difference. The commission undertook to give the subject further consideration.[518]

The Commission did not recommend that Lloyds Registry and Lloyds Register and Salvage Association; 'any of these admirable voluntary associations should be converted into authorized establishments for the compulsory survey of all merchant ships.'

With reference to Inquiries by the Board of Trade and Plimsoll's claim; "there had been few inquiries [into the loss ships] until the pressure of public opinion had constrained the Board of Trade to undertake these duties", evidence from wreck returns was analysed by the Commission for 1869, with it being established that 87 inquiries had been held, not the three claimed by Plimsoll. The Commission agreed that there were many undesirable features of current courts of enquiry and agreed that;

'...amendment of the courts of inquiry is an object of great importance, but it is a matter which would require careful consideration, and we have not taken sufficient evidence upon the subject to justify our making and recommendations.' They did, however, give Plimsoll qualified credit;

> We might, if necessary, point out many other inaccuracies in his statements, but he has the merit of having called attention to the loss of life which occurs in the Mercantile Marine from the culpable neglect of shipowners, as well as from other preventable causes. Some allowance may therefore be made for mis-statement and exaggerations which we are obliged occasionally to notice.[519]

Chapter 18

Royal Commission on Unseaworthy Ships[520]

FINAL REPORT[521]
TO THE QUEEN'S MOST EXCELLENT MAJESTY

WE, Your Majesty's Commissioners appointed to inquire into the alleged unseaworthiness of British registered ships, humbly beg leave to present to Your Majesty the following Report on the several matters referred to us.

Much misconception appears to exist as to what is meant by seaworthiness. We think it therefore necessary before offering any recommendation with a view to the preservation of human life at sea, that we should preface our observations with a few words on this subject.

The safety of a ship at sea cannot be secured by any one precaution or set of precautions, but requires the unceasing application of skill, care, and vigilance from her first design to her unloading at the port of destination. She must be well designed, well-constructed, well equipped, well stowed, or she is not seaworthy. She must be also well manned and well navigated, otherwise all precautions as to her construction and as to her stowage will be unavailing.

These remarks are obvious enough when stated, but there is abundant proof that while public attention has been eagerly directed to some of the above precautions, other sources of danger have been altogether unnoticed. A summary of official inquiries into wrecks and casualties, excluding collisions, shows that from the year 1856 to 1872 inclusive, a period of 17 years, while 60 ships were known to have been lost from defects in the vessel or in the stowage, 711 ships were lost from neglect or bad navigation.

Without placing too much reliance on this tabular statement, which, especially in the earlier years, may be imperfect, we shall be justified in ascribing a large portion of the casualties at sea to preventable causes other than the faulty construction, the insufficient repair, and overloading of ships.

We have endeavoured to obtain more complete statistics on this subject, in order to ascertain how far the loss of life at sea is to be ascribed to the several matters into which we have been commanded to inquire.

We have been furnished by the committee of Lloyds and the Registrar General of Seamen with elaborate statistics relating to casualties and loss of life at sea; but, as these statistics were only produced at our last meeting, we have been unable to examine them sufficiently to test their accuracy or to form any definite conclusions upon them. They will be found in the Appendix.

LOAD LINE

In our former Report, which was a summary of the evidence collected during last year, we stated that we had, in obedience to Your Majesty's commands, taken much evidence on the subject of overloading, but that we were unable to recommend any enactment for establishing a fixed load line founded on the proportion of freeboard to the depth of the hold of the vessel. The additional evidence which we have received confirms us in that opinion. At the same time we reserved for future consideration the question, whether any other scale of measurement could be either enforced by law, or adopted as a guide for the safe loading of merchant ships.

The information which we have obtained leads us to the conclusion, that the settlement of a load line should be mainly guided by the consideration of the reserve buoyancy, that is to say, of the proportion which the capacity of the watertight and solidly constructed part of the ship which is above water bears to the capacity of the part immersed.

Mr. Martell, chief surveyor to Lloyd's registry, after obtaining information from many shipowners, and having consulted with some of Lloyd's surveyors, submitted to us a scheme, not indeed for a compulsory load line, to which he objected, but for a mode of judging the depth to which a merchant ship might be safely laden. Witnesses who have examined this scheme say that if such a test were applied and enforced ships which have hitherto made their voyages in perfect safety, could no longer be profitably employed.

We referred in our former Report to a scheme which Mr. Rundell, secretary to the Liverpool registry, submitted to us for indicating the proper freeboard of first class vessels. Coasting vessels and many other ships must, he said, be altogether exempted from this scale, and a large discretion must be allowed to the Government surveyor in applying such a rule of freeboard.

Another scheme, founded on the same principle, but allowing a wider margin for different seasons of the year, has been brought to our notice. This mode of marking a merchant ship was intended to indicate the greatest amount of cargo which the ship might safely carry, when all the circumstances, that is, the season of the year, the length of the voyage, and the nature of the cargo, were favourable. These circumstances must continually vary, and under a charter this mode of marking would have a dangerous tendency of inducing the charterer to insist on the vessel being laden up to the line of deepest immersion, and thus imperiling the safety of the ship.

Any rule of freeboard founded on surplus buoyancy gives to a vessel of light scantling an advantage over a stronger vessel. Thus, the inferior ship would by law be allowed to carry the heavier cargo. Such an enactment would not contribute to the safety of life at sea.

From all the evidence which we have collected on this subject, we are of opinion that an Act of Parliament enforcing any scale of freeboard would be mischievous. The rough rule of three inches of freeboard to every foot of hold is easily applied, and may be practically convenient, but in our former Report we pointed out the objections to fixing by law such a scale for regulating the loading of all vessels.

Some witnesses suggest that there should be an elasticity in the law, which should be left to the discretion of the surveyor. The existence of such opinions shows the inexpediency of legislating either to secure freeboard in proportion to the depth of hold, or to provide some fixed percentage of spare buoyancy in every vessel.

There is no general agreement as to a rule by which the requisite amount of reserve buoyancy could be determined, and it appears that except under definite circumstances it is not a determinable problem.

The proper load line in each particular case depends not only upon the principal dimensions of the ship, but also upon her form and structural strength, the nature of her cargo, the voyage, and the season of the year.

Discretion as to the proper loading of his ship must be left to the shipowner, or, under his directions, to the manager, on whom the responsibility rests for sending the ship to sea in a seaworthy condition, which responsibility it is inexpedient to diminish. We have, therefore, come to the conclusion, though not without regret, that we cannot prescribe any universal rule for the safe loading of all merchant ships.

In a subsequent part of our Report we shall offer some suggestions for rendering the responsibility of the shipowner more complete, but, as regards freeboard, we would now recommend that every merchant ship should have marked upon each of her sides, amidships, a vertical scale of feet downwards from the edge of her main deck. To explain our view more precisely, the zero point of the scale should be at the lowest part of the upper side of the highest deck, that is, of the deck up to which the ship is completely strong and watertight.

A note of this reading should be entered in the log book, after the vessel has received her full load, immediately before the time of her starting on her voyage, and should, wherever practicable, be left with the officer of customs or with the British Consul, by whom it should be recorded.

Since the appointment of this Commission, the Canadian Legislature has prohibited the carriage of deck loads in timber ships across the Atlantic from the 1st October to the 16th March, with an important exception, however, in favour of deals.

This exception was reluctantly made as a concession to certain shipowners, and materially diminishes the value of the enactment.

The evidence of Mr. Fry, President of the Dominion Chamber of Commerce, proves the danger arising from deck loads during the winter months, and although the efficacy of the law depends on its enforcement at the port of departure, yet a similar enactment by the British Parliament would sanction the views of the Canadian Legislature, and might induce other timber exporting countries to consider favourably the propriety of such legislation. The rules of several mutual insurance clubs forbid such cargoes during the winter months, and as these rules are prescribed by the shipowners themselves, it cannot be supposed that the timber trade would be injuriously affected by the law.

The opinion of some witnesses is that all deck loads should be prohibited. Bales of cotton, it is said, are frequently piled up on the deck, seriously interfering with the working of the ship, and increasing the dangers of navigation.

Merchant ships would undoubtedly be safer if they were lightly laden and carried no deck cargoes but a merchant ship is a machine employed for earning freight, and we are of opinion that it would be unwise for the legislature absolutely to prohibit deck cargoes, except in the special case of the timber trade.

We recommend, however, that whenever a deck cargo is carried, the quantity and character of such cargo should be stated in the log, and a copy of such statement left at the Custom House. In case of non-compliance with this provision, the shipowner, if he be in fault, or the master, should be liable to penalties.

Grain cargoes are attended with danger to life, and require exceptional care. The rapid mode lately adopted for loading the grain ships adds to the danger. There are, however, well-known precautions tending to diminish this danger, but the application of these will be best left to the responsibility of the shipowner, and to the practical knowledge of the captain.

The powers granted to naval courts by the Acts of 1854 and of 1871 provide an imperfect remedy for these evils, but there are serious objections to conferring on courts abroad the extensive powers which the Board of Trade possess in the United Kingdom,— —powers which it requires great judgment and the utmost caution even on the part of the Board of Trade to exercise without injury to the shipowner and serious prejudice to commercial interests.

SURVEY OF BRITISH MERCHANT SHIPS

We have taken further evidence as to the practicability of instituting a survey of all British merchant ships.

The policy of instituting a Government survey for the purpose of securing the sea-worthiness of ships is more than questionable. It would tend to remove responsibility from those persons on whom it should rest, and would render the Government nominally responsible for the form, the materials, and the whole construction of our merchant ships.

With the view of providing for the greater safety of life at sea, it has been suggested that the Board of Trade should superintend the construction, the periodical inspection, the repair, and the loading of all British merchant ships.

There is now an official survey of emigrant and passenger ships, and it has been proposed that a similar survey should be extended to all merchant ships. The system pursued in reference to passenger and emigrant ships is chiefly valuable for securing arrangements conducive to the health and accommodation of the passengers.

The surveyor under the Board of Trade inquires into a variety of details in regard to the ship and her equipments, and, being familiar with the requirements needed, his suggestions are advantageous, but when he interferes with the steam engines, boilers, and safety valves, he hampers the shipowner, and increases the cost of navigation, while he takes upon the Government an undue responsibility. We even consider it to be a question worthy of serious consideration, whether, in the case of passenger ships, the certificate of the Board of Trade, so far as regards specific approval, should not be expressly confined to the number of passengers to be allowed, and to the accommodation for their health, comfort, and general security; all questions of seaworthiness of hull, machinery, and equipment being left to the owners, subject only to a general power of interference in case of a danger sufficiently apparent to justify special intervention.

This alteration would take away many grounds of complaint against the interference of the Government and of the surveyors of the Board of Trade, who are now not unfrequently accused of enforcing upon shipowners and marine engineers special views of their own, which are not always in accordance with the best judgment of the professions.

If a similar survey were applied to all British ships, the number of surveyors requisite to inspect all new ships, and all ships under repair, and the number of dry docks necessary in the ports of the United Kingdom, would present serious difficulties to the satisfactory fulfilment of the law; but, what is worse, the mischievous con-sequences to the future progress of shipbuilding would, we believe, be actually calamitous. Ships would be built and repaired so as to pass the examination of the official surveyor, and any additional outlay beyond what was indispensable to secure a certificate would be rejected as useless. Under the present enactments shipowners justly complain that their business is seriously inconvenienced, and that foreign ships are already gaining the trade which the British shipowner has been compelled to relinquish.

The official survey of merchant ships has been adopted in France, in Belgium, and in Italy, but the inspection is said to have been superficial: it was disregarded by underwriters, and, according to the statement of Monsieur C. Bal, the Director of the Bureau Veritas, it has now become a mere formality.

In our former Report we referred to a suggestion that the Government should adopt the machinery of Lloyd's registry for the survey and classification of British merchant ships, or that the registries of Lloyd's and of the Liverpool Association should be in some way amalgamated and be legalised as a Government system.

The classification of ships opens another question, which, although important to the mercantile community, has no direct reference to the safety of life at sea.

The Government is not concerned, as these registries are, to ascertain whether a ship is fit for the conveyance of dry and perishable goods, but merely whether the ship is seaworthy.

A Government certificate would therefore include a lower grade of ship than would be admitted, at least in the higher classes of these registries. Such a system, by including under one certificate the inferior as well as the best vessels, would dis– courage improvements in ship building. Some of the companies do not class their steam ships in any register, although these vessels are of acknowledged efficiency. Doubts have been suggested whether the rules laid down by either of these registries are sufficient to secure the requisite structural strength in very long iron ships. It is admitted, that, for this class of vessel, the rules both of Lloyd's and of the Liverpool registry have been recently under revision, with the view of providing additional strength.

Voluntary associations may modify their rules as experience may guide them, and shipowners can withdraw their ships from the register, or adopt the new requirements. If, however, a public department, having imposed compulsory rules, were suddenly to change them, great inconvenience would ensue to the whole mercantile community. On the other hand, if the Government or any authorised body could say, this or that mode of construction is legally sufficient, and shall receive our certificate, the ship-owner, on compliance with the law, would be relieved from all further care in this respect, and would seek nothing beyond its requirement. Some witnesses state that disadvantages have arisen from the rivalry and competition between Lloyd's and the Liverpool registers. Both these societies, however, direct the attention of shipowners to faults in construction and to insufficiency of repair: both have therefore contributed to the greater efficiency of merchant ships.

We are of opinion that it would be equally inexpedient to attempt to supersede these societies by a public department, or to amalgamate them with the view of investing the combined body with legal powers.

While considering this subject, our attention has been directed to the limited system of survey which is now in operation.

In our former Report, we alluded to a law which Parliament had recently enacted. The Merchant Shipping Act of 1873 (36 & 37 Vict. c. 85) made an important alteration of the laws into which we were appointed to inquire. The Board of Trade are by this Act empowered, at their discretion, to detain any British vessel which " they have reason to believe is by reason of the defective condition of her hull, equipment, or machinery, or by reason of overloading or improper loading, unfit "to proceed to sea without serious danger to human life." Power is also given to the Board of Trade to detain a ship for the purpose of survey, to impose conditions as to the repair of a ship, and to enforce alterations in the loading of a ship.

The officers of the Board of Trade state that no extension of these stringent and arbitrary powers is necessary or desirable in order to prevent unseaworthy ships leaving any port in the United Kingdom.

The various instructions issued by the Board of Trade for the guidance of their surveyors, with the orders and forms annexed, will be found in the Appendix to this Report. During the first nine months that this Act was in operation 286 ships were surveyed; and of these 256 were found to be unseaworthy; 234 from defects in the ship or equipments, and 22 from being overladen.

The officers of the Board of Trade state that in the exercise of the new power entrusted to them the greatest difficulty arises in deciding as to overladen ships. They have allowed vessels to leave the port more deeply laden than would have been permitted under any rule of freeboard, and vessels so laden have continued to make their voyages in safety.

Such a discretionary exercise of power is not free from objections, and although witnesses testify to the care and caution which the chief officers of the department endeavour to impress on their surveyors, yet shipowners feel aggrieved, and say that they would rather be governed by some definite law, or if that be not practicable, then that there should be some ready means of appeal to a competent authority.

We have already expressed our opinion that a definite rule of freeboard for all merchant ships is at present unattainable.

The power given to the Board of Trade of detaining a merchant ship is already qualified by a provision for an appeal (section 14) to any court in England having Admiralty jurisdiction, and in Scotland to the court of the sheriff.

The delay, anxiety, and expense of proceedings against a public department are, however, such serious hindrances to the business of the shipowner, that in most instances he would rather submit to injustice than resort to such a remedy. Ships have been detained which have been afterwards acknowledged to be seaworthy, but the shipowners then find themselves involved in another dispute as to the amount of compensation for such detention. Here, again, a shipowner is placed at great dis– advantage in contending with a public department, which naturally strives to reduce the cost of its administrative errors.

We are of opinion that an immediate appeal, such as is desired by the shipowners, should be given, and that it might be obtained by investing the shipping master or collector of customs with the power of summoning, on the application of the master of the detained vessel, two or more competent shipmasters, to constitute a court whose decision should be final.

The shipowners complain that the Merchant Shipping Act of 1873 was passed in the month of August of that year, without the examination and full discussion which it would have received at an earlier period of the session. The officers of the Board of Trade, who are entrusted with the execution of the Act, admit that it is of a new and tentative character. They express a hope that the detention of vessels notoriously overladen or otherwise unseaworthy will gradually compel negligent shipowners to be more attentive or to abandon the trade: worthless vessels will be broken up, and the eventual weeding out of such ships will not only add to the safety of a seafaring life, but will be a benefit to the careful shipowner, who will find his business increase, while the premiums to be paid on insurance will be reduced.

The Act of 1873 has, however, been in operation for so short a time that it is difficult to pronounce any certain opinion as to its probable effect upon our mercantile marine.

REMEDIAL LEGISLATION

Parliament has during many years been engaged in attempting to regulate minute details connected with shipping. Shipowners reasonably complain that they have been harassed in their business by well-intended but ill-contrived legislation, and that this legislation is enforced by a department imperfectly acquainted with the science of shipbuilding and with the interests of our commercial marine.

The officers of the Board of Trade admit that many enactments, designed to secure safety of life at sea, have been mischievous, and should be modified or repealed.

The amount of legislation, and the multiplicity of details connected with shipping, which are now regulated by law, have not been altogether successful, and it seems that the results aimed at are hardly attainable by Acts of Parliament.

The obligation to carry boats in proportion to tonnage was regulated by the Merchant Shipping Act of 1854; but the law was found to be impracticable, and was not enforced. By the Act of 1873 the Board of Trade have taken a discretionary power in this matter. The surveyors, however, sometimes differ in their views, and the number of boats sanctioned at one port are afterwards disallowed at another, occasioning thereby expense to the owner and obstruction to trade.

It would appear reasonable that the number and size of the boats should be in proportion to the number of persons on board, and that a vessel should not be forced to carry boats which could not be manned.

A complaint is also made against the requirement as to lights. The ships' lights are most important for the avoidance of collisions; but shipowners complain that lights approved by one surveyor are disapproved by another. The Board of Trade have not as yet prescribed any satisfactory standard of efficiency, but tell the shipowners that they must obey the statute. No coloured lamps have, until recently, been found on trial equal to the requirements of the statute, and meanwhile the shipowner is subject to the capricious decisions of surveyors.

Water-tight bulkheads are, undoubtedly, a security against a ship's foundering at sea, and a law prescribing two bulkheads as a minimum was enacted by Parliament, but the effect of this enactment was to increase the risk, and to give a false notion of security. Although, therefore, we attach great value to water-tight bulkheads, we see great practical difficulty in legislation upon this subject.

Sea-cocks have probably, it is said, occasioned the foundering of some vessels. The position of the sea-cocks and the arrangements for controlling them from the upper deck in case of leakage have been brought to our notice. The suggestions offered on this subject deserve the serious attention of shipowners, but these are not matters which legislation can beneficially control.

Double bottoms for water ballast are attended with danger, because when the cargo is taken on board these spaces are emptied of water, and this may tend to capsize the ship. There are, however, many cases where the double bottom affords additional security. Any legislation on this matter would therefore be inexpedient.

It is probable that some missing steamers may have been lost from the hatchways necessary for the ventilation of the engine-room and the stoke hole being insufficiently guarded against the admission of water in heavy weather.

In our former Report we stated that the law intended to secure the efficiency of chain cables had not been successful. The bad effects of a law requiring a mere tensile strain by hydraulic pressure were in some degree modified by an alteration of the system of testing the cables, and the application of the breaking test. The Board of Trade now recommend that the compulsory clauses of the Act should be repealed, and that the testing should be voluntary. As this subject is now under the consideration of the House of Commons we have not thought it necessary to take further evidence upon it.

The increased employment of iron ships, and the more frequent conveyance of iron in ships, render the adjustment of the compasses, and an acquaintance with the errors of the compass, essential to the safety of merchant ships. The Board of Trade instituted in July 1870 a system of voluntary examination on this subject, accompanied by certificates, with a view to extend a knowledge of the errors and deviations of the compass among the officers of the mercantile marine. It is desirable that adjusters of compasses should be required to pass an examination before they are entitled to certify that compasses have been properly adjusted.

The legislation as to safety valves should, it is said, be materially altered. Ship– owners state that the practice of the Board of Trade in reference to the boilers of passenger steamers is vexatious and inconsistent. Restrictions are imposed which unnecessarily limit the power of the engines and the speed of steam vessels. This limitation interferes seriously with the economical working of the vessel.

The evidence upon all these matters evinces the inexpediency of incessant interference in details connected with shipping. The Board of Trade have now large discretionary powers, and the judicious exercise of those powers will check negligent shipowners, without harassing the whole mercantile community. We believe that much legislation upon matters of detail might be advantageously dispensed with.

We are of opinion that the present system of compulsory pilotage is not conducive to the security of life or property at sea, and from the evidence we have taken, we believe it would be, upon the whole, advantageous to get rid of it. We do not consider that it falls within the scope of our Commission to go beyond this statement, or to discuss its bearing upon individual or corporate interests and privileges. But we think that all systems which tend to remove responsibility from shipowners and their paid servants are against the true principles of public policy, and we consider that compulsory pilotage is one of these systems.

INQUIRIES BY THE BOARD OF TRADE

In our former Report we referred to the importance of instituting a better system of inquiry into losses and casualties at sea, as affording the best means of discovering the cause of loss, and thereby contributing to the greater safety of navigation. We have taken further evidence upon this subject, and we will now briefly advert to the imperfections of the present system, and to the amendments which have been suggested.

The officers of the Board of Trade, the solicitors of the Customs, who act for the Board of Trade in these inquiries, and the shipowners, have all stated serious objections to the present mode of conducting these inquiries. The tribunal does not command general confidence, the mode of procedure is said to be dilatory and expensive, the power of the court is ill defined, and in some cases cannot be enforced.

The present mode of conducting these inquiries assumes the shape of a criminal proceeding against the captain, rather than a careful investigation into the cause of the disaster. The chief point at issue seems to be whether the captain is to be acquitted or punished; and, inasmuch as he is on his trial, he may, if he pleases, volunteer a statement, but cannot be examined.

The court, again, has no power over the shipowner; he may be culpable, but he is altogether beyond the jurisdiction of the court.

It is a matter of public interest, with a view to the preservation of human life, that these inquiries should be conducted in such a manner as may best disclose the circumstances to which every disaster at sea should be ascribed.

We attach, therefore, great importance to instituting such a searching and impartial inquiry as may elicit the facts of the case, and may show whether the casualty is owing to the faulty construction of the vessel, to bad stowage, to circumstances connected with the navigation, to the incompetency of officers, or to the neglect or misconduct of the crew.

The first proceeding in these inquiries is the taking of a deposition under the powers of the Merchant Shipping Act of 1854.

The Receiver of Wrecks, who is usually an officer of the Customs, or in his absence any justice of the peace, is empowered to examine upon oath any person as to matters connected with the loss, abandonment, or material injury of any vessel. In practice the Receiver of Wrecks always takes these depositions.

By a circular of 1869 the Board of Trade issued new instructions as to the matters to be inquired into, and the mode of taking the depositions. The points to which the attention of the receiver is directed are set forth in the Appendix.

The solicitors of the Customs recommend that the preliminary inquiry should be limited to a few important points, such as would enable the Board of Trade to decide upon the expediency of ordering a further investigation. If the Board consider such an investigation desirable, they should lose no time in at once ordering the witnesses to be detained.

Under the present system there is much time lost before the Board of Trade decide whether or not there shall be a further inquiry. In some instances there is a delay of weeks or months; meanwhile the master may have gone away on another voyage, and the crew may be abroad or dispersed through the country. It then becomes necessary to collect the witnesses wherever they can be found, and to await the return of the master.

In former years the official inquiries were few in number. Mr. Hamel states that before the year 1872 they did not exceed on the average 37 per annum. In the year ending December 1872 there were 50 inquiries. In the year 1873 there were 195 inquiries, of which however 34 were abandoned.

It is admitted that a legal adviser at the Board of Trade would easily perceive whether a case was such as demanded an inquiry. Thus expense and delay would be avoided. When an inquiry has been resolved upon, the object should be to ascertain the cause of the casualty.

The constitution of the court should, it is said, be altered, and the practice made uniform.

As to the court, Mr. O'Dowd suggests that the kingdom should be divided into districts, and a competent barrister appointed as a judge for each district. The judge would require one, or perhaps two, nautical assessors to assist him in the inquiry. They should be men whose skill and character would inspire general confidence. Mr. Farrer considers the creation of these new courts unnecessary, and suggests another mode of meeting the difficulty.

Founding our opinion on the evidence which we have obtained, we recommend that the preliminary inquiry by the Receiver of Wrecks should be limited to such a narrative statement as would enable the Board of Trade, with the aid of their legal adviser, to decide upon the propriety of an official inquiry.

If such an inquiry is deemed advisable, with the view of ascertaining the cause of the disaster, and thereby guarding against future casualties, we recommend that there should be a complete severance between this inquiry and any proceedings of a penal character: it should be a mere inquest into the cause of the loss or casualty. The result should be reported to the Board of Trade, and the Board should have power to prosecute the shipowner, or to proceed criminally against the master, mate, or any member of the crew whose neglect of duty may have occasioned the disaster. We think that the 11th section of the Merchant Shipping Act, 1871, should be amended, and be made expressly to extend to the master of the vessel; for it is very important to avoid any doubt that the master who without justifiable excuse leaves port with his vessel in an unseaworthy condition, renders himself amenable to the criminal law.

On comparing the accidents occurring at sea with those taking place on land, and especially on railways, we are struck by the fact that, whereas in the latter cases it is usual to prosecute those servants whose negligence has occasioned loss of life, there is scarcely a single instance of a prosecution of a master or mate, or a man on the look-out or at the helm of a vessel, although the cases have undoubtedly been numerous in which vessels have been lost either by the negligence of the master or crew. We think that enactments relating to the punishment of the master or crew, whose negligence has occasioned loss of life or property, should be framed of a more definite and stringent character than those now in existence. We are of opinion that the present system, under which the certificate of a master or other officer is suspended, very frequently only for an error of judgment, should be entirely discontinued, and that neither the court of inquiry, nor the Board of Trade, should have the power of dealing with the certificate. We think that the certificate of the officer should never be suspended, but that, in cases to be provided for by express enactment, the tribunal before which the officer is tried should have the power of cancelling either all his certificates, or, at its discretion, his higher certificates, leaving him in these cases the power of finding employment in a lower grade.

The constitution of the court of inquiry must rest with the executive Government. The evidence of Mr. O'Dowd, of Mr. Hamel, and of Mr. Farrer indicates the nature of the change required, in order to secure a tribunal commanding public confidence.

We attach great importance to these inquiries, as affording the best means of ascertaining on whom the culpability rests for losses at sea, and we believe that such inquiries, followed by the proceedings which we have suggested, would be more conducive to the safety of life at sea, than many of the complex and minute regulations which Parliament has heretofore enacted.

UNDER-MANNING

In connection with the subject of under-manning we have taken further evidence as to the present condition of our merchant seamen.

The growth of trade, and the consequent additional opportunities for employment on shore, as well as at sea, have increased the difficulty of obtaining able seamen. The wages of seamen have risen largely within the last few years, but yet shipowners complain that they are often compelled to take such men as present themselves, of whom many prove to be incompetent to discharge properly the duties of seamen. The ignorance and incapacity of these men throw additional work on the good seamen, cause dissatisfaction in the ship, and enhance the dangers of navigation.

It is admitted that the coasting trade, and some of the great lines of steamers attract the steadiest and best seamen. Voyages in which men are not long absent from home, and where vessels return periodically to the same port, are naturally preferred. The wages, the accommodation, and the food, are generally better in the large steamers.

The general tendency of the evidence, however, leads to the conclusion that there is a deficiency of British able seamen; captains of merchant ships could not, it is said, man their vessels without Swedes, Norwegians, and Lascars. The rating of able seaman is often given without sufficient consideration by the masters of merchant ships.

The British seamen at the present time are not, it is said, wanting in elementary education. It is a rare exception when they cannot write; but nevertheless the men do not always seem to have received the benefits which are commonly supposed to belong to education in early life. They are often deficient in thrift, in sobriety, in discipline, and in that self-control which education is intended to promote. Parliament has endeavoured, by various enactments, to ameliorate the condition and improve the character of merchant seamen.

The examination of masters and mates, the regulation of space for crews, the insertion of the scale of food in the articles, the means of remitting wages, the allotment note, the establishment of seamen's saving banks, and various other important measures, indicate the earnest wish of the legislature to secure the welfare of the sailor.

SHIPPING OFFICES, AND DISCIPLINE

Shipping offices were originally established at Liverpool by the shipowners, in order to abolish crimping. These offices were encouraged by the Board of Trade with the same view. In the large ports they are managed by the local marine board, a body partly elected by the shipowners, and partly selected by the Board of Trade. Some shipowners now state that the system does not work well, and that it would be better if they were allowed to engage seamen as other employers engage their workmen, without the presence of the officer called the shipping master.

This arrangement was, however, made for the protection of the seamen, in order that they might be acquainted with the articles to be signed by them, with their pay, the duration of the voyage, and other details.

The practices by which sailors were obtained before the establishment of shipping offices were corrupt and degrading, and it appears from the evidence that if the captain of a merchant ship will take trouble in seeking out eligible men, he can arrange to meet them at the shipping office, or even engage them on board under a special application. We do not therefore recommend the abolition of shipping offices; but it must be remembered that these offices were not intended to relieve captains from the trouble of seeking out men fitted for service at sea.

The anxiety of Parliament to protect the seaman, to treat him as incompetent to take care of himself and as requiring the special interference of the legislature, has exercised a bad influence on his character. It has tended to destroy confidence between the captain and the crew, and to promote insubordination where good discipline is essential to safety.

The rule that any act of misconduct on the part of a seaman, if entered in the log, must be immediately read to the offender, is a contrivance so ill calculated to promote good behaviour, that captains leave the offence unnoticed rather than resort to such a proceeding. We are of opinion that this rule should be modified.

To secure fair treatment for the British seaman, without destroying discipline by weakening the authority of the master, should be the object of the legislature.

When a merchant ship leaves the port, the lives of the passengers and crew, as well as the safety of the ship, are entrusted to the skill and judgment of the master.

It is essential, therefore, that the authority of the master should be upheld, and any interference tending to impair his authority and to lower his position adds seriously to the dangers of navigation.

The evidence which we have taken shows that the masters of ships have no longer the control over the crew which is necessary, and was formerly usual. It is certainly not to be regretted that the increased independence of seamen (which we attribute chiefly to the increased demand for their services) has rendered tyranny and cruelty both difficult and unprofitable. But there is reason to doubt whether the change has not been such as practically to deprive the master of the control necessary to the security of his own vessel and to that of other vessels which he may chance to meet. There appears, practically, to be very little power of punishing the sailor for anything but mutinous conduct. The consequence of this is that he can be guilty, with virtual impunity, of many gross derelictions of duty, some of which tend directly to the loss of property and of life. We are informed that it is impracticable to punish a sailor for such a gross breach of trust as neglecting to keep a look-out, except by some extreme process, such as charging him with manslaughter after loss of life.

Such offences as drunkenness on duty, neglect to place a look-out or to relieve it, sleeping on the look-out, neglect of machinery, disobedience and insubordination, appear to us to require more direct penalties, and a less cumbrous remedy, than that of being treated as mutiny, or of being only punished when they have produced fatal results.

COMPULSORY APPRENTICESHIP

With a view to remedy the existing deficiency of able seamen, several witnesses recommend the adoption of compulsory apprenticeship.

A system of compulsory apprenticeship was established in the year 1844, but was abolished in the 1849, on the repeal of the Navigation Laws. Some shipowners subsequently desired to restore the system, but the measure was successfully opposed by others who were interested in steamships.

The increased employment of steamers has diminished the opportunities for training sailors, and although steam vessels engaged in the coasting trade and in short voyages attract many of the best men, they train up few for the service. Different schemes have been suggested to supply this acknowledged evil. Firstly, compulsory apprenticeship; secondly, training ships; thirdly, a combination of both schemes. This last plan may be understood from the following outline.

It is proposed that every vessel above 100 tons register, whether propelled by sail or steam, should be required to carry apprentices in proportion to her tonnage (the number to be fixed hereafter), or to pay a small contribution annually (such as 6d. per ton register), this sum to be applied towards the maintenance of training ships in all the principal ports of the United Kingdom. The apprentices should, it is said, be indentured at or about the age of 14 to the master of the training ship for five years, and after serving in this ship for one or two years, the indenture should be transferred to any shipowner who would be willing to take the apprentice, and with whom the apprentice might be willing to serve until the completion of his term. In order that these training ships might fit the boys for service at sea, a small vessel should, it is suggested, be attached to each ship, so that, with other instruction, the habit of a sea life might be acquired. These school ships should receive grants from the State according to their efficiency.

In the report of the Commission on Manning the Navy in the year 1859, training ships were proposed to be maintained at the public expense. The cost of every boy so trained was estimated at 25*l*. a year. This sum would he increased by the additional cost of sailing tenders, and without this preparation for a sea life shipowners would not so readily take the boys.

The system of apprenticeship undoubtedly affords the best means of training boys for a service in which fitness can only be acquired during early life, and if shipowners were willing to contribute, as suggested above, it would, in our opinion, be a wise policy for the Government to aid these industrial schools of the mercantile marine.

Some of the most respectable shipowners take apprentices, and from among these apprentices they frequently choose officers, so that this system must have worked well. It is said, however, to be a drawback to the system that there is a practical difficulty in getting quit of a disorderly and worthless apprentice. As it is desirable to encourage the system of apprenticeship, this inconvenience should be remedied.

As this scheme for schools and apprentices must depend upon the support which it may receive from the shipowners, we have not entered further into the details of the plan. The number of lives entrusted to British ships and the annual value of property afloat impress us with the importance of securing so far as possible not only that the ships shall be seaworthy, but that seamen also shall be well trained and disciplined for the merchant service.

The system of training boys for the Royal Navy has been successful, and if a somewhat similar plan could be adopted for the mercantile marine, the sailors and shipowners would be benefited, while many sources of danger to the merchant service would be diminished or removed.

A self-supporting pension fund for the benefit of seamen, as suggested by the Manning Commission of 1859, might prove of great value in creating a tie to bind the British seaman to the merchant service of his own country. The subject does not lie strictly within the scope of our inquiry; but we are of opinion that it well deserves the attention of the Government.

DESERTION IN FOREIGN PORTS

Our attention has been drawn to the large pecuniary loss inflicted on shipowners, and to the serious deterioration of the character of the seamen, resulting from desertion abroad.

There is great difficulty in preventing desertion, and in enforcing discipline, in foreign ports, and shipowners have urgently pressed upon us the necessity for some international conventions for this purpose.

It appears that we have not adopted in this country such measures as would entitle us to ask for the requisite authority in foreign states.

This matter deserves the serious attention of the Government, inasmuch as British ships are now often obliged to sail on their return voyage, when heavily laden, with insufficient or incompetent crews.

ADVANCE NOTES

The evidence before us leads to the conclusion that the system of advance notes is one great obstacle to the amelioration of the condition of merchant seamen. All the witnesses whom we have examined admit that the system is most pernicious, but it is defended on the ground that without this advance the sailor could not pay for his lodging on shore, or procure the clothes requisite for him when he joins a ship.

In practice it seems that the advance note is handed over to the lodging-house keeper, not usually in exchange for cash, but in discharge of debts which the sailor has been induced to incur. The lodging-house keeper charges a heavy discount, and the sailor is frequently brought on board half-clad and intoxicated.

Shipowners and captains of merchant ships concur in stating that a large portion of the ship's crew is very often brought or even lifted on board in a condition of helpless drunkenness, that the vessel must often be detained for twenty-four hours in order that the men may be so far recovered as to be able to get her under weigh, and that there is great risk of life and property at the commencement of the voyage from the consequent inefficiency of the seamen.

The advance note is not payable until some days after the sailing of the ship; but if the ship then puts back or touches at another port, the seaman often takes the opportunity of making some complaint, in order to get free from his engagement, and will even incur a month's imprisonment with this object, whilst the shipowner or the person who has cashed the note loses the money which has been paid in advance.

It is said that if there were no advance note, the crimp in a foreign or colonial port would not have the same inducement to entice the sailor to desert.

After careful consideration of the numerous evils attending this mode of prepayment, we recommend that advance notes should be declared illegal, that no payment or order for payment made in advance for wages shall be a discharge for the payment of any portion of a seaman's wages, when due, and that no money paid by a shipowner to or for a seaman shall be debited to the seaman, except wages already earned, the allotment notes, and the cost of such supplies as the seaman may receive after joining the ship.

There will be some inconvenience felt at first from the abolition of the existing system, and there will be perhaps considerable opposition to the change in the ports, and amongst the lodging-house keepers, who profit by the advance notes. We feel, however, convinced that unless this mischievous mode of payment be discontinued, the seamen will never be raised from their servile dependence on crimps, and taught to rely on their own industry and intelligence.

The crimping system at Quebec was brought to our notice by witnesses well acquainted with the disgraceful practices in that port. The disorderly proceedings consequent upon it require stringent, measures for their repression, and deserve the attention of the colonial as well as of the home Government; but we have not entered further into matters which belong directly to colonial administration.

MARINE INSURANCE

We have taken further evidence on the important subject of marine insurance, with a view to ascertain whether any alteration of the law which now governs marine insurance is desirable.

The system of marine insurance, while it protects shipowners against losses which would otherwise be ruinous, tends to render them less careful in the management of their ships.

Underwriters and insurance companies have, however, a direct interest in the sea-worthiness of ships, and in the honesty of shipowners. Confidence is the foundation of an underwriter's business; and in accepting or rejecting a risk, the prudent under-writer is to a great extent guided by his knowledge of the persons with whom he has to deal.

The large capital which is now invested in marine insurance would be unprofitable, unless the great majority of shipowners and merchants were known to be deserving of trust.

It is said that the profits derived by prudent underwriters have led speculative persons and new companies to engage in the business. Competition in insurance encourages carelessness in shipowners, and thus increases disasters at sea.

The law has operated in the same direction, not merely by relieving the shipowner from all loss when his ship has foundered at sea, but by even enabling him in some cases to derive a pecuniary profit from the shipwreck.

We examined many witnesses on this subject, because the whole commerce of the British empire may be affected by a change in the existing system of insurance, and in attempting to check some possible evils we may embarrass the honest shipowner and interfere with the convenient usages of trade.

It is argued that under the existing law a shipowner can insure himself against every loss which can occur to his vessel, and that consequently he is rendered indifferent to the proper maintenance of his ship and to the arrangements necessary for her safe navigation.

In order to illustrate this matter by a simple case, let us assume that the owner of the ship is also the owner of the cargo; he can insure his ship for her full value, he can also insure the cargo, he can insure the freight, and beyond these insurances he can insure 10 percent profit on the cargo. In such a case it is impossible to deny that the interest of the shipowner in the safety of his vessel is seriously diminished. Another illustration of the operation of the law is given by Mr. Farrer. A ship is bound from London to Calcutta and back. She is lost in the Bay of Biscay on her outward voyage. In this case the owner, if he has insured prudently, though not exorbitantly, may recover the value of the ship at the commencement of the voyage, and the freight on the outward and homeward voyages, while he would be exempted from paying seamen's wages from the date of the disaster, the expenses at Calcutta, including purchase of provisions, and the expenses in London on the ship's return. To this extent the shipowner would be an actual gainer by the loss.

The contract of marine insurance is in its essence a contract of indemnity, and the spirit of the contract is violated if the assured can make the occurrence of a loss the means of gain. The law has, however, allowed a considerable deviation from this fundamental principle.

Property can now be insured against perils of the seas by a valued policy, that is, by a policy in which the value of the property is fixed beforehand by agreement between the assured and the underwriter. The effect of this is, that unless the policy is altogether void on account of fraud or of concealment of a material fact, the assured can, in the case of a total loss, receive the value which has been stated in the policy, however much it may exceed the actual worth of his property.

Thus the shipowner has, in certain decided cases, been allowed to recover 50, even 100, percent more than the value of his vessel.

It has been suggested that, in the case of a total loss, the underwriter should be allowed to open a valued policy when he considered that the value had been overstated. Many shipowners and underwriters object to this proposal. They contend that where a value has been agreed upon between the shipowner and the underwriter, subsequent interference would be mischievous, or futile, as it might induce shipowners to insure abroad. The value of a ship may indeed depend upon a variety of circumstances; for instance, the loss of a steamer to a shipowner who is starting a new line of steam communication is inadequately replaced by the cost of the vessel. It is true that the existing law induces the shipowner to prefer a total loss, or a constructive total loss, to a partial loss. A ship is said to have sustained a constructive total loss when she has been damaged to such an extent that the cost of repairs will exceed the value of the ship when repaired, and in such case the owner is, under the present law, entitled to receive the value stated in the policy, however much it may exceed the real value of the vessel.

It is to the interest of the underwriter that a ship should be insured for her full value, first, because he receives a larger amount as premium, and, next, because, in a case of partial loss, a clause of the policy exempts him from liability for all damage which amounts to less than three per cent of the amount insured. On the other hand the shipowner has an interest in undervaluing his ship, because he would have a less premium to pay, and a better chance of his partial losses, which are far more likely to occur than a total loss, being borne by the underwriter.

As regards the insurance of freight, it has been suggested that the shipowner should not, in case of total loss, be entitled to recover the freight, without deducting the expenses saved to him by reason of the loss of the vessel. If these expenses could be fairly estimated, the assured would in this manner be indemnified against the loss he has sustained, without deriving from that loss the profit which undoubtedly accrues to him in some cases under our present system of insurance.

It is, however, urged that the necessity of estimating these un-incurred expenses would often give rise to doubt, difficulty, and litigation, and that, if the suggestion just referred to were adopted, the shipowner would be, to a great extent, deprived of the legitimate advantage he now enjoys of being able to obtain with facility an advance on his freight.

It is above all important to bear in mind that, if valued policies on ships were allowed to continue in force without the underwriter being at liberty to open them, the above suggestion would prove completely futile as against the negligent shipowner who is desirous of obtaining by insurance more than a complete indemnity, for he would be able to attain the same object by over-insuring his vessel in a valued policy to the extent of the freight.

It thus appears that the question relating to insurance on freight must at any rate depend on the answer to the question whether or not valued policies should be rendered illegal, or, at least, whether the underwriter should be allowed to open them.

The evidence which has been presented to us clearly proves that valued policies are extremely useful and convenient in the insurance of goods and profits, and in the insurance of ships in cases of partial loss, without, at the same time, giving rise to any serious evils.

After much consideration, we have arrived at the conclusion that we ought not to recommend any alteration of the law relating to valued policies in cases of total 1oss-cases which are shown to bear to those of partial losses only the proportion of 1 to 20.

There are weighty reasons, why the legislature should not interfere with contracts made by persons who are capable of taking care of their own interests, without carefully ascertaining the effect which this interference is likely to produce on the entire system of law relating to such contracts.

It appears to us that our whole system of insurance law requires complete revision, for not only does it allow the assured in some cases to recover more than the amount of the loss actually sustained by him, but it also, on the other hand, deprives him of an. indemnity in cases in which he ought to be protected by his insurance.

For instance, the shipowner is held not to be entitled to recover from the under- writer the wages he has to pay to the master and crew whilst the damage sustained by his ship is being repaired, and in this respect our law differs from that of almost all other countries. Again, in the case of voyage policies, any defect in the vessel which renders her unseaworthy at the commencement of the voyage, even if it has been made good long before the occurrence of the loss, as well as any deviation, however slight, from the voyage named in the policy, vitiates the insurance, although the defect in the vessel and the deviation in the voyage could not in the least have occasioned or affected the subsequent loss.

It is difficult to interfere in the complex arrangements which have grown up with the growth of trade, without the risk of incurring some new danger while we are endeavouring to promote safety at sea. It appears to us therefore that it would be unjust and unwise to interfere with the contract between the assured and the under writer, unless our whole system of marine insurance were to be completely revised and amended so as to restore marine insurance to what is its true character and only legitimate object, namely, a contract of indemnity which should protect the assured from losses occasioned by events over which he has no control.

A complete and thorough revision of our law relating to marine insurance is, however, a task of equal importance, difficulty, and delicacy, requiring evidence of an extensive character and necessitating a very lengthy and careful investigation, and it touches directly on so many subjects unconnected with the security of life at sea, on which it has only an indirect and somewhat remote bearing, that we do not think it properly falls within the scope of our commission. We should also have been reluctant to undertake the complete revision of our system of marine insurance law, because for many reasons it appears to us to be important that, before such a task is undertaken, an attempt should be made to induce foreign nations to concur with us in framing and adopting a general code of insurance law. To alter the English law of marine insurance to any considerable extent might have the effect of throwing the business of insurance into the hands of foreigners, and there is so much insurance of foreign property in England, as well as of English property abroad, that it is most desirable that the law of insurance should, as far as possible, be the same amongst all commercial nations. An examination of the foreign codes leads us to hope that there would be found no insuperable difficulty in the way of attaining this important object.

In connection with this subject, it should be observed that the shipowner can by a bill of lading exempt himself from liability to the owner of the cargo for loss occasioned by the negligence of the master or crew, the unseaworthiness of the vessel, or any other cause whatever.

Beyond this, there are societies which undertake to protect shipowners against extra risks not covered by ordinary marine policies.

In an ordinary Lloyd's policy the underwriter engages to make good three-quarters of the amount which the ship insured may have to pay to the ship with which she comes into collision. The shipowner in this case is not completely indemnified, but he may secure himself still further by belonging to a protection society.

Under the existing law, and by means of these various contrivances, the shipowner can so far release himself from all liability that the cost of every casualty at sea is borne by underwriters and not by the shipowners.

Although we do not think, for the reasons already stated, that we can advise any alteration to be made at present in the law relating to valued policies, there are some recommendations which in our opinion can be safely and usefully adopted with a view of checking the evils caused by insurance.

We think that in analogy to the principle involved in the 11th section of the Merchant Shipping Act Amendment Act, 1871, the shipowner's liability for damage to property or person should be unlimited in cases where the death of the seaman or the damage to person and property has been occasioned by the ship having been sent to sea in an unseaworthy condition, unless he proves that he, or those to whom he commits the management of his business, used all reasonable means to make and keep the vessel seaworthy. He should also, in these eases, be made liable, under Lord Campbell's Act, to the family of the deceased seaman.

We are also of opinion that any provision in a bill of lading or other agreement having for its object or effect to avoid or limit the liability of the shipowner in the cases just referred to ought to have no legal validity.

We think that the shipowner should not be enabled to recover his insurance, whether under a time or voyage policy, when it could be shown that he or his agent had not done everything reasonably within their power to make and maintain the ship in a seaworthy condition, and that unseaworthiness occasioned the loss.

The evidence presented to us clearly proves that the present system, under which insurance cases are tried before a judge and jury, is extremely unsatisfactory, and we think that a judge and two assessors would constitute a far better tribunal.

The evidence taken respecting mutual insurance clubs, together with the rules of mutual insurance which have been submitted to us, prove that in general these clubs are societies honestly united for mutual insurance against sea risks. Their rules are framed with the view of checking overloading, and of securing seaworthy vessels, and we are of opinion that the general principle upon which they have been founded is calculated to promote prudent management among the members of the club.

CONCLUSION

In closing our report at the termination of this prolonged inquiry, it may be convenient that we should recapitulate briefly the general principles on which our recommendations are founded.

The Board of Trade possess under the recent Act ample power to survey and to detain any British ship which they may have reason to believe is overladen, or is in any respect of hull or of equipment unseaworthy.

This large discretionary power renders it in our opinion unnecessary and inexpedient to subject all British shipowners to the delay and annoyance of official surveys and inspections. We believe the wisest policy will be for the Board to interfere only where there is ground for suspecting some gross mismanagement, and wherever the case for detention may appear doubtful, to direct the attention of the ship-owner or manager to the circumstances which have attracted official notice.

We consider that an improved system of inquiry into casualties at sea, such as we have above indicated, will afford the best means of guarding against future disasters. So far as we have been able to ascertain, the losses of life and property at sea, which may be directly ascribed to negligence of the shipowner, are few in comparison with those which are caused by subsequent neglect, or by events over which the ship-owner has no control. A more searching system of inquiry may elicit the truth upon this subject. The statistics which we endeavoured to obtain on this head were not prepared in time to assist our investigations.

We attach great importance to our suggestion that the marine department of the Board of Trade should be revised and strengthened.

Some additional nautical assistance is requisite for the due performance of the duties now entrusted to the Board.

A legal adviser exclusively belonging to the Department is also essential for the conduct of the business.

It will be the duty of the Board of Trade to check the negligent, and to punish the culpable shipowner, but it is desirable that these functions should be performed without harassing the great body of shipowners, who, by their ability and indefatigable energy, have contributed to the prosperity of the Empire.

In accordance with these views we have been anxious throughout our Report not to transfer responsibility from the shipowner to the executive government. It is the duty of the shipowner to keep his ship in a seaworthy condition, and to select competent officers and crew. We believe that under the arrangements suggested in our Report, the Board of Trade will have the means of ascertaining how far this duty has been fulfilled, and will then have the power to punish those persons who have been neglectful.

Such a policy, judiciously administered by the Board of Trade, will contribute to the greater safety of life at sea, and will thus tend to

> produce the results which this Commission was appointed to secure.
>
> All which we humbly submit to Your Majesty's gracious consideration.

The Commissioner's conclusions were disappointing and did not satisfactorily address more relevant and urgent matters such as seaworthiness, overloading and the statutory and ethical responsibility of the Government to intervene legislatively in matters of safety of life, as had long been done in less unsafe industries such as mining and railways.

There can be no argument regarding the responsibility of the shipowner to ensure that his ships are in a seaworthy condition but he cannot, for example, remain as the sole arbiter of how deeply the ship can be laden. There can only be clear, proactive and unambiguous requirements in law, applicable and enforceable for all ships, to settle this vexed matter. The conclusions regarding casualty inquiries, and addition of a legal and nautical assistance to the Board of Trade were readily accepted and put in place.

The maritime press generally found these conclusions confusing and perplexing and but gave grudging support to the status quo regarding surveys and inspections;

> And, as regards this terrible bugbear of rules..., to suppose that a large staff of technical and as, someone has said "capricious", officers are to work all over the country without strict rules, it is sheer nonsense. If there is a survey at all, that is not a sham, there must be rules, let the survey be called a "general" survey or a specific survey; and while the survey exists at all, the tendency of the surveyors, as well as of the public, is to go into detail. And now the point comes, and this is the critical question, what ought those rules to be? But it must not be forgotten that the more minute are rules, the less there can be room for inequality, favouritism, subsequent detention, or individual eccentricity[522]

The Western Daily Mail stated that "Mr. Plimsoll need not be discouraged" and Punch believed that "though [Plimsoll] failed the other night, he'll gain his object nearly, if not quite, and the Government will take his cause in hand"[523]

Chapter 19

Conflagrations and Chain Cables

Eighteen hundred and seventy-four did not start well for Plimsoll. The Prime Minister, William Gladstone, who had strongly supported Plimsoll's proposal for a royal commission on unseaworthy ships, resigned in January 1874. He had previously offered to resign in March 1873 when an Irish University Bill failed to pass in the Commons, but continued in office when Disraeli refused to form a Government. Through his resignation in 1874 he effectively dissolved Parliament but his Liberal party were soundly defeated in the ensuing election in February. Although the Liberals lost fifty seats, Plimsoll survived with an increased majority due, in no small part, to his well-known campaign on behalf of seamen. One benefit from the election was that Chichester Fortescue, no friend of Plimsoll's, lost his seat. However, this was offset by the appointment of Sir Charles Adderley as President of the Board of Trade who promptly announced that he had no intention of bringing in a new shipping Bill. He set the tone for his new role in declaring; "he would be sorry to see seaworthiness defined by an Act of Parliament", deploring the expense that "Plimsoll's misinformation had already incurred to the Board of Trade" and advising the Board to be cautious in dealing with such complaints received from Plimsoll.[524]

Ships crossing the North Atlantic during the winter of February/March 1874 experienced extreme weather resulting in the loss of some and long passages for others; steamers and sailing ships alike. The North German steamship ***Nurnberg*** experienced a 'terrific gale' on February the 23rd which tore four lifeboats from the davits, one of which smashed a skylight resulting in flooding of the passenger accommodation.[525] The sailing ship ***Alsen*** from Rotterdam, on passage to New York, rescued the crew of the bark ***Auguste*** which had sailed from Liverpool on the 1st of February. Captain Siebert of the ***Auguste*** reported that he'd encountered a violent gale from East to North-East lasting from the 5th to the 7th of March during which the ship sprung a leak which could not be controlled in spite of all hands being constantly at the pumps. When the crew were taken off the ship had water ten feet deep in her hold and the crew were completely exhausted.[526] The

Captain of the bark ***Victoria*** from Hamburg reported, on arrival in New York on the 31st of March, that on the 22nd he'd passed the waterlogged and abandoned sailing ship ***Lila*** of St. Johns. Another North German steamship, the ***Hermann***, arrived in New York on the 29th of March after a stormy passage of 18 days during which 'remarkably heavy weather was experienced'. The Captain reported that he'd never experienced heavier weather than from the 21st to 24th of March during the whole of his professional experience.[527]

On the 21st of February a young master mariner boarded the American Line passenger ship ***Pennsylvania*** (1871) of 3,016 ton, as passenger for a voyage to Philadelphia. The ship was certified to carry 76 first-class and 854 steerage passengers, but on this mid-winter sailing she carried only 2 saloon and twelve steerage passengers. The master mariner was Cornelius Brady, who the previous year had served as Third Officer aboard the ill-fated ***Atlantic***. The ***Pennsylvania*** soon encountered bad weather in the North Atlantic which developed into storm force North-westerlies, with very heavy seas breaking on deck and carrying everything moveable away. During the night of the 27th the first of several huge seas broke on her foredeck, staving in the forward end of the passenger accommodation, and allowing water to enter and flow down the entire length of the passenger deck. The crew and several male passengers, including Brady, worked frantically to shore up the forward bulkhead in an attempt to prevent more seas from flooding the accommodation. By midnight, when the ship was experiencing very heavy confused seas from North-west and South-west, a mountainous sea hit the starboard bow and came aboard, completely carrying away a portion of the bridge, the wheelhouse, the mate's accommodation, four of the lifeboats and all the life rafts. The sea also stove in all four forward hatches and flooded the saloon and steerage accommodation. There was no trace left of the bridge, with the Captain, First and Second Officers and two quartermasters lost overboard with the wreckage.

The ship was left wallowing beam on to the seas, not under command and rolling heavily. The Third Officer was completely out of his depth, stating; "he did not understand the handling of steamships", having spent his whole career before the ***Pennsylvania*** in sailing ships, and refused requests from the crew and passengers to take command of the ship. Brady, with a Master's certificate in steam, gained the support of all aboard and took command of the ship, immediately ordering the crew to bring the lower deck hatch covers up on deck to make the forward hatches watertight. He reduced speed and brought the ship head into the weather to lessen the chance of water on deck until the hatches were secure; a task that wasn't completed until the following morning. After consulting with the Chief Engineer as to the amount of coal remaining, no doubt with his experience aboard the ***Atlantic*** in mind, he set course for Philadelphia where a pilot boarded on the 10th of March after a seventeen-day passage from Liverpool. For his superb demonstration of seamanship and leadership in saving the ship and cargo, jointly worth $850,000, the American Line offered Brady a paltry reward of $1,000, which he refused. He took the company to court to claim compensation based upon the value of the ship, the cargo and the costs and expenses he sustained in pursuing the matter. The 'reward' was increased by the court to $4,200.[528]

In March 1874, the first prosecution in an Irish court for 'sending an unseaworthy ship to sea' under section 11 of the Merchant Shipping Act, 1871, took place in Belfast. The case turned upon whether the two owners of the small coastal sailing vessel ***Nimrod*** (1847) of 103 tons, had sent her to sea in an unseaworthy condition. Neither the ship nor any members of the crew were lost. In instructing the jury the judge made it clear that, under the Act, they were only to consider two matters; '…whether the ship was sent to sea in an unseaworthy state, and, if they came to the conclusion that she was, then they were to consider whether the traversers [owners] used every reasonable means to make the ship seaworthy and to keep her so…'. The Jury found both prisoners guilty on both counts. In his sentencing that Judge stated;

> …both of you have been convicted of a most serious offence – namely, sending a ship to sea in an unseaworthy state, calculated to endanger the lives of those aboard. The evidence was clear to my mind that you [both] knew perfectly well the condition of that ship, and that you were determined to run her as long as you could earn money thereby

Taking into account a plea for clemency from the jury, the sentence of the Court was that 'you and each of you be sentenced to imprisonment for two calendar months, and that you each pay to the Queen a fine of £150'.[529]

Parliament resumed after the election for the 1874 Session on the 6th of March and, after dealing with the formalities of bedding in a new Government for the first five sitting days, turned on the 29th to their business at hand. Plimsoll wasted no time in gaining; "leave ... to bring in a Bill to provide for the periodical Survey of Merchant Ships, and for so marking Ships as to diminish the practice of overloading." The Merchant Shipping Survey Bill (No. 11) was presented and read for the first time.[530] On the 13th of April Adderley, in reply to a question from Mr. Gourley, advised that the long postponed consolidation of all Mercantile legislation was dead in the water, and fired a few opening salvoes across Plimsoll's bow, in stating that;

> The Government have no present intention of introducing a Bill for consolidating the Merchant Shipping Acts. I hope they will never attempt, by any measure, to specify in detail what is meant by seaworthiness as to model, hull, &c, or to affirm that seaworthiness should depend on any prescribed model. The erroneous information given by the hon. Member for Derby (Mr. Plimsoll) in the case of the Parga cost the country £1,239 11s. 7d. The Board of Trade have never stopped any ship named the Western Chief; but in the case of the Western Ocean. which was stopped, the sum of £600 was paid as compensation. These and all other cases are stated in the Appendix to the evidence given before the Royal Commission. There are the Somerset. £7 16s; Effort. £40; Lady Head. £30; and Fountain. £50. The Board of Trade exercise a discretion as to the information upon which to take the proceedings which Parliament has imposed upon them by the Act of 1873, and will be cautious in acting upon information coming from quarters from which previous informations have failed of proof. Their principle is to prosecute the worse, and clearest cases as examples, and to interfere as little as possible with the legitimate course of trade.[531]

The Chain Cables and Anchor Act, 1871, came in for renewed scrutiny by Parliament on the 1st of May when a Bill to amend the Law respecting the proving and sale of Chain Cables and Anchors was ordered to be brought in by Sir Charles Adderley and Mr. Cavendish Bentnick. The Bill was presented, and read the first time. In response to a request for more time for this matter to be considered Adderley explained on the 5th of May that; "...The Bill is not, as described, for substituting voluntary for compulsory testing of cables and anchors, but for abolishing legislative penalties on the sale of untested chains, which so far from proving compulsory, have proved abortive and yet indirectly mischievous. No signs of opposition, but only of general concurrence, have yet appeared..."[532] On the 8th of June a Select Committee was appointed, led by Adderley, with the power to send for persons, papers, and records.[533]

In reply to a question in the House from Mr. Cowper-Temple on the 7th of May as to; "...whether any steps have been taken to require passenger ships to carry a number of boats, rafts, or other appliances for saving life, sufficient for the persons carried on board each ship?", Adderley replied that;

> ...the question of compelling large passenger ships with numerous passengers to carry boats sufficient for all the persons on board has been frequently considered by the Emigration Commissioners and by the Board of Trade. But it is impossible; because there is not room for such boats, and because by encumbering the decks they would render the safe working of the ship impracticable. Further, even the boats now required are seldom found to be practically available in those cases of wreck in which they are most required. No rafts or other appliances for saving life have yet been discovered which would be practically available; and attempted contrivances might lead to more lives being lost by needlessly leaving a ship, than to any increase of lives being saved in real emergencies.[534]

Plimsoll's Merchant Shipping Survey Bill received its second reading on the 24th of June; the very day that the Royal Commission concluded and signed their report; a fact not lost on the majority of members contributing to the debate on the Bill. During a lengthy introduction, Plimsoll summarized the purpose of the three clauses in the Bill.

> The Bill proposed to authorize the Board of Trade to direct the survey of all unclassed ships, instead of their having to wait, as they had to do under the present Act, until an allegation of unseaworthiness was made against a particular ship, and to relieve the Department from having to pay damages, to which they were liable under that Act, for the detention of any ship which was found fit to proceed to sea... By the second provision of his Bill it was proposed to prohibit deck loading between the 1st of September and the 31st of March in each

> year—a restriction which was generally enforced by marine insurance societies...The third proposal in his Bill was to require a broad white streak, showing the proper load line, for the protection of the crew, to be painted on the side of a vessel, by which a moral influence would be brought to bear on shipowners, who would thus be shamed into not overloading their ships, for it was perfectly obvious that ships being only a foot, and sometimes not more than an inch, above the waterline, must in bad weather, inevitably go to the bottom.... He proposed that in all cases of this kind the Board of Trade should have power to interfere and prevent these ships going to sea. In that case many causes of disasters would be prevented.

In reply, a number of Members, for example; "....confessed to feeling some surprise that the hon. Gentleman had chosen that particular time to bring forward the Bill, for they would, he hoped, soon have before them the final Report of the Royal Commissioners. Their preliminary Report—cautious, moderate, and prudential as it was—furnished a strong warning to the House to exercise great caution in dealing with a matter which was surrounded with great difficulties." One M.P. commented; "... The practices complained of by the hon. Gentleman were condemned by the shipowners themselves; but they could not support the hon. Gentleman, because his zeal and philanthropy had overstepped the bounds of reason at times." Surprisingly, the Chairman of the Royal Commission, Lord Eslington, entered the debate; expressing his opinions on the Bill in no uncertain terms, and giving Members a good indication of the contents of the final report, in the course of which he; "...gave the hon. Member for Derby full credit for the motives which actuated him; but could not think that the Bill he had introduced was not calculated to fulfil the purpose its framers had in view. Any person of intelligence reading the Bill, and being unacquainted with the agitation which had produced it, could only come to one conclusion—namely, that it was a measure expressly and designedly framed, and ingeniously worded, to relieve shipowners from responsibility, and to place such responsibility upon the shoulders of the Board of Trade."

Mr Samuda made a valuable contribution in supporting the Bill by producing statistics to demonstrate that, proportionally, losses of ships were worse than they had ever been;

> ...it could not be denied that there had for years past been an increase

> of losses at sea enormously disproportionate to the increase of our shipping. The total losses which had not been accidental but the consequences of neglect, had gone on in an increasing ratio year by year for a considerable period. Abstracts from The Wreck Register showed that in the four quinquennial periods of the last 20 years the losses on the average had been for the first period 970; the second, 1,118; the third, 1,488; and the fourth, 1,741. These were absolutely total losses. During the same period the number of ships had only increased from 27,000 to 29,000. So that, while the increase in the number of our mercantile ships during that period had only been 8 per cent the increase in the number of total losses had been about 50 per cent. During a period of 10 years the average total losses of vessels from all causes, were 2,700 per annum, while the average total loss of vessels during that period from carelessness and neglect was 1,100 per annum. Consequently, half the total number of losses arose from preventable causes, and legislation might improve that state of things.

The contentious matter of the danger of deck cargoes, in particular timber deck cargoes during the north Atlantic winter, was addressed by another member in reminding the House: "… An Act was passed in 1840, prohibiting the carrying of deck-loads of timber between the 1st of September and the 1st of May. The Act remained in force until 1862, when, in consequence of the differential duties on foreign timber having been repealed, the Board of Trade thought it impossible to enforce the law, and by a clause in the Act passed in 1862, removed that restriction upon loads of timber carried on deck. But the danger arising from carrying excessive deck-loads of timber had been so conspicuously illustrated within the last year or two, that he sincerely hoped the Legislature might at an early date take steps for prohibiting this most dangerous class of ships from navigating the Atlantic during the winter months".

The President of the Board of Trade, Sir Charles Adderley made his opposition to the Bill clear in no uncertain terms; "…It was both an impracticable thing, and false in theory, that the Board of Trade should be called upon to assume an indefinite control over the Mercantile Marine of this country. Strange, that the Board of Trade which, it was said, had shown itself unequal to its present task, was called upon so largely to increase the task imposed upon it… What did the Bill propose? Simply this, that no ship should be allowed to clear from any port of this Kingdom until it had received a certificate from the Board of Trade of the safety of its construction, its hull, its equipment, and all its details, down to the stowage of its cargo, and that not only upon its first starting, but upon every voyage it made. The second part of the Bill dealt with the much-vexed question upon which Parliament had to reverse its policy more than once—namely, that a Government Department should certify whether a ship should be allowed a deck-load in the case of every voyage in which it was required. Thirdly it was proposed that a load-line should be ascertained, which in the opinion of most nautical authorities was impossible... It would be quite sufficient to induce the House to reject the second reading to be reminded that the subject was before a Royal Commission, which had only concluded its Report today".

Adderley was, therefore, greatly surprised when the motion that the Bill should be read for a second time was put to a vote and lost narrowly; 170 Ayes and 173 Noes. Plimsoll must have been heartened by this strong cross party support, and the Prime Minister, Disraeli, amazed that the vote was lost by only three votes urged Adderley to draw up a measure after all. *Punch* commented on Plimsoll's speech;

> To lose a Bill by a majority of three under such circumstances (that is, with some MP's anxious to await the report of the Commission) was to carry it. The House, like the Country, has made up its mind against further toleration of floating coffins. Mr Plimsoll deserves the credit of having brought England to this mind. Of course, Mr Plimsoll has been indiscreet. People who attack great evils and large interests always are – more power to such indiscretion...At the same time, in this as in all war upon evil, the less mud flung and the less ill-blood stirred the better; and so *Punch* congratulates his friend Plimsoll on the most moderate measure, and the least aggressive speech, yet made on a subject fit to provoke a saint and make an angel aggressive.[535]

The annual wreck returns, compiled by the Board of Trade, were very late for the calendar years 1873 and 1874 due to a decision by the Board in 1873 to move from calendar years to annual statistics from the 1st of July to the 30th of June in order to include all winter casualties into one twelve month period. Accordingly, the wreck return for 1873/1874 was not published until July 1875. Statistics produced, not only for 'Wrecks &c of British and Foreign ships at home' but also for the same categories of ships in

British waters abroad, and for 'British ships in foreign countries and on the high seas' showed the loss of life to be unprecedented and alarming, with 1,991 more seamen being lost than average, and 150 ships with their entire complements totaling 2,381 men reported as missing.

A letter from the Permanent Secretary of the Marine Department, Mr. Thomas Gray of the Board of Trade to the Nautical Magazine, dated 27 July 1875, attempted to set the record straight on two interpretations of statistics included in the Wreck Return for 1873/1874;

> Will you allow me to say a few words as to the passage in your leader of today, in which you say that 'five thousand *seamen* go to the bottom every year'? Mr. Plimsoll puts the number at 6,927. The average number of *all* persons drowned at sea, taking into account the returns for the years ended December 1872, is 2,425, and that number includes *passengers* as well as crew lost or missing from British ships all over the world. The number of lives lost by casualties to British ships during the year ended June 1874, is 4,416, including passengers and including missing crews. It is thus, 1,991 above the annual average. Of this excess of 1,991 lives lost in the year, I may mention that 821 and 420 respectively were lost in Coolie ships abroad. These two losses alone account for 1,241 of the 1,991 lives. As regards the loss of 2,381 lives in 150 missing ships, I should like to point out that the 150 ships and the 2,381 missing men are included in the 4,416 and also that 69 of these ships were known to be classed ships; the remainder were not known to be classed but many of them might have been. It is a fact, that with the 150 missing ships there are 2.381 missing men. Of these 1,462 are missing in classed ships, and 919 in the others. The whole number of seamen's lives lost is 2,958, not 6,927...[536]

Statistics showed that the most dangerous cargoes being carried were; coal, 36 ships and 525 lives; grain; 23 ships and 710 lives, and timber; 12 ships and 167 lives. The complete disappearance of so many ships in one twelve month period was unprecedented, and occasioned the following comment in the maritime press;

> The most unsatisfactory feature in the present wreck register is the number of *missing* vessels. Notwithstanding the reasons we have given for the exceptional increase in the receipt of reports of this class of

> losses [a reference to requirement of the 1873 Act for owners to report lost or missing vessels] in this year, the numbers are truly alarming. Let us think what the numbers are! *Missing vessels;* vessels that no one knows anything about! Besides all the *known* and described vessels with their 2,100 lives lost, 150 British ships disappeared, clean gone, wiped out like a grease spot, never heard from after leaving port; and this in one year's records. With the 150 missing ships there are also 2,381 missing men – a good many struck off the muster-roll in one year from one "class" of casualty only.[537]

The first annual report from the Board of Trade to Parliament on unseaworthy ships indicated the effectiveness of section 12 of the Merchant Shipping Act, 1873, – *Survey of ships suspected of being unseaworthy;*

> From this it appears that 440 vessels have been surveyed for defects in either hull, equipments, or machinery, and that of this number 17 only were steam vessels. Fourteen [of the 440] only were found seaworthy, upon survey 404 were pronounced unseaworthy, and the remaining 22 cases were pending. In 25 cases the vessels were broken up or dismantled after survey. Government officers are stated to be the source information in 408 cases, crews in 13, and "other persons" in 24 cases. The return accounts for 34 cases of overloading only, and it is satisfactory to find that the action taken by the Board of Trade was justified as each vessel appears to have been unloaded or reloaded to the satisfaction of their surveyors…the return is a very complete one, carefully summarized, and shows very clearly the tonnage of every vessel surveyed, which ranges from 15 to 1,500 tons.[538]

Edward Bates, the Member of Parliament for Plymouth, whom Plimsoll would cross swords with in the House in 1875, owned the Liverpool based shipping company Edward Bates and Sons, operating a number of sailing ships converted from iron steam ships with their engines removed, primarily involved in carrying coal around the Cape of Good Hope to Aden, a bunkering station for ships on passage to the Far East through the Suez Canal. Bates was to lose six ships between 1873 and 1875; five carrying coal and one homeward bound from Calcutta.[539] One of these ships; the ***Euxine,*** an iron hulled ex-paddle steamer built in 1847, departed from Newcastle on the 11th June and experienced good weather until the 1st of August when, during a storm, a heavy sea washed one of the crew overboard, washed away the quarter boat, and shifted the cargo. The crew re-trimmed the cargo to bring the ship upright and on the 3rd of August made sail. Shortly afterwards smoke was seen coming out of the fore and main ventilators. Course was altered to make for St. Helena, and the crew commenced discharging coal overboard, in an attempt to locate the seat of the fire, and pumped water into the holds. By the 6th of August the fire had still not been located but, as the ship and accommodation were full of smoke and gas, the ventilators were closed all day. At seven that evening there was an explosion which blew off the hatch covers. On the 7th the ship hove to, but the hatches covers were again blown off a number of times and fire was discovered alongside the wooden ventilator in the main hatches. The crew turned the boats out and provisioned them, but were forced to abandon ship that evening, standing by the ship in the boats observing flames coming out of the hatches. The following morning the Captain, First Mate and Bosun re-boarded the ship but, finding the fire out of control returned to their respective boats, bringing with them more provisions.

The boats set course for St. Helena, 850 miles away, and agreed to stay together, although the Captain's was the fastest. The Captain's and Chief Mate's boats arrived at St. Helena two weeks later. On the 12th day after leaving the ***Euxine*** the Second Mate estimated that his boat was in the latitude of St. Helena and 30 miles to the east, after which they steered westward for two days, but with no sighting of the island. The bold decision was then made to steer for the long coastline of Brazil, 2,000 miles away, and rations were reduced from two biscuits and one pint of water per day to one biscuit and a half a pint of water. During this passage the boat capsized twice, drowning two of the crew the first time and forcing the remainder to spend the night in the water the second time before they could right the boat. They had lost all supplies, their sail and navigation equipment, and a further two crew in the course of the second capsize. By the 30th of August thirst drove the remaining crew to drink seawater. One drank too much, went mad the following day and suggested to the others that they kill and eat him. Instead they decided on who should die by drawing straws. A young Italian lost and resigned himself to his fate. His throat was cut and his head severed and thrown overboard. One person held a bowl to catch the blood which they all drank and then mixed with seawater and small pieces of his heart and liver. The rest of the body was saved for future use. Tragically for the Italian, their boat was sighted only three hours later by the ***Java Packet*** of Amsterdam which carried the four survivors to her next port, Batavia, where they arrived on the 2nd of November. The four survivors made frank depositions about their ordeal upon which the Attorney General in Singapore decided to not prosecute for murder. The Colonial Office disagreed and insisted upon a trial which failed due to a matter of invalidity of the evidence.[540] Echoes of this example of 'the custom of the sea' were to later reverberate between Parliament and the Board of Trade in mid-1875, at a time of unprecedented political upheaval in the House.

Work continued on the Chain Cables and Anchors Bill with the Select Committee reporting on the 30th of June, the third reading taking place on the 6th of July and the Bill being passed to go up to the House of Lords. The first reading of the Bill by the Lords took place on the 7th of July, with the second reading on the 14th of July being preceding by an explanation of the reason for the amendment to the 1871 Act;

> ...The Chain Cables Act of 1864 required that all anchors made in in this country for the use of the merchant service should be subjected to what was known as the tensile strain. No anchors which were not up to that strain could be sold in this country. That Act expired on the 1st of July, 1872, and in the Session of 1871, a Bill was brought in having for its object, not only to perpetuate the clauses of that Act, but to make certain important additions to them. By the provisions of that Bill, which was now an Act of Parliament, there was another test besides the tensile strain applied to cables. The whole of the cable was subjected to that strain, but, in addition, there was a special and more severe test applied to five links in every 15 fathoms. An objection to the existing Act was this—that it prohibited any maker selling, even to a foreign shipowner, for use out of this country a cable not tested in our way; while some of those shipowners preferred other systems of testing, such, for instance, as the Dutch system which was applied at Amsterdam. The object of this Bill was to enable chain-cable makers to manufacture cables for the foreign market without subjecting them to the statutory test or any test applied in this country. The 3rd clause, therefore, confined the test to anchors and chain cables "for the use of any British ships," so that henceforward the foreign purchaser would have the option of having his chain cable tested according to our system, or having it tested elsewhere. The 6th clause repealed the section of the 34 & 35 Vict., which directed the nature and amount of

> the test, and substituted any test approved of by the Board of Trade as a test equal or superior to the existing tests.[541]

A House of Lords committee reported back on the 17th and 20th of July, with the Bill being read for the third time and passed the following day. Royal assent for the amended Act was received on the 30th.[542] The Act made some administrative changes to s.5 of the Chain Cable and Anchor Act, 1864; *Fees payable on licenses*, and s.6; *As to the Remuneration of Inspectors*. Section 12 of the Merchant Shipping Act, 1872; *Fees and expenses in relation to testing of chain cable and anchors by Trinity House to be paid and charged on the mercantile marine fund* was repealed. The Chain Cables and Anchors Act, 1874[543], entered into force on the 30th of July; *An Act to amend the Law respecting the Proving and Sale of Chain Cables and Anchors.*

Towards the end of 1874 there occurred the tragic loss of an emigrant ship on passage from Great Britain to New Zealand and almost her entire complement of 477, save for three of her crew. News of the tragedy didn't reach Great Britain or New Zealand until the New Year due to the ship's very isolated location. The ***Cospatrick***, built in India in 1856, was a three masted 'Blackwall frigate' of 1,199 ton that had spent most of her life carrying cargo, troops and emigrants to India. In 1873 she was taken over by Shaw Savill & Co and had completed one voyage to New Zealand with emigrants before sailing from London for Auckland on the 11th of September 1874 carrying 433 passengers and 44 crew, including 124 women and 126 children. The ***Cospatrick*** carried five boats capable of holding 187 people, plus a small Captain's gig. Most of the passengers were labourers or relatives of people who had already emigrated to New Zealand.[544]

On the 17th of November, when the ship was in the South Atlantic about 400 miles south-west of Capetown, fire broke out in the bosun's store in the forepart of the ship just after midnight.[545] The store contained many inflammable items, and the fire soon took hold. The crew attempted to turn the ship downwind to isolate the fire but could not do so and the fire spread the length of the ship, burning through two boats and hampering efforts to launch boats. Other boats were launched with some difficulty, but the starboard lifeboat capsized, throwing its occupants into the sea. The longboat caught fire while the crew were trying to launch it, then the Captain's gig was launched without anyone tying it on, and it drifted away, empty. That left just the port lifeboat, which could accommodate thirty people. In the end, 35 survivors, including fourteen crew, were packed into the 7.5 metre boat. A group of twenty-six survivors had also managed to right the starboard lifeboat, and once the two boats came together the passengers were distributed so there were 32 in one boat, skippered by the First Mate Charles Romaine, and 30 in the other, led by the Second Mate, Henry MacDonald.[546]

These boats, standing by the ship, saw the main and mizzen masts fall, crushing many people seeking refuge from the flames on the poop, and watched it sink in flames on the 19th. During a gale on the 21st of November the boats were separated, and the First Mate's boat was never seen again. The sole remaining boat, with 30 aboard, was in a desperate and helpless situation with no water, food, masts, or sails and only one oar. One after another most of those aboard succumbed to thirst, starvation or madness. Early on the morning of the 26th a ship passed not more than 50 yards away, close enough for the boat to hail, with no response. The boat was sighted and picked up by the ***British Sceptre*** on 27 November, by which time there were only five men left alive, who had been reduced to drinking the blood and eating the livers of their dead companions. The boat had drifted about 500 miles north-east from where the ***Cospatrick*** had sunk. Two of the survivors died shortly after being rescued. A court of inquiry in England found that the fire probably started when one of the crew or a passenger pilfering cargo set fire to straw or some similar material with a match or candle, and that the fire gained a rapid hold due to the flammable goods stored in the forehold – coal, turpentine, palm oil and other oils.[547]

Recalling that the ***Cospatrick*** was equipped with five boats of a total capacity of 187 persons, plus a non-mandatory small Captain's gig, it's instructive to recall the legal requirements for carriage of boats applicable to such a ship at the time of her loss. These requirements had not been reviewed or amended since the Merchant Shipping Act, 1854, and the Passengers Act, 1855, in spite of a steady increase in the tonnage and passenger carrying capacity of ships over this period. Both Acts used tonnage as the principal criteria for determining the number of boats to be carried regardless of the number of people aboard. In the case of a ship, such as the ***Cospatrick*** of 1,199 ton, the Merchant Shipping Act, 1854, required 4 boats for sailing ships greater than 800 ton. The Passenger Act, 1855, clause XXVII, required

6 boats for ships between 1,000 and 1,500 ton;– provided that no "Passenger Ship" shall be required to carry a greater Number of Boats than are sufficient in the judgement of the Emigration officer at the Port of Clearance to carry all the Persons on board such ship. Clause XXVII went on to state that;

> ...One of such Boats shall in all Cases be a Long Boat and one shall be a properly fitted Life Boat, which shall be carried in such a Manner as to be, in the Opinion of the Emigration Officer, most available for immediate Service: Each of such Boats shall be of a Size and Description to be approved by the Emigration officer at the Port of Clearance, and properly supplied with all Requisites and kept clear at all Times for immediate Use at Sea...

Putting aside the different requirements for boats under each Act, and the question of primacy; as a sailing ship carrying emigrants, the ***Cospatrick's*** boats were clearly not sufficient '*...to carry all the Persons on board such ship*' in spite of their presumed approval by the Emigration officer at the port of clearance.

The matter of the ***Cospatrick*** was brought up in the House on the 22nd of February, 1875, when the President of the Board of Trade was asked; "... whether in view of the great loss of life attendant upon the burning of the "Cospatrick," he will undertake to insist upon a system of fire-drill, similar to that practised on board Her Majesty's men-of-war, being adopted on board of all emigrant ships; that the crew be practised in lowering the boats, and that a proper supply of provisions, with oars and rudders, be kept at all times in each of the boats?" Adderley's reply revealed the tentative and cautious approach generally taken by the Board of Trade to regulation of matters of critical to the safety of ships and all aboard, in stating that;

> Among the suggestions, Sir, issued by the Board of Trade to the captains of emigrant ships, there is one that a crew of picked men should be assigned to each boat, under the charge of an officer, a steady person, who is responsible for everything being kept at hand and ready for use, and that the men should be exercised in lowering the boats at sea when opportunities occur. It is also suggested that the fire engines which by law must be carried should be likewise under special charge, and worked once or twice a-week, so as to be kept in proper order. Every equipment—oars, rudder, sails, hatchets, &c.—must be in every

> boat before it is passed by the Board of Trade surveyor. As to provisioning boats, which the best Lines do, a further suggestion is now being made by the Board of Trade. With regard to the suggestions as to drill, no law enables the Board of Trade to enforce them; nor, if there were a law, would it probably be possible practically to enforce it.[548]

In reply to a question in the House on the 23rd of March on the dangers of carrying dangerously flammable cargoes, Adderley referred to s. 9 of the Passengers Act, 1855, which gave '*...power to the Board of Trade both to stop passenger ships if loaded with such shipments dangerous to the health or lives of the passengers or safety of the ship, or if the cargo is not stowed and secured to the satisfaction of the officers of the Board of Trade*' He also noted that; "...it has since the case of the Cospatrick been under the consideration of the Board of Trade whether any general regulations on the subject can be made in the interests of safety compatible with the necessities of the trade".[549]

In reply to a further question in the House on the 11th of August 1875, Sir Charles Adderley stated;

> ...the Court which inquired into the loss of the Cospatrick by fire made three recommendations. The first was, that in wooden vessels there should be bulkheads to cut off communication with the hold as in iron ships, and that has been seen to as far as possible. The second was, that there should be better stowage of boats, and that they should not be stowed keel upwards. That point is under consideration of a Departmental Committee; but its decision has been delayed by the illness of Captain Forster, the Chief Emigration Officer of the Board of Trade. The third was, that there should be a [weekly] boat drill on board emigrant ships. To these recommendations we have called the attention of shipowners throughout the country; but, at the same time, I beg to state that we do not think it desirable that imperative orders should be issued for compliance with them, and much less that compliance with them should be enforced by special legislation directed to that end.[550]

Chapter 20

Competing Bills, Coal Cargoes, and Custom of the Sea

Board of Trade officials had clearly been busy during the second half of 1874, when Parliament was in recess, as on the 5th of February, 1875, the Queen informed her Lords and Gentlemen that; "A Bill for the amendment of the Merchant Shipping Acts will be laid before you".

On the next sitting day, the 8th of February, Sir Charles Adderley introduced a Merchant Shipping Acts Amendment Bill. In the course of a long introduction it was explained that the Bill dealt with four recommendations of the Royal commission that required legislation; discipline on board merchant ships, the safety of ships and those on board, improved inquiries into casualties at sea and the training of boys for service at sea. In response to the Commission's finding that 'evidence affords ample proof that masters of vessels have not at this moment sufficient control over their men, and that the men can be guilty with impunity of the grossest dereliction of duty' the Bill would propose that the system of advance notes would be rendered illegal. Further, that the criminal code of the merchant service would be 'recast' in that charges against certified officers would be dealt with by stipendiary magistrates or the local Admiralty Court, rather than the Board of Trade or local Marine Boards. Assessors would be appointed by the High Court of the Admiralty and incompetent officers would not have their certificates suspended, but either cancelled or substituted by a lower certificate. The only additional offence proposed was that of neglect to keep a proper lookout or sleeping on watch. A new principle was introduced whereby; 'double punishment would be inflicted in cases of drunkenness and other offences committed under circumstances which endanger the ship, or the lives of those on board'. Adderley also advised Members that the recommendations regarding expertise within the Board of Trade had been adopted through the appointment of a second nautical adviser; a law adviser who would conduct prosecutions, and improved organization of the surveying staff.

Regarding surveys for seaworthiness by the Board of Trade, the Bill didn't depart from the existing reactive measure of acting only on 'good and trustworthy information' dealing with suspicious cases. Adderley agreed with the Royal Commission that;

> ...a general periodical Government survey of all ships would, 'even if possible, be most mischievous and vexatious, and not only that, but I would go further and say that it would be fatal to its object; because if the Government were to certify continually all ships in the Merchant Service, it would be impossible, in the case of any casualty, that anyone but the Government should be made responsible...We altogether decline to certify the whole Mercantile Navy; a course which would not only be vexatious in itself, impede improvement, and shackle our commerce in foreign competition, but which would relieve shipowners of the liabilities which are the chief security of public safety

Adderley saw no possibility of making a compulsory load-line; "On the contrary, the attempt would be most mischievous and delusive", but he did adopt the suggestion of the Commissioners that there should be an added scale of feet downwards amidships to test the buoyancy of ships, as a caution against overloading, as affording instructions to the surveyors, and as a record and evidence in case of casualty. The recommendations of the Commissioners regarding deck loads were not entirely accepted but it was proposed that every ship carrying a deck load should report to the Customs 'the weight, bulk and character of any such cargo' and enter this information in the log book.

One very positive and long overdue proposal in the Bill was the consolidation of the various regulations for provisions of boats to 'a uniform principle', but this proposal was unfortunately qualified by inclusion of the principle of 'elastic rules to meet special cases'. Adjustment of compasses was addressed through a proposal that it only be carried out by persons 'examined and certified as competent for such a duty'. Responsibility, and liability, for knowingly and without excuse sending an unseaworthy ships to sea would be firmly sheeted home to ship owners.

Lastly, it was proposed to separate the first inquiry into the circumstances and causes of any casualty from any criminal proceedings subsequently taken against all who appeared to have been culpable. The preliminary inquiry by the Receiver of Wrecks would remain the same. "The formal inquiry which may follow the preliminary one will be simply an inquest, and taken altogether out of the hands of ordinary justices and placed in the hands of stipendiary magistrates with Assessors appointed by the Admiralty, so that the Board of Trade will stand altogether clear of any judicial action, ready to take criminal proceedings in the ordinary Courts of Law as prosecutor against guilty parties". Adderley concluded his introduction by explaining;

> These are the main enactments proposed by this Bill, which is a measure entirely independent of party. Drawn up with careful attention to the Report and collection of evidence of the Royal Commission on the subject, I hope it will, with perhaps some modifications, be accepted by the House. The question, though not a party one in any way, is one of great national interest; and I believe, after having carefully considered the matter with those who are best able to give advice, that the Bill will be found calculated to ameliorate the condition and character of our merchant seamen, place the shipowner in a sounder and more satisfactory position before the law, and at the same time enable the Department, on which a delicate and difficult task is imposed, to develop more vigorously the powers with which it has been entrusted.[551]

Plimsoll, who had been eagerly anticipating the Bill, was the first Member to respond to Adderley's introduction and stated, amongst other things, that;

> ...when first he heard the Government intended to bring in a Merchant Shipping Bill his hopes were highly raised, and he felt like a shipwrecked sailor who saw a sail in the horizon bearing down towards him; but now he had ascertained what kind of a measure it was, he felt like that shipwrecked sailor would feel when, the ship having come quite close to him, it suddenly altered its course and left him to his fate, with the only consolation that his case would be inquired into when the vessel reached home. Since he had listened to the speech of the right hon. Gentleman, he must confess his hopes and the expectations in which he had indulged had undergone a similar diminution.... On the whole, the measure introduced by the President of the Board of Trade was weak and ineffectual, and seemed to fall lamentably short of meeting the requirements of the case, for the reason mainly that it

contained no provision for the surveying of ships and none to prevent overloading.

A member of the Royal Commission; Mr. T. Brassey, echoed statements made by Adderley in his address; "the condition of the law in reference to marine insurance lay at the very root of this most important subject. In the present state of the law, there were many cases in which the insured could recover more than the value of his ship if it happened to be lost, and it was most desirable that the law should, if possible, be amended, and marine insurance limited to indemnity for losses actually sustained." A strong supporter of Plimsoll was disappointed with the Bill as being too severe and recommended that preference be given to the Bill introduced by Plimsoll in 1874; a view supported by another Member, along with a Member representing a large ship-owning community who believed that the proposals by Plimsoll's Bill were more likely to preserve life at sea than those of the President of the Board of Trade; "...Prevention was better than cure, and if a survey was to be of any real practical use, it ought to be made before the vessel was sent to sea, and not after the mischief was done". He also stated that there was not the slightest difficulty in fixing a load line and that practical men and shipowners would be "much better pleased if such a course were adopted".

Adderley's Motion for "leave be given to bring in a Bill to amend the Merchant Shipping Acts" was agreed to and a Bill was ordered to be brought in. The Bill was presented and read for the first time. Taking note of the debate, Plimsoll successfully reintroduced the Bill that was thrown out in 1874, with the House in Committee *resolving* "That the Chairman be directed to move the House that leave be given to bring in a Bill to amend the Acts relating to Merchant Shipping". The Resolution was *reported and the* Bill *ordered* to be brought in by Mr. Plimsoll, Mr. Roebuck, Mr. Samuda, and Mr. Kirkman Hodgson. The Bill was *presented*, and read the first time.[552] Parliament then found itself in the unusual situation of having to consider two Bills presenting opposing views on the same matters; the Merchant Shipping Acts Amendment Bill (Government), and the Merchant Shipping Acts Amendment (No.2) Bill (Plimsoll).

A question to the President of the Board of Trade in the House on the 23rd of February recounted a mournful toll of steamships lost or abandoned during the Parliamentary recess; "have inquiries been held to ascertain the cause of loss of the following steamers: ***Alice*** 975 tons, ***Bride*** 1,341 tons, ***King Leopold*** 867 tons, ***Scorpio*** 885 tons, ***Stad Brugge*** 1,128 tons, ***Viceroy*** 1,139 tons, ***George Batters*** 1,116 tons, ***Berar*** 1,033 tons, ***Kathleen Mary*** 1,268 tons, ***Thornaby*** 1,472 tons, reported as missing, and supposed to have foundered, with all hands, in the months of October, November, and December 1874, and January 1875, and the reasons for holding or not holding inquiries in each case?" A further part of the question enquired about ships abandoned during the same period; "similar information as to the following steamers; ***La Plata*** 1,218 tons, ***Clifton*** 543 tons, ***Precursor*** 791 tons, ***Violet*** 1,281 tons, ***Alpha*** 1,292 tons, ***Emma David*** 1,733 tons, ***Cortes*** 1,517 tons, abandoned, in some cases with loss of life, during the same period of time". Adderley could only ineffectively reply that the ships lost had been reported to the Board of Trade by their owners.[553]

A further question during the same sitting focused on prosecutions for sending an unseaworthy ship to sea, and resulting from the above losses;

> How many prosecutions there have been under Clause 11 of the Merchant Shipping Amendment Act of 1871; and what have been the results of such prosecutions; if he is aware that ten British steamers have foundered in the Bay of Biscay during the last six months, drowning upwards of two hundred people; and how many inquiries have been held or are likely to be held in regard to these disasters; and, whether, supposing any of these vessels to have been unseaworthy, it is proposed to prosecute anybody; and, in such event, how he proposes to reach the persons responsible for the improper condition in which vessels that have gone to the bottom, with all hands, sailed from foreign ports homeward bound?

Adderley advised that there had been four prosecutions and that others were in progress. Of the 10 steamers named, five were reported as having foundered in the Bay of Biscay, with 100 lives lost; five are missing. Inquiries have been held in the first five cases namely; the ***La Plata, Cortes, Mary, Clifton,*** and ***Alpha*** and inquiries will be held in the other cases if any trustworthy evidence should be forthcoming. Of the first five, the ***Mary*** was found by the Court to have been unseaworthy, and the case is in the hands of the Lord Advocate for a criminal prosecution. As to homeward-bound ships from foreign ports; "it is the Consul's business to report any suspicious cases and he may summon a Naval Court which can order survey. Owners of unseaworthy ships would be prosecuted on evidence sent home by the Consul". Plimsoll took the opportunity to peevishly state that; "...to-morrow I shall ask the President of the Board of Trade, on what authority he imputes to me. any responsibility for the inquiry into the case of the ***Viceroy***, as at the present moment I am entirely unaware of having had anything to do with it; and, whether he thinks it wise on the part of the Board of Trade to parade themselves before the public continually by attacking me without just reason?"[554]

On the 25th of February, in response to a question about "the large number of coal ships that have recently been burnt at sea" Adderley replied; "...The Government have lately resolved to advise the issue of a Royal Commission to inquire into the causes and remedies of the spontaneous combustion of coal ships, which has so much increased...".[555] Pressure was maintained on the Board of Trade throughout March with four questions in the House on alleged overloading, carriage of inflammable cargoes on passenger ships, and lack of boats on coasting vessels. The parliamentary calendar was further encumbered on the 23rd of March with a third Bill on load lines and surveys; "On Motion of Mr. Norwood, Bill to provide for the marking of a Load Line on British Ships; and for other purposes relating to the Survey of Ships, *ordered* to be brought in by Mr. Norwood, Mr. Ashley, Mr. Edward Reed, and Mr. Eustace Smith". The Bill was *presented*, and read the first time – the Merchant Shipping (Load Line) Bill. [Bill 106.][556] Pressure was kept on Adderley with a Member threatening to bring in yet another Bill on the 6th of April if the Board of Trade were not to proceed with the Merchant Shipping Acts Amendment Bill [No.4]. The Member was assured by Adderley that the "Notice Paper, on which the second reading of this Bill was the First Order of the Day for Thursday..." and "...he believed he had the concurrence of the seamen's best friends and of the best shipowners throughout the country".[557] The promised second reading of Bill No.4 took place two days later.

Adderley summarized the changes made to the first draft of the Bill as being; "substitution of the existing clause relating to shipowners' liablity with a new clause relating, and introduction of a voluntary load line clause", emphasizing that in so doing;

> ...the object of the measure was to secure increased safety at sea and a diminution of the unnecessary perils to which seamen were now exposed, while avoiding at the same time any mischievous interference with shipowners in carrying on their business. ...shipowners were not necessarily experts, and their ships often came to grief with no criminal intention on their part, or even knowledge of the cause. He therefore thought that, alone of all trades, the shipowner should have guaranteed to him the profits arising from his trade, while the Government should be responsible for supplying him with the requisite knowledge for conducting it.

The Bill was drafted by Board of Trade officials, with Adderley's support, to firstly provide for improvement in the discipline and condition of seamen through removal of advances on wages; secondly, for better equipping of ships, particularly with regard to the supply of boats which ships would be obliged to carry and thirdly to prevent unseaworthy ships from going to sea. The amended Bill proposed the status quo on this matter; intervention on receipt of complaints rather than compulsory surveys. It also proposed to deal with and improve the system of inquiry into casualties at sea and, lastly, to amend the law as to the liabilities of shipowners. The second object to which he had referred namely, the better equipment of ships, had regard, among other things; "to the supply of boats which ships would be obliged to carry". The existing law on this point was, by the Bill, adapted to present circumstances; "that is to ships of larger tonnage and carrying more passengers".

In speaking to the Motion that the Bill be read for a second time, Sir Charles Norwood, representing a large constituency of shipowners, objected to; "the peremptory abolition of advances to sailors ...and proposed instead that the advance given in British ports "...might be limited to a certain sum. He ventured to suggest £1 but he was of opinion that there should be no limit at all to the right of giving advances in foreign ports". In addressing the proposed discipline causes he considered; "the Bill was that it was too much a Bill of Pains and Penalties. It contained too much in the shape of coercion, and too little in the shape of encouragement". Firm views were expressed by other Members on the generally poor standard, and shortage of, able bodied seamen and that this contributed to unseaworthy ships as espoused by the Royal Commission. Lord Eslington, of the Royal Commission, in stating that the public's concern simply with statistics for loss of life, did not take into account the growth of the shipping industry;

> ... An analysis of loss of life by shipwrecks in the six years from 1867 to 1872 showed that the whole number of lives lost was 12,048, or about 2,000 per annum; and of that entire number 6,105 were lost in classed ships, while 5,943 were lost in unclassed ships. That was a curious state of things, when it was said it would be a great preventive of loss of life at sea to have a compulsory classification of ships. With regard to our coasting trade, the Returns were so accurate, that the calculation of the loss of life could be made to a nicety. In 1856 the tonnage entered and cleared in the United Kingdom was 10,970,000 tons; and in 1872 it was 25,714,270. In 1856 the number of lives imperilled on the coast of the United Kingdom was 2,764. The lives saved were 2,243, and the lives lost were 521. In 1872, when their tonnage had increased by 15,000,000 of tons, the number of lives imperilled upon their coast was 5,224. The number of lives saved was 4,634, and the number of lives lost was 590; so that only 69 lives were lost more than in 1856, though the tonnage had increased by 15,000,000 of tons.

The constant concerns of Members of Parliament and the Government about the availability and standard of merchant seamen in wartime underlaid the comments of one Member; "No Government or Board of Admiralty would think of entering upon a great European war unless the Mercantile Marine of this country was in a sound and prosperous state". More than one MP disagreed with the severe increase in penalties in the Bill; arguing that, for example; "there had not been a single prosecution to date for the offence of not keeping a proper lookout, and the penalties in the 1854 Act which it were proposed to increase were perfectly adequate". After stating that he felt ill and was "desirous to proceed home" Plimsoll made a relatively brief intervention which he summarized as; "...in conclusion, [he] stated that in Committee he would give the House the opportunity of voting on the following points: The survey of unclassed vessels' adoption of a load-line; a test for iron; prohibition of deck loads except within certain limits and the prohibition of grain cargoes in bulk. He informed the House that until 1872 there had been great fatality among vessels bringing cargoes of bulk grain from Canada; a fact that had lead Canada to pass a law that required shipowners to stow such cargoes to the satisfaction of port authorities. Since this time, in the words of a Member of the Canadian Government; "Not one single vessel sailing from those ports with grain has met with any accident whatever". A cogent comparison was made by another Member regarding differing standards for passenger and non-passenger ships, and also in rebutting long-standing received wisdom that it was impossible to determine how the location of a load line could be determined;

> ...there was another point which had been entirely overlooked, and that was, that they [the Board of Trade] did not allow any passengers to go to sea without their being protected by a Government survey; and it was only when it came to a question of the lives of seamen that the Government stopped short, and said it was not necessary to take any steps in the matter, and they would leave the seamen to take care of themselves. That Bill, with its penal enactments, treated seamen as persons who were not only to be drowned without consideration, but to be punished without mercy and almost without consideration.... He saw no insuperable difficulty in the way of deciding upon a form of load-line which would be simple and easily understood, but which, at the same time, would answer all practical purposes.

Mr. Charles McIver MP, managing owner of Cunard, who spoke from the experience of having been responsible for the carriage of 72,000 passengers the previous year, accepted that occasional disasters might occur to the best of ships and that notwithstanding the greatest care, such ships might sometimes unaccountably go to the bottom. This did not always mean that the owner had been to blame. But, he believed that, in the previous few months, about a dozen steamers that had foundered in the Bay of Biscay; "had gone to the bottom from causes which might have been prevented; and, as he thought, from causes preventable by legislation such as might fairly be held to be in harmony with the principle of the Government Bill". To prevent such losses he supported the marking of load line and adoption of the survey for passenger ships for cargo ships.

A motion to adjourn the debate was opposed by Disraeli who stated; "he thought the proposal was not in accordance with Parliamentary usage. The principle of the Bill had been accepted on both sides of the House, and the speeches which had been made in the course of the discussion, however interesting and ingenious, were, with very rare exceptions, Committee speeches; and even the hon. Member for Derby, whose general views might be supposed to form a system opposed to the policy of the Government, had announced it to be his intention to move amendments at a future stage of the measure. He, therefore, trusted the debate would not be adjourned. Ample opportunity would be afforded to hon. Members to express their opinions on the Bill both in Committee and on other occasions, and it was therefore to be hoped that the House would proceed at once with the second reading". The debate continued.

The controversial shipowner, Eduard Bates, made a short and pertinent contribution to the debate in stating that he believed that shipowners of Liverpool and other ports would agree that in general that the Bill; "was in the right direction", although there were one or two points which might require revision in Committee; for example, those referring to advance notes. Iron used in the construction of ships should be subjected to a Government test as it had been recently found out that the iron in some ships, damaged through collision, was as brittle as cast iron. He believed that no grain should be carried in ships in bulk, unless at least half of the cargo was in bags. With some alterations the Bill would be a good one, and he would therefore generally support it. The debate was then adjourned with the Bill being read for the second time and committed to the following day.[558]

The dangers involved in making a landfall in fog after a long ocean passage were tragically demonstrated by the loss of the German trans-Atlantic passenger liner Schiller on the 7th of May 1875. The ***Schiller*** of 3,421 tons; built in Glasgow in 1873 for the German Transatlantic Steam Navigation Line, had operated successfully between Hamburg and New York since her maiden voyage in February 1874 until departing New York on the 27th of April for Plymouth, Cherbourg and Hamburg on, what was to be, her final voyage. Carrying a total of 378 souls, comprising 140 cabin and 120 steerage passengers and 118 crew she approached the English coast on the evening of the 7th of May in thick fog. Due also to rain and haze, an accurate position had not been obtained for three days, but the Captain, calculating that the ship, on a course of East by South, was approaching the Scilly Islands, posted extra lookouts to sight the Bishop Rock lighthouse or hear its fog signal. At 9.00pm speed was reduced to four knots and sails furled. At 9.30pm, as testified later under oath by both the First Mate and Fourth Mate, the Captain ordered a large course alteration to South-south-west, heading slowly into a moderate South-westerly wind to seek clear water in mid-channel. At 10.00pm the ***Schiller*** struck the Retarrier Ledges, to the East-south-east of the Bishop Rock lighthouse. The engines were given full power astern, to no avail, and the ship filled rapidly.

The Captain ordered the six boats to be launched amongst scenes of chaos, confusion and panic. Two lifeboats were crushed and many passengers killed when one of the two funnels fell on them. Two other boats were filled with males and, in spite of the Captain threatening them with his revolver, and shooting at them, none of the males left the boats, which subsequently capsized killing all aboard them. Most of the women and children took shelter in the deckhouse and were all lost when a sea tore the roof off and swept all inside overboard. As the tide came in and covered the wreck survivors climbed the rigging but many were maimed and killed by falling rigging. The mainmast fell at 7.30am taking all who had taken refuge on it to their deaths, with the foremast, and the thirty-four people clinging to it, falling a half hour later. Out of the one boat and two gigs successfully launched, one was badly damaged with the eleven survivors being transferred to another boat. The remaining two boats eventually ended up on the island of Tresco. Of the twenty-seven aboard these boats, there was only one female and no children. Local boats became aware of the wreck in the morning and managed to rescue a number of survivors from floating wreckage and the rocks. Out of the 378 souls aboard the ship, 335 perished.[559]

Questions inevitably followed this disaster in the maritime press and Parliament. Why was the lead not used; why was allowance not made for a well-known current; was the ship purposely taken close to the Scillies so that her position could have been signalled to the telegraph station, as was the practice of many ships; was there confusion between the guns fired and rockets legally sent up by the Schiller as signals of distress until midnight, and the guns fired illegally by ships to announce their arrival, or to signal other ships belonging to the same company; why was the fog signal on the Bishop Rock lighthouse not heard?[560] An inquest into the deaths of some of those lost was held in the Scilly Islands soon after the tragedy at which the 'Coroner recommended that telegraphic communication be established between the Bishop lighthouse and the shore, which would in this case have resulted in saving all on board'. The Chief and Second Officers of the ***Schiller*** concurred in this opinion, and the Coroner was requested to forward a copy of the verdict to the proper quarter.[561] The Court of Inquiry attributed the loss of the ***Schiller*** to the Captain's 'benign neglect.

At the beginning of June 1875, a passenger steamer was lost through striking ice whilst trying to carefully navigate an extensive icefield on the eastern extremity of the Grand Banks about 120 miles South-east from St. Johns, Newfoundland. The ***Vicksburg*** of 2,484 gross tons had been built in Glasgow in 1872 for the Dominion Line service between Liverpool, Quebec and Montreal, with accommodation for 80 cabin and 600 steerage passengers. On her last voyage the ***Vicksburg*** was carrying only seven cabin and twenty-five steerage passengers, along with sixty crew, when departing Quebec on the 27th of May for Liverpool. As testified by one of the surviving crew; "fair weather was experienced until the evening of the 30th of May when a large ice field was encountered, surrounding the ship. Engines were stopped until the following morning when all hands were called to shorten sail as she encountered large masses of heavy ice about the ship on all sides, and cakes of great weight bearing down upon her. Course was altered to the south and all steam put upon her in a determined attempt to break through the field of ice". At midnight a floe of ice struck under the stern heavily, breaking off the propeller and knocking a large hole in the port quarter.

Sails were used to try and stem the inrush of water but the Captain's hopes of proceeding to St. Johns under sail were dashed when it was reported that the rising water had extinguished the boiler fires. In seas that had become heavy only three boats were launched, mainly occupied by crew. One boat capsized after being launched with five crewmembers but was righted, and, after four days was sighted and rescued by the ship ***State of Georgia*** bound for New York. The crew of this boat saw the Second Mate's boat launched with a total of ten persons aboard, and saw another boat float off the ship as it sank; 'containing the Chief Officer and about thirty people'. All three boats were rescued but forty-seven souls were lost.[562]

On the 2nd of June a Petition from the Working Men's Association connected with the shipping trades at Liverpool was presented to Parliament urging inspections of ships, and responsibility being sheeted home to shipowners for the standard of their ships and prevention of overloading;

> To the Honourable the Commons of the United Kingdom of Great Britain and Ireland, in Parliament assembled. The humble petition of the United Shipping Trades Council, being the representatives

> of working men engaged in trades connected with the Shipping of the Port of Liverpool. Respectfully showeth— That your petitioners earnestly desire to call the attention of your honourable House to the great and, as your petitioners believe, preventable loss of life which occurs by the foundering of vessels. That, in the judgment of your petitioners, much of this loss of life arises from the absence of a proper system of inspection in regard to the conditions under which vessels go to sea. That your petitioners believe many Shipowners are personally unacquainted with practical details either in regard to the construction and repairing of vessels, or in regard to their loading. That your petitioners desire to see Shipowners made responsible for the condition in which their vessels go to sea; but cannot close their eyes to the fact that it is very seldom done. That your petitioners believe many Shipowners are beyond the reach of such legislation, but that their vessels would not be equally beyond the reach of a proper system of Government inspection. Wherefore your petitioners humbly pray that your honourable House will be pleased to provide such inspection, and will during the present Session of Parliment enact a short measure such as shall not merely prevent overloading, but shall also cause the vessels themselves to be built of sufficient strength and to be maintained in a proper state of repair. And your petitioners as in duty bound will ever pray, &c.[563]

Legislative building blocks were provisionally put in place while amendments to the Bill were being considered. It was resolved in the House on the 17th of June that money would be provided by Parliament for remuneration to; 'any Magistrate or Assessor for investigation into the causes of Shipping casualties, in pursuance of any Act of the present Session for amending the Merchant Shipping Acts'.[564] On the same day, and the following two sitting days, the House debated the re-introduced Government Bill, meeting in Committee to consider proposed amendments in detail, a process made more difficult and lengthy by addition to the original Bill of thirty-four pages of amendments submitted by forty-four people.

On the 9th of July the four survivors from the ***Euxine*** arrived back in England from Singapore to face trial for murder through cannibalism, although only one, the Second Mate, James Arthur, was English. Their continued detention was arguably illegal and was weakened by disagreements between the Home Office and the Colonial Office as to whether there should have been an unsuccessful prosecution for murder in Singapore. The main purpose of the proposed trial in England was to settle, once and for all, whether cannibalism was legally acceptable in the circumstances they found themselves in, or was the 'custom of the sea' argument acceptable. Implicated by association in the whole matter was 'Bully Bates', Member of Parliament and owner of the ***Euxine***, who was to incur Plimsoll's wrath in the House on the 22nd of July over the loss of five of his ships in a year. Bates had actually lost six ships in a year, but failed to mention the ***Euxine***. The Home Office advised the Board of Trade; "…after careful consideration of all the circumstances the Secretary of state does not consider that this is a case in which it would be advisable to institute proceedings against these men". Involved in the final decision not to proceed were Charles Adderley, Thomas Gray and Thomas Farrar of the Board of Trade; Gray stating; "the details are too disgusting to take to court". Farrar supported the 'custom of the sea' argument in that; "it would only harrow the feelings of the public and that punishment would have no effect on future cases, since only exceptional necessity would prompt such action". Adderley agreed with these views and the four survivors were quietly set free, with the three foreign seamen being required to sign an official form absolving the ship's officers and Edward Bates from any legal liability.[565]

The Royal Commissioners appointed to inquire into spontaneous combustion of coal cargoes, after hearing a great deal of evidence and visiting the chief coal loading ports concluded;

1. That certain descriptions of coal are intrinsically dangerous for shipment on long voyages

2. That the breakage of coal in its transport from the pit to the ship's hold, the shipment of pyritic coal in a wet condition, and especially ventilation through the body of coal cargoes, conduce spontaneous combustion, even though the coal may not be unfit for conveyance on long voyages

3. That spontaneous combustion in coal cargoes would be less frequent, if regard were to be had by shipowners and underwriters to these facts

4. That where coal is being carried on long voyages the temperature of the various portions of the cargo should be tested periodically by thermometer, and registered in the log

5. That, with a view to guard against explosion, fire and continuous egress to the open air; independently of hatchways, should be provided for the explosive gasses by means of surface ventilation, which would be effective in all circumstances of weather

6. That in order to make known the descriptions of coal liable to combustion, the Inspectors of Mines should be instructed to hold inquiry into all cases of spontaneous combustion occurring in cargoes of coal taken from their respective districts; exporters being required always to record on their specifications the denominations of coal forming the cargo

7. That no additional legislation with reference to the carriage of coal by sea is required, unless for the purpose of giving effect to our proposals with regard to enquiries by Inspectors of mines, and to the fuller specifications for coal entered outward at Her Majesty's customs

In scientific advice attached to the report it was shown that; '…the chief agent in developing heat in coal cargoes is air, and therefore the [current] system of passing currents of air through the body of the coal is injurious in the extreme. This [is] directly opposed to the view which has prevailed among coal shippers [and seamen] for many years; it having been considered a measure of safety to provide a system of through ventilation for coal cargoes. The surface ventilation referred to in the 5th paragraph of the summary is intended to guard against explosion, an effect produced by causes differing from those which bring about spontaneous combustion'.

Thus, by the careful inquiries of a Royal Commission, supported by sound scientific advice, was the traditional method of carrying and ventilating coal done away with, to be replaced by a sound knowledge of methods of safe carriage of this dangerous cargo that had cost the loss of many ships and countless seamen. Recommendation seven was welcomed by the maritime industry as; '…we have no doubt that a knowledge of the dangers will operate more effectually to reduce the number of casualties from spontaneous combustion than any quantity of legislation'.[566]

Chapter 21

The 'Stop-gap Act'

With the 1875 Session drawing to a close, concern started to be expressed in the House as to when the final Bill would be considered. Disraeli, who was ambivalent about the Bill, started to mount his case for delay when replying to a question on this matter when stating; "it is difficult to fix a day now for the discussion of the Bill, but after the Labour Laws and Agricultural Holdings Bills are passed, or a considerable advance is made with them, the Merchant Shipping Acts Amendment Bill is the measure I shall endeavour to bring before the consideration of the House".[567] On the 22nd of July Plimsoll rose in the House and 'with great excitement' stated;

> ...I beg, Sir, to move the adjournment of the House. Sir, I earnestly entreat the right hon. Gentleman at the head of Her Majesty's Government not to consign some thousands of living human beings to undeserved and miserable death. Sir, I believe, and I have not hesitated to say—and I told the President of the Board of Trade him-self at an early period of the Session—I do not for a moment charge him with anything like breach of faith or treachery—that the Bill, of which the first 30 clauses were merely re-enactments—with unimportant exceptions—was so drawn as to afford unlimited facilities for death-dealing volubility and hypocritical Amendments. I adhere to that opinion... The Secretary of Lloyd's tells a friend of mine that he does not know a single ship which has been broken up voluntarily by the owners in the course of 30 years on account of its being worn out. Ships gradually pass from hand to hand, until bought by some needy and reckless speculators, who send them to sea with precious human lives. On the 3rd of this month I had a list carefully prepared of 15,000 vessels on Lloyd's Register; and ongoing over these what does the House think was the result? It was found that no fewer than 2,654 of the classed ships had gone off their class and forfeited their position. And what is the consequence that ensues? It is that continually, every winter, hundreds and hundreds of brave men are sent to death, their wives are made widows and their children are made orphans, in order that a few speculative scoundrels, in whose hearts there is neither the love of

> God nor the fear of God, may make unhallowed gains. There are ship-owners in this country of ours who have never either built a ship or bought a new one, but who are simply what are called "ship-knackers," and I accidentally overheard a Member of this House described in the Lobby by an ex-Secretary to the Treasury as "a shipknacker".

The Speaker reminded Plimsoll that as; "his speech, and all the references of his speech, relate to a Bill which is on the Order Book, and which is set down for consideration this very day …he is not at liberty to discuss, on a Motion for adjournment, the merits of any Bill which is on the Orders of the House". Plimsoll went on to ask the Speaker to inform the House of the facts surrounding the loss of five named ships in twelve months, and also asked the Speaker, as recorded in Hansard; "whether the registered owner of these ships, Edward Bates, is the Member for Plymouth, or if it is some other person of the same name. ["Order!"] And, Sir, I shall ask some questions about Members on this side of the House also. I am determined to unmask the villains who send to death and destruction" —*Loud cries of* "Order!" and much excitement.

The Speaker also questioned Plimsoll's use of the word 'villain' and, twice, presumed that Plimsoll did not apply that expressions to any Member of this House. Upon replying; "I did Sir, and I do not mean to withdraw it" Plimsoll was advised that "The expression of the hon. Member is altogether un-Parliamentary, and I must again ask him whether he persists in using it". After Plimsoll repeatedly declined to either retract or withdraw his expression the Speaker advised him that he must submit his conduct to the judgment of the House. "I shall be happy to submit to the judgment of the House, and this is my Protest. (The hon. Member placed a paper on the Table.) ["Order, Chair!"]. Disraeli rose; "to say – under a sense of deep pain—and I am sure every Member of the House will have experienced the same feeling—that a brother Member should have conducted himself in a manner almost unparalleled" to which Plimsoll, to calls of 'Chair' and 'Order' retorted "And so has the Government". This was too much for Disraeli;

> I desire, as far as I can, to do that which will conduce to the dignity of the Chair, and to the honour of this House and its Members, and I think the conduct of the hon. Member cannot be passed without

> notice. It is of the most violent and offensive kind. Although I do it with great reluctance, I feel I am only expressing the sense of the whole House when I say that this is an occasion on which you, Mr. Speaker, must exercise one of your highest duties, and that is that you should reprimand the hon. Gentleman for conduct so disorderly and violent as that we have just witnessed. I beg accordingly to move that the hon. Member for Derby be reprimanded by you, Sir, for his violent and disorderly conduct.

The Motion was made and question proposed; "That Mr. Plimsoll, the Member for Derby, for his disorderly conduct, be reprimanded, in his place, by Mr. Speaker". Instead of 'replying in his place' Plimsoll withdrew from the House to the lobby with the parting shot; "Do you know that thousands are dying for this?" The motion was then debated with the Marquess of Hartington suggesting; "I cannot help thinking it will be very much to the advantage and dignity of our proceedings if action in this matter could be postponed for a short time, during which I have no doubt—or at least I have great reason to hope—that the hon. Member for Derby may be induced to see the impropriety of his conduct and to set himself right with the House". This idea was supported by another Member who sought indulgence for Plimsoll who was extremely ill. Disraeli welcomed these observations as a way of defusing and resolving an unprecedented incident and "...thought it would be best that the hon. Member for Derby should not be required to attend in his place till this day week. I beg, therefore, to move that the debate be adjourned for a week". The debate was adjourned until the following Thursday.[568]

Rather than being a spontaneous outburst of frustration there was the possibility that Plimsoll, with his now vast experience of public speaking and displays of emotion, carefully planned and staged his intervention that morning. As Plimsoll was leaving the House he gave a prearranged signal to his wife in the Ladies Gallery who immediately dropped copies of the protest he'd tabled in the House onto the Press Gallery, thus ensuring ample coverage of the incident. A contributing factor to suspicions of a staged event is that Plimsoll would have been well aware that the Government Bill was on the order paper for consideration later that same day. There were also reports at the time that Plimsoll had heard earlier that day that 'he was to be disappointed' (with passage of the Government Bill). Plimsoll absented himself from the house for the stipulated week and made a contrite apology upon his return. The papers published Plimsolls 'protest' in full, engendering even more public support for his cause;

> ...they [the Government] are wittingly and unwittingly – for there are both – playing into the hands of the maritime murderers inside the House and outside the house, to secure a further continuance of the present murderous system. What is demanded by humanity is that rotten ships should be broken up or repaired; that ships should not be overloaded; that grain cargoes should not be carried in bulk, so as to expose the lives of those on board to deadly peril, and deck cargoes, the source of unutterable agony to many and death to so many more, should be put an end to. The Government Bill provides for none of these things; it provides only heavier penalties and severer punishments against our unfortunate fellow-subjects whose necessities take them to sea. [569]

The protest went on to 'urging in the name of our common humanity' the immediate adoption of the Merchant Shipping Bill, and desiring to 'unmask the villains who sit in the House, fit representatives of the more numerous, but no greater villains who are outside the House'. Plimsoll laid 'upon the head of the Prime Minister and his fellows, the blood of all the men who shall perish next winter from preventable causes' and concluded with a fervent plea reminiscent of that in Our Seaman – An Appeal, but even more intemperate;

> Ye shall not afflict any widow, or fatherless child. If thou afflict them in any wise, and they cry at all unto me, I will surely hear their cry; and My wrath shall wax hot, and I will kill you with the sword and your wives shall be widows and your children fatherless' (Exodus 22: verses 22-34). How much hotter, then, shall be His indignation and wrath against those who reduce unhappy women and children to that deplorable condition, and who leave their own fellow-creatures, guilty of no crime, to a violent and sudden death.[570]

Unbeknownst to Plimsoll; Machiavellian manoeuvring was taking place within Government circles to thwart the passage of the Government Bill, no matter how imperfect he may have considered it to be. On the day of Plimsoll's expulsion from Parliament, the shipowning MP and Chancellor of the Exchequer, Sir Stafford Northcote, wrote to Disraeli with a suggested strategy for scuppering the Government Bill. Commencing cynically with; "May I make the following suggestions as to the process of massacre?" Northcote wrote;

> When the orders of the day are called you might rise and say that, after carefully considering the state of public business, you had come to the conclusion that it would be impossible to find time for a full discussion of the Merchant Shipping Bill; that you thought it undesirable to attempt to pass a mere fragment of so important a measure; and that you therefore moved to discharge the order, promising at the same time, that the bill should have a first place among the measures of next session. (This would be quite in order, but, of course, it might lead to some debate both on merchant shipping in particular and on the course of business in general; but I do not see how you can avoid it under any circumstances.)

Northcote's advice was carried through to the letter. The House spent seven hours during the day of Plimsoll's outburst discussing 'questions of manurial value' and tenant's rights as the Government, 'on a point of obstinate pride, was persisting with a Bill which many of their own supporters opposed, which was not urgently called for by the country, and for which they were sacrificing this vital measure'; the Agricultural Holdings (England) Bill. Members were resigned to the withdrawal of the Government Bill, but very critical of the Government's delays in dealing with the Bill, the ineptness of Adderley in shepherding it through Parliament, and the fact the Bill, in spite of its avowed number two priority in the Queen's speech, had been side-lined in favour of Bills of far lesser importance. In closing the debate Northcote cynically stated; "It was with the greatest regret that the Government found it necessary at the last moment to move that this Order be discharged. They found the Merchant Shipping Bill in such a position that even if the Agricultural Holdings Bill were out of the way there was not time to consider it fully. The postponement of the Bill till next Session would forward the solution of the question rather than hinder it". The Merchant Shipping Amendment Bill (the Government Bill) was withdrawn.

On the 24th of July Northcote explained his reasons to Disraeli as being; 'Plimsoll's Bill was not a bill for applying a direct and simple remedy to an admitted evil. The direct and simple remedy of authorising the Board of Trade to stop unseaworthy ships had already been applied by the Act of 1873; and the other direct and simple remedy which Plimsoll desired, of instituting a Government survey of all seagoing ships, we were not prepared to adopt". Disraeli had stated his political philosophy during a debate in Parliament a month earlier as;

Permissive legislation is the characteristic of a free people. It is easy to adopt compulsory legislation when you have to deal with those who only exist to obey. But in a free country, and especially in a country like England, you must trust to persuasion and example as the two great elements, if you wish to effect any considerable change in the manners and customs of people.[571]

Following newspaper reports of the events in Parliament on the 22nd very large crowds gathered in London to express their support for Plimsoll and meetings were held throughout the country expressing dismay at the inadequacy of the Government Bill and the urgency need for legislation to protect the lives of seamen. During these events Disraeli wrote, in a weak and self-serving style, to the Queen, condemning Adderley, in stating that "...He thinks he shall be able to steer through all the difficulties of Merchant Shipping, though Sir Charles Adderley is a weak vessel, and Mr D. [Disraeli] ought to have taken the subject out of his hands, but, as your Majesty once deigned to say; 'Mr D. is too good-natured' – that is to say, he cannot bear to hurt anybody's feelings, which is a mistake in politics and war...". Her Majesty replied that she was sorry to hear; "how hard worked and fatigued Disraeli was" and she clearly thought that Plimsoll had a case; "...She trusts that all will be satisfactorily settled. There is no doubt that the state of Merchant Shipping vessels is very disgraceful and dangerous and many lives are lost thereby".[572]

On the 26th of July, while Plimsoll was still 'out of the House', Mr. Dillwyn moved a motion that; "the Merchant Shipping Acts Amendment (No. 2) Bill be fixed for second reading on Thursday next"; Plimsoll's Bill. Immediately after this motion was agreed to Adderley rose to give notice to the House that on the following Wednesday he would move for leave to introduce a Bill; "for giving further powers to the Board of Trade for stopping Un-seaworthy Ships". This Bill; the genesis of the 'stop-gap Act' and a clear reaction to public clamour, clearly caught Members by surprise with another Member immediately rising to ask the Prime Minister, if he will give precedence over the other Orders of the Day to the Merchant Shipping Acts Amendment (No. 2) Bill, which has been introduced by the hon. Member for Derby, and which will stand for second reading on Thursday next'.[573]

There had been a clear message to Disraeli from the Queen and her subjects that something must be done. Accordingly, by the 28th of July, before Plimsoll re-entered Parliament, the Board of Trade had hastily cobbled together a 'stop-gap Bill' (as referred to in the House on the 26th), to block Plimsoll's Merchant Shipping Amendment (No.2) Bill. Later in the day the long-standing question of consolidation of all Merchant Shipping Acts arose when Addderley was asked whether he would introduce a relevant Bill during the next Session. Adderley replied that this was not his intention as he had prepared and published a Digest of all existing Merchant Shipping Acts which; "may to a great extent serve the purpose of a Consolidation Act".

On the 27th of July Mr. Dillwyn again asked whether the Prime Minister; "would give precedence over the Government Orders of the Day to the Merchant Shipping Acts Amendment (No. 2) Bill, which was introduced by the honourable Member for Derby, and which stands for Second Reading on Thursday next?". Disraeli's reply drew heavily upon the advice given him by Northcote on 'the process of massacre' and his letter of the 24th in replying initially that;

> ...Her Majesty's Government are not prepared to give precedence to the Bill of the hon. Member for Derby on Thursday next, and for two reasons. In the first place, they could not support that Bill, because, however excellent its motives, it is their opinion that the tendency of that measure, if it were carried, would be to aggravate the evils it affects to remedy; and, secondly, because the Bill would lead, from its very character and the important principles which it involves, to a protracted discussion, which would require time, the want of which has obliged Her Majesty's Ministers to relinquish for the present the Bill they themselves brought forward this year...What, in their opinion, is required at this moment is a temporary measure—a short and temporary measure—which will give more rapid and direct action to the Government in the way of stopping unseaworthy ships, and a

> measure having that effect will almost immediately be introduced by the President of the Board of Trade. When I say a temporary measure, I mean a measure limited in its operation to one year—first, because the measure may involve powers which the House may not choose to grant to a Ministry for a permanent measure; and, secondly, because a temporary measure, or measure for one year, will be a material guarantee for the introduction, at the earliest possible opportunity next Session, of a permanent measure on the subject.

With only fourteen sitting days remaining in the Session there was considerable debate and scepticism that Disraeli's motion would give adequate time to debate either Plimsoll's Bill or Disraeli's proposed Bill the following day. A question was put that 'Government Orders of the Day shall have precedence on Tuesdays and Wednesdays for the remainder of the Session'. Disraeli's responded that; "he hoped the Agricultural Holdings (England) Bill would be got through that day. If that were done, then they could go on to-morrow with Supply, and continue until about half-past 4 o'clock, when his right hon. Friend the President of the Board of Trade could introduce his Bill". Out of 192 Members present, 173 voted in favour of the question.[574]

The following day, with Plimsoll still 'out of the House', the first reading took place of the Unseaworthy Ships Bill (No.274); '...a Bill to make provision for giving further powers to the Board of Trade for stopping Unseaworthy Ships...framed on the principle on which all our legislation has hitherto been based—namely, that of enforcing responsibility on those who conduct the Mercantile Marine service of this country to take all reasonable precaution or means in their power to protect the lives of those who are employed by them at sea.'. Upon members taking offence at his claim that Plimsoll's Bill was based on the wrong principles Adderley tried to recover by stating; "I point out the different principles of the two Bills brought before Parliament this year for the purpose of showing that, while in the case of the Government Bill we were unable to proceed this Session, yet, considering the other Bill, we were unable to adopt it in lieu of the Government measure, because we believe that it proceeds on a wrong and dangerous principle". In supporting the effectiveness of existing provisions. Adderley quoted statistics showing that the Board of Trade had stopped 558 ships under the powers of the 1871 and 1873 Acts, of which 515 were unseaworthy; including 58 which were overloaded, all of which 'had to be lightened of their cargoes'. The two main provisions of the Bill proposed to;

> ...enable the Government to appoint a sufficient number of officers forthwith, and from time to time, to detain unseaworthy ships—that is, ships in defective condition, or overloaded, or improperly loaded—for the purpose of being surveyed, and not allowed to go to sea till set right, without waiting for authority from the Board of Trade, but immediately reporting. The House is aware that the Surveyors of the Board of Trade can only now report; upon which authority is sent down to the officers of Customs, and the proposal of the Bill is to give the Government the right to delegate such powers...The Bill also proposes to allow one-fourth of any crew to demand a survey of an alleged unseaworthy vessel without the preliminary of desertion, and without even the necessity of giving security for costs incident to the prosecution of the complaint, precautions, of course, being taken against frivolous or vexatious allegations.

Among concerns expressed by Members about the unfortunate processes taken to withdraw the Government Bill without any intent of introducing another, and to then suddenly produce another due to pubic pressure with very little time left to properly consider it, one Member stated; "...there should be before us one or other of these courses—either to give up the Bill of the hon. Member for Derby, and endeavour to engraft on the Government Bill such Amendments as may bring it nearer perfection than it is in its present state; or, should the Bill of the Government be found incapable of satisfactory Amendment, to stand by the Bill of the hon. Member for Derby"; a proposal that achieved wide support. The member also pointed out that the Board of Trade had failed to notice two important points; "that were least debated on this sore question—namely, they do not deal with the question of deck-loading, nor with the carrying of cargoes of grain in bulk". Another Member commented on the fact that; "...In eight weeks of 1873 no less than 30-odd grain-laden steamers were reported sunk or missing, and all had been built within five or six years. Why did that immense fleet go to the bottom? The underwriters said that the expenditure of £50 upon each of those vessels for the purchase of sacks would, in all probability, have saved two-thirds of those vessels". The Prime Minister concluded the debate by attempting to reassure members that the second reading should be fixed for Friday morning, and I hope that the Bill will be in the hands of hon. Members to-morrow morning. A Bill to make provision for giving further powers to the Board of Trade for stopping Unseaworthy Ships, [was] *ordered* to be brought in by Sir Charles Adderley, Mr. Disraeli, and Mr. Chancellor of the Exchequer [Northcote]. Bill 274 was presented and read for the first time.

Having served his Parliamentary punishment, Plimsoll returned to the House on the following day, well aware of the proceedings of the 28th. The second reading of the now printed Unseaworthy Ships Bill took place on the following day, but not before Bates had asked the Prime Minster if the Government would; "assent to the appointment of a Select Committee to inquire into the allegations of the honourable junior Member for Derby regarding my conduct as a shipowner?" Disraeli was reluctant to do so, referring to Plimsoll's proper and ample apology to the House, and to the proper and dignified manner in which Bates had vindicated himself in the House at the time, but; "...if my hon. Friend still feels it would be a satisfaction to him, as a Member of this House and the Representative of a large constituency, that there should be an investigation into this matter by a Committee of this House, I shall not only not oppose such a Motion, but shall give every facility to my hon. Friend in the formation of the Committee for such an inquiry". Bates did not pursue the matter. However, early in the debate on the proposed Bill he took the opportunity to make a lengthy and very detailed intervention on the condition and history of all six of the ships his company lost, including that they; "...were classed Al. They were so classed; but, in addition to this, I find four of the six were also classed double A 1 in Lloyd's Register, three of them with a star, and which denotes they were constructed of heavier or stronger material than required by Lloyd's rules... the accusation brought against me by the hon. junior Member for Derby is as unjust as it is untrue".

Speaking next, Plimsoll ignored Bates's remarks apart from the pointed comment; "...that when silence was desirable and seemed likely to facilitate the progress of the Bill brought in by the Government to remedy the state of things which existed in the Merchant Marine, he observed silence...". Regarding the proposed Bill; "...he could assure the House that he had read the Bill with the utmost possible pleasure, because it appeared to him that if the clauses of which his hon. Friend the Member for Pembroke (Mr. E. J.

Reed) had given Notice [deck cargoes and stowage of grain cargoes] were adopted, they would form just the other half of the measure, for the matter as it now stood before the House seemed like a steam-engine with-out a governor". In referring to quiet repeal of the Timber Ships Act in 1862 and those responsible in the Board of Trade, he believed that;

> ...there were other smaller men of shallower capacity who were not so easily impressed by the circumstances, and one of those unfortunately acquired considerable power in one of the administrative Departments of the Government; and in 1862 the legislation, the effects of which he had described, was swept away without notice to the public. He had turned to the debates upon the subject, and he found, that with the exception of a word or two uttered by the then President of the Board of Trade in the House of Commons, on leave to bring in a Bill, no word of reference was made to such a vital change in the law. Yet he might say, without exaggeration, that it might be computed that nearly 20,000 of Her Majesty's subjects had been drowned in consequence of that night's work in the House, when a Schedule of the Act passed in silence, and, probably, nearly £30,000,000 of property had gone to the bottom of the sea...In conclusion, he would ask the House to put down their foot firmly upon any attempt to kill the proposals of the Government by talking against time. [*Ministerial Cheers.*]'.[575]

After praising Plimsoll at length for all of his efforts to save the lives of seamen, Northcote made a very long intervention in which he disagreed with most of his proposals, with one exception; the proposal by another MP for an amendment to make it illegal for any ship-owner or any other person to send, or take part in sending, an unseaworthy ship to sea. Peel, dismayed by the Government's statement that they 'were not willing to entertain the questions of survey and load line during the present Session' took the opportunity to reiterate his views stated at the first reading on load lines and seaworthiness. He considered that; "a moment's reflection, however, would show that the measure must imply a definition of load line, and the question of soundness or unsoundness... the President of the Board of Trade could not stop a ship on the ground of unseaworthiness without being in a position to show that she was unseaworthy. Why, then, should not that also be done long before the vessel was ready to proceed to sea?" Other members reminded the Government of their promise to take Plimsoll's Bill into account in their consideration of the final Bill, and that '...In regard to load line, the opinion of the Royal Commissioners was equally decided, and he thought equally without foundation'.

In concluding the second reading Disraeli defensively reminded the House; "that on the day when I had the mortification to announce to the House that it was impossible for the Government to proceed with this measure, the number of Amendments on this [Government] Bill was 178, and that 140 of them were suggested by hon. Gentlemen opposite, I think the House will acknowledge that on the 22nd of July that was evidence that could not be disregarded in coming to a conclusion on this subject... I trust—and indeed know—that we are all agreed upon one point—namely, that we should read the Bill a second time, and therefore I must point to the clock as showing that there are 'breakers ahead', and that we must not lose any time in doing so. I hope, on Monday, we shall go into Committee—the most important part of the proceedings on the Bill—and arrive on that day at conclusions which will give satisfaction to the country".[576]

Bates would not let go of his request for appointment of a select committee to look into the matter of Plimsoll's 'untrue and unjust accusations' against him as a shipowner. On the next sitting day he moved a motion; "That a Select Committee be appointed to inquire into certain charges made by Mr. Plimsoll, Member for Derby, against Mr. Bates, Member for Plymouth". In the course of a lengthy debate Members pointed out that Plimsoll had not apologised to Bates in the House, but it was claimed that he had made a satisfactory apology to the Prime Minister. Also, that Bates had been vindicated in the House through the opportunities to make two lengthy interventions to defend his 'fair fame'. The resolution of the debate was; 'That, in the opinion of this House, no stain rests upon the character of the honourable Member for Plymouth in consequence of the statements made in this House by the honourable Member for Derby on the 22nd of this instant July'.[577]

On the 2nd of August a debate in the House took place after Reed, who spoke on behalf Plimsoll; absent through illness, moved that; "the overloading of merchant ships cannot he effectually restrained unless owners and captains are prohibited from loading their ships beyond a load-line limit of safety which has either been sanctioned by the Government or submitted to the Government for record" and that "it was very desirable it should make provision for the regulation of deck cargoes and cargoes of grain, for the restriction of ships within a reasonable draught of water, when laden, and for a compulsory survey". He further; "asked the House to declare that no ship should be allowed to proceed to sea with cargo or human beings on board unless she bore upon her side a load line drawn by her owner beyond which he himself did not propose to load her". In the course of the ensuing debate Adderley clarified; "The Government had not proposed either that the load line should be sanctioned by Government or submitted to the Board of Trade for record. They proposed that a voluntary load line should on every voyage be fixed by the owner of the ship, and that this load line should be described in the form of entry outwards, and in the articles of agreement with the crew and in the official log-book; but care was studiously taken that the Government should have nothing to do with fixing or accepting the load line. It was intended to be a sort of contract between the owner and the crew, that the owner did not intend to load beyond it, and that if he did, it would amount to absolute fraud". After mixed and confused interventions Reed stated that; "as a division was desired by the House, to take it at that time, even if it were successful, would delay the Bill. He therefore would withdraw his Amendment". The House then moved into Committee to consider the draft Unseaworthy Ships Bill in detail, after which the 'Bill [was] *reported;* as amended, to be considered upon *Thursday,* and to *be printed.* [Bill 281.] [578] Plimsoll's Bill – The Merchant Shipping Act Amendment Bill (No.2), was withdrawn.

With only seven sitting days remaining in the 1875 Session the pressure came on for the Unseaworthy Ships Bill to move through all of its stages in both Houses as quickly as possible. On the 6th of August the Bill, as amended, was considered; with its third reading taking place the following day, at the end of which the Bill was passed and sent up to the House of Lords where it was given its first reading. On the 9th the Duke of Richmond, in introducing the Bill stated; "...in moving that the Bill be now read the second time, [said]: Her Majesty's Government feel strongly the necessity of dealing with this subject. They have so felt for some period, believing that few subjects which come under the attention of Parliament require more careful consideration". The 'Bill [was] read 2nd accordingly, and *committed* to a Committee of the Whole House *To-morrow,* when further consideration was briefly given before the Bill had its third reading in the Lords the following day, was passed and sent to the Commons. On the 13th of August, the last day of the Session, Unseaworthy Ships [38 & 39 *Vict* c.

88], received Royal assent.

The short title was The Merchant Shipping Act, 1875[579] – *An Act to make provision for giving further powers to the Board of Trade for stopping unseaworthy ships*, with s.11 clarifying that the Act ...*may be construed as one with the Merchant Shipping Act, 1854, and the Acts amending the same, and the said Acts and this Act may be cited collectively as the Merchant Shipping Act, 1875.*

The Act provided for; 1. *Appointment of powers and officers having the authority to detain unseaworthy ships; 2. Ship to be detained on complaint of crew; 3. Cargo of grain etc; 4. Penalties on sending unseaworthy ships to sea; 5. Marking of deck-lines; 6. Statement of load-line; 7. Penalty for offences in relation to marks on ships; 8. Proceedings may be taken against the Board of Trade by action against the principal secretary; 9.Laibility of shipowner to crew; 10. Short title; 11. Duration of Act.*

Section 1 provided that;

The Board of Trade may forthwith and from time to time by special order appoint a sufficient number of fit and proper persons, from their own staff or otherwise, to be officers having the authority to detain unseaworthy ships, and may from time to time revoke any such appointment.

Grounds for detention 'for the purpose of being surveyed' were; defective condition of the hull, equipments, or machinery, overloading or improper loading, or unfitness to proceed to sea without serious danger to human life. If one fourth of the crew complained to the Board of Trade or one of its appointed officers that there were grounds for detention the Board or officer had a duty to inspect the ship. However, the powers of detention and survey were circumscribed by a provision that the ship must not be unnecessarily delayed through an inspection to determine whether it is unseaworthy.

Concerns about the well proven dangers associated with carrying grain in bulk were addressed through s.3; applicable from the 1st of October, 1875;

> ...no cargo of which more than one third consists of any kind of grain, corn, rice, paddy, pulse, seeds, nuts or nut kernels be contained in bags, sacks or barrels, or secured from shifting by boards, bulkheads, or otherwise...

Section 4(1), that repealed s.11 of the Merchant Shipping Act, 1871, made it very clear that any person, including the managing owner of a ship, had a clear responsibility to ensure that their ship was not intentionally sent to sea in an unseaworthy state;-

> Every person who sends a ship to sea in such unseaworthy state the life of any person would be likely to be endangered, and the managing owner of any British ship sent to sea from any port in the United Kingdom, shall be guilty of a misdemeanour unless he can prove that he used all reasonable means to ensure her being sent to sea in a seaworthy state, or prove that her going to sea in an unseaworthy state was, under the circumstances reasonable and justifiable; and for the purpose of giving such proof, such person may give evidence in the same manner as any other witness.

To avoid doubt, and to sheet home responsibility, s.4(4) stated that;

> The owner of every British ship shall from time to time register at the customs house of the port in the United Kingdom at which such ship is registered, the name of the managing owner, and if there be no managing owner, then the person to whom the management of the ship is entrusted by and on behalf of the owner…

Sections 5 and 6 required the marking, from the 1st of November, 1875, of the level of each deck as the upper margin for measurement of free-board, and, for the first time, with a form of mark indicating the maximum depth the ship to which the ship could be loaded; the "Plimsoll Line", the enduring and universally recognised legacy of Samuel Plimsoll;

> …the owner of every British ship shall, before entering his ship outwards from any port in the United Kingdom upon any voyage for which he is required so to enter her, or if that is not practicable, as soon after as may be, mark upon each of her sides amidships, or as near thereto as practicable, in white or yellow on a dark ground, or black on a light ground, a circular disc, twelve inches in diameter, with a horizontal line eighteen inches in length drawn through its centre… the centre of this disc shall indicate the maximum load line in salt water to which the owner intends to load the ship for that voyage… he shall also, upon entering her…deliver a statement in writing of the distance in feet and inches between the disc and the upper edge of

> each of the line indicating the position of the ship's decks which is above that centre.
>
> The owner was also required to enter a copy of this statement in the crew agreement before any crew were engaged, and also in the official logbook. And – *she shall be kept so marked until her next return to a port of discharge in the United Kingdom.* Accordingly, the owner could arbitrarily determine the position of the load line from voyage to voyage, so long as it remained unaltered for the duration of the round voyage. 'The attitude of some shipowners to this long overdue legislation is reflected in the fact that, as the Act did not specify where the load line should be painted, some derisorily painted it on the funnel. It would not be until 1890 that the Board of Trade would eventually specify exactly where the load line should be marked'.[580]

The Merchant Shipping Act, 1875, although brief and of short duration, was significant and overdue recognition by Parliament and the Board of Trade of the importance and relevance of Plimsoll's crusade on seaworthiness. The objective of the Act gave recognition to the matter of unseaworthy ships, and to the inadequacy of the Board of Trade's centralised power of detention. For the first time a form of load line; the 'Plimsoll Line', was required, albeit with its location to be subjectively determined by the owner on a voyage-by-voyage basis. Plimsoll's plea for the inclusion of provisions relating to deck cargoes and compulsory surveys of all unclassed ships were ignored; possibly to be revisited during the twelve months the 'stop-gap Act' would be in force. The Board of Trade had snatched a hollow victory from the jaws of defeat to meet the some of the expectations of the Queen, Parliament and the public. Some incremental improvements had been made to ensure seaworthiness and responsibility pending a more substantial piece of legislation the following year. Plimsoll was sanguine about the situation and, once again, looked forward to more substantial progress the following year.

Eighteen seventy-five ended with the stranding of another German passenger steamer off the coast of Great Britain, with significant loss of life. The Norddeutscher Lloyd Line passenger ship ***Deutschland*** of 2,800 gross tons, had been built in Scotland in 1866 for the emigrant trade from Bremehaven to New York via Southampton. On the 4th of December the ship sailed from Bremen with 107 emigrants, a number of cabin passengers and ninety-nine crew, but anchored overnight in the river due to heavy weather. She got underway the following morning, for her short passage across the North Sea and down-Channel to Southampton, in a fresh North-easterly and light snow, which worsened during the day to a strong gale with thick snowstorms. The following morning the ship was running on dead-reckoning towards the mouth of the English Channel in very poor visibility, with four lookouts on the bridge and two posted forward. Due to uncertainty as to her position soundings were taken a number of times between four and five o'clock on the morning, with speed being reduced to half ahead (9.5 knots) and, before the last sounding of 17 fathoms about five o'clock the engine was stopped. Breakers were then sighted ahead and full astern ordered whereupon the propellor shaft broke and the ship drifted onto a sandbank. The ***Deutschland*** had ran aground only 3 miles from the lightship on the Kentish Knock shoal; 23 miles off Harwich and 22 miles from Margate. At the time she was 30 miles from where the Captain estimated she was. The ship touched lightly before becoming firmly aground, and came to rest beam on to the sea, resulting in seas sweeping the deck, washing several people and one boat overboard and wrecking three other boats. Rockets were let off and lifebelts issued to all passengers.

The visibility during the Monday was clear, with a heavy sea and strong winds, and signals of distress were made all day to passing ships, to no avail. The crew set a foresail during Monday morning in an unsuccessful attempt to drive the ship through the breakers, and then spent all day lightning the ship forward by jettisoning cargo; dropping both anchors when the ship was well onto the shoal. Rockets were set off again during Monday evening and were finally sighted by the Sunk and Cork lightships, with Harwich sighting the rockets. At about two o'clock on Tuesday morning the Captain ordered all passengers on deck and into the rigging as the aft cabin flooded at high tide. Many passengers fell to their deaths from the rigging due to cold and exposure. At first light Tuesday a tug was dispatched from Harwich to determine the cause for the rockets by visiting the three lightships; finally locating the wreck and rescuing the 138 people still alive.[581] An enquiry was held by the Board of Trade in London on the 20th of December, not least but to address the concerns of the German Government that 'a large steamer with upwards of 200 persons aboard should have lain on a dangerous sand close to the English coast for thirty hours before any assistance came to her'. The enquiry concluded that the

Master 'had let the vessel get ahead in its reckoning' and had 'shown a very great want of care and judgement'. The Master subsequently requested an official German investigation, but this was ruled out.[582]

In February 1876, a collision occurred in the Straits of Dover between a British and a German ship, the aftermath of which was to have far reaching consequences. On the late afternoon of the 17th of February two ships were proceedings westwards just off Dover. The passenger steamer ***Strathclyde*** (1871) of 1,951 tons had departed Dover after dropping a pilot, on passage from London to Bombay with 23 first class passengers and 47 crew. Steaming at nine knots in fine and clear weather, she set her course for Ushant. At this time she was about two and a half miles off Dover, being overtaken, fine on her port quarter, by the German passenger liner ***Franconia*** (1872) of 3,098 tons bound from Hamburg to New York. It became apparent to the ***Strathclyde*** that the ships were on a collision course but, as the ***Franconia*** was clearly the give way vessel, the ***Strathclyde*** maintained her course and speed. When it became apparent to the ***Strathclyde*** thirty minutes later that collision was imminent, she altered her course to port but, at the same time, the ***Franconia*** altered course to starboard and struck the ***Strathclyde*** between her funnel and mainmast cutting into her hull for a distance of about four feet, then backing off and striking her again abreast of the mainmast, cutting another deep hole.

The ***Strathclyde*** managed to launch a boat with fifteen woman aboard but it capsized and most of those aboard were lost. A second boat was successfully launched and saved two of the drowning women from the first boat. By this time, the seas were breaking over the vessel as high as the bridge and washing many of those on deck overboard. The Captain, 2nd Engineer, and a fireman were the last to leave, jumping overboard as the ***Strathclyde*** sank by the stern ten minutes after the collision, her boilers and decks blowing up as she went down. In the short time the two ships were locked together, five of the crew of the ***Strathclyde***, including the Chief Officer, clambered aboard the ***Franconia*** and, upon seeing that her crew were making no attempt to launch boats, tried to do so themselves but could not achieve this before the ***Strathclyde*** sank. They were then carried aboard the ***Franconia*** to the Downs where the badly damaged ship anchored. Thirty-eight of the 70 persons aboard the ***Strathclyde*** were lost.

Captain Ferdinand Keyn of the ***Franconia*** was arrested and charged in the Central Criminal Court with the manslaughter of Jessie Dorcas Young, a passenger of the ***Strathclyde***. At the close of the prosecution Keyn's counsel submitted that, as a question of law, Keyn could not be considered amenable to British law as he was a foreigner in command of a ship and 'was merely proceeding upon the high seas, the general highway of nations'. The Judge of the refused to stop the case, but reserved the point of law for consideration by the Court of Appeal. Keyn was found guilty of manslaughter and released on bail.[583]

Keyn's appeal was heard in the Court of Appeal before Lord Chief Justice Cockburn and twelve other Judges. The majority (7-6) decision of the Court for Crown Cases Reserved held that the Central Criminal Court had no jurisdiction to try the offence. Cockburn clarified in his summation that although customary law might recognise a three-mile territorial limit there was no penal law applicable in Great Britain;

> The legislature has omitted to adopt the alleged sovereignty over the littoral sea, to the extent of making our penal law applicable generally to foreigners passing through it for the purpose of navigation... We must take this, I think, as an exposition of the opinion of Parliament that specific legislation is here necessary, and consequently, that without it the foreigner in a foreign vessel will not come within the general law of this country in respect of matters arising on the sea... All the writers upon public law agree that every nation has exclusive jurisdiction to the distance of a cannon-shot or marine league over the waters adjacent to its shores"... As to the question, how far our legislature could properly affect the rights of foreign ships within the limits of three miles from the coast of this country, there can be no possible doubt that the water below low-water mark is part of the high seas. But it is equally beyond question that for certain purposes every country may, by the common law of nations, legitimately exercise jurisdiction over that portion of the high seas which lies within the distance of three miles from its shores... It is not questioned that there is a right of interference for defence and revenue purposes; and it is difficult to understand why a country, having this kind of territorial jurisdiction over a certain portion of the high road of nations, should not exercise the right of settling the rules of the road in the interests of commerce. An exercise of jurisdiction for such a purpose would be, at least, as beneficial as for purposes of defence and revenue

In supporting the Chief Justice's summation, Lusk J summarised the existing position in law regarding Britain's 'three mile limit' and stressed that it was a matter for Parliament alone to ensure there was appropriate penal law enacted to provide territorial jurisdiction in those waters; "...I think that usage and the common consent of nations, which constitute international law, have appropriated these waters to the adjacent State to deal with them as the State may deem expedient for its own interests. They are, therefore, in the language of diplomacy and of international law, termed by a convenient metaphor the territorial waters of Great Britain, and the same or equivalent phrases are used in some of our statutes denoting that this belt of sea is under the exclusive dominion of the State. But the dominion is the dominion of Parliament, not the dominion of the common law..."[584]

The *Franconia* decision was clearly not expected by the British Government, and two years later English law was brought back into line with the view of international law that Great Britain had taken throughout the nineteenth century, by the enactment of the Territorial Waters Jurisdiction Act, 1878.[585] That Act reaffirmed the 'rightful jurisdiction' of the Crown over territorial waters, which were 'deemed by international law to be within the sovereignty of Her Majesty '...although... the Act was the subject of much critical comment, and there were occasional doubts on the question expressed privately within the British Government.[586]

> The Act stated in its preamble that the jurisdiction of the Crown – ... extends and always has extended over the open sea adjacent to the Coasts of the United Kingdom and all other parts of her Majesty's dominion to such distance as is necessary for the defense and security of such decisions.[587] Section 2 of the Act – *Amendment of law as to jurisdiction of the Admiral* – provided that;
>
> An offence committed by a person, whether he is or is not a subject of Her Majesty, on the open sea within the territorial waters of Her Majesty's dominions, is an offence within the jurisdiction of the Admiral, although it may have been committed on board or by means of a foreign ship, and the person who committed such offence may be arrested, tried, and punished accordingly.

Chapter 22

Merchant Shipping Bill, 1876

Resentment amongst shipowners over some requirements of the 'stop-gap' Act, which they saw as an 'unwarrantable interference with the shipping business', had been simmering during the 1875 Parliamentary recess and came to a head early the following year. A mass meeting of shipowners, from all ports of the country, was held in London before the 1876 Session commenced and heard strong opinions that the powers of Board of Trade surveyors under their new powers were 'detrimental to the British shipping trade and opened the door to the competition of foreigners who were not hampered by such surveillance and restrictions'. The meetings view was also that 'the large body of shipowners who conducted their business properly and honestly were being hampered and punished for a small body of reckless, if not dishonest shipowners'. The chairman, Lord Eslington MP and member of the Royal Commission, summed up the feeling of the meeting in stating; "...let the responsibilities of shipowners be clearly defined. If any man sent a ship to sea in an unseaworthy condition – that was a crime and ought to be punished; then make the punishment certain and severe, but take care to make that man only responsible for acts over which he had control". The matter of lack of consolidation and codification of the forty-one merchant shipping Acts passed since 1849 also came in for criticism, along with a general reference to the decrease and deterioration in the quality a British seamen as a cause of loss of life at sea.

Lord Eslington summarised the matters discussed at the meeting as; "recent changes in legislation had been most inconvenient and harassing to shipowners – that it had been fragmentary and ill-considered – but the shipowners were willing to accord their support to any well considered measure for saving life at sea. They were desirous to give their best assistance to the Government in passing necessary legislation, but they trusted that they would have means afforded to them of making known their opinions", particularly on the resolutions passed at the meeting;

That there should be local appeal against arbitrary decisions of the

> Board of Trade surveyors in the various ports,
>
> That they entered 'a protest against Clause 4 of the Act of 1875 (as to unseaworthy ships), which imposes on shipowners a responsibility hitherto unknown in the jurisprudence of the country,
>
> That a large proportion of casualties, etc, were caused by the inefficiency, intemperance, and negligence, or insubordination of crews,
>
> Also 'a protest against section 2 of the same Act, which permitted a ship to be detained upon complaint of one-fourth of the crew,
>
> And 'against a hard and fast load-line'

A deputation of shipowners was received by the Prime Minister a few days before the opening of the 1876 Session at which he assured them; "Government had no desire to do anything which would militate against so vast and important an interest, and that what had been done seemed necessary". He didn't miss the opportunity to remind them that; "the Merchant Shipping Act could have been consolidated at any time during the past seven years had it not been for the opposition raised not only by shipowners, but in many other quarters" and concluded by informing them; "he would take care that their resolutions had the careful consideration of the Government prior to any future legislation, but that he could not promise to deal with the Merchant Shipping Acts, as a whole as it would take up too much time, to the detriment of other important matters".[588]

In her speech from the throne at the opening of the 1876 Session of Parliament on the 8th of February, 1876, the Queen made it clear to the Lords and Gentlemen of the House of Commons that; "...Bills...for the amendment of the Merchant Shipping Laws will be immediately submitted to you". During the Commons' address in answer to the speech the same day the Marquis of Huntingdon proposed a realistic and conciliatory approach to the fraught question of effective legislation for safety at sea;

> Merchant Shipping legislation is also expected by Parliament and the country. The Report of the Royal Commission and the discussions which arose in this House and in the country during the last Session have, I think, done much to clear the way of the Government with

> reference to the introduction of this measure; and I do not think, therefore, that the Government will fall into either of the mistakes which they made last year. They will neither underrate the difficulties with which the subject is surrounded, nor the interest with which the subject is regarded by the House and the country. As has been remarked by the hon. Gentleman the Mover of the Address, the interest which was manifested on this subject in the country during the last Session of Parliament has been adequately sustained during the Recess, and the tone which has animated the discussion, both on the part of the shipowners—who are personally and directly interested in the subject—and of those who have more especially taken up the cause of the seamen, shows a most satisfactory desire not to interpose unnecessary difficulties, but to meet each other in a spirit of conciliation.

No time was lost, with leave being given the following day to bring in a Bill to amend the Acts relating to Merchant Shipping and not one but two complementary Bills being read during the first sitting of the House on the 10th of February; the Merchant Shipping Bill and the Maritime Contracts Bill. In introducing the Merchant Shipping Bill the President of the Board of Trade, Sir Charles Adderley, took the opportunity to disabuse Members of any intention by the Board of Trade to complete the long pending codification of all merchant shipping law while amendments were continuing to the existing law. He then went on to summarise the proposed changes from the standpoint of the 1875 Merchant Shipping Bill and the 'stop-gap' Act.

It was proposed to strengthen the obligation of the shipowner to his crew that he, or his agent, should take all reasonable precautions to make and keep the ship in a seaworthy state, by adopting 'Section 9 of the temporary Act of 1875, which gave the seaman a civil remedy for injury sustained by the unseaworthiness of a ship, thus imposing on the owner an obligation to the crew out of which he could not contract himself'. If a seaman lost his life his widow would have a claim against the shipowner, but the owner's liability would be kept limited. Regarding existing detention provisions it was Adderley's view that an easier system should be introduced for shipowners to appeal against the judgement of surveyors than through the local Admiralty, or County Court. Instead, it was proposed that a Court of Survey be established, consisting of a Judge and two assessors; one the nominee of the Board of Trade and the others of the local Marine Board or Association of Shipowners. The example was given of shipowners being able to appeal against a surveyor's charge of overloading, or to have an assessor accompany the surveyor and 'settle the point at once' before appealing to the Court. In other cases the Court could appoint scientific referees or persons of 'nautical, engineering, or other special skill and experience'. He hoped that these provisions would 'fairly meet the wishes of the shipowners for a more easy and satisfactory Court of Appeal and the just demands of the case'.

Adderley informed the House of the measures taken by the Board of Trade to address the issue of proper stowage of bulk cargoes of grain. Immediately after the passing of the 1875 Act, the Board had sent a copy of the Act to British Consuls at all grain exporting ports in the Baltic, Black Sea and America (seven eighths of grain loading ports), requesting them to report any violations of s.3 of the Act, followed by a circular of instructions and orders to report monthly to the Board of Trade, or, in special cases, immediately; also calling the masters or his agent's attention to any violation. This circular was followed by another in December, 1875, empowering a selected list of Consuls, Vice Consuls and Agents to employ persons to inspect grain loadings, and to forward reports of all British ships loading or unloading grain at their ports. Instructions were also given to Board of Trade surveyors to inspect grain laden ships upon arrival which had been reported to be in transgression of the regulation and to enforce penalties if required.

The next proposed clause would deal with deck cargoes. 'It was intended specifically to exempt some cargoes from prohibition—such as cattle, meat, and several things which must be carried on deck; but with regard to un-exempted cargoes carried on deck, or in any space not included in tonnage measurement, such space would be measured into tonnage measurement and uncovered cargo on the open deck would be measured by its area and the rectangle of its bulk. This, he thought, 'was a very feasible plan, and would provide an effective check on deck cargoes, or, at least deprive them of their present unfair advantage, while at the same time it would not do more than was in itself reasonable'. This provision would not apply to coastal ships. The Master of every ship would also be required to record the quantity and quality of the deck cargo carried.

Referring to what he called 'one of the most difficult and most vexed questions connected with the Merchant Shipping Laws' Adderley turned to the matter of load lines. In order to determine whether a general rule could be developed to assist surveyors in their judgement of overloading Adderley had formed a committee of twelve persons equally from Lloyds of London, Lloyds of Liverpool and the Board of Trade to decide 'whether any such general rules and principles could be laid down'. After three days of discussions the committee concluded that such general rules were impossible for every voyage, every cargo, and every season. Accordingly he proposed to make permanent ss. 5 & 6 of the 1875 Act, stating that he'd received satisfactory reports from all ports in England with regard to the enacted load line, with the exception of Liverpool 'where some attempts were made to render the provisions of the Act ridiculous, if not nugatory, by fixing the load line absurdly high'; but after a little reflection;

> ...the shipowners found it was not quite such a trifle as they had imagined. In the first place, the load-line by the words of the Act indicated the point up to which the owner intended to load, and, consequently, if the vessel were lost he would have to prove to the underwriters that he had not really loaded the ship up to that point—for the underwriters, of course, had a right to assume he had done so. Again, in the agreement with the crew it was a very important check, as it gave them a right, which they would not otherwise possess, to make claims and remonstrances. Besides, for marking so as to mislead there was a penalty of £100, which might be repeated any number of times. Consequently, it had been found at Liverpool that the matter was serious, and practical, and evasive load-lines had been changed.

Turning to the constitution of enquiries into wreck Adderley proposed to follow the recommendations of the Royal Commission through the appointment of a superior class of Judges to be called Wreck Commissioners who would be able to take depositions in the same manner as Receivers of Wreck. Initially only one would be appointed in London and the existing tribunals would continue with this addition. As an example he referred to the last important wreck which had occurred; '...that of the ***Deutschland***—showed the importance and illustrated the usefulness of such a step. It was most important that an inquiry should take place quickly, and before the very best authorities, but it turned out that there was no police-court in London which was ready to undertake such an inquiry. Under these circumstances, the Board of Trade commissioned Mr. Rothery, Registrar of the Admiralty Division of the High Court of Judicature, and he undertook the inquiry as an Inspector of the Board of Trade under the Act of 1854. He believed that anyone who had followed the proceedings would agree with him that the inquiry was in all respects a full and satisfactory one'. The remaining two proposed clauses provided support for the concept of training ships, and for a certificate of health to be procured by seamen on their engagement.

Plimsoll's contribution to the short introductory debate opened with a positive and supportive statement; "...He should meet the Bill with every disposition to see an opportunity of amending it rather than of embarrassing the Government and seeking to keep open the question a day longer than was absolutely necessary". Plimsoll raised issue briefly with most of Adderley's proposed clauses and in particular deck cargoes and load lines. Regarding the former he expressed astonishment at Adderley's view that; "the legislation that existed before 1862 prohibiting deck cargoes had been absolutely nugatory", reminding him that; "a Circular was issued by the Board of Trade itself to Lloyd's in 1874, asking for information on this very subject. Lloyd's employed two gentlemen of great ability—namely, Messrs. Jansen and Wakefield—who examined the records of over 6,800 voyages of timber-loaded ships for 10 years during which deck-loading was prohibited, and for the 10 years after the prohibition was removed in 1862, and they reported to Lloyds, who, he presumed, reported to the Board of Trade, that the loss of life since 1862 was vastly greater than when the deck loading was prohibited'. On Adderley's views on load lines Plimsoll reminded him that he had; "...expressed himself satisfied with the legislation of last year as to the load-line; but upon that point he should be prepared to join issue with him in Committee; because one of the right hon. Gentleman's own supporters had said, with regard to many of the ships sailing from the port he belonged to, that the load-line might just as well be put upon the funnel as where it was placed under last year's statute. Shipowners who placed a very fair load-line on their ships in our ports buried that line completely when they got into the Black Sea, and thus it became utterly valueless". And tellingly, that; "...In the present Act there was no penalty for submerging the load-line, such as it was".

It was Resolved, that the Chairman be directed to move the House, that leave he given to bring in a Bill to amend the Merchant Shipping Acts. Resolution *reported*:—Bill *ordered* to be brought in by Mr. Raikes, Sir Charles Adderley, and Mr. Edward Stanhope. Bill *presented*, and read the first time. [Bill 49.]

The second reading of the Merchant Shipping Bill took place on the 17th of February. One of Plimsoll's often stated claims that all ships would be built to a better standard and be safer if they were built and maintained to the standards of either Lloyds of London or Lloyds of Liverpool was refuted by the first speaker; Mr. T. Rathbone, who pointed out that, of the 750,000 tons of ships represented by the Liverpool Steamships Owner's Association, more than 400,000 tons was not in class as the owners; "wished to build them in a different and superior manner, and to have their hands free to introduce such improvements as they thought desirable, without having to consult the Committee of either Lloyd's or of the Liverpool Registry as to whether they might do so or not". Further, as an example that compulsory classification was undesirable, that all ships of the Peninsula and Oriental Company, Royal Mail and other large London companies were unclassed. He supported this claim by referring to the report of the Royal Commission which stated that 'there were in six years 5,316 lives lost by ships where the cause of loss was ascertained; but of these 5,153, or 97 per cent, were lost in vessels which there was every reason to believe were seaworthy, and only 163 were lost in vessels from unseaworthiness. Besides these lives lost from known causes, there were 5,345 lost in missing ships, the cause being unknown, and of these 4,223, nearly four-fifths, were lost in classed ships, and only 1,122 in unclassed ships'. In conclusion he stated that; "he had tried to show that, in the legislation which was desirable to prevent loss of life and property at sea, it was not necessary—nay, that it would be dangerous—to deviate from the English principles of leaving the action and energy of our citizens free and unfettered by minute Government direction; but holding them to a strict account for the use of that freedom, when they injured or attempted to injure others thereby".

Plimsoll was not at all happy with most of the proposed provisions in the Bill; "with which he was not at all surprised to find that the shipowners were not displeased, for from beginning to end of it the shipowner appeared to him to count for everything and the sailor for nothing…he did not think seamen were proper judges of the seaworthiness of vessels, and it was unfair to shipowners that they should be exposed to great loss by giving to ignorant men the opportunity of stopping vessels. The law committed this ridiculous folly—first of all it made the seaman a judge, and then if, however sincere he might be, he made an error, it treated him as a criminal and sent him to gaol". He was particularly scathing about the proposed Courts of Survey, sincerely hoping they would not be established; and with the Board of Trade:

> It would be the Board of Trade over again, and in its dealing with the Mercantile Marine that Department seemed to have united the maximum of meddling with the minimum of management. He wondered that shipowners had not insisted long ago on the total re-organization of the Board of Trade and demanded a special Board of Commissioners, consisting of retired shipowners and shipbuilders, who knew all about their business, and who would be able in a very short time to bring about the necessary alterations with the least possible trouble. Such a body ought to have power to make bye-laws about under manning, boats, and other matters which were essential, but which could not be crystallized in an Act of Parliament. When this was done we should see daylight, and he was persuaded that in a very short time there would be a wonderful diminution in the loss of life at sea, and such an addition to the comfort and safety of the men as would make it no longer difficult to man our vessels, while respectable men would not be ashamed, as they were at present, of beginning life as sailors.

Plimsoll criticised the lack of any supervison of loading at either at the port which a vessel was cleared outwards, or at the port of unloading; and considered that the clause as to grain-loading as it stood in the Bill would be perfectly valueless. Also; "the load-line proposed by the Bill seemed to be an owner's load-line, but there was no principle laid down for guidance, and if he chose to put it on the bulwarks probably no one would interfere with him…he objected to the proposal, because owners were often shop-keepers, without the special and technical knowledge requisite for that purpose. It was his intention, instead of recognizing the owner's load-line, to ask for the appointment of a Commission to examine all such load-lines, with power to provide a proper freeboard wherever necessary". He proposed to deal with the lack of any penalty for an incorrect load line in Committee. He concluded by once again by sailing very close to the wind in his criticism of ship-owning Members in stating; "he had heard of one shipowner, a Member of that House, who had lost 28 men within the last year, and of another, also a Member, who had lost seven ships, whereby 100 seafaring lives were sacrificed. If there were to be such a waste of the raw material as this, he thought the House would pause before it expressed satisfaction with, or assented to, any arrangement such as the Government proposed".[589]

In reply to a question in the House on the 22nd of February, the President of the Board of Trade clarified that of the 550 ships detained between August 1873 and June 1875, all were unseaworthy and they would not have been detained unless there were allegations of unseaworthiness imperiling life or property, such as defective hull or equipment or alleged overloading. On the 9th 0f March Adderley stated, in reply to a question, that;

> I have Returns for the half-year which has elapsed since the adoption of the load line, and Returns for the corresponding period of the preceding year, in relation to disasters happening in the Bay of Biscay. From November 1, 1874, till February 28, 1875, six steamers were lost in the Bay of Biscay, involving the loss of 175 lives; from November 1, 1875, when the use of the owner's load line was begun, till February 29 of this year, two steamers were lost in the Bay of Biscay, involving a loss of 26 lives. I have good reason to believe that the use of the load line has materially contributed to this gratifying diminution in the loss of life and property at sea.[590]

Regardless of this news there had been little enforcement under Clause 11 of the Merchant Shipping Amendment Act of 1871 for an owner sending a ship to sea in an unseaworthy condition; whether for unseaworthiness or overloading. Adderley advised Parliament on the 23rd of March that, before the "stop-gap" Act passed in 1875 there had been only two prosecutions since the 1871 Act had been passed. Eight prosecutions by the Board of Trade had taken place since the 1st of January 1874, of which three resulted in convictions, the magistrates failed to commit in three cases, and two were pending.

Also on the 23rd of March, further debate took place on the Merchant Shipping Bill. The first speaker, Mr. Gorst, made a lengthy and impassioned plea that the longstanding injustice of imprisonment of seamen for refusing to sail on an unseaworthy ship should be abolished;

> the Merchant Shipping Acts should be so amended that the breach of a contract of service not involving danger to life or injury to the ship on the part of a seaman should be no longer punishable with imprisonment and forfeiture, and should no longer render such seaman liable to be arrested without warrant within the United Kingdom'. A motion to this effect was then debated in Committee. In the course of a debate that was generally supportive of the motion Adderley reminded Members that; '...The general purport of the clauses in the Bill of last year was to give the sailor, convicted of the offences now under consideration, an alternative of fine and forfeiture of wages instead of imprisonment; and to limit the powers given to the shipowners, as to arrest without warrant, so that they should not go beyond what the circumstances of the case rendered necessary'. The Member for Bradford, W.E. Forster cautioned that if the proposed amendment went to a vote, in spite of both sides of the House being in its favour, '...it would be sure to be defeated, and a false impression might thereby be created'. He suggested that the Member for Chatham, Mr Gorst, should withdraw the Motion and bring up the clauses at a later stage of the Bill'. This proposal was supported by the Chancellor of the Exchequer and the proposed amendment was withdrawn. The remainder of the debate dealt with a proposal, under Clause 3 of the Bill – *Sending unseaworthy ships to sea a misdemeanor*, to insert the word 'wilfully' before 'sending'; 'the object being to limit criminal liability for sending a ship to sea which might prove unseaworthy to those who did so wilfully'. This amendment, which was not supported, was withdrawn. The amendment had been proposed due to decision by '... the high authority of Mr. Justice Brett, who...had in his charge to the Grand Jury at Liverpool, held that day, used words which had an important bearing upon the Amendment. They amounted, in effect, to a condemnation of the clause as it stood in the Bill. The learned Judge, referring to the Act passed last year, observed upon the absence of the word "intentional" in reference to the sending of unseaworthy ships to sea, and stated that such omission would change the principle of our criminal law.[591]

On the following Monday debate resumed on the Merchant Shipping Bill with the first speaker being Samuel Plimsoll who, in a long address, reiterated his long-standing belief that compulsory survey of unclassified ships would be the most effective solution to the problem of unseaworthy ships being sent to sea. He claimed that his views were supported by;

> ...a Petition from Bristol shipowners, who suggested that seaworthiness would be secured by survey and Lloyd's classification. The Chamber of Commerce of Newcastle and Gates head recommended that there should be inspection of all sailing ships unclassed at Lloyd's or at Liverpool, and urged that, while boats and lights were looked after, it could not be of less importance to take security that a ship itself was seaworthy. They stated further that it was much better to prevent the sailing of unseaworthy ships than to punish the shipowner after they were lost. The Town Council of Leeds had also presented a similar Petition. There had also been a great meeting of the Associated Chambers of Commerce held in the Westminster Palace Hotel. The first resolution they passed was that a periodical inspection of sailing ships and steamships that were unclassed at Lloyd's or elsewhere should be compulsory. The second resolution was that, owing to frequent losses of vessels at sea, the attention of the Government ought to be given to the subject, with a view of fixing the maximum load-line...The resolution of the Associated Chambers of Commerce described the same ships as he wished to include, and he preferred, indeed, their words to his own, because they effected the object in a manner less open to objection than his own Resolution.

In further support Plimsoll presented statistics he'd prepared in mid-1875 which showed that '...the total loss of British ships of 100 tons and upwards was in 1874, according to the Board of Trade Return, 593, of which number 181 were classed at Lloyd's and 412 not classed. The proportion of ships which foundered was 1.68% of ships classed and 3.26 % of ships not classed; while the proportion of losses during the first six months of 1875 was 1.3% of ships classed, and 2.25% of ships unclassed'. .

Adderley, scathing in his contemptuous refutation of all Plimsoll had said and referring to the amendment as "infatuated folly", was supported by Lord Eslington; "...upon two grounds: first, because it was unsafe; and second, because, [strangely] if adopted, it would be destructive of all improvement in the construction of ships". Other interventions were more measured and cogent with Plimsoll's supporter, Reed, stating that "...after having listened to the speech of the right hon. Gentleman, [Adderley] he felt that they were still as far as ever from a settlement of the question; for it seemed so contrary to the conditions under which they were discussing the subject, that he confessed he had heard it with considerable astonishment". Shaw-LeFevre, late of the Board of Trade, reminded members that; "...either the shipowners must be left free to adopt their own means, and afterwards be held responsible for whatever mishaps might occur, or the means must be prescribed for them, and they must be held blameless as long as they complied with the law. They must therefore decide which of the two principles they would adopt". After a debate lasting eight hours the amendment was lost on a vote of 110 Ayes and 247 Noes. Adderley had the last word, reminding Plimsoll that his second amendment, which ought to have preceded the first, was informal as it then stood upon the paper. Plimsoll, accordingly, yielded and withdrew the second amendment.[592]

There were further debates on Clause 3 (*Sending unseaworthy ships to sea a misdemeanor.*) and Clause 4 (*Obligation of shipowner to crew with respect to use of reasonable efforts to secure seaworthiness*)[593] of the Bill on the 30th of March, and the 3rd of April on Clause 5 (*Power to detain unsafe ships and procedure for such detention.*) and Clause 6 (*Constitution of court of survey for appeals*) [594] without any significant amendments. Clauses 7 (*Power and procedure of court of survey*), 8 (*Rules for procedure of court of survey, &c.*), 9 (*Liability of Board of Trade and shipowner for costs and damages*), 10 (*Power to require from complainant security for costs*), 11 (*Supplemental provisions as to detention of ship*), 12 (*Appeal to court of survey on survey of passenger steamer or emigrant ship*), 13 (*Reference in difficult cases to scientific persons)* and 14 (*Stowage of cargo of grain, &c*) were debated and agreed to on the 6th of April.[595]

Plimsoll opened the debate on the Bill on the 24th of April to put forward an amendment to Clause 14 of the 1875 Act (*Stowage of cargo of grain, &c*) to provide more specificity in arrangements to prevent the shifting of cargoes of bulk grain; "...Shifting boards not less than two and a half inches in thickness, running from the keelson or screw tunnel, as the case may be, longitudinally throughout the part of the ship so loaded, and up to the underside of the planking of the deck next above the top of such grain cargo, and also by having not less than one-fourth of such grain cargo in sacks or bags laid upon the surface of the remaining three-fourths of such cargo loaded in bulk". He explained that these standards were those adopted at the main grain exporting ports in the Black Sea, as supervised by the British Consuls, and were the reason that fewer grain ships had been lost in the Bay of Biscay, as claimed by the President of the Board of Trade. Plimsoll had visited many of these ports and British grain ships during the Parliamentary recess and claimed that in spite of the owners; "a great number of captains adopted the recommendations which he made, and employed shifting boards". After a short debate during which the proposed amendment was referred to by one Member as vexatious and injudicious, and other Members thought it inflexible, unnecessary and expensive, Plimsoll withdrew the proposed amendment.

Plimsoll proposed a further amendment that; "...before 'master', to insert 'managing owner or', with the object of making not only the master of a ship, as proposed by the clause as it stood, but also the managing owner, liable for improper loading". This amendment was agreed to with the inclusion of Adderley's suggestion that the word 'agent' be included after 'managing owner'. Plimsoll then went on to ask leave to introduce a verbal amendment regarding deck cargoes to Clause 15 (*Space occupied by certain deck cargo to be liable to dues*); repeating his arguments put forward in 1875 regarding the increased loss of life in the North Atlantic timber trade during winter months after the Timber Ships Act, 1845, was quietly repealed in 1862. During a fractious debate the Attorney General ingenuously reminded members that; "...the scope of the clause was misapprehended. It did not deal with deck cargoes in the way of prohibition; but whatever its effects might be, it was simply a tonnage clause". Plimsoll resignedly stated; "...Whatever became of it, even if it were carried, he should treat it as a mere tonnage clause, and bring up another one on the Report to deal with deck cargoes". He lost his proposed amendment that the words; "If any ship, British or foreign" be replaced by "no British ship" by a majority of thirty-three votes.

After an inconclusive debate on the effectiveness of the proposed tonnage tax on deck cargoes in achieving safe stowage of such cargoes, it was proposed by Mr. Grieve that the following clause should be included; "...Provided always, That it shall not be lawful for a vessel leaving North America between the first day of September and fifteenth day of April, nor from the North of Europe between the first day of October and the fifteenth day of April to carry deck cargo". This was withdrawn after an intervention by

Sir Henry James, who clearly had no knowledge of the Timber Deck Cargo Acts and had not paid attention during the debate on the loading of grain on British ships at overseas ports, in stating; "… the hon. Member for Greenock (Mr. Grieve) was proposing to do what the House found out 100 years ago that it could not do—namely, legislate for North America. How could any Act that they might pass be enforced on vessels starting from foreign ports? He suggested that his hon. Friend should withdraw his Amendment".

Sir William Harcourt, in expressing his dismay at the lack of any meaningful progress; "on the important subject of deck cargoes" stated; "…The question of deck cargoes had not been advanced that night one inch, and therefore it would be better to reserve it for future consideration, unless the Government were prepared to deal with it by an effective clause. England, as the first maritime nation of the world, ought not to shrink from laying down a rule upon this question that should set an example to the whole world". A vote on whether 'it would be far better to reject the clause altogether' was taken and agreed to by a majority vote of 37.[596]

Most of the debate on the Bill on the 27th of April was taken up with the vexed question of applying British law to foreign ships in the matter of the loading of timber deck cargoes. In his opening address the Chancellor for the Exchequer gave notice; "…that it was the intention of the Government to propose an additional clause with regard to deck loads, and to state that such clause would apply, not only to British, but also to foreign ships". He admitted that; "…It was a serious and difficult matter how to deal with foreign ships, in consequence of the questions that might arise in connection with International Law from British shipping going into the ports of all the nations in the world, and that the same rules and laws this country might lay down for the treatment of foreign ships in our ports might be applied to British ships in foreign ports. They must, however, run the risk of having to contend with these difficulties…" and went on to propose that the existing, and successful, Canadian law that banned deck cargoes over the winter period be made the basis of the British legislation. There was general agreement with this view, particularly as the Canadian Parliament had agreed quite recently that they would have no problem with such a law, but that it must apply equally to all foreign ships including Canadian ships which would be at a clear disadvantage if treated differently. Norwood concluded his address by stating that due to the; "exceeding delicacy and difficulty from its having a considerable bearing on our Treaty relations and of International Law, he would not then mention the terms of the clause which the Government had under consideration upon the subject". He also revealed that, in the course of the debate on the bill in March, the Board of Trade received a letter from the Colonial office enclosing a Resolution passed by the Canadian Government stating that had received correspondence from Canada that firmly indicated that;

> ... in the opinion of this House, the right of legislation to affect Canadian ships and the rights and liabilities of the owners thereof, belongs exclusively to the Parliament of Canada, and that any legislation on these subjects by the Imperial Parliament, except so far as it may equally affect Canadian ships with the ships of all other countries in the ports of Great Britain, would be inconsistent with the exclusive rights of the Canadian Parliament.

Norwood explained that the position the Canadian Parliament took was that they said; "We are perfectly willing that you should legislate for us and for the rest of the world. Make your own rules; but if you claim to legislate for us as British subjects, we say we have a Parliament of our own; and you must not interfere with us as British subjects, apart from legislation affecting foreign subjects also". The Canadian Government clearly did not want Canadian ships to be disadvantaged by losing their trade to foreign ships and to being treated differently in British ports. Norwood's proposal regarding application to foreign ships was met with general agreement but concerns were expressed as to how the provision could be applied to foreign ships loading in British ports. It was clarified that such a clause would apply to all Atlantic ports, not just Canada. He then moved to postpone debate on Clause 15 to allow Board of Trade officials time to prepare such a clause at the earliest opportunity. This was eventually agreed after members urged the Board of Trade to 'lay the proposed clause on the Table as soon as possible'.

The debate then moved on to consider Clause 17 *Marking of Deck Lines*. Plimsoll proposed an amendment to extend application of the clause to coastal ships as well as foreign-going ships by introducing a bottom limit of 80 tons referring to a statement in the annual Wreck Registers year after year that 'about half of this loss is occasioned through the unseaworthy, ill-found, and over laden state of the vessels employed in the coasting trade of Great Britain'. This amendment was immediately agreed to. A similar amendment was agreed to for Clause 18 *Marking of Load Line*. The debate concluded with Plimsoll losing a vote on a proposed amendment to require ships to transmit a copy of the position of a load line to the Board of Trade. Plimsoll was absent when a debate took place the following day on Clause 19 *Penalty for offences in relation to marks on ships*. Mr. E. Jenkins (for Mr. Plimsoll) moved, as an Amendment, in page 11, line 8, after «marked,» to insert «or who allows the ship to be so loaded as to submerge the centre of the disc". Adderley immediately opposed the amendment as; "the clause was of the nature of a contract by which the shipowner, who himself fixed the disc, undertook that his maximum loading should not exceed its centre, and, if it did, he would be liable to a civil action, or a prosecution for misdemeanour, besides vitiating his insurance'. Wiser heads prevailed after the Attorney General summarized the intent of the clause;

> Under the 18th clause the shipowner was required to put a load line on his ship at the maximum point to which he intended to load his ship. If he loaded the ship beyond that point he would break the contract into which he had entered with the sailors. If no damage thereby ensued to a seaman he could not recover more than nominal damages, but he would have a perfect right to refuse to proceed to sea, and the owner would be unable to compel him. Even if the vessel went to sea, and an accident occurred in consequence of her being overloaded, the mere fact of the load line having been submerged would be most cogent evidence of negligence on the part of the owner. There would be one great advantage which they would have, and which it was intended they should have. If a seaman was drowned his family might sue the owner for compensation for loss of his life, and if the submerging of the load line made the ship unseaworthy, the owner would further expose himself to a charge of manslaughter.

Plimsoll's amendment was agreed to, with inclusion of the words "in sea water" after the word "submerge", after Lord Eslington's intervention that; "the discussion was, in his opinion, a waste of time. The Government had accepted the Amendment, and they had, in his opinion, acted rightly in so doing. It would be an absurdity to establish a load line if it were not made a line for ensuring safety".

After Clause 20 *Appointment, duties, and powers of wreck commissioners for investigating shipping casualties,* as previously amended was *agreed to,* and consideration was given to Clause 21 *Assessors and rules of procedure on formal investigations into shipping casualties'* a proposal that 'Where an investigation may involve the cancellation or suspension of the certificate of the master or mate, one of the assessors shall, if practicable, be a person having experience in the merchant service' was agreed to without debate. Clauses 22 *Power for wreck commissioner to institute examination with respect to ships in distress under 17 & 18 Vict. c. 104. s. 448,* and Clause 23(*Power to hold inquiries or formal investigations as to stranded and missing ships* were *agreed to without amendment.* Due to lack of time debate on Clause 24 *Contribution from Mercantile Marine Fund to training ships* was postponed.[597] Clauses 24 and 25 *Expenses incurred for seamen left abroad who have been engaged without certificates of health,* were, by agreement, *withdrawn* from the bill the following day as it was considered that the Merchant Shipping Bill should be confined to matters of the safety of ships.

A proposal by Adderley to qualify Clause 26 *Enforcing detention of ship;* 'the master of the ship and also the owner and any person who sends the ship to sea' by addition of the words 'if party or privy to the offence' was objected to by Plimsoll as providing a loophole for escape, but was agreed to after Adderley's comment that; "the penalty should not attach if there was no privity to the offence". Clauses 27 *Ship's managing owner or manager to be registered,* 28 (*Fees, salaries, and costs* and 29 *Legal proceedings in cases of offences* were *agreed to without amendment.* Clause 30 *Application of Act to Scotland* was amended to ensure that the Bill applicable to the law of Scotland, Clause 31 *Application of Act to Ireland* being *agreed to.*

The debate then turned to matters outstanding and proposed additional clauses. Adderley's proposal to withdraw the postponed clause 16 *Entry of deck cargo in official log* on the grounds that it served no useful purpose *was agreed without debate.* Adderley then moved the addition of a new clause dealing with deck loading of timber that would not be limited to the Atlantic trade and would provide that;

> ...during the winter months a ship, British or foreign, arriving at any port in the United Kingdom should not, while subject to British jurisdiction, carry upon or above any part of the upper deck any heavy

> timber as cargo or any light timber to a height exceeding three feet above the deck, under a penalty of £5 for every cubic foot of timber so carried; the penalties not to exceed £100 and to be recovered on summary jurisdiction, the clause not to apply to any ship putting into port through stress of weather or for repairs.

Adderley explained; "he had adopted for imposts, as far as he could, the exact terms of the Canadian Law prohibiting the export of deck-loaded timber", and hoped that; "as it was not proposed that the clauses should come into operation before the 1st of January, he had no doubt that foreign Governments would make arrangements to meet the change". He then brought up the new clause and read it for the first time. Plimsoll's response was; "to prohibit deck loads of timber or wood goods altogether in winter, in which case he ventured to think that there would be such a diminution in the loss of life as would fully justify the prohibition. He thought it would be better to fix the prohibition from the 15th of September than from the 1st of October in each year, the former date being that fixed upon by the insurance companies as the beginning of the dangerous season". Opinions were mixed on the proposed clause with a common concerns being upon the application to foreign ships and to cargoes loaded in Scandinavian ports. One MP expressed serious fears on the subject. "He believed it would be found that the attempt to put penalties upon ships entering our ports which had loaded according to the laws of their own country, and which had safely crossed the sea, could not be sustained. It was, in his opinion, contrary to the principles of International Law and to the stipulations for equal treatment in all treaties with other Powers'. The Chancellor of the Exchequer thanked the committee for the manner in which they had generally received the clause and took the opportunity to remind Members of the predominant position held by British merchant shipping law;

> The hon. Member for Liverpool (Mr. Rathbone) had on the Paper a clause of a very excellent character, dealing with the possible case of arranging by Treaty with foreign countries for the acceptance by them of our Merchant Shipping Acts; and at one time the Government were disposed to think that all the objects in view might be met in that way; but while they would endeavour by negotiation, by persuasion, and by a proper use of their legitimate influence as the first great maritime Power in the world to induce foreign countries to come into arrange-

ments with them, the Government felt that in bringing forward the clause, which they did with considerable anxiety, they were doing what was best for the promotion of the great objects of the Bill and for the interests of the country.

After a brief debate some minor amendments were agreed to the proposed Clause which was *read* the third time and *added* to the Bill.

Adderley then proposed a new clause on the application of detention powers to overloaded and improperly loaded foreign ships in British ports, adding; "as soon as the provisional order for detention of a foreign ship was made notice was to be given to the Consul of the nation to which the ship belonged; and if the foreigner disputed the order, then the Consul would name a competent surveyor to decide between the master and the Board of Trade'. The clause was read for the second time without amendment, but there was not sufficient time for a third reading.[598]

On the 4th of May Adderley brought up a new version of the clause which was read for the first and second times;-

> *Foreign Ships, Overloading* – Application to foreign ships of provisions as to detention.
>
> Where a foreign ship has taken on board all or any part of her cargo at a port in the United Kingdom, and is whilst at that port unsafe by reason of overloading, the provisions of this Act with respect to the detention of ships shall apply to that foreign ship as if she were a British ship, with the following modifications:
>
> (1.) Sub-sections (4), (5), (6), and (7), of section five of this Act shall not apply;
>
> (2.) A copy of order for the provisional detention of the ship shall be forthwith served on the consular officer for the State to which the ship belongs at or nearest to the place where the ship is detained;
>
> (3.) If the owner or master of the ship is dissatisfied with the order for provisional detention the consular officer may, on his request and at any time within twenty-four hours after the service of the order 54 on the master, appoint some competent person to survey the ship; and if

> on survey that person decides that the ship ought to be released, she shall be released accordingly

The clause was amended slightly, agreed to, and added to the Bill. In a wide ranging debate on all provisions of the Bill it was agreed that, as the provisions made for protection of the lives of seamen were sufficient for a limited number of passengers, Clause 13 would be amended so that 'Any steam ship may carry passengers not exceeding twelve in number although she has not been surveyed by the Board of Trade as a passenger ship, and does not carry a Board of Trade certificate as provided by the Merchant Shipping Act of 1854 with respect to passenger steamers'.

An opportunity to enshrine in legislation a provision that passenger ships should carry lifeboats and deck rafts for all aboard was once again defeated by the entrenched views of many Members, including Plimsoll. Colonel Beresford had proposed a clause on a matter he'd raised in the House many times, that provision should be made that; "certificates should not be granted to passenger ships unless they were provided with lifeboats and deck rafts sufficient to save all on board in case of disaster or shipwreck". Adderley immediately responded with the Board of Trade's long held view on the matter;

> ...the clause would not effect the object which his hon. and gallant Friend had in view. In the great disasters which had occurred lately all the boats on board had not been used. In very rare cases had the boats been of any use. But suppose a ship wrecked in the middle of the Atlantic, with all the lifeboats and deck rafts proposed by the clause on board, and that all the passengers were lowered safely into them, what would become of them? They would simply be starved and die by inches instead of being drowned in the ship. Boats and rafts were useful to take passengers to any near shore, or ship, by relays such as there were seamen enough to manage: but more boats than there were men to manage were useless. A great number of boats and rafts would be the worst kind of deck-loading, and would impede the working and navigation of the ship. He considered that the existing law and the powers possessed by the Board of Trade were sufficient to effect the purpose in view. One Act stated a proportion of boats to tonnage very ample, if not excessive; and another Act enabled the Board of Trade to alter the scale, or to substitute rafts or life-boats.

...to which Beresford responded that the Baronet had little experience at sea, or he would not have opposed the clause on such grounds. Common experience showed that there was a lamentable deficiency of life-saving appliances'.

Plimsoll then entered the debate; "agreeing that in many cases—perhaps in 99 cases out of 100—boats proved useless, but rafts would not be open to the same objections, and would not be liable to be stove in as boats were in being lowered. There were rafts which could be easily stowed that were fitted up in the centre so as to carry preserved meats whereby people might be kept alive for a long time. Of course, there was no necessity for any alteration if the argument of the right hon. Gentleman [Adderley] were sound, and if it were better for the passengers to be drowned at once instead of dying a lingering death in the boats". Other Members expressed opinions that 'it would be impracticable to have on board a crew sufficiently large to man the boats, or even to lower them. Even if the passengers were got in, the only difference would be that they would be drowned in the boats, instead of being drowned in the ship' and 'There were exceptions to all rules; but, upon the whole, he thought ships' boats had lost more lives than ships' boats would ever save. A vote was taken and the motion was inevitably lost with Ayes 46, Noes 103.[599]

A motion to give colonial certificates equal weight to British certificates was agreed to and incorporated into the Bill. Motions to introduce new clauses dealing with seamen's diets to prevent scurvy, and making conditional advance notes illegal were not supported. A motion to replace Clause 25 with a new clause which would require a seaman to prove he was healthy before signing articles as, 'if the clause were rejected the Bill would be a most one-sided one, for, while penalties and restrictions were heaped upon the shipowner, nothing was done to insure the seaworthiness of the seaman', was rejected.[600]

The Merchant Shipping Bill was again considered in committee on the 8th of May with Plimsoll moving to introduce a new clause 27 (Registered British ships if disclassed to be deemed unseaworthy until surveyed by Board of Trade). He had reduced the scope of his long-proposed survey regime saying; "that he had carefully considered the objections that had been urged against a clause which he had previously proposed upon the subject, and he believed that by the clause which he now proposed it would be possible to reach unseaworthy ships without the clause being open to the objections which had been previously raised. The clause, no doubt, would not reach ships which had never been classed at all, yet it would reach most of the vessels which would have been reached by the fuller treatment which he had previously suggested". The motion received very little support and was soundly defeated in a vote. A proposed new clause, put forward to cease duplication of certification for passenger ships under the Passenger Acts and the Merchant Shipping Act was readily accepted by the President of the Board of Trade and incorporated into the Bill.[601]

Final consideration of the draft Bill, as amended, took place on the 22nd of May with Adderley introducing a new Clause 17 (*Provisions of signals of distress, inextinguishable lights, and life buoys in passenger steamers and emigrant ships*) which was considered, amended and added to the Bill;-

> Every sea-going steamship and every emigrant ship shall be provided to the satisfaction of the Board of Trade—
>
> (1.) With means for making the signals of distress at night specified in the First Schedule to 'The Merchant Shipping 1055 Act, 1873,'or in any rules substituted therefor, including means of making flames on the ship which are inextinguishable in water, or such other means of making signals of distress as the Board of Trade may previously approve; and
>
> (2.) With a proper supply of lights inextinguishable in water and fitted for attachment to life buoys.
>
> If any such ship goes to sea from any port of the United Kingdom without being so provided as required by this section, for each default in any of the above requisites the owner shall, if he appears to be in fault, incur a penalty not exceeding one hundred pounds, and the master shall, if he appears to be in fault, incur a penalty not exceeding fifty pounds.

Colonel Beresford again raised the question of adequate boats or rafts for all on board, moving a clause to the effect that; "in all vessels with a passenger certificate from the Board of Trade when the passengers are in excess of the number which can be carried in the ordinary boats in the event of disaster at sea, such vessels should, in addition to such boats, be required to provide means for saving life by rafts or other appliances in such proportion as the Board of Trade might deem sufficient, and it should be in the discretion of the Board of Trade to allow shipowners to substitute rafts for a portion of the boats, such rafts to be approved by the Board, of Trade".

Adderley was the first to respond commenting that the clause; "would require the deck to be crowded with a number of boats, two-thirds of which probably would become rotten and unusable, and certainly all of them could not be lowered or manned in case of emergency". In reply to this view the President of the Board of Trade was accused of not being aware of the progress of invention in life-saving appliances…and…the indifference and ignorance of the Board of Trade would continue the wasteful loss of life which might be easily prevented. Other Members thought encouragement should be given to the carrying of large life rafts on board ship, and that ships should be allowed to carry no more than a certain number of passengers, and 'that life belts should be added to the proposal of the hon. and gallant Member, so that some second chance of safety should be provided for all', but, in spite of support from a few Members the amendment was soundly beaten in a vote.

A proposal; "That from and after the first day of January, 1877, every British ship exceeding 100 tons register shall be provided with a certificate of classification or of survey from Lloyd's Register of British and Foreign Shipping, or the Liverpool Underwriters' Registry, or the Bureau Veritas, or from such other association or associations as the Board of Trade may from time to time sanction for the purpose…" met the same fate in spite of spirited support from Plimsoll. An amendment was agreed to that would enable the owner of a [detained] passenger steamer, instead of going to a Court of Inquiry, to ask the Board of Trade surveyor to survey the vessel in company with an assessor. If the two agreed it would not be necessary to go to a Court of Inquiry; but if they disagreed, that course would be necessary. Other minor amendments of detail were agreed. During the debate Plimsoll put forward four amendments, all of which either lost on a vote or were withdrawn.[602] The Bill was then considered amended with the third reading scheduled for the following Thursday, the 26th of May, at which the Bill was read the third time; verbal amendment made and *passed*.[603] The first reading of the Bill took place in the House of Lords on the following sitting day; the 29th of May.[604]

On the 23 of June, in the House of Lords, the Duke of Richmond and Gordon in moving that the Bill be read a second time explained that it; "was to provide additional security for the lives of our sailors from the avoidable risks which attended their calling. He was perfectly aware that in dealing with the matters embraced in this Bill—namely, the questions of unseaworthy ships and of overloading—the Government were only dealing with a part of a very large question; but that part was by no means an unimportant part, and they felt that it was better to confine themselves to it for the present rather than to extend the area and operation of the Bill to a large extent". Lord Carlingford, the late President of the Board of Trade, Chichester Fortescue, disagreed with the provision for deck cargoes of timber to a maximum height of three feet as; "...with regard to deck loading, the Canadian law, which till now we had looked up to with satisfaction and admiration, was satisfied with saying that deck cargoes from the 1st of October to the 16th of March should be prohibited, save and except deck loads not exceeding 3 feet high and consisting of light timber. That Act had been in operation for some time, and he was informed that ships built and loaded in accordance with its provisions were perfectly safe. This was the original provision of the clause; but in consequence of the defeat of the Government on this proposal, as mentioned by the noble Duke, the clause had assumed its present shape, and our law came into direct collision with the law of Canada on this matter. Such a conflict of laws should not be allowed to arise without such a necessity as he did not believe existed in the present case. He hoped the Government would amend the Bill in this particular". Lord Hampton was dismayed about the clause relating to deck cargo and load line as being; "of hardly any value, while the Duke of Somerset stated that shipowners had expressed strong objection to the 4th clause "which made the sending of unseaworthy ships to sea a misdemeanour". The Earl of Carnarvon supported application of Canadian Law; namely that; "at a certain season no ship should go to sea with a deck loading exceeding 3 feet of light timber" but was concerned about 'the grave and delicate nature of the clause relating to detention of foreign ships". Otherwise, the Bill was reasonably well received, apart from a few concerns to be dealt with in committee, the motion *agreed to, and the* Bill...'*committed* to a Committee of the Whole House on *Monday* the

3rd of *July'*.[605]

The Bill was considered in Committee on the 7th of July with all clauses being agreed to without amendment except 'Clause 21 Penalty for carrying deck loads of timber in winter [which was] *struck out,* and the following new clause *inserted* in lieu thereof;-

> After the 1st day of January, 1877, if a ship, British or foreign, arrives between the last day of October and the 16th day of April in any year at any port in the United Kingdom from any port out of the United Kingdom, carrying as deck cargo, that is to say, in any uncovered space upon deck or in any covered space not included in the cubical contents forming the ship's registered tonnage, any wood goods coming within the following description; that is to say—
>
> (a) Any square, round, waney, or other timber, or any pitch pine, mahogany, oak, teak, or other heavy wood goods whatever; or
>
> (b) Any more than five spare spars or store spars, whether or not made, dressed, and finally prepared for use; or
>
> (c) Any deals, battens, or other light wood goods of any description to a height exceeding three feet above the deck.
>
> The master of the ship, and also the owner, if he is privy to the offence, shall be liable to a penalty not exceeding five pounds for every hundred cubic feet of wood goods carried in contravention of this section, and such penalty may be recovered by action or on indictment or to an amount not exceeding one hundred pounds) (whatever may be the maximum penalty recoverable) on summary conviction. Provided that a master or owner shall not be liable to any penalty under this section—
>
> (1) In respect of any wood goods which the master has considered it necessary to place or keep on deck during the voyage on account of the springing of any leak, or of any other damage to the ship received or apprehended; or
>
> (2) If he proves that the ship sailed from the port at which the wood goods were loaded as deck cargo at such time before the last day of

> October as allowed a sufficient interval according to the ordinary duration of the voyage for the ship to arrive before that day at the said port in the United Kingdom, but was prevented from so arriving by stress of weather, or circumstances beyond his control. Provided further, that nothing in this section shall affect any foreign ship coming into any port of the United Kingdom under stress of weather, or for repairs, or for any other purpose than the delivery of her cargo.

There was to be no ban upon deck cargoes of timber during the winter months, but an alignment with the Canadian Law. Plimsoll later spoke of; "the malign and homicidal influence of Lord Carlingford" in removing the deck loading clause, and declared him to be; "morally responsible for the deaths of thousands of men".[606] It was however agreed; 'The Report of the Amendments to be received on *Friday* next; and Bill to be *printed,* as amended'.[607]

The Report of Amendments was considered on the 14th of July. The words suggested by Plimsoll; "and the managing owner of any British ship so sent to sea from any port in the United Kingdom" in Clause 4 – (*Sending unseaworthy ships to sea a misdemeanour* were struck out as, 'the omission of these words made it clear that 'every person' who sent, or was party to sending, a ship to sea in such unseaworthy condition as to endanger the life of any person was guilty of a misdemeanour.' 'If he proves that the ship sailed from the port at which the wood goods were loaded as deck cargo at such time before the sixteenth day of April as allowed a reasonable interval according to the ordinary duration of the voyage for the ship to arrive after that day at the said port in the United Kingdom, and by reason of an exceptionally favourable voyage arrived before that day' was added to Clause 24 – *Penalty for carrying deck loads of timber in winter* along with a proviso; 'that nothing in this section 'shall affect any foreign ship coming into any port of the United Kingdom under stress of weather, &c,' [is] amended by leaving out the words 'foreign ship coming, and inserting in lieu thereof, 'ship not bound to any port in the United Kingdom which comes'. The Bill [was to] to be read 3a on *Friday* next; and to be *printed* as amended.[608] The third reading took place on the 21st of July and the Merchant Shipping Bill was passed;[609] receiving Royal Assent on the last day of the 1876 Session on the 15th of August, 1876, as the Merchant Shipping Act Amendments Act, 1876.

In her speech, read at closure of the Session, the Queen stated that;

> The Act which you have passed for the amendment of the Laws relating to Merchant Shipping will, I trust, promote the safety of our ships and seamen, without imposing unnecessary restrictions upon the conduct of a service in the prosperity of which our national interests are in so many ways involved.[610]

Chapter 23

Merchant Shipping Act, 1876

The Merchant Shipping Act, 1876;[611] *An Act to amend the Merchant Shipping Acts;* one of the watershed Acts of the nineteenth century, amended a number of Acts from the Merchant Shipping Act, 1854, onwards, and would be the last significant amendment Act until 1894. The Act, which came into operation on the 1st of October; the date that the 'stop-gap' Act of 1875 ceased to be effective, consolidated, broadened and strengthened the remarkable progress made in the 1870s towards safe and seaworthy ships as a result of the combined effects of 'Plimsoll', public pressure, and political ideology being largely tempered with pragmatism.

The Act was made up of a number of Parts; *Unseaworthy Ships* (Clauses 1 – 12); *Foreign Ships Overloading* (Clause 13); *Appeal of Refusal of certain Certificates to Ships* (Clause 14); *Scientific Referees* (Clause 15); *Passenger Steamers and Emigrant Ships* (Clauses 16 – 21); *Grain Cargoes* (Clause 22); Deck Cargoes (Clauses 23 – 24); *Deck and Load Lines* (Clauses 25 – 28); *Investigations into Shipping Casualties* (Clauses 29 – 33) and *Miscellaneous* (Clauses 34 – 45. A Schedule contained two Tables; Part 1, *Enactments Repealed from commencement of the Act,* and Part II, *Enactments repealed from 1st January 1877.* The final draft of the associated Merchant Shipping Bill underwent some significant amendments in the House of Lords.

Clause 4 – *Sending an Unseaworthy Ship to Sea a Misdemeanour;* remained the same as in the 1875 Act, after Plimsoll's amendment '...and the managing owner of a British ship so sent to sea from any port in the United Kingdom' had been struck out by the Lords. Due to concerns raised regarding extra-territorial jurisdiction, the provision in Clause 4 that 'A prosecution under this section shall not be instituted except by or with the consent of the Board of Trade ' had the words'*...or of the Governor of the British possession in which such prosecution takes place* added.

Clause 6(4) – *Power to detain unsafe Ships, and Procedures for such Detention;* which provided that; *Before the order for final detention is made, a copy of the report shall be served upon the master of the ship, and within seven days after such service the owner or the master of the ship may appeal in the prescribed manner to the Court of Survey (hereinafter mentioned) for the port or district where the ship is detained* – had been amended in the House of Commons to add;

> Where the ship has been provisionally detained on the ground that she is unsafe by reason of overloading, and with the consent of the Board of Trade, where a ship has been provisionally detained on any other ground, the owner or the master of the ship may, within three days after the service of the order on the master, appeal in the prescribed manner to the Court of Survey for the port or district where the ship is detained.

This addition to the clause was struck out by the Lords.

Clause 6(5) opened with; '*Where a ship has been provisionally detained the owner or master of the ship <u>may require that the person appointed by the Board of Trade to survey the ship</u> shall be accompanied by such person as the owner or master of the ship may select out of the list of assessors for the Court of Survey…*'. The underlined words were amended by the Lords to read; '*,at any time before the person appointed under this section to survey the ship makes such survey, may require that he…*'.

Clause 7; *Constitution of Court of Survey for Appeals,* in addressing requirements for assessors *to be summoned in accordance with the rules under this Act by the registrar of the court out of a list of persons periodically nominated for the purpose,* was amended by the Lords to widen the scope and range of the provision by expansion of the inclusion of the provision that; *…if a Secretary of State thinks fit at any time, on the recommendation of the Government of any British possession or any foreign State, to add any persons or persons to any such list, such persons or persons shall, until otherwise directed by the Secretary of State, be added to such list, and if there is no list shall form such list.*

The Lords amended wording in Clause 10; *Liability of Board of Trade and Shipowner for Costs and Damages;* from *If it appears that <u>a ship provisionally detained was not, at the time of such detention, unsafe within the meaning of this Act that [and]</u> there was not reasonable and probable cause by reason of the condition of the ship, or the act or default of the owner, for the provisional detention of the ship, the Board of Trade shall be liable…*by striking out the underlined words.

Clause 11; *Power to Require from Complainant Security for Costs,* was a clause first introduced through the 1873 Act, and repeated in 1875, to deter frivolous or vexatious complaints about unseaworthy British ships, by the requirement, if considered necessary, for a complainant to provide security for costs and compensation, to be paid to the Board of Trade if the complaint proved groundless. If the complaint had been made by one-fourth of the crew, and was proven to be not frivolous or vexatious, such security was not required. The third section of the clause, as sent to the Lords, stated;

> Where a ship is detained in consequence of any complaint <u>and it appears that she was not at the time of such complaint unsafe within the meaning of this Act</u>, and the circumstances are such that the Board of Trade are liable under this Act to pay the owner of the ship any costs and compensation, the complainant shall be liable to pay to the Board of Trade all such costs and compensation as the Board incur or are liable to pay in respect of the detention and survey of the ship.

The Lords struck out the words underlined.

Clause 12(1); *Supplementary Provisions as to Detention of Ships,* was amended by the Lords to remove a wordy provision regarding timing of a detention order and replace it with a new Clause 12(2) simply stating; – *An order for detention of a ship, provisional or final, and an order varying the same, shall be served as soon as may be on the master of the ship.*

The controversial provision allowing for detention of overloaded foreign ships was enacted unchanged from that agreed in the House of Commons, with sections (2) and (3) reflecting the concerns of the Parliament and the Board of Trade about detention of foreign flagged ships, albeit limited to overloading; the first tentative and cautious exercise by Great Britain of port State control;

Foreign Ships Overloading

> 12. Application to Foreign Ships of Provisions as to Detention – Where a foreign ship has taken on all or any part of her cargo at a port in the United Kingdom and is whilst at that port unsafe by reason of overloading, or improper loading, the provisions of this Act shall apply as if she were a British ship, with the following modifications:-

(1) A copy of the order for the provisional detention of the ship shall be forthwith served on the Consular officer for the State to which the ship belongs at or nearest to the place at which the ship is detained

(2) Where a ship has been provisionally detained, the Consular officer, on the request of the owner or the master of the ship, may require that the person appointed by the Board of Trade to survey the ship shall be accompanied by such person as the Consular officer may select, and in such case if the surveyor and such person agree, the Board of Trade shall cause the ship to be detained or released accordingly, but if they differ, the Board of Trade may act as if the requisition had not been made, and the owner and master shall have the appeal to the Court of Survey touching the report of the surveyor which is provided for by this Act; and

(3) Where the owner or master of the ship appeals to the Court of Survey the Consular officer, on the request of such owner or master, may appoint any competent person who shall be assessor, who, if the ship were a British ship, would be appointed otherwise than by the Board of Trade

In this section the expression "Consular officer" means any consul-general, vice-consul, consular agent, or other officer recognised by a Secretary of State as a Consular officer of a foreign State.

Issues arising from duplication of jurisdiction under the extant Merchant Shipping Acts and Passenger Acts, and the question of refusal by an official, under either Act, to issue a certificate to enable the ship to lawfully sail, particularly in the case of schedule passenger steamers, were addressed by Clause 14; *Appeal on Refusal of certain Certificates to Ships.* The aggrieved owner was given a right to appeal to the local Court of Survey and, when the Board of Trade was satisfied that the requirements of the report of the Judge and other provisions of the Acts had been complied with, could, in the case of a passenger steamer (including refusal to give a certificate as to lights and fog-signals) issue a certificate under the Merchant Shipping Act, 1854. In the case of an emigrant ship the Board could give, or direct the emigration officer to give, a certificate of clearance. The final section of clause 14, as drafted by the House of Commons, explained the process to be followed in such cases;

> In cases of urgency the owner may, instead of appealing as aforesaid, require that the Board of Trade surveyor shall again make a survey accompanied by such persons as the owner may select out of the list of assessors (nominated as herein mentioned) or out of any list approved by the Board of Trade, and in such case if the surveyor and such person agree in their report the Board of Trade shall act in the same manner as if the report had been made by the judge of the Court of Survey under the provisions of this section, but if they differ the Board of Trade may act as if the requisition had not been made, and the owner shall have the appeal as is here-before provided by this section

The Lords struck out this section and replaced it with a less explicit provision very much in the interests of the shipowner;-

> Where the survey of a ship is made for the purpose of a declaration or certificate under the above-recited enactments, the person appointed to make the survey shall, if so required by the owner be accompanied on the survey by some person [not an assessor approved by the B. of T.] appointed by the owner, and in such case if the said two persons agree there shall be no appeal to the Court of Survey in pursuance of this section

Clauses 16 – 21, additional to those in the 1875 Act, provided for certification and certain safety requirements for *Passenger Steamers and Emigrant Ships*; British, Colonial and Foreign.

Clause 16; *Exemption of certain Steamers from Passenger Certificates* allowed cargo ships to carry passengers as it was considered that the safety equipment requirements for the crew were adequate to cater for a maximum of twelve passengers.

Clause 17; *Colonial Certificates for Passenger Steamers* were, under certain conditions of equivalency, given the same force as certificates issued under the British Acts of Merchant Shipping.

Clause 18; *Provision against Double Survey in cases of Passenger Steamers and Emigrant Ships* allowed for mutual recognition of the requirements of the Merchant Shipping Act, 1854, and the Passenger Act, 1855, and the Acts amending them.

The primacy of equivalent flag State regulation was acknowledged under clause 19; *Provision as to Survey of Foreign Passenger Steamer or Emigrant Ship.* The Board of Trade could recognise certificates issued by foreign Governments if they had the same effect as if given under the Merchant Shipping Act, 1854, or Passenger Act, 1855. The Government reserved the right to direct, through Order in Council, that the section '...shall not apply in the case of an official survey at a foreign port at which it appears to Her Majesty that corresponding provisions are not extended to British ships'.

Power was given to the Board of Trade under clause 21 to exempt emigrant ships from requirements of the Passengers Act, 1855, if the ship met superior food, space, accommodation standards or any other particular thing. Clauses 19 and 20 were added bodily by the Lords. The last clause in this Part; clause 21; *Provision of Signals of Distress, Inextinguishable Lights and life Buoys* updated the requirements of the Merchant Shipping Acts; 1854 and 1873.

Conditions for the carriage of deck cargoes were provided by Clauses 23 and 24. Clause 24; *Penalty for carrying Deck Loads of timber in Winter* was incorporated to the same effect as summarized earlier with the exception that the date of introduction was changed from '...*After the 1st day of January, 1877, if a ship, British or foreign, arrives between the last day of October and the 16th day of April in any year at any port in the United Kingdom from any port out of the United Kingdom..*' to '...*After the first day of November, one thousand eight hundred and seventy-six, if a ship, British or foreign, arrives between the last day of October and the sixteenth day of April in any year at any port in the United Kingdom...*'. Application of clause 24 was qualified by addition of a provision that '...*nothing in this section shall affect any ship not bound to any port in the United Kingdom which comes into any port in the United Kingdom under stress of weather, or for repairs or for any purpose other than the delivery of cargo*'.

Provisions for Deck-Lines and Load Lines included Clause 25; *Marking of Deck-Lines,* Clause 26; *Marking of Load-line on Foreign-going British Ships,* Clause 27; *Marking of Load-line in case of Coasting Vessels* and Clause 28; *Penalty for Offences in relation to Marks on Ships.* Plimsoll's amendment to require ships of 80 ton or more to have a deck line was provided for through Clause 25. The wording for Clause 26 was amended slightly from that in the 1875 Act to include '...*except ships under eighty tons register employed solely in the coasting trade, ships employed solely* in fishing...'.

Clause 27 was similar to the provisions in clause 26 for foreign-going ships, except that reporting on the location of the load line was not required every one of the ship's frequent coastal voyages. Instead, the owner was required to report annually to the collector or other principal officer of Customs at the ship's port of registry as to 'the distance in feet between the centre of the disc and the upper edge of each of the lines indicating the positions of the ship's decks which is that centre'. A similar written report was required, before the ship proceeded to sea, after any 'renewal or alteration of the disc'.

Clause 28 provided the disincentive for any ship, British or foreign but excluding home trade ships, of tonnage being paid on the cubic contents of any deck cargo. The tonnage of space occupied by the deck cargo was to be determined by the Board of Trade or a Customs Officer and entered by him in the ship's official log-book. The Lords added to this requirement; '...*and also in a memorandum which he shall deliver to the master, and the master shall, when the said dues are demanded, produce such memorandum in like manner as if it were the certificate of registry, or, in the case of a foreign ship, the document equivalent to a certificate of registry, and in default shall be liable the same penalty as if he had failed to produce the said certificate or document'.*

Clauses 29 – 33; *Investigations into Shipping Casualties,* were enacted with minor amendments to the corresponding clauses in the Merchant Shipping Act, 1854, as was Clause 34; *Enforcing Detention of Ship* under Miscellaneous.

A new Clause 35; *Service of Order on Master etc* was added in the Lords providing that; *in the absence of the master, any document required to be served on the master could, in the United Kingdom, be served on the managing owner, or his agent, be affixed to the mast of the ship, or by leaving it for the master 'on board the ship with the person being or appearing to be in command or charge of the ship*. Clause 36 was also a new clause that required the name of the ship's managing owner, manager, or ship's husband or other person to whom the management of the ship was entrusted by or on behalf of the owner, to be registered at the Customs House of the port of registry.

Clause 37; *Power for Her Majesty by Order in Council to apply certain provisions of Merchant Shipping Acts to Foreign Ships,* enacted a new provision, no doubt brought about by the application of British law to foreign ships through the 1876 Act in the matter of timber deck cargoes arriving in British ports, and to overloading, but with a potentially far wider scope;

> Whenever it has been made to appear to Her Majesty that the Government of any Foreign State is desirous that any of the provisions of the Merchant Shipping Acts, 1854 – 1876, or of any Act hereafter passed amending the same, shall apply to the ships of such State, Her Majesty may, by Order in Council, declare that such of the said provisions as are in such Order specified shall (subject to the limitations, if any, contained in the Order) apply, and thereupon so long as the Order remains in force, such provisions shall apply (subject to the said limitations) to the ships of such State, and to the owners, masters, seamen and apprentices of such ships when not locally within the jurisdiction of such State, in the same manner in all respects as if such ships were British ships.

Clause 38, inserted by the Lords, ensured that where Her Majesty made, revoked or altered such Orders in Council they were lawful. The remaining clauses provided for *Fees, Salaries and Costs* (Clause 39), *Legal Proceedings in case of Offences* (Clause 40), *Application of Act to Scotland* (Clause 41), *Application of Act to Ireland* (Clause 42),), *Application of Act to Ilse of Man* (Clause 43), *Saving for Colonial Inland Waters* (Clause 44), and *Repeal of Acts* (Clause 45).

The 'circular disk twelve inches in diameter with a horizontal line drawn through its centre'; the visible legacy of Plimsoll's long crusade on behalf of 'our seamen', has come down through history, internationally and fittingly, as the Plimsoll Line. It was not perfect as the owner could place it where he wished as many did, particularly in foreign ports, but the penalties placed upon the master and the owner for not using it, or misusing it, were deterrent enough for it to obtain widespread usage. Plimsoll himself recognized its shortcomings in stating publicly that 'An Act of Parliament is now on the Statute book, which although by no means without defects, is still one that, zealously and faithfully administered, will be found to remedy the evils which afflict our sea-going population. My special work, therefore, I regard as done'.[612]

In the address in answer to Her Majesty's speech to Parliament at the commencement of the 1877 Session, the Chancellor of the Exchequer explained that it was not the intention of Her Majesty's Government to drop the Maritime Contracts Bill. '…It stood upon the Paper for a considerable time last Session, and towards the close of the Session I gave Notice of a Motion to refer it to a Select Committee; but as it was found impossible, from circumstances that occurred, to get the Bill through the second reading stage we were obliged to let it stand over till this year. It is, however, our intention to re-introduce it, and I hope, after it has been read a second time, to ask the House to send it to a Select Committee'.[613]

One of the most fraught questions regarding losses of unseaworthy ships was the long-standing allegation that insurance was the prime factor, in that owners would buy unseaworthy ships, over-insure them, and the cargo, and then send them to sea in the hope that the ship would be lost – becoming a 'coffin ship'. The Royal Commission had given this matter long consideration and, on this matter, had concluded that;

> We think that the shipowner should not be enabled to recover his insurance, whether under a time or voyage policy, when it could be shown that he or his agent had not done everything reasonably within their power to make and maintain the ship in a seaworthy condition, and that unseaworthiness occasioned the loss.

The Board of Trade had taken notice of this conclusion but had determined that it was a matter of contract between the shipowner and a private party and not one which sat easily within a Merchant Shipping Act dealing with the safety of ships and seafarers. Accordingly, the Maritime Contracts Bill had, in February 1876, been introduced the same day as the Merchant Shipping Bill.

In his introduction of the Bill the Chancellor of the Exchequer, Sir Stafford Northcote, explained the Government's philosophy on how to deal with this matter legislatively as '…

> I think we may say that our seamen and all connected with ships would naturally have their great protection in the interest the shipowner must have in the preservation of his ship. Naturally, and in the absence of any legislation or of any system which might prevent the operation of that law, there would be a law by which the shipowner is more desirous of preserving his ship than any other person can be, because if his ship is lost he loses that which constitutes his property.

> But there has long prevailed in this country and elsewhere a system of insurance the effect of which is that if a man partially insures his ship he mitigates his loss; if he wholly insures her he covers his loss; and if he over-insures her it is possible that his loss may even become his gain. Therefore, unless proper attention is paid to this subject, and care is taken to prevent as far as possible the over-insurance of ships, it is possible that a system most excellent in its intentions, most valuable in its working, may be the cause of great abuse and evil. Therefore, unless proper attention is paid to this subject, and care is taken to prevent as far as possible the over-insurance of ships, it is possible that a system most excellent in its intentions, most valuable in its working, may be the cause of great abuse and evil'.

Northcote went on to explain the structure of the short Bill of twelve clauses; 'two or three of which are merely formal and the others only consequential'. The questions of warranty and those stipulations in bills of lading by which shipowners were able to contract themselves out of their liability to the shippers of cargo were addressed. A novel feature in law was proposed whereby, in the 4th clause, the shipowner would be responsible for the safety of passengers as well as cargo. Accordingly, '... in every contract after the commencement of the Act for the carriage of goods or persons at sea there shall, by virtue of this Act, be an implied warranty by the shipowner, charterer or other person contracting, that the ship is seaworthy at the commencement of the voyage to be performed under the contract. This is a novelty, for the passenger, in short, is here put on the same footing as cargo'. Provision was also proposed 'for rendering this warranty efficacious—that is to say, for preventing the shipowner from contracting himself out of his liability'. In describing 'the most important and striking provision in the Bill', Northcote deemed it necessary to quote the exact wording of the proposed ['coffin ship'] Clause 8 which '...It goes upon the principle that the natural kind of policy is the open one, which, as construed by successive decisions, gives to the insurer the amount to which he is fairly entitled as compensation for the loss of his ship, and no more';

> Where, in an action on a contract of insurance on ship or freight made after the commencement of this Act by a Valued policy, it appears to the Court, at any stage of the action, whether application in this behalf is made by the defendant or not, that there is ground to believe that the valuation is unreasonably in excess of the real value of the subject-

> matter of insurance, the Court may, if it thinks fit, direct an inquiry before referees, on such terms and conditions respecting costs and other matters as to the Court seem just, to ascertain what would have been the value of the interest of the insured, if the policy had been an open one. If, on the report of the referees, it appears to the Court that the valuation is unreasonably in excess of the real value of the subject-matter of insurance, then the insured shall not be entitled to recover in the action more than the value as ascertained by the referees.

The next clause related to freight in that it was proposed to provide in the following clause that;...Where there is an insurance on freight effected after the commencement of this Act, the insured shall not be entitled to recover in respect of any freight lost without allowing for the proportion of expenses remaining, at the time of the loss, to be incurred in earning such freight.

Clause 10 contained a proposal central to the issue of seaworthiness; not only for the existing practice of a warranty of seaworthiness at the commencement of a proposed voyage, but for a longer period under a time policy, in that;

> Where an insurance on behalf of a shipowner on ship or freight by time is effected after the commencement of this Act, the insured shall not be entitled to recover in respect of any loss occurring, if the loss would not have occurred but for the unseaworthiness of the ship, and that unseaworthiness existed at the time of the ship leaving the port or place of safety (if any) in which she was at the commencement of the risk, or the port or place of safety in which she was last before the commencement of the risk, and could have been prevented by the exercise of reasonable care on the part of the owner or of the master of the ship, or of any agent of the owner, charged, as such, with the loading of the ship, or with the sending of her to sea from that port or place.

An associated provision would make it clear; '...For the purposes of this section, unseaworthiness arising from the defective condition of the hull, equipments, or machinery of the ship, or by reason of overloading or improper loading, shall alone be deemed unseaworthiness'. After a short debate, with mixed views, it was resolved, '...That the Chairman he directed to move the House that leave he given to bring in a Bill to amend the Law relating to Insurances and other Maritime Contracts. The Bill was ordered to he brought in by Mr. Raikress, Mr. Chancellor of the Exchequer, and Mr. Attorney General; …presented, and read the first time.[614]

In the course of a progress report on the Merchant Shipping Bill on the 24th of April, the Chancellor emphasized the importance of the Maritime Contract Bill and its synergy with the Merchant Shipping Bill; '...We could not prevent all danger, but he maintained that by the legislation proposed this year, in the present measure and the Maritime Contracts Bill, Her Majesty's Government were making a very earnest, and, he hoped an effective move in the right direction of limiting those dangers to which the hon-Member for Derby had called the attention of the country—namely, the dangers to which our seamen were exposed'. On the 20th of July, when discussing the amount of business that could be completed during the Session, the Marquess of Hartington made the observation that;

> There was a very important measure which was introduced at the commencement of the Session—the Maritime Contracts Bill—and which we were informed was intimately connected with and even as important as the Merchant Shipping Bill, and we understood that both Bills were to be proceeded with together. No progress was made with the Maritime Contracts Bill, and a short time ago the Order for the Second Reading of the Bill was discharged without any Notice being given to the House of the intention of the Government.

The Prime Minister replied that '…The noble Lord complains that the Maritime Contracts Bill… [has] been withdrawn without Notice from the Paper. Now, I think the noble Lord is under a mistake in that respect. My memory is that the Chancellor of the Exchequer, with respect to the Maritime Contracts Bill made [a]statement to the House; and that ample Notice was given to the House of the intentions of the Government'.[615] There was no further consideration of the Bill during the 1876 Session.

During the Address in Answer to Her Majesty's Gracious Speech on the opening day of the 1877 Session, the Marquess again raised the question of the status of the Maritime Contract Bill;

> There is one other omission from the Speech which I can hardly

> help thinking is accidental, but which appears to me remarkable. The House will remember that the subject of the amendment of the laws relating to Merchant Shipping was only partially dealt with last Session. Equal importance was attached by Her Majesty's Government to the Merchant Shipping Bill and to the Maritime Contracts Bill. The Merchant Shipping Bill passed, but the Maritime Contracts Bill was postponed until this Session, and it is rather surprising that neither in the Speech from the Throne nor in the speeches of the noble Mover and Seconder of the Address is there any reference to the latter measure, or, any expression that would lead us to suppose that it is the intention of Her Majesty›s Government to legislate further upon the subject.

The Chancellor explained that "…it is not the intention of Her Majesty's Government to drop that measure. It stood upon the Paper for a considerable time last Session, and towards the close of the Session I gave Notice of a Motion to refer it to a Select Committee; but as it was found impossible, from circumstances that occurred, to get the Bill through the second reading stage we were obliged to let it stand over till this year. It is, however, our intention to re-introduce it, and I hope, after it has been read a second time, to ask the House to send it to a Select Committee".[616] On the 16th of February it was resolved that a Bill to amend the Law relating to Insurances and other Maritime Contracts be brought in, with the Maritime Contracts Bill being read for the first time as Bill 90. Questions were asked in the House three times during March as to when the Bill would have its second reading, to no avail. To a further question on the 28th of June as to 'whether it is his intention to proceed with the Maritime Contracts Bill this Session', the Chancellor effectively signed a death warrant for the Bill in replying that;

> This is a Bill which touches such large interests, and raises such important questions that, although it had been carefully considered by the Government before it was introduced, we feel it will be only right before proceeding with it to give an opportunity of discussing it before a Select Committee. We have not been able to find a day for the second reading, and at this period of the Session it is almost impossible to get the Bill read a second time and carried through a Select Committee and the subsequent stages. Under those circumstances we propose to discharge the Order.[617]

The Maritime Contracts Bill was not given the urgent attention accorded to it by the Chancellor. The opportunity to address the issue, identified by the Royal Commission and acknowledged by the majority of Parliamentarians and shipowners, of the linkage between maritime insurance and unseaworthy ships was lost. The Bill disappeared from the Order Paper and did not reappear again, in a different guise, until 1884.

A large number of shipmasters met in London on the 5th of May 1876 to express their unanimous indignation and protest against the injustice of a decision taken by a Magistrate of the Thames Street Police Court that called into question a shipmaster's authority and ability to maintain discipline. Captain Barnes of the ship ***Locksley Hall*** had brought a seamen named Allen before the Magistrate and charged him with assaulting the Chief Officer on the high seas, gross insubordination and refusal of duty. The punishment provided for these offences was imprisonment for any period not exceeding twelve weeks, and also, at the discretion of the Court, forfeiture, for every twenty-four hours of such disobedience or neglect, of six days pay.[618] The seaman brought a counter charge against the Master of illegal assault for placing him in irons. The Magistrate agreed that Captain Barnes's case was fully proven, but in passing judgement said; "he had taken into consideration what Allen had already suffered by having been confined to irons on board the ship" and, "for the refusal of duty he inflicted a nominal punishment of one day's imprisonment, and for the assault another day's imprisonment." Captain Barnes was sentenced to be imprisoned for twenty-one days without the option of a fine for having placed Allen in irons.

A powerful deputation of shipmasters met the Prime Minister, Disraeli, and presented a unanimous protest against such injustice, resulting in the intervention of the Home Secretary and the release of Captain Barnes. The Magistrate's ruling had, however, called into question the powers legitimately exercised by the Master in maintaining discipline and a further deputation of shipmasters and others met Disraeli again to demand a change to the law to prevent the recurrence of such judgements. The Prime Minister was unsympathetic, stating that "the law gave the shipmaster full power on board his ship at sea. What more could they want?" and went on to state that in the particular case it was not the law that was at fault but the Judge; "…an error had been committed, and would be remedied". The

Magistrate was removed from the Thames Street Police Court.

This case was the catalyst for the formation of a country wide organization, the Shipmasters' Society', to monitor legislation and, in particular, the constitution, proceedings and decisions of Courts of Inquiry, and to highlight the lack of any Court of Appeal in doubtful cases. By 1879 the need for a Court of Appeal had become very apparent resulting in enactment of the Shipping Casualties Investigation Act, 1879 [619] which created a Court of Appeal re-hearing any case in which 'new and important evidence which could not be produced at the investigation is discovered, or if for any other reason there has been in their [the Board of Trade's opinion] ground for suspecting a miscarriage of justice.' Under this Act the Lord Chancellor established new rules as to assessors on Courts of Inquiry, with their appointment being by the Home Secretary. If the Court was considering suspension of on officer's certificate of competency not less than two assessors having experience in the merchant service were required to be appointed. For example, in the case of an engineer's certificate, at least one assessor was required to hold a First Class Certificate and have accumulated at least five years' sea service. In 1880 further rules were introduced applying principally to the re-hearing of cases in the Court of Appeal.[620]

In the second half of the 1870s there was increasing concern that the stowage requirements of the 1876 Act for bulk cargoes of grain were ineffective. A large number of grain-laden steamships were being either lost or missing. In the case of the latter it was very difficult, if not impossible, to determine the exact circumstances of the loss of the ship. A paper, presented to the Institution of Naval Architects in April, 1880, by a Lloyd's senior surveyor, discussed possible causes, and identified the most probable as being 'the want of proper care in loading' and 'a want of initial stability'. The author referred to 'the hasty dispatch required by owners' as being partially responsible for bad stowage, citing 'the greater original cost, and the expense in working steamers, as compared to sailing ships' as having made rapid despatch a question of greater importance, with too little attention being paid to proper stowage of the cargo. The report also stated;

> '...when we come to consider the causes of loss arising from overloading and improper stowage, it will be impossible to acquit shipmasters of all blame; but it must be remembered of them that, what-

> ever their faults of omission, or of commission, they always risk, and too often have to pay the penalty with, their lives for their mistakes, whether they arise from ignorance or inadvertence'

In support of his jaundiced view of shipmasters, the Lloyds surveyor drew upon the example of how the port of Montreal dealt with uncooperative masters who were imperiling their grain laden ships, many of which were lost after departing Montreal, a situation that lead to introduction of rules to ensure that grain cargoes were correctly stowed, under a penalty of $40. 'This fine was so ridiculously low that the shipmasters paid it as a matter of course, loaded their ships as they liked, and numerous losses used to ensue'. In 1873 the fine for evading the Port Warden's regulations was increased to $800 and 'since that time not a single grain-laden vessel from the port has foundered at sea';

> This story tells its own tale and teaches its lesson to shipmasters. Whatever they may choose to risk for themselves, they have no right to imperil the lives of their crews. How many lives have they sacrificed, as well as committed moral suicide themselves, to satisfy the greed of unscrupulous owners? A small fine was paid with a light heart, but when it was made heavy enough to make it no longer worth while to risk it, the evil was cured.[621]

The British Government took note of the Montreal solution and enacted the Merchant Shipping (Carriage of Grain) Act, 1880,[622]which came into operation on the 1st of January 1881 and laid down stringent rules for the stowage of grain cargoes, with associated heavy penalties;

> s.3 *Where a grain cargo is laden on any British ship, all necessary and reasonable precautions (whether prescribed by this Act or not) shall be taken in order to prevent the grain cargo from shifting. If such precautions have not been taken in the case of any such ship, the master of the ship, and any agent of the owner who was charged with the loading of the ship or sending her to sea, shall be liable to a penalty not exceeding three hundred pounds, and the owner of the ship shall also be liable to the same penalty, unless he shows that he took all reasonable precautions to enforce the observance of this section, and was not privy to the breach thereof.*

While the arguments over load lines raged during the early 1870s technical developments led to more powerful and economic steam engines, radical changes to ship design and many other innovations.

The year of 1871 had seen the introduction of another competitor in the passenger/emigrant trade across the North Atlantic; the Oceanic Steam Navigation Company of Liverpool. T H Ismay, a shipbroker who'd established a successful shipping company operating small sailing vessels to Mexico and the West Indies, was given the opportunity to purchase the name, flag and goodwill of a bankrupt line of clippers; the White Star Line known as such through their red swallow tailed house flag with a white star, and assistance with funding to build new iron ships of a radical design. He changed from wood to iron construction for his new sailing ships and, two years later, entered the North Atlantic passenger trade.[623] The first ship for the White Star Line, the ***Oceanic***; 420 feet long and only 41 feet beam, of 3707 gross tons, was launched in Glasgow in 1871. Her radically narrow beam to length ratio of 1 - 10, designed for speed, enabled her, with a four-cylinder compound engine delivering 1990 indicated horsepower, to achieve a speed of fourteen and a half knots, becoming the fastest steamship afloat, carrying a total of 1166 passengers and 143 crew. She was soon joined by five sister ships; ***Atlantic, Baltic, Republic, Celtic*** and ***Adriatic*** operating a weekly service between Liverpool and New York. The long, lean and easily driven design of the White Star ships; modelled by her designers and builder Harland and Wolff on their recent Bibby Line ships,[624] become the template for future North Atlantic passenger ships for the remainder of the nineteenth century and beyond.

The 1870s were a time of constant technical innovation. The first steam powered ice breaker was built for the Russians in 1871; unimaginatively named ***Eisbrecher*** in German, and the first steamship specifically designed for bulk carriage of oil, the ***Vaterland,*** was built on the Tyne in 1872. A steam steering gear engine was developed in 1873 leading on to small steam engines being used for operating capstans, bilge pumps, gun turrets and hoists. Two British warships were fitted with steam-driven direct-current generators for electric arc searchlights in 1876; the same year that more ocean-going steamships were built than sailing ships. In 1879, electric arc lamps were installed in the ***City of Berlin*** for internal lighting and incandescent filament lamps installed in the Inman Line passenger liner ***City of Richmond.***[625]

Another major development in the construction of ships took place during the 1870's; the transition from iron to steel construction. 'Just as an iron ship was both lighter and stronger than a wooden vessel of the same size, steel offered the same advantages over iron; but, like iron, for years it was resisted by shipowners as too expensive, of uncertain quality, and unfamiliar and difficult to handle.'[626] Improvements in the manufacture of steel on an industrial scale were introduced during the 1850s by Bessemer (blowing air through fluid pig iron); a process improved by the Seimens-Martin technique, which resulted in improvements in the quality and a lowering of cost of steel, but, the major impediment for shipowners was the fact the by the late 1870s steel was still twice the cost of iron. However, a steel ship was 14% lighter than its iron counterpart, resulting in fuel savings, more internal volume for accommodation and cargo, and extra strength.[627] Weighing up these pros and cons, the newly established Union Steamship Company of New Zealand took the bold decision in 1879 to order the world's first all steel ship; the ***Rotomahana***, from William Denny's yard in 1879. The first all-steel Cunarder, ***Servia,*** was launched in 1881.[628]

Throughout the 1870s, ideas were also being developed on an improvement to the double expansion (compound) engine; the triple expansion steam engine, which gained more power and efficiency through the addition of a third, larger, lower pressure cylinder to the compound engine. An associated requirement, to cope with the even higher pressures of a triple expansion engine, was a boiler of adequate strength. The first triple expansion engine with water tube boilers was installed in 1873 aboard a ship owned by shipbuilder Alex Kirk; the ***Propontis***. It was not until 1881 that engine designer Robert Napier persuaded the Aberdeen Line that steel made by the Siemens process was of sufficiently high standard for the boiler that a triple expansion engine was installed in their flagship, the ***Aberdeen.***[629] The resultant considerable increase in power and savings in fuel, coupled with the benefits of steel construction, paved the way for previously unimaginable increases in the size and speed of passenger ships, on the North Atlantic in particular. The Inman Line passenger ships ***City of Paris*** and ***City of New York*** (1888); both fitted with triple expansion engines, and first ships of their type to have twin propellors, set the standard for trans-Atlantic crossings with record crossings of less than six days. Towards the end of a century of dramatic technical progress, quadruple expansion engines were fitted to four German liners.[630]

Chapter 24

Ineffective Legislation

Looking back from the mid-1880s at the effectiveness of merchant shipping legislation enacted between 1870 and 1876 it was clearly apparent that it had been ineffective. The decade from 1874 saw an overall increase in numbers of ships and seafarers lost, or missing, rather than the decrease anticipated from the many provisions enacted during this period through the Merchant Shipping, Passenger, and Chain Cable and Anchors Acts regarding safety and seaworthiness. Additionally, the Shipping Casualties Investigation Act, 1879; and the Merchant Shipping (Carriage of Grain) Act, 1880 had been enacted during this period to reinforce and improve the measures provided in the earlier Acts.

Two of 699 missing steamships, along with their crews totaling 95, were owned by the same shipping company and had both been lengthened from their original design. The ***City of London*** (1863/1869) of 2,765 tons, owned by the Thistle Line, had been launched in 1863 for the Inman Line then lengthened by 42 feet and re-engined with a compound engine in 1869. The ship departed London on 13 November 1881 with 52 crew bound for New York and sailed into 'ferocious weather of hurricane strength that caused devastation to shipping from the USA to Europe. Dozens of ships were damaged, several sunk and several others went missing' including the ***City of London***. Shortly afterwards, in January 1882, the ***City of Limerick*** (1863) of 1,550 tons, also built for the Inman Line, and bought by the Thistle Line in 1879, disappeared in the North Atlantic with 43 persons on board.

An answer to a Parliamentary question in February 1882 regarding the loss of these two ships provided more detail with the President of the Board of Trade, Mr. Chamberlain replying;

> My attention has been called to the paragraph stating that the agents of the steamship City of Limerick, 47 days out, believe she is lost. My attention has long been directed to this ship. She is, or was, an iron steamer, was lengthened and otherwise altered by Messrs. Inman, in 1870, and a spar deck added. She was sold by them in 1880 to a Mr.

Thompson, of New York. In his hands she was altered for the carriage of cattle, and a superstructure added above the spar deck. The Board of Trade were advised that after these alterations her peculiar proportions and structure rendered her an unsafe ship. A passenger certificate was refused to her, and ultimately the Board of Trade detained her at Sunderland in May last, in order to have the question of her safety determined by a Court of Survey. The owner appealed to a Court of Survey, and this Court, consisting of the Wreck Commissioner and two Assessors, after hearing the Board of Trade evidence, and without hearing the other side, pronounced her to be safe, and released her unconditionally. The owner brought an action against the Board of Trade under the Merchant Shipping Act, 1876, for having detained the ship without reasonable and probable cause. The case was tried at Liverpool before the Lord Chief Justice, and resulted in a verdict for the plaintiff, with full damages. The Board of Trade applied for a rule for a new trial, which was refused by the Divisional Court. The Board then appealed, and the Court of Appeal has granted a rule nisi, which now stands for argument. On the 8th of January last the City of Limerick left New York for London with a full crew and cargo, besides 275 head of cattle. I have inquired at Lloyd's, and she is not insured there, nor is she yet posted as "missing;" but she has not been heard of since she sailed, and it is feared she has gone to the bottom with all hands. I have communicated with the registered owner, both at Liverpool and New York, but have not yet heard from him. The City of London has not been heard of since the 14th of November, 1881, and is supposed to have been lost. I do not know, from any official records, whether the ownership or management of the City of Limerick is the same as that of the City of London. Both are lengthened ships. If any ships similar in construction to the City of Limerick are known to be sailing from ports in this country, I shall, notwithstanding the decision of the Wreck Court, and of the Assize Court already referred to, feel it my duty to order a survey upon them.[631]

An ongoing stability issue, typified by the lengthening and structural additions to the ***City of London*** and ***City of Limerick***, was heightened when a newly built steamship, the ***Daphne***, was launched in Glasgow on the 4th of July 1883 and immediately capsized with the loss of 124 out of 200 shipyard workers, many of them boys.[632] A Commission of Inquiry was appointed by the Home Secretary into the circumstances of the ***Daphne*** disaster chaired by the eminent naval architect Sir Edward Reed who stated in his report;

> I venture to add…that with the large number of ships afloat possessing so little stability as to make their safety at sea dependent upon the judicious stowage of cargo, arrangements of coal [bunkers] and use of water ballast, it would appear to be high time that some knowledge of the elements of a ship's stability was imparted to the officers of the Mercantile Marine, and required of them by the Board of Trade examiners. I must be excused for further adding that the recent legislation of Parliament has, in my opinion, been *much less efficient* in preserving life and property at sea *than it might have been* had the Board of Trade *understood and recognized* the very large extent to which this question of stability of necessity enters into the design, construction, stowage, load line, freeboard, and almost every other subject with which the Board of Trade has to deal in regulating shipping matters[633]

On the 19th of January, 1883, a collision occurred off the North Sea island of Borkum between a small British steam collier, the ***Sultan,*** and the German passenger ship ***Cimbria*** (1867) of 3,037 gross tons, resulting in the loss of the ***Cimbria,*** most of her complement of 91 crew, 401 Slovenian emigrants and a French pilot. The ***Cimbria*** had sailed from Hamburg on a cold, foggy winters morning on the 17th of January bound for New York. At 2.00am on the 19th, steaming at reduced speed in dense fog, a lookout saw a faint green light and the ship immediately altered course to port. The other ship proved to be the British collier ***Sultan*** from Hull which also altered course to port. Moments later the Sultan struck the ***Cimbria*** on her port side, cutting a deep hole into the hull. Upon immediately going astern the ***Sultan*** pulled plating off the ***Cimbria's*** hull which increased the catastrophic flooding taking place. The still navigable ***Sultan*** disappeared into the fog without coming to the aid of the doomed passenger ship, the Captain later claiming that he had no idea that the ***Cimbria,*** being the far larger ship, was so badly damaged. The ***Cimbria*** sank within fifteen minutes. Three boats were launched in this very short time with one capsizing through overcrowding. Thirty-nine passengers were later rescued from the lifeboats and a further seventeen persons from the rigging which was out of the water after the ship sank in a depth of 25 metres. Four hundred and thirty-seven souls were lost including nearly all the 72 women and 87 children aboard. The subsequent inquiry found that both ships had taken the wrong action to prevent collision by turning towards each other.[634]

The Board of Trade turned its attention at the beginning of 1884 to a question that many in the shipping industry, particularly the Board and shipowners, had long believed to be insoluble; a calculation for the location of the load line that could be universally applied to all ships. Board of Trade officers were empowered to prevent 'overladen' ships from proceeding to sea, but an absolute answer to what was an overladen ship was not available; a problem exacerbated by the legal right of the master or shipowner to site the load line on his vessels wherever he deemed appropriate. A committee of Lloyd's Register had developed a voluntary method of determining freeboard during the 1830s, known as 'Lloyd's Rule', based on three inches of freeboard per foot depth of hold. For the average merchant ship of 600 – 1400 tons, with a length five or six times longer than beam, this formula would require a freeboard of 28% of the depth of hold to prevent overloading and ensure adequate stability.[635] 'In 1882 Lloyds Register [had] published, for the benefit of those fixing freeboards, reserve buoyancy tables. These were not enforceable in law, but they had behind them an institution whose influence among the shipping community was very powerful, and whose decisions could not be lightly disregarded. Indeed, within two years the Committee assigned freeboards to no less than 1200 vessels.'[636] To re-address and solve this thorny issue, the Board of Trade established a load line committee in January, 1884, consisting of thirteen of the most eminent Government officials, professors of naval architecture, Lloyds and practical shipbuilders to consider 'whether it is now practicable to frame any general rules concerning freeboard which will prevent dangerous overloading without unduly interfering with trade…'

The Board of Trade disagreed with Lloyd's recent reserve buoyancy tables, which were made available to the committee, but after a 'long and patient inquiry' a solution was reached. The committee reported to the President of the Board of Trade that;

1. We are of opinion that it is now practicable to frame general rules concerning freeboard, which will prevent overloading without unduly interfering with the trade

2. We have the pleasure to submit herewith tables which we consider

should be adopted

3. They would be available to all existing types of cargo vessels, and for some years to come.

The committee cautiously added that 'if rigidly applied to some cases that might arise' such as new types of ship not presently inexistence, or perhaps not contemplated by Lloyds and other classification societies, which would have to be dealt with on their merits...'injustice might be done'. When legislation was finally enacted in 1890 to introduce rules regarding freeboard such special cases were to be left to the discretion of the Board of Trade. The committee's new freeboard rules were accepted by the Board of Trade and introduced as guidance in 1886.

The Board of Trade's response to the grim statistics of lost ships and seafarers was to introduce a Bill on the second day of the 1884 Session 'to provide for the greater security of life and property at sea'. The Merchant Shipping Bill (No.1) was introduced, read for the first time and distributed to Members on the 23rd of February.[637] The Bill had two main thrusts; unseaworthiness and, the long dormant Maritime Contracts Bill regarding over insurance. In moving that the second reading take place on the 23rd of May, Chamberlain explained; "the main principle of this Bill... is that it is a wrong, an inexpedient, and an immoral thing that a man should be able to make a profit out of the loss of his ship, with the lives he has in his charge..." He went on to remind Members of the exact words of the current Leader of the Opposition who was entrusted with leading the introduction of the Maritime Contracts Bill in 1876;

> ...there has long prevailed in this country and elsewhere a system of insurance, the effect of which is that if a man partially insures his ship he mitigates his loss; if he wholly insures her he covers his loss; and if he over-insures her it is possible that his loss may become his gain. Therefore, unless proper attention is paid to this subject, and care is taken to prevent, as far as possible, the over-insurance of ships, it is possible that a system most excellent in its intentions, most valuable in its working, may be the cause of great abuse and evil...God forbid that I should impute to shipowners as a class, or, indeed, to any man, that he would deliberately send his ship to sea overvalued, in the hope that she may be lost; but I would point out that this practice of over-

> valuation exposes shipowners to very great temptation. And not only has it that effect, but it produces on seamen and the public at large an unsatisfactory feeling—namely, that the loss of a ship may be an actual gain to her owner—a feeling which cannot be at all good for the service. It cannot be satisfactory that that which is loss of life and property to a great mass of the population should be not only no loss, but a subject of gain, to any one class of that population.

Chamberlain supported his allegations of over insurance by quoting statistics of ships lost by certain shipowners present at a stormy public meeting he attended in Birmingham; "...Of the 59 picked men present 49 were shipowners in their own names, others were shipowners not registered in their own names, and many held shares in Shipping Companies... I have looked up the matter, and I find that in the last five years these 49 owners, who, it must be remembered, were picked men, have lost 65 ships and 367 lives; and that, of the 49, nine alone have lost 36 ships and 177 lives". Referring to another public meeting in Liverpool, Chamberlain went to the extent of naming "a certain Captain Hatfield who expressed violent opposition to the Bill, as having since 1877, in less than seven years, owned 12 ships, and in the course of that time lost 11 of them".

Chamberlain demonstrated that loss of life at sea had been increasing by quoting statistics from the previous twelve years from Wreck Returns. These reported that the total loss of life was 9,314 in the first three years; in the next there was a slight falling off to 9,181; in the third period the total was 7,612; but in the last three years 9,553; the highest figure in the series. The reduction in fatalities in the third period was explained as being due to following; "...almost immediately on the Plimsoll agitation; and although I do not myself think the legislation of that time can be said to have produced any very great result, yet I think that the attention which was called to the matter, and the self-examination of shipowners themselves in view of the agitation going on around them, had a very advantageous effect in diminishing the loss of life". Figures from the most recent return, 1883, showed the loss of 3,304 lives, more than in any previous year of the series, excepting 1872, 1874, and 1881. Summarising, Chamberlain stated that; "during those 12 years 36,000 men suffered violent deaths; and of the whole number one in six lost his life; ...one in six of the average number employed of every man, every boy, every officer, and every seaman, lost his life in the British Merchant Service. Go on, and carry that a step further. If you assume that the average working life of the seaman is 24 years, then you will find that one in every three will, in the course of his working life, perish by a violent and dreadful death".[638]

A later study showed that the fatality rate from work-related accidents in British merchant ships between 1875 to 1883 was 1,367 per 100,000 seafarer-years at risk, or one in 73 deaths from accidents per year, with a higher rate for those serving on sailing ships; about one in 40. Crew berthed forward were at higher risk of death from collision. At this time the fatal accident rate in merchant ships was 'six times greater than that in coal mining, 10 times higher than for railway workers and ◎150 times that for factory and shop operatives. The major cause of the excess mortality among the seafarers—55% of 26,188 deaths—was disasters involving the ships rather than individual accidents affecting the seafarers'.[639] The causative factors for this unexpected and unprecedented increase in losses of ships and seafarers were not clear. Many of the missing ships were proven to be steamships carrying cargoes of bulk wheat or coal; issues that had been attended to by measures enacted to prevent cargoes of bulk wheat from shifting and the Commission on Carriage of Coal. Chamberlain reported that, regarding seafarers lost in other countries, the Foreign Office had obtained figures showing that; "in Italy, for five years past, the loss of life was one in 454 of the seamen employed; in the Netherlands, one in 232; in Norway, during a period of eight years, one in 277; and in Germany, the worst case I could find, one in 123 on an average of five years".[640]

Referring to the cause of losses and culpability of shipowners, Chamberlain advised the House that Mr. Rothery, Wreck Commissioner, "had presented a Report which has examined into all the cases which have come before him since his appointment as Wreck Commissioner, and he has made an analysis and given the result, which has been laid before the House. He says, in the course of his Report, February 22, 1884, in connection with strandings and collisions";

> We also find, on examining the Returns more closely, that in cases of stranding or collision the fault, as might naturally be expected, rests in general either with the master or with some person on hoard the vessel; but even in these cases the owner is not always entirely free

> from blame. The casualty may have been due to her having been sent to sea in an unseaworthy condition, or badly equipped, or with an insufficient crew, or without proper charts; and, in these cases, the owner must bear his share of the responsibility. Again, in many of these cases, the casualty may have been due to the expressed or implied instruction of the owner that the master should make a quick passage; for I find, in a great number of these cases, the casualty is due to reckless navigation, arising either from the vessel having been run at too great a speed on a dark night or in a fog, or from the unwillingness of the master to lose time by stopping his vessel to take a cast of the lead, even though in entire ignorance of his true position.[641]

Some notable shipowners gave their opinions on the principal causes of losses of ships. The manager of the British India Steam Navigation Company; -"I am myself fully persuaded that a very large proportion of the losses at sea are preventable. The chief causes of the disasters are overloading, under-manning, and over-insuring". Mr. James Harrison, a well-known shipowner of Liverpool; "...this terrible loss of life through foundering, &c. is, to a very large extent, a preventable loss". The Managing Director of the Glen Line, pointed to under-manning as an evil only in degree less than that of unfair loading, and called attention to over-insurance as a question of paramount importance. A shipowner at Leith observed; "...vessels going to sea out at Shields laden down to the gunwale. Instead of going across the Atlantic he would not go to London in them. Neither the lives of those on board nor the thought of desolate homes affected the cupidity of such owners".

Chamberlain then turned to the failure of existing legislation, admitting that it had not succeeded due to having proceeded on wrong methods and principles. Firstly, giving power to the Board of Trade to detain ships which their officers determined to be unseaworthy; and secondly, endeavouring to fix criminal liability upon shipowners proven to have been in default in respect of precautions which they ought to have taken. With regard to the first point; 832 ships had been detained since 1876 on various grounds; with only 13 having been released unconditionally. Secondly; "...we have also endeavoured by legislation to fix criminal liability upon the owners. This has failed in practice, and no recent prosecution has succeeded..." He quoted a very experienced lawyer as stating that ...the present law says to the shipowner – 'Buy your ship as cheaply as you can, equip her as poorly as you can, load her as fully as you can, insure her as highly as you can, and send her to sea. If she gets to the end of her voyage you will have made a very good thing of it; if she goes to the bottom you will have made a very much better thing of it'.

Chamberlain also explained, what was to him, an extremely important feature of the proposed Bill, the application of the Employers' Liability Act to seamen. This Act gave *employees* compensation, under certain limitations, for all damage, or injury, or loss of life arising from the negligence of the employer, or defective equipment of his works, or the defective condition of his machinery. It also prevented the employer from pleading the doctrine of common employment, under limitations, where the accident arose from the negligence of some person in authority, who might be called a servant. The proposed clauses, 22 to 26, would apply precisely the same law to seafarers, with one exception; it would not apply to officers as well as seamen as persons in authority were expressly excluded. Shipowners had pointed out that their supervision was less direct than on the land, and they urged that in particular classes of cases, as, for instance, stranding, or collision which arise from errors of navigation on the part of officers or seamen, that they ought not to be held liable. Chamberlain concurred with this view and agreed to add a proviso to the clause which would exempt cases of error of navigation from the causes of accidents which are to involve liability.

Chamberlain summarized the intent of the Bill as simply being; "…that the insured person shall not gain by the loss of the thing insured" and was not dismissive of the suggestion by a Member that;

> … the whole question of Merchant Shipping be put before a Royal Commission. That will enable hon. Members representing shipowners, or anybody else concerned, to attack the Board of Trade to their heart's content; and if, after the statement I have made tonight, there remains in the mind of any shipowner the idea that he has been wrongfully charged, that I have brought against his class anything which he can justly resent, let that also be brought before the Royal Commission, by whom, as I have already said, I am perfectly prepared that the whole matter shall be fully and carefully considered… [642]

Following the adjourned debate on the second reading there were frequent questions in the House as to when there would be further consideration of the Maritime Contracts Bill, and whether it should go to a Select Committee, a Grand Committee or a Royal Commission. The matter was still unresolved on the 30th of June when an Order for resuming Adjourned Debate on Amendment on Second Reading [19th May] was read. The opening speaker was concerned about rumours that that the Government did not intend to proceed further with the Bill; '...and if they had arrived at that conclusion it was time they should take the House into their confidence, and not hang up such important interests as those which were concerned. If they had made up their minds and intended to proceed with, it no further, the sooner it was taken off the Paper the better'. [643] A few days later Chamberlain admitted defeat, claiming that although he had support for the amended Bill from London and Liverpool shipowners, their colleagues in North-eastern ports and on the Clyde were implacably opposed. Lacking this support and recognizing the lack of time for the very complex Bill to go through its necessary stages he; "reluctantly came to the conclusion that the Bill must be withdrawn, and when on Monday it comes on I shall move that the Order be discharged". He had not, however, ruled out the possibility of a Royal Commission stating that it; "is a matter which will have the immediate attention of the Government, and at a later stage I hope to be able to state the intentions of the Government".[644]

On the 7th of July 1884 the Merchant Shipping Bill (No.1) was withdrawn. When asked by a member; "...whether he is still of opinion that the present state of the Law occasions a preventable loss of life, he will take care that competent officials of the Board of Trade carry out to the letter their duties, with a view to preventing unseaworthy or overladen ships leaving our ports?"; Chamberlain resignedly replied; "I have to say that the officials of the Board of Trade will continue to carry out their arduous duties to the best of their abilities; but I have already given my reasons, in the debate upon the second reading of the Merchant Shipping Bill, for thinking that it is impossible for them to exercise such a supervision as would effectually prevent unseaworthy or overladen ships from leaving our ports".[645] Many portions of it were dealt with in the following years, but little alteration in the mode of insurance has been achieved; neither has the Employers' Liability Act been extended to seamen.[646]

On the 24th of October Chamberlain advised the House that the names of the Commissioners for the Royal Commission on the Saving of Life at Sea had been submitted to Her Majesty and approved of, and he hoped that the names of the Commissioners and the terms of the Reference will be gazetted in the course of the next day or two. The Commission would include the functions and administration of the Marine Department of the Board of Trade.

Chapter 25

Saving of Life at Sea Commission

The terms of reference of the Royal Commission on the Saving of Life at Sea, granted at the end of 1884, required the Commissioners to;

> Inquire into the extent and cause of the loss of ships and lives at sea since the Report of the Royal Commission on Unseaworthy Ships, and to report on the remedies for such losses, having special but not exclusive regard to the following subjects, viz,:-
>
> The laws concerning marine insurance and the liability of the ship-owners;
>
> The functions and administration of the Marine department of the Board of Trade;
>
> The functions of the Courts before whom wreck inquiries are conducted; and
>
> The condition and efficiency of merchant marine officers and seamen, and the best means of improving same.

The Royal Commission issued a summary of the evidence taken during 1885, but without any recommendations, as the hearings were not finished. Parliament had been dissolved in November and the old Commission was superseded by a new one, chaired by Mr. Shaw Lefevre. The Commission continued its work throughout 1886, with its final report being released on the 27th of August 1887. Their review of recent Merchant Shipping legislation led them to the conclusion;

> ...When we look at the general results of the legislation thus referred to, upon the loss of life and property at sea in British vessels, it is most unsatisfactory to find that no sensible effect has been produced in reduction of their loss. From the returns laid before this Commission by the Board of Trade, the substantial accuracy of which has not been questioned, it appears that from 1874 to 1883 inclusively, there was a

> marked increase in the losses of British ships, and of the lives of those employed in them... The most serious losses occurred in respect of vessels (excluding fishing vessels) reported as missing. No less than 699 vessels, with 8475 hands on board, were reported as missing during this period of nine years, the cause of whose loss was unknown.

In spite of the Permanent Secretary of the Board of Trade, Thomas Gray, who compiled the wreck reports disagreeing with the Commission's calculations as to the number of seamen employed; as did shipowners, the Commission stood by its findings; '...but, whichever method of comparison be taken, the proportion of deaths by drowning of seamen was very high, and had undoubtedly increased during the period under consideration –viz., from 1 in 81 in 1875, to 1 in 56 in 1883...'. A vastly experienced master mariner, shipowner and Member of Parliament commented; '...To outside observers there is no reason to suppose that Mr. Gray was actuated by malice towards the shipowners, and that he wished to exaggerate the truth; whereas it is very evident from the course of the evidence that, by every device possible, they endeavoured to minimize the truth, and to show that the ordinary perils of the sea alone were responsible for the loss, and not, as was alleged from preventable causes'.[647] The report also made particular mention of the numbers of seafarers who had been saved from shipwreck for the nine years ending 30 June 1883; '...no less than 96,494 lives were saved at home and abroad, chiefly by lifeboats, rocket apparatus, ships' boats etc'.[648]

The Commission on the Saving of Life at Sea had initially considered statistics included in the annual wreck reports produced by the Board of Trade that showed a steady increase in serious casualties to steamships; from 406 in 1877 to 656 in 1883 -1884; or more than 50 per cent. The loss of life in 1883-1884 was 2245; less than the preceding year but above the average of the preceding seven years. The number of ships missing during the 1883-1884 period was 121 of which 109 were sailing ships with a loss of 1044 lives, and 12 steamships with 238 lives, including a total of 197 passengers lost aboard missing sailing ships and steamers.[649] When statistics became available during the long duration of the Commission's activities it was shown that loss of life at sea actually lessened during the three year period from 1884-1886; from 1181 in 1884, to 1190 in 1885 and 1067 in 1886; a reduction of 42% from the average of the preceding three years. Thomas

Gray believed that there were three reasons for this; comparatively favourable weather over the period; an almost general decrease in the value of ships in insurance policies, and the close attention paid to overloading and general seaworthiness by both shipowners and the Board of Trade. The Commission concluded;

> To whatever cause this diminution of loss of life during the years 1884 – 1886 may be due, it cannot be contended that it was in any way the result of the legislation of 1875-6; and the fact remains indisputable that, in spite of all the provisions made by Parliament, and the great increase in the staff of the Board of Trade, entailing a very large charge upon the country, there was not only no diminution in the loss of life at sea in merchant vessels in the years following upon this legislation, and up to the year 1883, but a considerable increase

Regarding the increased annual cost for Board of Trade officials to determine the seaworthiness of vessels; from £12,000 to £50,000, the Commission dealt with the question of whether this had been value for money. '…The action of the surveyors led to the breaking up of a considerable number of vessels of the lowest grade…if these vessels had not been interfered with, it might have been that the loss of life would have been greater even than it proved to be…On the other hand, it is equally clear that the surveyors of the Board of Trade were unable to prevent a large number from going to sea in a state which undoubtedly contributed to, if it was not the immediate cause of, disaster and loss'.

Many shipowners presented their long-held view at hearings that the fault for loss of their ships lay with their Masters and officers; a fact they claimed to have no control over. The Commissioners took qualified heed of these views, while at the same time justly criticizing shipowners, in concluding;

> Of all the vessels lost by strandings and by collisions, it is undoubtedly the fact that a very great number were due to the misconduct, or neglect, or error of judgement, of the officers or persons in charge of the ships; and we are satisfied that in a large proportion of these cases the loss was due not to mere error of judgement, but to the neglect by the master or officers of the most ordinary rules and requirements of navigation. We notice habitual neglect of the use of the lead, and omission to slacken speed in fog. We think, however, owners may do

> much to prevent this class of accident by a careful selection of officers, and by insisting on the strict observance of recognized rules and precautions, especially as masters undoubtedly feel the pressure of the demand for quick passages, We also think that the neglect of the lead is sometimes attributable to an insufficient number of hands in the watches, and that this also sometimes affects the character of the steering and look-out, and thus has a bearing upon both strandings and collisions.

The Report recognized the difficulty of legislating to bring home responsibility to shipowners, in that; '...the very important provision of the Act of 1876, which made it a misdemeanor for the owner or manager to send a ship to sea in an unseaworthy condition, in consequence of the legal and other difficulties attending its enforcement, have been such that it has almost become a dead letter...the alternative produced by the Acts of 1875-6, viz., that by which the Board of Trade is empowered to detain vessels which are unseaworthy, and to prevent them from going to sea, is attended with the utmost difficulty, and in practice has proved inefficacious...we do not see that any good results can be got from the extension of the system of surveys and from the increase of power of detention...it would almost necessarily result either in the surveys becoming mere formalities, as in the case of France, or in the management of ships and everything connected with them being transferred from the owners to Government officials...it would tend still more to level down, than to level up, the average condition of vessels'.

With regard to the standard of officers and men the Commission was; '... unable to come to the conclusion that there was any just foundation for the allegations that British seamen have deteriorated in quality...in view of the facts of the case we are unable to advise any interference by law with the employment of foreign seamen...it is almost universally admitted by the witnesses that these men from the north of Europe are excellent seamen'. The Commission did not recommend returning to the system of compulsory apprenticeship which had abandoned 'owing to the abuses it had given rise to'. They recommended; '...a simple professional examination should be required for the ratings of carpenter and boatswain and that seamen with the rating of A.B. should be required to have continuous records of their service'. One commentator observed that; '...the meagerness of the result of two and a half years inquiry will undoubtedly be apparent...it seems a miserable and unsatisfactory compromise of the truth. Nevertheless, some good resulted, for it set many of our shipping authorities, naval architects, and others upon the alert'.[650]

There was no doubt at the time that there were significant problems with the design of steamships and the carriage of grain and coal cargoes. Scientific evidence of these issues was available during the course of the Royal Commission. A paper was presented to a meeting of naval architects in the autumn of 1886 on 'Losses at Sea in 1881 to 1885', in which a Professor Elgar had 'treated the question very exhaustively, and accompanied it by a set of admirable drawings and tables'. He determined that the majority of the missing vessels were of the 'most modern building and type' and carrying cargoes of grain or coal. His conclusion was that they foundered from the cargo shifting, or, especially in the case of steamers of the then fashionably narrow-beamed three deck type, from absolute lack of stability. Another paper in the spring of 1887 by a Professor Jenkins; 'On the Shifting of Cargoes', considered the action of various cargoes under stress of weather and rolling and heeling motions and concluded that coal and grain cargoes would undoubtedly shift, stating that;

> Notwithstanding the enforcement of the stringent regulations of the Grain Acts of 1876 and 1880...the annual loss of life continues to be very large. During the three years ending 1877, 93 grain-laden British ships foundered or were missing, the number of lives lost being 833. In the next three years the number of vessels so lost rose to 111 and the lives to 946; but in the next triennial period, during the whole of which the Carriage of Grain Cargoes Act (1880) was in force, the numbers were reduced to 74 ships and 854 lives'.

He then considered the dangers associated with carriage of coal cargoes, which, unlike grain were subject to no restriction, but; '...statistics appear to show that they need it quite as much. During the three years ending 1877, 200 coal-laden British vessels foundered or were missing and with them were lost 991 lives. During the following three years the number of vessels so lost fell to 184 and the lives lost to 912; but in the triennial period ending 1883 the number of vessels rose to of 314, and the lives [lost] reached the melancholy total of 1849, or more than twice as many as were lost during the same period from grain-laden vessels...The subject is one that has no doubt received the attention of the Royal Commission now sitting on 'Loss of Life at Sea' and it is to be hoped that that body will not fail to recommend some plan under which the annual loss of life resulting from shifting of cargoes will become much reduced'.

This hope was not fulfilled. The narrow scope of their terms of reference did not include such matters and the general outcome of their inquiry was the Life-Saving Appliances Act, 1888, which 'did not touch the root of all evil, but only makes provision for the saving of life when accidents do occur'.[651]

In despair, Blackmore commented; "...The coal is literally poured into the ships from shoots and staithes, and the moment the lading is finished the vessel is hustled off to sea, neither the owner, master, or charterer taking the least care of proper trimming or stowage, each party trying the throw the blame on the other, and so between them valuable lives are lost, the master sacrificing his own with those of the crew. As Admiral De Horsey remarked, 'With unskilled stevedores, and fully insured ships and cargoes, the safety of the ship appears to be a matter of secondary importance', and there can be no doubt that morally the possibility of full insurance of ship and cargo is, notwithstanding all the owners may say against it, a very important and undeniable cause of loss of life. The false competition of managing owners makes it imperative to save expense in the treatment and loading of cargoes, and although their great outcry is for seamen to command their ships, seamen are useless to prevent this dangerous practice of taking ships to sea improperly stowed, and all their experience stands for nought as against this cruel saving of expense".[652]

A novel approach was taken by Parliament when considering the Merchant Shipping (Life Saving Appliances) Bill in 1888. The report of the select committee on saving life at sea recommended that a standing committee, representing all parties interested, be appointed to frame rules for carrying out the provisions of the resultant Act; the Merchant Shipping (Life Saving Appliances) Act, 1888.[653] The Act, accordingly, provided for a comprehensive committee of fifteen members namely; three shipowners selected by the Council of the Chamber of Commerce; one shipowner by the Owners' Association of Glasgow and one each selected by the Liverpool Steam Shipowners' Association and the Liverpool Shipowners' Association. Two shipbuilders to be selected by the Council of the Institution of Naval Architects;

three persons practically acquainted with the navigation of vessels selected by the Shipmasters' Societies recognized by the President of the Board of Trade; three persons being, or having been, able-bodied seamen, selected by Seamen's Societies similarly recognized and two persons selected by the Committee of Lloyd's along with the Committees of Lloyds Register Society and the Committee of the Institute of London Underwriters. All the members of the resultant Life Saving Appliances Committee were to hold office for two years and to be eligible for re-appointment.

The Committee's duties, as prescribed in the Act, were to be; firstly, the arranging of British ships into classes having regard to the services in which they are employed, the nature of the voyage, and the number of persons carried; secondly, the number and description of the boats, lifeboats, rafts, life-belts and life-buoys, to be carried by each class, with their equipment, means of putting into the water, and thirdly; the quantity and quality of buoyant apparatus to be carried in addition to, or in lieu of, boats, rafts, jackets, or buoys. The Committee was established in November, 1888, and submitted its work to the Board of Trade in April, 1889.

The Committee initially divided all shipping into six classes, numbered from one to six. These classes were again divided into subdivisions lettered A and B, and in one case C. The first class comprised vessels carrying emigrants subject to all conditions of the "Passenger Acts;" subdivision A being steamers, and B sailing ships.

Class 2, similarly subdivided, comprised foreign going and sailing ships carrying passengers. Class 3 included steamers and sailing ships not certified for carrying passengers. Class 4. included A, steam-ships certified for carrying passengers anywhere in the home trade limits; i.e., anywhere in the United Kingdom, or between the United Kingdom and ports in Europe between the river Elbe and Brest, B, steam-ships in the same trade not certified for passengers, and C, sailing ships in the same trade not carrying passengers.

Class 6, included steamers carrying passengers on short excursions or pleasure trips to sea, or in estuaries or mouths of rivers during daylight, or across the Straits of Dover with Class 7 including steamers carrying passengers on rivers or lakes, but not going to sea or into rough waters.

The general rules under these categories classified the different boats to be carried, the method for calculating their cubical contents, the numbers of persons each was deemed fit to carry, the appliances for putting the boats under davits into the water, the equipment each boat was required to carry, the number of people that life-rafts were deemed capable of carrying, also the capacity of and the rules for testing other buoyant apparatus, life-belts and lifebuoys, and the stowage of life-belts and buoys.

The number of boats to be carried were divided into five classes, lettered from A to E. 'A' signified a life-boat with extra buoyancy by air-cases equal to nearly its cubical contents and placed inside the boat. 'B'; a life-boat with the same extra buoyancy, at least one-half of which must be attached to the outside of the boat. 'C' was styled a life-boat, but was required to have only one half of the additional buoyancy prescribed for 'A' and 'B', which could be inside or outside the boat, provided at least one-half is outside. 'D' was an ordinary ship's boat without any additional buoyancy, and 'E', a collapsible boat of an approved pattern. The number of persons each boat was to carry was calculated by finding the boat's cubical contents by a simple rule given, and dividing that amount by ten in the case of boats coming under class 'A', and by eight in those under classes 'B', 'C', 'D' and 'E'.

Then followed clear and precise rules for fitting the boats' davits and lowering gear, also the outfit or equipment for each boat. The equipment was divided into two parts; 1st, that which is compulsory in all boats, and comprised oars, thole pins or crutches, two plugs for each plug-hole, a sea anchor, a baler, rudder and tiller or yoke, a boat-hook, and a vessel to be kept filled with fresh water for each boat. The 2nd or additional equipment for boats of classes 'A' and 'B', comprised two hatchets or tomahawks, mast or masts with at least one good sail, and proper gear for each, a lifeline in loops round the boat outside, an efficient compass, one gallon, of oil in a vessel of approved pattern for distributing it in the water in rough weather, and a lantern ready trimmed to burn for eight hours.

The following shows the tonnage divisions, number-of boats under davits required to be carried by vessels of different sizes, and the average number of persons they were computed to carry. The number of persons was an average as it varied by the reason of the option being given of carrying 'A' or 'B' boats, the former of being allotted one-tenth of their cubical contents, and the latter one-eighth per man.

Figures refer to; (gross tonnage – number of boats required to be carried – total capacity of persons carried by boats) i.e. (9,000 -14 – 620), (8,000 – 14 – 580), (7,000 -12 – 530), (6,000 -12 – 470), (5,000 – 10 – 420), (4,000 – 8 – 340), (3,000 – 8 – 280), (2,000 – 6 – 210), (1,000 – 4 – 130), (500 – 4 – 90), (100 – 2 -33).

All steamers in the various classes carrying passengers were required to comply absolutely with the above requirements, and if the boats required to be carried were not enough to carry all the people on board the ship had to carry '…additional wood, metal, collapsible, or other boats or life-rafts, all of approved pattern, as conveniently placed for putting into the water as the ship's arrangements admit of'. If necessary to provide for all on board, these additional boats had to equal in cubical capacity those under davits. Ships were also obliged to carry a life-buoy for each boat under davits, and a life-belt of approved pattern for each person in the ship. Sailing ships carrying passengers had to possess the same amount of boat accommodation as steamers, except where they could not be placed under davits they were to be carried so that they could easily be got into the water to the satisfaction of a Board of Trade officer. Steamers (foreign going) not carrying passengers were required to carry, on each side, sufficient boats to accommodate all persons on board, one of which was to be a life-boat.

Sailing ships (foreign going) not carrying passengers were required to carry boats enough for all on board up to the conditions of the Table, and one additional good serviceable boat of class 'D'. Steamers carrying passengers within Home Trade limits were required to carry the same boat accommodation as other passenger steamers; but when it was not practicable for them to carry the additional boats or life-rafts, they had to substitute buoyant deck seats or other fittings of an approved pattern. Steamers in the home trade not carrying passengers came under the same conditions as similar vessels in the foreign trade. Sailing vessels in the home trade had to carry sufficient boats for all on board, and each boat had to be provided with one gallon of oil for distributing in the water in rough weather. The conditions for steamers carrying passengers from one part of the United Kingdom to another, and steamers carrying passengers on short excursions to sea by daylight, or across the Straits of Dover, were similar to those for other passenger steamers.

In addition to the above requirements for boats, every vessel was required to carry a sufficient number of life-buoys and an approved life-belt or other similar approved article of equal buoyancy suitable for being worn on the person for every person on board. All life-buoys and life-belts had to be so placed as to be readily accessible to the persons on board, and so that their position was known to those for whom they are intended. [654]

With hindsight, it's surprising that the widely experienced members of the Life Saving Appliances Committee settled upon a figure of 9,000 gross tons and upwards as being the maximum parameter for carriage of lifeboats. This tonnage had already been exceeded when Committee was drafting the rules by the launching of the ***City of New York*** in March 1888, followed by her sister-ship the ***City of Paris*** in November, 1888. Each ship was of 10,699 gross tons and capable of carrying 1,740 passengers along with 362 crew for a total complement of 2,102 persons. According to the proposed rules, these ships would be required to carry 14 lifeboats under davits capable of carrying 620 persons, with the remaining 1,482 persons being dependent upon 'wood, metal, collapsible, or other boats or life-rafts, all of approved pattern, as conveniently placed for putting into the water as the ship's arrangements admit of'. White Star Line had launched the ***Teutonic*** and ***Majestic***, each of 9,984 gross tons in 1889, with passenger capacities of 1,498; the first British trans-Atlantic liners to dispense with yards and sails due to the reliability of separate engine rooms driving twin propellers.

The Life Saving Appliances Committee's report, submitting the rules, contained a postscript calling attention to a matter outside the scope of their terms of reference; the question of any necessity for watertight bulkheads;

> We have shown some appreciation of the importance of efficient subdivision of ships in Class I, Division (AX paragraph (g) of these rules, but we consider it our duty to further express our sense of the importance of the question, and to recommend that it should be investigated by a committee of duly qualified persons, the subject as a whole, having been held to be outside the scope of the reference to this Committee." With this view we entirely agree, and have only to remind our readers of the frequently recurring great loss of life through the immediate sinking of iron vessels after collision. Amongst others, we may mention the Kapunda, with her 311 souls on board, of which 296 perished on a fine night off the coast of Brazil, whilst the colliding ship, if we mistake not, kept afloat for many hours. It is true that if the

> new rules respecting ships' boats had then been in force and carried out on board the colliding ship, her boats would have been in the water much sooner than they were, and doubtless would have saved many of the unfortunate passengers of the ill-fated Kapunda; but the collision was so sudden and so destructive that the vessel sank almost immediately, and we very much doubt, however well-prepared the Kapunda's boats might have been, whether time and circumstances would have admitted of their being taken advantage of as a means of rescue; but if she had had efficient watertight bulkheads so placed as to provide for her floating with any two compartments (to use the words of the Committee) " in free communication with the sea," the loss of life must have been very much smaller. Another casualty, in which the loss of life was probably greatly increased by the same cause, was the loss of the large steamer belonging to the Glen line, which during the past winter was run into and sunk, with all hands, not far from Dungeness, No one having been saved, this is to a certain extent conjecture, but reasonable conjecture, because, if she had not sunk immediately, one or more boats from a large and well-found steamer must surely have succeeded in getting away. That the dividing bulkheads, even when put in, may prove a delusion in the hour of need, unless their construction is closely watched, seems also to be pointed at by the circumstances attending the loss of H.M.S. Sultan, when a large quantity of water certainly found its way into compartments other than those injured by the rocks she struck on. The composition of this Committee gives the greater force to their recommendations from the fact that they could not but be alive to the point that any action in this direction would tend to increase the expense of shipbuilding, besides possibly interfering with the facilities for loading, unloading and carrying cargo, and therefore add to the charges laid upon the British shipowner, which are already considered onerous enough, and will be increased in some cases by the rules under consideration.[655]

It will be recalled that the requirement s.300 of the Merchant Shipping Act, 1854 for all iron ships to be subdivided into three equal parts by watertight partitions had been repealed through the Merchant Shipping Act, 1862. However, the Board of Trade considered the Life Saving Appliances Committee's views on watertight bulkheads and commissioned an investigation into the matter of watertight bulkheads by a separate committee; the Bulkhead Committee, appointed for a two year renewable term. The terms of reference of the committee are indicative of the Board's increasing awareness of the importance of properly designed and installed watertight bulkheads and their contribution to safety of life at sea;

> To be a Committee to consider and report upon the following matters, viz.: -
>
> 1. As to the manner in which ships shall be subdivided so that they may float in moderate weather with any two compartments in free connection with the sea, and what Rule there should be as to the proportion of freeboard of the watertight deck next above to which such bulkheads are attached, as shall be sufficient to enable the ship so to float.
>
> 2. As to the description of ship to which such should apply, in regard to size, or what difference, if any, as between Paddle or screw Steamers, or sailing Ships or as to Ocean Voyagers, or Cross-Channel Steamers.
>
> 3. Upon the construction and fitting of watertight bulkheads with a view to their being able to sustain the necessary strain, particularly when the ship is rising and falling in a seaway, without shoring or other adventitious aid, should it so happen that two adjoining compartments are in free communication with the sea, regard being given to the support of any 'tween decks abutting thereto.
>
> 4. In what manner the surveyors of the Board of Trade can best determine the sufficiency of such Bulkheads.
>
> 5. Under what restrictions may passageways be permitted through such bulkheads as closable by portable plates, or so-called watertight doors, self-acting or otherwise, and what precautions are necessary as to openings in longitudinal bulkheads, to enable the water to pass freely or under control from one side to the other in case of the ship showing signs of instability, as might readily be the case should she be struck on a transverse bulkhead, and two compartments, both on one side, be in free communication with the sea.
>
> 6. Whether a transverse compartment divided into two by a longitudinal bulkhead should be treated as one or two compartments.

7. What particulars, drawings, and calculations should be furnished by the owners of ships to the Board of Trade when they desire to take advantage of the following paragraph in the Rules made under the Merchant Shipping (Life-saving Appliances.) Act, 1888 (51 and 52 Vict., cap. 24.): -

(13.)Watertight Compartments.

When ships are divided into efficient watertight compartments, so that, with any two of them in free communication with the sea, the ship will remain afloat in moderate weather, they shall only be required to carry additional boats or life-rafts of one-half of the capacity required by Paragraph (f.), Class 1, Division A, of these Rules.

8. Whether, independently of the precise requirements of the fore-going paragraph the Committee have any recommendations to make with reference to bulkheads which would, in their opinion, contribute to the safety of life at sea.

(Signed.) M. E. Hicks-Beach.

The Bulkhead Committee produced a comprehensive technical report which became the standard for Board of Trade surveyors when deciding whether the watertight bulkheads voluntarily fitted to a ship were 'efficient' and 'to their satisfaction', as detailed in paragraph 4 of the report;

The surveyors of the Board of Trade may accept the designs and scant-lings contemplated in the tables above referred to as a standard of sufficiency, but other modes of construction may be allowed provided that it be shown to the satisfaction of the Board of Trade that the strength will not be less than it would have been if the bulkheads had been constructed as in Appendix B. In all cases regard is to be had to any collateral support given by decks, partial decks, longitudinal bulkheads, bunkers, etc.

Paragraph eight, dealt with conflation by the Board of Trade of approved watertight bulkheads and benefits to shipowners of reduced additional boats and life rafts to that required by General Rule 13;

Having regard to the great additional safeguard which such subdivision as we recommend would provide against loss not only by collision or stranding, but also by fire, we would suggest that the Board of Trade might well offer a larger concession than that mentioned in Section 7 of the Reference to this Committee, as an inducement to owners to subdivide their vessels to the extent that we have indicated under the several grades. We therefore submit that in such case owners might be relieved of the obligation to carry any part of the additional boats, rafts, and other life-saving appliances required by the Rules issued by the Board of Trade under the Merchant Shipping (Life Saving Appliances) Act, 1888.

The Board of Trade amended their draft General Rule Number 12; effective from the 1st of November 1890, but were not so bold as to completely accept the Bulkhead Committee's suggestion that no additional boats and rafts would be required; reducing the existing requirement from three-quarters to half as suggested in their terms of reference;

Watertight compartments.—When ships of any class are divided into efficient compartments to the satisfaction of the Board of Trade they shall only be required to carry additional boats, rafts, and other life-saving appliances of one half of the capacity required by these Rules

In a reply to a question in the House that expressed; '…serious concern at the inconvenience to shipowners through the uncertainty with regard to the Rule 12...' the President of the Board of Trade in February, 1891 explained that; '….The Board of Trade are not in a position to arrive at a decision with regard to this Rule until they receive the Report of the Bulkheads Committee appointed to inquire into the matter. This, I hope, will be about the end of next month…'[656]

The report of the Bulkhead Committee, received by the Board of Trade in June, 1891, advised the Board that;

Vessels may be considered able to float in moderate weather with any two adjacent compartments in free communication with the sea, if fitted with efficient transverse water tight bulkheads, so spaced that when two such compartments are laid open to the sea the uppermost watertight deck to which all bulkheads extend and which we shall call the bulkhead deck, is not brought nearer to the water surface than would be indicated by a line drawn around the side as a distance amidships of 3/100ths of the depth at the side at that place below the bulkhead deck, and gradually approaching it towards the ends, where it may be 2/100ths of the same depth below it. This line we call the margin-of-safety line.

The Board of Trade did not provide any regulations to enforce such requirements but depended upon the report of the Bulkhead Committee for guidance to surveyors and classification societies as to interpretation of the standard. Questions were still being asked in Parliament a year later as to; '…whether Her Majesty's Government intend to take any, and what, steps to carry out the recommendations contained in the Report of the Committee appointed to consider the spacing and construction of water-tight bulkheads in ships of the Mercantile Marine?'; to which Hicks Beach reiterated his earlier statement; "…The Board of Trade are acting upon the recommendations of the Bulkheads Committee, and in every case in which they are satisfied that those recommendations have been complied with, they authorise a reduction of the life-saving appliances otherwise required by the Statute to be carried on board every British merchant ship".[657]

Introduction of the rules concerning life-saving appliances proposed by the Life Saving Appliances committee had been delayed throughout 1889 due primarily to concerns expressed about their impact on coastal ships and questions regarding accuracy of calculations for cubic capacity of lifeboats. The proposed rules were still undergoing debate in Parliament in 1890 and awaiting final approval by the Board of Trade. In reply to a question in the House on the 20th of February, 1890, as to; '…if it is true that the enforcement of the rules under the Saving life at Sea Act, 1888, have been postponed by the Board of Trade until June, and if it is well understood that they will not be longer delayed?' the President of the Board of Trade, Sir M. Hicks Beach, replied; "…It is true that the rules in question have been delayed in order to refer a point raised to the Committee. I hope it may not be necessary to further postpone them, and as far as it depends upon me it shall not be done".[658] The Act came into force on the 1st of November, 1890.

On the 17th of July, 1890, concerns were raised in the House regarding application of such rules to coastal ferries carrying a large number of passengers. Mr. McCartney, the Member for Antrim was concerned about; "the injurious effect upon ferries between England and Ireland";

> ...Last year Rules identical with these were made, but were not carried into effect, in consequence of the representations made. The objections are two, and the first relates to the regulations as to boats, the second to life belts and other appliances. In the first place, I contend that the provision for new boats is unnecessary, and, in the second place, if a vessel is equipped with boats according to the scale laid down the result will be illusory. I may illustrate this by reference to particular steamers running between this country and Ireland. Owing to the number of boats being made dependent upon the cubic measurement, a magnificent ship like the Ireland, which runs between Holyhead and Dublin and generally carries about 200 passengers, will have to carry six more boats than it now does, although it is a new vessel and fully equipped with six boats; whereas the Mayo, a smaller vessel, but one which sometimes carries 1,000 passengers, will only be required to have three boats altogether. The objection to many boats is that they occupy deck space, and further, the crew will be insufficient to man so many boats...

McCartney suggested; "the number of life-belts in each vessel should be in proportion to the tonnage, and I have placed the proportion at 10 to every 100 tons, or the Board of Trade should use its existing discretionary power as to the number of lifebelts to be carried in the case of such vessels which were very different to trans-Atlantic liners". He proposed an amendment to the draft rules to state; "... Provided that where in existing ships the boats are in good order and of sufficient capacity they shall not be required to be altered under this section". After a rebuttal by the President of the Board of Trade, which concluded by stating that "...The matter was one of great technical difficulty and of the gravest importance to the saving of life at sea, and I should be sorry if the House rejected the recommendation of the Committee....there is a clause which provides that no ship shall be called on to carry more boats and rafts than are sufficient for the accommodation of all the persons on board. The sole objection to these rules is on the part of a few interested traders, who object to some extra expense which will be thrown on them..." The motion was withdrawn.[659]

After a long hiatus since the Report of the Load Line Committee had been adopted by the Board of Trade in 1886, a Merchant Shipping Acts Amendment Bill was brought in at the very beginning of the 1890 Parliamentary Session; '...to amend the Merchant Shipping Acts relating to load-line, &c...'. The Bill was presented and read for the first time.[660] On the 5th of March a proposed second reading of the amended Bill was deferred as one Member objected that '...Members for Liverpool and opponents of the Bill have not yet seen the amendments".[661] After another deferment on the 12th of March an order was made on the 20th for the second reading of the Bill. The President of the Board of Trade informed the House that; "...Great care has been taken in drafting the proposed Amendments to the Bill, which include reference to the recommendations of the Load Line Committee, and which have the approval of the Board of Trade and the shipping interest". The Bill was read for the second time and 'committed for Monday next'.[662] Considering the Bill in committee on the 14th of April, Mr Baird, Member for Glasgow, proposed a new clause reading; "The registered owner of any ship shall have a right of appeal from the decision of the Board of Trade, or of any corporation, association, or committee appointed by the Board of Trade for the purpose of fixing the disc of any such ship as aforesaid, to a committee, which shall he appointed from time to time by the President of the Board of Trade in accordance with the [proposed] schedule to this Act [attached]". The proposal was withdrawn after the President of the Board of Trade stated;

> I quite recognise the object of my hon. Friend in moving this clause, and entirely agree with him in the desire that the load-line should be fixed by some body of experts rather than by the Board of Trade. But the proposal of my hon. Friend is that, when the shipowner has chosen his own tribunal for the fixing of the load-line, if he is dissatisfied with the decision of that tribunal he should have an appeal to another tribunal. I hope my hon. Friend will not press this Amendment. If he will withdraw it, I will undertake on Report to obviate one of the objections he has raised as to the shortness of the term before which this Bill comes into effect. I will move to substitute six months for three. That will give a longer time for the formation of any such Association as is contemplated in the Bill, and will enable the shipowners on the north-west coast to form a Committee to fix a load-line for their ships.[663]

The Bill, which was read for the third time and passed on the 16th of April, had a straightforward passage through the House of Lords before being reported back to the Commons with the Lords' amendments agreed to by the House of Commons on the 3rd of June. The resultant Merchant Shipping Act, 1890,[664] made the marking of load lines compulsory in accordance with associated rules and regulations and, '...when the Bill became law there were three authorities licenced to assign load lines: Lloyd's Register, the British Corporation and the British Committee of the Bureau Veritas, and the British Corporation' [later amalgamated with Lloyds].[665] To protect British ships against competition, the Act required all foreign ships departing British ports to be similarly marked with the load line required by the Act; thus encouraging international standardisation of Plimsoll's load line. The Act received Royal Assent on the 9th of June, 1890 and was, without a doubt, the most significant contribution to the prevention of overloading and saving of life at sea during the nineteenth century, and far beyond.

Chapter 26

The "Grand Act"

The last decade of the nineteenth century was to see five more merchant shipping Acts[666] come into effect, including a major consolidation of almost all merchant shipping and mercantile shipping law. A significant and unprecedented increase in the number, size and capacity of steamships would have a long-term detrimental effect on the appropriateness of some safety legislation. Crew sizes would decrease per ton on all types of ship due to increased efficiencies and a large degree of under manning, but, the tragic loss of ships, seamen and passengers experienced throughout the century would continue unabated during the last decade, particularly as a result of two collisions, each resulting in catastrophic loss of life.

In March 1891, the Master of a British passenger ship carrying a large number of emigrants from Italy to New York made a grievous error of judgement that resulted in the deaths of 562 passengers and crew. The steamship ***Utopia*** (1874) of 2,371 gross tons had been built in Scotland for the Anchor Line and spent most of her career carrying a small number of first and second class passengers, and large numbers of emigrants, from Britain to America. In 1882 the first class accommodation was reduced from 120 to 45 and the second class accommodation removed, allowing steerage accommodation for emigrants to be increased from 600 to 900. Under this configuration the ship commenced a new service carrying emigrants from Trieste to New York via Naples, Genoa and Gibraltar. On the evening of the 17th of March, with a total of 880 souls aboard, including 85 women and 67 children, along with 3 Saloon passengers, 815 emigrants, 59 crew and 3 stowaways, the ***Utopia*** entered Gibraltar harbour to anchor for bunkers. It was dark, with a strong South-westerly wind. In command was Captain John McKeague, the holder of an Extra Master's Certificate and a commission as Lieutenant in the Royal Naval Reserve.

During the Court of Inquiry, held in Gibraltar on the 24th of March to '…

inquire into the casualty and shipwreck of the British steamer 'Utopia', whereby a considerable loss of life was occasioned...' Captain McKeague described to the Court the fatal situation into which he placed his ship;

> ...After rounding Europa Point I steered North (Magnetic) until I came halfway between Europa Point and New Mole light. I then stopped engines altogether. Five minutes before they had been going slow. I stopped them to get the way off the ship. I then steered to keep the 'Anson' right ahead, as she occupied the position outside the berth [anchorage] I was making for. I then observed the 'Rodney' outside her again, and they appeared to be very close together. I thought that the berth outside the 'Rodney' would be too deep to let go my anchor. Thinking the inside berth was all clear, I kept nearer to the breakwater. As I drew up towards the breakwater, the brilliant lights from the vessels dazzled me, and I could not see objects inside the 'Anson'. As I got clear of the rays from these vessels that were inside the moles, I suddenly discovered that the inner anchorage was full of ships. The stern of the 'Anson' seeming to overlap the ship inside appeared to give me room to pass in. I might say that I was close to the breakwater when these vessels came fully into my sight, and from the position I occupied, they appeared to be very close together. As I considered I had more way on my ship than I expected, making it imprudent to let go the anchor, I found myself placed upon three evils. The first was, if I came full astern, my ship being light her head would have canted to starboard, and before I got the way off her most likely would have grounded on the breakwater, or if by any possibility she had gained sternway before reaching the breakwater and being sufficiently distant from the breakwater to turn with the engines ahead, I should have drifted onto the 'Anson'. The second difficulty appearing to me, on the spur of the moment was that, as the current was carrying me with such velocity, and the current being a very bad factor in causing the ship to steer, I thought if I reversed my engines slowly I might have stopped her steerage way, as it was the current that was giving me the headway. I knew most assuredly that I would have lost control of my ship and smashed her into one of the ships inside. From my standpoint, thinking that the 'Anson' was further off than she really was, I considered that the least of the three evils was to come out again. I put my helm hard-a-starboard, my engines ahead, and did all that was possible to clear the 'Anson'

> by passing ahead of her. When I had the 'Anson' abreast of my bridge I put my helm hard-a-port so as to throw my ship's stern clear of the bows of the 'Anson', which she would most assuredly have done if it had not been for some obstacle which caught the ship about the after part of the engine room, which I first thought was the cable-chain of the ship, but which I found by the ship sinking, must have been something else.

The 'obstacle' was the ram bow of ***HMS Anson***, protruding underwater well forward of the ship's stem; which carried out its lethal purpose by opening up the ***Utopia*** in way of the engine and after hold to such an extent that the ship listed very heavily to port and sank within twenty minutes, coming to rest upright on the sea floor with the masts and funnel visible. All of the port boats were rendered useless after they were submerged by the capsize, and it was impossible to launch the starboard boats due to the heavy port list. In answer to questions from the Court, the Captain explained that the ***Utopia*** normally carried seven boats, of which four were lifeboats, which could in total hold 460 people in moderate weather but "...she had six boats available. We lost one, but intending replacing it at Gibraltar, it was ready for us there...I had no life rafts on board... and sufficient lifebelts but could not say the number". The Chief Officer testified that there were 200. The Captain also confessed that he "...had no idea how far a ram projects from a man-of-war. I could not tell a ram ship from another vessel". Three hundred and eighteen persons survived including 290 steerage passengers, 2 saloon, 3 Italian interpreters and 23 crew members.

The decision of the Court was that;

> The master of the steamship 'Utopia' committed a grave error of judgement, by which his ship was sunk and loss of life occurred –
>
> Firstly, In attempting to enter the anchorage behind the New Mole without having first opened out and ascertained what vessels were there
>
> Secondly, In attempting to turn his ship across the bows of Her Majesty's ship 'Anson'

The following day a Marine Court was convened to consider a charge of 'grave error of judgement'. The Court, made up of the same persons who comprised the Court of Inquiry, were unanimously of the opinion that '…it is not deemed necessary …to deal in any way with the master's certificate'.[667]

In March 1892, the President of the Board of Trade informed the House that "…the number of British vessels reported missing during the year of 1891 for which accounts are available is 79. Inquiry was made by the Board of Trade officers in every case, but official inquiries were held in only seven cases. I have no reason to believe that an official inquiry could have been usefully held in any case in which it was not actually ordered.'[668] It was not reported how many lives were lost. However, during an address to the Chamber of Shipping of the United Kingdom a few days earlier Hicks Beach had stated that the rate of loss of life at sea had reduced from 1 in 79 in 1881 to 1 in 256 in 1891. This statistic was questioned in the House on the 17*th* of March as to whether "…he was speaking of the total loss of life at sea from all causes, or whether he was speaking of the loss of life under two headings alone of several under which the loss of life at sea is classified; and what were the headings under which loss of life at sea are classified which were not included by him in the figures he gave?" It would appear from the President's reply that losses of life from missing ships were not included in his figures;

> When speaking on the occasion to which the hon. Member refers, I was not stating the "total loss of life at sea from all causes," but, as I clearly explained, only the loss of life among seamen arising from wrecks and casualties at sea to merchant ships registered in the United Kingdom—namely, lives lost in direct consequence of accidents causing total loss or damage to the ships. The corresponding figures for 1881 are 1 in 79. The loss of life which is not included in the foregoing figures was that which occurred from drowning and other accidents, although the ships were in no way damaged or in danger.[669]

As early as December 1890 questions were being asked of the President of the Board of Trade as to the nature of instructions to surveyors, and about doubts regarding application of the load line requirements of the 1890 Act to vessels already sailing and marked under Lloyd's freeboard rules. Hicks Beach replied; "...The instructions to Surveyors include the tables of the Load Line Committee, with a Memorandum on their application and directions as to the course to be followed when owners apply for load lines to be fixed by the Board of Trade. The provisions of the law apply to all British vessels, whether previously marked by Lloyd's or not, and I have not heard of any real difficulties having arisen in the matter…"

Regardless of this reassurance it was clear by 1892 that not all ships were compliant with the load line provisions of the 1890 Act and, accordingly, the Board of Trade introduced a short Bill to provide heavier penalties for non-compliance. The requirement of the 1890 Act for compulsory marking of load lines in accordance with associated rules and regulations was to contribute greatly to improved safety. Although the number of steamships increased by 10% in the decade 1890-1900, the mean percentage of their losses fell from 2.12% to 1.41%, with the number of deaths by wreck, drowning and accident decreasing by 20% between 1891 and 1900.[670]

The other long-standing issue addressed by the Merchant Shipping Act Amendment Bill, 1892 was the matter of seamen's rations, particularly for protracted voyages, which were still based upon either the old Liverpool Scale or the Board of Trade Scale of 1867 – 68. It was not possible for Board of Trade officials to obtain the agreement of shipowners to a statutory food scale for all voyages but a compromise was reached through section 3(1) of the resultant Merchant Shipping Act, 1892;[671] *An Act for the detention of unsafe overloaded ships and inspection of crew's provisions'*. The Act required food and water provided for ships making passages through the Suez Canal, or around the Cape of Good Hope, to be inspected by a Board of Trade inspector before departure. During the first year the Act was in force inspectors carried out 273 inspections between the 17th of July and 2nd of September 1893 and condemned the stores aboard 96 ships; a 35% condemnation rate. [672]

Between 1840 and 1893 no less than eighty-one Acts referring to merchant shipping and mercantile shipping law had been passed, making it difficult to determine the actual law in force. The long-standing call from politicians, the merchant shipping industry and the legal profession for all of these Acts to be consolidated into one easily accessed and understandable statute had not been achieved due to a focus upon amendment rather than consolidation. Finally, a Merchant Shipping Bill was introduced by Mr. Mundella, President of the Board of Trade, on the 22nd of August, 1893, "...to consolidate enactments relating to Merchant Shipping". The Bill was presented and read for the first time.[673] On the 4th of September, in reply to a question in the House, Mundella clarified that;

> There is no intention of hurrying this Bill through the House. We have circulated over 70 copies of the Bill to bodies and authorities interested in its administration, and have invited their observations from the point of view of consolidation only. We propose now merely to read the Bill a second time, with a view to its reference to a Committee of both Houses, who will consider the suggestions received, and who will satisfy themselves that the Bill in no substantial sense increases the powers of the Board of Trade, imposes new penalties, or creates new offences.[674]

This assurance was supported by the Chancellor of the Exchequer who, in discussing the business of the House observed; "...With regard to the Bills the Government desire to keep on the Paper, I prefer to mention the names of those which we hope may live rather than those which we fear may die...Then I come to ... Bills of an extremely useful and non-contentious character, mostly Consolidation Bills, which are of immense convenience to all classes of the community. They have been prepared with great care, and, as they merely re-enact the present law, I hope the House will allow them to be taken in the interstices of business. They [include]... the Merchant Shipping Bill".[675]

With these reassurances the Bill had a swift and non-contentious passage through the Commons and the Lords. On the 18th of December, 1893, a Joint Committee of six Members of the House of Commons and six Lords reported that the Bill had been completed without amendment, and their Report and Special Report were to lie upon the table and be printed, ready to be considered by the next session of Parliament.[676]

The Merchant Shipping Act, 1894;[677] *An Act to consolidate Enactments relating to Merchant Shipping*, was passed on the 25th of August 1894; effective from the 1st of January 1895. Containing 14 Parts, 748 sections and 700 pages; it was the largest statute to have ever be enacted by the British Parliament, consolidating maritime legislation stretching as far back into the history of England as the reign of Edward II in the fourteenth century[678]. The Act remained the cornerstone of maritime legislation for upwards of 100 years,[679] provided a framework of law which served as a model for principal maritime States, and repealed all or part of 48 Acts.

The 14 Parts of the Act were; I – Registry; II – Masters and Seamen; III – Passengers and Emigrant Ships; IV – Fishing Boats; V – Safety; VI – Special Shipping Inquiries; VII – Delivery of Goods; VIII – Liability of Shipowners; IX – Wreck and Salvage; X – Pilotage; XII – Mercantile Marine Fund; XIII – Legal Proceedings and XIV – Supplemental.

Twenty-one Schedules covered; I – Documents for ship registration; II – Measurement of tonnage; III – Fees for tonnage measurement and examinations; IV – Fees for examinations; V – Regulations for anti-scorbutics; VI – Regulations with respect to accommodation aboard ships; VII – Constitution of local Marine Boards; VIII – Records to be kept by Master of births and deaths at sea; IX – Fees for Passenger Steamers' certificates and surveys of emigrant ships; X – Regulations as to numbers of persons carried on emigrant ships; XI – Regulations as to accommodation for steerage passengers; XII – Water and provisions; XIII – Carriage of horses and cattle in emigrant ships; XIV – Forms (under Part III) passenger and emigrant ships; XV – Number and dimensions of boats for fishing ships; XVI – Fees for inspections of lights and fog signals; XVII – Life savings appliances; XVIII – Precautions as to carriage of grain cargoes; IXX – Statements in case of salvage by Her Majesty's ships; XX – Fees and remuneration of receivers of wreck; XXI – Maximum rates of pilotage to be demanded and XXII – Repeal.

Part V – Safety; which incorporated, with one critical amendment, all the matters of importance to the safety of ships, their cargoes, and their complements, included; ss.418 – 424, *Prevention of Collision;* ss. 425 – 426, *Report of Accidents and Loss of Ship;* ss. 427 – 431, *Life Saving Appliances,* ss. 432 – 433, *Signals of Distress,* ss. 436 – 445, *Draught of Water and Load line;* ss. 446 – 450, *Dangerous Goods;* s. 451, *Loading of Timber;* ss. 452 – 456, *Carriage of Grain; and* ss. 457 – 463, *Unseaworthy Ships.*

Details of provisions of Part V of particular interest to the longstanding issues of seaworthiness, overloading, crewing and safety included;

418 Collision regulations

(1) Her Majesty may, on the joint recommendation of the Admiralty and the Board of Trade, by Order in Council, make regulations for the prevention of collisions at sea, and may thereby regulate the lights to be carried and exhibited, the fog signals to be carried and used, and the steering and sailing rules to be observed, by ships, and those regulations (in this Act referred to as the collision regulations), shall have effect as if enacted in this Act.

(2) The collision regulations, together with the provisions of this Part of this Act relating thereto, or otherwise relating to collisions, shall be observed by all foreign ships within British jurisdiction, and in any case arising in a British court concerning matters arising within British jurisdiction foreign ships shall, so far as respects the collision regulations and the said provisions of this Act, be treated as if they were British ships.

419 Observance of collision regulations

(1) All owners and masters of ships shall obey the collision regulations, and shall not carry or exhibit any other lights, or use any other fog signals, than such as are required by those regulations.

(2) If an infringement of the collision regulations is caused by the wilful default of the master or owner of the ship, that master or owner shall, in respect of each offence, be guilty of a misdemeanour.

(3) If any damage to person or property arises from the non-observance by any ship of any of the collision regulations, the damage shall be deemed to have been occasioned by the wilful default of the person in charge of the deck of the ship at the time, unless it is shown to the satisfaction of the court that the circumstances of the case made a departure from the regulation necessary.

(4) Where in a case of collision it is proved to the court before whom the case is tried, that any of the collision regulations have been infringed, the ship by which the regulation has been infringed shall be deemed to be in fault, unless it is shown to the satisfaction of the court that the circumstances of the case made departure from the regulation necessary.

(5) The Board of Trade shall furnish a copy of the collision regulations to any master or owner of a ship who applies for it.

424 Application of collision regulations to foreign ships

Whenever it is made to appear to Her Majesty in Council that the Government of any foreign country is willing that the collision regulations, or the provisions of this Part of this Act relating thereto or otherwise relating to collisions, or any of those regulations or provisions should apply to the ships of that country when beyond the limits of British jurisdiction, Her Majesty may, by Order in Council, direct that those regulations and provisions shall, subject to any limitation of time conditions and qualifications contained in the Order, apply to the ships of the said foreign country, whether within British jurisdiction or not, and that such ships shall for the purpose of such regulations and provisions be treated as if they were British ships.

427 Rules as to life-saving appliances

(1) The Board of Trade may make rules (in this Act called rules for life-saving appliances) with respect to all or any of the following matters; namely,—

(a) The arranging of British ships into classes, having regard to the services in which they are employed, to the nature and duration of the voyage, and to the number of persons carried;

(b) The number and description of the boats, life-boats, life-rafts, life-jackets, and life-buoys to be carried by British ships, according to the class in which they are arranged, and the mode of their construction, also the equipments to be carried by the boats and rafts, and the methods to be provided to get the boats and other life-saving appliances into the water which methods may include oil for use in stormy weather; and

(c) The quantity, quality, and description of buoyant apparatus to be carried on board British ships carrying passengers, either in addition to or in substitution for boats, life-boats, life-rafts, life-jackets, and life-buoys.

(2) All such rules shall be laid before Parliament so soon as may be after they are made, and shall not come into operation until they have lain for forty days before both Houses of Parliament during the session of Parliament; and on coining into operation shall have effect as if enacted in this Act.

(3) Rules under this section shall not apply to any fishing boat for the time being entered in the fishing boat register under Part IV of this Act.

Although the Act was one of consolidation rather than amendment, there was one small, but inadequate, nod to progress when the General Rule made under the Merchant Shipping Act, 1890, for carriage of boats under davits was amended under section 427(b) of the 1894 Act from an upper limit of 9,000 gross tons and upwards to 10,000 gross tons and upwards. The Life Savings Appliances Committee and the Board of Trade had paid no heed to the reality that Cunard had launched the sister ships Campania and Lucania in 1892 and 1893 respectively; both of 12,590 gross tons and certified to carry 2,000 passengers, with crew totalling 424. The maximum number of boats required to be carried under davits for these ships, and those of any tonnage upwards, only increased by two; from 14 to 16.

428 Duties of owners and masters as to carrying life-saving appliances

It shall be the duty of the owner and master of every British ship to see that his ship is provided, in accordance with the rules for life-saving appliances, with such of those appliances as, having regard to the nature of the service on which the ship is employed, and the avoidance of undue encumbrance of the ship's deck, are best adapted for securing the safety of her crew and passengers.

The loosely worded section 428, clearly reflecting the influence of shipowning Members of Parliament and pressures from shipowners in its reference to 'avoidance of undue encumbrance of the ship's deck,' gave considerable licence to the owners of increasingly large passenger ships in their interpretation of the law. Before the turn of the century the White Star Line were planning four sister ships of a greater tonnage and longer than Brunel's leviathan, the Great Eastern. The first of this quartet, the Celtic (1901) of 20,904 gross tons became, at the time of her launch, the largest ship in the world and set the pattern for exponential increases in tonnage, size, speed and passenger capacity over the following few years. The Celtic and her sisters had a capacity of 300 First Class, 160 Second Class and 2,350 Steerage Class passengers, along with about 350 crew, for a total complement of 3,169.

439 Ships with submerged load-lines deemed unsafe

If a ship is so loaded as to submerge in salt water the centre of the disc indi-

cating the load-line, the ship shall be deemed to be an unsafe ship within the meaning of the provisions hereafter contained in this Part of this Act, and such submersion shall be a reasonable and probable cause for the detention of the ship.

457 Sending unseaworthy ship to sea a misdemeanor

(1) If any person sends or attempts to send, or is party to sending or attempting to send, a British ship to sea in such an unseaworthy680 state that the life of any person is likely to be thereby endangered, he shall in respect of each offence be guilty of a misdemeanor, unless he proves either that he used all reasonable means to insure her being sent to sea in a seaworthy state, or that her going to sea in such an unseaworthy state was, under the circumstances, reasonable and justifiable, and for the purpose of giving that proof he may give evidence in the same manner as any other witness.

(2) If the master of a British ship knowingly takes the same to sea in such an unseaworthy state that the life of any person is likely to be thereby endangered, he shall in respect of each offence be guilty of a misdemeanor, unless he proves that her going to sea in such an unseaworthy state was, under the circumstances, reasonable and justifiable, and for the purpose of giving such proof he may give evidence in the same manner as any other witness.

(3) A prosecution under this section shall not, except in Scotland, be instituted otherwise than by, or with the consent of, the Board of Trade, or of the governor of the British possession in which the prosecution takes place.

(4) A misdemeanor under this section shall not be punishable upon summary conviction.

(5) This section shall not apply to any ship employed exclusively in trading or going from place to place in any river or inland water of which the whole or part is in any British possession.

458 Obligation of shipowner to crew with respect to use of reasonable efforts to secure seaworthiness

(1) In every contract of service, express or implied, between the owner of a ship and the master or any seaman thereof, and in every instrument of apprenticeship whereby any person is bound to serve as an apprentice on board any ship, there shall be implied, notwithstanding any agreement to the

contrary, an obligation on the owner of the ship, that the owner of the ship, and the master, and every agent charged with the loading of the ship, or the preparing of the ship for sea, or the sending of the ship to sea, shall use all reasonable means to insure the seaworthiness of the ship for the voyage at the time when the voyage commences, and to keep her in a seaworthy condition for the voyage during the voyage.

(2) Nothing in this section—

(a) shall subject the owner of a ship to any liability by reason of the ship being sent to sea in an unseaworthy state where, owing to special circumstances, the sending of the ship to sea in such a state was reasonable and justifiable ; or

(b) shall apply to any ship employed exclusively in trading or going from place to place in any river or inland water of which the whole or part is in any British possession.

458 Obligation of shipowner to crew with respect to use of reasonable efforts to secure seaworthiness

(1) In every contract of service, express or implied, between the owner of a ship and the master or any seaman thereof, and in every instrument of apprenticeship whereby any person is bound to serve as an apprentice on board any ship, there shall be implied, notwithstanding any agreement to the contrary, an obligation on the owner of the ship, that the owner of the ship, and the master, and every agent charged with the loading of the ship, or the preparing of the ship for sea, or the sending of the ship to sea, shall use all reasonable means to insure the seaworthiness of the ship for the voyage at the time when the voyage commences, and to keep her in a seaworthy condition for the voyage during the voyage.

(2) Nothing in this section—

(a) shall subject the owner of a ship to any liability by reason of the ship being sent to sea in an unseaworthy state where, owing to special circumstances, the sending of the ship to sea in such a state was reasonable and justifiable ; or

(b) shall apply to any ship employed exclusively in trading or going from place to place in any river or inland water of which the whole or part is in any British possession.

459 Power to detain unsafe ships, and procedure for detention

(1) Where a British ship, being in any port in the United Kingdom, is an unsafe ship, that is to say, is by reason of the defective condition of her hull, equipments, or machinery, or by reason of overloading or improper loading, unfit to proceed to sea without serious danger to human life, having regard to the nature of the service for which she is intended, such ship may be provisionally detained for the purpose of being surveyed, and either finally detained or released as follows:—

(a) The Board of Trade, if they have reason to believe, on complaint or otherwise, that a British ship is unsafe, may order the ship to be provisionally detained as an unsafe ship for the purpose of being surveyed.

(b) When a ship has been provisionally detained there shall be forthwith served on the master of the ship a written statement of the grounds of her detention, and the Board of Trade may, if they think fit, appoint some competent person or persons to survey the ship and report thereon to the Board.

(c) The Board of Trade on receiving the report may either order the ship to be released or, if in their opinion the ship is unsafe, may order her to be finally detained, either absolutely, or until the performance of such conditions with respect to the execution of repairs or alterations, or the unloading or re loading of cargo, as the Board think necessary for the protection of human life, and the Board may vary or add to any such order.

(d) Before the order for final detention is made a copy of the report shall be served upon the master of the ship, and within seven days after that service the owner or master of the ship may appeal to the court of survey for the port or district where the ship is detained in manner directed by the rules of that court.

(e) Where a ship has been provisionally detained, the owner or master of the ship, at any time before the person appointed under this section to survey the ship makes that survey, may require that he shall be accompanied by such person as the owner or master may select out of the list of assessors for the court of survey, and in that case if the surveyor and assessor agree, the Board of Trade shall cause the ship to be detained or released accordingly, but if they differ, the Board of Trade may act as if the requisition had not been made, and the owner and master shall have the like appeal touching the report of the surveyor as is before provided by

this section.

(f) Where a ship has been provisionally detained, the Board of Trade may at any time, if they think it expedient, refer the matter to the court of survey for the port or district where the ship is detained.

(g) The Board of Trade may at any time, if satisfied that a ship detained under this section is not unsafe, order her to be released either upon or without any conditions.

(2) Any person appointed by the Board of Trade for the purpose (in this Act referred to as a detaining officer) shall have the same power as the Board have under this section of ordering the provisional detention of a ship for the purpose of being surveyed, and of appointing a person or persons to survey her; and if he thinks that a ship so detained by him is not unsafe may order her to be released.

(3) A detaining officer shall forthwith report to the Board of Trade any order made by him for the detention or release of a ship.

(4) An order for the detention of a ship, provisional or final, and an order varying the same, shall be served as soon as may be on the master of the ship.

(5) A ship detained under this section shall not be released by reason of her British register being subsequently closed.

(6) The Board of Trade may with the consent of the Treasury appoint fit persons to act as detaining officers under this section, and may remove any such officer; and a detaining officer shall be paid such salary or remuneration (if any) out of money provided by Parliament as the Treasury direct, and shall for the purpose of his duties have all the powers of a Board of Trade inspector under this Act.

(7) A detaining officer and a person authorised to survey a ship under this section shall for that purpose have the same power as a person appointed by a court of survey to survey a ship, and the provisions of this Act with respect to the person so appointed shall apply accordingly.

462 Application to foreign ships of provisions as to detention

Where a foreign ship has taken on board all or any part of her cargo at a port in the United Kingdom, and is whilst at that port unsafe by reason of overloading or improper loading, the provisions of this Part of this Act with respect to the detention of ships shall apply to that foreign ship as if she were a British ship, with the following modifications:—

(i)A copy of the order for the provisional detention of the ship shall be forthwith served on the consular officer for the country to which the ship belongs at or nearest to the said port;

(ii) Where a ship has been provisionally detained, the consular officer, on the request of the owner or master of the ship, may require that the person appointed by the Board of Trade to survey the ship shall be accompanied by such person as the consular officer may select, and in that case, if the surveyor and that person agree, the Board of Trade shall cause the ship to be detained or released accordingly, but if they differ, the Board of Trade may act as if the requisition had not been made, and the owner and master shall have the like appeal to a court of survey touching the report of the surveyor as is herein-before provided in the case of a British ship ; and

(iii) Where the owner or master of the ship appeals to the court of survey, the consular officer, on his request, may appoint a competent person to be assessor in the case in lieu of the assessor who, if the ship were a British ship, would be appointed otherwise than by the Board of Trade.

The detail of requirements under all provisions of the Merchant Shipping Act, 1894, such as numbers of lifeboats, were contained in General Rules issued by the Marine Department of the Board of Trade. These Rules were drafted and, on the authority of the President of the Board of Trade, laid before Parliament. They lay 'on the Table' for 40 days and, if objected to were dealt with by an Address to the House. If the House had no objections to the Rule after 40 days it had the force of a statute.

Chapter 27

Lack of Crew and Loss of Life

The year that the Merchant Shipping Act, 1894, came into force there was a collision in the North Sea between a large German passenger ship and a small British cargo ship, with an uncanny resemblance to that between the German passenger ship ***Cimbria*** and the small British collier ***Sultan*** eleven years earlier. Both collisions resulted in the rapid sinking of the large passenger ships with catastrophic loss of life, and survival of the small cargo ships.

The North German Lloyd ship ***Elbe*** (1881) of 4,510 gross tons sailed from Bremerhaven for New York, via Southampton on the evening of the 29th of January 1895. Due to the winter sailing she carried only 50 first class passengers, none in second class and 149 emigrants in steerage instead of her maximum capacity of 1,117 passengers in all three classes. The officers and crew brought the total aboard to 352 people. About the same time the small Scottish steamship ***Craithie*** of 475 gross tons with a crew of 12 departed Rotterdam bound for Aberdeen with general cargo. The weather in the North Sea was very bad, with freezing temperatures, rough seas and a heavy swell, although it was clear with a strong Easterly wind. At five o'clock the next morning, about 30 miles off the coast of the Dutch island of Terschelling the ***Elbe's*** officer of the watch sighted the green light of an approaching ship broad off the port bow. The Mate of the ***Craithie*** didn't sight the ***Elbe*** as he'd gone down to the galley to chat with the crew, leaving only the helmsman on the bridge. As the ship with right-of-way the ***Elbe*** maintained her course and speed, sending up rockets to alert the approaching ship to no avail. The ***Craithie*** struck the Elbe just aft of the after engine room bulkhead at a slight angle opening up a long gash towards the stern. There had been no time to close the ***Elbe's*** seven watertight doors and, when the ***Craithie*** pulled astern, the sea rushed in flooding the engine room and after compartments, causing the ship to immediately list heavily to port. Amidst a scene of great confusion and panic, the crew managed to launch two boats from the port side, one of which was overloaded with passengers and immediately capsized with the loss of all aboard. The second boat was launched with twenty persons; fifteen crew and four passengers. The Captain ordered the women and children to muster at the starboard boats but, due to the heavy port list, they couldn't be launched; a problem exacerbated by frozen boat falls. The ***Elbe*** sank twenty minutes after the collision. The ***Craithie***, badly damaged forward, steamed slowly back to Rotterdam having offered no assistance to the few survivors. Six hours later the sole lifeboat was sighted by a trawler from Lowestoft which, under great difficulty, brought the survivors aboard. A total of 332 souls were lost including all children, all women apart from one, and the entire bridge crew. At the subsequent inquiry by the Board of Trade the Mate and all eleven other crew of the ***Craithie*** stated that there had been thick fog at the time of collision; a claim soundly refuted by survivors from the ***Elbe*** and the many fishing boats in the area. The inquiry found the Mate of the ***Craithie*** to have been in default, solely responsible and cancelled his certificate. The American nautical journal Seaboard reflected public opinion in stating; 'A more shocking and, apparently, a less excusable collision never occurred. The grossest neglect of the rules of the road, and the most heartless disregard for the promptings of humanity, controlled the actions of the officers in charge of the ***Craithie*** before and after the disaster'.[681]

Two years later a British passenger liner was wrecked, with the loss of almost all on board. On the 28th of May 1896 the ***Drummond Castle*** (1881) of 3,706 gross tons, operated by the Castle Mail Packet Company, sailed from Capetown for London with 143 passengers and 102 crew. Two and a half weeks later she was approaching the island of Ushant, a well-lit landmark with a fog signal, at the southwestern entrance to the English Channel, with the presumed intention of taking the normal route for ocean steamers of passing to the north-west (outside) of the island. There was speculation after the event that the master was taking a short cut, known by local vessels, inside Ushant, or had been set to the south-east and was, unwittingly, proceeding inside Ushant. The weather was reported by other ships in the vicinity to be hazy due to drizzle and fog, with a heavy sea. At about 11.00pm the ***Drummond Castle*** struck a submerged reef between Ushant and the island of Molene at full speed, tearing the bottom out of the ship for its full length. A report of the wreck, gleaned from accounts from the three survivors, described the event;

> The rent in the stricken steamer was so wide and deep that but few of the passengers had time to scramble on deck before she gave two or three heavy rolls and then an awful lurch, accompanied by some

> interior explosions, and then she sank, with a moaning, hissing sound, beneath the angry waves, which were beating mercilessly over her.[682]

The two seamen who survived, along with one male passenger, recounted that there was no time to launch any boats and the ship sank off the reef into deep water within about three minutes with loss of 244 souls. The finding of the Court of Inquiry into the disaster was that the loss was due to 'careless or unskillful navigation'.

Of increasing concern during the 1890s was the issue of inadequate manning for merchant ships and its implication for seaworthiness. At this time the only legal requirement regarding manning was that emigrant ships should have an 'efficient crew' as required by s.28 of the Passenger Act 1855. The number of qualified officers was not negotiable; masters and mates had been required to hold certificates of competency from 1850, and marine engineers from the 1860s. Cooks and Able-bodied Seamen were also brought into this fold in 1880. However, regarding the remainder of the crew necessary for the efficient and safe operation of his ship, a shipowner was free to choose whatever number he believed were required to have an 'efficient crew'; quite often deciding upon fewer than were required to efficiently operate the ship and, in particular, to keep effective watches. In the twenty years between 1860 and 1880 the mean number of crew employed per hundred tons of steam shipping fell by almost a half while in all classes of ships the manning ratio was down by a quarter. Larger vessels provided economies of scale, and labour-saving devices also had an effect, but with regard to manning the objective and subjective evidence was that owners were increasingly following a policy of minimum, or less than minimum, manning during this period.[683]

A statistic that demonstrates the continuing decrease in size of crew, against increased size of ship, throughout the nineteenth century is that of the number of crew per 100 ton. In 1815 the average ship was 113 tons with an average of 6.6 men per hundred ton. By 1835 ships averaged 116 tons with 6.2 men per hundred ton. In 1855 British ships averaged 145 tons with 4.85 men per hundred ton. Ten years later ships averaged 250 tons and 3.65 men per hundred tons; figures which changed to 292 and 3.4 in 1875, and 377 and 2.75 in 1885. In 1894 the average ship was 527 tons with an average of 2.65 men per hundred ton. Taking foreign going ships alone; in 1894 sailing ships averaged 1,240 tons, with 1.6 men to every 100 tons, with the steamships averaging 1,462 tons with 2.24 men to every 100 tons. 'The average number of hands in steamships includes the crews of the large passenger steamers with their numerous stewards and servants, all of whom count. As a fact there are many cargo steamers sailing on long voyages with less than one man for every 100 gross tons, seamen and engineers all told'. The average size of size of ships in 1894 were three times those of 1865, yet there had been a 39% decrease in the number of ships. In 1850 there was not a registered ship larger than 2000 tons. In 1894 the largest ships were the passenger liners ***Campania*** and ***Lucania*** of 12,950 tons. [684]

The fifth and final report of a long-standing Royal Commission on Labour recommended in 1894 that a departmental inquiry should be carried out into the safe manning of merchant ships. When the Board of Trade was also confronted with evidence showing that, of 80 steamships and 65 sailing vessels with regard to which the question of manning was raised at wreck inquiries between 1878 and 1894, 45 steamships and 24 sailing vessels were found to be undermanned, it was decided to form a departmental committee to examine the question of safe manning under the chairmanship of Sir Edward Reed.

The resultant Manning Committee heard evidence from seamen, shipowners and maritime unions. Seamen of all ranks were overwhelmingly in favour of a compulsory manning scale. Captain E.B. Hatfield, a Liverpool shipowner and master mariner, stated that that there had been; "a more or less reckless disregard for keeping up what I should call a sound standard of manning". George Robinson, an Able Seaman with eighteen years at sea, testified that "the majority of vessels going to sea now are under-manned". The Merchant Service Guild, an officers' trade union, called for four hands in each watch when giving evidence to the committee. Captain George Groot, forty-three years in command, believed that sailing ships were "not half manned to what they were years ago" and Joseph Korzeniowski (Joseph Conrad), formerly a master in sail, believed that foreign-going steamers having only three men to a watch were undermanned. Williams, a seaman, explained what happened in coasting steamers when only two men were on watch:

> You must understand that whenever a light is passed – a lightship or a light on shore – the man is called off the lookout to look at the log and see what the vessel has gone at that particular point. Of necessity

> that man is called off the lookout to do that particular duty, unless the officer takes the wheel and lets the man at the wheel go to look at the log, or unless the officer goes himself; and it is always necessary for one man to leave the deck, whether from the wheel or lookouts to call the watch below, which invariably takes ten minutes to do.

Shipowners were against any system whereby manning was determined by the Board of Trade.

The committee also heard concerns that one result of having only two men on watch at night was that if the lookout had to go forward to tend the sidelights when the officer of the watch and the helmsman were preoccupied with a potential collision situation, there was no-one available to call the master.[685]

In its final report the association between hours of work and a manning scale was emphasised by four members of the Manning Committee who, in disagreeing through a minority report, believed a comprehensive manning scale would eventually result in an eight-hour day [instead of the long-standing watch-and-watch system which resulted in an 84 hour week]. However, there was recognition given to the importance of keeping an effective navigational watch; '…Every foreign-going vessel shall, when under weigh, at all times and places have a minimum effective watch on duty on deck to secure her safe navigation, and in default of such effective watch the master, owner, or officers in default should he held liable to the consequences of the failure of duty, and the ship regarded as in default and undermanned'. George Laws, a member of the committee, refused to sign the final report on behalf of the Shipping Federation because he believed, probably correctly, that a tonnage-based method of determining manning took no account of differences between individual ships. However, he also insisted that the report contained a phrase indicating that undermanning did not, of itself, amount to unseaworthiness.[686] In spite of this particular, and incorrect, view, when introducing the second reading of the Merchant Shipping (Safe Manning) Bill on the 3rd of May 1897, the President of the Board of Trade, Mr. C. T. Ritchie established a definite association between undermanning and seaworthiness;

> …the Second Reading of the Bill…had been promoted with the view of remedying what he could not help thinking was an omission on the part of the authors of the Merchant Shipping Acts when they dealt with the subject of unseaworthy ships. An ordinary individual would

> certainly have imagined that an undermanned ship would have been included in the term "unsafe ship," but the Board of Trade had been advised that, although a vessel might be detained for defects in hull equipments or machinery, or for being overloaded or improperly loaded, no ship could be detained under the 459th Section of the Act of 1894, no matter how much she was undermanned. Undermanning was a source of unseaworthiness, not only to the ship herself, but to all other ships on the high seas. The object of the present Bill was to remedy that defect of the law and to include in Section 459 under-manning as one of the reasons for which a ship might be detained.

In considering the preferred option of many of a fixed manning scale for all ships based upon tonnage, rig and trade, the Board of Trade had come to the view that a '...hard-and-fast manning scale was not reasonably possible'. Accordingly their preference was for undermanning to be a detainable deficiency, a proposal given enthusiastic support by Members;

> The procedure proposed to be adopted if the Bill became law was that, if the Board of Trade or any detaining officer of the Board had reason to believe that a vessel was undermanned, the vessel should be detained until the matter was examined into; and if after examination the Board of Trade decided that the vessel should be detained until the defect was remedied, and if the owner demurred to the course, the matter would go before a Court of Survey, composed of a Judge and two Assessors, who would decide the issue. It might be objected that that provision would place great power in the hands of the Board of Trade and their officers; but that power was hedged round by another provision that, if a ship were detained unreasonably, costs and damages could be obtained by the owner of the ship against the Board of Trade for such detention.

There was further debate on a hesitant proposal by the Board of Trade to apply the same provisions to foreign registered ships loading in British ports; '...It would no doubt add to the difficulties of administering the law, but it would be the duty of the Board of Trade to try to work it with as little friction as possible, and with as much consideration as was compatible with the carrying out of the provisions of this Measure...'.[687] Ritchie need not have been concerned. There was no opposition to this principle during the passage of the short Bill through the Commons and the Lords and the Merchant Shipping Act, 1897,[688] *An Act to amend the Merchant Shipping Act*

1894, with respect to the Power of Detaining for Undermanning, was passed on the 6th of August 1897. The very brief Act of two sections read;

> *Section four hundred and fifty-nine of the Merchant Shipping Act 1894 (which gives power to detain unsafe ships), shall apply in the case of undermanning, and accordingly that section shall be construed as if the words "or by reason of undermanning" were inserted therein after the word "machinery", and as if the words "or for ascertaining the sufficiency of her crew", were inserted after the word "surveyed", and as if the words "or the manning of the ship" were inserted therein after the words "reloading of cargo", and the powers exercisable under or for the purposes of that section shall include power to muster the crew.*
>
> *Section four hundred and sixty-two of the Merchant Shipping Act 1894 (which relates to foreign ships), shall also apply in the case of undermanning, and accordingly that section shall be construed as if the words "or by reason of undermanning" were inserted therein after the words "improper loading".*

There was a view expressed that the 1897 Act, that was supposed to implement the recommendations of the Manning Committee, proved to be 'dead letter', for while section one gave power to detain undermanned ships and treat them as unsafe there was no statutory definition of undermanning, and the section could not be employed unless ships were so weakly manned that they could scarcely leave port.[689] However, as with many safety provisions in the Merchant Shipping Act, 1894, the mere existence of this detention power would have weighed heavily upon the minds of shipowners regarding the crewing of their vessels and reduced the likelihood of them being undermanned.

In the very last months of the nineteenth century and in spite of comprehensive prevention of collision rules observed by all maritime States, a collision between a British sailing ship and a French passenger liner, resulted in the rapid sinking of the French ship and the largest loss of life in any collision at sea between two merchant ships during the entire century. The ***La Bourgogne*** (1885) of 7,395 gross tons had been built for the Compagnie Generale Transatlantique for their Le Havre to New York service with a service speed of 17 knots and capacity for 390 First Class, 65 Second Class and 600 Third Class passengers. At 5 o'clock on the morning of the 4th of July 1898 the ***La Bourgogne*** was about 60 miles south of Sable Island on the Grand Banks heading for Le Havre with 506 passengers and 220 crew aboard and steaming at full speed in dense fog. The British iron sailing ship ***Cromartyshire*** was also in the vicinity bound from Glasgow to New York, sailing under reduced canvas and sounding her foghorn. The ships saw each other at the last minute but the ***Cromartyshire*** struck the ***La Bourgogne*** under the bridge on her port side. Both ships were badly damaged with the ***Cromartyshire's*** bow stove in to the collision bulkhead but she drifted off into the fog and remained afloat. The ***La Bourgogne*** was fatally damaged, sinking in thirty minutes.

> The last few minutes on board the Bourgogne witnessed some of the most terrible scenes of horror and cruelty that have blotted the history of a civilized race. Instead of the heroic discipline which so often has been one of the bright features of such awful moments, the crew of the steamer fought like demons for the few lifeboats and rafts, battering the helpless passengers away from their only means of salvation, with the result that the strong overcame the weak and the list of [162] saved contains the name of but one woman.

There were 300 women aboard and no children survived. 549 were lost.[690]

On the 27th of February, 1899, the President of the Board of Trade rose in the House to seek permission to introduce a Bill to consolidate two extant Acts dealing with chain cables and anchors, enacted in 1864 and 1871.[691] The Bill would be to 'simplify and amend the law relating to testing and sale of anchors and chain cables…the law now provides that anchors and chain cables used on board ship shall be subjected to the test, but the law has been found to be extremely unsatisfactory. It is contained in three or four Acts of Parliament, and it has been pointed out to the Board of Trade that this renders the law extremely uncertain, because these Acts are not altogether in accord the one with the other. Thus the law is very easily evaded, and it is also very difficult to enforce'. The only amendment to extant law would be to ensure there was no confusion as to which body had tested anchors, as some private testing firms were marking anchors in a manner similar to those tested under the auspices of the Board of Trade. The consolidated Act; the Anchors, Chains and Cables Act, 1899,[692] would require that such testing marks were distinctive and unmistakable.

Chapter 28

Conclusions

With enactment of the Merchant Shipping Acts of 1894 and 1897, and consolidation of the various Acts on anchors, chains and cables in 1899, the building blocks for effective legislation to ensure the seaworthiness of ships, and safety and welfare of their crews and passengers, put into place slowly, hesitantly, reactively and often reluctantly since the Passenger Vessels Act, 1803, were finally in place. Realism, pragmatism and common sense had slowly overcome an entrenched laissez faire philosophy and resultant reluctance of politicians to use the 'evil', 'vicious' and 'mischievous' tool of legislation, for fear of relieving shipowners of their responsibilities. It is incomprehensible, from a modern perspective, that legislation that had been proven to save life at sea, such as watertight bulkheads and timber deck cargo restrictions, could be arbitrarily repealed on the entirely subjective view that they were a 'dead letter'. During the last quarter of the nineteenth century the suspicion and predominantly negative influence of shipowning members of Parliament largely mellowed into a willingness to work with all involved in the shipping industry, but their legacy of ineffective and qualified legislation for provision of life-saving appliances and watertight bulkheads would come home to haunt them during the early years of the twentieth century.

Masters, and deck and engineer officers, had become more competent through examinations and certification. The longstanding problem of overladen ships had finally been resolved through effective load line requirements which were adopted internationally as customary law; as had international cooperation regarding common steering and sailing rules, led by the United Kingdom. Steamships of all types had become larger, safer and more reliable mechanically, albeit with fewer crew per ton due to economies of scale, increases in efficiency and availability of labour-saving devices.

Passenger ships were carrying far greater numbers of passengers and crew with the associated risk of far greater loss of life if accidents should occur through shipwreck, collision or any of the many other perils of the sea, including sometimes the hubris and folly of shipmasters. A long history of reluctance and inaction by the Board of Trade to address endemic problems in the shipping industry still prevailed as evidenced by their folly throughout the nineteenth century of basing requirements for carriage of lifeboats upon tonnage, and not amending upper tonnage limits as passenger ships became much larger, particularly towards the end of the century.

A total of 67 merchant shipping Statutes addressing safety had been enacted in the course of the nineteenth century and consolidated into the 'Grand Act' of 1894; a model for merchant shipping legislation adopted by many of the world's principal maritime nations. But were ships, their crews and their passengers safer as a result of this vast body of legislation? There was no question that seafaring was a very hazardous occupation. In terms of raw numbers it was estimated that an average of at least 1,000 seamen were lost at sea every year throughout the entire nineteenth century. It is pertinent to recall the mournful toll of lost ships and seafarers; seamen and passengers, throughout the nineteenth century and to reach a conclusion as to whether victims of maritime disasters would eventually have a better chance of survival due to effective safety legislation. Effective, and very limited, legislation was not enacted until mid-century.

From records published by the Board of Trade losses for the consecutive periods of five years ending in 1853, 1858, 1863, and 1868 were respectively 969 ships, 1,118 ships, 1,488 ships, and 1,744 ships. In 1858 the total number of ships registered in the United Kingdom was within 100 of 27,000, while in 1868 there were 29,000. Accordingly, while the increase in the number of ships during these 10 years was only 8 per cent, the increase in the number of losses was at the rate of 50 per cent. Wrecks and casualties for the 10 years ending 1871 increased to a total of 13,300, of which those resulting from stress of weather numbered 7,300; those resulting in wreck from various other causes, or from causes unknown, numbered 2,500; while not less than 3,400 were set down as being lost from inattention, carelessness, neglect, and defective equipment. In plain language meaning that nearly one-half of the losses arose from preventable causes.

The average number of all persons drowned at sea, taking into account the returns for the years ended December 1872, was 2,425; a number that included passengers as well as crew lost or missing from British ships all over the world. The number of lives lost by casualties to British ships during the year ended June 1874, was 4,416, including passengers and including missing crews. It was thus, 1,991 above the annual average. Of this excess of 1,991 lives lost in the year, 821 and 420 respectively were lost in Coolie ships abroad. These two losses alone accounted for 1,241 of the 1,991 lives. As regards the loss of 2,381 lives in 150 missing ships; the 150 ships and the 2,381 missing men were included in the 4,416.

In 1876 Plimsoll referred to a report of the Royal Commission on the Saving of Life at Sea which stated; 'there were in six years 5,316 lives lost by ships where the cause of loss was ascertained; but of these 5,153, or 97 per cent, were lost in vessels which there was every reason to believe were seaworthy, and only 163 were lost in vessels from unseaworthiness. Besides these lives lost from known causes, there were 5,345 lost in missing ships, the cause being unknown, and of these 4,223, nearly four-fifths, were lost in classed ships, and only 1,122 in unclassed ships'.

In 1881, a total of 3,278 seamen aboard British and colonial ships were lost through shipwreck or shipboard accidents resulting in a mortality rate in 1881 of one in 57 of the 187.000 seafarers. In 1883 a further Royal Commission stated; 'From the returns laid before this Commission by the Board of Trade, the substantial accuracy of which has not been questioned, it appears that from 1874 to 1883 inclusively, there was a marked increase in the losses of British ships, and of the lives of those employed in them. The most serious losses occurred in respect of vessels (excluding fishing vessels) reported as missing. No less than 699 vessels, with 8475 hands on board, were reported as missing during this period of nine years, the cause of whose loss was unknown. The majority of which were in class and of a good standard.[693]

Figures from the 1883 Wreck Return showed the loss of 3,304 lives, more than in any previous year of the series, excepting 1872, 1874, and 1881. Chamberlain explained to the House that; "during those 12 years 36,000 men suffered violent deaths; and of the whole number one in six lost his life; ...one in six of the average number employed... of every man, every boy, every officer, and every seaman, lost his life in the British Merchant Service. Go on, and carry that a step further. If you assume that the average working life of the seaman is 24 years, then you will find that one in every three will, in the course of his working life, perish by a violent and dreadful death".

In 1887 the Commission stood by its findings; '...but, whichever method of comparison be taken, the proportion of deaths by drowning of seamen was very high, and had undoubtedly increased during the period under consideration –viz., from 1 in 81 in 1875, to 1 in 56 in 1883...'. The report also made particular mention of the numbers of seafarers who had been saved from shipwreck for the nine years ending 30 June 1883; '...no less than 96,494 lives were saved at home and abroad, chiefly by lifeboats, rocket apparatus, ships' boats etc'.[694]

The Commission concluded that;

> To whatever cause this diminution of loss of life during the years 1884 – 1886 may be due, it cannot be contended that it was in any way the result of the legislation of 1875-6; and the fact remains indisputable that, in spite of all the provisions made by Parliament, and the great increase in the staff of the Board of Trade, entailing a very large charge upon the country, there was not only no diminution in the loss of life at sea in merchant vessels in the years following upon this legislation, and up to the year 1883, but a considerable increase.

Out of all these tragic statistics, the causative factors for this unexpected and unprecedented increase in losses of ships and seafarers were not clear. Many of the missing ships were proven to be steamships carrying cargoes of bulk wheat or coal; issues that had been attended to by measures enacted to prevent cargoes of bulk wheat from shifting and recommendations of the Commission on Carriage of Coal.

By 1896 the mortality rate had, however, improved significantly, particularly for the crews of steamships. Out of a total workforce aboard British ships of 218,000, 1,859 crew were lost; a rate of one in 117. Of these, one in 180 were lost aboard steamships while the mortality rate was three times higher in sailing ships, at one in 60; little better than in 1881[695]. Regardless of the jaundiced view of the Royal Commission for the Saving of Life at Sea in 1887, there is no doubt that legislation had proven beneficial in finally turning the mournful rising tide of lost seafarers throughout most of the nineteenth century.

Credit for this improvement can be largely sheeted home to increased detention powers for unseaworthy ships, compulsory load lines, more effective regulations for the carriage of bulk grain and coal, along with an increase in size of steamships, more appropriate manning and a reduction in the total number of sailing ships. Collisions and speed in fog were, however, two issues that could only be resolved through adherence by Masters and officers to the collision regulations. Dedicated efforts by long-standing Board of Trade officials had solved politician's long-standing problem of how to effectively consolidate a large number of extant Acts into one comprehensive and clear Statute. However; two significant and closely associated issues remained. Inadequate standards for watertight bulkheads, and for determining numbers of life boats and deck rafts to be carried.

It will be recalled that the requirement of s.300 of the Merchant Shipping Act, 1854 for all iron ships to be subdivided into three equal parts by watertight partitions was arbitrarily repealed through the Merchant Shipping Act, 1862. The 1888 report of a select committee on saving life at sea recommended that a standing committee, representing all parties interested, be appointed to frame rules for carrying out the provisions of the Merchant Shipping (Life Saving Appliances) Act, 1888.

The committee was also asked for '…any recommendations to make with reference to bulkheads which would, in their opinion, contribute to the safety of life at sea'. The resultant Bulkhead Committee produced a technical report which became the standard for Board of Trade surveyors when deciding whether the watertight bulkheads voluntarily fitted to a ship were 'efficient' and 'to their satisfaction…' Ship designers and owners had the ability to influence this subjective standard. Section eight of the report introduced conflation of approved watertight bulkheads and carriage of lifeboats by considering the benefits to shipowners of reduced additional boats and life rafts to that required by a draft Board of Trade General Rule.

> The Board of Trade duly issued General Rule Number 12; effective from the 1st of November 1890, but were not so bold as to completely accept the Bulkhead Committee's recommendation that; '…as an inducement to owners to subdivide their vessels… owners might be relieved of the obligation to carry any part of the additional boats, rafts, and other life-saving appliances required by the Rules issued by the

> Board of Trade under the Merchant Shipping (Life Saving Appliances) Act, 1888; reducing the allowance from three-quarters to one half as suggested in their terms of reference for the Life Saving Appliances Committee.

Section 428 of the Merchant Shipping Act, 1894, clearly reflected the influence of ship owning Members of Parliament, and pressures from ship-owners, in its reference to *'avoidance of undue encumbrance of the ship's deck'*; giving considerable license to Board of Trade officers in their interpretation of the law for increasingly large passenger ships.

> *428 Duties of owners and masters as to carrying life-saving appliances*
>
> *It shall be the duty of the owner and master of every British ship to see that his ship is provided, in accordance with the rules for life-saving appliances, with such of those appliances as, having regard to the nature of the service on which the ship is employed, and the avoidance of undue encumbrance of the ship's deck, are best adapted for securing the safety of her crew and passengers.*

The Life Savings Appliances Committee and the Board of Trade had paid no heed when drafting the Act to the reality that Cunard had launched the sister ships ***Campania*** and ***Lucania*** in 1892 and 1893 respectively; both of 12,590 gross tons and certified to carry 2,000 passengers, with crew totalling 424. The maximum number of boats required to be carried under davits for these ships, and those of any tonnage upwards, only increased by two; from 14 to 16.

Before the turn of the century the White Star Line were planning four sister ships of a greater tonnage and longer than Brunel's leviathan, the ***Great Eastern***. The first of this quartet, the ***Celtic*** (1901) of 20,904 gross tons became, at the time of her launch, the largest ship in the world and set the pattern for exponential increases in tonnage, size, speed and passenger capacity over the following few years. The ***Celtic*** and her sisters had a capacity of 300 First Class, 160 Second Class and 2,350 Steerage Class passengers, along with about 350 crew, for a total complement of 3,169.

These fatal flaws in the Merchant Shipping Act, 1894, that perpetuated inadequate tonnage limits for determination of numbers of lifeboats and rafts; compounded by ineffective oversight of tonnage limits for carriage of lifeboats by Board of Trade officials; exacerbated by conflation of life saving appliances requirements and watertight bulkheads, and made worse by legislation allowing owners to subjectively influence the number and type of watertight bulkheads and the capacity of life saving appliances, remained unchanged at the turn of the century and would inevitably result in unprecedented loss of life at sea in the early twentieth century.

References

Chapter 1 – Seaworthiness

1 United Nations Convention on the Law of the Sea, Montego Bay, 10 December 1982. In force 16 November, 1994. 21 ILM 1245 (1982)
2 Ibid, Article 94, *Duties of the flag State*
3 Boisson P, *Safety at Sea, Policies, Regulations and International Law*, Paris, Edition Bureau Veritas, 1999, ISBN 2-86413-020-3
4 *The Monthly Review*, 1838, Vol. II (https://archive.org/details/monthlyreviewfr00google)
5 Bell J D, *The Role of Classification in Maritime Safety*, 9th Chua Chor Teck Annual Memorial Lecture, Singapore, 13 January 1995, IMO Library.
6 Ibid. p. 2
7 Lloyds Register: A Brief History
8 Report of the Select Committee on Shipwreck, 1836
9 Ibid.
10 Ibid.
11 Captains exercised absolute authority at sea and so were dubbed 'Master under God' by early insurance writs, agreements with shipowners and passengers, and the Board of Trade
12 Harvey C & Matthew H, *Nineteenth Century Britain*, Oxford University Press, 2000, p.11
13 Jenkins S, *A Short History of England*, Profile Books Ltd., London, 2011, p.185
14 Dixon C, *Seamen and the law; an examination of the impact of legislation on the British merchant seaman's lot*, 1588 – 1918, PhD Thesis, University College, London, 1980
15 Mitchell B R , *British Historical Statistics*, Cambridge University press, Cambridge, 1988, p.535
16 43 Geo III, C.56
17 https://opentextbc.ca/preconfederation/chapter/10-3-immigration/
18 Kitchen J, *The Employment of Merchant Seamen*, Taylor and Francis Group, Oxfordshire, 1980, p.81
19 53 Geo.3, c.36
20 56 Geo 3, c.83
21 56 Geo.3, c.83
22 57 Geo.3, c.10
23 4 Geo.4, c.84
24 6 Geo.4, c.116
25 Haydn J, A *Dictionary of Dates Relating to all Ages and Nations*, Ninth Edition, Edward Moxon and Co., London, 1860, p.718
26 The Percy Anecdotes, 1823 – Loss of the East Indiaman, Earl of Abergavenny 1805
27 TheShipsList, Loss of the Aurora, 1805
28 Bryant A, *Years of Victory*, Collins, London, 1945, p.186
29 Ibid, p.42
30 Ibid, p.325

31 Clayton T, *Waterloo – Four Days that Changed Europe's Destiny*, Little Brown, London, 2014, pp.53-54
32 Bryant, p.90
33 Clayton, pp.53-54
34 Blackmore, p.52
35 Treaty of Ghent, 24 December 1814 (8 Stat. 218)
36 Ibid
37 Woodman R, *Masters Under God*, The History Press, 2009, p.13
38 Blackmore E, *The British Mercantile Marine*, Griffiths and Company Ltd, London, 1897, p.54
38 *New Monthly Magazine and Universal Register*, Vol. II, July to December, 1814, p.123
39 Ibid
40 Dickinson HW, *A Short History of the Steam Engine*, The MacMillan Company, New York, 1938
41 Crump, p.65
42 English Historical Documents, Vol. XI, p.556 (388G)
43 Campbell, RD, *The Ship's Register: a History of British Ship Status and Registration Procedures including their adoption in New Zealand*, Ministry of Transport, - Marine Division, New Zealand, 1980, p.11
44 Lindsay W.S, *A History of Merchant Shipping and Ancient Commerce*, Vol IV, Sampson Low, Marston, Low and Searle , London, 1876, p.73
45 Robins, p.5
46 Crump, pp, 284-5
47 Keble Chatterton E, *The Mercantile Marine*, William Heinemann Ltd.,, London, 1923, p.172
48 Unwin P, *The Narrow Sea*, Headline Book Publishing, London, 2003, p.184
49 Fox S, *The Ocean Railway*, HarperCollinsPublishers, London, 2003, p.31
50 Campbell, pp. 11-12
51 Fox, p.34
52 Crump, p.287
53 Mansell J N K , *Flag State Responsibility*, Springer, 2009, p.26 ['The "Tonnage Laws" refers to the Navigation Acts that]…encompassed ownership, marking of the ship's name and port of registry, transfer of ownership, proof of location of build, tonnage, record of the identity and changes of master, and provision of a unique registration number carved into the main beam of the ship to provide indisputable evidence of identity of the ship in case of shipwreck.
54 Clark AH, *The Clipper Ship Era*, G.P.Putnam & Sons, New York and London, 1912, p.20
55 Ibid pp. 22-31
56 Lindsay, pp. 38-40
57 Fox, p.15
58 Lindsay, pp. 45-46
59 Robbins, p.43
60 Ibid
61 Fox, pp. 50-51
62 Ibid, pp. 51-53

63 The Steam Navigation Act, 1846, introduced a requirement for two watertight bulkheads in steam vessels to separate the engine room from cargo spaces.

64 Evidence of Robert A. Gray, shipowner, to the 1833 Select Committee on Manufactures, Commerce and Shipping. Report of the Select Committee on Manufactures, Commerce and Shipping, BPP 1833 (690) VI 231

65 Dixon C, pp.35 & 36

66 Ibid. p.38

67 Woodman, p.7

68 Jenkins S, p.190

69 Importation, etc., in Foreign Vessels Act, 1823 (4 Geo.IV. c.77) and Duties on Foreign Vessels Act, 1824 (5 Geo. IV. C.1)

70 Blackmore, p.55

71 2 & 3 Ann. c.6

72 3 & 4 Will. IV. c.88

73 http://www.discovertranmore.ie/history

74 British Parliamentary Papers; Report of the Select Committee on Shipwrecks, 1836 XVII

75 Ibid.

76 Boisson P, p.365

77 Hadyn J, p. 718

78 9 Geo.4 c21

79 Lindsay, pp. 497-498

80 Blane G, *Observations on the Diseases Incident to Seamen,* 1785, p.211.

81 Coggeshall G, *Thirty-Six Voyages to Various Parts of the World,* Geo. P Putnam, New York, 1858 (1974 edition) p. 61

82 5 & 6 Will. IV. c.19

83 An Act for prevention of Frauds and Regulating Abuses in the Plantation Trade, 1696 (7 & 8 Will. 3, c.22)

84 https://archive.org/details/treatiseonlawrel00abbo

85 *Outrageous Seas,* Baehre R., Ed., Carleton University Press, 1999, p.35

86 Newfoundland's Grand Banks, genealogical and historical data

87 http://www.stpaulisland.net/shipwrecks.html

88 5 & 6 Wm.4. c.55

89 HC Deb 19 March 1835 vol 26 cc1235-9

90 Woodman, pp. 63-64

Chapter 2 – Shipwreck and Cannibalism

91 Report from Select Committees on the Causes of Shipwrecks and on Shipwrecks of Timber Ships, with minutes of evidence, appendices and indices, 1836-1839. First and Second Report from the Select Committee on Shipwrecks, with minutes of evidence, appendix and index, 1843. Preliminary Report from the Royal Commission on the Alleged Unseaworthiness of British Registered Ships, with minutes of evidence, digest of oral evidence and appendix, 1873. Final Report from the Royal Commission on the Alleged Unseaworthiness of British Registered Ships, with minutes of evidence, digest of evidence taken in 1874, First Report from the Royal Commission on

the Loss of Life at Sea, with minutes of evidence and appendix, 1884–85, Final Report from the Royal Commission on the Loss of Life at Sea and Report from the Board of Trade Committee on Merchant Shipping (Life Saving Appliances) Act, 1887–89, with minutes of evidence, digest of evidence, and appendix, 1887–1889

92 Dixon C, Appendices 1 & 2. A Statistical Department administered by the Board of Trade was established in 1832

93 Ibid., p. 68

94 'On the Frequency of Shipwrecks' *Edinburgh Review* LX, 1834-35, 339-340.

95 Dixon, p.41, fn. The Times of 10 June 1831 shows that a general association of shipowners had been formed following a meeting in London the previous day. Aaron Chapman, M.P. for Whitby, and George Frederick Young, MP for Tynemouth, were the leading lights. An article 'The General Ship Owners Society' - in the October 1832 issue of The Nautical Magazine Vol.1 420-423 shows the organisation was created because trade was depressed, and that it's foundation derived from a provisional meeting of shipowners on 10 April 1828. A small reform group was led by James Silk Buckingham, the Member for Sheffield. The reformers were only able to defeat the combined strength of the Admiralty and the shipowners over one issue - the contribution made by merchant seamen for the upkeep of Greenwich Hospital.

96 *The Monthly Review*, Vol. 146, p.134

97 It would not be until July 1998 that ships were required to be "...designed, constructed and maintained in compliance with the structural, mechanical and electrical requirements of a classification society..." through an amendment to SOLAS Chapter II-1, Part A-1, Reg. 3-1

98 Lindsay, pp. 497-498.

99 Blackmore E, p.60

100 Clarke, pp. 19-20

101 Report of the Select Committee on Shipwrecks, BPP 1836 (567) XVII 373.

102 Dixon, p. 69

103 Ibid

104 Blackmore, pp. 62-63

105 Ibid, p.63

106 Dixon., pp. 75-76

107 Ibid., p. 77

108 Report of the Select Committee on Shipwrecks of Timber Ships 1839, p.xvii

109 Ibid., p.xviii

110 Dixon, pp. 78 & 79

111 Report of 1839 committee, p. xviii

112 Dixon, p. 78

113 Report of 1839 Committee, p.xix

114 2 & 3 Vict. c.44

115 Tames R, *Isambard Kingdom Brunel*, Shire Publications, Oxford, 2010, p.25

116 Ibid. Brunel proved that 'whereas the carrying capacity of a hull increases as the *cube* of its dimensions, its resistance (the power needed to dive it through the water) increases only as the *square* of those dimensions'

117 Fox, p.71

118 Tames, p.26
119 Lindsay, p.80
120 Fox. p.87
121 Ibid. pp. 92-93
122 Ibid. p.94
123 Tomalin C, *Charles Dickens – a Life*, The Penguin Press, New York, 2011, pp. 128-129 and 138

Chapter 3 – Logs, Lifeboats and Laissez Faire

124 Burgess, p. 177
125 3 & 4 Vic. c.36
126 5 & 6 Vic. c.17
127 8 & 9 Vic. c.14
128 3 & 4 Vict. c.21
129 5 & 6 Victoria, c.107. The Act repealed a number of earlier Passenger Acts.
130 Passenger ships engaged in voyages to North America of more than 12 weeks were not required to carry "medical men"; a provision belatedly amended through Part XXXVIII of the Passengers Act, 1852
131 Captain of HMS Beagle during its three year scientific circumnavigation between December 1831 and October 1836 with Charles Darwin aboard.
132 Dixon C, pp. 80-81
133 Ibid, pp.80-84
134 Blackmore, p.75
135 *Nautical Magazine and Naval Chronicle*, 1843, pp.683-684
136 *Nautical Magazine and Naval Chronicle*, p.683-684
137 5 & 6 Vict. c.102
138 The only maritime legislation at this time dealt with the carriage of passengers, their allocated space per ton, victualling etc.
139 Blackmore, pp.66-67
140 Ibid., p.72
141 Woodman, p.73
142 Blackmore, p.72
143 *The Spectator* Archives
144 9 & 10 Vic. c.100
145 Mitchell, p.537
146 *Journal of the Society of Arts*, February 23, 1866
147 Boisson
148 *Journal of the Society of Arts*, 1866, p. 240
149 Jenkins, p.199
150 Ibid, p.200
151 Fox, p.15
152 Rogers S, *The Atlantic*, George G Harrap and Company Limited, London, 1930, pp. 153-154
153 Phillips-Birt D, *A History of Seamanship*, George Allen & Unwin, London, 1971, p.280
154 Atkinson N, *Crew Culture*, Te Papa Press, Museum of New Zealand, Wellington, 2001, p.17

[155] Ibid, pp. 44-45
[156] Bullen F T, *The Men of the Merchant Marine,* Frederick A Stokes Company, New York, 1900, 323-324
[157] Atkinson, pp. 19-20
[158] Ibid, pp. 22-23
[159] Ibid, p.24
[160] Keble Chatterton, pp 178-180
[161] Robins, p.64. Iron construction was very much the exception to the rule of all wooden construction which was to remain dominant throughout the 1850s; the first ship of composite construction – iron frames with wooden hulls - the Tubal Cain of 737 ton, being built in Liverpool in 1859. After operating ever larger wooden paddle-steamers across the North Atlantic from 1840 Cunard finally built their first iron-hulled paddle steamer, the Persia of 3300 ton, in 1855
[162] Ibid. pp. 145-146
[163] Fox, pp. 148-149
[164] Tames, p.28
[165] Fox, pp. 153-154
[166] Kirkaldy, pp.57-58
[167] Fox, pp. 114-115

Chapter 4 – Fire, Famine and Free Trade

[168] Canadian Immigration History – The arrival of the Irish
[169] Page T W, *The Transportation of Immigrants and Reception Arrangements in the Nineteenth Century,* Journal of Political Economy, Vol. 19, No. 9 (Nov., 1911), pp. 732-737
[170] Fox S, pp. 76-78
[171] *The Times,* Tuesday 4 May, 1847, p.4
[172] 5 & 6 Victoria, c.107. The Act repealed a number of earlier Passenger Acts.
[173] Passenger ships engaged in voyages to North America of more than 12 weeks were not required to carry "medical men"; a provision belatedly amended through Part XXXVIII of the Passengers Act, 1852
[174] Villiers P, *Joseph Conrad, Master Mariner,* Seafarer Books, Rendlesham, England, 2006, p.50
[175] Conrad J, *Youth and Gaspar Ruiz,* J.M. Dent and Sons Ltd., London, 1920, pp. 35, 48, 52, 53
[176] The Ocean Monarch was one of nine large packet ships built by the famous shipbuilder Donald McKay in Boston for Enoch Train's White Diamond Line of Boston-Liverpool vessels, measuring 179 feet in length and 1,301 tons and launched in July 1847
[177] *The New York Times,* "The loss of the Ocean Monarch" – Report
[178] "An Emigrant Ship on Fire", *Colonial Times,* Hobart, 5 April 1850, p.4
[179] As reported in the *Shipping Gazette and Sydney General Trade List*, Vol. 5, Page 265, 4 Nov 1848
[180] 11 & 12 Vict. c.81
[181] Dixon C, p.85,
[182] 8 & 9 Vict. c.14

183 10 & 11 Vict. c.103
184 11 & 12 Vict. c.6
185 12 & 13 Vict. c.33
186 Campbell, p.18
187 English Historical Documents, Vol, IX, p.353 (51A—E)
188 12 Cha. 2 c.18
189 7 & 8 Will. 3 c.22
190 26 Geo. 3 c.60
191 Geo III, c.95
192 4 Geo.4 c.41, An Act for the Registering of Vessels
193 6 Geo. 4 c.110, An Act for the Registering of Vessels
194 3 & 4 Will.4 c.55, An act for the Encouragement of British Shipping and Navigation
195 8 & 9 Vict. c.89
196 13 & 14 Vict. c.93
197 11 & 12 Vict. c.33
198 *Nautical Magazine and Marine Quarterly*, Vol.18, 1849, pp.151-152
199 Kirkaldy AW, *British Shipping - its history, organisation and importance,* Kegan Paul, Trench, Trubner & Co., Ltd, London, 1914, pp 26 – 32
200 17 & 18 Vict, c.5

Chapter 5 – Collision and Consolidation

201 Kirkaldy, Appendix XVIII
202 Ibid, p.60
203 Fox, pp.125-128
204 Ibid, p. 31
205 Haydn J, A *Dictionary of Dates Relating to all Ages and Nations,* Ninth Edition, Edward Moxon and Co., London, p.722
206 *The Argus, Melbourne,* 13 November 1851, p.4
207 17 & 18 Vict. c.104
208 13 & 14 Vict. c.93
209 14 & 15 Vict. c.96 The Act was largely a tidy-up of the 1850 Act
210 *New Zealander,* Volume 6, Issue 457, 31 August 1850, p.2
211 "Wreck of the Orion", *Liverpool Journal,* 22 June 1850
212 "Wreck of the "Edmund"." *Illustrated London News* (7 December 1850): 436. Hathi Trust Digital Library
213 14 & 15 Vict. c.79
214 *Nautical Magazine and Naval Chronicle,* 1851, pp.99 - 100
215 14 & 15 Vict. c.1
216 15 & 16 Vict. c.44
217 Kipling, *Collected Verse of Rudyard Kipling,* Kessinger, 2005,p. 305.
218 Hansard, HL Debate 28 June 1852, Vol. 122, cc 1333-6, p.1333
219 The Passenger Act, 1852 was amended by Passenger Act Amendment Act, 1853 (16 & 17 Vict. c.84) – *An Act to Amend the Passenger Act, 1852, so far as relates to the Passage of Natives of Asia or Africa and also Passages between the Island of Ceylon and certain Parts of the East Indies*
220 "A Sample of Shipwreck Statistics within 10 miles of the British Coast",

http://freepages.rootsweb.com
221 https://www.wrecksite.eu/wreck.aspx?117989
222 Haydn. p. 722
223 "Wreck of a Steamer – Loss of Life", *Maori Messenger*, Te Karere Maori, Vol. VI, Issue 136, March 1854
224 "Wreck of the Dalhousie", *Southport Visitor*, October 28th 1853
225 *Journal for the Society of Arts, and the Institutions in Union*, Volume II, November 11, 1853, to November 19, 1854, George Bell, London, p.123
226 Rogers, p. 164
227 Ibid

Chapter 6 – Prevention of Collision

228 Ashburner W. Ed. *The Rhodian Sea-Law*, The Lawbook Exchange Ltd., 2001. As with the loss of the ship Northfleet, January 22nd 1873
229 McGuffie, pp.131-132
230 Boisson P, Safety At Sea. *Policies, Regulations and International Law*. Paris, Edition Bureau Veritas, 1999, ISBN 2-86413-0 S20-3
231 The Corporation of Trinity House, incorporated by Royal Charter in 1514 to regulate pilotage on the River Thames and provide for aged mariners, is a charity dedicated to safeguarding shipping and seafarers, providing education, support and welfare to the seafaring community and with a statutory duty as a General Lighthouse Authority to deliver a reliable, efficient and cost-effective aids to navigation for the benefit and safety of all mariners.
232 Unwin, p. 191
233 Loss of the steamer Mercury, SG & SGTL Vol 12, Page 90, 14 May 1855
234 Cockcroft A N and Lameijer J N K, *A Guide to the Collision Avoidance Rules*, 4th Edition, Butterworth-Heinemann, Oxford, 1990, p. xiv
235 Unwin, p.191
236 Haydn, p.660
237 *Nautical Magazine and Naval Chronicle*, 1852, pp.257-262
238 *Shipping Gazette & Sydney General Trade List*, Vol 12, Volume 12, Number 558 (15 January, 1855)
239 Hearn CG, *Tracks in the Sea*, International Marine/McGraw-Hill, 2002, pp. 207 - 208
240 Seymour W. D., Ed, *The Merchant Shipping Act, 1854*, W G Benning, London, 1855, p.236
241 *Shipping Gazette & Sydney General Trade List, The Times,* Sep 22 1854 - Oceanus - Collision and Loss of Life in the Channel off Start Point
242 HL Deb 08 July 1862 vol 168 cc1-41
243 Ibid, p.677
244 Boyd A C, *The Merchant Shipping Laws* – being a consolidation of all the Merchant Shipping and Passenger Acts from 1854 to 1876 inclusive with notes of all the leading English and American cases on the subjects affected by the legislation, Stevens & Sons, London, 1876, fn p.263
245 Ibid, p.266, fn., *The Rona*, 2 Asp. Mar. Law. Cas. (P. C.) 182
246 *Nautical Magazine and Naval Chronicle*, 1870, pp.26-27
247 Boyd, p.277, fn., *The Anglo Indian*, 3 Asp. Mar. Law. Cas. (P. C.) 4, 33 L.T.N.S.

235)

[248] Cockroft A N and Lameiger J N F, p.xv

[249] The *Sydney Morning Herald*, 26 November 1866, p.3

[250] HC Deb 06 December 1867 vol 190 cc642-3642

[251] Hughes T, *The Blue Riband of the Atlantic*, Patrick Stephens, Cambridge, 1973, p.50

[252] Boyd, pp.275-276, fn., *The Westphalia*, 1 Asp. Mar. Law. Cas. 24; 24 L. T. N. S. (Amer.) 75

[253] Ibid, *The Pensylvania*, 19 Wallace (Amer. Rep.) 133

[254] Ibid, *The Pensylvania*, 3 Mar. Law. Cas. (P. C.) 47; *The Pensylvania*, Wallace (Amer. Rep.) 125; 2 Asp. Mar. Law. Cas. 378; *The Great Eastern*, Br. & L. 287

[255] *The Rose*, 2W, Rob.1; *The Vivid*, Swa. 88; *The Nothern Indianna*, 3 Blatchford (Amer. Rep.) 92

[256] Hughes, p.70

[257] Fox, p.341

[258] *New York Times*, May 23, 1887

[259] Ibid

[260] Gault S, Ed., *Marsden on Collisions at Sea*, Thirteenth Edition, Sweet & Maxwell, London, 2003, p.218, see fn. 77

[261] As reported in the Times of February 22nd 1896

[262] (Ad. Ct. Feb. 1896)

[263] 'Similarly, the "Commercial Code of Signals for the Use of Nations" published by Great Britain in 1857, formed the basis of the work of the Washington Conferences of 1889 and 1927, and of the London Conference of 1948, and is now in universal use'. Colombo CJ, *The International Law of the Sea*, 6th Edition, Longmans, United Kingdom

[264] For example; By Order in Council, September 5 1880, the Collision Regulations, 1879, with the exception of Article 10, apply to the ships of Cochin, Kattyawar, Kelat, Kutch, Muscat, Travecore and Zanzibar. By Order in Council, 27 November 1880, the rules of 1879 apply to ships of Hawaii. By Order in Council, 9 July 1885, the rules of 1884 apply to ships of Turkey. Article 10 of the rules of 1879 and 1884 apply to ships of the following countries: Austria-Hungary, Belgium, Brazil, Chili, Ecuador, France, Germany, Greece, Italy, Japan, Netherlands, Norway, Portugal, Russia, Spain, Sweden, United States. By Order in Council, 7 July 1897, the Collision Regulations apply to ships of the following countries: Argentine Republic, Austria-Hungary, Belgium, Brazil, Chili, China, Costa Rica, Denmark, Ecuador, Egypt, France, Germany, Greece, Guatemala, Italy, Japan, Mexico, Netherlands, Norway, Peru, Portugal, Russia, Siam, Spain, Sweden, USA.

[265] Merchant Shipping Act 1894, s.424

[266] Colombo, p. 60

[267] Cockroft, pp. xiv-xv

[268] Ibid

[269] Ibid

[270] Ibid

Chapter 7 – Merchant Shipping Act, 1854

271 Haydn, p.792 (Wrecks)
272 Ibid. Arctic 300+, Favourite 210, Lady Nugent 400, City of Glasgow 480
273 "Loss of the Iron Ship Tayleur off Lamby", *Colonial Times*, Hobart, 5 April 1850, p.2
274 "Loss of the John [sic] Tayleur and 300 lives", *Southport Visiter*, Jan. 27th 1854
275 Ibid
276 Loss of the City of Glasgow 1854 – *Daily Missouri Republic*, April 12th 1854
277 Missing Steamer – City of Glasgow, *New York Herald*
278 Dixon p.109
279 Ibid
280 Ibid. p.110. (Hansard 3 112 1070)
281 Ibid, fn. p.110, Thomas Henry Farrer was a barrister who served at the Board of Trade for almost forty years. Later raised to the peerage, he was a life-long advocate of laissez-faire and put his views plainly in a book entitled The State in its Relation to Trade. According to his obituary in The Times of 18 March 1890, he was 'the last of the Cobdenites'.
282 Ibid. (Hansard 3 130 246)
283 Ibid, fn. p.112, Joseph Warner Henley, (1793-1884), was MP for Oxfordshire from 1841-78. He was briefly President of the Board of Trade in 1852, and again in 1858-59. An Oxfordshire country gentleman whose father had been a shipowner and coal merchant, Henley was an arch-conservative.
284 Ibid. Edward Cardwell, (1813-86), was MP for Oxford in 1854. He had been unseated as Liverpool's MP in 1852 because of his free trade stance and his support for the repeal of the Navigation Laws.
285 Ibid. p.111
286 Seymour D. Ed., *The Merchant Shipping Act, 1854*, W.G. Benning & Co., London, 1855, Preface
287 Kirkaldy, p.130
288 Fox, p.131
289 Kirkaldy, p.62
290 "Island's forgotten disaster", *The Oban Times*, 22 Nov. 2017
291 Hadyn, p.752

Chapter 8 – Continuing Calamities

292 *Quebec Mercury*, Tuesday, May 29th, 1855. Page 3, Col. 1C.
293 SG & SGTL Vol 12 ; Page 204; 3 Sep 1855
294 18 & 19 Vict. c.91
295 18 & 19 Vict. c.119
296 "Shipping Intelligence", *The Maitland Mercury and Hunter River General Advertiser*, Sat. 6 Jan. 1855, p.2
297 Robins, p.61
298 Crump, pp.297-298
299 Fox, p. 273
300 Crump, p.298
301 Fox, pp. 137-138
302 *New York Daily Times*, New York, N.Y. Jun 23, 1856 p. 3, Jul 7, 1856 p. 1, Jul

12, 1856 p. 4

303 The Ships List. "Never heard of" – Mysteries of the Atlantic Ferry, C.L. Davis, Esq., 1900

304 Ibid

305 Ibid

306 Ibid

307 Cox W. T, *The Life of Robert Fulton and a History of Steam Navigation*, G. P. Putnam's Sons, New York and London, 1886, p.361

308 Rogers, pp. 173–174

309 *Sacramento Daily Union*, Volume 11, Number 1593, 3 May 1856

310 For example - one of the author's ancestors undertook a passage on the maiden sailing of the full rigged ship Fifeshire of 557 tons; departing London 17 September 1841, the Downs on 2 October and arriving at Nelson on 1 February 1882; a passage of 143 days. The Fifeshire ran aground upon departure from Nelson and became a total loss.

311 UNSW Press, Sydney, 2006

312 Bound for South Australia – Shipwreck, accessed 27 May 2018

313 Fox, pp.365/366

314 A Sample of Shipwreck Statistics within 10 miles of the British coastline

315 "Shipwreck off the Irish Coast", *Wexford Constitution*, April 30th 1859

316 Baynes N, *An Account of the Wreck of the "Royal Charter*, Wyman and Sons, London, 1859

317 "The Royal Charter Gale, Met Office, London

318 Fitzroy R, *The Weather Book; a Manual of Practical Meteorology*, Volume II, Longman, Green, Longman, Roberts and Green, London, 1863, pp. 321/322

Chapter 9 – Chain, Cables and Casualties

319 HC Deb 02 February 1860 vol. 156 cc497-501

320 *Canadian News and British American Intelligencer*, Mar.14 1860, pp. 3-4

321 Jones N, *The Plimsoll Sensation*, Little, Brown, London, 2006, p.11

322 *The Newfoundler*, August 1, 1859

323 The Ships List, Galway Line/Royal Atlantic Steam Navigation Company

324 *New York Times*, 09 October 1860

325 *Nautical Magazine and Naval Chronica*l, 1860, p.540

326 Ibid p.541

327 Ibid, p.542

328 Ibid, p.544

329 HC Deb 31 January 1860 vol. 156 cc332-78

330 http://www.robertsewell.ca/canadian.html

331 25 & 26 Vict. c.63

332 See Chapter 28 for detail of these provisions

333 16 & 17 Vict. c.107

334 Masters D, *The Plimsoll Mark, Cassell*, London, 1955, pp.132-133

335 Ibid

336 HC Deb 21 March 1862 vol 165 cc1931-6

337 *Nautical Magazine*, October, 1876, pp. 222 – 259, Report to the President of the Board of Trade on the legislation concerning merchant shipping and

seamen enacted during the last forty years, 1835 – 1875, T.H. Farrer

338 Alderman G, Joseph Chamberlain's Attempted Reform of the British Merchant Marine , *Journal of Transport History*, New Series, 1 (1972) pp.169-184

339 *Journal of the Society of the Arts*, XIV, (1863-6) p.239. Thomas Gray was Permanent Secretary of the Maritime Department, Board of Trade from 1869 to 1889

340 TheShipsList, Official Report into the Loss of the Anglo Saxon

341 "Total Wreck of the Anglo Saxon – Loss of 250 Lives" *Liverpool Mercury*, May 11th 1863

342 26 & 27 Vict. c.51

343 27 & 28 Vict. c.27

Chapter 10 – Loss of the London

344 Chatterton, p.222

345 Kirkaldy, Appendix XVII, Net tonnage of the leading mercantile fleets of the world from 1850 - 1910

346 Robins, pp 64-66

347 "The Loss of the SS London", *The Argus*, Melbourne, 16 Mar. 1866, p.5

348 Jones N, p.2

349 HC Deb 19 March 1866 vol 182 cc524-53524

350 Ibid

351 *Nautical Magazine and Naval Chronicle*, 1866, p.166

352 Ibid

353 Jones, p.8

354 *Journal of the Society of Arts*, 1866, p.243

355 HC Deb 23 February 1866 vol 181 c1060

356 Harvie and Matthew, p.73

357 HC Deb 17 July 1866 vol. 184 cc943-71

358 HC Deb 19 July 1866 vol. 184 c1072

359 HC Deb 07 February 1867 vol. 185 c8383

360 30 & 31 Vict. c.124

361 Dixon, p.155

362 Ibid, fn 'Originally, the clause had called for twelve superficial feet, but the Liverpool Shipowners Association used the 'hot bunk' argument, saying that twelve feet was excessive because 'not more than half the crew are ever below at one time'

363 Ibid, fn p.156. See Hepworth Dixon John Howard and the Prison World of Europe (1850 edition) 136.

364 Ibid, p.157

365 Rowland KT, *Steam at Sea: A History of Steam Navigation*, Newton Abbot, 1970, pp.119-120.

366 Dixon, p.165

367 5 & 6 Will. IV c.19

368 7 & 8 Vict. c.112

369 5 & 6 Will. IV c.53

370 14 & 15 Vict. c.96

371 17 & 18 Vict. c.120

372 Dixon, p.167, fn. 'A petition to Queen Victoria in 1855 complained that seamen were being compelled to sail in unseaworthy ships under threat of imprisonment. The Board of Trade obtained a legal opinion to the effect that seaworthiness was implied when a man signed-on, but that proof of unseaworthiness lies with the man who refuses duty - PRO MT/9 60 M.70151 1871. The civil liability of a shipowner to provide a seaworthy ship was finally established by Steel v. State Line Steamship Co. in 1877 (3 App. Cas. 72).

373 HC Deb 07 June 1867 vol. 187 cc1731-21731

Chapter 11 – Overladen and Unseaworthy

374 *Nautical Magazine and Naval Chronicle*, 1867, pp.380 - 387

375 HC Deb 12 August 1867 vol 189 c1337

376 HC Deb 13 August 1867 vol 189 cc1487-98

377 Woodman, *The History of the Ship*, p.187

378 *Nautical Magazine and Naval Chronicle*, 1867, pp. 603-609

379 Ibid

380 HC Deb 19 May 1868 vol 192 c513

381 HC Deb 25 June 1868 vol 192 c2136

382 *Nautical Magazine and Naval Chronicle*, 1869, p.584

383 Ibid, p.586

384 Ibid, p.587

385 Mitchell, p.536

386 HC Deb 09 August 1869 vol 198 cc1499-517

387 Ibid, pp.1500-1501

388 Ibid, p.1502

389 Ibid, 1503-1504

390 Ibid, 1508

391 *Nautical Magazine and Naval Chronical*, 1869, p.523

392 Ibid, p.524

393 *Nautical Magazine and Naval Chronicle*, 1870, p.38

394 Ibid, p.640

395 32 & 33 Vict. c.11

396 Crump, p.298

397 Blackmore, p.104

Chapter 12 – The Seaman's Friend

398 HC Deb 14 February 1870 vol 199 cc286-316

399 Ibid, p.289

400 Ibid, p.291

401 Ibid, p.301

402 Jones, *The Plimsoll Sensation – The Great Campaign to Save Lives at Sea*, Little Brown, 2006, p.66

403 Ibid. pp.66-68

404 Dixon, pp.169-170

405 HC Deb 31 March 1870 vol 200 cc990-1

406 Jones, pp. 52-55
407 Ibid
408 Ibid
409 Blackmore, p.104
410 30 & 31 Vict. c.102
411 Jones, pp.46 -47
412 Ibid, pp.55-56
413 Ibid. p.65
414 HC Deb 20 May 1870 vol 201 cc1094-123
415 HC Deb 13 May 1870 vol 201 c729
416 Jones, p.65
417 HC Deb 13 June 1870 vol 201 cc1987-2008
418 HC Deb 04 July 1870 vol 202 c1426
419 HC Deb 28 July 1870 vol 203 cc1102-11
420 Ibid
421 Ibid
422 Ibid
423 33 & 34 Vict. c.95
424 *Nautical Magazine*, 1871, pp. 858-859
425 *Lloyd's Weekly Newspaper*, London, October 23, 1870.

Chapter 13 – A Contemporary View

426 The *Nautical Magazine* 1871, v.40, pp.217 – 242
427 The List contained the names, tonnage, owners and date of loss of nine ships, ranging from 51 to 1,235 tons, owned by Berwick and Holdsworth and lost at sea between 1844 and 1866

Chapter 14 – Mr. Fortescue's Act

428 *Nautical Magazine*, 1871, p.126
429 Jones, p.70
430 Scarborough Maritime Heritage Centre, A Great Storm in 1871 in Bridlington Bay
431 Jones, pp.80-81
432 HC Deb 10 February 1871 vol 204 c1531
433 HC Deb 13 February 1871 vol 204 cc231-2
434 HC Deb 22 February 1871 vol 204 cc662-91
435 HC Deb 14 March 1871 vol 204 cc1981-2
436 HC Deb 28 March 1871 vol 205 cc768-70
437 HC Deb 21 April 1871 vol 205 c1469
438 HC Deb 03 July 1871 vol 207 c1077
439 HC Deb 07 August 1871 vol 208 cc1061-4
440 HC Deb 09 August 1871 vol 208 c1194
441 HL Deb 21 August 1871 vol 208 c1888
442 *Nautical Magazine*, 1872, p.884
443 HC Deb 15 June 1871 vol 207 c121
444 34 & 35 Vict. c.101

445 *Shipping and Mercantile Gazette*, 16th December, 1871
446 *Nautical Magazine*, 1873, pp. 974-975

Chapter 15 – Procrastination, Plimsoll and Passengers

447 *Nautical Magazine*, 1873 p.548
448 HC Deb 16 May 1870 vol 201 c790 - Select Committee appointed, «to inquire into the cause of Steam Boiler Explosions, and as to the best means of preventing them."
449 Jones, p.33
450 HC Deb 12 February 1872 vol 209 cc232
451 Until the early 19th century mines were largely unregulated, but by the end of the century there was considerable government control from legislation supported by an inspection structure. Legislation often followed from government enquiries, which also provide a detailed contemporary assessment of those aspects of mining within their remit. North of England Institute of Mining and Mechanical Engineers Nicholas Wood Memorial Library Government and Mining: Legislation, Inspection, Enquiries a resource list. www.mininginstitute.org.uk Accessed 08.04.2019
452 HC Deb 16 May 1870 vol 201 c790
453 Bindon E B, *Records of Steam Boiler Explosions*, E. and F.N. Spon, Charing Cross, London, 1872
454 The Steam Boiler Explosions Bill, introduced and first read on the 7th of March 1872 – *A Bill to provide a more efficient remedy to Persons injured and property damaged by the Explosion of Boilers from negligence* was enacted on the 10th August 1872 as the Coal Mines Regulation Act, 1872. (Vict.35 & 36, c.76)
455 HC Deb 19 June 1851 vol 117 cc998-1000
456 Berry C D, *Loss of the Sultana and Reminiscences of Survivors*, Darius D Thorpe, Lansing, Michigan, 1892, pp. 7-9
457 HC Deb 19 June 1851 vol 117 cc998-1000
458 HC Deb 23 February 1872 vol 209 cc1008-17
459 HC Deb 04 July 1872 vol 212 cc640-63
460 HC Deb 15 February 1872 vol 209 cc467
461 *Nautical Magazine*, June 1872, pp.453-458
462 HC Deb 27 June 1872 vol 212 c33
463 HL Deb 10 August 1872 vol 213 c857
464 35 & 36 Vict. c.73

Chapter 16 - Load Line, Libel and Shipwreck Commission

465 The Ships List, Loss of the Northfleet
466 HL Deb 07 February 1873 vol 214 cc144-50
467 *Nautical Magazine*, 1874, pp.175-176
468 Jones, p.84
469 Plimsoll, p.38
470 Ibid. p.40
471 Ibid. p.74
472 Ibid. p.40

473 Ibid. p.56
474 Ibid. p.101
475 Ibid. p.113
476 Ibid. p.124
477 Ibid. p.128
478 Ibid. p.90. Comment attributed to George Howells in his handwritten history of the Plimsoll Movement
479 Jones, p.92.
480 HC Deb 10 February 1873 vol 214 cc273-4
481 HC Deb 17 February 1873 vol 214 cc542
482 HC Deb 20 February 1873 vol 214 cc733-43
483 Jones, pp.92-93
484 Ibid, p.92
485 Ibid, p.94
486 Ibid, pp.95-96
487 HC Deb 04 March 1873 vol 214 cc1319-62
488 Fox, p.243

Chapter 17 – Merchant Shipping Act, 1873

489 Flayhart, pp.43-44
490 Fox, pp.245-246
491 Ibid, pp.247-249
492 Flayhart, pp.44 -46
493 Ibid, p.52
494 Ibid, pp.48-53
495 *Nautical Magazine*, 1873, p.579
496 HC Deb 24 March 1873 vol 215 cc9-11
497 HC Deb 25 March 1873 vol 215 cc105-9
498 HC Deb 28 March 1873 vol 215 cc298-9
499 HC Deb 07 April 1873 vol 215 cc639-44
500 Jones, p.121
501 *Nautical Magazine*, 1873, p.608
502 Ibid, p.680
503 HC Deb 13 May 1873 vol 215 c1961
504 HC Deb 14 May 1873 vol 215 cc1987-97
505 Jones, p.135
506 HC Deb 20 May 1873 vol 216 cc167-9
507 Jones, p.138
508 HC Deb 05 June 1873 vol 216 c515
509 Jones, p.149
510 36 & 37 Vict. c.87
511 *Nautical Magazine*, 1873, pp.701-702
512 Flayhart, pp.61-66
513 Jones, p.147
514 *Nautical Magazine*, 1873, pp.878
515 Ibid
516 Ibid, p.879

517 Ibid, pp.879-880
518 Ibid, p.880
519 Ibid, p.881

Chapter 18 - The Royal Commission on Unseaworthy Ships - 1874

520 The Appendices referred to in the report are not included but are available on line – see below
521 The Final Report, Minutes of Evidence and Appendix is available at https://babel.hathitrust.org/cgi/pt?id=mdp.35112203984325;view=1up;seq=10
522 *Nautical Magazine*, 1874, p.991
523 Jones, p.156

Chapter 19 – Conflagrations, Chain cables and Cannibalism

524 Jones, p.155
525 *New York Times*, 12th of March, 1874
526 Ibid, 31st of March, 1874
527 Ibid, 30th of March, 1874
528 Flayhart, pp.69-78
529 Unseaworthy Ships Commission Report, Appendix LV, p.420
530 HC Deb 20 March 1874 vol 218 c191
531 HC Deb 13 April 1874 vol 218 c495
532 HC Deb 05 May 1874 vol 218 c1676
533 HC Deb 05 May 1874 vol 218 c1676
534 HC Deb 07 May 1874 vol 218 cc1838-9
535 Jones, pp.155-156
536 *Nautical Magazine*, 1875, p.798
537 *Nautical Magazine*, 1875, p.645
538 Ibid, p357
539 Jones, p.202
540 *Rockhampton Bulletin* (Qld) 18 February 1875, p.2
541 HL Deb 14 July 1874 vol 220 cc1616-7
542 HL Deb 30 July 1874 vol 221 c957
543 37 & 38 Vict. c.51
544 Clark, C. R. *Women and Children Last - The Burning of the Emigrant Ship Cospatrick*. Dunedin, New Zealand: Otago University Press, 2006
545 "Burning of the Emigrant-Ship Cospatrick at Sea". *Illustrated London News*. 2 January 1875. .
546 Ell S, Ocean – *Tales of voyaging and encounters that shaped New Zealand*, Penguin Random House, New Zealand, 2018, p.105
547 Brett H, *White Wings* (vol. I), The Brett Printing Company Limited, Auckland, 1924, pp.64- 65
548 HC Deb 22 February 1875 vol 222 c626
549 HC Deb 23 March 1875 vol 223 c221
550 HC Deb 11 August 1875 vol 226 cc858-9

Chapter 20 – Competing Bills, Coal cargoes and Custom of the Sea

551 HC Deb 08 February 1875 vol 222 cc124-38
552 Ibid
553 HC Deb 23 February 1875 vol 222 cc751-2
554 HC Deb 23 February 1875 vol 222 cc754-5
555 HC Deb 25 February 1875 vol 222 c847
556 HC Deb 23 March 1875 vol 223 c297
557 HC Deb 06 April 1875 vol 223 cc363-4
558 HC Deb 08 April 1875 vol 223 cc505-73
559 *The Guardian*, 10 May 1875, p.8; 11 May 1875, p.5 and 30 June 1875, p.5. *Nautical Magazine*, 1875, pp.517-520
560 *Nautical Magazine*, 1875, pp.517-518
561 *Western Morning News*, 11 May 1875
562 *Rockhampton Bulletin*, 30 June 1875, p.3
563 *HC Deb 02 June 1875 vol 224 cc1294-5*
564 HC Deb 17 June 1875 vol 225 c140
565 Jones, pp.200-201
566 *Nautical Magazine*, 1876, pp905-906

Chapter 21 – The Stop-gap Act

567 HC Deb 12 July 1875 vol 225 cc1325-6
568 HC Deb 22 July 1875 vol 225 cc1822-9
569 Jones, pp.169-170
570 Ibid, pp.176-177
571 Ibid, pp171-172
572 Ibid, pp.187-188
573 HC Deb 26 July 1875 vol 226 c43
574 HC Deb 27 July 1875 vol 226 cc92-9
575 HC Deb 30 July 1875 vol 226 cc225-67
576 Ibid
577 HC Deb 31 July 1875 vol 226 cc340-66
578 HC Deb 02 August 1875 vol 226 cc379-431
579 38 & 39 Vict. c.88

580 Mansell, p.48
581 *Nautical Magazine*, 1875, pp. 19-21
582 "The Loss Of The Deutschland [Inquiry 1st day]". *The Times* (28504). London. 21 December 1875. p. 8.
583 *Nautical Magazine*, 1876, p.395
584 (L.R.2 Ex. D. 63; 13 Cox C.C.403) R.v Keyn (The Franconia, The Strathclyde)
585 41 & 42 Vict. c.73
586 Churchill R R & Lowe A V, *The Law of the Sea*, Third Edition, Manchester University Press, Manchester, 1999, p.73
587 McGuffie K C, *Marsden: The Law of Collisions at Sea*, Stevens & Sons Ltd., London, 1961, p.21

Chapter 22 – Merchant Shipping Bill, 1876

588 Blackwood, pp.109-111
589 HC Deb 17 February 1876 vol 227 cc428-66
590 HC Deb 09 March 1876 vol 227 cc1707-8
591 HC Deb 23 March 1876 vol 228 cc518-51
592 HC Deb 27 March 1876 vol 228 cc627-87
593 HC Deb 30 March 1876 vol 228 cc884-912
594 HC Deb 03 April 1876 vol 228 cc1147-61
595 HC Deb 06 April 1876 vol 228 cc1367-77
596 HC Deb 24 April 1876 vol 228 cc1580-622
597 HC Deb 28 April 1876 vol 228 cc1879-85
598 HC Deb 01 May 1876 vol 228 cc1913-49
599 HC Deb 04 May 1876 Vol. 229 c.69
600 HC Deb 04 May 1876 vol 229 cc53-96
601 HC Deb 08 May 1876 vol 229 cc208-35
602 HC Deb 22 May 1876 vol 229 cc1054-82
603 HC Deb 26 May 1876 vol 229 cc1334-7
604 HL Deb 29 May 1876 vol 229 c1340
605 HL Deb 23 June 1876 vol 230 cc317-35
606 Jones, p.235
607 HL Deb 07 July 1876 vol 230 cc1130-3
608 HL Deb 14 July 1876 vol 230 cc1432-4
609 HL Deb 21 July 1876 vol 230 c1681
610 HL Deb 15 August 1876 vol 231 c1224 (39 & 40 Vict. c.80)
611 39 & 40 Vict. c.80

Chapter 23 – Merchant Shipping Act, 1876

612 Jones, p.243
613 HC Deb 08 February 1876 vol 232 cc59-121
614 HC Deb 08 February 1876 vol 227 cc52-114
615 HC Deb 20 July 1876 vol 230 cc1631-40
616 HC Deb 08 February 1877 vol 232 cc59-121
617 HC Deb 28 June 1877 vol 235 c409
618 Merchant Shipping Act, 1854, s.243
619 42 & 43 Vict. c.72
620 Blackmore, pp.113-115
621 Ibid, p116
622 43 & 44 Vict. c.43
623 Fox, p.239
624 Ibid, p.240
625 Crump, p.303
626 Fox, p.292
627 Ibid, p.293
628 Crump, p.302
629 Ibid, pp.303-304
630 Ibid

Chapter 24 – Ineffective Legislation

631 HC Deb 28 February 1882 vol 266 cc1835-6
632 *The Glasgow Herald*, 4 July 1883, p.9, *Apalling Disaster on the Clyde. Vessel capsized at launch. Great Loss of Life*
633 Blackmore, p.117; from the report of the Commission of Inquiry, chaired by the 'eminent naval architect Sir Edward Reed' into the circumstances of the capsizing, upon her launch in 1883
634 https://maritimecyprus.com/2020/01/19/flashback-in-maritime-history-the-cimbria-disaster-19-jan-1883-the-story-of-the-german-titanic/
635 Jones, p.266
636 Kirkaldy, p.234
637 HC Deb 06 February 1884 vol 284 c155
638 HC Deb 19 May 1884 vol 288 cc685-787
639 Jones S E, *Fatal work-related accidents in UK merchant shipping from 1919 – 2005. Occupational Medicine*, Vol. 58, Issue 2, March 2008, pp.129-132
640 Ibid
641 Ibid
642 HC Deb 19 May 1884 vol 288 cc685-787
643 HC Deb 30 June 1884 vol 289 cc1736-40
644 HC Deb 03 July 1884 vol 289 cc1889-91
645 HC Deb 07 July 1884 vol 290 cc217-9
646 Blackmore, p.121

Chapter 25 – Saving of Life at Sea Commission

647 Ibid, p.122
648 Ibid
649 Ibid, p.119
650 Ibid, pp.122-125
651 Ibid, pp.125-126
652 Ibid
653 51 & 52 Vict. c.24
654 *The Lifeboat Journal*, Royal National Lifeboat Institution, Vol.XIV, No.153, 01 August 1889
655 *The Lifeboat Journal*
656 HC Deb 12 February 1891 vol 350 c497
657 HC Deb 10 June 1892 vol 5 cc696
658 HC Deb 20 February 1890 vol 341 cc746-7
659 HC Deb 17 July 1890 vol 347 cc184-8
660 HC Deb 12 February 1890 vol 341 c179
661 HC Deb 05 March 1890 vol 342 cc59-60
662 HC Deb 20 March 1890 vol 342 cc1355
663 HC Deb 14 April 1890 vol 343 cc539
664 53 & 54 Vict. c.9
665 Kirkaldy, p.235

Chapter 26 – The Grand Act - 1894

666 Three of these Acts are not covered; the Merchant Shipping (Exemption from Pilotage) Act, 1897, (60 & 61 Vict. c.61) which abolished certain exemptions from compulsory pilotage under the Pilotage Act,1825; the Merchant Shipping (Liability of Shipowners) Act, 1898 (61 & 62 Vict. c.14) extended Part VIII (limitation of liability provisions) of the Merchant Shipping Act, 1894, to ships in the course of construction and to the owners, builders and other parties interested in such ships, and the Merchant Shipping (Mercantile Marine Fund) Act, 1898, (61 & 62 Vict. c.44) which amended that law with regard to provision of payment of certain expenses under the Merchant Shipping Act, 1894, and with regard to the levying of light dues.

667 Report of the investigation into the shipwreck of the steamship "Utopia"

668 HC Deb 10 March 1892 vol 2 c513

669 HC Deb 17 March 1892 vol 2 c1059

670 Ibid

671 55 & 56 Vict. c.37

672 Dixon, p.227

673 HC Deb 24 August 1893 vol 16 c1067

674 HC Deb 04 September 1893 vol 16 cc1875-6

675 HC Deb 07 September 1893 vol 17 cc472

676 HC Deb 18 December 1893 vol 19 c1724

677 57 & 58 Vict. c.60

678 See Table of Acts Repealed by the Merchant Shipping Act, 1894 in Appendices

679 For example, the New Zealand Shipping and Seamen Act, 1952, repealed by the Maritime Transport Act, 1994, contained many references to the Merchant Shipping Act, 1894.

680 Thomas M & Steel D, p.127; 'Seaworthy' in this section means that a ship should be in a fit state, as to repairs, equipment and crew, and in all other respects, to encounter the ordinary perils of the voyage, and the negligence of the captain in not using with proper care the means of safety provided does not make the ship unseaworthy within the section: *Hedley* v. *Pinkney & Sons S.S. Co.* [1894] A.C. 222; affirming [1892] 1 Q.B. 58.

Chapter 27 – Loss of Life and Lack of Crew

681 Fox, pp.375-377

682 *The Times*, Philadelphia, Pennsylvania, 19 June, 1896, p.9

683 Dixon, p.229

684 Blackmore, pp.132-134

685 Ibid, p.228

686 Ibid, pp.227-233

687 HC Deb 03 May 1897 vol 48 cc1492-9

688 60 & 61 Vict. c.59

689 Dixon, p.231

690 *Kansas City Journal*, Kansas City, Missouri, Thursday 7 July 1898, p.1

691 Chain, Cables and Anchors Act, 1864, Chain, Cable and Anchor Act, 1871

692 62 & 63 Vict. c.23

Chapter 28 - Conclusion

693 Blackmore, p.122. *The Effects of late Legislation described*, from the Report of the Royal Commission on the Saving of Life at Sea

694 Ibid

695 Atkinson, pp.49-50

Principal Merchant Shipping Acts 1800 - 1899

1803	Passenger Vessels Act , 1803	43 Geo.III, c.56
1813	Passenger Vessels Act , 1813	53 Geo.III
1816	Shipping Act, 1816	56 Geo.III, c.114
1817	Passenger Vessels Act, 1817	56 Geo.III, c.83
1823	Registering of Vessels Act, 1823	4 Geo,IV, c.41
	Passenger Vessels Act, 1823	4 Geo.IV, c.88
1825	Passenger vessels Act, 1825	6 Geo.IV, c.116
	Pilotage Act, 1825	6 Geo.IV, c.125
1826	Merchant Seaman Act, 1826	6 Geo.IV, c.59
1827	Passenger Vessels Act, 1827	7 & 8 Geo.IV, c.19
1828	Passengers in Merchant Vessels Act, 1828	9 Geo.IV, c21
1833	Merchant Seaman Act, 1833	3 & 4 Will.IV, c.19
1835	Merchant Seaman Act, 1835	5 & 6 Will.IV, c.19
	Merchant Vessels, Etc Act, 1835	5 & 6 Will.IV, c53
	Tonnage, Etc, of Ships Act, 1835	5 & 6 Will.IV, c.56
1839	Timber Ships, British N. America Act, 1839	2 & 3 Vict. c.44
1840	Passenger Ships Act, 1840	3 & 4 Vict, c.21
1842	Timber Ships America Act, 1842	5 & 6 Vict. c.17
	Passengers in Merchant Ships Act, 1842	5 & 6 Vict. c.107
1844	Merchant Seaman Act, 1844	7 & 8 Vict. c.112
1845	Passenger Ships Act, 1845	7 & 8 Vict. c.14
	Merchant Seaman Act, 1845	7 & 8 Vict. c.27
	Timber Ships Act, 1845	7 & 8 Vict. c.45
1846	Steam Navigation Act, 1846	9 & 10 Vict. c.100
1847	Passenger Act, 1847	9 & 10 Vict. c.103
1848	Passengers to North America Act, 1848	11 & 12 Vict. c.6
	Steam Navigation Act, 1848	11 & 12 Vict. c.81
1849	Passenger Act, 1849	12 & 13 Vict. c.33
1850	Mercantile Marine Act, 1850	13 & 14 Vict. c.93
1851	Steam Navigation Act, 1851	14 & 15 Vict. c.79
	Mercantile Marine Act Amendment Act, 1851	14 & 15 Vict. c.96
1852	Passengers Act, 1852	15 & 16 Vict. c.44
1853	Pilotage law Amendment Act, 1853	16 & 17 Vict. c.129
	Merchant Shipping Law Amendment Act, 1853	16 & 17 Vict. c.131

1854	The Coasting Trade Act, 1854	17 & 18 Vict. c.5
	Merchant Shipping Act, 1854	17 & 18 Vict. c.104
	Merchant Shipping Repeal Act, 1854	17 & 18 Vict. c.120
1855	Merchant Shipping Act Amendment Act, 1855	18 & 19 Vict. c.91
	Passengers Act, 1855	18 & 19 Vict. c.119
1862	Merchant Shipping Amendment Act, 1862	25 & 26 Vict. c.63
1863	Passengers Act Amendment Act, 1863	26 & 27 Vict. c.51
1864	Chain Cable and Anchor Act, 1864	27 & 28 Vict. c.27
1867	Merchant Shipping Act, 1867	30 & 31 Vict. c.124
1869	Merchant Shipping (Colonial) Act, 1869	32 & 33 Vict. c.11
1870	Passengers Act Amendment Act, 1870	33 & 34 Vict. c.95
1871	Chain Cable and Anchor Act, 1871	34 & 35 Vict. c.101
	Merchant Shipping Act, 1871	34 & 35 Vict, c.110
1872	Chain Cable and Anchor Act, 1872	35 & 36 Vict. c.30
	Merchant Shipping Act, 1872	35 & 36 Vict. c.73
1873	Merchant Shipping Act, 1873	36 & 37 Vict. c.85
1874	Chain Cables and Anchors Act, 1874	37 & 38 Vict. c.51
1875	Merchant Shipping Act, 1875	38 & 39 Vict. c.88
1876	Merchant Shipping Act, 1876	39 & 40 Vict. c.80
1878	Territorial Waters Jurisdiction Act, 1878	41 & 42 Vict, c.73
1879	Shipping Casualties Investigation Act, 1879	42 & 43 Vict. c.72
1880	Merchant Shipping (Carriage of Grain) Act, 1880	43 & 44 Vict. c.43
1888	Merchant Shipping (Life Saving Appliances) Act	51 & 52 Vict. c.24
1889	Passengers Act Amendment Act, 1889	52 & 53 Vict. c.29
	Merchant Shipping Act, 1889	52 & 53 Vict. c.46
1890	Merchant Shipping Act, 1890	53 & 54 Vict. c.9
1892	Merchant Shipping Act, 1892	55 & 56 Vict. c.37
1894	Merchant Shipping Act, 1894	57 & 58 Vict, c.60
1897	Merchant Shipping Act, 1897	60 & 61 Vict, c.59
1898	Merchant Shipping (Liability of Shipowner) Act	61 & 62 Vict. c.14
1899	Chain Cables and Anchors Act, 1899	62 & 63 Vict. c.23

Acts repealed by the Merchant Shipping Act, 1894

Session and Chapter.	Short Title.	Extent of Repeal.
17 Edw. 2. Stat. 2. c. 11. (Prerog. Reg. Stat. temp. incert. c. 13 in Rev. Edition).	Prerogativa Regis	The words "wreck of the sea."
4 Geo. 4. c. 80.	An Act to consolidate and amend the several laws now in force with respect to trade within the limits of the charter of the East India Company, and to make, further provision with respect to such trade	Section twenty-seven, section twenty-eight, from "and for every omission" to "herein is required" and the word "omission" after "non-observance," and section thirty-four.
15 & 16 Vict. c. 26.	The Foreign Deserters Act, 1852.	The whole Act.
16 & 17 Vict. c. 84.	An Act to amend the Passengers Act, 1852, so far as relates to the passages of natives of Asia or Africa, and also passages between the Island of Ceylon and certain parts of the East Indies.	The whole Act.
17 & 18 Vict. c. 104.	The Merchant Shipping Act, 1854.	The whole Act.
17 & 18 Vict. c. 120.	The Merchant Shipping Repeal Act, 1854.	
18 & 19 Vict. c. 91.	The Merchant Shipping Act (Amendment) Act, 1855.	The whole Act.
18 & 19 Vict. c. 119.	The Passengers Act, 1855.	The whole Act.
19 & 20 Vict. c. 41.	The Seamen's Ravings Bank Act, 1856.	The whole Act.
24 & 25 Vict. c. 10.	The Admiralty Court Act, 1861.	Sections nine, twelve, and twenty-four.
24 & 25 Vict. c. 52.	The Australian Passengers Act, 1861.	The whole Act.
25 & 26 Vict. c. 63.	The Merchant Shipping Amendment Act, 1862.	The whole Act.

Session and Chapter.	Short Title.	Extent of Repeal.
26 & 27 Vict. c. 51.	The Passengers Act Amendment Act, 1863.	The whole Act.
30 & 31 Vict. c. 114.	The Court of Admiralty (Ireland) Act, 1867.	Sections, thirty-five and forty-five.
30 & 31 Vict. c. 124.	The Merchant Shipping Act, 1867.	The whole Act, except section one as far as "Act, 1867," and section twelve.
31 & 32 Vict. c. 45.	The Sea Fisheries Act, 1868.	Sections twenty-two to twenty-four.
31 &:32 Vict; c. 129.	The Colonial Shipping Act, 1868.	The whole Act.
32 & 33 Vict. c. 11.	The Merchant Shipping (Colonial) Act, 1869.	The whole Act.
33 & 34 Vict. c. 95.	The Passengers Act (Amendment) Act, 1876.	The whole Act;
34 & 35 Vict. c. 110.	The Merchant Shipping Act, 1871.	The whole Act.
35 & 36 Vict. c. 73.	The Merchant Shipping Act, 1872.	The whole Act, except sections one, ten, and seventeen.
36 &37 Vict. c. 85.	The Merchant Shipping Act, 1873.	The whole Act.
37 & 38 Vict. c. 88.	The Births and Deaths Registration Act, 1874.	Section thirty-seven, except sub-section (6), and except so far as the section relates to Her Majesty's ships.
38 & 39 Vict. c. 17.	The Explosives Act, 1875.	Section forty-two.
39 & 40 Vict. c. 27.	The Local Light Dues Reduction Act, 1876.	The whole Act.
39 & 40 Vict. c. 80.	The Merchant Shipping Act, 1876.	The whole Act.
40 & 41 Vict. c. 16.	The Removal of Wreck Act, 1877.	The whole Act.
42 & 43 Vict. c. 72.	The Shipping Casualties Investigation Act, 1879.	The whole Act.
43 & 44 Vict. c. 16.	The Merchant Seamen Payment of Wages and Saving Act, 1880.	The whole Act, except the first paragraph of Section one and section eleven.

Session and Chapter.	Short Title.	Extent of Repeal.
43 & 44 Vict. c. 18.	The Merchant Shipping; Act (1854) Amendment Act, 1880.	The whole Act.
43 & 44 Vict. c. 22.	The Merchant Shipping (Fees and Expenses) Act, 1880.	Sections two, five, sis, and seven.
43 & 44 Vict. c. 43.	The Merchant .Shipping (Carriage of Grain) Act, 1880.	The whole Act.
45 & 46 Vict. c. 55.	The Merchant Shipping (Expenses) Act, 1882.	The whole Act, except the first paragraph of section one and section eight.
45 & 46 Vict. c. 76.	The Merchant Shipping (Colonial Inquiries) Act, 1882.	The whole Act.
46 & 47 Vict. c. 22.	The Sea Fisheries Act, 1883.	Section eight.
46 & 47 Vict. c. 41.	The Merchant Shipping (Fishing Boats) Act, 1883.	The whole Act.
49 & 50 Vict. c. 38.	The Riot (Damages) Act, 1886.	In section six, Paragraph (a), and the words "plundering, damage," before "injury ; " and from " and as if" to the end of the section.
50 & 51 Vict. c. 4.	The Merchant Shipping (Fishing Boats) Act, 1887.	The whole Act.
50 & 51 Vict. c. 62.	The Merchant Shipping (Miscellaneous) Act, 1887.	The whole Act.
51 & 52 Vict. c. 24.	The Merchant Shipping (Life Saving Appliances) Act, 1888.	The whole Act.
52 & 53 Vict. c. 5.	The Removal of Wrecks Act, 1877, Amendment Act, 1889.	The whole Act.
52 & 53 Vict. c. 29.	The Passenger Acts Amendment Act, 1889.	The whole Act.
52 & 53 Vict. c. 43.	The Merchant Shipping (Tonnage) Act, 1889.	The whole Act.
52 & 53 Vict. c. 46.	The Merchant Shipping Act, 1889.	The whole Act.
52 & 53 Vict. c. 68.	The Merchant Shipping (Pilotage) Act, 1889.	The whole Act.

Session and Chapter.	Short Title.	Extent of Repeal.
52 & 53 Vict. c. 73.	The Merchant Shipping (Colours) Act, 1889.	The whole Act.
53 & 54 Vict. c. 9.	The Merchant Shipping Act, 1890.	The whole Act.
55 & 56 Vict. c.37.	The Merchant Shipping Act, 1892.	The whole Act.

Bibliography

Ashburner W, Ed. *The Rhodian Sea-Law*, The Lawbook Exchange Ltd., 2001

Atkinson N, *Crew Culture*, Te Papa Press, Museum of New Zealand, Wellington, 2001

Baehre R., Ed., *Outrageous Seas*, Carleton University Press, 1999

Baynes N, *An Account of the Wreck of the "Royal Charter"*, Wyman and Sons, London, 1859

Bell J D, *The Role of Classification in Maritime Safety*, 9th Chua Chor Teck Annual Memorial Lecture, Singapore, 13 January 1995, IMO Library

Berry C D, *Loss of the Sultana and Reminiscences of Survivors*, Darius D Thorpe, Lansing, Michigan, 1892

Bindon E B, *Records of Steam Boiler Explosions*, E. and F.N. Spon, Charing Cross, London, 1872

Blackmore E, *The British Mercantile Marine*, Griffiths and Company Ltd, London, 1897

Blane G, *Observations on the Diseases Incident to Seamen*, John Cooper, Edinburgh,1785

Boisson P, Safety at Sea, *Policies, Regulations and International Law*, Paris, Edition Bureau Veritas, 1999, ISBN 2-86413-020-3

Boyd A C, *The Merchant Shipping Laws* – being a consolidation of all the Merchant Shipping and Passenger Acts from 1854 to 1876 inclusive with notes of all the leading English and American cases on the subjects affected by the legislation, Stevens & Sons, London, 1876

Brett H, *White Wings* (Volume I), The Brett Printing Company Limited, Auckland, N.Z1924

Bryant A, *Years of Victory 1802 – 1815*, Collins, London, 1945

Bullen F T, *The Men of the Merchant Marine*, Frederick A Stokes Company, New York, 1900

Burgess D R, *Engines of Empire – Steamships and the Victorian Imagination*, Stanford university Press, Stanford, 2016

Campbell, R D, *The Ship's Register*, Ministry of Transport, - Marine Division, New Zealand, 1980

Churchill R R & Lowe A V, *The Law of the Sea*, Third Edition, Manchester University Press, Manchester, 1999

Clark A H, *The Clipper Ship Era*, G.P.Putnam & Sons, New York and London, 1912

Clark, C R, *Women and Children Last - The Burning of the Emigrant Ship Cospatrick*. Dunedin, New Zealand: Otago University Press, 2006

Cockcroft A N and Lameijer J N K, *A Guide to the Collision Avoidance Rules*, 4th Edition, Butterworth-Heinemann, Oxford, 1990

Coggeshall G, *Thirty-Six Voyages to Various Parts of the World*, Geo. P Putnam, New York, 1858

Colombo C J, *The International Law of the Sea*, Sixth Revised Edition, Longmans, 1968

Conrad J, *Youth and Gaspar Ruiz*, J.M. Dent and Sons Ltd., London, 1920

Cox W. T,, *The Life of Robert Fulton and a History of Steam Navigation*, G. P. Putnam's Sons, New York and London, 1886

Clayton T, *Waterloo – Four Days that Changed Europe's Destiny*, Little Brown, London, 2014

Crump, T, *The Age of Steam*, CPI Group (UK) Ltd., 2007

Dickinson H W, *A Short History of the Steam Engine*, The MacMillan Company, New York, 1938

Dixon C, *Seamen and the law; an examination of the impact of legislation on the British merchant seaman's lot*, 1588 – 1918, PhD Thesis, University College, 1980

Ell, S, *Ocean – Tales of voyaging and encounter that defined New Zealand*, Penguin Random House, New Zealand, 2018

Flayhart W,, *Perils of the Atlantic*, W. W. Norton & Co.,Inc., New York, 2003

Friendly A, *Beaufort of the Admiralty, The Life of Sir Francis Beaufort 1774 – 1857*, Random House, New York, 1977

Fox S, *The Ocean Railway*, HarperColliinsPublishers, London, 2003

Fitzroy R, *The Weather Book; a Manual of Practical Meteorology*, Volume II, Longman, Green, Longman, Roberts and Green, London, 1863

Gault S, Ed., *Marsden on Collisions at Sea*, Thirteenth Edition, Sweet & Maxwell, London, 2003

Haines R, *Life and Death in the Age of Sail: The Passage to Australia*, UNSW Press, Sydney, 2006

Harvie C & Matthew H, *Nineteenth Century Britain*, Oxford University Press, 2000

Haydn J, A *Dictionary of Dates Relating to all Ages and Nations*, Ninth Edition, Edward Moxon and Co., London, 1860

Hearn C G, *Tracks in the Sea – Matthew Fontaine Maury and the Mapping of the Oceans*, International Marine/McGraw-Hill, 2002

Hughes T, *The Blue Riband of the Atlantic*, Patrick Stephens, Cambridge, 1973

Jenkins S, *A Short History of England*, Profile Books Ltd., London, 2011

Jones N, *The Plimsoll Sensation*, Little, Brown, London, 2006

Jones S E, *Fatal work-related accidents in UK merchant shipping from 1919 – 2005*. Occupational Medicine, Vol. 58, Issue 2, March 2008

Keble Chatterton E, *The Mercantile Marine*, William Heinemann Ltd.,, London, 1923

Kirkaldy AW, *British Shipping - its history, organisation and importance*, Kegan Paul, Trench, Trubner & Co., Ltd, London, 1914

Kipling R, *The Collected Works of Rudyard Kipling*, Kessinger Publishing, 2005

Lindsay W.S, *A History of Merchant Shipping and Ancient Commerce*, Vol IV, Sampson Low, Marston, Low and Searle , London, 1876

McGuffie K C, *Marsden: The Law of Collisions at Sea*, Stevens & Sons Ltd., London, 1961

McLachlan D, *A Treatise on the Law of Merchant Shipping*, Third Edition, William Maxwell & Son, London, 1880

Mansell J N K, *Flag State Responsibility – Historical Development and Contemporary Issues*, Springer-Verlag, Berlin, 2009

Masters D, *The Plimsoll Mark*, Cassell, London, 1955

Mitchell B R , *British Historical Statistics*, Cambridge University Press, Cambridge, 1988

Moore P, *The Weather Experiment*, Vintage, London, 2015

Phillips-Birt D, *A History of Seamanship*, George Allen & Unwin, London, 1971

Plimsoll S, *Our Seamen - an Appeal*, Virtue & Co., London, 1873

Robins N, *The Coming of the Comet – The Rise and Fall of the Paddle Steamer*, Seaforth Publishing, Barnsley, 2012

Rogers S, *The Atlantic*, George G Harrap and Company Limited, London, 1930

Rowland K T, *Steam at Sea: A History of Steam Navigation*, Newton Abbot, 1970

Russell A, *Lord Kelvin – His Life and Work*, T.C. & E.C. Jack, London, 1912

Seymour D. Ed., *The Merchant Shipping Act, 1854,* W.G. Benning & Co., London, 1855

Tames R, *Isambard Kingdom Brunel*, Shire Publications, Oxford, 2010

Thomas M & Steel D, *Temperley - The Merchant Shipping Acts,* Volume II, Seventh Edition, Stevens & Sons, London, 1976

Tomalin C, *Charles Dickens – a Life,* The Penguin Press, New York, 2011

Unwin P, *The Narrow Sea,* Headline Book Publishing, London, 2003

Villiers P, *Joseph Conrad, Master Mariner,* Seafarer Books, Rendlesham, England, 2006

Wilson A N, *The Victorians*, Arrow Books, London, 2003

Whyte R, *1847 Famine Ship Diary – The Journey of an Irish Coffin Ship*, Mercier Press, Cork, 1994

Woodman R, *The History of the Ship*, Conway Maritime Press, London, 2005

Woodman R, *Masters under God – Makers of the Empire 1817 – 1884,* Endeavour Press Ltd., 201

Index

C

D

E

F

G

H

I

J

K

L

M

N

O

P

Q

R

S

T

U

www.ingramcontent.com/pod-product-compliance
Lightning Source LLC
LaVergne TN
LVHW102010210926
848483LV00010B/245